ADVANCES IN PSYCHOLOGICAL SCIENCE: BIOLOGICAL AND COGNITIVE ASPECTS

RÉCENTS DÉVELOPPEMENTS EN PSYCHOLOGIE SCIENTIFIQUE: ASPECTS BIOLOGIQUES ET COGNITIFS

T0347325

Advances in Psychological Science
Récents développements en psychologie scientifique

Volume 2

Biological and cognitive aspects
Aspects biologiques et cognitifs

Congress Proceedings / Actes du Congrès
XXVI International Congress of Psychology
XXVI Congrès international de psychologie

Montréal, 1996

Edited by / Sous la direction de:

Michel Sabourin
Fergus Craik
Michèle Robert

Psychology Press
Taylor & Francis Group

HOVE AND NEW YORK

Published 1998 by Psychology Press Ltd., Publishers
27 Church Road, Hove, East Sussex, BN3 2FA
711 Third Avenue, New York, NY 10017

First issued in paperback 2014

Psychology Press is an imprint of the Taylor and Francis Group, an informa business

British Library Cataloguing in Publication Data

A catalogue record for this book is available from the British Library

Typeset by Graphicraft Typesetters Ltd., Hong Kong

ISBN 13: 978-1-138-87712-2 (pbk)
ISBN 13: 978-0-86377-471-3 (hbk)

Contents

List of contributors

Renée Baillargeon, Department of Psychology, University of Illinois, 603 East Daniel, Champaign, IL 61820, USA

C. H. Bennett, Department of Experimental Psychology, University of Cambridge, Downing Street, Cambridge CB2 3EB, UK

Paul Bertelson, Laboratoire de Psychologie Expérimentale, Université Libre de Bruxelles, 50 Av. F. D. Roosevelt, B-1050 Bruxelles, Belgium

John T. Cacioppo, Department of Psychology, The Ohio State University, 1885 Neil Avenue, Columbus, Ohio 43210-1222, USA

Anne Christophe, LSCP, EHESS-CNRS, 54 Bd Raspail, 75270 Paris Cédex 06, France

Michael C. Corballis, Department of Psychology, University of Auckland, Auckland, New Zealand

Laila Craighero, Istituto di Fisiologia Umana, Università di Parma, via Gramsci 14, I-43100 Parma, Italy

Hervé Degrelle, Laboratoire d'Endocrinologie, UFR Biomedicale, Université Paris V-René Descartes, 45 rue des Saints Pères, 75006 Paris, France

Bennett G. Galef, Jr., Department of Psychology, McMaster University, Hamilton, Ontario L8S 4K1, Canada

Rochel Gelman, Department of Psychology, University of California, 1285 Franz Hall, Box 95163, UCLA, Los Angeles, CA 90095-1563, USA

Giyoo Hatano, Department of Human Relations, Keio University, 2-15-45 Mita, Minato-ku, Tokyo 108, Japan

Claes von Hofsten, Department of Psychology, Umeå University, S-90187 Umeå, Sweden

Marc Jeannerod, Institut des Sciences Cognitives, CNRS, 67 boulevard Pinel, 69500 Bron, Lyon, France

Nancy Kanwisher, Department of Brain and Cognitive Sciences, Massachusetts Institute of Technology, Cambridge, MA 02139, USA

Bryan Kolb, Department of Psychology and Neuroscience, University of Lethbridge, Lethbridge, Alberta T1K 3M4, Canada

Asher Koriat, Department of Psychology, University of Haifa, Haifa 31905, Israel

Isabelle Le Roy, UPR CNRS 9074, Génétique, Neurogénétique, Comportement, Institut de Transgénose du CNRS, 3B rue de la Ferollerie, 45071 Orléans Cédex 02, France

N. J. Mackintosh, Department of Experimental Psychology, University of Cambridge, Downing Street, Cambridge CB2 3EB, UK

Jacques Mehler, LSCP, MSH, 54 Bd Raspail, 75270 Paris Cédex 06, France

Ronald Melzack, Department of Psychology, McGill University, 1205 Dr. Penfield Avenue, Montreal, Quebec H3A 1B1, Canada

Stéphane Mortaud, UPR CNRS 9074, Génétique, Neurogénétique, Comportement, Institut de Transgénose du CNRS, 3B rue de la Ferollerie, 45071 Orléans Cédex 02, France

Risto Näätänen, Department of Psychology, P.O. Box 13 (Meritullinkatu 1), FIN-00014 University of Helsinki, Helsinki, Finland

J. Bruce Overmier, Center for Research in Learning, Perception, & Cognition, University of Minnesota, 75 East River Road, Minneapolis, MN 55455, USA

Christophe Pallier, Rutgers University, and LSCP, EHESS-CNRS, 54 Bd Raspail, 75270 Paris Cédex 06, France

Kim Plunkett, Department of Experimental Psychology, University of Oxford, South Parks Road, Oxford, UK

Robert A. Rescorla, Department of Psychology, University of Pennsylvania, 3815 Walnut Street, Philadelphia, PA 19104, USA

Anik de Ribaupierre, Faculté de Psychologie et des Sciences de l'Education, Université de Genève, 9, rte de Drize, CH-1227 Carouge, Switzerland

Giacomo Rizzolatti, Istituto di Fisiologia Umana, Università di Parma, via Gramsci 14, I-43100 Parma, Italy

Mark R. Rosenzweig, Department of Psychology-1650, 3210 Tolman Hall, University of California, Berkeley, CA 94720-1650, USA

Pierre L. Roubertoux, UPR CNRS 9074, Génétique, Neurogénétique, Comportement, Institut de Transgénose du CNRS, 3B rue de la Ferollerie, 45071 Orléans Cédex 02, France

Evgeny N. Sokolov, University of Wuppertal, Department of Physiological Psychology, Max-Horkheimerstr. 20, D-42119, Germany.

John E. R. Staddon, Department of Psychology: Experimental, Duke University, Box 90086, Durham NC 27708-0086, USA

Hannu Tiitinen, Department of Psychology, P.O. Box 13 (Meritullinkatu 1), FIN-00014 University of Helsinki, Helsinki, Finland

Sylvie Tordjman, UPR CNRS 9074, Génétique, Neurogénétique, Comportement, Institut de Transgénose du CNRS, 3B rue de la Ferollerie, 45071 Orléans Cédex 02, France

Endel Tulving, Rotman Research Institute of Baycrest Centre, University of Toronto, Toronto, Canada

XXVI International Congress of Psychology

XXVI Congrès international de psychologie

Montréal, Canada

August 16–21 août 1996

Under the joint sponsorship of/
Sous le parrainage conjoint de:

Canadian Psychological Association
Société canadienne de psychologie

National Research Council Canada
Conseil national de recherches Canada

Under the auspices of / Sous les auspices de

International Union of Psychological Science (IUPsyS)
l'Union internationale de psychologie scientifique (UIPsyS)

President / Président
David Bélanger

Congress Council/Conseil du Congrès

David Bélanger (President), John G. Adair (Scientific Program Committee), Sylvie Fafard, Alain Brissette (Montreal Convention Center), Laurier Forget (Congress Director), Terrence P. Hogan (Finance Committee), Pierre Lamoureux (Congress Manager), Pierre L.-J. Ritchie (Secretary-Treasurer), Mark J. Rosenzweig (IUPsyS Liaison), Michel E. Sabourin (Organizing Committee), John Service (CPA Liaison).

Scientific Program Committee/Comité du programme scientifique

John G. Adair (Chair), John W. Berry, Fergus I. M. Craik, Kenneth L. Dion, Michèle Robert, Gordon Winocur.

Organizing Committee/Comité organisateur

Michel E. Sabourin (Chair), Hélène Cauffopé, Marcelle Cossette-Ricard, François Doré, Jacques Forget, Andrée Fortin, Robert Haccoun, Jacques Lajoie, Luc Lamarche, Jean-Roch Laurence, Jean-Claude Lauzon, Paul Maurice, Stéphane Sabourin, Donald Taylor.

Scientific Advisory Council/Conseil consultatif scientifique

E. W. Ames, K. S. Bowers, A. S. Bregman, M. P. Bryden, C. A. Cameron, J. K. Chadwick-Jones, R. Cloutier, J. B. Conway, K. D. Craig, T. Gouin-Décarie, V. Di Lollo, K. K. Dion, A. R. Dobbs, P. C. Dodwell, V. I. Douglas, L. Dubé, N. S. Endler, R. C. Gardner, M. A. Goodale, J. Grusec, D. N. Jackson, L. Jacoby, D. Kimura, B. E. Kolb, J. De Koninck, W. E. Lambert, F. Lepore, R. S. Lockhart, J. A. McNulty, D. H. Meichenbaum, R. Melzack, P. M. Merikle, B. A. Milner, D. R. Olson, A. U. Paivio, A. Pinard, C. Porac, S. W. Pyke, B. Rusak, S. Shettleworth, L. S. Siegel, J. Stewart, F. Strayer, P. Suedfeld, R. C. Tees, E. Tulving, V. Vikis-Freibergs, T. MacBeth

IUPsyS Executive Committee—1992–1996—Comité exécutif de l'UIPsyS

Kurt Pawlik (President), Mark R. Rosenzweig (Past-President), Qicheng Jing (Vice-President), Lars-Göran Nilsson (Vice-President), Géry d'Ydewalle (Secretary-General), J. Bruce Overmier (Deputy Secretary-General), Michel E. Sabourin (Treasurer), Fouad A.-L.H. Abou-Hatab, Rubén Ardila, Derek Blackman, Michel Denis, Rochel Gelman, Terrence P. Hogan, Hiroshi Imada, Cigdem Kağitçibaşi, Durganand Sinha, Jan Strelau.

Introduction

Under the auspices of the International Union of Psychological Science (IUPsyS) and the joint sponsorship of the National Research Council Canada and the Canadian Psychological Association, the XXVIth International Congress of Psychology was held in Montréal, Canada, during the third week of August, 1996. Persons from more than 80 countries attended this session of Psychology's quadrennial international scientific congress, composed of 4,200 delegates and students, with another 600 individuals being distinguished guests, accompanying persons, and representatives of the large number (50) of exhibitors. Participants came from all regions of the world including some that have not always been present at the Congress.

Montréal displayed all of the charm for which it is renowned as the second largest French-speaking city in the world and one of North America's most cosmopolitan venues. The colorful Opening Ceremony presented a spectacular display of circus arts in a musical context for which the province of Québec has become famous. Officially opened by the Canadian Minister for International Cooperation, the Honorable Pierre Pettigrew, and the Québec Minister of State for the Métropole de Montréal, the Honorable Serge Ménard, the opening session was also addressed by Madame Francine Fournier, Deputy Director General, Social and Human Sciences, UNESCO.

Altogether more than 400 scientific program items arranged in 24 concurrent sessions for the duration of the Congress provided participants the latest research developments in psychology from around the world. Highlighting the program of invited speakers were 15 Keynote Addresses, 45 State-of-the-Art lectures, and the IUPsyS Presidential address. Covering a range of topics balanced across the entire discipline, 140 invited symposia and 49 submitted, integrated paper sessions contributed to the core of the scientific program. Individually submitted papers arranged into 116 thematic oral sessions and four days of more than 1,700 interactive posters provided an opportunity for individual psychologists from around the world to present and discuss their work with other colleagues.

Following the practice initiated at the 1992 Congress in Brussels, the Congress proceedings volumes present the contributions of the invited speakers. The balanced content of the scientific program has enabled us to arrange these in two equal-sized volumes. Volume 1 covers contributions to the social, personal, and cultural aspects of psychological science. It also features the address of Kurt Pawlik, the President of the International Union of Psychological Science, entitled "The psychology of individual differences: The personality puzzle". Volume 2 comprises the biological and cognitive aspects of the discipline.

Each volume is divided into parts reflecting the topical foci of the Congress. The first part of Volume 2 is devoted to psychobiological processes. After an initial chapter dealing with how behavior-genetic analysis can help discovering the physiological pathways from gene to behavior (Pierre Roubertoux, Stéphane Mortaud, Sylvie Tordjman, Isabelle Le Roy, and Hervé Degrelle), a description of the evolution of the human mind as a major focus of psychological enquiry (Michael Corballis) is presented. Two chapters on the psychological consequences of stress follow: the first attempts to identify the clues that the stress system and its disorders provide for the understanding of pain (Ronald Melzack), while the second discusses the important role played by the nature and amount of reactivity to acute psychological stressors and the long-term costs of excessive activation (John Cacioppo).

More central processes are then considered in the second part that deals with brain mechanisms. First, there is a chapter on the effects of experience on brain structure and synaptic organization and that of the associated behavioral changes (Bryan Kolb). Auditory attention capacities are then examined in relation to the mismatch negativity index, a potentially interesting tool to better comprehend central auditory function (Risto Näätänen and Hannu Tiitinen). This chapter is followed by one proposing that spatial attention results from the activation of the same "pragmatic" circuits that program motor activities (Giacomo Rizzolatti and Laila Craighero). From attention mechanims, we move on to human visual recognition and examine the evidence derived from functional brain imaging (Nancy Kanwisher). The last chapter of this part analyzes the different patterns of interaction between psychology and neuroscience and the respective contributions of each field to the other (Mark Rosenzweig).

A third part is devoted to the learning processes in both humans and animals. A first chapter attempts to explain how and why associative relations are learned and persist in the context of instrumental learning situations (Robert Rescorla). It is followed by the presentation of a dynamic model of memory that seeks to explain habituation and forgetting (John Staddon). The development of social learning and imitation in animals as a dynamic interdisciplinary area of inquiry is then discussed (Bennett Galef). Next, the evolution of the learned helplessness construct, its extension as a model of reactive depression, as well as its role in illuminating certain consequences of stress are reviewed (Bruce Overmier). Finally, a conditioning analysis of the different parameters of perceptual learning along with their effects (N. J. Mackintosh and C. H. Bennett) completes this part.

The next seven chapters that are devoted to cognition, perception, and memory, offer an excellent illustration of some of the major new directions research is taking in this most fundamental area of psychological science. Brain activation patterns during simulation, observation, or performance of mental actions (Marc Jeannerod) are first considered. This chapter is followed by the presentation of a four-dimension model that attempts to explain color perception and encoding, as well as other cognitive phenomena (Evgeny Sokolov). From a psycholinguistic point of view, the next chapter examines the plasticity displayed by infants in learning language and in discriminating among different languages (Jacques Mehler, Christophe Pallier, and Anne Christophe). Focusing on the involved cognitive processes, the following chapter offers an interpretation of comprehension activity in both individuals and groups (Giyoo Hatano). We then move on to perceptual issues, and more specifically to a discussion of the methodological and conceptual issues associated with the perception of multimodal events (Paul Bertelson). The results of the neurocognitive analysis of memory function based on brain imaging techniques is then presented, not only to help better locate remembering processes, but also attempt to solve certain theoretical issues (Endel Tulving). The last chapter of this part considers the metacognitive judgments associated with the feeling of knowing and the control one has over them (Asher Koriat).

Cognitive development is the unifying theme of the last part. After an examination of the early development of the visual system toward a sophisticated organ of exploration and manipulation (Claes von Hofsten), the very young child's understanding of the physical world and his or her knowledge of physical events are carefully scrutinized (Renée Baillargeon). This is followed by the analysis of individual differences in cognitive development (Anik de Ribaupierre) and the presentation of domain-specific theories of cognitive development (Rochel Gelman). Questions of central concern to developmental psychologists are then raised and some answers are proposed using computational modeling of developmental change (Kim Plunkett).

Although six invited speakers, Patrick Cavanagh, Martha Farah, Patricia Goldman-Rakic, Susan Iversen, John Krebs and Shepard Siegel could not, for different reasons, supply chapters to include in this volume, their contributions to the success of the Congress is gratefully acknowledged. In the weeks preceding the Congress, we learned about the sad and untimely death of Jean Requin. Professor Requin was to speak on the role of cognitive processes in movement organization. Considering the prominence of all the contributors, the quality of their chapters and the broad scope of the involved issues, the editors feel that this volume and its companion volume are aptly entitled *Advances in Psychological Science.*

The editors would like to acknowledge several persons and institutions who provided assistance in the preparation of this volume. The project greatly benefited from the technical skills of Josée Déziel and Georges Schwartz, both of whom assisted the senior editor. In addition, we wish to express our deepest appreciation to the Departments of Psychology in our respective universities, the Université de Montréal and the University of Toronto, for the resources and support they supplied. We especially want to thank all of the contributing authors for their prompt and efficient cooperation throughout the editing process.

The Editors:
Michel Sabourin
Fergus Craik
Michèle Robert

Introduction

Le XXVIe Congrès international de psychologie s'est déroulé à Montréal, au Canada, au cours de la troisième semaine du mois d'août 1996. Cet événement était placé sous les auspices de l'Union internationale de psychologie scientifique (l'UIPsyS) et sous le patronage conjoint du Conseil national de recherches Canada et de la Société canadienne de psychologie. Des participants venus de plus de 80 pays ont assisté à cette session quadriennale qui rassemblait 4200 délégués et étudiants, ainsi que 600 autres personnes, soit des invités d'honneur, des personnes accompagnant les congressistes et des représentants d'un nombre considérable (50) d'exposants. Toutes les parties du monde étaient représentées, y compris certaines n'ayant pas toujours figuré à un tel événement.

Montréal, la deuxième plus grande ville francophone au monde et l'un des sites les plus cosmopolites en Amérique du Nord, a su déployer tout le charme qu'on lui connaît pour accueillir ces invités. Une cérémonie d'ouverture toute en couleur fut marquée d'un spectaculaire assortiment de numéros de cirque artistique avec musique, numéros ayant fait la célébrité du Québec. L'Honorable Pierre Pettigrew, Ministre canadien responsable de la coopération internationale, et l'Honorable Serge Ménard, Ministre d'état québécois pour la métropole montréalaise, ont procédé à l'ouverture officielle du Congrès. Madame Francine Fournier, Directrice générale adjointe (Sciences sociales et humaines) de l'Unesco, a également pris la parole.

Plus de 400 présentations scientifiques, regroupées à l'intérieur de 24 séances simultanées pendant tout le Congrès, ont renseigné les participants sur les progrès les plus récents de la recherche en psychologie à travers le monde. Venaient en tête de ce programme d'éminents chercheurs invités qui ont présenté 15 grandes conférences et 45 exposés-synthèses, ainsi que la conférence présidentielle de l'UIPsyS. Couvrant une variété équilibrée de thèmes, 140 symposiums organisés sur invitation et 49 séances de communications orales intégrées dans des ensembles cohérents formaient le noyau du programme. Des communications individuelles furent présentées oralement au sein de 116 séances thématiques et, durant quatre journées, plus de 1,700 communications affichées donnèrent l'occasion à autant de psychologues provenant de toutes les parties du monde d'exposer leurs travaux à d'autres collègues et d'en discuter avec eux.

Suivant l'initiative lancée par les organisateurs du Congrès de Bruxelles en 1992, les volumes des Actes du Congrès présentent les contributions des con-férenciers invités. Le caractère équilibré du contenu du programme scientifique a permis de regrouper ces conférences en deux volumes d'égale ampleur. Le premier inclut les contributions aux aspects sociaux, personnels et culturels de la psychologie et le second, les contributions à ses aspects biologiques et cognitifs. Le premier chapitre du premier volume est consacré à l'allocution intitulée « The psychology of individual differences: The personality puzzle », faite par Kurt Pawlik, le président de l'Union internationale de psychologie scientifique.

Chaque volume est découpé de manière à refléter les principaux thèmes abordés durant le Congrès. La première partie de ce second volume est consacrée aux processus psychobiologiques. Après un premier chapitre portant sur la façon dont l'analyse génétique-comportementale peut contribuer à la découverte du passage physiologique des gènes aux comportements (Pierre Roubertoux, Stéphane Mortaud, Sylvie Tordjman, Isabelle LeRoy et Hervé Degrelle), on présente une description de l'évolution de l'esprit humain comme principal objet de l'investigation psychologique (Michael Corballis). Viennent ensuite deux chapitres sur les conséquences du stress: le premier tente d'identifier les indices que le système responsable du stress et ses perturbations apportent dans la compré-hension de la douleur (Ronald Melzack), alors que le second traite de l'important rôle de la nature et du degré de la réactivité aux agents de stress psychologique aigu et des conséquences à long terme d'une activation excessive (John Cacioppo).

La seconde partie aborde des processus plus centraux, les mécanismes cérébraux. On présente d'abord l'étude de l'influence de l'expérience sur la structure du cerveau et sur l'organisation synaptique, ainsi que l'étude des changements de comportement qui y sont associés (Bryan Kolb). L'intérêt se porte ensuite sur les capacités d'attention auditive en rapport avec la composante négative désassortie des potentiels évoqués, un outil plein de possibilités intéressantes en vue d'une meilleure compréhension du fonctionnement auditif central (Risto Näätänen et Hannu Tiitinen). Le chapitre qui suit soutient que l'attention spatiale résulte de l'activation des circuits « pragmatiques » mêmes qui programment l'activité motrice (Giacomo Rizzolatti et Laila Craighero). Des mécanismes de l'attention, nous passons au processus de reconnaissance visuelle chez l'humain pour étudier les données mises au jour par les techniques d'imagerie cérébrale (Nancy Kanwisher). Le dernier chapitre de cette partie analyse les diverses configurations de l'interaction psychologie-neurosciences et les contributions réciproques de chacun de ces domaines (Mark Rosenzweig).

Une troisième partie porte sur les processus d'apprentissage chez l'humain et l'animal. Le premier chapitre tente d'expliquer comment et pourquoi les relations associatives sont apprises et persistent dans des situations d'apprentissage instrumental (Robert Rescorla). Il est suivi de la présentation d'un modèle dynamique de la mémoire qui cherche à expliquer l'habituation et l'oubli (John Staddon). On traite ensuite du développement de l'apprentissage social et de l'imitation chez l'animal en tant que domaine actif en recherche interdisciplinaire (Bennett Galef). Puis vient un bilan de l'évolution de la notion d'impuissance acquise, de son application comme modèle de dépression réactionnelle, de même que de son rôle dans la compréhension de certaines conséquences du stress (Bruce Overmier). Cette partie se termine enfin par une analyse, basée sur le conditionnement, des divers paramètres de l'apprentissage perceptif, ainsi que de leurs effets (N. J. Mackintosh et C. H. Bennett).

Sept autres chapitres traitant de la cognition, de la perception et de la mémoire mettent en lumière quelques-unes des principales orientations de la recherche dans ce secteur vraiment fondamental de la science psychologique. On considère d'abord les patrons d'activation cérébrale durant la stimulation, l'observation ou l'exécution d'activités mentales (Marc Jeannerod). Vient ensuite la présentation d'un modèle à quatre dimensions qui tente d'expliquer la perception et l'encodage de la couleur, de même que d'autres phénomènes cognitifs (Evgeny Sokolov). Un autre chapitre examine, d'un point de vue psycholinguistique, la plasticité manifestée par les enfants en bas âge dans l'apprentissage du langage et la capacité à distinguer diverses langues (Jacques Mehler, Christophe Pallier et Anne Christophe). Se centrant sur les processus cognitifs en jeu, le chapitre suivant offre une interprétation de l'activité de compréhension, tant chez les individus que chez les groupes (Giyoo Hatano). Nous passons ensuite aux questions de perception et, plus précisément, à une discussion des problèmes méthodologiques et conceptuels associés à la perception d'événements faisant intervenir plusieurs modalités sensorielles (Paul Bertelson). Puis on présente les résultats de l'analyse neurocognitive du fonctionnement de la mémoire à partir des techniques d'imagerie cérébrale; cette approche n'a pas pour seul but d'aider à une meilleure localisation des processus mnémoniques, mais vise également à résoudre certaines questions d'ordre théorique (Endel Tulving). Le dernier chapitre de cette partie étudie les jugements métacognitifs associés au sentiment de savoir, ainsi que l'autocontrôle exercé sur ces jugements (Asher Koriat).

Le développement cognitif est le thème unificateur de la dernière partie. Après un examen du développement initial du système visuel pour aboutir à un subtil organe d'exploration et de manipulation (Claes von Hofsten), on scrute profondément la compréhension du monde physique que manifeste le très jeune enfant, de même que sa connaissance des événements physiques (Renée Baillargeon). Suivent l'analyse des différences individuelles dans le développement cognitif (Anik de Ribaupierre) et la présentation de théories du développement cognitif spécifiques à des domaines particuliers (Rochel Gelman). Enfin, on soulève des problèmes d'importance primordiale pour les psychologues du développement et on propose certaines solutions à l'aide de la modélisation computationnelle des changements prenant place dans le développement (Kim Plunkett).

Six conférenciers (Patrick Cavanagh, Martha Farah, Patricia Goldman-Rakic, Susan Iversen, John Krebs et Shepard Siegel) n'ont pu, pour diverses raisons, produire de chapitre à insérer dans ce volume; nous tenons cependant à leur exprimer notre profonde reconnaissance pour leur contribution au succès de ce Congrès. Nous devons signaler que, quelques semaines avant le début du Congrès, nous apprenions avec consternation le décès prématuré du regretté Jean Requin. Le Professeur Requin devait traiter du rôle des processus cognitifs dans l'organisation des mouvements. Etant donné l'éminente compétence de tous les collaborateurs, ainsi que la qualité de leur contribution et l'envergure des questions abordées, nous avons choisi de donner à ces deux volumes le titre approprié de *Récents développements en psychologie scientifique*.

En terminant, nous voulons souligner que la préparation de ce volume a bénéficié de la collaboration de plusieurs personnes et institutions. La réalisation de ce projet doit beaucoup à la compétence technique de Josée Déziel et de Georges Schwartz, qui ont tous deux assisté le rédacteur principal de ce volume. De plus, nous tenons à exprimer notre appréciation la plus profonde aux départements de Psychologie de nos universités respectives, l'Université de Montréal et l'Université de Toronto, pour les ressources mises à notre disposition et l'appui accordé. En particulier, nous remercions tous les auteurs de ce volume pour leur collaboration soutenue et la promptitude avec laquelle ils ont répondu à nos demandes.

Les rédacteurs:
Michel Sabourin
Fergus Craik
Michèle Robert

PART ONE

Psychobiological processes

CHAPTER ONE

Behavior-genetic analysis and aggression: The mouse as a prototype[1]

Pierre L. Roubertoux, Stéphane Mortaud, Sylvie Tordjman, and Isabelle Le Roy
UPR 9074 CNRS, Orléans, France

Hervé Degrelle
UFR Biomédicale, Université Paris V-René Descartes, Paris, France

Behavior-genetic analysis is now engaged in transferring both concepts and techniques from genetics to neuro-behavioral sciences. We are far from the Nature versus Nurture debate, Heredity-Environment controversy or computation of the percentages of variance due to genes or to milieu. The aim in the field is to find, to catch, to keep genes, involved either in behaviors or in physiological associated mechanisms. *Additions of genes* or of a chromosomal region (transgenesis), from one species to another (from human to murine genome) started several years ago and has pointed to several genes implicated in behaviors, providing the opportunity to discover the effect of a gene in a quite different genetic context and to test for the physiological pathways from gene to behavior. *Gene invalidation* has been proved to have neurobehavioral consequences. Genes coding for neurotransmitter receptors have been invalidated inducing behavioral modifications. *Gene mapping* or reverse genetic strategy is an alternative method. It takes advantage from the human or murine genome project advances. Several neurologic disorders have been mapped and the discovery of genes implicated in psychiatric disorders is still in progress. The Quantitative Trait Loci (QTLs) mapping strategy provides the means to map candidate genes for quantitative traits, which are the traits of most interest for psychologists, physiologists, and ethologists. We can expect an exhaustive knowledge of the basis carried by the human and the murin genome at the beginning of the 21st century. This is why accurate mapping strategies (mapping within the smallest confidence interval) is the main challenge in genetics today. Aggression has been selected to illustrate the main advances in this interdisciplinary field of research.

---

[1] This paper is dedicated to Professor Jerry Hirsch, friend and mentor.

L'analyse génétique appliquée aux comportements s'est maintenant impliquée dans le transfert des concepts et des méthodes de la génétique vers la neurobiologie comportementale. On est loin de la controverse hérédité-milieu ou des calculs de la part imputable aux gènes ou aux environnements dans un trait. Le but de la discipline est de trouver, attraper et garder des gènes impliqués soit dans les comportements soit dans leurs corrélats physiologiques. *L'ajout de gènes* ou de régions chromosomiques (transgénose) d'une espèce à l'autre (généralement de l'Humain vers la souris) a débuté voici quelques années et a permis d'identifier des gènes impliqués dans des comportements ainsi que des voies physiologiques entre ces gènes et ces comportements. *L'invalidation de gènes*, particulièrement de ceux codant pour des récepteurs à neuromédiateurs, a conduit à l'observation de modifications comportementales. *La localisation de gènes*, ou stratégie de génétique inverse, s'appuie sur les données des programmes génome humain ou génome murin. Les gènes de plusieurs troubles neurologiques ont été ainsi localisés et la recherche des gènes impliqués dans des troubles psychiatriques est en cours. La détection de polygènes (stratégie des Quantitative Trait Loci ou QTLs) fournit le moyen de localiser les gènes impliqués dans des traits quantitatifs, qui sont ceux que fournissent les études psychologiques, physiologiques et éthologiques. On peut s'attendre à une connaissance exhaustive des successions de bases portées par les génomes humain et murin dès le début du 21ième siècle. C'est pourquoi, la mise au point de techniques permettant une localisation précise (c'est-à-dire fournissant le plus petit intervalle de confiance) est le défi majeur de la génétique aujourd'hui. Le présent article illustre les avancées actuelles de ce secteur de recherche multidisciplinaire en présentant les travaux sur l'agression.

BEHAVIOR-GENETIC ANALYSIS: TO FIND, TO CATCH, TO KEEP GENES

The late Earl Green, who died last year and who directed for more than 20 years the Jackson Laboratory, said very often that the aim of genetics is "to find, to catch, to keep genes". We are far from the Nature versus Nurture debate, Heredity-Environment controversy or computation of the percentage of variance due to genes or to milieu. We are now engaged in applying genetics to neuro-behavioral sciences. So, our aim is to find, to catch, to keep genes involved either in behaviors or in associated physiological mechanisms. The task is perilous because we need expertise in both genetics and neuro-behavioral sciences. The tools and concepts in genetics advance very quickly. The analysis of behaviors reveals an unexpected complexity for behavioral traits under study. Psychiatric diagnoses are modified according to the periodic revisions of the DSM. It is not possible to have scientific credibility performing genetic analysis using old tests such as IQ or general factor of so-called intelligence, when psychology has demonstrated the complexity of cognitive processes.

What is at stake in the research of links between genetics and behavior or more generally between genes and integrated functions?

Behavioral, physiological, morphometric, biochemical characteristics of the individuals within a species are not transmitted from parents to the offspring. The chromosome included in the gametes, carries the genetic material and is indeed transmitted. It is made up of long sequences of chemical particles, the four bases (adenine, cytosine, guanine, and thymine), plus phosphodiester bonds and sugar-phosphate backbones. We transmit atoms and molecules, not traits. All cells of an individual carry identical genetic information because of the mitotic process. All the cells are genetic replicates of the original cell constituted by the fusion of the ovum and the spermatozoon. However, the cells have different shapes and functions and the same chain of amino acids is differentially expressed in the liver or the brain cells or in the cells of two different structures in the same brain. This is due to the regulation of gene expression, controlled by other genes and by the environments.

The incredible complexity of every living organism has roots in this original simplicity: the combination of four bases and 20 amino acids leads to a large number of proteins. Identification of a gene involved in a trait is the identification of a protein for the trait. Here, we have to make two points. First, it is impossible to recognize proteins or genes involved in functions or structures, but we can identify genes involved in individual differences, either in the normal or in the pathological range of variation. Hirsch (1963) and Hirsch and McGuire (1982) have stressed the differential aspect of genetic research several years ago. The genetic strategy consists of generating or observing meiotic recombinations and detecting co-segregations of identified genes with phenotypes. This strategy implies individual differences at both the genetic and phenotypic level. In these conditions, the identified gene or genes are correlated with observed differences in the population under study. Other genes may be discovered, with another population exhibiting other genetic differences. This is not specific for behavioral functions but is true also for every level of function. Second, there is probably no gene specific for behavioral differences or diffences in structure or function far from the primary effect of the gene. A gene code for a protein and most of the modifications occurring in its sequence (addition, deletion, substitution of bases) modify the protein. These changes may induce modification in the steps of cellular development and functioning. These modifications contribute to differences in shape, migration, and chemical communication within or between the cells, with consequences on behavioral differences. The genetic correlates of the behavioral differences that we observe are, at best, the indirect repercussions of the rearrangement observed in the sequences of the bases. This is why the study of the genetic correlates of behavior cannot be dissociated from the analysis of the neuronal pathways between genes and behavior.

Genetics and aggression illustrate the advances in behavior-genetic analysis

Twenty years ago, with Michèle Carlier we published a book, *Genetics and behavior* (Roubertoux & Carlier, 1976). It took 200 pages to present the state of the art. The phenotypes analyzed, the species used, and the methods employed have increased greatly. In 1995, more than 900 papers or chapters were published, written by specialists in behavioral sciences and genetics, biochemistry, and mathematics. We would not be able to produce a similar work again and, of course, we could not present a state-of-the-art lecture covering human abnormal and normal behavior (psychiatry, neurology, cognitive functioning, social relationships), and neurobehavioral traits in other species: mice, flies, rats, *Caenoabditis elegans.* Aggression should provide the way to survey the difficulties and to present the technical advances in the field of genetics applied to behavior and to neuronal correlates of behavior.

Aggression has been considered by classic ethology as the prime mover in the evolution of the species (Scott, 1992). The explanation not of why aggression occurs but how impulsive aggressive behavior happens is a crucial point in our societies. Farrington (1992) has stressed the growing number of crimes during the last 20 years in the US, increasing from 20 to 76 per 1000 population from 1969 to 1989. Moffit (1993) presents statistics showing that the FBI index of arrests (for homicide, rape, robbery, larceny, and car theft) is the highest (5000 per 100,000 population) for young people between 15 and 20 years of age. Several scientific meetings have been organized to discuss this point; one planned by NIMH was canceled due to protests, another that took place in 1995 was disturbed by demonstrators. The study of biological correlates of aggression, and particularly its genetic correlates, is a hot issue.

EVIDENCE FOR GENETIC CORRELATES OF AGGRESSION IN OUR SPECIES, ANIMAL MODELS

Difficulties in performing genetic analysis with social behaviors

Aggression is a social behavior and the first point is to ensure that performing genetic analysis of social behaviors is valid.

Social behavior is the succesion of behavioral sequences occurring between two or more individuals: care of pups, courtship, copulation, aggression, and so on. These sequences are the results of the aptitudes of the individuals. We can look for genes involved in aptitudes to initiate social behavior, because individuals exhibiting the aptitudes have genes; we cannot look for the genes of the product of the aptitudes. This point is ignored by researchers seeking genes for divorce or unfaithfulness and by that branch of sociobiology that tries to explain the social structure by genes. A social structure has no gene. This is the pitfall of most genetic studies of aggression. Several researchers have employed the homogeneous set pair test in mice. One individual from one strain is tested with an opponent from the same strain. The cues emitted by the opponent are strain-dependent and the measures performed with the male to be tested do not address the same aptitudes. Several strategies have been used to overcome this difficulty. The round robin test developed by Ginsburg and Allee (1942) has some drawbacks because the same tested male is successively exposed to different opponents and the defeat or the victory in one round modifies the behavior in the following rounds. For this reason, Roubertoux and Carlier (1987) developed a standard opponent test, where a male is tested with individuals from the same strain: same genotype kept in identical physiological conditions. With the standard opponent test the aptitude to initiate attack in reaction to the same set of stimuli is measured. The stimuli vary with the homogeneous set pair test and consequently different aptitudes are measured. This produces quite different scores for the strains.

Discrepancies reported in the genetic correlates from segregation analyzes with laboratory male mice are the result of a large range of protocols used to measure attack behavior and rearing conditions. Different protocols or rearing conditions result in different behaviors and different scores. In contrast, stable rearing conditions and identical protocols provide replicable results. Inbred strains provide the means to test for the reliability of traits because the mice within a strain have an identical genotype and maternal environment. We have measured initiation of attack behavior by a male against a conspecific male according the same protocol over eight years, in four strains. The results presented by Roubertoux et al. (1994a), are stable for the different measures of aggression. A strong stability has been reported for several behaviors: paw preference (Signore et al., 1991), vocalizations in one-day-old mice (number, length, frequency at the beginning, apex and end of whistles). The values are stable when compared to those obtained several years ago but also to values obtained in other laboratories (Roubertoux et al., 1996). Stable values were also obtained for biochemical measures: steroid sulfatase (Roubertoux et al., 1994b; Mortaud, Donzes-Darcel, Roubertoux, & Degrelle, 1995), or plasma serotonin (Tordjman, 1996; Tordjman et al., 1995). A stable phenotype is the prerequisite of any genetic or environmental analysis. Any modification of the conditions where the behavior is recorded modifies the behavior and either its genetic or environmental correlates. In our species, differences in the definition of the trait lead to different behaviors. Concordance drops from juveniles to adults for the two types of twins (monozygotic or dizygotic) as reported by Goldsmith and Gottesman (1995). The contrast is higher in adults than in juveniles crimes. Adult crimes are not the same as juvenile ones. In other words, the results of a genetic analysis provide restricted information irrespective of the background in which it was performed.

We can now consider the question: Is there evidence for genetic correlates of aggression in our own and in other species?

Aggression in human species

There is much more speculation than empirical evidence in the human species due to the use of inappropriate methodology. Figure 1.1, adapted from O'Connor (quoted by Rutter, 1996) shows that the within-pair correlation decreases as a function of genetic relatedness. But genetic relatedness in our species is associated

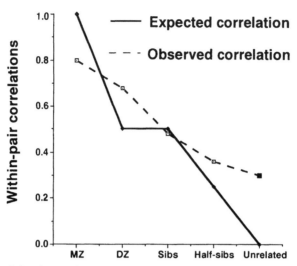

FIG. 1.1   Correlations by genetic relatedness, adapted from O'Connor et al., cited by Rutter (1996). Expected correlations are computed by the present authors, under additive hypothesis.

with environmental proximity and this kind of data cannot disentangle the two effects. Twin comparisons do not exhibit the significant differences that could suggest the contribution of genetic factors. The adoption method has been used for the study of petty criminality and a large number of psychiatric or psychological traits, including so-called intelligence. The adoption method does not permit distinguishing between genetics and environment, even when the children are adopted at birth. At birth, the child is not the product of genes only, because it has shared for nine months its mother's environment. Many people think that using tests with twins or adopted family will result in a genetic analysis. This is a delusion that is particularly strong in human behavior genetic analysis where researchers have no genetic training. Genetics needs the study of segregations.

Due to the paucity of evidence about genetic correlates of aggression in our species, we must turn to the results of animal studies. We could present embryologic, neuronal, developmental, and behavioral similarities between mice and humans. We are not naïve; there is no animal model for human behavior. A male mouse attacking another male in their cage is not a model for aggression in the Parisian metro. The socio-cultural framework of motivational factors is not to be denied in this field. However, the physiological mechanisms implicated in behavior are highly conserved in the species. The biochemical laws and their physiological outcomes are similar in every species. An enzymatic defect has the same biochemical and neuronal consequences in mouse and in human species. The interactions between hormones, immune system, and neurotransmitters follow invariant structures in vertebrates, providing similar direction in behavior. Clinical neurology has reported post-mortem hippocampal defects and impairment of memory in Alzheimer patients. Transgenic mice that had integrated one of the candidate genes for Alzheimer disease (the SOD-1 human gene) exhibit a reduction of terminal fields of hippocampal mossy fibers (Barkats et al., 1993). There is no murine model of human behavior, of course, but there are murine models of neurobiological pathways underlying behaviors that make rodents useful for the understanding of pathophysiological processes. As geneticists, we know the conservation of genomic organization in mammalian species. Comparative maps for mammalian genomes (DeBry & Seldin, 1996), and particularly for mouse and human (Nadeau et al., 1991), have been considered as a means to map human genes, taking advantage of existing homologies between the species. The discovery of a linkage in mouse indicates a candidate region for the homologous human gene. The best illustration for the use of the comparative maps is the homology between chromosome 21 in humans and 16 in mice, widely used to identify genes on the Down's syndrome region. This set of considerations suggests that results obtained with aggression in mouse genetics may not be neutral for understanding neurogenetics and aggression in our species.

Genetic analysis versus "an unfortunate short-cut": the heritability coefficient

Strain differences are known, but they are not a sufficient demonstration of a genetic contribution. Strains differ in their genes, but also in the maternal environment they provide to the pups (Carlier, Roubertoux, & Pastoret, 1991). This contribution is cytoplasmic, uterine, and post natal, including care to pups, milk quality and quantity. It interacts with the effects of the genotype. Breeding experiments consist of hybriding individuals to induce recombinations and observing the products of the meiosis at both the genetic and phenotypic levels.

Initial demonstrations of genetic correlates for aggression are derived from breeding experiments. Mendelian crosses, including backcrosses, intercrosses and diallel crosses, have lead to consideration that genetic variability is correlated with variability in aggression. Quantitative genetic analysis to partition the components either of the mean differences or of the variance provides information about the structure of the genetic correlates (additivity, dominance, epistatis-interactions between loci) as well as estimates for these components.

The best-known of these estimates is the heritability coefficient. Much has already been written on this estimate since Fisher (1951) warned about "the so-called coefficient of heritability, which I regard as one of those unfortunate short-cuts which have emerged in biometry for lack of a more thorough analysis of the data". However, we refer the reader to Wahlsten (1990) and the ensuing peer commentaries published in *Behavioral and Brain Sciences*, particularly those by McGuffin and Katz (1990). In short, heritability is part of the additive genetic contribution to the variability of the genotype. Its interpretation (and not its computation, unfortunately) implies several widely known assumptions: There is no dominance among allelic forms implicated in the phenotype, there is no epistasis, i.e. interaction between genes, and the matings are made at random. At this stage it is easy to consider how the model is unrealistic in describing the

TABLE 1.1

Three directional selection experiments in male mice: main results

Authors	Subjects	Selected variable	Generation of selection	Response to selection
Lagerspetz (1961); Lagerspetz and Lagerspetz (1971)	Males from an outbred laboratory stock (Swiss)	Composite score	19	Significant difference in the 2nd generation
Van Oortmerssen, Benus, and Dijk (1985); Van Oortmerssen and Bakker (1985); Sluyter et al. (1996).	Males from wild house colony	Attack latency	More than 36	The SAL (Short Attack Latency) line has been easily obtained; the LAL (Long Attack Latency) failed 5 times but succeeded at the 6th effort
Cairns et al. (1983); Gariepy (1995)	Males from ICR laboratory stock	Number of attacks	More than 20	The low and high lines differed at the 4th generation; the difference was due the rapid decrease of attacks of the low line

phenomenom in a natural setting. Another important issue to bear in mind is that this coefficient is the proportion of variance accounted for in the population, and not for an individual. Considering a value for a population, no prediction can be made for an individual taken from this population: Heritability is not heredity. Moreover, as heritability is specific to the population in which it is estimated, the value cannot be used to describe another population in which environmental factor and gene frequencies differ. Most geneticists and even psychologists working in behavior genetic analysis are aware of these points but some still continue to use heritability estimates. Why? If it is to predict the success (with farm or animal laboratories) of a selective breeding experiment, as illustrated by Roubertoux (1992) working with courtship behavior in the male guppy, they are right. Moreover, researchers cannot ignore that the misuse of heritability estimates may have catastrophic social consequences, especially in the field of intelligence (Hirsch, 1996; McGuire & Hirsch, 1977; Roubertoux & Carlier, 1996).

The most direct evidence is provided by divergent selections, resulting in high and low lines for attack latencies. Several studies presenting positive responses to pressure of selection have been reported (Table 1.1). These experiments could lead to identify genetic correlates of a trait under some conditions, particularly when combined with segregating analysis, as demonstrated by Jerry Hirsch's work with taxies. He started in 1958 a selective breeding for geotaxis (orientation and movement with respect to gravity) in *Drosophila melanogaster*. The high line had become stable in 1978 and the low line about 1982 (Ricker & Hirsch, 1985). Three allozymes were correlated with geotaxis expression: alcohol dehydrogenase (*Adh*, located on chromosome 2, region 2-50.1), amylase (*Amy*, chromosome 2-77.7), and 6-phosphogluconate dehydrogenase (*Pgd*, chromosome 1-0.5). However, by using hybrid subjects the authors observed the breaking up of the genotype-phenotype correlation for two markers, but not *Adh*. After crossing reciprocally the high and low lines at generation 699 they allowed free mating (i.e. absence of selection) during 66 generations in each of the reciprocal sublines (HL and LH). An association between *Adh* and geotaxis score was detected in the LH subline but not in the HL subline. The authors concluded that a previously unknown gene correlated with geotaxis was situated close to *Adh* gene, probably at one centiMorgan (Stoltenberg & Hirsch, 1996).

No similar experiments have been performed with selected lines for aggression to discover the genetic correlates of this trait, but other methods have lead to the discovery of genes implicated in different types of aggression in mice.

GENES IMPLICATED IN AGGRESSION: NEUROBEHAVIORAL CORRELATES OF PREVIOUSLY IDENTIFIED GENES

These genes are documented either by developing congenic strains or employing recombinant DNA methods.

The Y chromosome

Congenic strains were used to answer the question regarding the implication of genes carried by the Y chromosome in aggression. The association of differences in offensive behavior, defined as the initiation of attack behavior against a conspecific male, with the variants of the Y chromosome in mice is the subject of a long-standing debate, regarding both humans and mice (Carlier, Roubertoux, Kottler, & Degrelle, 1990, for a review). Briefly, correlated response for male and female aggression in lines differentialy selected only for female aggression has been reported by Cairns' group (Cairns, MacCombie, & Hood, 1983) suggesting that this behavior may not be transmitted by a locus linked to the Y chromosome. Several teams have, however, provided evidence for a contribution of the Y chromosome to male aggression against conspecific males. Our own story of the Y chromosome is of interest as it shows how difficult the investigation of a candidate gene is even with laboratory animals. The test previously described was used, and we must stress again how careful our attempts were to control the rearing conditions and to maintain the conditions constant over several years. The frequency of males initiating attack behavior is higher in the NZB strain than in CBA/H. We started a breeding experiments with reciprocal F_1s, showing a stable difference in the proportion of attacking male mice. Most authors would have concluded there was an effect of the Y as the HNF_1 group had received the Y from the strain that attacked most frequently. Several other factors contribute to the difference, including maternal effects plus genomic imprinting (Carlier et al., 1991). Only one solution was available to test for the Y effect: the development of congenic strains for the Y. The structure of the Y includes a specific part that is transmitted from father to son and a part that recombines with the X during the male meiosis and thus is partially transmitted from father to daughter. Performing repeated backcrosses between one parental female and the males from the cross, we obtained congenic strains for the specific part of the Y. No effect of the specific part of the Y was observed at the 45th generation. But the story is much more complex: When the homogeneous set pair test is used, the aggression effect of the specific part of the Y does appear (Table 1.2).

The specific part of the Y contributes aggression in interaction with autosomal effects. This conclusion is shared by three other independent research teams working in Storrs, Edinburg, and Gröningen (see Maxson, 1992a,b; 1996; Sluyter, Van Oortmerssen, Ruiter, & Koolhaas, 1996).

Recombinant DNA methods

These follow mirror strategies, either adding genes to a genome or preventing the expression of a defined gene in an organism. Transgenesis provides the means to integrate one gene from one specie into the genotype of another species. The transfer is generally from human to rodents, mostly mouse. The gene

TABLE 1.2
Implication of the two regions of the Y chromosome (the specific part $Y\text{-}^{NPAR}$,
and the pairing region $Y\text{-}^{PAR}$)

Authors	Strains and genetic design	Contribution to aggression
(a) effect of the $Y\text{-}^{NPAR}$		
Stewart, Manning, and Batty (1980)	C57BL/6Fa, CBA/FaCAM; congenic strains for $Y\text{-}^{NPAR}$ 2 generations	Decreased in fighting latency for mice bearing the $Y\text{-}^{NPAR}$ from the most rapidly attacking parental strain. Interaction with the autosomes (Carlier et al., 1990)
Maxson (1996); Maxson, Ginsburg, and Trattner (1979)	C57BL/10Bg, DBA/1Bg; congenic strains for $Y\text{-}^{NPAR}$ 20 generations	The effect of the $Y\text{-}^{NPAR}$ from the most attacking strain (DBA/1) is expressed only in males carrying 50% autosomes from DBA/1 (homogeneous set test: opponents from the strain of the tested male). No effect with the standard opponent test (Guillot et al., 1995)
Roubertoux et al. (1994a)	NZB and CBA/H; congenic strains for $Y\text{-}^{NPAR}$ 20 generations 25 to 26 generations	No effect of the $Y\text{-}^{NPAR}$ with the standard opponent test (Roubertoux et al., 1994) An effect of the $Y\text{-}^{NPAR}$ in interaction with the autosomes when the homogeneous set test is used (Guillot et al., 1995)
(b) effect of the $Y\text{-}^{PAR}$		
Roubertoux et al. (1994a)	Backcrosses keeping the maternal environment constant and comparisons of reciprocal F_1s from both parental and congenic strains	An effect of the $Y\text{-}^{PAR}$, plus the autosomes
Van Oortmerssen and Sluyter (1994)	Congenic strains compared with the F_1s from the parental strains	An effect of the $Y\text{-}^{PAR}$, plus the autosomes

is incorporated in the host's genotype and is transmitted according to Mendelian laws. Its expression induces phenotypes similar to those observed in the human species and provides the opportunity to follow the effects of this gene during development to analyze its effects. The alternative is preventing the expression of a gene by molecular methods. In this case, the gene is said to be knocked out. The consequence of the absence of the gene leads to recognition of its function. This strategy is of great interest because it shows up the physiological pathways between the gene and the behavioral trait.

A hypothesis about the protein implicated in the trait is a prerequisite to gene invalidation as the expressed protein depends on a gene. This hypothesis is

TABLE 1.3
Invalidation of genes with implication in aggression in mice

Authors	Target	Effect on aggression
Chen et al. (1994)	α-calcium-calmodulin kinase II	*Offensive aggression*: heterozygotes: normal, homozygotes: decreased; *Defensive aggression*: heterozygotes: increased, homozygotes: decreased
Saudou et al. (1994)	5-HT$_{1B}$	Homozygotes: attacks more rapidly and more frequently than heterozygotes and wild mice (resident intruder test)
Nelson et al. (1995)	Nitric oxide synthase	$nNOS^-$: mice display offensive aggressive behavior compared to wild mice
König et al. (1996)	Pre-proenkephalin	$enk^{-/-}$: mice attack more frequently and more rapidly during the first test. The difference disappears during the second test
Cases et al. (1995)	MAOA	$MAOA^{-/-}$: mice shorter attack latency (resident intruder test)

generally derived from the literature. The relationships between aggression and several transmitters is well documented and either correlations with transmitter concentrations or modulation of aggression by injection of agonists are reported: metenkephalin, ACTH, β-endorphins, GABA, and serotonin or 5-hydroxitryptamine (5-HT). They are released in the whole organism and particularly in the brain: cortex, hypothalamus, and spinal chord. The effect of a transmitter is the consequence of a balance between the quantity of transmitter and number or functionality of the receptors. For 5-HT, seven families of receptors are known: 5-HT$_{1A}$, 5-HT$_{1B}$, 5-HT$_{1C}$, 5-HT$_{1D}$, 5-HT$_3$, 5-HT$_4$, and 5-HT$_5$. The problem is that specific antagonists are not availlable for each receptor. Consequently the pharmacological tool is limited. René Hen's group invalidated gene coding for recptor 5-HT$_B$ (Saudou et al., 1994). This receptor is lacking in homozygous mice, which present the highest frequency of attack behavior in various tests, compared to both controls and heterozygous ones. Was the gene for aggression discovered? Five genes are now identified by the gene invalidation method as being involved in different types of attack behavior (Table 1.3).

The gene invalidation method has its own limits. (1) A gene has pleitropic effects, the invalidated gene too. Invalidated 5-HT$_B$ and α-calmodulin-kinase II genes are implicated in initiation of attack behavior and preference for alcohol and learning respectively (see Chen, Rainnie, Greene, & Tonegawa, 1994; Silva, Stevens, Tonegawa, & Yang, 1992) for α-Calcium-Calmodulin Kinase-II invalidation. This could suggest common physiological pathways between behaviors targeted by the artificial mutation. The interest of the conclusions depends on the more or less basic function of the gene; the more basic the function, the larger the number of traits that should be targeted. (2) The effect of invalidation is not tissue-specific. We know that 5-HT_{1B} is distributed in the gut and involved in its motility. It might induce nutritive defects that are known to increment aggression in rodents. The mechanisms involved in gene invalidation could be nonspecific. These methods are still current, the way to time-dependent and tissue-specific invalidations is open. (3) Results with invalidated genes suggest that the effect of invalidation depends on the genetic background. Transfer of invalidated genes onto different genetic backgrounds (strains) should reveal epistatic effects and provide information about single versus multiple genetic mechanisms. (4) Gene invalidation results in a null allele for this gene, and consequently the protein that would have been coded by the normal gene is lacking in the organism. The question remains as to how we can use conclusions from this pathological functioning to understand the effects of genes implicated in the normal range of variation. This is similar to researchers using observations from Down's syndrome or Phenylketonuria to understand normal cognitive processes. We know that compensatory processes are at work in the brain after lesions. When impaired after surgical destruction of a structure, a function can be replaced by another. A similar phenomenon cannot be excluded for the consequences of protein ablations following gene invalidation.

The prerequisite of classic genetics is the identification of a candidate gene. It implies the knowledge of the protein involved in the trait. Deficiency of enzymatic activity of monoamine oxidase A (Brunner, Nelen, Breakfield, Ropers, & van Oost, 1993) was found in a human family in which violent acts were observed. All the affected members of the family had a normal MAO B activity with a reduced activity for MAO A. The cause of the deficient activity was identified as a point mutation in the 8th exon and all the affected members carried the deficient allele. We do not know if this finding is general or whether it has a real bearing on violence. This approach implies a strong hypothesis about the protein involved in the trait. The difficulty lies in ignoring the protein involved in the trait under study for most of the behavioral studies. A complementary approach to identify genes involved in aggression consists of gene mapping.

GENES IMPLICATED IN AGGRESSION: GENE MAPPING

Reverse genetics and initiation of attack behavior in mice

It provides an exhaustive identification of the genetic correlates of a trait, including polygenic correlates (Quantitative Trait Loci, QTL). It takes advantage of information from human and murine genome sequencing project. One issue of these projects was mapping small noncoding sequences (SSLPs: short sequences for length polymorphism or microsatellites). They have a high level of polymorphism. They are not subjected to selection as they do not code for proteins.

More than 100,000 microsatellites are potentially available, 7000 are mapped in the mouse (Dib et al., 1996), 3000 in human (Weissenbach et al., 1992; Dietrich et al., 1994). Every individual can be identified according to the allele he or she carries for the typed locus; the distance to which DNA fragments migrate depends on their length (number of base pairs).

The first step in reverse genetics is fine-mapping of the gene. The second is gene identification (either by walking on the chromosome or by co-localisation of the gene to be identified with a previously identified gene). The abnormal protein is then deduced. After the mapping has been completed, two strategies are available to identify the gene(s): walking on chromosomes, which is time consuming, or co-mapping QTLs involved in a trait with previously identified genes. Besides, this may lead to the discovery of common QTLs for behavioral or neuronal traits contributing to establishing causal relationships between these traits.

We have employed QTLs detection in an F_2 design between NZB (initiating attack) and C57BL/6, which is pacific with a standard opponent test (A/jax male as opponent). Four to six microsatellites per chromosome were selected; together with Isabelle Le Roy we have thus performed about 40,000 typings. Analyses of the results are still in progress, but we can already conclude that microsatellites that are at the telomeric end of the X, close to the boundary of the pairing region, co-segregate with initiation of attack behavior. This finding fits with our previous results, which indicated that one of the genes involved in this behavioral difference in NZB and CBA/H was on the Y-X chromosome pairing region (Roubertoux et al., 1994a).

It is not surprising to discover more than one genetic correlate for one behavior.

Different measures of aggression have different genetic correlates. The specific part of the Y chromosome contributes to attack behavior in the homogeneous set test only when the effect of the opponent is pooled with ability to initiate attack behavior. The gene (or genes) linked to the pairing region are involved with standard opponent, when the males are not isolated, when the possible effect of stress due to isolation is eliminated. But we must protect ourselves against naïveté or reductionism: Both spontaneous attack behavior and attack behavior induced by isolation appear in mice without 5-HT_{1B} receptors and nitric oxide syntase. It is not specific of the specific part of the Y.

We should look to differences in the genetic pools for another explanation. A measured phenotype is a final pathway. It is the result of several physiological mechanisms. Let us assume each of them is controlled by one gene in this theoretical graph. This is no more than a hypothesis. The polymorphism of each gene depends on the genetic structure of the population (Fig. 1.2). Assuming that gene g1 is polymorphic in population 1, a one-gene mechanism could be discovered. In contrast, gene 1, 2, and 3 are not polymorphic in population 2, and thus the final pathway has a three-gene correlate, and so on. The trait has a four-gene correlate in the species; a limited number can be discovered in each

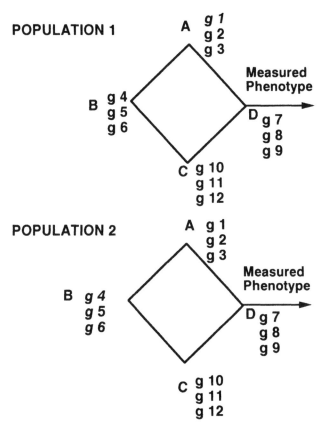

FIG. 1.2 Multigenic correlates in a species. The measured phenotype results of four hypothetical processes (A, B, C, and D), each of the processes is controlled by several genes. In population 1, the gene g1 carries different alles and thus will provide the mean to discover cosegregating phenotypic variations. In this population the phenotype is correlated to a single locus. In population 2, three loci are polymorphic (g1, g2, and g3). A three-gene correlate will be described.

population due to its limited polymorphism. This is the advantage of using inbred strains (providing the opportunity to identify genes by taking advantage of the restricted polymorphism observed within a pair of strains). However, this is also its limitation: Inbred strains are not representative of the genome in a species and provide a restricted number of genes correlated to a phenotype. As there are genes coding for variant proteins that have multiple consequences, some of them in the central nervous system inducing behavioral variations, this lead to the conclusion that the physiological correlates of aggression are not the same in different populations. It is necessary to investigate these correlates in several populations to get a picture of the genes involved in a trait in the species. Besides, the addition or the invalidation of one gene, wthin a population, induces dramatic effect. This can be due to the control of the effects of the other genes that are kept constant. The risk is to lead to the illusion that *the* gene involved in a behavior was discovered.

The task will be to identify these numerous genetic correlates in the near future. Is it possible and how?

Fine genetic mapping and the challenge of the 21st century

Recombinant Inbred Strains (RIS) may be used to map polygenic correlates of behaviors. Gora-Mazlak et al., 1991 were the first to suggest the use of RIS to map polygenic traits and to apply the method to behaviors in mice. QTL mapping has been carried out for most of alcohol-related traits: consequence of alcohol administration (Crabbe, Belknap, Mitchell, & Crawshaw, 1994); acceptance (Phillips & Crabbe, 1991; Phillips, Crabbe, Metten, & Belknap, 1994); preference (Phillips, Huson, Gwiazdon, Burkhart-Kasch, & Shen, 1995; Rodriguez, Plomin, Blizard, Jones, & McClearn, 1995). A large number of QTLs has been mapped for ataxic and hypothermic effects of alcohol (Crabbe, Phillips, Gallaher, Crawshaw, & Mitchell, 1996). All these studies have employed the Recombinant Inbred Strains (RIS). RIS are derived from intercrossed populations (F_2) that are maintained under brother × sister mating during several generations, providing inbred strains. In an RIS stock, the genotypes survive the individuals.

This method is popular because genotyping (tedious and expensive) is made once and is available in journals or on diskettes. A stock of RIS provides quickly candidate regions to locate QTLs. However, the method has strong and discouraging limitations for accurate QTL mapping. The number of strains is small in each set, reducing the number of QTLs that can be identified (Bayley, 1981). We must remember that one inbred strain is a replicated individual, and mapping a gene with a set of 25 inbred strains corresponds to a map with 25 individuals, even if the replicated individuals provide exceptionally high reliabilities for phenotyping and genotyping. The number of genes that can be detected decreases when the effect of the gene decreases. Consequently genes accounting for a small part of phenotypic variance can be ignored. Confidence intervals are generally wide and map positions based only on analysis of RIS should be interpreted with caution. This point is too often forgotten by most behavior scientists. Confirmation of one QTL should use linkage detection and congenic strains. This is done with too few exceptions (see Roubertoux, Raguenau, Baumann, & Semal, 1987, for an illustration of the joint strategies). The RIS between C57BL6 and DBA/2 strains are now used quasi-exclusively. They exhibit low average polymorphism for SSLPs (Dietrich et al., 1994) and for functional genes: 52% out of the 4006 available SSLPs differ. Researchers must move to more polymorphic strains and particularly to wild mice, which exhibit the highest polymorphisms compared to classic strains. The RIS method with the popular B6 and DBA/2 strains has provided some interesting candidate regions for genes involved in behavior but it will not provide the tool for accurate mapping. The stronger limitation is the large confidence interval obtained with RIS for candidate genes. This confidence interval is too large to permit co-detection of QTLs or walking on the chromosome. Confidence interval in RIS is not far from 12 centiMorgans, one centiMorgan being assumed to contain at least from 10 to 15 genes.

We can expect an exhaustive knowledge of the bases carried by the human and the murin genome (perhaps most of the genes) at the beginning of the 2nd millenium. Moreover, other genome projects that have started, with other species, will not be far behind in providing extensive maps. Mapping the candidate gene for a trait, at this time, will provide a candidate region. This region will include *n* genes. The function of every gene and thus its relevance for the trait will be investigated and tested either by transgenesis or by gene invalidation, according to the species. The larger the candidate region, the higher is the number of genes to test. The use of comparative mammalian maps requires very fine mapping too, to reach efficiency. This is why mapping within the smallest confidence interval is the main challenge in genetics today. RIS fails to met the challenge. The Advanced Intercross Lines were suggested first by Darvasi and Soller, (1995) to perform fine mappings (less than one centiMorgan). Advanced intercross lines are produced from an F_2 population generated from two inbred lines thus assumed homozygous for alternative alleles at a series of QTL and marker loci. The AILs, F3, F4, F5 . . . , are produced sequentially by randomly intercrossing the previous generation. For QTL mapping purposes, only the final generation is phenotyped and genotyped; the previous generations are only raised and reproduced. This method must be used with parental strains that exhibit large DNA polymorphisms, which is why C57BL6 and Castaneus strains, which present 98.5% SSLPs, were selected by P.L.R. to develop Advanced Intercross Lines. They have now reached the 10th generation. The fine-mapping strategy that will be offered by the Advanced Intercross Lines will provide progress.

HOW DO THE GENES ACT? CAN THEIR DISCOVERY TELL US SOMETHING ABOUT THE BIOLOGICAL MECHANISMS UNDERLYING AGGRESSION?

QTL detection leads to identify one candidate region and pave the road for walking on the chromosome to discover the gene. Sometimes the region where the QTL is mapped includes one identified gene that could be the gene implicated in the trait. We demonstrated that aggression in NZB and CBA/H is linked to gene(s) carried by the pairing region of the Y chromosome (see Table 1.2). The steroid sulfatase gene (*STS*) is mapped on this region and is a candidate gene. Several other genes have been described using recombinant DNA methods: receptor 1B for serotonin, nitric oxid syntase, α-Calcium-Calmodulin Kinase-II, and so on. Is the *STS* modulation involved in the mechanisms triggered by these genes?

Microsomal enzyme steroid sulfatase is expressed in the brain

The microsomal enzyme steroid sulfatase (STS, E.C.3.1.6.2) plays a central function in the neurosteroids mode of action because it is responsible for the switch between the sulfated and the free forms. This enzyme is ubiquitously distributed in mammalian tissues, where it hydrolyses several steroid sulfates, especially 3ß-hydroxysteroid sulfates. Human *Sts* gene has been cloned (Yen et al., 1987) and mapped to the distal portion of the short arm of the X chromosome that does not share recombination with the Y chromosome. The *Sts* gene is not functional on the Y chromosome. The situation is quite different in mice. Genetic studies using crosses of a STS-deficient mouse strain with normal animals in various combinations (Keitges, Rivest, Siniscalco, & Gartler, 1985; Soriano et al., 1987) have shown that the Y-linked gene is functional and undergoes obligatory recombination with its X-linked allele. Furthermore, the recent clonage of the murine *Sts* (Salido et al., 1996) confirmed that it escapes X-inactivation. All these studies were performed by estimating the STS enzymatic activity (i.e. the initial velocity of the steroid sulfate hydrolysis). There is no proof that this activity reflects a function of the gene, as the initial velocity of the substrate hydrolysis depends on several factors: individual tissue preparation, substrate concentration, presence of enzymatic inhibitors and integrity of the membrane structure, which regulates the function of the enzyme in its normal state as part of the microsomal membrane.

We started first with enzymatic activity of STS (Roubertoux et al., 1994a), then we purified the protein, then developed monospecific antibodies against murine steroid sulfatase to measure the protein itself (Mortaud et al., 1995). Both enzymatic activity and protein concentration are higher in the most attacking strain NZB compared to CBA/H. These measures were done with the liver. What happens with the brain? The concentration of aggressive strain is higher in the brain during development (Mortaud, Donzes-Darcel, Roubertoux, & Degrelle, 1996). A sexual dimorphism occurs at around 40 days. At this age, STS is higher in attacking males. Forty days is the time of puberty and, moreover, we have observed a peak of testosterone at this age. It was higher in NZB than in CBA/H. This might suggest that aggression was STS- and testosterone-dependant. But we found a co-segregation between aggression and the non-specific part of the Y, whereas aggression and the specific part of the Y did not co-segregate (see Table 1.2).

STS is involved in GABA A and N-methyl-D-aspartate receptor functioning

Attempts to establish causation between aggression and steroid measurement has provided contradictory conclusions (Arnold & Gorski, 1984; Carlier et al., 1990). The link is probably indirect. The recent discovery of steroids in the brain, either in free or in sulfated forms, exerting opposite effects, has put the focus on steroid sulfatase. The relationship between steroids and cerebral function may be reconsidered in light of the discovery of a biosynthetic pathway of steroidal compounds ensuring the synthesis of neurosteroids from cholesterol in the brain (Akwa et al., 1991). Steroids, such as 3β-hydroxy-5-pregnen-20-one (pregnenolone, Δ5P), 3β-hydroxy-5-androsten-17-one (dehydroepiandrosterone, DHEA), are present in the central nervous system of mammalian species as non-conjugated steroids, sulfate esters, and fatty acids esters (lipoidal derivatives). The brain accumulates substantial amounts of steroids metabolized from peripheral hormones or synthesized *de novo* in brain glial cells independently of peripheral steroidogenic sources, thus focusing on the possible physiological roles of neurosteroids (Akwa et al., 1991; Hawkinson et al., 1994). Several experiments have indicated the ability of neuroactive steroids to interfere with physiological, cellular, and behavioral phenomena (McEwen et al., 1995; Purdy, Morrow, Blinn, & Paul, 1990). Structure activity studies have established that several metabolites of progesterone, including 3α-hydroxysteroids (allopregnanolone, pregnanolone), bind to modulatory sites associated with the γ-aminobutyric acid (GABA$_A$)/ benzodiazepine receptor A complex. This effect is due to a stereoselective action of 3α-hydroxy A-ring reduced pregnane and androstane steroids on the GABA$_A$ receptor. These steroids are positive allosteric modulators of GABA$_A$ receptor-mediated Cl⁻ conductance (Koenig et al., 1995; Majewska, 1992). The GABA$_A$ receptor is an oligomeric protein complex that, when activated by agonists, increases neuronal membrane conductance to Cl⁻ ions, resulting in membrane hyperpolarization and reduced neuronal excitability. These neurosteroids have anxiolytic, anticonvulsant, and hypnotic properties that are related to their modulatory actions on GABA$_A$ receptors. The rates of average concentrations in the brain are identical in males and females, and given the probable compartmentalization of steroid distribution, this result implies the existence of rather high local concentrations (Arnold & Gorski, 1984; Corpéchot et al., 1981). An anti-aggressive effect of DHEA has been demonstrated in castrated male mice who attack in the presence of lactating females. This attack behavior, which does not appear in intact males, occurs in castrated animals and is suppressed by administering testosterone or estradiol. Small doses of DHEA could counteract the aggressiveness of castrated males. Δ5P is present in the olfactory bulb of male rats at a higher level than in the cerebral mean concentration. Δ5P levels selectively decrease in the olfactory bulbs of animals exposed to the scent of females in estrus. Furthermore, allopregnanolone (3α, 5α-THP) potentiates GABA agonistic activity and it has been reported that DHEA has a trophic effect on mouse neurons in culture and also reinforces long-term memory of active avoidance behavior (Kawashima & Takagi, 1994; Kawata, Yuri, & Morimoto, 1994; McEwen et al., 1995).

In contrast, the sulfate esters of pregnenolone (Δ5P-S) and DHEA (DHEA-S) as well as certain 3β-hydroxypregnane steroids have been shown to act as antagonists of the GABA$_A$ receptor complex. Δ5P-S and DHEA-S, which both specifically bind to synaptosomes, play a physiological role in the modulation of the $GABA_A$ receptor. Δ5P-S is also a positive modulator of the N-methyl-D-aspartate (NMDA) subtype of glutamate receptors (Mathis, Paul, & Crawley, 1994). They act as antagonists and block the effect of GABA on the chloride channel, reducing the frequency of openings in neurons in culture.

STS accounts for the switch between sulfated and free forms of steroids. The high level of STS concentration observed in the brain during pup development could be responsible for a regulation of the sulfated to free steroids ratio. High STS levels might lead to lower concentration of neurosteroid ester sulfates, inducing an increased GABAergic and a decreased glutamergic NMDA subtype activity. Thus, the antagonistic effect produced by neurosteroid sulfates on $GABA_A$ receptors would be reduced, whereas NMDA receptors would not be influenced by the agonistic effects of Δ5P-S. Cl⁻ chanel inhibiting function is predominant.

As pregnanolone has an agonistic effect on $GABA_A$ receptors, and as DHEA has a trophic effect on mouse neurons in vitro (Kawashima & Takagi, 1994; Kawata et al., 1994), it is possible that the switch carried out by STS towards nonsulfated neurosteroids plays a role in brain maturation after birth. Progesterone, which is produced from Δ5P, has potent neurotropic effects, regulating gene transcription in target neurons and glial cells (Kawashima & Takagi, 1994; Kawata et al., 1994). Differences observed between males and females during development may be explained by differential brain maturation. Indeed, the brain itself goes through a period of sensitivity to steroids. At this stage of development, the nervous tissue is highly plastic and some of the hormone effects are permanent.

DHEA and pregnanolone can potentially be involved in behavior. Several experiments have shown an anti-aggressive effect of DHEA in mice (Akwa et al., 1991). Several studies have suggested the implication of GABA in aggression (Majewska, 1992). Indirect suggestion of difference in NZB and CBA/H is provided by Martin, Desforges, and Chapouthier (1991). Chen et al. (1994) present evidence for implicating α-calmoduline-kinase II in both aggression and N-methyl-D-aspartate receptor functionning. We have no information about the possible implication of STS in 5-HT receptors.

These first indications suggest that STS plays a key role in aggression. STS acts as a modulator on different neurotransmitters. The potential modulation depends on allelic forms at the *Sts* locus and probably on genes at other loci that are involved in STS expression in the brain. Steroids have different effects on one receptor according to whether they are sulfated or not (Δ5P-S facilitates and Δ5P inhibits $GABA_A$ receptor, respectively). The effect of the same steroid is not in the same direction (Δ5P-S facilitates NMDA receptor and inhibits $GABA_A$ receptor). This consideration should be extended to the members of families or subfamilies of receptors of the same transmitter. The implication of STS in other transmitters or receptors, particularly those shown to be implicated in aggression by recombinant DNA methods, is still open.

These preliminary considerations concerning the physiological pathways between genes and behavior suggest that relationships between different biological levels of explanation and behavior are far from isomorphic. They should be considered in the near future in terms of patterns and not in terms of linear causation.

SOCIAL ISSUES FOR GENETIC ANALYSIS, THE LESSONS FROM THE WORK WITH MICE

Aggression has genetic correlates. This must not induce a false conception of these effects. Genes rarely act in a purely deterministic way. The effect is determinist for some diseases due to metabolic blocks. For most of the traits, this effect is probabilistic. It depends on several factors. An individual possesses an aptitude; he will exhibit the behavior if he is exposed to the events that will permit to display the behavior. Potentially aggressive mice could never display attack behaviors in a large terrarium where crowding is low. The environments act with the genotype effect in an additive or interactive way. Probability to display attack behavior depends in mice on preliminary exposure to male partners. This probability is strain-dependent, it is true for C57BL/6 and not for DBA/2. Carlier et al. (1991) have demonstrated that exposure to different maternal environments changes the genetic consequences of the gene carried by the pairing region of the Y in NZB and CBA/H crosses. Ovary transfer method was used, providing pups with well-defined genotypes, produced by mothers either from the isogenic genotype or from the hybrid genotype (F_1). The results are presented in Fig. 1.3. The proportions of attacking males are not the same for the same genotype (receiving the same pairing region of the Y) when it is exposed to different maternal environments. We have described several of these interactions between genotypes and well-identified components of maternal environments, for sensorial and motor measures of development and pup care behavior (see Roubertoux, Nosten-Bertrand, & Carlier, 1991, for a review). The main consequence of an interaction is to prevent any determinist prediction, either from an environmentalist or an hereditarist standpoint.

This experiment and the complexity shown for the physiological pathways between genes and behavior, described earlier, are of particular interest in behavior-genetic analysis due to possible racial and eugenic drifts.

First racial drift. Offending claims about the so-called genetic predisposition of African-American persons to crime, and particularly murder, are unfortunately well known. Rushton claims that African populations have evolved as a sub-species. Genes implicated in high testostrone concentration have been co-selected with genes for negritude. High testosterone concentration is related to lower intelligence and of course to aggression. Rushton has extended on the net similar claims to Gypsies. Last year, Whitney, as the Past President of the Behavior Genetics Association, delivered an unscientific address, in front of a captive audience, supporting the idea of a genetic basis for the high rate of crimes

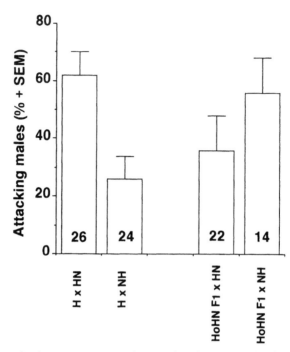

FIG. 1.3 Interaction between genotype and maternal environment. Males from two genotypes (H × HN and H × NH) were born and reared by two different mothers: H or HN F1. HoF1 HN mothers were HN females grafted with ovaries from the H strain (Carlier et al., 1991). Proportion of attacking males was measured with a standard opponent procedure with an A/J male. Sample sizes are shown in the columns.

among the African-American population in the US. This was published in *Mankind Quarterly*. Several members and officers left the audience. One of us (P.L.R.) resigned as President Elect and as member of the association. Other officers and members resigned too (Butler, 1995). These kinds of behavior could lead to the bankrupcy of our field of research. Remember the inconclusive results about the possible contribution of genes to aggression in our species. The difficulty of discovering genes for aggression in mice indicates how cautious we must be.

Second, possible eugenic drift. The discovery of numerous genetic correlates of aggression in mice and the multiple interactions between the different physiological mechanisms show a complicated picture. There is no reason to expect a simpler picture, in a more complex species, with nonexperimental situations. This should discourage any eugenic temptation and disgrace eugenics itself. Eugenics reduces one individual to one gene and one gene to one effect. Eugenics ignores pleiotropy and compensation by other genes. An individual is not reducible to one of his genes. He is the product of one genotype defined as a unique set of interacting genes. Both the genotype and the environment act to compensate the effect of most of the disfunctioning genes. An individual is also a personality resulting from the management of the difficulties produced by the gene. Assuming that there is one gene for aggression, eradication of the individuals carrying this gene would have erased Michelangelo, Caravaggio, Gesualdo, Jean Genet, Christopher Marlowe, Fernando de Roja, Cervantes, and many others.

ACKNOWLEDGEMENTS

UPR CNRS 9074 is affiliated with INSERM and Université d'Orléans. This research was supported by CNRS (UPR 9074), Ministry for Research and Technology (Université d'Orléans and Université Paris V-René Descartes), Région Centre and Préfecture de la Région Centre.

REFERENCES

Akwa, Y., Young, J., Kabbadj, K., Sancho, M. J., Zucman, D., Vourc'h, C., Jung-Testas, I., Hu, Z. Y., Le Goascogne, C., Jo, D. H., Corpéchot, C., Simon, P., Baulieu, E. E., & Robel, P. (1991). Neurosteroids: biosynthesis, metabolism and function of pregnenolone and dehydroepiandrostenone in the brain. *Journal of Steroid Biochemistry and Molecular Biology*, *40*, 71–81.

Arnold, A. P., & Gorski, R. A. (1984). Gonadal steroid induction of structural sex differences in the central nervous system. *Annual Review of Neurosciences*, *7*, 413–442.

Barkats, M., Bertholet, J. Y., Venault, P., Ceballos-Picot, I., Nicole, A., Phillips, J., Moutier, R., Roubertoux, P. L., Sinet P. M., & Cohen-Salmon, C. (1993). Hippocampal mossy fiber changes in mice transgenic for the human copper-zinc superoxide dismutase gene. *Neuroscience Letters*, *15*, 125–130.

Bayley, D. W. (1981). Recombinant inbred strains and bilineal congenic strains. In H. L. Foster, J. D. Small, & J. G. Fox (Eds.), *The mouse in biomedical research* (Vol. I, pp. 223–240). New York: Academic Press.

Brunner, H. G., Nelen, M., Breakfield, X. O., Ropers, H. H., & van Oost, B. A. (1993). Abnormal behavior associated with a point mutation in the structural gene for monoamine oxydase. *Science, 262,* 578–580.

Butler, D. (1995). Geneticists quit in protest at "genes and violence claims". *Nature, 378,* 224.

Cairns, R. B., MacCombie, J., & Hood, K. E. (1983). A developmental-genetic analysis of aggressive behavior in mice: I. Behavioral outcomes. *Journal of Comparative Psychology, 97,* 69–89.

Carlier, M., Roubertoux, P. L., Kottler, M. L., & Degrelle, H. (1990). Y chromosome and aggression in strains of laboratory mice, *Behavior Genetics, 20,* 137–156.

Carlier, M., Roubertoux, P. L., & Pastoret, Ch. (1991). The Y-chromosome effect on intermale aggression in mice is dependent upon the maternal environment, *Genetics, 129,* 231–236.

Cases, O., Seif, I., Grimsby, J., Gasper, P., Chen, K., Pournin, S., Müller, U., Aquet, M., Babinet, Ch., Shih, J. C., & De Mayer, E. (1995). Aggressive behavior and altered amounts of brain serotonin and norepinephrine in mice lacking MAOA. *Science, 268,* 1763–1766.

Chen, C., Rainnie, D. G., Greene, R. W., & Tonegawa, S. (1994). Abnormal fear responses and aggressive behavior in mutant mice deficient for α-Calcium-Calmodulin Kinase-II. *Science, 266,* 291–294.

Corpéchot, C., Robel, P., Lachapelle, F., Baumann, N., Axelson, M., Sjövall, J., & Baulieu, E. E. (1981). Characterization and measurement of dehydroepiandrostenone sulfate in the brain. *Proceedings of the National Academy of Sciences (USA), 78,* 4704–4707.

Crabbe, J. C., Belknap, J. K., Mitchell, S. R., & Crawshaw, L. I. (1994). Quantitative trait loci mapping of genes that influence the sensitivity and tolerance to ethanol-induced hypothermia in BXD recombinant inbred mice. *The Journal of Pharmacology and Experimental Therapeutics, 269,* 184–192.

Crabbe, J. C., Phillips, T. J., Gallaher, E. J., Crawshaw, L. I., & Mitchell, S. R. (1996). Common genetic determinants of the ataxic and hypothermic effects of ethanol in BXDTy recombinant inbred mice: genetic correlations and quantitative trait loci. *The Journal of Pharmacology and Experimental Therapeutics, 277,* 624–277.

Darvasi, A., & Soller, M. (1995). Advanced Intercross Lines, an experimental design for fine genetic mapping. *Genetics, 141,* 1199–1207.

DeBry, R., & Seldin, M. F. (1996). Human/Mouse homology relationships, *Genomics, 33,* 337–351.

Dib, C., Faure, S., Fizames, C., Samson, D., Drouot, N., Vignal, A., Millasseau, P., Marc, S., Hazan, J., Seboun, E., Lathrop, M., Gyapay, G., Morissette, J., & Weissenbach, J. (1996). A comprehensive genetic map on the human genome based on 5,264 microsatellites. *Nature, 380,* 152–154.

Dietrich, W., Miller, J., Steen, R., Merchant, M., Damron, D., Nahf, R., Gross, A., Joyce, D., Wessel, M., Dredge, L. D., Marquis, A., Stein, L. E., Goodman, N., Page, D. C., & Lander, E. S. (1994). A genetic map of the mouse with 4,006 simple sequence length polymorphisms, *Nature Genetics, 7,* 220–245.

Farrington, D. P. (1992). Trends in English juvenile delinquency and their explanation. *International Journal of Comparative and Applied Criminal Justice, 16,* 151–163.

Fisher, R. (1951). Limits to intensive production in animals. *British Agriculture Bulletin, 4,* 217–218.

Gariépy, J. L. (1995). The mediation of agressive behavior in mice. A discussion of approach/withdrawal processes in social adaptations. In K. E. Hood, G. Greenberg, & E. Tobach (Eds.), *Behavioral development. Research developmental and comparative psychology* (Vol. I, pp. 231–285). New York: Garland Publishing Inc.

Ginsburg, B., & Allee, W. C. (1942). Some effects of conditioning on social dominance and subordination in inbred strains of mice. *Physiology and Zoology, 15,* 485–506.

Goldsmith, D., & Gottesman, I. (1995). Heritable variability and variable heritability in developmental psychopathology. In M. F. Lenzenweger & J. J. Haugaard (Eds.), *Frontiers of developmental psychopathology.* New York: Oxford University Press.

Gora-Mazlak, G., McClearn, G. E., Crabbe, J., Phillips, T. J., Belknap, J. K., & Plomin, R. (1991). Use of recombinant inbred strains to identify quantitative traits loci in pharmacology. *Psychopharmacology, 104,* 413–424.

Guillot, P., Carlier, M., Maxson, S. C., & Roubertoux, P. L. (1995). Intermale aggression tested in two procedures using four inbred stains of mice and their reciprocal congenics: Y chromosome implications. *Behavior Genetics, 25,* 357–360.

Hawkinson, J. E., Kimbrough, C. L., McCauley, L. D., Bolger, M. B., Lan, N. C., & Gee, K. W. (1994). The neuroactive steroid 3α-hydroxy-5β-pregnan-20-one is a two-component modulator of ligand binding to the $GABA_A$ receptor. *European Journal of Molecular Pharmacology, 269,* 157–163.

Hirsch, J. (1963). Behavior genetics and individuality understood: behaviorism's counterfactual dogma blinded the behavioral sciences to the significance of meiosis. *Science, 142,* 1436–1442.

Hirsch, J. (1996). Défroquer les charlatans. *La Recherche, 283,* 78–79.

Hirsch, J., & McGuire, T. R. (1982). Introduction. In J. Hirsch & T. R. McGuire (Eds.), *Behavior-genetic analysis* (pp. 1–13). Stroudsburg, PA: Hutchinson Ross Publishing Company.

Kawashima, S., & Takagi, K. (1994). Role of sex steroids on the survival, neuritic outgrowth of neurons, and dopamine neurons in cultured preoptic area and hypothalamus. *Hormones and Behavior, 28,* 305–312.

Kawata, M., Yuri, K., & Morimoto, M. (1994). Steroid hormone effects on gene expression, neuronal structure, and differenciation. *Hormones and Behavior, 28,* 477–482.

Keitges, M., Rivest, M., Siniscalco, & Gartler, S. M. (1985). X-linkage of steroid sulphatase in the mouse is evidence for a functional Y-linked allele. *Nature, 315,* 226.

Koenig, H., Schumacher, M., Ferzaz, B., Do Thi, A. N., Ressouches, A., Guennoun, R., Jung-Testas, I., Robel, P., Akwa, Y., & Baulieu, E. E. (1995). Progesterone synthesis and myelin formation by schwann cells. *Science, 268*, 1500–1503.

König, M., Zimmer, A. M., Steiner, H., Holmes, P., Crawley, J., Brownstein, M. J., & Zimmer, A. (1996). Pain response and aggression in mice deficient in pre-proenkephalin. *Nature, 383*, 535–538.

Lagerspetz, K. (1961). Genetic and social causes of aggressive behavior in mice. *Scandinavian Journal of Psychology, 2*, 167–173.

Lagerspetz, K. M. J., & Lagerspetz, K. Y. H. (1971). Changes in the aggressiveness of mice resulting from selective breeding, training and social isolation. *Scandinavian Journal of Psychology, 12*, 241–248.

Majewska, M. D. (1992). Neurosteroids: endogenous bimodal modulators of the $GABA_A$ receptor. Mechanism of action and physiological significance. *Progress in Neurobiology, 38*, 379–395.

Martin, B., Desforges, C., & Chapouthier, G. (1991). Comparison between patterns of convulsions induced by two β-carbolines in 10 inbred strains of mice. *Neuroscience Letters, 133*, 73–76.

Mathis, C., Paul, S. M., & Crawley, J. N. (1994). The neurosteroid pregnenolone sulfate blocks NMDA antagonist-induced deficits in a passive avoidance memory task. *Psychopharmacology, 116*, 201–206.

Maxson, S. C. (1992a). Methodological issues in genetic analyzes of an agonistic behavior (offense) in male mice. In D. Goldowitz, D. Wahlsten, & R. Wimer (Eds.), *Techniques for the genetic analysis of the brain and behavior: Focus on the mouse* (pp. 349–374). Amsterdam: Elsevier.

Maxson, S. C. (1992b). Potential genetic models of aggression and violences in males. In P. Driscoll (Ed.), *Genetically Defined Animals Models of Neurobehavioral Dysfunctions* (pp. 174–188). Boston, MA: Birkhäuser.

Maxson, S. C. (1996). Searching for candidate genes with effects on an agonistic behavior, offense, in mice. *Behavior Genetics, 26*, 471–476.

Maxson, S. C., Ginsburg, B., & Trattner, A. (1979). Interaction of Y-chromosomal gene(s) in the development of intermale aggression in mice. *Behavior Genetics, 9*, 219–226.

McEwen, B. S., Gould, E., Orchinik, M., Weiland, N. G., & Woolley, C. S. (1995). Oestrogens and the structural and functional plasticity of neurons: implications for memory, ageing and neurodegenerative processes. In G. R. Bock & J. A. Goode (Eds.), *Non-reproductive actions of sex steroids. Ciba Foundation Symposium, 191* (pp. 52–73). Chichester, UK: Wiley.

McGuffin, P., & Katz, R. (1990). Who believes in estimates heritability as an end in itself? *Behavioral and Brain Sciences, 13*, 141–142.

McGuire, T. R., & Hirsch, J. (1977). General intelligence (g) and heritability (H2, h2). In I. C. Uzgiris, F. Weizmann, & J. McV. Hunt (Eds.), *The structuring of experience* (pp. 25–72). New York: Plenum.

Moffit, T. E. (1993). The neuropsychology of conduct disorders. *Developmental Psychopathology, 5*, 135–151.

Mortaud, S., Donzes-Darcel, E., Roubertoux, P. L., & Degrelle, H. (1995). Murine steroid sulfatase (*mSTS*): purification, characterisation and measurement by ELISA. *Journal of Steroid Biochemistry and Molecular Biology, 52*, 91–96.

Mortaud, S., Donzes-Darcel, E., Roubertoux, P. L., & Degrelle, H. (1996). Murine steroid sulfatase gene expression in the brain during post natal development and adulthood. *Neuroscience Letters, 215*, 145–148.

Nadeau, J. H., Davidson, M. T., Doolitle, D. P., Grant, P., Hilliard, A. L., Kosowsky, M., & Roderick, T. H. (1991). Comparative map for mice and humans, *Mammalian Genome, 1*, S461–S515.

Nelson, R. J., Demas, G. E., Huang, P. L., Fishman, M. C., Dawson V. L., Dawson T. M., & Snyder, S. H. (1995). Behavioral abnormalities in male mice lacking neironal nitric oxide synthase. *Nature, 378*, 383–386.

Phillips, T. J., & Crabbe, J. C. (1991). Behavioral studies of genetic differences in alcohol action. In J. C. Crabbe & R. A. Harris (Eds.), *The genetic basis of alcohol and drug actions* (pp. 25–104). New York: Plenum.

Phillips, T. J., Crabbe, J. C., Metten, P., & Belknap, J. K. (1994). Localization of genes affecting alcohol drinking in mice. *Alcoholism Clinical and Experimental Research, 18*, 931–941.

Phillips, T. J., Huson, M., Gwiazdon, C., Burkhart-Kasch, S., & Shen, E. H. (1995). Effects of acute and repeated ethanol exposures on the locomotor activity of BXD recombinant inbred mice. *Alcoholism Clinical and Experimental Research, 19*, 269–278.

Purdy, R. H., Morrow, A. L., Blinn, J. R., & Paul, S. M. (1990). Synthesis, metabolism and pharmacological activity of 3-α-hydroxy-steroids which potentiate GABA-receptor-mediated chloride ion uptake in rat cerebral cortical synaptoneurosomes. *Journal of Medical Chemistry, 33*, 1572–1581.

Ricker, J. P., & Hirsch, J. (1985). Evolution of an instinct under long-term divergent selection for geotaxis in domesticated populations of *Drosopila melanogaster*. *Journal of Comparative Psychology, 99*, 380–390.

Rodriguez, L. A., Plomin, R., Blizard, D. A., Jones, B. C., & McClearn, G. E. (1995). Alcohol acceptance, preference and sensitivity in mice. II. Quantitative trait loci mapping analysis using BXD recombinant inbred strains. *Alcoholism Clinical and Experimental Research, 19*, 367–373.

Roubertoux, P. L. (1992). Courtship behavior in the male guppy (*Pœcilia reticulata*): quantitative genetic analysis and directional selection, *International Journal of Comparative Psychology, 5*, 145–163.

Roubertoux, P. L., & Carlier, M. (1976). *Génétique et comportement*. Paris: Masson.

Roubertoux, P. L., & Carlier, M. (1987). Difference between CBA/H and NZB mice on intermale aggression. Maternal effects. *Behavior Genetics, 2*, 175–184.

Roubertoux, P. L., & Carlier, M. (1996). Le QI est-il héritable? Le consensus inventé par certains anglo-saxons n'existe pas. *La Recherche, 283*, 70–79.

Roubertoux, P. L., Carlier, M., Degrelle, H., Haas-Dupertuis, M. C., Phillips, J., & Moutier, R. (1994). Co-segregation of the pseudoautosomal region of the Y chromosome with aggression in mice. *Genetics, 135*, 254–263.

Roubertoux, P. L., Degrelle, H., Maxson, S. C., Phillips, J., Tordjman, S., & Dupertuis-Hass, M.-C. (1994a). Polymorphism for the alleles of the microsomal steroid sulfatase gene (*Sts*) in the pseudoautosomal region of the heterosomes of laboratory mice. *Comptes Rendus de l'Académie des Sciences, Paris, 317*, 523–527.

Roubertoux, P. L., Martin, B., Le Roy, I., Beau, J., Marchaland, C., Perez-Diaz, F., Cohen-Salmon, Ch., & Carlier, M. (1996b). Vocalizations in newborn mice: Genetic analysis. *Behavior Genetics, 26*, 427–437.

Roubertoux, P. L., Nosten-Bertrand, M., & Carlier, M. (1991). Additive and interactive effects between genotype and maternal environments, concepts and facts. *Advances in the Study of Behavior, 19*, 205–247.

Roubertoux, P. L., Raguenau, S., Baumann, L., & Semal, C. (1987). Early development in mice. IV. Age at disappearance of the rooting response; genetic analysis in newborn mice. *Behavior Genetics, 17*, 453–454.

Rutter, M. (1996). Introduction: concepts of antisocial behavior, of cause, and of genetic influences. In *Genetics of criminal and antisocial behavior. Ciba Foundation Symposium, 194* (pp. 1–20). Chichester, UK: Wiley.

Salido, E. C., Li, X. M., Yen, P., Martin, N., Mohandas, T. K., & Shapiro, L. J. (1996). Cloning and expression of the mouse pseudoautosomal steroid sulfatase gene (*Sts*). *Nature Genetics, 13*, 83–86.

Saudou, F., Amara, D. A., Dierich, A., Lemeur, M., Ramboz, S., Segu, L., Buhot, M.-C., & Hen, R. (1994). Enhanced aggressive behavior in mice lacking 5-HT$_{1B}$ receptor, *Science, 265*, 1875–1878.

Scott, J. P. (1992). Aggression: functions and control in social systems. *Aggressive Behavior, 18*, 1–20.

Signore, P., Nosten-Bertrand, M., Chaoui, M., Roubertoux, P. L., Marchaland, C., & Perez-Diaz, F. (1991). An assessment of handedness in mice. *Physiology and Behavior, 49*, 701–704.

Silva, A. J., Stevens, C. F., Tonegawa, S., & Yang, Y. Y. (1992). Deficient hippocampal long-term potential in α-calcium-calmodulin kinase-II mutant mice. *Science, 257*, 201–206.

Sluyter, F., Van Oortmerssen, G. A., Ruiter, A. J. H., & Koolhaas, J. M. (1996). Aggression in wild house mice: Current state of affairs. *Behavior Genetics, 26*, 489–495.

Soriano, P., Keitges, E. A., Schorderet, D. F., Harbers, K., Gartler, S. M., & Jaenisch, R. (1987). Hight rate of recombinaison and double crossover in the mouse pseudoautosomal region during male meiosis. *Genetics, 84*, 7218–7220.

Stewart, A. D., Manning, A., & Batty, J. (1980). Effects on Y chromosome variants on the male behavior of the mouse *Mus musculus*. *Genetic Research (Cambr.), 35*, 261–268.

Stoltenberg, S. F., & Hirsch, J. (1996). A gene correlate of geotaxis near *Adh* (2-50.1) in *Drosophila melanogaster*. *Journal of Comparative Psychology, 110*, 252–259.

Tordjmann, S. (1996). Association entre la sérotonine, les endorphines, les androgènes et le chromosome Y chez la souris: implication dans l'autisme infantile. UPR 1294. Thèse de doctorat de l'Université Paris XI.

Tordjmann, S., Roubertoux, P. L., Carlier, M., Moutier, R., Anderson, G., Launay, M., & Degrelle, H. (1995). Linkage between brain serotonin concentration and the sex-specific part of the Y-chromosome in mice. *Neuroscience Letters, 183*, 190–192.

Van Oortmerssen, G. A., & Bakker, T. C. M. (1981). Artificial selection for short and long attack latencies in wild *Mus musculus domesticus*. *Behavior Genetics, 11*, 115–126.

Van Oortmerssen, G. A., Benus, R. F., & Dijk, D. J. (1985). Studies in wild house mice: genotype-environment interaction for attack latency. *Netherland Journal of Zoology, 35*, 155–169.

Van Oortmerssen, G. A., & Sluyter, F. (1994). Studies in wild house mice. V. Aggression in selection lines for attack latency and their congenic for the Y chromosome. *Behavior Genetics, 24*, 73–78.

Wahlsten, D. (1990). Insensitivity of the analysis of variance to heredity-environment interaction. *Behavioral Brain Science, 13*, 109–161.

Weissenbach, J., Gyapay, G., Dib, C., Vignal, A., Morissette, J., Milasseau, P., Vaysseix, G., & Lathrop, M. (1992). A second-generation linkage map of the human genome. *Nature, 359*, 794–801.

Yen, P. H., Allen, E., Marsh, B., Mohandas, T., Wang, N., Taggart, R. T., & Shapiro, L. J. (1987). Cloning and expression of steroid sulfatase cDNA and the frequent occurrence of deletions in STS deficiency: Implications for X-Y interchange. *Cell, 49*, 443–454.

CHAPTER TWO

Evolution of the human mind

Michael C. Corballis
University of Auckland, Auckland, New Zealand

The hominids split from the apes some 5 million years ago. Evidence from modern African apes suggests that the pre-hominid apes probably possessed limited mind-reading skills and some form of communication through manual gestures. The early hominids were distinguished by bipedal locomotion, which would have imposed greater demands on parents in transporting and caring for their infants, enhancing mind-reading and perspective-taking. Bipedalism would also have freed the arms for a greater range of manual gestures for communication, allowing a sophisticated gestural language to emerge. In the early stages of hominid evolution, vocal communication was probably only a minor accompaniment to gesture, but may have assumed the dominant role with the emergence of *Homo sapiens* in Africa some 150,000 to 100,000 years ago. This switch may have been facilitated by the emergence and spread of a genetic allele that ensured that manual and vocal control emanated from the same (left) cerebral hemisphere in the majority of individuals. Vocal language again freed the hands and arms, leading to the development of more sophisticated technologies, allowing this species to radiate from Africa and replace the hominids, including the Neanderthals, who were descended from earlier migrants.

Les hominidés se sont séparés des primates il y a quelque 5 millions d'années. Des indices dégagés chez des primates africains modernes suggèrent que les primates antérieurs aux hominidés disposaient probablement d'habiletés limitées à discerner les états mentaux d'autrui, ainsi que d'une certaine forme de communication à l'aide de gestes manuels. Les premiers hominidés se sont distingués par la locomotion bipède, laquelle aurait imposé aux parents de plus grandes contraintes en ce qui a trait au transport de leurs jeunes enfants et aux soins à leur dispenser, d'où une amélioration de la capacité de discerner les états mentaux d'autrui et d'adopter différentes perspectives. La bipédie aurait aussi donné aux bras davantage de liberté pour exécuter une plus grande variété de gestes manuels à des fins de communication, ceci permettant l'émergence d'une langue gestuelle élaborée. Dans les premiers stades de l'évolution des hominidés, la communication vocale n'était probablement qu'un complément mineur du geste, mais elle a pu assumer le rôle principal avec l'apparition de l'espèce *Homo sapiens* en Afrique, il y a environ 100,000 à 150,000 ans. La transition a pu être facilitée par l'émergence et la diffusion d'un gène allélomorphe garantissant que contrôle manuel et contrôle vocal avaient pour origine le même hémisphère cérébral (le gauche) chez la majorité des individus. Encore ici, le langage vocal a libéré mains et bras, ce qui a conduit au développement de technologies plus complexes et permis à cette espèce de rayonner à partir de l'Afrique et de remplacer les hominidés, y compris les Néanderthaliens, qui descendaient de migrants plus anciens.

We humans have long considered ourselves to be fundamentally different from the other animals. Descartes (1647/1985), for example, argued that animals were mere automata, governed by mechanical principles, whereas humans were open to nonmaterial influences operating through the pineal gland. These influences allowed for free will, and an open-endedness of speech and action denied to other species. This idea of a fundamental discontinuity between humans and other animals was rudely shaken by Darwin's theory of natural selection, which implied that humans were descended from apes, and that the differences between humans and apes were ones of degree rather than kind. This issue remains as contentious as ever, and has profound implications for the way we treat other animals, the way we view death, the way we educate our children, and what we do at the weekend.

It also has profound implications for psychological theory. For a large part of the 20th century, Western psychology was in the grip of behaviorism, which carried the Darwinian assumption that there was nothing special separating us from other species. It mattered little whether we chose to study people, rats, or pigeons. Then, in the late 1950s, there came a Pied Piper called Noam Chomsky, who led all the rats away. Chomsky (1959), who has described himself as a Cartesian (Chomsky, 1966), showed that behaviorist principles could not capture the open-ended, generative, but rule-governed nature of human language, and the "cognitive revolution" was born. This re-established the human mind, rather than animal behavior, as the primary focus of psychological enquiry. In most important respects, the mind seemed to represent precisely what it was that separated humans from other animals.

More recently, the pendulum has begun to swing back. Genetic analysis has shown the extraordinary closeness of human and chimpanzee, dramatized chauvinistically in the title of one popular account, *The one percent advantage* by Gribbin (1988), and the question arises as to whether such a tiny difference in the genetic code can account for the evolution of such a momentous invention as mind. Research in animal cognition has led to a new respect for the mental capacities of animals, and in particular of our closest cousins, the African apes. Indeed, some see a greater discontinuity between the great apes and the other primates than between ourselves and the other apes, the most extreme manifestation being the "Great Ape Project", recently launched to confer on all great apes the ethical status of humans (Byrne, 1995).

HUMANS AS GREAT APES

The great apes comprise the orang-utans, gorillas, chimpanzees, and our own pre-human ancestors. As Fig. 2.1 shows, the great apes split from the other apes about 18 million years ago, and a second split about 16 million years ago separated the African apes, which include gorillas and two species of chimpanzees, from the line that led to the modern orang-utan (Friday, 1992). Including humans, the African apes comprise the superfamily known as *hominoids*. The precursors of humans, known as *hominids*, split from the chimpanzee line about 5 million years ago. These terms may change as increasing similarities between humans and apes are revealed. For example, it has been recently proposed that the term *hominoid* be extended back to include the orang-utans, that *hominid* include the chimpanzees and gorillas, and that humans and their precursors be known as *hominines* (Andrews, 1995; Martin, 1992). It would be premature for me to adopt this terminology, but it may be a sign of things to come.

In terms of DNA base sequences, humans appear to be closer to chimpanzees than chimpanzees are to gorillas (Diamond, 1988), but the anatomical similarity of chimpanzee to gorilla suggests that both have retained more "primitive" characteristics than have we humans. We can therefore expect to gain some appreciation of the mental capacities of the common ancestor of the apes and hominids from studies of the other African apes. The chimpanzee has commanded most interest, because it is our closest living relative. Molecular analysis shows that

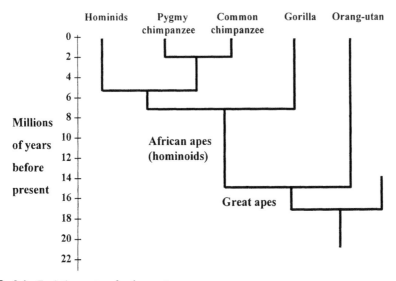

FIG. 2.1 Evolutionary tree for the great apes.

chimpanzees and humans are identical in 99.6% of their amino acid sequences and 98.4% of their DNA nucleotide sequences (Goodman, 1992).

Language

In assessing the mental capacities of the other African apes, investigators have not surprisingly focused on language, regarded by Descartes and many modern linguists, including Chomsky, as uniquely human. As this view has something of the quality of an edict, it may be seen as a challenge to prove that apes are capable of language. Attempts to teach chimpanzees to actually talk have never been successful (Kellogg, 1968). This need not mean that Descartes and Chomsky were right, because failure to talk might be due to deficiencies of the vocal tract rather than to the lack of any capacity for language. Greater success has been achieved in teaching a form of manual sign language, not only to a chimpanzee (Gardner & Gardner, 1969), but also to a gorilla (Patterson, 1978) and an orang-utan (Miles, 1990). Chimpanzees have also proven fairly adept at using plastic tokens (lexigrams) to represent objects and actions (Rumbaugh, 1977). But even the work on gestures and tokens has not been universally accepted as demonstrating true language, on the grounds that the animals' productions lack true syntax (Terrace, 1979), or are merely conditioned responses for food reward, without the generativity and spontaneity that characterize human language (Seidenberg & Pettito, 1987).

The most compelling evidence for something approaching genuine language in apes has come from the work of Savage-Rumbaugh on two young bonobos, or pygmy chimpanzees (*Pan paniscus*), named Kanzi and Mulika, who have learned to use gestures and lexigrams spontaneously while watching their mother being taught. Most of their productions are not random sequences or meaningless repetitions, but are spontaneous comments, requests, or announcements (Savage-Rumbaugh & Lewin, 1994). Kanzi even appears to have an understanding of spoken human language, with at least some regard to grammatical structure, at about the level of a two-year-old child (Savage-Rumbaugh et al., 1993). The common chimpanzee (*Pan troglodytes*) has also been observed to gesture spontaneously, and to teach signs spontaneously to a foster baby (Fouts, Fouts, & Van Cantfort, 1989).

Some are still not satisfied. Even after considering the exploits of Kanzi, Pinker (1994, p. 340) concludes that chimpanzees "just don't 'get it'". One of his counter-arguments is that many of the signs that chimpanzees have supposedly been taught actually occur naturally in the wild. But these signs may themselves hold the key to early language evolution. Chimpanzees in the wild extend hands in greeting, signal to others to halt, gesture for food or grooming, beckon for approach, and the stages in which these and other gestures emerge in young chimpanzees parallel closely those observed in human children (Plooij, 1978). It seems not unreasonable to conclude that our pre-hominid ancestors could have communicated with manual gestures, probably at the level of a pidgin language, and that this was the basis for the later evolution of more sophisticated language. The idea that language originated in manual gestures is a theme I shall develop later.

Mind-reading

Besides syntax, one of the properties of language is that it enables people to intentionally influence the *minds* of other people, implying an ability to mind-read. As Premack and Premack (1994) point out, we speak not merely to change the *behaviors* of others, but to change their *beliefs*. We attribute mental states to the people we talk to, and shape our language accordingly. It seems reasonable to assume that the ability to mind-read was a precursor to language (Baron-Cohen, 1995), which raises the question of whether great apes, even if they do not possess true language, might nevertheless be capable of mind-reading, or possess what Premack and Woodruff (1978) called a "theory of mind".

There is at least anecdotal evidence that they do. For example, animals often seem to indulge in tactical deception, where one individual acts so as to mislead another into believing something that is false. There are many instances of this in nonhuman species, but in many cases it can be attributed to simple association rather than mind-reading. A cat may go to the door and miaow loudly, deceiving its owner into thinking it wants to go outside. The owner goes to the door, and the cat quickly takes over the owner's warm chair by the fire. Tactical deception of this sort is quite widely observed in primates, and is also often seen in domestic cats and dogs, but seldom among nonprimates in the wild (Byrne, 1995). But the cat's deception is probably just a simple matter of learning that if it goes to the door and miaows, its owner will get up from the chair. To demonstrate that an animal is mind-reading, we need to know if its actions are *intentional* (Dennett, 1983).

It is not easy to infer intentionality, but there may be clues. For example, if the deceptive behavior is unusual, and therefore unlikely to be habitual or the result of trial and error, then it is reasonable to suppose that it is intentional. Byrne (1995) describes an instance recorded by Franz Plooij involving the behavior of chimpanzees being fed from a feeding box. A male chimpanzee arrived at the box just when a click at the box announced that food was available. Because a more dominant chimpanzee was also hovering nearby, the first chimpanzee acted as though he did not know food was there. His plan was evidently to return to the food later, when his more dominant rival had moved off. The dominant male did move away, but then hid behind a tree and peeped out at the first chimpanzee, who proceeded to open the box. The dominant chimpanzee was then able to relieve it of its food. Because the act of hiding and peeping is unusual for chimpanzees, Byrne suggests that it was genuinely intentional. Byrne and Whiten (1990) have collected over 100 anecdotes implying tactical deception in primates, but only 18 of those implied *intentional* deception. All were recorded in great apes, including orang-utans, gorillas, and both species of chimpanzee, except for one rogue event involving a baboon. This can be taken to imply that the great apes were capable of mind-reading, at some level at least, prior to hominid evolution.

Mind-reading also implies having the ability to represent one's *own* mind, and so to possess a concept of self. It has even been argued that knowledge of our own states of mind is no different in principle from knowledge of the states of mind of others, and depends on inference (e.g. Gopnik, 1993), suggesting that direct access to subjective experience is merely an illusion. If an ape can represent what is in the mind of another ape, then, it seems reasonable to expect it to also have a concept of self. One way to assess this is the mirror test, devised by Gallup (1970, 1977): If a mark is placed on an animal's forehead without its knowledge, and the animal is shown a reflection of itself in a mirror, does it then understand that the mark is on its own head? If so, it will presumably try to remove it. Monkeys evidently do not pass the mirror test, whereas at least some orang-utans and chimpanzees do (Gallup, 1977). Curiously, several gorillas have failed the test, leading to the suggestion that they may have lost this trait in the course of evolution (Povinelli, 1993). But not all chimpanzees pass the test (Swartz & Evans, 1991), and there is at least one home-reared gorilla who *is* vain enough to recognize his mirror reflection (Patterson, 1984). Human children pass the mirror test at around two years of age, although there is quite wide variation, depending in part on environmental influences (Lewis, Brooks-Gunn, & Jaskir, 1985). It seems reasonable to conclude that the common ancestor of the great apes was capable of some degree of self-recognition, perhaps at about the level of a two-year-old child, although a report that bottle-nosed dolphins pass the mirror test (Marten & Psarakos, 1994) raises the possibility of convergent evolution.

Humphrey (1976) has suggested that it was the complexity of the *social* world that shaped primate intelligence. Social pressures can be subtle, involving both co-operation and competition, leading to the emergence of what Byrne and Whiten (1988), in the title of their book, call "Machiavellian intelligence". The Machiavellian pursuit of individual gain in a social context would be greatly enhanced by the ability to mind-read: An animal with this ability could easily deceive its naive conspecifics for its own gain, or discern which are likely to be its friends. This in turn would favor selection of mind-reading in others, lest they be continually out-manoeuvred, with a consequent loss in reproductive fitness. Virus-like, the Machiavellian mind would have spread through the population.

Parker (1991) has a more benevolent view of primate intelligence, suggesting that the critical factor underlying the ability to mind-read might have been apprenticeship, especially in learning tool-aided extraction of food; an example is the use of twigs by chimpanzees to extract termites from their holes (Goodall, 1970). True apprenticeship implies awareness of oneself in relation to the other, whether as pupil learning from the instructor, or instructor tailoring actions to the needs of the pupil. The generality of Parker's hypothesis is unknown, as only chimpanzees and humans are known to engage in apprenticeship in extractive foraging (Parker & Mitchell, 1994).

It seems unlikely, though, that mind-reading was dependent entirely on social pressures, as social organization among chimpanzees, gorillas, or the relatively solitary orang-utans is no more complex than that of monkeys, who have not demonstrated any ability to mind-read (Byrne, 1995; Cheney & Seyfarth, 1988). Byrne (1995) has pointed out that intelligence in the great apes might reflect environmental as well as social challenges. Evidence for mental representation and intentionality in a nonsocial setting was first demonstrated by Kohler (1925), who recorded an incident in which a chimpanzee, finding that a stick was not long enough to rake in food, suddenly seized upon the idea of joining two sticks together. This kind of insight has since been observed in the other great apes as well (Byrne, 1995). It heralds the emergence of what might be called the *representational mind*, in which solutions to both social and practical problems can be found simply by thinking about them, without going through the painstaking process of trial and error.

It is dangerous to argue from ontogeny to phylogeny, but Premack (1988) nevertheless suggests as a useful rule of thumb that anything that cannot be done by a three-and-a-half-year-old child also cannot be done by a chimpanzee. This may actually be generous to the chimpanzee, since the three-and-a-half-year-old almost certainly outstrips the chimpanzee in grammatical sophistication. Pinker (1994, p. 276) describes the three-year-old as "a grammatical genius". A more conservative view, then, is that the chimpanzee is capable of a form of pidgin language and the ability to form mental representations, including those of their own and others' minds, at about the level of a two-year-old child. The child's mental development over the next two years may well hold the key to what distinguishes the human mind from the ape mind. This extra capacity must have arisen, in evolutionary terms, after the hominids split from the apes.

HUMANS AS HOMINIDS

In 1924, Raymond Dart came into possession of a skull with both human-like and ape-like features that had been found in a cave in Taung, South Africa. He christened it *Australopithecus africanus*, and hailed it as the "missing link" between human and chimpanzee (Dart, 1925, 1959). This momentous discovery has been followed by a great many other discoveries of hominid remains from Africa, so that the missing link has become not merely a chain, but a tangle of chains, all but one of which led to eventual extinction. Figure 2.2, adapted from Wood (1994), shows the hominid species thought to have occupied the time gap from the common ancestor of ourselves and *Pan*, the chimpanzee, some 5–6 million years ago, to the present-day survivor, *Homo sapiens*. There is some

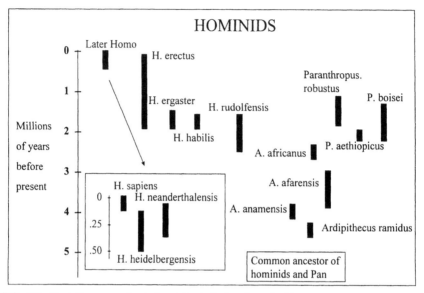

FIG. 2.2   Evolutionary tree for the hominids, including *Australopithecus anamensis*. Adapted with permission from "The oldest hominid yet", by B. Wood, 1994, *Nature*, 371, p. 280. Copyright 1994 Macmillan Magazines Ltd.

controversy over both the number and names of species involved, but Fig. 2.2 at least shows the complexity of the transitions from ape to human.

Bipedalism

The main characteristic that distinguishes the hominids from the apes is bipedalism, involving a reshaping of the pelvis to enable upright walking. Until recently, the earliest known hominid was *Australopithecus afarensis*, dating from about 3.6 million years ago, and there is clear evidence that this species was bipedal (Latimer & Lovejoy, 1990; Leakey, 1979). Evidence on the newly dis-covered *Ardipithecus ramidus*, the earliest species tentatively classified as a hominid, is not yet decisive as to whether or not it was bipedal, although the anterior placement of the foramen magnum (where the spine enters the skull) suggests that it might have been (White, Suwa, & Asfaw, 1994, 1995). Another recent discovery, *Australopithecus anamensis*, dating from 3.9 to 4.2 million years ago, does appear to have been bipedal (Leakey, Feibel, McDougall, & Walker, 1995). These two species lie very close to the common ancestor of the hominids and *Pan*; indeed, Wood (1994) suggests that if any species deserves to be called the "missing link", it is *Ardipithecus ramidus*.

There has been much speculation as to why bipedalism evolved. It is gener-ally assumed that it had to do with geological changes during the late Miocene and early Pliocene—a period during which there is a gap in the fossil record.

Up to about 8 million years ago, both East and West Africa consisted mainly of forests and woodlands, and the primates were adapted to brachiation—the ability to swing by the arms from the branches of trees. Then the continent of Africa collided with Eurasia, creating an upward pressure that formed the highlands of Kenya and Ethiopia. This eventually caused the earth's crust to crack, creating the Great Rift Valley, and much of the forest and woodland to the east gave way to savanna, or open terrain. The primates who inhabited this area evolved alternative forms of locomotion that enabled them to move through open spaces, as they could no longer rely on brachiation as the primary means of getting around.

But why bipedalism? Chimpanzees and gorillas adopt a quadrupedal method of locomotion known as knuckle-walking, but there must have been some factor that favored a switch to an upright stance. Lovejoy (1981) suggests that the inhabitants of the area east of the Great Rift Valley were forced into a nomadic existence, moving from one location to another in the search for food, and knuckle-walking may have been simply less efficient than upright walking, especially over long distances. A further advantage of bipedalism is that it would have freed the hands for carrying things, including the transportation of scavenged food to the home base.

Savage-Rumbaugh (1994) has made the radical suggestion that the hominids did not switch from knuckle-walking at all, but rather that bipedalism evolved directly from brachiation. Gibbons and siamangs, the modern lesser apes, are brachiators, but they walk bipedally when they cross open terrain. The common ancestor of humans and the great apes was therefore almost certainly a suspensory animal that spent most of the time in the trees, but moved bipedally when it became necessary. Knuckle-walking may therefore have been restricted to the gorilla and chimpanzee, evolving *independently* in these two species. From a cladistic point of view, this theory lacks parsimony, because it implies parallel evolution of knuckle-walking—although the alternative view that locomotion evolved from a mix of brachiation and bipedalism, through knuckle-walking, and back to bipedalism may seem equally unparsimonious (see Fig. 2.3). The fossil evidence is silent, because of the lack of fossils in East Africa between about 8 million and 4.5 million years ago.

There is much that is plausible about Savage-Rumbaugh's scenario. As we have seen, there may have been at least two bipedal hominids dating from at least 4 million years ago, namely *Ardipithecus ramidus* and *Australopithecus anamensis*, although the theory would prove to be wrong if *Ardipithecus ramidus* turns out to have been a knuckle-walker. Andrews (1995) raises the possibility that these early species may have been bipedal apes that were not part of the hominid line at all. Study of the ways in which monkeys, gibbons, chimpanzees, and humans walk has suggested that "the bipedal walking of the gibbon is closest to man" (Yamazaki, 1985, p. 129). Moreover, the fossil remains of a relatively large-brained (400cc) primate known as *Oreopithecus*, dating from 8–9 million years ago, reveal many of the characteristics of a common ancestor to the

Two Evolutionary Scenarios

1. Conventional   2. Savage-Rumbaugh (1994)

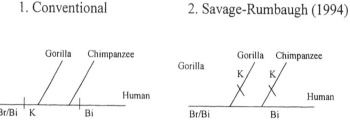

Br = brachiator; Bi = bipedal; K = knuckle walker

FIG. 2.3   Two different evolutionary scenarios for the evolution of knuckle-walking and bipedalism.

African ape and *Homo*, including skeletal adaptations for bipedalism (Pilbeam, 1972). Finally, the quadrupedal walking of the orang-utan involves the palms of the hands, not the knuckles (Savage-Rumbaugh, 1994), which is closer to the way that humans clamber if forced to move quickly on all fours.

In this view, then, it is gorillas and chimpanzees, not the bipedal hominids, who constitute the special case, by knuckling down. Why did they do so? Savage-Rumbaugh (1994) suggests that it had to do with the problem of transporting infants across open terrain. For a long-armed primate, one solution is to reach down with the arms and walk on all fours, so that the weight of the clinging infant is supported by the arms as well as the legs. The idea that this solution may have evolved independently in the gorilla and chimpanzee helps resolve one of the paradoxes of hominoid evolution. It is commonly assumed that chimpanzees are closer in evolutionary terms to the gorilla than to humans, because chimpanzees and gorillas appear to share more traits (including knuckle-walking), but the biomolecular evidence suggests that chimpanzees are closer to humans (Diamond, 1988; Sibley & Ahlquist, 1987). The apparent similarity of chimpanzees to gorillas, then, may be partly the result of convergent evolution rather than common ancestry.

With quadrupedal walking the infant can simply cling to the parent, and little parental monitoring is required. But if the infant is carried by a bipedal parent, there is a much greater onus on the parent to monitor it and ensure its well-being. If the infant is put down, it must be put in a safe place, and the parent must later remember to pick it up. The greater need for parental attention would have placed the infant at greater risk, but for those who survived and adapted there were longer-term gains. The foot was no longer involved in clinging, allowing it to become better adapted to bipedal walking. The parent could also cradle the infant's head, allowing for an increase in brain size that would not be possible if the infant had to support its own weight. More generally and importantly, survival would be enhanced to the extent that the parent was able to adopt the mental perspective of the child as well as of herself, and this may have been critical in the enhancement of the ability to mind-read (Savage-Rumbaugh, 1994).

Prolongation of infancy

One disadvantage of bipedalism is that it places limits on the width of the maternal pelvis, severely constraining brain size at birth. In humans, giving birth is a difficult and often hazardous business. But even this impediment seems to have been turned to advantage. Compared to human infants, the newborns of other primates are well developed at birth, whereas the human infant, relatively speaking, is born about nine months prematurely (Krogman, 1972); as Gould (1980) puts it, the child is effectively an embryo for the first nine months of its life. This results in a prolongation of infancy and childhood, and it is during growth that the brain is most receptive to environmental influences. The brain of the newborn chimpanzee is about 60% of its ultimate weight, compared with about 24% for the newborn human. The human brain is therefore much more open to environmental impact than is the chimpanzee brain. This is surely one of the major factors in the evolution of the human mind, and was probably critical to the evolution of language.

Brain size

The prolongation of infancy is not simply a matter of premature birth. The human brain also grows to a larger size than that of the other primates, even when taking body size into account. Passingham (1982) calculates that the human brain is about three times the size one would expect for a primate of our build, which he regards as "perhaps the single most important fact about mankind" (p. 78). A measure that is more suggestive of continuity, and one that may bear more relevance to the evolution of mind, is the so-called *neocortex ratio*, which is the ratio of the volume of neocortex to the volume of the rest of the brain (Dunbar, 1993). In humans, this ratio is 4.1:1, which is about 30% larger than that of any other primate. Dunbar suggests that an animal's cognitive capacity establishes an upper limit to the number of individuals with which the animal can maintain personal relationships, and presents evidence that the neocortical ratio correlates strongly with group size. Byrne (1995) further shows a linear relation in primates between the neocortex ratio and the prevalence of tactical deception.

The australopithecine brain was little larger in absolute terms than that of the chimpanzee, but it was clearly larger when body size is taken into account (Kappelman, 1996). Absolute brain size increased dramatically over the successive stages from *Homo habilis*, through *Homo erectus*, to *Homo sapiens* (Falk, 1987). Although the name *Homo habilis* means "handy man", and was derived from the association of this species with the earliest stone tools, it is unlikely that tools played a significant role in the expansion of the brain. For one thing, the increase in brain size may be misleading because of measurement problems. According to Kappelman (1996), when body mass is taken into account there was virtually no increase in brain size over nearly 2 million years of evolution in *Homo*, but then came a dramatic increase with the appearance of *Homo sapiens*, and even this last increase appears to have been driven by selection for smaller body mass than for a larger brain. Another reason to suspect that tools played little role is that the creation of simple Oldowan tools appears to be within the competence of modern chimpanzees (Toth, Schick, Savage-Rumbaugh, Sevcik, & Rumbaugh, 1993; Wynn & McGrew, 1989), and it has been claimed that the tool culture of Tai chimpanzees, although not involving the making of stone tools, represents a comparable stage of development (Boesch & Boesch, 1984). The Acheulian culture associated with *Homo erectus* around 1.6 million years ago was more sophisticated, but the development of tools was actually very slow, with little change for tens of thousands of years at a stretch (Foley, 1987). Only after the emergence of *Homo sapiens* did manufacture really begin to accelerate, to the extent that it now dominates our lives.

It is more likely, then, that the increase in brain size in hominid evolution was driven by social factors rather than by emerging technology. I argued earlier that the chimpanzee appears to be roughly comparable to a two- to three-year-old child in the capacity for mind-reading and self-awareness, and that the development over the next few years may hold the key to what distinguishes the human mind from that of the ape. What is the nature of that development?

Dissociation, episodic memory, and mental time travel

Three-year-olds are capable of some degree of mental attribution, but appear to be incapable of the degree of dissociation that enables them to simultaneously hold *different* mental states. For example, a child may believe there are smarties in a smarties box, but then is shown that there are pencils in the box. Three-year-olds fail to understand that this knowledge is not available to another person, and was not available to themselves before they were shown what the box contained; that is, they wrongly predict that another child will believe the box to contain pencils, and deny that they themselves once believed it to contain smarties.

These observations tie in with evidence that true episodic memory in children does not emerge until some time between the ages of three and four (Pillemer & White, 1989). At the age of two-and-a-half, infants may recall a few fragments of past episodes, but only between three and four do they begin to travel mentally into the past and construct episodes as narrative sequences. The failure of episodic memory in three-year-olds is further substantiated by the finding that they have severe difficulty recalling the source of their current knowledge, even though it may have occurred only minutes beforehand (Gopnik & Graf, 1988).

If true dissociation does not develop in the human child until about the age of four, we may then ask whether chimpanzees, or any other nonhuman animals, *ever* attain this level of cognitive development. Are nonhuman animals capable of episodic memory, for example? Tulving (1983, 1984) has suggested that they are not, but this has been disputed. Animal behavior often depends on the trace of an earlier event, as in delayed conditioned discrimination task, or when a foraging animal must remember not to go to the same flower twice to obtain nectar (Suddendorf, 1994). According to Olton (1984), such observations imply that the animal "represents" a past event, and therefore possesses episodic memory. But, as Dretske (1982) points out, this kind of representation may be causal rather than informational, and need not imply true episodic memory. In elaborating his view of episodic memory, Tulving (1993, p. 67) states:

> The owner of an episodic memory system is not only capable of remembering the temporal organization of otherwise unrelated events, but is also capable of mental time travel: Such a person can transport at will into the personal past, as well as into the future, a feat not possible for other kinds of memory.

The idea that mental time travel itself might be uniquely human is not without precedent. Although Kohler (1925) was able to show that chimpanzees could use mental processes such as insight to solve problems, he also noted that they apparently had little capacity to extrapolate into the past or future. Donald (1991) has remarked similarly that the lives of apes "are lived entirely in the present" (p. 149), and the same idea has been expressed by Bischof (1978), Savage-Rumbaugh (1994), and Suddendorf (1994, Suddendorf & Corballis, 1997).

Language

In contrast, we humans make frequent reference to events in the past and future, and this is nowhere more obvious than in our language. This suggests that language itself may be intimately related to the emergence of dissociation and mental time travel. If the dissociation that allows for mental time travel does not emerge until the third or fourth year, it may therefore be no coincidence that language also undergoes major development over the same period, with rapid increase in vocabulary, sentence length, and syntactic complexity, and is essentially established in about the fourth year (Pinker, 1994). In evolutionary terms, that aspect of language that gives expression to mental time travel may have emerged only after the split of the hominids from the apes.

There is a common belief, implicit in the writings of Chomsky, that language emerged fully fledged, presumably late in hominid evolution, and that there can have been no intermediate steps. Premack (1985), for example, remarks that "nature provides no intermediate steps, nothing between the lowly call system and the towering human language" (p. 276). He nevertheless speculates about the possibility of an intermediate stage that was lost in antiquity. Bickerton (1986) suggests that we do not need to search in the mists of antiquity—an intermediate stage that is higher than the call systems of animals can be discerned in pidgin languages prior to creolization, in the best efforts of Kanzi and other trained apes or dolphins, and in the speech of the two-year-old child, or of children deprived of linguistic input, such as Genie (Fromkin, Krashen, Curtiss, Rigler, & Rigler, 1974). Premack (1986) adds a further example—the drunken teenager. But even this concession implies that the emergence of language from this relatively primitive state was an all-or-none affair, a "big bang" (Bickerton, 1995). Another member of the "big bang" club, Piattelli-Palmarini (1989), states that the fossil record is incomplete, "not because the intermediate forms have been lost *for us*, but because they simply never existed" (p. 8).

This neo-creationist doctrine has been effectively challenged by Pinker and Bloom (1990), who argue cogently for the gradual evolution of language through natural selection, while still maintaining that language is a uniquely human adaptation. Others have explicitly linked the emergence of language to the gradual increase in brain size, and especially to the expansion of frontal and parietal neocortex, over the past 2 million years (Greenfield, 1991; Wilkins & Wakefield, 1995). These developments are challenging the view that language is special, a view still held by authors such as Pinker (1994) who even proposes specialized "grammar genes" (p. 299).

Language as gesture

A gradualist account of language evolution gains a good deal of support from the notion that language emerged, not from vocal calls, but from manual gestures. This idea has a long history. It was proposed in the 18th century by Condillac (1746/1947), and further discussed by Degerando (1800/1969) in a book designed to help explorers communicate with primitive peoples. It was revived by Hewes (1973), given slightly different shape by myself (Corballis, 1991, 1992) and others (e.g. Kendon, 1991), and developed into coherent if radical scenarios in recent books by Givon (1995) and Armstrong, Stokoe, and Wilcox (1995). The evidence for it is, I believe, almost overwhelming.

First, some anatomical considerations: As in present-day apes, the dominant sensory modality of the early hominids was undoubtedly vision. The capacity to analyze acoustic signals was comparatively limited, as was the vocal repertoire. Lieberman (1984, 1991) has claimed that the production of speech was not possible until the larynx descended in the neck, and that this adaptation, as well as concomitant changes in the brain mechanisms involved in producing speech, occurred only recently in human evolution, and perhaps only with the emergence of *Homo sapiens*. According to Lieberman, even the Neanderthals of 30,000 years ago would have suffered gross speech deficits that not only kept them apart from anatomically modern humans, but led to their eventual extinction (Lieberman, 1992). Lieberman's claims are controversial. Falk (1975), for example, has argued that if the reconstruction of the Neanderthal vocal tract proposed by Lieberman, Crelin, and Klatt (1972) were accurate, the creature would have been unable to swallow—although Lieberman (1982) has retorted that if Falk were right the chimpanzee would be unable to swallow either! Duchin (1990) has argued that the evolution of the tongue was more critical than that of the larynx, and her analyses suggest that the tongue would have been capable of producing articulate speech sounds in *Homo erectus*.

Whatever the precise timing of changes to the vocal tract, there can be little doubt that the evolution of a vocal tract capable of producing articulate speech lagged behind the evolution of a manual system capable of producing articulate gesture. Monkeys and apes are already partly bipedal, and the hands and arms are well adapted for activities requiring considerable flexibility, such as picking fruit, manipulating objects, making tools, throwing, and even gesturing. It is not surprising, then, that great apes have shown virtually no capacity for vocal speech (Hayes, 1952), but have been moderately successful in producing coherent manual gestures, numbering in the hundreds (Gardner & Gardner, 1969; Patterson, 1978; Savage-Rumbaugh & Lewin, 1994). The emergence of a fully bipedal stance in the early hominids would have enhanced an already considerable potential for generating communicative gestures.

Givon (1995) makes the additional point that the brain centers involved in the comprehension of language, including areas that make up what is loosely known as Wernicke's area, straddle visual areas in the cortex, especially those along the so-called ventral stream that runs from the visual cortex to the inferior temporal region. This stream is associated in the monkey with the recognition of visual form (Ungerleider & Mishkin, 1982). This suggests that the initial codes for language may have been visual rather than auditory, but the point is a fine one as the language-decoding areas also lie close to primary auditory cortex. Similarly Broca's area, now thought to be largely involved in the coding and decoding of grammar, lies close to the areas involved in both articulatory motor control and control of the arms and hands. The neurological evidence does not clearly support a visuo-manual over an audio-oral basis for language, in my view, but does support a close relation between the two.

Next, the linguistic argument: Research over the past three decades has established beyond reasonable doubt that American Sign Language (ASL) is a natural human language, and not the "You Tarzan, me Jane" sort of pidgin it was once thought to be (Klima & Bellugi, 1979; Poizner, Klima, & Bellugi, 1987). It is acquired by children in very much the same way that speech is acquired. For example, deaf infants exposed to ASL babble in the same way that hearing children do, except that they babble with elements of sign (Pettito & Marentette, 1991), and there is evidence for a sensitive period in the learning of ASL just as there is for spoken language (Newport, 1990). Like speech, ASL also depends primarily on the left cerebral hemisphere (Neville, 1991; Poizner et al., 1987). Indeed, the discovery that sign language is truly linguistic reinforces the idea, attributed to Neisser (1976), that even *spoken* speech might be better regarded as comprised of gestures rather than as sequences of abstract phonemic segments (e.g. Mowrey & MacKay, 1990; Studdert-Kennedy, 1987).

The linguistic argument can be taken further. One of the barriers to understanding the evolution of spoken language is its highly abstract nature. With rare exceptions, the "bow-wow" theory of the origin of speech does not work—the sounds of words bear no resemblance to the things they represent. The signs of ASL, in contrast, include a much higher proportion of elements that are iconic (Armstrong et al., 1995). For example, the sign for *I know that* consists of bending the right hand and touching the forehead with the fingertips—tapping one's head to show that the message has sunk in. Of course, the bow-wow theory does work for some words that describe sounds, like *snap*, *crackle*, and *pop*, but it so happens that most of the things we talk about are spatial rather than acoustic, and do not lend themselves to vocal mimicry. If the origins of language did lie in manual gestures, then the bow-wow theory should perhaps be replaced by what I like to call the "wag-wag" theory.

Another property of spoken language is what is known as *duality of patterning*, which refers to the fact that the rules governing the assemblage of phonemes into morphemes are independent of the rules for generating meaningful utterances from morphemes. Duality is seen by some as the critical step in language evolution (e.g. Pulleyblank, 1986). However, it does not appear to exist in ASL. Individual signs have the same compositional structure whether they are regarded as word or sentences. For example, the sign for *catch* involves moving one arm around the front of the body so that the hand grasps the upright finger of the other hand. This action can be seen equally as a sentence: *I catch it*. As Armstrong et al. (1995) point out, "an action of the hand and arm (or hands and arms) has the potential for symbolizing *either* a word *or* a sentence" (p. 21, emphasis in original). Duality of patterning may therefore not be intrinsic to language itself, but may have arisen as a consequence of the switch from manual to vocal communication. Because vocal communication lacks the iconic component, it was necessary to develop arbitrary conventions and rules of assembly.

ASL is therefore more iconic than spoken language, and is without the duality of patterning that characterizes speech. It includes a strong three-dimensional, spatial component, adding to its iconicity, whereas spoken language is rigidly linear. Given that most of the things we talk about involve space as well as time, gesture provides a more direct and easily interpretable medium of communication than does speech, and we all resort to mime and gesture when trying to communicate with those who speak another language. Other authors, including Kendon (1991) and Donald (1991), have proposed similarly that mime was critical to the transition from ape to hominid, and it seems likely that early gestures were primarily mimes, although they would no doubt have become more abstract and conventionalized over time. The transition from iconic to abstract representation is a well-established principle in the evolution and development of animal communication. It probably applied to the development of grammar as well as the lexicon, and it also characterized the development of writing systems from early pictograms to the abstract graphemes of present-day scripts (Givon, 1995).

One particular gesture that would almost certainly have played an important role in the early evolution of language is pointing (Hewes, 1981; Kendon, 1991). Human infants seem to understand the pointing of others by about 12 months of age, and can themselves point intentionally by about 14 months (Butterworth & Grover, 1988). Chimpanzees can be taught to respond to pointing by looking in the direction of a pointing finger, but have not themselves been successfully taught to point (Woodruff & Premack, 1979). The index finger became progressively longer relative to the other fingers in hominid evolution from about 4 million to 1.7 million years ago (Hilton, 1986). It has been argued that pointing was a precursor to the use of words to refer to objects (Bruner, 1983), but it may equally have served as the primary means of referring to objects in early gestural language. Hewes (1981) notes that pointing or pointing movements make up some 20–30% of the signs in existing sign languages.

We still gesture as we speak—some, it must be said, more than others. These gestures are often regarded as not linguistic, but as merely ancillary to speech, serving emotional or metalinguistic functions. This has been disputed, however, by McNeill (1985), who has documented the close correspondences between speech and gesture, arguing that they form a single, unified system. Kimura (1992) notes that one cannot dissociate the left-hemispheric lesions responsible for aphasia for sign language from those responsible for (nonlinguistic) manual apraxia. Even so, the gestures we make while speaking are unlike conventional sign languages in that they are holistic and imagistic, serving to complement the segmental, combinatorial properties of the speech itself. Unlike sign languages, they cannot be understood in the absence of speech. Goldin-Meadow, McNeill, and Singleton (1996) have shown, however, that when hearing adults are forced to communicate with sign, abstaining from speech, their gestures then do begin to assume the combinatorial structure of conventional sign language. That is, it is the act of speaking itself that "handcuffs" (p. 34) the accompanying gestures, restricting them to global and impressionistic forms.

I propose, then, that the origins of language lie in gesture and mime, going back to the pre-hominid apes, but receiving a special impetus with the emergence of a fully bipedal stance. Early gestural language was no doubt punctuated by vocalizations, just as present-day speech is embellished by gesture. The vocal component probably grew in importance, and at some stage took over the dominant role. I shall suggest later that this occurred with the emergence of *Homo sapiens*. First I need to consider another characteristic that is sometimes thought to differentiate the hominids from other primates.

Laterality

The great majority of humans are right-handed and have language represented primarily in the left cerebral hemisphere. Until quite recently, it has been supposed that these population biases are species-specific, but there is growing evidence for related asymmetries in other species, including nonhuman primates. MacNeilage, Studdert-Kennedy, and Lindblom (1987) argued that at least some nonhuman primates show a slight but consistent preference for the *left* hand, especially in visually guided reaching. While it might seem perverse to suppose that this might bear on human *right*-handedness, MacNeilage et al. suggest that in our primate ancestors, as in modern monkeys, the right hand played the supporting role while the left hand was used for catching insects or reaching for berries, and that, with the evolution of bipedalism, it was the right hand that was freed for more manipulative actions.

Chimpanzees in the wild show no consistent handedness in using tools, either to crack nuts (Boesch, 1991; Sugiyama, Fushimi, Sakura, & Matsuzawa, 1993) or to extract termites using twigs (McGrew & Marchant, 1992). There is nevertheless some evidence for a trend toward right-handedness in great apes when they are required to reach from a bipedal rather than a quadrupedal posture (Hopkins, 1993; Hopkins, Bennett, Bales, Lee, & Ward, 1993), and there is also evidence that in gorillas (Byrne & Byrne, 1991), bonobos (Hopkins & de Waal, 1995), and chimpanzees (Hopkins, 1994) the right hand takes the more active, manipulative role in feeding. These biases are slight relative to human hand preference. Hopkins (1994) found that just under 50% of chimpanzees preferred the right hand in feeding, compared with about 20% preferring the left hand, with the remainder being ambidextrous. Similarly, Hopkins (1995) tested 110 chimpanzees for hand preference in extracting peanut butter from a tube, and found that 67% of them used the right hand while holding the tube in the left hand.

These data suggest a bias that, when present, favors the right hand over the left in about a 2:1 ratio. There are also many asymmetries in humans that approximate this ratio (Previc, 1991). These include the enlargement of the left temporal planum relative to the right (Geschwind & Levitsky, 1968), an enlargement of the left side of the face relative to the right (Burke, 1971), an advantage of the right ear in monaural sensitivity (Ward, 1957), a tendency for neonates to lie with their heads to the right (Goodwin & Michel, 1981), and many others—all of which might be related to a leftward positioning of about 67% of fetuses in the final trimester of pregnancy (Churchill, Igna, & Senf, 1962). Previc (1991) suggests that there may be two independent sources of asymmetry arising from asymmetric prenatal development, a craniofacial asymmetry and a left-otolith dominance. A similar ratio also occurs in data from hominid artifacts going back to the lower Pleistocene of about 1.9 million years ago. Toth (1985) found that the shapes of flakes struck from stones by early hominids were characteristically asymmetrical. Those suggestive of right-handed operation outnumbered left-handed flakes by about 57:43 among the earliest samples, increasing to about 61:39 by 300,000 years ago.

Previc suggests that the higher incidence of right-handedness in modern humans might have to do with cultural bias, raising the ratio from 2:1 to about 8:1. The 8:1 bias, however, appears to be more or less constant across diverse human cultures (Corballis, 1983). More tellingly, the bias in favor of the left hemisphere for the representation of speech is if anything even higher (Milner, 1975), which is difficult to explain in terms of cultural bias. An alternative possibility is that the more pronounced bias underlying handedness and cerebral dominance for language depends on some additional genetic influence that emerged at some point in hominid evolution, to be superimposed on the already existing 2:1 bias.

The most compelling genetic models of laterality are those proposed by Annett (1985) and McManus (1985). Both assume that right-handedness and left cerebral dominance are controlled by a single gene locus. The important point about these models is that one genetic allele codes for right-handedness and left-cerebral dominance, and the other is neutral with respect to handedness or cerebral asymmetry. McManus refers to the two alleles of this gene as *dextral (D)* and *chance (C)*, and proposes that the percentage of right-handers is 100% among *DD* homozygotes, 75% among *DC* heterozygotes, and 50% among *CC* homozygotes. Annett's theory is similar, especially in that those lacking what Annett calls the "right shift" (p. 1) *(RS)* gene have no genetic predisposition toward either right- or left-handedness. Annett suggests that the *RS* gene influences cerebral dominance rather than handedness *per se*, but fits of both models to data have focused almost exclusively on handedness, presumably because there are no adequate population data on the frequency and inheritance of cerebral dominance. Both theories provide good fits to the data on the inheritance of handedness, and accord well with other facts about handedness, such as the common finding that left-handers are less lateralized than right-handers on measures of dominance, including cerebral dominance (e.g. Kim et al., 1993) and handedness itself (Annett, 1985).

I suggest that the default condition implied by the absence of the *RS* gene, or in McManus's terminology by the *C* allele, may not be one of equal probabilities of right- and left-handedness, but rather a 2:1 bias in favor of right-handedness. Annett (1995) herself provides support for this: In fitting her model to data, she has estimated that the proportion of right-handed writers among those lacking the *RS* gene is 66%, not the 50% that one would expect if handedness were determined at random, although she attributes the discrepancy to environmental bias rather than to a pre-existing biological asymmetry. If the laterality gene emerged relatively late in hominid evolution, this might explain why other primates, as well as hominids prior to *Homo sapiens*, show the 2:1 bias rather than the more extreme 8:1 bias evident in modern humans, and the 2:1 ratio might underlie the distribution of handedness in those lacking the gene.

Annett (1985, 1995) has argued that the *RS* gene is sustained by a relative advantage in the fitness of heterozygotes over homozygotes. This *heterozygotic advantage* implies that both alleles will be maintained in the population in a steady state, consistent with evidence that the proportion of left-handers in the human population has remained approximately constant for at least 5000 years (Coren & Porac, 1977). It also implies that the *RS* allele was beneficial to fitness, but only in a single dose. As it is associated with left-hemispheric dominance, it seems reasonable to suppose that the advantage had to do with either language or manual control—or both, as I shall suggest later. There is some evidence that left-hemispheric dominance is achieved at the expense of right-hemisphere function by a process of pruning (Galaburda, Rosen, & Sherman, 1990), which is perhaps why a double dose is disadvantageous. Assuming that the effects of the gene are additive, individuals homozygous for the lateralizing allele (*DD*, in McManus's terminology) might therefore run the risk of sacrificing spatial skills for verbal ones. Conversely, *CC* individuals who lack the lateralizing allele might have superior spatial abilities, but run the risk of language difficulties. Annett (1995) has summarized research findings on the relation of spatial ability to handedness, concluding that "*spatial ability declines from left to right along the continuum of R-L hand skill . . .*" (p. 451, her emphasis). There is also a long history of evidence that speech deficits, including stuttering, might be linked to the lack of cerebral dominance (Brain, 1945; Corballis, 1983; Orton & Travis, 1929). The optimal genetic endowment, then, might be heterozygosity—the possession of an allele of each type.

It takes only a tiny advantage in reproductive fitness to produce what is, on an evolutionary time scale, a rapid spread of a mutant allele through the population (Corballis, 1997). Figure 2.4 plots a simulation of the spread of a

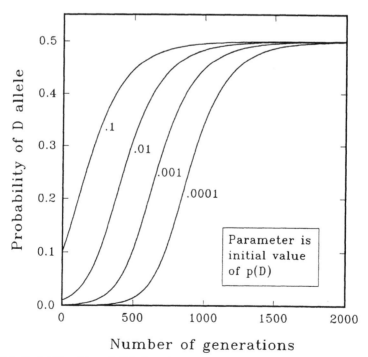

FIG. 2.4 Probability of dextral allele through succeeding generations, given initial probabilities of .1, .01, .001, and .0001, assuming that the fitness of homozygotes is 0.99 that of heterozygotes.

hypothetical D allele through a population given a relative fitness of homozygotes to heterozygotes of 0.99; that is, the relative number of offspring contributed by homozygotes is 99% of that contributed by heterozygotes. Suppose that this allele appeared in one of a group of 50 individuals comprising a breeding population, so that its initial probability was .01 (because each individual carries two alleles). Fig. 2.4 shows that this probability rises to its asymptote of .5 after about 1250 generations, or about 30,000 years. Dividing the initial probability by 10 displaces the curve to the right by about 330 generations. Figure 2.5 shows that only a slight drop in relative fitness can produce a dramatic change in the rate at which the allele spreads. For example, holding the initial probability at .01 and dropping the relative fitness to 0.96 produces the asymptote after only about 300 generations, or about 7500 years.

These simulations depend on the assumption that the relative fitnesses of DD and CC genotypes are equal. As shown in Fig. 2.6, dropping the fitness of CC homozygotes relative to DD homozygotes results in increasing probabilities of the D allele. So long as there is an overall heterozygotic advantage, the probability will reach a steady state between 0 and 1. But if the fitness of heterozygotes falls below that of either of the homozygotes, then one of the alleles will eventually disappear; the population will either be taken over by right-handers, or

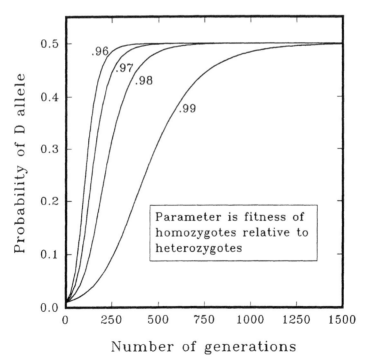

Number of generations

FIG. 2.5   Probability of dextral allele through succeeding generations, given initial probability of .01, with fitness of homozygotes relative to that of heterozygotes varying from 0.99 to 0.96.

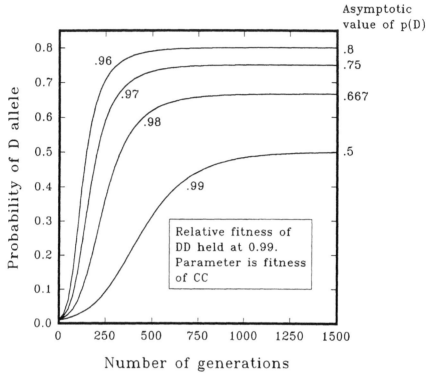

FIG. 2.6 Probability of dextral allele through succeeding generations, given initial probability of .01, with fitness of *DD* homozygotes held at 0.99 of *CD* heterozygotes, and fitness of *CC* homozygotes varying from 0.99 to 0.96.

handedness will revert to the default option, which may comprise a 2:1 ratio favoring right handers.

What was the advantage of the dextral allele that might have led to its rapid dispersal and ultimate stability in the human population? Annett (1985) suggests it may have conferred an advantage in learning to speak, as it effectively guaranteed that the production and perception of speech would be subserved by the same (left) hemisphere, creating a shorter and more reliable feedback from motor speech output to auditory input than if these functions are carried out in opposite hemispheres. Wilkins and Wakefield (1995) suggest similarly that lateralization may have facilitated manual activities, such as manipulation and throwing, by shortening the feedback from somatosensory to motor areas. Lateralization would also eliminate the possibility of interhemispheric conflict, especially in praxic functions (Corballis, 1991).

Another possibility can be derived from the theory, outlined earlier, that language originated in manual gesture, but was increasingly accompanied by vocalization. Kimura (1973a,b) observed that right-handers make many more gestures with the right hand than with the left hand when speaking, whereas left handers make more bilateral movements and show a more mixed pattern. This is consistent with the idea that the dextral allele underlies the left-hemispheric control of both speaking and gesturing, whereas in the absence of dextral allele the two activities may sometimes be controlled by opposite hemispheres. The importance of cerebral dominance may therefore have been to ensure that manual and vocal control were located in the *same* cerebral hemisphere. This may have been most critical at a time when spoken language began to emerge as an alternative to manual language, and this in turn may have been restricted to the next player in the unfolding drama. That player is familiar to us all.

HOMO SAPIENS

There have been two different scenarios as to the emergence of anatomically modern humans, or *Homo sapiens*. According to the "multiregional" model, championed by Wolpoff (1989), *Homo erectus* migrated from Africa to the Old World from close to 2 million years ago, and gradually evolved into the larger-brained *Homo sapiens*. The main evidence for this is the supposed continuity of the morphology of East Asian skulls over a period of more than a million years. The weight of evidence, however, lies with the "Out of Africa" model, which holds that *Homo sapiens* emerged in Africa some 100–150,000 years ago, and migrated from there to the Old and New Worlds, beginning somewhere between 100,000 and 60,000 years ago (Cavalli-Sforza, Menozzi, & Piazza, 1993). This species replaced the descendants of the earlier migrants. The "Out of Africa" model was developed from analysis of mitochondrial DNA, which implied that all modern humans were descended from Africa (Cann, Stoneking, & Wilson, 1987). This model was earlier suggested by analysis of the diversity of nuclear allele frequencies (Nei & Roychoudhury, 1982), and has continued to receive support, not only from more recent analysis of mitochondrial DNA (Penny, Steel, Waddell, & Hendy, 1995), but also from chromosomal analyses (Dorit, Akashi, & Gilbert, 1995; Hammer, 1995; Tishkoff et al., 1996), and from independent analysis of fossil and subfossil remains (Stringer & Andrews, 1988).

What was it that led to the subsequent dominance of *Homo sapiens* over the other hominids, including the Neanderthals, who are presumed to have descended from the earlier migrants? I suggest that the critical factor was speech. However, it emerged not as the result of a "big bang" that suddenly resulted in fully fledged language, but rather as a switch from manual to vocal language. This occurred some time prior to the migration of *Homo sapiens* out of Africa. It may have been facilitated by the emergence and spread of a dextral allele, which ensured that manual and vocal dominance were generally located in the same (left) cerebral hemisphere. As we have seen, the spread of the dextral allele could have taken place quite quickly on an evolutionary time scale, within tens of thousands of years at most. Equipped with speech, and perhaps brandishing weapons in the right hand, *Homo sapiens* advanced out of Africa, and conquered.

In what has been termed the "emerging synthesis" (Renfrew, 1992, p. 445), there is growing support for the "Out of Africa" scenario from the study of comparative linguistics (Cavalli-Sforza et al., 1993). Shevoroshkin (1990) and Ruhlen (1994), among others, have argued on the basis of the similarities among them that the spoken languages of the world must have evolved from a single language that Shevoroshkin (1990) calls "mother tongue" or "Proto-World" (p. 20). For example, the word pronounced with relatively minor variations as *akwa* occurs in a great many language families, and was probably a root word meaning *water*. Just as genetic diversity is greater in Africa than in any other region, so linguistic diversity is greatest there, supporting the idea that spoken language came out of Africa. Ruhlen (1994) notes that linguistic analysis is largely uninformative as to the dates of early linguistic evolution, but nevertheless "supports a recent, as opposed to a very ancient, date for the origin of modern languages" (p. 163). He is of course referring to *spoken* language, and he admits that it might have emerged from an earlier form based on manual gestures.

There are several advantages to a spoken language over a gestural one. One is that it allows communication at night, or over distances at which manual signs would be visually indiscriminable, or when obstacles prevent the communicating parties from seeing each other. Goldin-Meadow et al. (1996) make the more subtle point that communication is more effective if the voice takes care of the grammatical, combinatorial aspect of language, while the hands provide the more global, imagistic aspect. Reversing these roles would be less effective, because the hands and arms lend themselves more readily to holistic expression. But more importantly, perhaps, the switch to a dominantly vocal language freed the hands for other activities, including tool making (Corballis, 1991, 1992; Givon, 1995), and it may demonstrate tool-making techniques while at the same time verbally explaining them. This could be why the manufacture of tools, having been relatively static for 2 million years, suddenly launched on an upward curve *after* the emergence of *Homo sapiens*.

Archeologists have documented what they call an "evolutionary explosion" in artifacts in Europe and the Near East dating from about 35,000 years ago (Pfeiffer, 1985). It is characterized by cave drawings, the crafting of ornaments and objects that display visual metaphor (White, 1989), and more sophisticated manufacture than was evident at earlier Eurasian sites. It might be argued that the evolutionary explosion was too late to be attributable to a switch to vocal language that took place in Africa prior to the migration of *Homo sapiens*. There is, however, good reason to suppose that the evolutionary explosion actually began earlier in Africa, and eventually expanded into Eurasia. Mellars (1989, p. 367) writes that:

[I]t is possible to point to at least certain features of the archeological record of the Middle Stone Age (roughly between 100,000 and 40,000 years ago) in Southern Africa which suggest a significantly more "complex" (and perhaps more "advanced") pattern of behavior than that reflected in the parallel records of the Middle Paleolithic in northern Eurasia over the same time range.

Evidence of a sophisticated bone industry, including the possible manufacture of harpoons to catch fish, has been recently discovered in Zaire, and dates from some 90,000 years ago (Yellen, Brooks, Cornelissen, Mehlman, & Stewart, 1995).

The Neanderthals, who were presumably descendants of an earlier migration from Africa, had inhabited Europe and Western Asia from about 150,000 years ago until about 34,000 years ago, and their disappearance coincides at least roughly with the appearance of sophisticated technologies associated with the anatomically modern Cro-Magnons. There was nevertheless a period of co-existence, lasting from perhaps 40,000 to 34,000 years ago in France, during which the Cro-Magnons may have even traded technology to the Neanderthals (Hublin, Spoor, Braun, Zonneveld, & Condemi, 1996). Although the status of the Neanderthals remains controversial, the evidence largely supports the theory that they were a subspecies distinct from *Homo sapiens* (Hublin et al., 1996) and were eventually replaced by the invading Cro-Magnons (Mellars, 1996).

That prophetic switch from hand to mouth shaped our destinies in ways that our African forebears cannot have dreamed of. One of the remarkable characteristics of the human biological condition is that we possess a cognitive capacity that extends well beyond our immediate needs. The release of the hands from primary language duty allowed us to indulge in art, music, and manufacture, and later in writing, which in turn made possible philosophy, science, mathematics, and yet more sophisticated technology. These activities all exhibit a representational, generative character that evolved in the more restricted context of manual communication, which in turn evolved from the increasing complexities of hominid interactions. They comprise most of what is meant by the term *civilization*, and although they were made possible by biological evolution, they are shaped and maintained by culture, not biology. The biological evolution of the human mind was probably complete with the emergence of *Homo sapiens*.

CONCLUSIONS

My story has, wherever possible, emphasized continuity rather than discontinuity. The emergence of limited mind-reading skills and some form of gestural communication seems to exist in modern African apes, and so probably existed in the common ancestor of the African apes and humans. The bipedalism of the hominids may have evolved more or less continuously from brachiation, without an intervening stage of knuckle-walking that has hampered the cognitive evolution of our cousins, the African apes. Whether or not this is true, bipedalism would also have imposed greater demands on parents in transporting and caring for their infants, increasing the selective pressure for mind-reading and perspective-taking, and leading perhaps to the ability to dissociate from one's current state of mind, enabling mental time travel and the ability to converse. Bipedalism would also have freed the hands and arms, allowing the development of mime and manual gesture in communication. Then, among a group of late African hominids, vocalization may have gradually assumed the dominant role in communication, facilitated by the emergence and spread of a dextral allele that captured manual and vocal control in the same (left) cerebral hemisphere. This development would have freed the hands yet again, leading to further developments of technology. Thus equipped, *Homo sapiens* migrated from Africa, replacing those hominids, including the Neanderthals, who were descended from earlier migrants. The linguistic and technological developments, along with the later development of writing, laid the foundations for human culture, and for what we are pleased to call civilization. To quote Kurt Vonnegut, "so it goes". Just so, I like to think.

ACKNOWLEDGEMENTS

This is a slightly expanded version of a "State of the Art" talk delivered at the XVI International Congress of Psychology, held in Montreal, Quebec, from 16 to 21 August 1996. I thank Richard W. Byrne, Tom Givon, and Thomas Suddendorf for helpful discussion.

REFERENCES

Andrews, P. (1995). Ecological apes and ancestors. *Nature, 376*, 555–556.
Annett, M. (1985). *Left, right, hand and brain: The right shift theory.* Hove, UK: Lawrence Erlbaum Associates Ltd.
Annett, M. (1995). The right shift theory of a genetic balanced polymorphism for cerebral dominance and cognitive processing. *Current Psychology of Cognition, 14*, 427–480.
Armstrong, D. F., Stokoe, W. C., & Wilcox, S. E. (1995). *Gesture and the nature of language.* Cambridge: Cambridge University Press.
Baron-Cohen, S. (1995). *Mindblindness.* Cambridge, MA: Bradford/MIT Press.
Bickerton, D. (1986). More than nature needs? A reply to Premack. *Cognition, 23*, 173–221.
Bickerton, D. (1995). *Language and human behavior.* Seattle, WA: University of Washington Press/ UCL Press.
Bischof, N. (1978). On the phylogeny of human morality. In G. Stent (Ed.), *Morality as a biological phenomenon* (pp. 53–74). Berlin: Abakon.
Boesch, C. (1991). Handedness in wild chimpanzees. *International Journal of Primatology, 6*, 541–558.
Boesch, C., & Boesch, H. (1984). Mental map in wild chimpanzees: An analysis of hammer transports for nut cracking. *Primates, 25*, 160–170.
Brain, W. R. (1945). Speech and handedness. *Lancet, 249*, 837–841.
Bruner, J. S. (1983). *Child's talk: Learning to use the language.* Oxford: Oxford University Press.
Burke, P. H. (1971). Stereophotogrammetric measurement of normal facial asymmetry in children. *Human Biology, 43*, 536–548.

Butterworth, G., & Grover, L. (1988). The origins without language of referential communication in human infancy. In L. Weiskrantz (Ed.), *Thought without language* (pp. 5–24). Oxford: Clarendon Press.

Byrne, R. W. (1995). *The thinking ape: Evolutionary origins of intelligence.* Oxford: Oxford University Press.

Byrne, R. W., & Byrne, J. M. E. (1991). Hand preferences in the skilled gathering tasks of mountain gorillas (*Gorilla g. beringei*). *Cortex, 27,* 521–546.

Byrne, R. W., & Whiten, A. (Eds.) (1988). *Machiavellian intelligence: Social expertise and the evolution of intellect in monkeys, apes, and humans.* Oxford: Oxford University Press.

Byrne, R. W., & Whiten, A. (1990). Tactical deception in primates: The 1990 data base. *Primate Report, 27,* 1–101.

Cann, R. L., Stoneking, M., & Wilson, A. C. (1987). Mitochondrial DNA and human evolution. *Nature, 325,* 31–36.

Cavalli-Sforza, L. L., Menozzi, P., & Piazza, A. (1993). Demic expansions and human evolution. *Science, 259,* 639–646.

Cheney, D. L., & Seyfarth, R. M. (1988). *How monkeys see the world: Inside the mind of another species.* Chicago: University of Chicago Press.

Chomsky, N. (1959). A review of B. F. Skinner's "Verbal behavior". *Language, 35,* 26–58.

Chomsky, N. (1966). *Cartesian linguistics: A chapter in the history of rationalist thought.* New York: Harper & Row.

Churchill, J. A., Igna, E., & Senf, R. (1962). The association of position at birth and handedness. *Pediatrics, 29,* 307–309.

Condillac, Etienne Bonnot de (1947). *Oeuvres philosophiques de Condillac* [The philosophical writings of Condillac]. Paris: Georges Leroy. (Originally published 1746.)

Corballis, M. C. (1983). *Human laterality.* New York: Academic Press.

Corballis, M. C. (1991). *The lopsided ape: Evolution of the generative mind.* New York: Oxford University Press.

Corballis, M. C. (1992). On the evolution of language and generativity. *Cognition, 44,* 197–226.

Corballis, M. C. (1997). The genetics and evolution of handedness. *Psychological Review, 104,* 714–727.

Coren, S., & Porac, C. (1977). Fifty centuries of right-handedness: The historical record. *Science, 198,* 631–632.

Dart, R. A. (1925). *Australopithecus africanus*: The man-ape of South Africa. *Nature, 115,* 195–199.

Dart, R. A. (with D. Craig) (1959). *Adventures with the missing link.* London: Hamish Hamilton.

Degerando, J.-M. (1969). *The observations of savage peoples* (F. C. T. Moore, Trans.). London: Routledge & Kegan Paul. (Original work published 1800.)

Dennett, D. C. (1983). Intentional systems in cognitive ethology: The "Panglossian paradigm" defended. *Behavioral and Brain Sciences, 6,* 343–390.

Descartes, R. (1985). *The philosophical writings of Descartes* (J. Cottingham, R. Stoothoff, & D. Murdock, Eds. and Trans.). Cambridge: Cambridge University Press. (Original work published 1647.)

Diamond, J. M. (1988). DNA-based phylogenies of the three chimpanzees. *Nature, 332,* 685–686.

Donald, M. (1991). *Origins of the modern human mind.* Cambridge, MA: Harvard University Press.

Dorit, R. L., Akashi, H., & Gilbert, W. (1995). Absence of polymorphism at the ZFY locus on the human Y chromosome. *Science, 268,* 1183–1185.

Dretske, T. (1982). The informational character of representations. *Behavioral and Brain Sciences, 5,* 376–377.

Duchin, L. E. (1990). The evolution of articulate speech: Comparative anatomy of the oral cavity in *Pan* and *Homo. Journal of Human Evolution, 19,* 687–697.

Dunbar, R. I. M. (1993). Coevolution of neocortical size, group size and language in humans. *Behavioral and Brain Sciences, 16,* 681–736.

Falk, D. (1975). Comparative anatomy of the larynx in man and chimpanzee: Implications for language in Neanderthal. *American Journal of Physical Anthropology, 43*, 123–132.

Falk, D. (1987). Hominid paleoneurology. *Annual Review of Anthropology, 16*, 13–30.

Foley, R. (1987). Hominid species and stone tool assemblages. *Antiquity, 61*, 380–392.

Fouts, R. S., Fouts, D. H., & Van Cantfort, T. E. (1989). The infant Loulis learns signs from cross-fostered chimpanzees. In R. A. Gardner, B. T. Gardner, & T. E. Van Cantfort (Eds.), *Teaching sign language to chimpanzees* (pp. 280–292). New York: State University of New York Press.

Friday, A. E. (1992). Human evolution: The evidence from DNA sequencing. In S. Jones, R. Martin, & D. Pilbeam (Eds.), *The Cambridge encyclopedia of human evolution* (pp. 316–321). Cambridge: Cambridge University Press.

Fromkin, V. A., Krashen, S., Curtiss, S., Rigler, D., & Rigler, M. (1974). The development of language in Genie: A case of language acquisition beyond the critical period. *Brain and Language, 1*, 81–107.

Galaburda, A. M., Rosen, G. D., & Sherman, G. F. (1990). Individual variability in cortical organization: Its relationship to brain laterality and implications to function. *Neuropsychologia, 28*, 529–546.

Gallup, G. G., Jr. (1970). Chimpanzees: Self-recognition. *Science, 167*, 86–87.

Gallup, G. G., Jr. (1977). Self-recognition in primates: A comparative approach to the bidirectional properties of consciousness. *American Psychologist, 32*, 329–338.

Gardner, R. A., & Gardner, B. T. (1969). Teaching sign language to a chimpanzee. *Science, 165*, 664–672.

Geschwind, N., & Levitsky, W. (1968). Human brain: Left-right asymmetries in temporal speech region. *Science, 161*, 186–187.

Givon, T. (1995). *Functionalism and grammar*. Philadelphia, PA: Benjamins.

Goldin-Meadow, S., McNeill, D., & Singleton, J. (1996). Silence is liberating: Removing the handcuffs on grammatical expression in the manual modality. *Psychological Review, 103*, 34–55.

Goodall, J. (1970). Tool use in primates and other vertebrates. In D. S. Lehrman, R. A. Hinde, & E. Shaw (Eds.), *Advances in the study of behavior* (Vol. 1, pp. 195–249). New York: Academic Press.

Goodman, M. (1992). Reconstructing human evolution from proteins. In S. Jones, R. Martin, & D. Pilbeam (Eds.), *The Cambridge encyclopedia of human evolution* (pp. 307–312). Cambridge: Cambridge University Press.

Goodwin, R. S., & Michel, G. F. (1981). Head orientation position during birth and in infant neonatal period, and hand preference at nine weeks. *Child Development, 52*, 819–826.

Gopnik, A. (1993). How we know our own minds: The illusion of first-person knowledge of intentionality. *Behavioral and Brain Sciences, 16*, 1–14.

Gopnik, A., & Graf, P. (1988). Knowing how you know: Young children's ability to identify and remember the source of their belief. *Child Development, 59*, 1366–1371.

Gould, S. J. (1980). Human babies as embryos. In S. J. Gould (Ed.), *Ever since Darwin* (pp. 70–75). Harmondsworth, UK: Penguin Books.

Greenfield, P. M. (1991). Language, tools, and the brain: The ontogeny and phylogeny of hierarchically organized sequential behavior. *Behavioral and Brain Sciences, 14*, 531–595.

Gribbin, J. (1988). *The one percent advantage: The sociobiology of being human*. Oxford: Oxford University Press.

Hammer, M. F. (1995). A recent common ancestry for human Y chromosomes. *Nature, 378*, 376–378.

Hayes, C. (1952). *The ape in our house*. London: Gollancz.

Hewes, G. W. (1973). Primate communication and the gestural origins of language. *Current Anthropology, 14*, 5–24.

Hewes, G. W. (1981). Pointing and language. In T. Myers, J. Laver, & J. Anderson (Eds.), *The cognitive representation of speech* (pp. 263–269). Amsterdam: North-Holland.

Hilton, C. E. (1986). *Hands across the old world: The changing morphology of the hominids.* Unpublished manuscript, University of New Mexico at Albuquerque.

Hopkins, W. D. (1993). Posture and reaching in chimpanzees (*Pan*) and orangutans (*Pongo*). *Journal of Comparative Psychology, 17,* 162–168.

Hopkins, W. D. (1994). Hand preferences for bimanual feeding in 140 captive chimpanzees (*Pan troglodytes*): Rearing and ontogenetic factors. *Developmental Psychobiology, 27,* 395–407.

Hopkins, W. D. (1995). Hand preference for a coordinated bimanual task in 110 chimpanzees (*Pan troglodytes*): Cross-sectional analysis. *Journal of Comparative Psychology, 109,* 291–297.

Hopkins, W. D., Bennett, A., Bales, S., Lee, J., & Ward, J. P. (1993). Behavioral laterality in captive bonobos (*Pan paniscus*). *Journal of Comparative Psychology, 107,* 403–410.

Hopkins, W. D., & de Waal, F. D. (1995). Behavioral laterality in captive bonobos (Pan paniscus): Replication and extension. *International Journal of Primatology, 16,* 261–276.

Hublin, J., Spoor, F., Braun, M., Zonnefeld, F. W., & Condemi, S. (1996). Late Neanderthal associated with Upper Paleolithic artefacts. *Nature, 381,* 224–226.

Humphrey, N. K. (1976). The social function of intellect. In P. P. G. Bateson & R. A. Hinde (Eds.), *Growing points in ethology* (pp. 303–317). Cambridge: Cambridge University Press.

Kappelman, J. (1996). The evolution of body mass and relative brain size in fossil hominids. *Journal of Human Evolution, 30,* 243–276.

Kellogg, W. N. (1968). Communication and language in the home-based chimpanzee. *Science, 162,* 423–427.

Kendon, A. (1991). Some considerations for a theory of language origins. *Man, 26,* 199–221.

Kim, S.-G., Ashe, J., Hendrich, K., Ellerman, J. M., Merkle, H., Ugurbil, K., & Georgopoulos, A. P. (1993). Functional magnetic resonance imaging of motor cortex: Hemispheric asymmetry and handedness. *Science, 261,* 615–616.

Kimura, D. (1973a). Manual activity during speaking—I. Right-handers. *Neuropsychologia, 11,* 45–50.

Kimura, D. (1973b). Manual activity during speaking—II. Left-handers. *Neuropsychologia, 11,* 51–56.

Kimura, D. (1992). *Neuromotor mechanisms in human communication.* Oxford: Oxford University Press.

Klima, E., & Bellugi, U. (1979). *The signs of language.* Cambridge, MA: Harvard University Press.

Kohler, W. (1925). *The mentality of apes.* New York: Routledge & Kegan Paul.

Krogman, W. M. (1972). *Child growth.* Ann Arbor, MI: University of Michigan Press.

Latimer, B., & Lovejoy, C. O. (1990). Metatarsophalangeal joints of *Australopithecus afarensis. American Journal of Physical Anthropology, 83,* 13–23.

Leakey, M. D. (1979). Footprints in the ashes of time. *National Geographic, 155,* 446–457.

Leakey, M. G., Feibel, C. S., McDougall, I., & Walker, A. (1995). New four-million-year-old hominid species from Kanapoi and Allia Bay, Kenya. *Nature, 376,* 565–571.

Lewis, M., Brooks-Gunn, J., & Jaskir, J. (1985). Individual differences in early visual self-recognition. *Developmental Psychology, 21,* 1181–1187.

Lieberman, P. (1982). Can chimpanzees swallow or talk? A reply to Falk. *American Anthropologist, 84,* 148–152.

Lieberman, P. (1984). *The biology and evolution of language.* Cambridge, MA: Harvard University Press.

Lieberman, P. (1991). *Uniquely human: The evolution of speech, thought, and selfless behavior.* Cambridge, MA: Harvard University Press.

Lieberman, P. (1992). On Neanderthal speech and Neanderthal extinction. *Current Anthropology, 33,* 409–410.

Lieberman, P., Crelin, E. S., & Klatt, D. H. (1972). Phonetic ability and related anatomy of the newborn, adult human, Neanderthal man, and the chimpanzee. *American Anthropologist, 74,* 287–307.

Lovejoy, O. C. (1981). The origin of man. *Science, 221,* 341–350.

MacNeilage, P. F., Studdert-Kennedy, M. G., & Lindblom, B. (1987). Primate handedness reconsidered. *Behavioral and Brain Sciences, 10*, 247–303.

Marten, K., & Psarakos, S. (1994). Evidence of self-awareness in the bottlenose dolphin (*Tursiops truncatus*). In S. T. Parker, R. W. Mitchell, & M. L. Boccia (Eds.), *Self-awareness in animals and humans* (pp. 361–391). Cambridge: Cambridge University Press.

Martin, R. (1992). Classification and evolutionary relationships. In S. Jones, R. Martin, & D. Pilbeam (Eds.), *The Cambridge encyclopedia of human evolution* (pp. 17–23). Cambridge: Cambridge University Press.

McGrew, W. C., & Marchant, L. F. (1992). Chimpanzees, tools, and termites: Hand preferences or handedness? *Current Anthropology, 33*, 114–119.

McManus, I. C. (1985). Handedness, language dominance and aphasia: A genetic model. *Psychological Medicine* (Suppl. 8), 1–40.

McNeill, D. (1985). So you think gestures are nonverbal. *Psychological Review, 92*, 350–371.

Mellars, P. (1989). Major issues in the emergence of modern humans. *Current Anthropology, 30*, 349–385.

Mellars, P. (1996). *The Neanderthal legacy: An archaeological perspective from Western Europe.* Princeton, NJ: Princeton University Press.

Miles, H. L. (1990). The cognitive foundations for reference in a signing orangutan. In S. T. Parker & K. Gibson (Eds.), *"Language" and intelligence in monkeys and apes: Comparative developmental perspectives* (pp. 511–539). New York: Cambridge University Press.

Milner, B. (1975). Psychological aspects of focal epilepsy and its neurosurgical management. In D. P. Purpura, J. K. Penry, & R. D. Walters (Eds.), *Advances in neurology* (Vol. 8, pp. 299–321). New York: Raven.

Mowrey, R. A., & MacKay, R. A. (1990). Phonological primitives: Electromyographic speech error evidence. *Journal of the Acoustical Society of America, 88*, 1299–1312.

Nei, M., & Roychoudhury, A. K. (1982). Genetic relationship and evolution of human races. *Evolutionary Biology, 14*, 927–943.

Neisser, U. (1976). *Cognition and reality.* New York: Freeman.

Neville, H. J. (1991). Whence the specialization of the language hemisphere? In I. S. Mattingly & M. Studdert-Kennedy (Eds.), *Modularity and the motor theory of speech perception* (pp. 269–294). Hillsdale, NJ: Lawrence Erlbaum Associates Inc.

Newport, E. L. (1990). Maturational constraints on language learning. *Cognitive Science, 14*, 11–28.

Olton, D. R. (1984). Comparative analysis of episodic memory. *Behavioral and Brain Sciences, 7*, 250–251.

Orton, S. T., & Travis, L. E. (1929). Studies in stuttering. IV. Studies of action currents in stutterers. *Archives of Neurology and Psychiatry, 21*, 61–68.

Parker, S. T. (1991). A developmental approach to the origins of self-consciousness in great apes. *Human Evolution, 6*, 435–449.

Parker, S. T., & Mitchell, R. W. (1994). Evolving self-awareness. In S. T. Taylor, R. W. Mitchell, & M. L. Boccia (Eds.), *Self-awareness in animals and humans* (pp. 413–428). Cambridge: Cambridge University Press.

Passingham, R. E. (1982). *The human primate.* San Francisco: Freeman.

Patterson, F. (1978). Conversations with a gorilla. *National Geographic, 154*, 438–465.

Patterson, F. (1984). Self-recognition by *Gorilla. Gorilla, 7*, 2–3.

Penny, D., Steel, M., Waddell, P. J., & Hendy, M. D. (1995). Improved analyses of human mtDNA sequences support a recent African origin for *Homo sapiens. Molecular and Biological Evolution, 12*, 863–882.

Pettito, L. A., & Marentette, P. F. (1991). Babbling in the manual mode: Evidence for the ontogeny of language. *Science, 251*, 1493–1496.

Pfeiffer, J. E. (1985). *The emergence of humankind.* New York: Harper & Row.

Piattelli-Palmarini, M. (1989). Evolution, selection and cognition: From "learning" to parameter setting in biology and the study of language. *Cognition, 31*, 1–44.

Pilbeam, D. (1972). *The ascent of man: An introduction to human evolution.* New York: Macmillan.

Pillemer, D. B., & White, S. H. (1989). Childhood events recalled by children and adults. In H. W. Reese (Ed.), *Advances in child development and behavior* (Vol. 21, pp. 297–240). New York: Academic Press.

Pinker, S. (1994). *The language instinct: How the mind creates language.* New York: Morrow.

Pinker, S., & Bloom, P. (1990). Natural language and natural selection. *Behavioral and Brain Sciences, 13,* 707–784.

Plooij, F. X. (1978). Some basic traits of language in wild chimpanzees. In A. Lock (Ed.), *Action, gesture, and symbol: The emergence of language.* New York: Academic Press.

Poizner, H., Klima, E. S., & Bellugi, U. (1987). *What the hands reveal about the brain.* Cambridge, MA: MIT Press/Bradford.

Povinelli, D. J. (1993). Reconstructing the evolution of mind. *American Psychologist, 48,* 493–509.

Premack, D. (1985). "Gavagai!" or the future history of the animal language controversy. *Cognition, 19,* 207–296.

Premack, D. (1986). Pangloss to Cyrano de Bergerac: "Nonsense, it's perfect!" A reply to Bickerton. *Cognition, 23,* 81–88.

Premack, D. (1988). "Does the chimpanzee have a theory of mind?" revisited. In R. W. Byrne & A. Whiten (Eds.), *Machiavellian intelligence* (pp. 94–110). Oxford: Clarendon Press.

Premack, D., & Premack, A. J. (1994). How "theory of mind" constrains language and communication. In D. C. Gajdusek, G. M. McKhann, & L. C. Bolis (Eds.), *Discussions in neuroscience: Vol. X. Evolution and neurology of language* (pp. 93–105). Amsterdam: Elsevier.

Premack, D., & Woodruff, G. (1978). Does the chimpanzee have a theory of mind? *Behavioral and Brain Sciences, 4,* 515–526.

Previc, F. (1991). A general theory concerning the prenatal origins of cerebral lateralization in humans. *Psychological Review, 98,* 299–334.

Pulleyblank, E. G. (1986). The meaning of duality of patterning and its importance in language evolution. *Sign Language Studies, 51,* 101–120.

Renfrew, C. (1992). Archeology, genetics, and linguistic diversity. *Man, 27,* 445–478.

Ruhlen, M. (1994). *The origin of language: Tracing the evolution of the mother tongue.* New York: Wiley.

Rumbaugh, D. (1977). *Language learning by a chimpanzee: The LANA Project.* New York: Academic Press.

Savage-Rumbaugh, E. S. (1994). Hominid evolution: Looking to modern apes for clues. In D. Quiatt & J. Itani (Eds.), *Hominid culture in primate perspective* (pp. 7–49). Niwot, CO: University of Colorado Press.

Savage-Rumbaugh, E. S., Murphy, J., Sevcik, R. A., Brakke, K. E., Williams, S. L., & Rumbaugh, D. M. (1993). *Language comprehension in ape and child.* Chicago: University of Chicago Press.

Savage-Rumbaugh, S., & Lewin, R. (1994). *Kanzi: An ape at the brink of the human mind.* New York: Wiley.

Seidenberg, M. S., & Pettito, L. A. (1987). Communication, symbolic communication, and language. *Journal of Experimental Psychology: General, 116,* 279–287.

Shevoroshkin, V. (1990). The mother tongue. *The Sciences, 30(3),* 20–27.

Sibley, C. G., & Ahlquist, J. E. (1987). DNA hybridization as evidence of hominoid phylogeny: Results from an expanded data set. *Journal of Molecular Evolution, 26,* 99–121.

Stringer, C. B., & Andrews, P. (1988). Genetic and fossil evidence for the origin of modern humans. *Science, 239,* 1263–1268.

Studdert-Kennedy, M. (1987). The phoneme as a perceptuomotor structure. In D. A. Allport, D. G. Mackay, W. Prinz, & E. Scheerer (Eds.), *Language perception and production: Relationships between listening, speaking, reading and writing* (pp. 67–84). London: Academic Press.

Suddendorf, T. (1994). *Discovery of the fourth dimension: Mental time travel and human evolution.* Unpublished master's thesis, Waikato University, Hamilton, New Zealand.

Suddendorf, T., & Corballis, M. C. (1997). Mental time travel and the evolution of the human mind. *Genetic, Social, and General Psychology Monographs, 123,* 133–167.

Sugiyama, Y., Fushimi, T., Sakura, O., & Matsuzawa, T. (1993). Hand preference and tool use in wild chimpanzees. *Primates, 34,* 151–159.

Swartz, K. B., & Evans, S. (1991). Not all chimpanzees show self-recognition. *Primates, 32,* 483–496.

Terrace, H. S. (1979). Is problem solving language? *Journal of the Experimental Analysis of Behavior, 31,* 161–175.

Tishkoff, S. A., Dietzsche, E., Speed, W., Pakstis, A. J., Kidd, J. R., Cheung, K., Bonne-Tamir, B., Santachiara-Benerecetti, A. S., Moral, P., Krings, M., Paabo, S., Watson, E., Risch, N., Jenkins, T., & Kidd, K. K. (1996). Global patterns of linkage disequilibrium at the CD4 locus and modern human origins. *Science, 271,* 1380–1387.

Toth, N. (1985). Archeological evidence for preferential right-handedness in the lower and middle Pleistocene, and its possible implications. *Journal of Human Evolution, 14,* 607–614.

Toth, N., Schick, K. D., Savage-Rumbaugh, S., Sevcik, R. A., & Rumbaugh, D. M. (1993). Pan the toolmaker: Investigations into stone tool-making and tool-using capabilities of a bonobo (*Pan paniscus*). *Journal of Archeological Science, 20,* 81–91.

Tulving, E. (1983). *Elements of episodic memory.* New York: Oxford University Press.

Tulving, E. (1984). Precis of *Elements of episodic memory. Behavioral and Brain Sciences, 7,* 223–268.

Tulving, E. (1993). What is episodic memory? *Current Directions in Psychological Science, 2,* 67–70.

Ungerleider, L. A., & Mishkin, M. (1982). Two cortical visual systems. In D. G. Ingle, M. A. Goodale, & R. J. Q. Mansfield (Eds.), *Analysis of visual behavior* (pp. 549–586). Cambridge, MA: MIT Press.

Ward, W. D. (1957). Hearing of naval aircraft maintenance personnel. *The Journal of the Acoustical Society of America, 29,* 1289–1301.

White, R. (1989). Visual thinking in the ice age. *Scientific American, 261(1),* 74–81.

White, T. D., Suwa, G., & Asfaw, B. (1994). *Australopithecus ramidus,* a new species of early hominid from Aramis, Ethiopia. *Nature, 371,* 306–312.

White, T. D., Suwa, G., & Asfaw, B. (1995). Corrigendum to "*Australopithecus ramidus,* a new species of hominid from Aramis, Ethiopia". *Nature, 375,* 88.

Wilkins, W. K., & Wakefield, J. (1995). Brain evolution and neurolinguistic preconditions. *Behavioral and Brain Sciences, 18,* 161–226.

Wolpoff, M. H. (1989). Multiregional evolution: The fossil alternative to Eden. In P. Mellars & C. Stringer (Eds.), *The human revolution: Behavioral and biological perspectives on the origins of modern humans* (pp. 62–108). Edinburgh: University of Edinburgh Press.

Wood, B. (1994). The oldest hominid yet. *Nature, 371,* 280–281.

Woodruff, G., & Premack, D. (1979). Intentional communication in the chimpanzee: The development of deception. *Cognition, 7,* 333–362.

Wynn, T. & McGrew, W. C. (1989). An ape's view of the Oldowan. *Man, 24,* 383–398.

Yamazaki, N. (1985). Primate bipedal walking: Computer simulation. In S. Kondo (Ed.), *Primate morphophysiology, locomotor analyses, and human bipedalism* (pp. 105–130). Tokyo: University of Tokyo Press.

Yellen, J. E., Brooks, A. S., Cornelissen, E., Mehlman, M. J., & Stewart, K. (1995). A Middle Stone Age worked bone industry from Katanda, Upper Semliki Valley, Zaire. *Science, 268,* 553–556.

CHAPTER THREE

Pain and stress: Clues toward understanding chronic pain

Ronald Melzack
McGill University, Montréal, Québec, Canada

The neuromatrix theory of pain proposes that pain is a multidimensional experience produced by characteristic neurosignature patterns generated by the body-self neuromatrix in the brain. These patterns may be dependent on sensory inputs or may be generated independently of them. In particular, most chronic pain syndromes defy explanation in terms of peripheral sensory causes and present a challenge to current theories of pain. However, recent research on the stress system and its disorders provides valuable clues toward understanding pain. We are so accustomed to considering pain as a purely sensory phenomenon that we have ignored the obvious fact that injury disrupts the body's homeostatic regulation systems, thereby producing stress and initiating complex programs to restore homeostasis. I propose that particular neuromatrix output patterns, which activate and maintain these programs, become the neurosignature patterns that are the basis of pain experience. Moreover, prolonged stressors, physical as well as psychological, may produce a variety of disorders, including the destruction of muscle, bone, and nerve tissue, thereby contributing additional inputs to the neuromatrix. Injury and the stress it produces, therefore, may trigger a cascade of events in which activation of homeostatic regulation programs that contribute to the neurosignature for pain also, concurrently, produce destructive physical conditions that intensify the initial pathology and provide the basis for prolonged, chronic pain. The neuromatrix theory of pain places the neural-hormonal mechanisms of stress on a level of importance equal to the neural mechanisms of sensory transmission. This new approach has important implications for research and therapy.

La théorie neuromatricielle de la douleur voit la douleur comme une expérience multidimensionnelle produite par certains modèles de signature neurale caractéristiques générés dans le cerveau par les neuro-matrices corps-moi. Ces modèles de signature peuvent dépendre des entrées sensorielles ou être générés d'une façon indépendante. Il faut noter, en particulier, que la plupart des syndromes de douleur chronique résistent à toute explication en termes de causes sensorielles périphériques et présentent un défi aux théories actuelles sur la douleur. Cependant, la recherche récente sur le fonctionnement du stress et des troubles qui en découlent fournit des indices intéressants pour la compréhension de la douleur. Nous sommes tellement habitués à considérer la douleur comme un phénomène purement sensoriel que nous avons ignoré le fait évident qu'une blessure perturbe les systèmes corporels de régulation homéostatique, produisant ainsi du stress et mettant en branle des programmes complexes pour rétablir l'homéostasie. L'auteur soumet que certains modèles de débit neuromatriciel, qui active et maintient ces programmes, deviennent des modèles de signature neurale qui sont à la base de l'expérience de la douleur. De plus, des stresseurs persistants, aussi bien physiques que psychologiques, peuvent produire une variété de désordres, incluant la destruction de tissus musculaires, osseux et neuraux, contribuant ainsi à des entrées additionnelles dans la neuromatrice. Les blessures et le stress qui les accompagnent peuvent, par conséquent, déclencher une cascade d'événements dans lesquels l'activation des programmes de régulation homéostatique qui contribuent également et concurremment à la signature neurale de la douleur va produire des conditions physiques de destruction qui intensifient le désordre initial et fournissent la base à une douleur chronique et prolongée. La théorie neuromatricielle de la douleur place les mécanismes neuro-hormonaux du stress sur un pied d'égalité avec les mécanismes neuraux de la transmission sensorielle. Cette nouvelle approche a des implications importantes pour la recherche et la thérapie.

The neuromatrix theory of pain (Melzack, 1991, 1995) proposes that pain is a multidimensional experience produced by characteristic neurosignature patterns generated by the body-self neuromatrix in the brain. These patterns may be dependent on sensory inputs, but they may also be generated independently of them. Input-dependent pains have been meticulously investigated by neuroscientists, and sensory transmission mechanisms (see Melzack & Wall, 1996) are generally well understood. In contrast, chronic pain syndromes, which are characterized by severe pain associated with little or no injury or pathology, remain a mystery. The neuromatrix theory, however, provides a new approach: It proposes that the output patterns of the neuromatrix are comprised of commands to activate homeostatic and behavioral programs after injury or pathology. Particular portions of these output patterns are, concurrently, the neurosignature patterns that give rise to pain experience.

We are so accustomed to considering pain as a purely perceptual phenomenon that we have ignored the obvious fact that injury also disrupts the body's homeostatic regulation systems, thereby producing stress and initiating complex programs to restore homeostasis. By recognizing the role of the stress system in pain processes, the scope of the puzzle of pain is greatly expanded and new pieces of the puzzle provide valuable clues in our quest to understand chronic pain.

Hans Selye (1950), who founded the field of stress research, studied stress as a biological response to a wide range of stressors. They include physical injury, infection, and other pathology as well as psychological stressors, such as the loss of a job or the death of a friend. Recently, stress has been defined (Chrousos, 1992) as a state of threatened homeostasis—that is, a disruption by stressors of physiological processes such as blood sugar level and body temperature that are normally maintained at a fixed, delicately balanced set-point.

The disruption of homeostasis by a stressor, either physical or psychological, activates programs of neural, hormonal, and behavioral activity aimed at restoring homeostasis. The particular programs that are activated are selected from a genetically determined repertoire of programs (which have been modified by events such as earlier exposure to stress), and are influenced by the extent and severity of the perceived stress.

Given the multiplicity of interacting neural and hormonal factors that contribute to homeostasis, it is not surprising that programs to reinstate homeostasis may go awry. The consequence is a variety of stress-related disorders, which include several chronic pain syndromes (Chrousos, 1992; Chrousos & Gold, 1992; Sapolsky, 1992). It is important, therefore, to examine the hypothesis that stress may produce the conditions that give rise to some forms of chronic pain.

THE STRESS SYSTEM

When injury occurs, sensory information is projected rapidly to the brain and, in parallel with the neuromatrix activities that usually lead to pain perception (Melzack, 1991, 1995), the stress system (Fig. 3.1) initiates the complex sequence of events to restore biological homeostasis. Activities in the injured tissues produce cytokines, which are complex molecules produced by the interaction of transformed white blood cells known as macrophages and injured tissues. These cytokines are released within seconds after injury and take part in producing a local inflammatory response. Within minutes, cytokines such as gamma-interferon, interleukins 1 and 6, and tumor necrosis factor enter the bloodstream and travel to the brain, where they breach the blood-brain barrier at specific sites and have an immediate effect on hypothalamic cells (Sapolsky, 1992). The cytokines together with the perception of pain—a stressor—rapidly begin a sequence of activities aimed at the release and utilization of glucose for necessary actions such as the repair of tissues and "fight or flight" responses to survive the threat to the body-self.

Cytokines that penetrate the hypothalamus activate the hypothalamic-pituitary-adrenal (HPA) system, in which corticotropin releasing hormone (CRH) produced in the hypothalamus is released into the local blood stream that carries it to the pituitary. There, the CRH causes the release of adrenocorticotropic hormone (ACTH) and other substances (Chrousos, 1992; Sapolsky, 1992). The ACTH then activates the adrenal cortex to release cortisol (in humans; corticosterone in animals), which plays a powerful role in the stress response.

At the same time that the HPA system carries out these processes, the autonomic system is activated: The powerful locus coeruleus/norepinephrine (LC/NE) system in the brainstem acts upward on neural mechanisms throughout the brain and hypothalamic and other limbic areas act downward through the descending autonomic (sympathetic and parasympathetic) nervous system (Chrousos, 1992). During the stress response, the sympathetic system predominates and produces readiness of the heart, blood vessels, and other viscera for complex action programs to respond appropriately to the stressor and to reinstate homeostasis.

As the stress response continues, it has a powerful impact on multiple additional systems. The immune system is suppressed and major portions of the limbic system (mesocorticolimbic areas as well as the amygdala and hippocampus), which play a role in emotional, motivational, homeostatic, and cognitive processes, are activated. Furthermore, the endogenous opioids such as endorphin are released within minutes. Their initial function may be primarily to inhibit or modulate the release of cortisol (Chrousos, 1992; Sapolsky, 1992).

This highly simplified description does not include multiple other neural and hormonal systems, and the complex interactions among them, that take part in the stress response (Chrousos, 1992). Figure 3.1 provides a schematic representation of the major components that comprise the stress system and the checks and balances among them. Figure 3.2 is a more simplified diagram of these components and their interactions.

The stress and pain-perception systems, therefore, have complex interactions. Injury produces information that feeds into the body-self neuromatrix that generates the output patterns that comprise the neurosignature for the perception of the extent and severity of the injury, and, concurrently, activate the appropriate action patterns to be chosen from the available pool (Melzack, 1995). This output, together with information generated by the neuromatrixes that receive inputs from the other sensory and cognitive systems, acts on the stress-regulation mechanisms that are part of the limbic system—the HPA and LC/NE-sympathetic systems—and determines whether or not pain will be experienced or suppressed. It is well known (Melzack, Wall, & Ty, 1982; Melzack & Wall, 1996) that people who undergo severe injury may not feel any pain for as long as hours, even days, afterwards. Because the stress system requires about 1–4 minutes to be activated, the endorphin and other opioid substances released by stressors cannot be the determinant of the complete suppression of pain after injury. Rather, the neuromatrixes that generate sensory-evaluative information regarding the body and the circumstances of injury (for example, an injury in an automobile accident, a gash in the leg of a zebra by a hungry lion) determine the initial activation or suppression of the pain, inflammation processes, and immune systems (Sapolsky, 1992).

Prolonged activation of the stress-control systems produces breakdown of muscle, bone, and neural tissue. Excessively long or intense activation of these systems, therefore, can have disastrous consequences. They may set the stage for fibromyalgia, osteoporosis, and other chronic pain syndromes (Chrousos & Gold, 1992).

To recapitulate, the HPA and LC/NE-sympathetic systems are activated by perceived pain or other forms of stress on the basis of sensory and cognitive

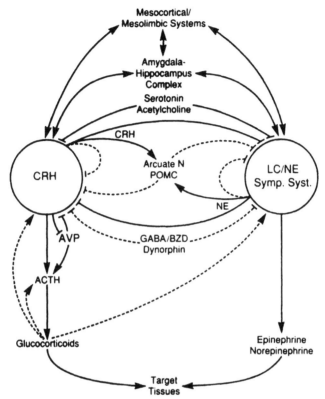

FIG. 3.1   A simplified, heuristic representation of the central and peripheral components of the stress system, their functional interrelations, and their relation to other CNS systems involved in the stress response. The hypothalamic corticotropin releasing hormone (CRH) neuron in the paraventricular nucleus and the centers of the arousal and autonomic systems (LC = locus coeruleus; sympathetic system) in the brainstem represent major centers of this system, connected anatomically and functionally to each other in a positive feedback cycle, with CRH stimulating the latter and brainstem norepinephrine (NE) the former. Local negative feedback loops are present in each center, with CRH and NE inhibiting their own secretion via a presynaptic mechanism. The CRH neuron and the LC receive stimulatory cholinergic and serotonergic innervation as well as inhibitory opioid peptidergic and gabaergic influences. Most opioid peptides inhibiting CRH originate from arcuate nucleus neurons that produce the proopiomelanocortin (POMC)-derived peptides beta-endorphin and ACTH, which are also inhibitory to CRH secretion. Glucocorticoids inhibit the activity of the CRH neuron and the arousal or sympathetic system centers. Vasopressin, a factor that markedly synergizes with the effects of CRH, must also be considered an important component of this system. From Chrousos, G. P. & Gold P. W., The concepts of stress and stress disorders. *JAMA*, *267*, 1244–1252, 1992, with permission.

input to the body-self neuromatrix. At the same time, when injury or other pathology occurs, cytokines are released into the blood stream and are carried to the hypothalamus, where they act directly on the HPA and LC/NE-sympathetic systems, which are the two major pillars of the stress system. Activation of

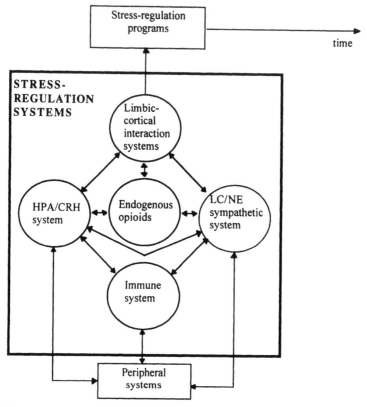

FIG. 3.2 A simplified schematic diagram of the components of the stress system and the interactions among them.

the stress system also influences several other powerful systems, including the immune system, the endogenous opiates, and major portions of the limbic system (mesocorticolimbic areas as well as the amygdala and hippocampus). All of these systems interact with each other and are characterized by multiple checks and balances (Chrousos & Gold, 1992; Fuchs & Melzack, 1997; Fuchs, Kerr, & Melzack, 1996; Harbuz & Lightman, 1992; Lariviere, Fuchs, & Melzack, 1995; Sapolsky, 1992). It is not surprising, then, to find great variability among studies. Nevertheless, particular effects of the stress system are firmly established.

The inhibitory effect of cortisol on the immune system and the serious effects of prolonged immune suppression are fully documented (Chrousos, 1992; Sapolsky, 1992). The opiates appear to modulate the effects of cortisol but their full function is not understood. The programs aimed at a return to homeostasis are only partly known; their relation to chronic pain must, because of our lack of knowledge, be surmised.

PROGRAMS INVOLVING THE STRESS SYSTEM

Cortisol, together with the activation of the sympathetic system, sets the stage for the stress response. Cortisol plays an essential role because it is responsible for producing and maintaining high levels of glucose for the response. At the same time, cortisol is potentially a highly destructive substance because, to ensure a high level of glucose, it breaks down the protein in muscle and inhibits the ongoing replacement of calcium in bone. It can also have a marked deleterious effect on neurons in the hippocampus (Sapolsky, 1996). As a result, if the output of cortisol is prolonged, excessive, or abnormally patterned, it may produce destruction of muscle, bone, and neural tissue and produce the conditions for many kinds of chronic pain.

The deleterious effect on hippocampal neurons during aging is particularly serious because the hippocampus acts as a natural brake on cortisol release. As aging proceeds, therefore, cortisol is released in larger amounts, producing a cascading destructive effect (Sapolsky, 1992) that could contribute to the increase of chronic pain problems known to occur among older people.

It is possible that any site of increased cytokine activity and inflammation, including sites of strain, sprain, or spasm of muscles and tendons could become the focus of cortisol action and muscle destruction. This could mark the beginning of trigger zones at sites that tend to become inflamed due to minor injury (Sola, 1994), and may become particularly vulnerable to cortisol's destructive effects. The breakdown of muscle protein could also be the basis for fibromyalgia and other muscle pains. At the same time, calcium replacement in bone is inhibited (Sapolsky, 1992). If the inhibition is prolonged, it may become the basis of osteoporosis, which may produce deformities and fractures, particularly of the vertebrae and hip, that are often extremely painful. Rheumatoid arthritis, interestingly, is associated with hypoactivity of the HPA axis, and has been attributed to an abnormality of hypothalamic regulation (Tsigos & Chrousos, 1994).

The cortisol output by itself may not be sufficient to cause chronic pain problems, but rather provides the background conditions so that other contributing factors may, all together, produce them. Estrogen levels, genetic predispositions, psychological stresses derived from social competition and the hassles of everyday life may act together to influence the effects of cortisol on the target organs.

A high proportion of cases of chronic back pain may be due to more subtle causes (Jayson & Freemont, 1995). The perpetual stresses and strains on the vertebral column (at discs and facet joints) produce greatly increased vascularization and fibrosis of the area. As a result, there is a release of substances such as bradykinen, which are known to produce inflammation and pain, into local tissues and blood stream. As a result, the whole HPA cascade may be triggered repeatedly.

The effect of stress-produced substances—such as cortisol and noradrenalin—at sites of minor lesions and inflammation may, if it occurs often and is prolonged, activate a neuromatrix program that anticipates increasingly severe damage and attempts to counteract it. The program, to reduce strain and inflammation, could generate the neurosignature for pain, which induces rest, the repair of injured tissues, and the restoration of homeostasis.

This speculation is supported by strong evidence. Chrousos and Gold (1992) and Tsigos and Chrousos (1994) have documented the effects of dysregulation of the cortisol system, to which they attribute fibromyalgia, rheumatoid arthritis, and chronic fatigue syndrome (which is often painful). They propose, on the basis of experimental data, that they are associated with *hypo*cortisolism—that is, reduced release of cortisol during stress. However, hypocortisolism may also reflect a higher level of utilization and metabolism of cortisol, which may appear as a depletion due to prolonged stress. Indeed, an important problem that requires investigation is the effect of a prolonged series of brief stresses— that is, brief spurts of hypo- or hypercortisolism over a long period of time— compared to prolonged, continuous stress. Whatever the mechanism, myopathy, bone decalcification, fatigue, and accelerated neural degeneration during aging are produced by prolonged exposure to stress.

A better understanding of the multiple modulation effects among the components of the stress system, as well as the effects of long durations of abnormal patterns of secretion of cortisol, may reveal the underlying interactional mechanisms (Chrousos & Gold, 1992; Sapolsky, 1992). For example, the endogenous opioids that are released by stress produce a further reduction in cortisol output. Cortisol levels are also decreased by sympathetic activity. The temporal patterns of output of different substances may determine hypo- versus hypercortisolism and, therefore, the resultant painful conditions. Diabetes mellitus, especially with diabetic neuropathy, is associated with *hyper*cortisolism (Tsigos & Chrousos, 1994). Research is therefore needed especially to investigate these deleterious effects on tissues in relation to pain.

PROGRAMS INVOLVING THE IMMUNE SYSTEM

A major effect of stress is the suppression of the immune system, which normally attacks invading bacteria and viruses (Steinman, 1993). However, this suppression may induce the immune system to attack the body itself, which would produce autoimmune diseases, many of which are also chronic pain syndromes. A possible mechanism is that prolonged suppression may result in dangerous levels of infection and an accumulation of toxins. Conceivably, the release from suppression may lead to a rebound, excessive, autoimmune response.

Concurrently with the suppression of the immune response, stress also suppresses the perception of pain and inflammation at the site of injury. The value of suppressing pain is clear: A wounded zebra, for example, needs to run from an attacking lion, and pain as well as inflammation would hamper running speed and could lead to death (Sapolsky, 1992). However, this suppression of pain,

TABLE 3.1
Autoimmune diseases with a prominent pain component and painful diseases
with a suspected autoimmune component

Autoimmune diseases with a prominent pain component	Painful diseases with a suspected autoimmune component
Autoimmune arthropathy: rheumatoid synovitis	Endometriosis
Autoimmune polyneuropathies	Fibromyalgia
Dermatomyositis	Osteoarthritis
Inflammatory bowel diseases (Crohn's disease; ulcerative colitis)	
Inflammatory myopathy	
Insulin-dependent diabetes (Diabetic neuropathy and pseudo-tables lightening pains)	
Interstitial cystitis	
Mixed connective tissue disease (polyarthritis, diffuse scleroderma, trigeminal neuropathy)	
Multiple sclerosis	
Polymyositis	
Rheumatoid arthritis	
Scleroderma	
Sjögren's syndrome	
Systemic lupus erythematosis	
Systemic sclerosis	

inflammation, and immune-system activity could also produce increased levels of tissue damage and infection. The suppression of pain may persist for hours, sometimes days, yet the pain returns (Fuchs et al., 1996; Fuchs & Melzack, 1997; Melzack et al., 1982), indicating that the mechanisms that produce pain and inflammation remain intact. It is possible, therefore, that the immune system may rebound with excessive vigour.

Consequently, the initially protective mechanisms may produce autoimmune diseases that are associated with significant levels of pain (Table 3.1). Some are also categorized as chronic pain syndromes—such as Crohn's disease, multiple sclerosis, rheumatoid arthritis, scleroderma, and lupus (Merskey & Bogduk, 1994).

The mechanisms that relate immune suppression and chronic pain are not understood. One possible mechanism is that immune suppression, which prolongs the presence of dead tissue and invading bacteria and viruses, could produce a greater output of cytokines, with a consequent increase in cortisol release and its destructive effects. Another possibility, as I have already suggested, is that prolonged immune suppression may give way to a rebound, excessive immune response that may lead to autoimmune disease and chronic pain syndromes. Thorough investigation may provide valuable clues for understanding at least some of the chronic pain syndromes that perplex us and are beyond our

TABLE 3.2
Sex prevalence of various painful disorders

Female prevalence	Male prevalence	No sex prevalence
Atypical facial pain (odontalgia) (F>>M)	Ankylosing spondylitis (9:1)	Acute herpes zoster
Burning tongue syndrome (F>M)	Cluster headache (9:1)	Chronic gastric ulcer
Chronic tension headache (1.5:1)	Hemophilic arthropathy (M>>F)	Cluster-tic syndrome
Fibromyalgia syndrome (7:1)	Postherpetic neuralgia (M>F)	Crohn's disease
Interstitial cystitis (10:1)	Posttraumatic headache (M>F)	Thoracic outlet syndrome
Irritable bowel syndrome (5:1)		
Migraine with aura (2:1)		
Migraine without aura (7:1)		
Multiple sclerosis (2:1)		
Raynaud's disease (5:1)		
Rheumatoid arthritis (F>M)		
Scleroderma (3:1)		
Systemic lupus erythematosis (9:1)		
Temporomandibular joint disorder (F>M)		
Tic douloureux (2:1)		

Age-dependent sex differences

Female prevalence	Male prevalence
Gout (after age 60)	Erythromelalgia (over age 50)
Livedo reticularis (under age 40)	Gout (before age 60)
Osteoarthritis (after age 45)	Osteoarthritis (before age 45)
Reflex sympathetic dystrophy (under age 18 (6:1) and after age 50)	

This table is adapted from Berkley (1997), with additional information from Merskey and Bogduk (1994). The ratios shown in brackets are the best estimates available in Merskey and Bogduk or Wall and Melzack (1994). The "greater than" sign (> or >>) is used when ratios are not available.

control. For example, it is well known that estrogen promotes the release of the cytokine, gamma-interferon, which in turn produces increases in cortisol output as well as autoimmune diseases (Steinman, 1993). This may explain why more females than males suffer from most kinds of chronic pain as well as painful autoimmune diseases such as multiple sclerosis and lupus.

In general, more women than men have autoimmune diseases and chronic pain syndromes (Table 3.2). Among the 5% of adults who suffer from an autoimmune disease, two out of three are women. Pain syndromes also show sex differences, as Berkley (1997) has argued, with the majority prevalent in women, and a much smaller number prevalent in men. Of particular importance are the increases and decreases in chronic pain among women concurrently with changes in estrogen output as a function of age. The relationship between autoimmune diseases and some forms of chronic pain leads to a search for possible causes. It is well known that estrogen produces an increase in cortisol levels for a brief period prior to menstruation. If this happens each month, the repetitive pattern could produce a cumulative destructive effect. Because these differences are small, they tend to be discounted, but they should not be. Abnormal patterns of cortisol release may produce myopathy, osteoporosis, neural dysfunction during aging, and autoimmune diseases (Sapolsky, 1992).

However, the role of estrogen in stress-regulation programs is obviously very complex. Estrogen has been implicated by Steinman (1993) as playing a role in several autoimmune syndromes, whereas Chrousos (1992) and Sapolsky (1992) believe that there is not sufficient free estrogen to have a significant effect on stress-dysregulation syndromes. Estrogen, in fact, presents a paradox: It increases the output of cortisol, which diminishes calcium replacement, yet estrogen replacement therapy after menopause is widely used to prevent osteoporosis. It is possible, though unlikely, that estrogen plays only a minor role in stress-related dysfunctional syndromes. It is more likely that its effects are modulated, inhibited, or facilitated by genetic determinants, other concurrently circulating hormones such as vasopressin, as well as the levels of estrogen receptors and even the patterns of change of all of these factors. It is also possible that, under some conditions, estrogen may have an inhibitory effect on the cascade of events that leads to stress-related syndromes. Clearly, this is a potentially important field for research, with many tantalizing clues.

Three additional clues reveal the relationship between stress and chronic pain. First, in addition to a higher incidence of autoimmune diseases and chronic pain syndromes, women also have a disproportionately higher incidence (3:1) of depression, which is strongly influenced by stress. Second, as we have seen, antidepressants are often highly effective for the treatment of chronic pain. Third, antidepressants act on the hippocampus, which acts as a brake on cortisol release during stress. Smith (1991) has made a strong argument that macrophages such as interleukin-1 provoke depression. As the hippocampus plays a powerful role in the affective dimension of pain and acts as a brake on stress, the effect of antidepressants on the neural activity of the hippocampus would be expected to modify the output neurosignature pattern and influence both pain and depression.

PROGRAMS INVOLVING HOMEOSTATIC REGULATION

Pain and other stressors produce changes in every physiological activity that is under homeostatic control, such as blood pressure, blood sugar level, and body temperature. A major stressor produces marked changes in one or more of these activities, and homeostatic programs are activated to bring about a return to normal set-point levels. The relationship between pain sensitivity and several homeostatic physiological activities provides valuable evidence that the body-self neuromatrix contains programs that exert a continuous influence on pain sensitivity in order to maintain homeostatic equilibrium. At least, this is a reasonable assumption. Consider the following examples.

Hypertension and pain

It is now well established (France & Ditto, 1996) that chronic hypertension is associated with decreased sensitivity to pain. The current explanation is that baroreceptors are stimulated by increased blood pressure to bring about a reduction in pain sensitivity. However, in place of this stimulus-response interpretation, it is more plausible to propose a genetically determined neuroendocrine program that regulates both hypertension and pain. The decreased sensitivity to pain, I assume, decreases the possibility that severe pain will raise blood pressure to dangerous levels that threaten survival of the body-self. Hypertensive people are less sensitive to pain in a variety of experimental and clinical situations. Remarkably, even the adult children of hypertensive parents, who show no signs of hypertension, are also less sensitive to pain. This points to a genetically determined program that is influenced by the concurrent genetic predisposition to hypertension and its potential danger to survival. The neuroendocrine program, the evidence suggests, produces a continuously lowered sensitivity to pain.

Further evidence (reviewed by France & Ditto, 1996) supports this concept. Hypertensive people who were placed on anti-hypertensive medication for three months showed significant decreases in blood pressure but no significant change in pain sensitivity. Lowered pain sensitivity, evidently, was maintained by a mechanism independently from the hypertension, although the strong link between the two has been confirmed by a large number of excellent studies. Interestingly, specially bred hypertensive rats also show a decreased sensitivity to pain, which develops as early as three weeks of age and precedes the later development of elevated blood pressure. It is reasonable, then, to propose a genetic mechanism for a neuroendocrine program that anticipates the development of hypertension and maintains a decreased sensitivity to pain in order to prevent bombardment of the brain when injury occurs, thus diminishing pain, stress, and a consequent reflex increase in blood pressure.

Blood sugar levels and pain

Several studies (reviewed by Morley, Mooradian, Levine, & Morley, 1984) found that diabetic patients, in contrast to hypertensive patients, were less able to tolerate pain than control subjects who did not have diabetes. Furthermore, when non-diabetic subjects were infused with glucose, they showed an increased sensitivity to pain. To explain this unusual observation, it is conceivable that increased sugar levels in diabetics activates a neuroendocrine program that produces increased pain in order to make diabetics more careful about sustaining an injury (because an injury hurts more). As a result, the sensory bombardment of the brain by pain-producing input would be diminished, which would also decrease stress and the disruption of metabolic homeostasis.

Brain temperature and pain

A major aim of homeostatic programs after moderate to severe injury is to prevent large increases in brain metabolism and the consequent rise in brain temperature produced by injury from reaching dangerous levels. It is a fact that a rise in brain temperature of a few degrees produces convulsions, and a few degrees more results in death. To achieve the goal of maintaining brain temperature within a narrow range, a number of strategies are available to the brain: (1) decrease of brain activity by direct neural inhibition or by the local constriction of blood vessels; (2) dilation of blood vessels in the brain to increase blood flow to remove the heat produced by brain metabolism; (3) decrease of blood flow to sensory nerves (which may destroy them); and (4) the destruction of transmitting nerve cells (apoptosis) by commands from program centers.

Inhibition of activity in widespread areas of the brain, including portions of the visual system, may be induced by cutaneous stimulation (such as rubbing the skin) under particular conditions (light anesthesia) (Melzack & Casey, 1967; Melzack, Konrad, & Dubrovsky, 1968, 1969). The mechanisms that underlie this inhibition are not known. The large decrease (and occasional increase) in metabolic activity reflect both neural metabolic changes and blood flow. The inhibition, moreover, may persist for long durations after brief periods of stimulation. The brain, therefore, possesses a system capable of exerting strong, widespread inhibition that is normally held under control but is available as a program to modulate brain metabolism.

Recent evidence using elegant brain imaging techniques supports the concept of inhibition of brain metabolism during pain. Jones and his colleagues (Di Pierro et al., 1991) found that patients with severe, persistent pain due to cancer showed a significantly *lower* level of blood flow in the thalamus compared to pain-free control subjects. Even more impressive is the fact that a cordotomy (which cuts the sensory pathways from the cancerous areas to the thalamus) produced relief of pain and a striking *increase* in blood flow to the thalamus until local temparatures reached normal levels. A further recent study (Canavero et al., 1993) found that two patients with central pain syndromes showed a decrease of blood flow in the parietal lobe, with still further decreases after nonpainful stimulation. These results provide powerful evidence that pain is associated with a homeostatic *decrease* in blood flow in a major sensory transmission relay, which returns to normal, higher levels when pain is relieved. This may seem anomalous, but is consistent with the idea of long-term homeostatic programs to prevent an excessive increase in brain temperature.

The dilation or constriction of blood vessels to the brain is a well-known accompaniment of the sequence of events that occurs during most migraines. Migraines are subjectively undesirable but represent a powerful program by which the brain, because of a perceived threat, can diminish activity in a large part of the brain and, by inducing pain, can force the organism to rest and decrease all inputs to the brain.

The possible strategy of prolonged, reduced blood flow to nerves and apoptosis ("suicide") of neurons in response to the anticipated danger of a rise in brain temperature may seem drastic, but it is a reasonable strategy to cope with a perceived threat of a prolonged rise in brain temperature that could eventually produce convulsions and incapacitate an animal seeking to escape a deadly predator. Apoptosis of neurons could occur at any level; in the brain itself, in the cord, and in peripheral nerves. It could explain spontaneous neuropathies (as a program gone wrong) or diabetic or other neuropathies related to conditions involving abnormal stimulation of peripheral nerves. For example, as the lower limbs in diabetics may develop circulation problems that would produce massive input and pain, the brain may activate an anticipatory program to destroy the potentially offending nerves by restricting blood flow to them or by apoptosis. Misinformation, or misinterpretation of information, or misresponse to information could all lead to inappropriate spontaneous neuropathy. Apoptosis, in this case, is akin to the immune system behaving inappropriately and producing some of the autoimmune diseases.

IMPLICATIONS OF STRESS REGULATION

By unifying the perceptual and stress systems involved in pain, we immediately expand our available knowledge related to pain and open the door to new therapies. Our present understanding of receptor and spinal mechanisms, which is the basis of the gate control theory of pain (see Melzack & Wall, 1996) and its more recent extensions (Melzack, 1971; Melzack & Casey, 1968), is not diminished. Rather, the data and the gate control theory now fit into the broader framework of the neuromatrix theory of pain.

The intimate relationship between the perceptual and stress systems is not surprising. The limbic system, which receives the projections of the medial sensory transmission pathways, is the neural substrate of the affective-motivational dimension of pain (Dennis & Melzack, 1977; Melzack & Casey, 1968), and a portion of the system, including the hypothalamus, is an integral part of the stress system. The two systems are so interdependent that they should be considered as components of a single system (Fig. 3.3). This close relationship is further indicated by observations that pain exhibited by rats in the formalin test is abolished by a lesion of the medial projection system at the level of the thalamus, but is unaffected by a lesion of the lateral system at the same level (McKenna & Melzack, 1994). The lateral system has the important role of

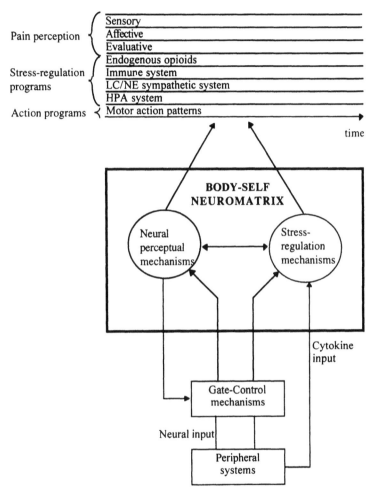

FIG. 3.3 A schematic diagram of the components of the neuromatrix theory of pain. The body-self neuromatrix comprises (a) neural perceptual mechanisms and (b) the stress-regulation system. Neural perceptual mechanisms incorporate the mechanisms of the gate theory (see Melzack & Wall, 1996) as well as the conceptual model of parallel, distributed processing systems described by Melzack and Casey (1968). The stress system comprises the components systems and their interactions shown schematically in Figs. 3.1 and 3.2. Both parts—perceptual and stress systems—produce actions and perceptions that persist in time and are shown as a "vivigram" of the components of the action systems. Also shown is the perceptual experience produced concomitantly with the action system activities by the output neurosignature patterns generated by the body-self neuromatrix. The influences of other sensory and cognitive processes on the generation of the neurosignature are not shown.

conveying precise information to the body-self neuromatrix and generates the information needed for the localization and evaluation of the input. Both kinds of information are projected to the limbic system, which is prepared to generate the affective-motivational response to perceived injury and stress. We now have a new conceptual model of the brain in which limbic structures, the cerebral cortex, and all major components of the stress system play key roles. The new concept has important implications for the study of pain.

Rationale of pain therapies

First, let us look at therapies that make sense within the framework of the new concept. For example, tricyclic antidepressant drugs relieve some forms of chronic pain even though the pain is not caused by depression. However, cytokines, particularly interleukin-1, interferon-alpha, and tumor necrosis factor, have been shown to produce the symptoms of major depression, including the hormone abnormalities associated with depression (see Smith, 1991), and they also activate the stress system, which may produce the basis for chronic pain syndromes. Conceivably, antidepressants may act on hormones and neurotransmitters, such as noradrenalin and serotonin, that play a role in both depression and pain. Smith (1991) also notes that major depression is as much as two to three times more common among women than men. Moreover, estrogen increases the production of cytokines, which produce an almost fourfold increase in cortisol production. Rheumatoid arthritis, which is associated with dysregulation of cortisol output, also has a female: male ratio in young adults of 5:1. Beyond age 60, this drops to 2:1, and major depression also drops dramatically in women after age 65 (from 5.8% in women aged 18–44 to 1.6% in women over 65). As migraine, lupus, and a variety of stress- and immune-system diseases also show ratios of women:men that range from 2:1 to 9:1, it is reasonable to assume that a large number of chronic pain syndromes as well as depression are linked to the stress-regulation systems.

A variety of well-known facts that had no place in the Cartesian paradigm now have plausible, meaningful roles. For example, the high rate of pain relief after lesions of the pituitary in cancer patients now becomes comprehensible (Miles, 1994), because it is a major link in the HPA system. This dramatic relief is reported by patients with hormone-related cancers but also occurs in a variety of nonhormone-related chronic pains. Lesions of the hypothalamus can also produce relief of some kinds of chronic pain (Bouckoms, 1994). Even the excellent pain-relieving effects of lesions of the cingulate cortex and cingulum bundle (Bouckoms, 1994) become comprehensible in view of their strategic location as part of the limbic system and, therefore, of the stress/immune systems.

The neuromatrix theory of pain also fits with observations that a program involving steroid injections can have powerful pain-relieving effects (Kozin, McCarty, Sims, & Genant, 1976; Kozin, Ryan, Carerra, Soin, & Wortmann,

1981). These effects cannot be attributed simply to the local control of inflammation. Steroid injections for reflex sympathetic dystrophy (RSD) can have very dramatic effects, revealing mechanisms that must involve widespread neural, adrenergic, and hormonal mechanisms. The effects of steroids for rheumatoid arthritis are explicable in terms of the dysfunctional HPA system in these patients. But the excellent effects of steroids on RSD cannot be so easily explained. Steroids are potentially dangerous substances, yet can dramatically relieve pain. Conceivably, as we learn more about augmenting steroids with other substances that are part of the whole stress system, we will learn to do even better. This approach toward controlling the stress system has, I believe, tremendous potential. There is, to be sure, the complexity of the inhibitory, excitatory, and modulatory interactions. However, research will undoubtedly reveal them and our armamentarium for pain therapy will be greatly enriched.

Determinants of chronic pain

An important source of individual differences in the effects of stress—why some people and not others develop autoimmune diseases—is genetic. In the case of systemic lupus erythematosus (SLE), for example, a genetic factor is definitely involved; if one member of a set of twins has SLE, there is a 30% chance that the other twin will also develop it (far higher than the appearance in the general population). In addition to this genetic contribution to individual variation of response to injury is the variable response to stress due to the enhancement of a given stress by (1) other concurrent stress; (2) the cumulative effect of prior stresses (partly determined by their pattern of appearance); and (3) the kinds of concurrent or prior stresses or stress-effects: psychological versus physical, severity and duration of the stresses, the degree of effects due to prenatal stress of the mother (Meaney et al., 1993).

It is well known that adaptation to repetitive stressors occurs, so that chronic or repeated stress is generally associated with normal circulatory levels of ACTH and corticosterone (the rat's equivalent of cortisol). There is good evidence, however, that the system may become more sensitive to other types of acute stressors during this period. For example, the pituitaries of chronically stressed animals may be hypersensitive to the effects of vasopressin, which is an important regulator of pituitary responsiveness to chronic stress (Harbuz and Lightman, 1992).

Genes and sensory inputs may both play synergistic roles in determining the development of a chronic pain syndrome. Consider the following experiment: Mayeux et al. (1995) and Mayeux (1996) examined the risk of developing Alzheimer's disease (AD) in elderly people who had sustained a head injury and possessed the gene known as apolipoprotein-epsilon 4. They found that a "ten-fold increase in the risk of AD was associated with both apolipoprotein-epsilon 4 and a history of traumatic head injury, compared with a two-fold increase in risk with apolipoprotein-epsilon 4 alone. Head injury in the absence of an apolipoprotein-epsilon 4 allele did not increase risk. These data imply that the biological effects of head injury may increase the risk of AD, but only through a synergistic relationship with apolipoprotein-epsilon 4." In other words, after a physical head injury, the gene may turn a normal repair process into a step toward disease of far greater complexity.

It is reasonable to suspect a similar synergistic relationship between other genes and physical injuries as a causal factor in some chronic pain syndromes. For example, multiple sclerosis—which is often a painful syndrome—has been shown to have a genetic contribution and very often develops a few weeks after a routine illness. These combinations merit further investigation in the attempt to understand chronic pain syndromes. Many syndromes, such as reflex sympathetic dystrophy, causalgia, postherpetic neuralgia, or diabetic peripheral neuropathy, develop in some people and not others, even though the nerve injury is apparently the same in both groups. Why should two people receive virtually identical gunshot wounds, yet one develops horrible, persistent burning pain and the other heals without any subsequent pain? Or, why should two people have the same degree of diabetes, yet one person develops peripheral neuropathy and the other does not? Conceivably a genetic predisposition exerts a synergistic effect together with sensory input following an injury. This hypothesis is highly speculative, but merits consideration because chronic pain syndromes are so debilitating and most have, so far, defied all the traditional sensory approaches in the attempt to understand them.

The place of psychological factors in producing pain and relieving is clear. Cortisol is released by either psychological stress or physical injury, and Sapolsky (1992) has proposed that the cumulative release of pulses of cortisol is a major determinant of pathology. All psychological stresses may contribute to the neuroendocrine processes that give rise to pain syndromes, and psychological therapies that control stress ultimately affect cortisol release and, therefore, influence the development of chronic pain. A decrease in cortisol output by psychological therapy may not by itself be sufficient to produce a major reduction in pain, but it should be part of multiple therapies that can have additive effects in decreasing the destructive effects of cortisol.

Each kind of stressor can produce physiological effects that are additive with the effects of other stressors. The patterns of stress responses, moreover, may vary for each (Sapolsky, 1992). It is essential, therefore, in the context of injury and pain, to recognize that the stress effects of an injury can vary, in severity and pattern, as a function of other stresses, such as loss of self-esteem, employment, or other security symbols.

These shared mechanisms of stress produced by psychological causes and physical injury help make sense of data that are otherwise difficult to understand. Patients with chronic pain, as a group, typically report higher than usual incidence of childhood abuse, or rape, or other stresses. This result is easily interpreted to mean that the abusive or stressful event produced neurotic traits which made the person more prone to chronic pain. However, instead of invoking neuroticism, it is sufficient to recognize the additive effects of psychological and physical stresses in producing the conditions for chronic pain.

Studies with animal subjects throw light on these additive effects. Meaney and his colleagues (1993) demonstrated the effects of prenatal stress on HPA function in the adult. Pregnant female rats were subjected to the stress of physical restraint during the third trimester of pregnancy and the offspring were studied when they were fully mature adults. Interestingly, the effects of prenatal stress were pronounced in female offspring but not in males. The females showed sharply enhanced responses to stress. Similarly, prenatal alcohol intake by the mothers resulted in increased HPA responses to stress in female offspring, but not in males. These investigators also found that handling or "gentling" in early postnatal life produced substantial decreases in the response to stress at maturity —a positive effect that occurred in males as well as females. Meaney and his colleagues (1993, p. 83) conclude that "the early environment is able to 'fine-tune' the sensitivity and efficiency of certain neuroendocrine systems that mediate the animal's response to stimuli that threaten homeostasis."

The neuromatrix theory, therefore, provides a reasonable mechanism whereby psychological stresses may provide the basis for chronic pain. Stressors have destructive effects on muscle, skeletal, and hippocampal neural tissue, which may become the immediate basis of pain or provide a basis for the devastating effects of later minor injuries in which the severity of pain is disproportionately far greater than would be expected from the injury.

It is possible that psychological stress alone can become a cause of chronic pain because it produces substances that have destructive effects on body tissues. Prolonged stressful events, it is now evident, can leave a memory etched into bone, muscle, and nerve tissue, just as an injury sculpts a neuronal pattern into the neuromatrix. Stress, however, is a subjective experience. Threatening sensory or cognitive events may or may not be perceived as a stressor, just as the sensory input from an injury may or may not be perceived as pain. Even when pain is experienced, it may be a stressor if it implies danger and threat to survival of the self physically or psychologically. In contrast, a major injury may evoke little or no stress if it is perceived as a successful escape from danger, such as a battlefield.

The neuromatrix theory of pain also has implications for understanding the origins of reflex sympathetic dystrophy (RSD). It is has long been assumed that RSD is primarily a disease of overstimulation of the sympathetic nervous system. However, I propose that after a period of time, the HPA axis takes over, and the destructive signs observed after several months are the result of dysregulation of the cortisol system rather than the noradrenergic system. This could explain the observation (Hannington-Kiff, 1994) that sympathetic blocks may prevent RSD if administered early in the disease but not if given after the signs are well under way.

Hannington-Kiff (1994) has observed that the "early", mainly autonomic, features are usually clinically obvious by about 3–6 weeks after a minor injury. After this time, major dystrophic changes occur in the skin and nails, with muscle and joint stiffness, skin swelling, excessive heat and sweating, abnormal blood flow and skin color, and abnormal skin sensitivity and pain. At this stage, treatment with sympathetic blocks is rarely effective. The reason, I propose, is that the HPA axis has superseded the sympathetic system and now dominates the stress response to the injury that initiated the cascade of events. For this reason, it is possible that psychological stress and stressful events at earlier stages in life contributed to the sequence of events. Current stress also aggravates the course of the disease. This does not mean that RSD is due to "psychogenic" causes. Rather, it may be a stress-related disease, in which all types of stress produce cumulative actions and in which the HPA axis and the destructive effects of cortisol predominate.

These considerations suggest lines of therapy for RSD that differ from those now generally in use. Decreases in stress and manipulation of the HPA component of the stress system are more likely to produce pain relief for these people who suffer so terribly. Kozin has achieved generally excellent results with RSD patients by using steroid injection therapy, and he notes wistfully (1993, p. 1670) that "unlike the interruption of sympathetic pathways, no currently known theoretic mechanisms explain the efficacy of corticosteroids in RSD". The powerful role of the stress system in chronic pain provides a plausible mechanism.

A further important feature of chronic pain that implicates the stress system is the fact that the severity of pain during an injury or infection is a major predictor of the occurrence of subsequent persistent pain. Dworkin and Portenoy (1996) have identified six factors that predict those patients with shingles (herpes zoster) who are most likely to develop chronic pain (postherpetic neuralgia) that persists long after the infection has healed. The predictors are: more severe pain during the initial acute stage, greater severity of the infection of the nerve and its effects on the adjacent skin, greater sensory dysfunction of the affected dermatome, greater magnitude and duration of the humoral and immune response during the acute stage, pain in the dermatome before the appearance of the rash (painful prodrome), and fever greater than 38°C during the acute stage. Clearly, these factors include signs of activity of the stress system in addition to the greater pain, which is itself a stressor. Further evidence of acute pain intensity as a predictor of later persistent pain is the observation by Malenfant et al. (1996) that patients with severe burns who suffer the most intense pain in the initial stages of recovery and healing are the ones most likely to have persistent pain that continues for years after full healing has occurred. Finally, Katz, Jackson, Kavanagh, and Sandler (1996) found that patients with intense pain during the first two days after a chest operation (thoracotomy) are much more likely to report persistent chest pain a year-and-a-half after the operation than patients who were pain-free after the operation. Katz concludes that "aggressive management of early post-operative pain may reduce the likelihood of long-term post-thoracotomy pain". It is evident, then, that severe pain, which is a powerful stressor, is a major determinant of chronic pain after healing has occurred and there are no obvious physical causes of the severe pain suffered by the patients. The initial pain and stress, it is reasonable to assume, produced changes in both the perceptual and stress systems that contributed to the abnormal output patterns of the body-self neuromatrix.

SUMMARY

In summary, the neuromatrix theory of pain proposes that the neurosignature for pain experience is modulated by sensory inputs and by cognitive events, such as psychological stress. It may also occur because stressors, physical as well as psychological, act on stress-regulation systems, which may produce lesions of muscle, bone, and nerve tissue, thereby contributing to the neurosignature patterns that give rise to chronic pain. In short, the neuromatrix, as a result of homeostasis-regulation patterns that have failed, produces the destructive conditions that may give rise to many of the chronic pains that so far have been resistant to treatments developed primarily to manage input-dependent pains. The stress-regulation system, with its complex, delicately balanced interactions, is an integral part of the multiple contributions that give rise to chronic pain.

The neuromatrix theory of pain—which places the neural-hormonal mechanisms of stress on a level of importance equal to the neural mechanisms of sensory transmission—has important implications for research and therapy. Some of these have been sketched out here. Others will become evident to endocrinologists and immunologists and, perhaps, to pain specialists with a knowledge of the field of stress. An immediate recommendation is that interdisciplinary pain clinics should expand to include specialists in endocrinology and immunology. Such a collaboration may lead to insights and new research strategies that may reveal the underlying mechanisms of chronic pain and give rise to new therapies to relieve the tragedy of unrelenting suffering.

ACKNOWLEDGEMENTS

This study was supported by Grant A7891 from the Natural Sciences and Research Council of Canada. I am grateful to Dr Kirk Osterland for his generous help in developing Table 3.2, and to Ms Lucy Gagliese and Dr Geoffrey Schultz for their valuable suggestions. Portions of this paper are derived from a chapter in a forthcoming book by the author.

REFERENCES

Berkley, K. J. (1997). Sex differences in pain. *Behavioral and Brain Sciences, 20*, 1–10.

Bouckoms, A. J. (1994). Limbic surgery for pain. In P. D. Wall & R. Melzack (Eds.), *Textbook of Pain* (pp. 1171–1187). Edinburgh: Churchill Livingstone.

Canavero, S., Pagni, C. A., Castellano, G., Bonicalzi, V., Bello, M., Duca, S., & Podio, V. (1993). The role of cortex in central pain syndromes: preliminary results of a long-term technetium-99 hexamethylpropyleneamineoxine single photon emission computed tomography study. *Neurosurgery, 32*, 185–207.

Chrousos, G. P. (1992). Regulation and dysregulation of the hypothalamic-pituitary-adrenal axis. *Endocrinology and Metabolism Clinics of North America, 21*, 833–858.

Chrousos, G. P., & Gold, P. W. (1992). The concepts of stress and stress system disorders. *JAMA, 267*, 1244–1252.

Dennis, S. G., & Melzack, R. (1977). Pain-signalling systems in the dorsal and ventral spinal cord. *Pain, 4*, 97–132.

Di Piero, V., Jones, A. K. P., Iannotti, F., Powell, M., Perani, D., Lenzi, G. K., & Frackowiak, R. S. J. (1991). Chronic pain: a PET study of the central effects of percutaneous high cervical cordotomy. *Pain, 46*, 9–12.

Dworkin, R. H., & Portenoy, R. K. (1996). Pain and its persistence in herpes zoster. *Pain, 67*, 241–251.

France, C. R., & Ditto, B. (1996). Risk for high blood pressure and decreased pain perception. *Current Directions in Psychological Science, 5*, 120–125.

Fuchs, P. N., Kerr, B., & Melzack, R. (1996). Delayed nociceptive response following cold-water swim in the formalin test: possible mechanisms of action. *Experimental Neurology, 139*, 291–298.

Fuchs, P. N., & Melzack, R. (1996). Restraint reduces formalin-test pain but the effect is not influenced by lesions of the hypothalamic paraventricular nucleus. *Experimental Neurology, 139*, 299–305.

Fuchs, P. N., & Melzack, R. (1997). Repeated cold water swim produces delayed nociceptive responses, but not analgesia, for tonic pain in the rat. *Experimental Neurology, 145*, 303–307.

Hannington-Kiff, J. G. (1994). Sympathetic nerve blocks in painful limb disorders. In P. D. Wall & R. Melzack (Eds.), *Textbook of Pain* (pp. 1035–1052). Edinburgh: Churchill Livingstone.

Harbuz, M. S., & Lightman, S. L. (1992). Stress and the hypothalamo-pituitary-adrenal axis: acute, chronic and immunological activation. *Journal of Endocrinology, 134*, 327–339.

Jayson, M. I. V., & Freemont, A. J. (1995). The role of vascular damage in the development of nerve root problems. In R. M. Aspden & R. W. Porter (Eds.), *Lumbar Spine Disorders: Current Concepts* (pp. 132–144). River Edge, NJ: World Scientific Publishing Co.

Katz, J., Jackson, M., Kavanagh, B. P., & Sandler, A. N. (1996). Acute pain after thoracic surgery predicts long-term post-thoracotomy pain. *The Clinical Journal of Pain, 12*, 50–55.

Kozin, F. (1993). Painful shoulder and reflex sympathetic dystrophy syndrome. In D. J. McCarty & W. J. Koopman (Eds.), *Arthritis and Allied Conditions* ((12th ed.), pp. 1643–1676). Philadelphia, PA: Lea and Febiger.

Kozin, F., McCarty, D. J., Sims, J., & Genant, H. (1976). The reflex sympathetic dystrophy syndrome. I. Clinical and histological studies: evidence for bilaterality, response to corticosteroids and articular involvement. *The American Journal of Medicine, 60*, 321–331.

Kozin, F., Ryan, L. M., Carerra, G. F., Soin, J. S., & Wortmann, R. L. (1981). The reflex sympathetic dystrophy syndrome (RSDS). III. Scintigraphic studies, further evidence for the therapeutic efficacy of systemic corticosteroids, and proposed diagnostic criteria. *The American Journal of Medicine, 70*, 23–30.

Lariviere, W. R., Fuchs, P. N., & Melzack, R. (1995). Hypophysectomy produces analgesia and paraventricular lesions have no effect on formalin-induced pain. *Experimental Neurology, 135*, 74–79.

Malenfant, A., Forget, R., Papillon, R., Amsel, R., Frigon, J.-Y., & Choinière, M. (1996). Prevalence and characteristics of chronic sensory problems in burn patients. *Pain, 67*, 493–500.

Mayeux, R. (1996). Reply from the author. *Neurology, 45*, 891–892.

Mayeux, R., Ottman, R., Maestre, G., Ngai, C., Tang, M. X., Ginsbert, H., Chun, M., Tycko, B., & Shelanski, M. (1995). Synergistic effects of traumatic head injury and apolipoprotein-epsilon 4 in patients with Alzheimer's disease. *Neurology, 45*, 555–557.

McKenna, J. E., & Melzack, R. (1994). Dissociable effects of lidocaine injection into medial versus lateral thalamus in tail-flick and formalin pain tests. *Pathophysiology, 1*, 205–214.

Meaney, M. J., Bhatnagar, S., Larocque, S., McCormick, C., Shanks, N., Sharma, S., Smythe, J., Viau, V., & Plotsky, P. M. (1993). Individual differences in the hypothalamic-pituitary-adrenal stress response and the hypothalamic CRF system. *Annals of the New York Academy of Sciences, 697*, 70–85.

Melzack, R. (1971). Phantom Limb pain: implications for treatment of pathological pain. *Anesthesiology, 35*, 409–419.

Melzack, R. (1991). The gate control theory 25 years later: new perspectives on phantom limb pain. In M. R. Bond, J. E. Charlton, & C. J. Woolf (Eds.), *Proceedings of the VIth World Congress on Pain* (pp. 9–21). Amsterdam: Elsevier.

Melzack, R. (1995). Phantom limb pain and the brain. In B. Bromm & J. E. Desmedt (Eds.), *Pain and the Brain* (pp. 73–82). New York: Raven Press.

Melzack, R., & Casey, K. L. (1967). Localized temperature changes evoked in the brain by somatic stimulation. *Experimental Neurology, 17*, 276–292.

Melzack, R., & Casey, K. L. (1968). Sensory, motivational, and central control determinants of pain: a new conceptual model. In D. Kenshalo (Ed.), *The Skin Senses* (pp. 423–443). Springfield, IL: Thomas.

Melzack, R., Konrad, K. W., & Dubrovsky, B. (1968). Prolonged changes in visual system activity produced by somatic stimulation. *Experimental Neurology, 20*, 443–459.

Melzack, R., Konrad, K. W., & Dubrovsky, B. (1969). Prolonged changes in central nervous system activity produced by somatic and reticular stimulation. *Experimental Neurology, 25*, 416–428.

Melzack, R., & Wall, P. D. (1996). *The challenge of Pain* (updated 2nd ed.). London: Penguin Books.

Melzack, R., Wall, P. D., & Ty, T. C. (1982). Acute pain in an emergency clinic: latency of onset and descriptor patterns. *Pain, 14*, 33–43.

Merskey, H., & Bogduk, N. (1994). *Classification of Chronic Pain*. Seattle: IASP Press.

Miles, J. (1994). Pituitary destruction. In P. D. Wall & R. Melzack (Eds.), *Textbook of Pain* (pp. 1159–1170). Edinburgh: Churchill Livingstone.

Morley, G. K., Mooradian, A. D., Levine, A. S., & Morley, J. E. (1984). Why is diabetic peripheral neuropathy painful? The effects of glucose on pain perception in humans. *American Journal of Medicine, 77*, 79–83.

Sapolsky, R. M. (1992). Neuroendocrinology of the stress-response. In J. B. Becker, S. M. Breedlove, & D. Crews (Eds.), *Behavioral Endocrinology*. Cambridge, MA: MIT Press.

Sapolsky, R. M. (1996). Stress, glucocorticoids, and damage to the nervous system: the current state of confusion. *Stress, 1*, 1–19.

Selye, H. (1950). *Stress*. Montreal: Acta Medical Publisher.

Smith, R. S. (1991). The macrophage theory of depression. *Medical Hypotheses, 35*, 298–306.

Sola, A. E. (1994). Upper extremity pain. In P. D. Wall & R. Melzack (Eds.), *Textbook of Pain* (pp. 457–474). Edinburgh: Churchill Livingstone.

Steinman, L. (1993). Autoimmune disease. *Scientific American, 269*, 107–114.

Tsigos, C., & Chrousos, G. P. (1994). Physiology of the hypothalamic-pituitary-adrenal axis in health and dysregulation in psychiatric and autoimmune disorders. *Endocrinology and Metabolism Clinics of North America, 23*, 451–466.

Wall, P. D., & Melzack, R. (Eds.) (1994). Textbook of Pain. Edinburgh: Churchill Livingstone.

CHAPTER FOUR

Somatic responses to psychological stress: The reactivity hypothesis

John T. Cacioppo
The Ohio State University, Columbus, Ohio, USA

Traditionally, tonic autonomic or neuroendocrine states have been thought to predict if not mediate the effects of stress on health. Research is reviewed suggesting that the nature and amount of *reactivity* to acute psychological stressors should not be overlooked. The very concept of stress connotes the exposure of an individual to a threatening stimulus or potentially overwhelming event. Autonomic and neuroendocrine activation in response to stressors is beneficial up to a point, but excessive activation may also have long-term costs. The metabolic requirements posed by the psychological stressors to which people are typically exposed in contemporary society are often minimal. Consequently, strong autonomic and neuroendocrine activation to psychological stressors is often not needed for effective coping but instead may affect cellular aging and health across time.

Traditionnellement, on pensait que les états toniques neuroendocrinien ou autonomique pouvaient prédire, voire médier, les effets du stress sur la santé. Une recension des recherches en ce domaine suggère que la nature et la quantité de réactivité à des stresseurs psychologiques aigus ne devraient pas être négligées. Le concept même de stress inclut l'exposition de l'individu à un stimulus menaçant ou à un événement potentiellement accablant. L'activation autonomique ou neuroendocrinienne en réponse à des stresseurs est avantageuse jusqu'à un certain point, mais une activation excessive peut également comporter des coûts à long terme. Surtout que les exigences métaboliques des stresseurs psychologiques auxquels les gens sont habituellement exposés sont minimales. En conséquence, une activation autonomique et neuroendocrinienne forte à des stresseurs psychologiques n'est souvent pas requise pour une adaptation efficace, mais peut, au contraire, avec le temps, réduire la dégénérescence cellulaire et la santé.

Conflicting choices, unexpected obstacles, overwhelming challenges, and uncontrollable events in contemporary society are an inescapable part of everyday life. When demands are perceived to exceed our ability or willingness to cope, the experiences they evoke are labeled as stress (Lazarus & Folkman, 1984). Whether or not one is able to cope, however, the demands, hassles, and irritations of daily life can activate autonomic and neuroendocrine responses. These responses often provide more than enough metabolic support for the behavioral demands of the situation but may have hidden costs in the long run.

Anecdotal evidence abounds for the influence of social and psychological stress on health. A supervisor on a construction crew exudes hostility, berating everyone with whom he comes into contact. His hostility carries over into his personal life, creating an atmosphere of animosity that reinforces his anger and hostility. He dies of a heart attack as he gets up to go to work one morning before his 50th birthday. A woman diagnosed as having breast cancer develops feelings of helplessness and hopelessness. Although her cancer is detected at an early stage, the disease progresses more quickly than in her more optimistic counterparts. She fails to survive five years. An otherwise healthy widower grieves over the loss of his long-time spouse. Within a year he dies, some say of a broken heart. An individual, depressed and lonely over becoming unemployed, engages in a series of predictably detrimental behaviors; she smokes incessantly, lives on sweets and fast food, becomes sedentary, has poor hygiene, and fails to comply with the prescribed medical regimens. She becomes vulnerable to various infectious diseases and dies in her sleep of pneumonia.

As we approach the 21st century the world is increasingly burdened by preventable illness, injury, and disability. Heart disease, for instance, accounts for approximately three-quarters of a million deaths annually in the US, cancer more than another half million, and respiratory and viral infections remain a major cause of morbidity and mortality among older adults (Baum, Cacioppo, Melamed, Gallant, & Travis, 1995; McGlone & Arden, 1987). In 1960, 5% of the US Gross National Product (GNP) went to medical services; in 1990 this share had grown to 12% (US Public Health Service, 1990). Injury now costs more than $100 billion annually, cardiovascular disease about $135 billion, and cancer over $70 billion.

Many of these health problems, and the consequent human, societal, and economic costs, have affective bases ranging from anxiety, anger, and depression to unrealistic or drug-induced feelings of euphoria and invulnerability. According to the US Public Health Service, of the 10 leading causes of death, at least seven could be reduced substantially if people at risk would change just five behaviors: compliance (e.g. use of anti-hypertensive medication), diet, smoking, exercise, and alcohol and drug abuse. For instance, approximately 65% of instances of cancer are thought to be caused by smoking, diet, and exposure to sun; workplace carcinogens, chemical interactions among compounds like tobacco, asbestos or alcohol, and viruses such as hepatitis B are thought to account for another 20–30%. Epidemological studies have established a relationship between such social factors as social isolation and health. In a recent review of prospective studies, for instance, House, Landis, and Umberson (1988) found social isolation to be a major risk factor for morbidity and mortality from widely varying causes, even after statistically controlling for known biological risk factors, social status, and baseline measures of health. The strength of social isolation as a risk factor is comparable to health risk factors such as smoking, blood pressure, obesity, and physical activity (House et al., 1988).

With the aging of the world population, the development of antibiotic-resistant strains of bacteria and viruses, and the rising costs of health care, attention has turned to identifying emotional and behavioral factors that may increase a person's resiliency to infectious diseases. Stress may actually promote health in some circumstances. The stress of learning of a friend's demise may be a sobering experience that alters a wide range of health behaviors. Stress can foster adaptive actions and stimulate autonomic, neuroendocrinological, and immunological reactions to support these actions. It can enhance one's sense of personal mastery or efficacy and help individuals minimize the negative outcomes of future stress. Thus, new challenges and demands can be a source of growth as well as a source of stress.

STRESS AND IMMUNE FUNCTION

Although stress may be necessary for survival, it can also alter susceptibility to disease. Stress, particularly if prolonged or repeated, can produce cardiovascular changes that can contribute to a narrowing of blood vessels and to heart attacks or strokes and reduce the strength of immunological activities in the body (Baum, 1994). Stress may alter cardiovascular function, immune function, and health through various pathways (Glaser & Kiecolt-Glaser, 1994; Rabin, Cohen, Ganguli, Lyle, & Cunnick, 1989). Stress may obscure symptoms, increase appraisal and patient delays and reduce medical compliance (Andersen & Cacioppo, 1990; Andersen, Cacioppo, & Roberts, 1995; Cacioppo, Andersen, Turnquist, & Petty, 1986). Stress can activate maladaptive behaviors that reflect attempts to cope with negative emotional responses. Persons experiencing psychological stress may engage in unhealthy practices such as smoking, not eating or sleeping properly, and not exercising, and these behaviors may foster accidents, cardiovascular disease, and suppressed immune function (Baum, 1994; Rabin et al., 1989). Nerve fibers connecting the central nervous system and immune tissue provide another path by which stress may influence immunity (Cohen, 1996).

Stress also evokes a variety of adaptational somatic responses, including stimulation of the hypothalamic-pituitary-adrenal axis (HPA) and the sympathetic adrenal medullary (SAM) system. The pituitary and adrenal hormones and other neuropeptides play an important role in the modulation of the immune system (Munck, Guyre, & Holbrook, 1984). Hormones such as epinephrine, norepinephrine, and cortisol circulate in the blood and can act on visceral as well as cellular immune receptors. These neuroendocrines, therefore, are an important gateway through which psychological stressors affect the cellular immune response (Ader, Felton, & Cohen, 1991).

The association between stress and immune function has received considerable attention in recent years. Spousal caregivers of dementia patients, relative to control participants, report longer episodes of infectious illness, primarily upper respiratory tract infections, and a diminished proliferative response to the mitogens concanavalin A (Con A) and phytohemagglutinin (PHA) (Kiecolt-Glaser, Dura, Speicher, Trask, & Glaser, 1991). In addition, caregivers show higher levels of antibody titers to latent Epstein-Barr virus (EBV) than controls, reflecting diminished control of the cellular immune response over the steady-state expression of latent EBV (Kiecolt-Glaser et al., 1991). Caregivers of relatives with a progressive dementia, compared to controls, also show a poorer humoral and virus-specific T-cell response to influenza virus vaccination and have lower *in vitro* interleukin-1β (IL-1β) (Kiecolt-Glaser, Glaser, Gravenstein, Malarkey, & Sheridan, 1996). Because respiratory and viral infections remain a major cause of morbidity and mortality among older adults (McGlone & Arden, 1987), these differences in immune response to influenza virus vaccination may be significant. Furthermore, the health consequences of stress may extend beyond infectious diseases. Recent research has shown that caregivers of relatives with a progressive dementia are characterized by impaired wound-healing relative to controls matched for age and family income (Kiecolt-Glaser, Marucha, Malarkey, Mercado, & Glaser, 1995). These results are not limited to the stress of caregiving, as the suppression of immune function has also been observed among persons in marital conflict (e.g. Kiecolt-Glaser et al., 1987), taking important examinations (e.g. Kiecolt-Glaser et al., 1984), and living near the site of a serious nuclear power plant accident (McKinnon, Weisse, Reynolds, Bowles, & Baum, 1989). Clinical depression (Herbert & Cohen, 1993a) and psychological distress (Herbert & Cohen, 1993b) have also been associated with decreased immune function. Finally, psychological distress has been found to covary with self-reported (Cohen & Williamson, 1991) and biologically verified (e.g. Graham, Douglas, & Ryan, 1986) upper respiratory disease.

This research is consistent with stress-induced susceptibility to infectious disease but much of it is not definitive. Self-report measures of illness episodes may be unreliable, individuals who are more ill may also report higher levels of stress, and individuals who are more stressed may increase their exposure to infectious agents (Cohen, 1996). A recent study by Cohen and colleagues is especially interesting in this regard. Cohen, Tyrrell, and Smith (1991, 1993) quarantined 420 healthy volunteers, measured their level of stress, exposed them to saline or one of five upper respiratory viruses, and monitored for the development of disease. After seven days of quarantine, each participant was classified as not infected, infected but not ill, or infected and ill. No participant who was exposed to saline became ill, and about a third of the participants exposed to the cold viruses became ill.

Three measures of stress were related to disease onset: (1) a stressful life event scale to measure the cumulative event load; (2) a perceived stress scale to assess perceptions of overload-induced stress; and (3) a measure of negative affect. For each measure, participants were categorized as under high or low stress according to whether their score on each scale fell above or below the median score. For all three measures, paticipants who reported high stress were more likely to develop an infectious disease than those who reported low stress.

Although these data provide strong evidence for an association between stress and infectious disease, the mechanism by which stress influenced health could not be identified in this research (Cohen et al., 1991, 1993). Among the mechanisms examined were differences in health behaviors, white blood cell populations, total (nonspecific) antibody levels, age, sex, education, and personality factors such as self-esteem or personal control. Furthermore, Cohen and colleagues found that more stressful life events were associated with greater susceptibility to disease whether or not these stressors elicited perceptions of stress or negative affect. Indeed, perceptions of stress or negative affect were not required for stressful life events to enhance susceptibility to disease. That is, people who confronted many stressors recently were more likely to become ill whether or not they rose to the challenge posed by the stressors.

The nature and amount of *reactivity* to acute psychological stressors may help illuminate the effects of stress on immune function and health. As noted earlier, the concept of stress implies the exposure of an individual to a threatening stimulus or overwhelming event. Autonomic activation in response to stressors is beneficial up to a point, but excessive autonomic activation may also have hidden costs. Because the metabolic requirements posed by the psychological stressors are often minimal (Cacioppo, 1994; Turner, 1989), the metabolic support provided by the differential physiological reactivity to stressors may not be needed for effective coping and instead may take a toll on cellular aging and health across time.

In discussing general principles of behavior, Kimble (1990, p. 36) noted that "up to a point, in obedience to Newton's second law, the greater the irritation, the greater the change". This fundamental principle of the excitatory response of the nervous system served as a basis for two postulates in our work on reactivity within the context of our psychophysiological activation theory (Cacioppo et al., 1992): (a) individuals are comprised of partially interacting neurophysiological (e.g. HPA, SAM) systems, each with response potentialities that are stable until ignited to action, and (b) the greater the stimulation of an excitatory neural system, the greater the output from that system tends to be. Accordingly, prior research on stress and health has tended to contrast individuals who are high versus low in basal physiological activation or high versus low in their exposure to a stressor.

The study of autonomic, neuroendocrine, and immune response as a function of *stress reactivity* represents a complementary approach. The same excitatory stimulus (e.g. stressor) can have profoundly different effects on physiological activation across individuals or life circumstances even when coping, performance, and perceived stress are comparable. That is, the gain, or increment of response per quantum of stimulation, can vary dramatically across individuals or conditions, with resulting differences in reactivity and profiles of physiological activation (see Cacioppo et al., 1992). This heterogeneity in stress response may hold a key to understanding what makes some individuals (or individuals in some circumstances) susceptible to disease and others (or the same individuals at other times) resilient to disease. That is, although higher levels of stress are associated with susceptibility to disease, it may also be the case that individuals who show relatively large physiological stress responses to the threats and irritations of everyday life (high stress reactivity) may be at greater risk for disease susceptibility even though their affect and perceptions of coping and stress are comparable to individuals who show relatively muted physiological stress responses (low stress reactivity).

INVESTIGATION OF STRESS REACTIVITY

To go beyond anecdotal evidence and investigate the effects of stress reactivity, we developed a set of brief laboratory stressors representative of everyday events that were tailored to hold performance constant and to be perceived as moderately engaging and stressful by all participants (Saab, Matthews, Stoney, & McDonald, 1989; Turner, 1989; see review by Cacioppo, 1994). Briefly, participants in our studies are exposed to speech and math stressors. In the math stressor, particip- ants are asked to perform six 1-minute serial subtraction problems continuously for 6 minutes. Participants are instructed that any error they made would be corrected by the experimenter, and that they should continue from the correct number. The minuend for minute 1, for instance, might be 297, for minute 2 might be 688, and so on. Results from our prior research on mental arithmetic indicates that participants average approximately 10 serial subtractions per minute when they are engaged in the task (Uchino, Kiecolt-Glaser, & Cacioppo, 1992). Thus, the subtrahend for minute 1 might be 3, but to maintain maximal task involvement and moderate task difficulty (i.e. approximately 10 correct answers per minute), the subtrahend specified for each subsequent minute is contingent on the participant's performance during the preceding minute (see Table 4.1; Cacioppo et al., 1995).

In the speech stressor, participants might be asked to imagine that they are asking a new acquaintance for a date, or that they are in a department store shopping when a security guard falsely accuses them of shoplifting (Saab et al., 1989), or that a bill collector is pursuing them for a medical bill that they have already paid (Cacioppo, Poehlmann, et al., in press). Participants are instructed to give intelligent and well-thought out answers because their speech will be re- corded and compared with the speeches of others. Participants are given 3 minutes to prepare and 3 minutes to present their speeches. Because we are interested in the reactions to acute psychological stressors generally, the results are aggreg- ated across these laboratory stressors.

In an illustrative study, 44 healthy undergraduate men participated in a pre-screening study in which heart rate (HR) reactivity to a brief speech stressor was assessed (Sgoutas-Emch et al., 1994). Following adaptation to the lab, HR and blood pressure were recorded continuously over a 3-minute baseline period and in response to a speech stressor (Saab et al., 1989).

We first examined the internal consistency of HR, systolic blood pressure (SBP), and diastolic blood pressure (DBP) from the pre-screening component. The two sets of data included in the analyses were baseline and speech periods. Cronbach alphas for the measure of HR, SBP, and DBP over these periods were satisfactory, and a repeated measures ANOVA confirmed that the speech stressor elevated HR. We identified individuals in the top or bottom quartiles in HR reactivity ($M_{HR\ reactivity}$ = 30.1 and 5.3 bpm, respectively) and conducted ancillary analyses to ensure high and low HR reactors were comparable in terms of basal HR and health-related behaviors. High and low HR reactors were then recruited to participate in the follow-up study in the Ohio State University Hospital.

The main study was run in the morning and consisted of four components: (1) informed consent, explanation of task, and insertion of an indwelling catheter into the antecubital vein; (2) a 30-minute supine adaptation period followed by a blood draw; (3) a 5-minute baseline period; and (4) a 12-minute mental arithmetic task followed by a post-stress blood draw. During the last 6 minutes of the stressor, participants were also exposed to random 100dB noise blasts. The participants were told that the noise blasts were designed to make the task more challenging. HR and blood pressure were recorded continuously during the 5-minute resting baseline and during the 12-minute mental arithmetic task. The blood draws prior to and following the experimental stressor provided the materials for the neuroendocrine and immune assays.

Test-retest correlations showed that the HR reactivity to the speech stressor in the prescreen predicted well the HR reactivity to the mental arithmetic stressor 3 weeks later (r = +.62, P < .01). Furthermore, high HR reactors—as defined by their HR response to the speech stressor in the prescreening—displayed larger HR increases to the mental arithmetic stressor in the subsequent session (Sgoutas-Emch et al., 1994). Thus, participants differed reliably in terms of HR reactivity.

Intense physical and psychological stressors can activate the autonomic nervous system (fight-or-flight response) and promote the release of pituitary and adrenal hormones, reflecting the activation of the HPA and SAM systems, respectively (cf. Cacioppo, Berntson, & Crites, 1996). These hormones have diverse effects that aid the body in coping with stressors. These include promoting alertness, enhancing muscular efficiency, elevating energy resources and cellular metabolism, and reducing inflammatory and allergic responses.

As illustrated in Table 4.1, we replicated prior research showing that brief psychological stressors increase norepinephrine and epinephrine activity but not cortisol levels. It is this observation that has led others to suggest that brief psychological stressors activate the SAM system but *not* the HPA system. A bit

TABLE 4.1
Mean response as a function of
psychological stressor

Measure	Baseline	Post-stressor
Epinephrine	31.50	33.70
Norepinephrine	250.80	356.00
Cortisol	12.00	12.80
CD4+/CD8+	2.81	2.29
Cell Proliferation to Con A	4.14	4.09
NK Cytotoxicity	47.50%	68.20%

more detective work, however, has revealed HPA activation, and its associated glucocorticoid reactivity, to be present and important. I will return to this point after summarizing the effects of stressors on immune function.

THE EFFECTS OF STRESSORS ON IMMUNE FUNCTION

The immune system is comprised of different cell types, each with its own effects, yet orchestrated to defend the body against antigens and pathogens. The human immune response can be functionally divided into two categories: non-specific and specific response (Kennedy, Kiecolt-Glaser, & Glaser, 1990). Non-specific responses refer to the general bodily defenses that result from exposure to a pathogen and include the activation of natural killer (NK) cells, which monitor the body and destroy virally infected and tumor cells, and the activation of macrophages, which engulf and destroy foreign substances. Specific immune responses include T-lymphocyte-mediated responses involving helper/inducer and suppressor/cytotoxic T-lymphocytes (i.e. cellular immune response) and antibody production by B-lymphocytes (i.e. humoral immune response). A T-lymphocyte gives rise to a large clone of cells when activated by an antigen. Suppressor/cytotoxic T-cells and helper/inducer T-cells migrate to the site of infection and act to destroy the invading pathogens. Among the actions of helper/inducer T-lymphocytes are the activation of antibody production by B-lymphocytes, stimulation (by the release of lymphokines) of T-helper cell and cytolytic T-cell production, and enhancement (via the release of gamma-interferon) in the lytic power of NK cells. Suppressor/cytotoxic T-cells help regulate the magnitude or duration of an immune response by suppressing T-helper cells and antibody production by B-lymphocytes. Because the cells of the immune system are pooled in diverse locations throughout the body, circulating blood plays an important role in transporting the immune cells between organs (e.g. spleen, thymus, bone marrow) and sites of antigens.

The percentage of various kinds of blood cells can be quantified *in vitro* by using commercially available monoclonal antibodies. For instance, the CD4+ marker on the cell surface identifies helper/inducer lymphocytes, whereas the

CD8+ marker identifies suppressor/cytotoxic lymphocytes (Kennedy et al., 1990). Because a balance of helper/inducer and suppressor/cytotoxic T-lymphocytes is important in mounting an effective immune response (Herbert & Cohen, 1993a), the ratio of CD4+/CD8+ cells is often of interest. The brief psychological stressor resulted in more circulating suppressor/cytotoxic T (CD8+) cells, a reduction in the ratio of circulating helper to suppressor/cytotoxic T cells (CD4+/CD8+), and more circulating NK cells.

NK cell activity (cytotoxicity) can also be measured by incubating NK cells with radioactively labeled target (e.g. tumor) cells and, following incubation and harvesting, measuring the radioactivity released from the lysed cells (Kennedy et al., 1990). The functional status of cellular immunity is typically examined by measuring the lytic power of cells or by quantifying *in vitro* the cell proliferation to the mitogens concanavalin A (Con A) and phytohemagglutinin (PHA), which can stimulate T-lymphocyte proliferation and is thought to model how cells respond to antigens *in vivo* (Kennedy et al., 1990). Cancer cells, for instance, develop daily in most individuals. These cells have different surface proteins than normal body cells, and these proteins act as antigens and stimulate an immune response that destroys these abnormal cells. Normally, suppressor/cytotoxic T-cells, macrophages, and NK cells attack and destroy cancer cells. According to the theory of immunosurveillance, immune cells sometimes fail to recognize cancer cells as foreign, or are unable to destroy them as fast as they reproduce, resulting in the uncontrolled growth of these abnormal cells. Patients with advanced cancer, for instance, have diminished NK cell activity. Analyses in our study revealed that the cell proliferation to Con A decreased and NK cell activity increased as a result of exposure to the acute psychological stressors (see Table 4.1).

In sum, autonomic and neuroendocrinological activation in response to stressors serves to mobilize metabolic resources to support the requirements of fight or flight. The stressors of contemporary society, however, often do not require or even allow behavioral fight or flight, and the autonomic and neuroendocrine reactions shown in response to acute psychological stressors substantially exceed metabolic requirements. Thus, although somatic activation in response to stressors is beneficial up to a point, excessive autonomic and neuroendocrine activation can diminish health across time. That is, a design for the brain and stress physiology that worked well in human evolution may have maladaptive aspects that manifest as life expectancy has increased well beyond the reproductive years. Indeed, according to the disposable soma theory of aging, it may be "disadvantageous to increase maintenance beyond a level sufficient to keep the organism in good shape through its natural life expectancy in the wild, because the extra cost will eat into resources that in terms of natural selection are better used to boost other functions that will enhance fitness" (Lithgow & Kirkwood, 1996, p. 80). Given the metabolic requirements posed by the psychological stressors in today's society are often minimal, the differential responses of high versus low reactors may shed light on what these long-term costs might be and on possible mechanisms underlying the effects of stress on cellular aging and health.

LOW AND HIGH REACTORS TO STRESS

The pattern of neuroimmune responses described thus far, for instance, can be explained in terms of the activation and immunoregulatory effects of the SAM axis (e.g. Crary et al., 1983). However, when we contrasted the high and low HR reactors' neuroendocrine and immune response to stressors, another pattern emerged. The stressor elevated plasma catecholamine levels comparably in high and low HR reactors, but high HR reactors showed higher stress-related levels of plasma cortisol than low HR reactors. As illustrated in Fig. 4.1, analyses also indicated that the high HR reactors showed larger stress-related increases in NK cell lysis. These data suggest that the HPA axis should not be ignored and that variations in HPA activation by brief psychological stressors may help explain why it is that daily irritations and stressors have greater health consequences for some individuals than others, or for individuals in some life circumstances but not in others. The finding that cortisol concentration was heightened in

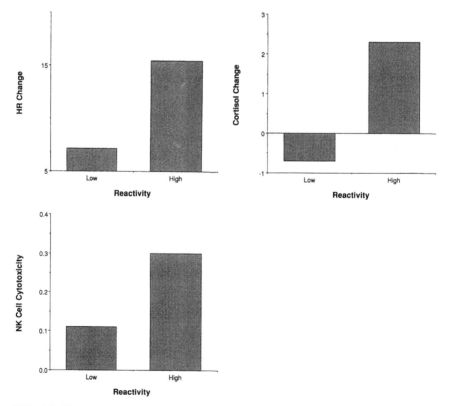

FIG. 4.1   Heart rate, plasma cortisol concentration, and natural killer cell response to acute psychological stress in low and high reactors.

high reactors is particularly provocative in view of the extensive literature linking cortisol with the down-regulation of multiple aspects of cellular immune function *in vitro* (Cohen, Evans, Stokols, & Krantz, 1986; Glaser & Kiecolt-Glaser, 1994).

Prior research has failed to find a relationship between cortisol and immune response *in vivo*, but these studies have focused on tonic cortisol concentrations (e.g. Glaser, Pearl, Kiecolt-Glaser, & Malarkey, 1994). We, too, found no relationship between basal levels of cortisol and immune response; however, the observation that high reactors showed differential cortisol changes and NK cytotoxicity to the acute psychological stressors suggests that stress reactivity may be an important factor to consider. If the glucocorticoid receptors on immune cells are sensitive to phasic changes in cortisol concentrations, short-term modulations of plasma cortisol levels by daily psychological stressors may influence cellular immune function even though these stress-induced changes in plasma cortisol levels are more likely to occur repeatedly over the course of the day in only some individuals and are relatively small.

Hypothalamic mechanisms and corticotropin-releasing hormone (CRH) not only affect endocrine function but can affect heart rate (HR) reactivity by altering the sympathetic and/or parasympathetic activation of the heart. An individual's classification as high or low in HR reactivity in a given situation ignores possible differences in the autonomic origins of this reactivity, however. An individual's classification as high in HR reactivity in a given situation could originate in elevated sympathetic reactivity, vagal withdrawal, or reciprocal activation of the sympathetic and vagal outflows to the heart. Research on cardiac reactivity has generally emphasized variations in HR reactivity rather than variations in the autonomic origins of HR reactivity (Cacioppo, Uchino, & Berntson, 1994a). This classification of participants in terms of HR reactivity relegates variations in the autonomic orgins of HR reactivity to the error term, a practice that may obscure the relationship between autonomic responses to stressors and behavioral, humoral, or clinical outcomes.

INVESTIGATION OF HEART RATE REACTIVITY

Quantifying differences in the autonomic determinants of heart rate (HR) reactivity across situations or individuals requires replacing the concept of HR reactivity as being a unidimensional (e.g. sympathetic activation) vector with a two-dimensional autonomic space. We recently outlined such an autonomic space (Berntson, Cacioppo, & Quigley, 1991) and reviewed the evidence consistent with the notion that HR reactivity can derive from multiple modes of autonomic control (Berntson, Cacioppo, & Quigley, 1993). According to this concept, reliable differences exist not only in HR reactivity to psychological stressors, but also in sympathetic cardiac reactivity and in vagal cardiac reactivity. This concept also requires a means of measuring the separable autonomic origins of HR reactivity.

We have relied on the noninvasive measures of respiratory sinus arrhythmia (RSA) and cardiac pre-ejection period (PEP) because both psychometric (e.g. Cacioppo et al., 1994a) and autonomic blockade research (e.g. Berntson et al., 1994; Cacioppo et al., 1994b) indicate that these measures represent noninvasive indices of the autonomic control of the heart in the context of our stress-reactivity protocol.

We have demonstrated in research on psychological stressors that the interrelationships among HR, RSA, and PEP reactivity measures are consistent with the use of RSA and PEP reactivity as noninvasive indices of the vagal and sympathetic determinants, respectively, of stress-induced HR reactivity (Cacioppo et al., 1994a). We correlated basal HR, task HR, and HR reactivity (calculated as a simple change score and as a residualized change score) during sitting with the corresponding index during standing to determine test-retest reliabilities, and we performed comparable analyses for the indices based on RSA and on PEP. Results revealed that these test-retest correlations ranged from .53 to .82 ($Ps < .01$). The finding that HR, RSA, and PEP reactivity indices during sitting were highly predictive of the corresponding reactivity measures during standing provided support for the use of PEP and RSA as indices of the autonomic substrates of cardiac reactivity in our stress-reactivity paradigm. Subsequent analyses (whether we used simple change scores or residualized change scores) provided additional evidence. First, the correlations between stressed-induced changes in RSA and in HR were all negative, reflecting the negative chronotropic effects of vagal input to the heart. That is, individuals who displayed stress-induced increases in RSA also were likely to show small increases in HR, whereas individuals who showed stressed-induced decreases in RSA (reflecting vagal withdrawal) also displayed large increases in HR. Furthermore, the median correlation among these measures was statistically significant (median $r = -.53$, $P < .01$). Second, the correlations among stressed-induced changes in PEP and in HR were uniformly large and negative, consistent with the notion that stress-induced sympathetic cardiac activation shortens PEP and elevates HR. The median correlation among these measures was also statistically significant (median $r = -.54$, $P < .01$). Third, the correlations between the RSA and PEP reactivity measures revealed that these indices did not consistently covary across individuals, and the median correlation among these measures was not significant (median $r = .29$, n.s.). These results are consistent with the notion that stress-induced changes in RSA and in PEP can vary independently and that each predicts unique autonomic determinants of HR reactivity (Cacioppo et al., 1994a).

Our psychometric and autonomic blockade studies of RSA and PEP (Berntson et al., 1994; Cacioppo et al., 1994a,b) also indicated that when high and low HR reactors are identified based on extreme scores from the HR reactivity distribution, these group differ in both sympathetic cardiac reactivity *and* vagal cardiac stress reactivity. However, if sympathetic cardiac reactivity is the better marker of HPA activation by brief psychological stressors, then variations in sympathetic

TABLE 4.2
Mean response as a function of
psychological stressor

Measure	Baseline	Post-stressor
HR	60.8	83.5
PEP	101.3	93.4
RSA	6.9	6.5
SBP	110.4	118.5
DBP	69.3	76.1
Epinephrine	24.5	29.5
Norepinephrine	280.3	404.1
ACTH	14.3	15.6

cardiac reactivity should be related more strongly to stress-induced changes in plasma cortisol concentrations and cellular senescence than vagal reactivity.

In a test of this hypothesis, 24 healthy undergraduate women participated in the study (Uchino, Cacioppo, Malarkey, & Glaser, 1995). The study was run in the morning and consisted of a 30-minute adaptation period followed by a blood draw, a 6-minute baseline (prestress) period, and a 12-minute mental arithmetic task, during the last 6 minutes of which participants were exposed to 100dB noise blasts. Autonomic measurements were made during baseline and stressor periods, and blood draws were obtained during baseline and following the stressor.

Recall that the laboratory stressors were developed to assess reactions to the irritations and stressors people face numerous times in their daily lives. The psychological stressors evoked a large increase in HR that was accompanied by a diminution of PEP and RSA. The analyses of blood pressure provided additional evidence that the brief psychological stressor activated the cardiovascular system (Table 4.2). Together, these data suggest that, at least at the group level, the stressors produced a reciprocal sympathetic activation and parasympathetic withdrawal. Also summarized in Table 4.2 is our finding that the acute psychological stressor again produced an increase in the norepinephrine and epinephrine plasma levels but appeared to have no effect on HPA activation.

When we focussed on stress reactivity in our prior study, we found evidence for differential HPA activation by the stressor: SAM activation was comparable for high and low HR reactors, but high reactors showed relative HPA activation. Analyses of autonomic-neuroendocrine relationships in this study replicated these results: HR reactivity was significantly correlated with stress-related changes in plasma ACTH and cortisol (rs = +.50 and +.62, respectively, Ps < .02). Furthermore, and consistent with our hypothesis, it was sympathetic cardiac reactivity that was underlying these relationships: PEP reactivity was significantly correlated with cortisol reactivity ($r = -.45$, $P < .05$) but RSA reactivity was unrelated to cortisol changes ($r = -.18$, n.s.), and none of these autonomic measures were correlated with plasma catecholamine reactivity to the psychological stressor ($-35 < rs < .20$, n.s.).

Analyses of NK cell activity replicated the elevation in NK cytotoxicity that was observed in response to the brief stressor. Analyses aimed at examining the autonomic substrates of this association confirmed our expectation that stress-induced PEP reactivity was a strong predictor of NK cell activity ($r = -.56$, $P < .01$) whereas RSA reactivity was uncorrelated with changes in NK cell activity ($r = -.12$, n.s.). As might be expected, we also observed a positive correlation between cortisol and NK cell activity changes ($r = .51$, $P < .02$).

To examine directly potential mediational processes, we used ROMONA PC (Browne & Mels, 1990) to test the the hypothesis that cardiac sympathetic reactivity (as indexed by PEP changes) was having an effect on NK cell activity via stress-related changes in SBP. Recall that a shortening of PEP is associated with greater beta-adrenergic activation of the heart and an increase in both the rate and force of contractility. SBP reactivity, in turn, may impact on short-term NK cell activity through mechanical or soluble immune factors (Ottaway & Husband, 1992). The increased vascular pressure, for instance, may lead to a migration of NK cells from lymphoid tissues into the peripheral circulation, which may elevate overall NK cell activity. Results of the path analysis provided evidence for this mechanism of action: (a) PEP reactivity was a significant predictor of SBP reactivity; (b) SBP reactivity was a significant predictor of NK cell activity even after controlling for the effects of PEP; and (c) the direct path between PEP and NK cell activity became nonsignificant when controlling for the effects of SBP reactivity (i.e. the mediator).

Considerable evidence has now accumulated suggesting that sympathetic cardiac reactivity marks HPA activation to brief psychological stressors (al' Absi et al., in press; Cacioppo, 1994; Cacioppo et al., 1995; Lovallo, Pincomb, Brackett, & Wilson, 1990; Uchino et al., 1995). The health consequences of these differences may be more evident in older than in younger individuals, however. Therefore, we studied 22 elderly women to examine the generalizability of this effect and to explore possible differences in response to an influenza vaccine in high and low reactors (Cacioppo et al., 1995). The study was run in the morning and consisted of a 30-minute supine adaptation period followed by a blood draw, a 5-minute baseline period, and a 6-minute mental arithmetic task and a 6-minute speech task. Our laboratory stressor was adapted slightly to investigate the typical reactions that these elderly individuals show to irritations and stressors in their daily lives. Autonomic measurements were made during baseline and stressor periods, and blood draws were obtained at baseline, mid-stressor, and post-stressor periods. Immunological data were obtained from the pre- and post-stress blood draws, and neuroendocrine measures were obtained from pre-, mid-, and post-stress blood draws. That afternoon, a subset of the participants received an influenza vaccine, and blood was drawn that afternoon, two weeks later, and 3 months later to determine their response to the vaccine (Kiecolt-Glaser et al., 1996).

TABLE 4.3
Mean response as a function of psychological stressor

Measure	Baseline	Mid-stressor	Post-stressor
HR	68.0	79.0	80.4
PEP	95.5	85.8	86.2
RSA	5.0	4.3	4.2
SBP	128.5	141.0	136.4
DBP	78.3	85.0	83.1
Epinephrine	22.2	42.3	35.2
Norepinephrine	454.1	609.8	595.5
ACTH	11.2	16.3	14.8
Cortisol	12.2	12.1	11.7

As in our prior research, the psychological stressor evoked a large increase in HR that was maintained across the 12-minute stress period. Furthermore, just as we had observed in our prior studies, the psychological stressor resulted in a diminution of PEP and RSA. Analyses of blood pressure again revealed significant pressor responses, consistent with the notion that brief psychological challenges that require active coping can produce a reciprocal sympathetic activation and parasympathetic withdrawal. In addition, we again found that the psychological stressor elevated epinephrine and norepinephrine plasma levels, and we found that the stressor elevated ACTH levels. Cell means are summarized in Table 4.3.

Analyses of the lymphocyte and NK cell numbers also revealed the same pattern of results as found in our study of undergraduate men. The psychological stressor increased the number of circulating T-cells and NK cells, elevated the number of circulating suppressor/cytotoxic (CD8+) cells, and reduced the ratio of circulating helper to suppressor/cytotoxic T-cells (CD4+/CD8+). Analyses of the functional measures of cellular immune response also revealed a similar pattern of results: The acute psychological stressor decreased the blastogenic response to Con A and increased NK cell activity. The magnitude of the effects of stress on cellular immune responses is especially impressive, given cellular immune activity is diminished in the elderly.

Limited *in vivo* samples of cortisol may not be an optimal approach for investigating the relationships among autonomic, neuroendocrine, and immune function because cortisol varies in a pulsatile fashion and is subject to large diurnal variations. Nevertheless, we conducted regression analyses to examine whether the sympathetic substrate of HR reactivity (as indexed by PEP reactivity) might be more strongly related to stress-related neuroendocrine and immune changes than the vagal substrate of HR reactivity. In our prior studies (Sgoutas-Emch et al., 1994; Uchino et al., 1995), the pre- and post-stress levels of plasma cortisol were comparable, but variations in cardiac reactivity predicted stress-related changes in plasma cortisol levels. We again found that the higher the HR reactivity, the greater tended to be the stress-induced change in cortisol ($r = .31$). More interestingly, sympathetic cardiac reactivity predicted the stress-induced changes in plasma cortisol concentrations ($r = -.62$), whereas vagal cardiac reactivity was unrelated to cortisol responses ($r = .18$). This is precisely the pattern of results one would expect if sympathetic reactivity were underlying the relationship between HR reactivity and cortisol, and is a relationship we replicated in a study of undergraduate men (Uchino et al., 1995). To test this hypothesis further, we conducted hierarchical regression analyses. Results confirmed that the relationship between stress-induced PEP and cortisol changes was highly significant ($P < .01$), and that the relationship between HR reactivity and cortisol changes was completely eliminated when statistically controlling for PEP reactivity ($F < 1$). These data, therefore, indicate that brief psychological stressors have an impact on the HPA axis in *some* situations and individuals—specifically, when sympathetic cardiac reactivity is also high.

OTHER NEUROENDOCRINE CHANGES

To examine what other neuroendocrine changes covaried with cardiac sympathetic reactivity, we conducted analyses based on a median split on stress-related PEP changes. The results, depicted in Fig. 4.2, showed that both low and high reactors showed stress-related elevations in epinephrine, but that low reactors showed relatively muted SAM activation and no stress-related increases in HPA activation. To the extent that catecholamines and glucocorticoids can have long-term suppressive effects on the immune response to viral and infectious agents, low reactors may show superior immunosurveillance.

In a pilot study headed by Jan Kiecolt-Glaser to examine this hypothesis, a subset of these participants received an influenza vaccine the afternoon of their participation in our reactivity protocol. The T-cell response to this vaccine was measured by an influenza virus-specific interleuken-2 (IL-2) response *in vitro*. Analyses of the IL-2 response revealed the expected inverted U-shaped cellular immune response across time, with a decline in the T-cell response clearly evident by 3 months following vaccination.

Differences in the maintenance of an immune response to an influenza vaccine may have health relevance because the elderly already exhibit diminished immune function involving T-cells and cytokine response, and respiratory and viral infections remain a major cause of morbidity and mortality among older adults (McGlone & Arden, 1987). Consistent with the stress-reactivity hypothesis, high sympathetic cardiac reactivity was associated with diminished immune response in this pilot study. The T-cell response declined more completely 3 months after the vaccination in individuals who exhibited high sympathetic cardiac reactivity to representative psychological hassles and challenges in our laboratory stress-test ($r = .68$). HR and cardiac vagal reactivity, on the other hand, did not predict IL-2 levels (rs $= -.17$ & $-.12$, respectively). These data

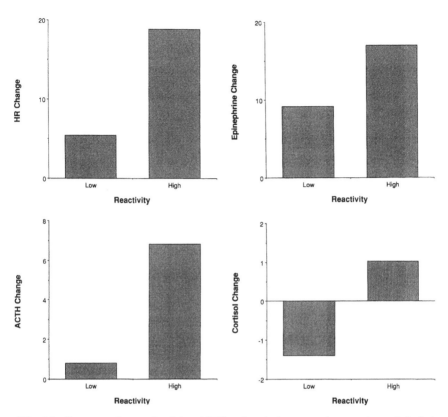

FIG. 4.2   Heart rate, plasma epinephrine, ACTH, and cortisol concentration to acute psychological stress in low and high reactors.

suggest that the autonomic and neuroendocrine changes we assessed in the lab 3 months earlier indexed how these individuals responded on a daily basis to irritations and stressors, given their life circumstances over this period.

If sympathetic cardiac reactivity to brief laboratory stressors reflects differences in the impact of daily stressors on the activation of the HPA axis, then stress-related variations in plasma cortisol may better predict the virus-specific T-cell response (IL-2 production) to the vaccine 3 months later than changes in plasma epinephrine. Although results should be considered preliminary, the analyses provided support for this reasoning: Stress-induced changes in plasma cortisol levels predicted IL-2 levels 3 months later, with individuals showing stress-related increases in plasma cortisol characterized by lower IL-2 levels ($r = -.56$); in contrast, stress-induced plasma epinephrine levels were positively and nonsignificantly related to IL-2 levels ($r = +.13$). That is, the psychological stressors activated the SAM system in the elderly participants generally, but these stress-induced plasma epinephrine levels were unrelated to the virus-specific

T-cell response to the influenza vaccine 3 months later; the activation of the HPA system by acute psychological stressors, on the other hand, predicted maintenance of the T-cell response to the viral antigen.

REACTIVITY AND EPSTEIN-BARR VIRUS

The studies presented thus far have demonstrated that psychological stressors can activate the autonomic nervous system and promote the release of adrenal and pituitary hormones. To the extent that catecholamines and glucocorticoids can have long-term suppressive effects on the immune response to viral and infectious agents, low reactors may show superior immunosurveillance. The results of our pilot study of responses to an influenza vaccine in an elderly population were consistent with this hypothesis. In a follow-up test of our hypothesis that high reactivity is associated with immunosuppression, we recently examined the association between reactivity and antibody titers to EBV (Cacioppo et al., submitted).

The competence of the cellular immune response is a critical factor in controlling primary herpes virus infections such as EBV and maintaining virus latency (Glaser & Kiecolt-Glaser, 1994). Considerable evidence has accumulated linking stress with the appearance, duration, and intensity of herpes virus infections, and the modulation of the steady-state expression of latent EBV (e.g. Glaser & Kiecolt-Glaser, 1994; Glaser et al., 1987). When latent EBV is reactivated, the memory immune response reacts to the increased synthesis of viral proteins resulting in heightened antibody levels to the virus. Reliable changes in antibody titers to EBV virus capsid antigen (VCA) IgG have been found concomitant with the down-regulation of different aspects of the cellular immune response (Glaser et al., 1991, 1987; Kiecolt-Glaser et al., 1984).

Data were obtained from 54 elderly women who participated in a larger study. The study was run in the morning and consisted of a 30-minute adaptation period followed by a blood draw, a 6-minute baseline (pre-stress) period, and a 12-minute psychological stressor that again consisted of a 6-minute mental arithmetic task and a 6-minute speech task. Autonomic measurements were made during baseline and stressor periods, and blood draws were obtained during baseline, immediately following the stressor, and 30 minutes following the stressor.

As in the previous studies, the psychological stressors evoked a large increase in HR that was accompanied by a diminution of PEP and RSA. The analyses of blood pressure again provided converging evidence that the brief psychological stressor activated the cardiovascular system, and analyses of the recovery period showed that these changes were short-term (Table 4.4).

To examine what effects covaried with cardiac sympathetic reactivity, we conducted a median split on stress-related PEP changes. Recall that the laboratory stressors were designed to be comparably and moderately engaging for all participants. Consistent with this design, high and low reactors rated the laboratory

TABLE 4.4
Mean response as a function of psychological stressor

Measure	Baseline	Mid-stressor	Post-stressor	Recovery
HR	65.7	75.6	75.2	66.7
PEP	95.5	88.8	88.2	97.0
RSA	5.5	5.1	5.3	5.3
SBP	138.3	142.3	145.7	132.4
DBP	81.5	82.8	82.4	79.1

stressor as equally unpleasant, mentally effortful, and frightening. High and low reactors also expressed comparable basal levels in state anxiety and changes in state anxiety following exposure to the laboratory stressor.

Because high and low reactors were defined based on a median split on PEP reactivity, PEP reactivity was, of course, larger in the high reactors than low reactors. High and low reactors did *not* differ in terms of basal cardiac sympathetic activation, as indexed by pre-stress PEP; basal cardiac parasympathetic activation, as indexed by pre-stress RSA; or basal HR or blood pressure. More interestingly, analyses of autonomic reactivity revealed that (a) the laboratory stressor produced significant cardiac sympathetic activation (i.e. reduction of PEP) in the high reactor group but no significant change in cardiac sympathetic activation in the low reactor group; (b) these autonomic differences in high and low reactors were also evident in HR reactivity, systolic blood pressure reactivity, and diastolic blood pressure reactivity; and (c) these autonomic differences were not manifest in cardiac parasympathetic (RSA) activity. Together, these results indicate that the laboratory stressor produced large and significant increases in the sympathetic activation of the autonomic nervous system in high reactors, whereas the stressor did not alter sympathetic activation in low reactors. Furthermore, the effect of the stressors on parasympathetic activation was comparable for high and low reactors.

As can be seen in Fig. 4.3, cardiac sympathetic reactivity was associated with elevated NK cell activity, an effect that as our prior research has shown is transient and due largely to changes in cell trafficking (e.g. Uchino et al., 1995). In earlier research, no relationship was found *in vivo* between EBV VCA IgG antibody titers and basal plasma cortisol levels (Glaser, Kutz, MacCallum, & Malarkey, 1995) even though glucocorticoids can reactivate EBV *in vitro* (Bauer, 1983; Glaser et al., 1994). Because cortisol fluctuates over 24 hours in the plasma, we explored the possibility that the pulsing characteristic of glucocorticoid hormones in high versus low reactive individuals might reveal the relationship of these hormones and the steady-state expression of latent EBV *in vivo*. Results confirmed that high reactors showed higher EBV antibody titers than low reactors. Differences between low and high reactors in the steady-state expression of latent EBV are likely to reflect biologically significant changes in the status of

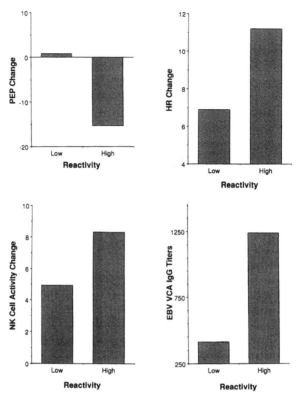

FIG. 4.3   Pre-ejectin period (PEP), heart rate, NK cytotoxicity, and Epstein-Barr virus (EBV VCA) IgG antibody titers in high and low reactors.

the latent EBV genome and differences in the cellular immune response in high and low reactors rather than transient reactions to the laboratory stressor *per se*, because EBV antibody titer levels were determined prior to the laboratory stressor.

Previous studies showing the induction of EBV from latently infected Daudi cells have been performed using single concentrations of a given hormone over time. Results showed that glucocorticoids but not catecholamines reactivated latent EBV (Glaser et al., 1995). Given the prior work linking cortisol and sympathetic cardiac reactivity to psychological stressors (al' Absi et al., in press; Cacioppo et al., 1995; Lovallo et al., 1990; Sgoutas-Emch et al., 1994; Uchino et al., 1995) and the association found in this study between sympathetic cardiac reactivity and the steady-state expression of latent EBV, we explored the possibility that varying dexamethasone (a glucocorticoid) concentrations over a 72-hour period might influence the expression of the latent EBV genome in Daudi cells in a different way (Cacioppo et al., submitted). In one set of cultures run in Ron Glaser's laboratory, the concentration of dexamethasone was varied from 10^{-5}M to 10^{-9}M every 24 hours for 3 days. The control cells were exposed to media or a single concentration of the hormone for 3 days.

Confirming previous reports, we found cells grown in media without hormone showed approximately 3–5% antigen positive cells, and an enhancement of the percentage of EBV antigen positive cells when the cells were exposed to 10^{-9}M dexamethasone, 10^{-7}M dexamethasone, 10^{-5}M dexamethasone after 72 hours of incubation. This dose-response curve replicates prior research. Extending this research, we found that the cultures that were exposed to the varying concentrations of dexamethasone over a 24-hour period for 3 days showed approximately 36% EBV antigen positive cells.

CONCLUSION

The effects of stress on health have traditionally been conceptualized as operating through tonic (e.g. basal) autonomic and neuroendocrine states. The thesis outlined here is that *stress reactivity* represents an important but often overlooked perspective in this area. The same stressor can have profoundly different effects on physiological activation across individuals or in individuals across different life circumstances even when comparable levels of coping, performance, and perceived stress are expressed. This heterogeneity in stress response may help explain what makes some individuals susceptible and others resilient to disease. Although higher levels of stress are associated with susceptibility to disease, the series of studies described here suggest that individuals who show relatively large physiological stress responses to the hassles, challenges, and frustrations of everyday life (high stress reactivity) may be at higher risk for disease susceptibility even though their affect and perceptions of coping and stress are comparable to individuals who show relatively muted physiological stress responses (low stress reactivity). These data also provide clues for understanding how the modulation of physiological responses induced by psychological stress can mediate immune function and health. Both low and high reactors exhibited stress-related elevations in SAM activity but the elevations shown by low reactors tended to be smaller. More strikingly, low reactors showed little or no stress-related change in HPA activation compared to high reactors. High reactors may therefore show poorer immunosurveillance because of the long-term suppressive effects of sympathetic activation and pituitary hormones on the immune response to viral and infectious agents.

To summarize, the economic and social costs of health problems in society today are staggering. With the aging of the world population and the rising challenges and demands of contemporary civilization, these costs are expected to become an increasingly heavy burden unless we can learn how to manage better the negative impact of stress on health. Six misconceptions are now evident regarding the relationship between stress and health that may contribute to this end-point. First, the notion that health/medical problems begin at disease onset is incorrect. The processes that produce chronic as well as acute health problems can be in place long before disease manifests itself. Second, the belief that the detrimental effects of psychological stressors and the salubrious effects of social factors are minor relative to genetic and biological factors (e.g. obesity, high blood pressure) is incorrect. As noted earlier, epidemiological studies have found that loneliness is as big a risk factor for all-cause mortality as smoking, obesity, and high blood pressure (House et al., 1988). Third, the notion that autonomic responses to psychological stressors vary in a unidimensional manner is incorrect. Our research indicates that psychological stressors can produce cardiac activation via vagal withdrawal as well as sympathetic activation, and that it is the latter rather than the former changes that are related most closely to neuroendocrine and immune responses to stressors. Fourth, the notion that the SAM and HPA systems respond similarly to acute psychological stressors, except for differences in thresholds and response recovery, may be an over-simplification. Evidence, including the results of our studies using dexamethasone (Malarkey, Lipkus, & Cacioppo, 1995) indicate instead that the activation of the SAM and HPA systems (and, presumably, the neural control of these responses) differ for metabolic and psychological stressors. Fifth, the conception that the heterogeneity of the stress response across individuals in a situation simply reflects error variance may be misleading. Nomethetic analyses in our research consistently indicated that psychological stressors produce reciprocal sympathetic activation, whether the stressor was metabolic (e.g. orthostasis) or psychological (e.g. mental arithmetic, speech stressor). Idiographic analyses revealed different neural substrates for these types of stressors, however (e.g. see Berntson et al., 1994), and further showed that measures of these neural substrates (e.g. cardiac sympathetic activation) were more predictive of the neuroendocrine and immune responses to stress than were the functional outcomes of these inputs (e.g. heart rate reactivity). A final misconception is that it is only the tonic, autonomic or neuroendocrine states that predict if not mediate the effects of stress on health. The present research suggests that we should not overlook the nature and amount of *reactivity* to acute psychological stressors. In retrospect, this point seems obvious. The very concept of stress connotes a person's re-action to an threatening stimulus or potentially overwhelming event. Autonomic and neuroendocrine activation in response to stressors is beneficial up to a point, but excessive activation may also have long-term costs. The metabolic requirements posed by the psychological stressors to which people are typically exposed in contemporary society are minimal. Consequently, strong autonomic and neuro-endocrine activation to psychological stressors is often not needed for effective coping but instead may affect cellular aging and health across time.

ACKNOWLEDGEMENTS

This paper is based on an Invited Address at the XXVI International Congress of Psychology, Montreal, Canada, August 1996. The research described in this paper is the result of an interdisciplinary collaboration with Janice K. Kiecolt-Glaser in the Department of Psychiatry, William B. Malarkey in the Department of Medicine, Ronald Glaser in the Department of Medical Microbiology and Immunology, and Gary G. Berntson in the Department of Psychology. This research would not have been possible without their collaboration and support, and their contributions and friendship are gratefully acknowledged. In addition, Kirsten A. Poehlmann, Bert N. Uchino, Karen S. Quigley, John A. Ernst, David L. Lozano, Daniel A. Litvack, Annette Fieldstone, and Robert C. MacCallum, Department of Psychology; Issac M. Lipkus, Department of Medicine; John Sheridan, Department of Oral Biology; Philip F. Binkley, Division of Cardiology, Department of Internal Medicine; Dennis Pearl, Department of Statistics; and Mary H. Burleson, Sandra A. Sgoutas-Emch, and Leigh Ann Kutz, Department of Medical Microbiology and Immunology, were important contributors to many aspects of this research. This research was supported partially by the John D. and Catherine T. MacArthur Foundation, National Science Foundation Grant Nos. DBS-9211483 and SBR-9512459, National Institute of Aging Grant No. PO1-AG11585, National Institute of Mental Health Grant Nos. T32-MH19728 and T32-MH18831, and National Center for Research Resources Grant No. M01-RR00034.

REFERENCES

al' Absi, M., Bongard, S., Buchanan, T., Pincomb, G. A., Licinio, J., & Lovallo, W. R. (in press). Cardiovascular and neuroendocrine adjustment to public-speaking and mental arithmetic stressors. *Psychophysiology.*

Ader, R., Felton, D. L., & Cohen, N. (1991). *Psychoneuroimmunology.* San Diego, CA: Academic Press.

Andersen, B. L., & Cacioppo, J. T. (1990). Secondary and tertiary prevention: Psychophysiological comparison theory and its role in understanding patient delay. *Cancer Prevention, 1,* 122–126.

Andersen, B. L., Cacioppo, J. T., & Roberts, D. C. (1995). Delay in seeking a cancer diagnosis: Delay stages and psychophysiological comparison processes. *British Journal of Social Psychology, 34,* 33–52.

Bauer, G. (1983). Induction of Epstein-Barr virus early antigens by corticosteroids: Inhibition by TPA and retinoic acid. *International Journal of Cancer, 31,* 291–295.

Baum, A. (1994). Behavioral, biological, and environmental interactions in disease processes. In S. Blumenthal, K. Matthews, & S. Weiss (Eds.), *New research frontiers in behavioral medicine: Proceedings of the national conference.* Washington, DC: NIH Publications.

Baum, A., Cacioppo, J. T., Melamed, B. G., Gallant, S. J., & Travis, C. (1995). *Doing the right thing: A research plan for healthy living.* Human Capital Initiative Strategy Report, Washington, DC: American Psychological Association.

Berntson, G. G., Cacioppo, J. T., & Quigley, K. S. (1991). Autonomic determinism: The modes of autonomic control, the doctrine of autonomic space, and the laws of autonomic constraint. *Psychological Review, 98,* 459–487.

Berntson, G. G., Cacioppo, J. T., & Quigley, K. S. (1993). Cardiac psychophysiology and autonomic space in humans: Empirical perspectives and conceptual implications. *Psychological Bulletin, 114,* 296–322.

Berntson, G. G., Cacioppo, J. T., Binkley, P. F., Uchino, B. N., Quigley, K. S., & Fieldstone, A. (1994). Autonomic cardiac control. III. Psychological stress and cardiac response in autonomic space as revealed by autonomic blockades. *Psychophysiology, 31,* 599–608.

Browne, M. W., & Mels, G. (1990). *RAMONA PC user's guide.* Technical report, Ohio State University.

Cacioppo, J. T. (1994). Social neuroscience: Autonomic, neuroendocrine, and immune response to stress. *Psychophysiology, 31,* 113–128.

Cacioppo, J. T., Andersen, B. L., Turnquist, D. C., & Petty, R. E. (1986). Psychophysiological comparison processes: Interpreting cancer symptoms. In B. L. Andersen (Ed.), *Women with cancer: Psychological perspectives* (pp. 141–171). New York: Springer-Verlag.

Cacioppo, J. T., Berntson, G. G., Binkley, P. F., Quigley, K. S., Uchino, B. N., & Fieldstone, A. (1994b). Autonomic cardiac control. II. Basal response, noninvasive indices, and autonomic space as revealed by autonomic blockades. *Psychophysiology, 31,* 586–598.

Cacioppo, J. T., Berntson, G. G., & Crites, S. L., Jr. (1996). Social neuroscience: Principles of psychophysiological arousal and response. In E. T. Higgins & A. W. Kruglanski (Eds.), *Social psychology: Handbook of basic principles* (pp. 72–101). New York: Guilford Press.

Cacioppo, J. T., Kiecolt-Glaser, J. K., Malarkey, W. B., Kutz, L. A., Poehlmann, K. M., Burleson, M. H., & Glaser, R. (submitted). *Autonomic and glucocorticoid associations with the steady state expression of latent Epstein-Barr virus.*

Cacioppo, J. T., Malarkey, W. B., Kiecolt-Glaser, J. K., Uchino, B. N., Sgoutas-Emch, S. A., Sheridan, J. F., Berntson, G. G., & Glaser, R. (1995). Cardiac autonomic substrates as a novel approach to explore heterogeneity in neuroendocrine and immune responses to brief psychological stressors. *Psychosomatic Medicine, 57,* 154–164.

Cacioppo, J. T., Poehlmann, K. M., Kiecolt-Glaser, J. K., Malarkey, W. B., Burleson, M., Berntson, G. G., & Glaser, R. (in press). Cellular immune response to acute stress in caregivers and matched controls. *Health Psychology.*

Cacioppo, J. T., Uchino, B. N., & Berntson, G. G. (1994a). Individual differences in the autonomic origins of heart rate reactivity: The psychometrics of respiratory sinus arrhythmia and pre-ejection period. *Psychophysiology, 31,* 412–419.

Cacioppo, J. T., Uchino, B. N., Crites, S. L., Jr., Snydersmith, M. A., Smith, G., Berntson, G. G., & Lang, P. J. (1992). Relationship between facial expressiveness and sympathetic activation in emotion: A critical review, with emphasis on modeling underlying mechanisms and individual differences. *Journal of Personality and Social Psychology, 62,* 110–128.

Cohen, S. (1996). Psychological stress, immunity, and upper respiratory infections. *Current Directions in Psychological Science, 5,* 86–90.

Cohen, S., Evans, G. W., Stokols, D., & Krantz, D. (1986). *Behavior, health, and environmental stress.* New York: Plenum.

Cohen, S., Tyrrell, D. A. J., & Smith, A. P. (1991). Psychological stress and susceptibility to the common cold. *New England Journal of Medicine, 325,* 606–612.

Cohen, S., Tyrrell, D. A. J., & Smith, A. P. (1993). Life events, perceived stress, negative affect and susceptibility to the common cold. *Journal of Personality and Social Psychology, 64,* 131–140.

Cohen, S., & Williamson, G. M. (1991). Stress and infectious disease in humans. *Psychological Bulletin, 109,* 5–24.

Crary, B., Borysenko, M., Sutherland, D. C., Kutz, I., Borysenko, J. Z., & Benson, H. (1983). Decrease in mitogen responsiveness of mononuclear cells from peripheral blood after epinephrine administration in humans. *The Journal of Immunology, 130,* 694–697.

Glaser, R., & Kiecolt-Glaser, J. K. (1994). *Handbook of human stress and immunity.* San Diego, CA: Academic Press.

Glaser, R., Kutz, L. A., MacCallum, R. C., & Malarkey, W. B. (1995). Hormonal modulation of Epstein-Barr virus replication. *Neuroendocrinology, 62,* 356–361.

Glaser, R., Pearl, D. K., Kiecolt-Glaser, J. K., & Malarkey, W. B. (1994). Plasma cortisol levels and reactivation of latent Epstein-Barr virus in response to examination stress. *Psychoneuroendocrinology, 19,* 765–772.

Glaser, R., Pearson, G. R., Jones, J. F., Hillhouse, J., Kennedy, S., Mao, H., & Kiecolt-Glaser, J. K. (1991). Stress related activation of Epstein-Barr virus. *Brain, Behavior, and Immunity, 5,* 219–232.

Glaser, R., Rice, J., Sheridan, J., Fertel, R., Stout, J., Speicher, C. E., Pinksy, D., Kotur, M., Post, A., Beck, M., & Kiecolt-Glaser, J. K. (1987). Stress-related immune suppression: Health implications. *Brain, Behavior, and Immunity, 1,* 7–20.

Graham, N. M. H., Douglas, R. B., & Ryan, P. (1986). Stress and acute respiratory infection. *American Journal of Epidemiology, 124,* 389–401.

Herbert, T. B., & Cohen, S. (1993a). Depression and immunity: A meta-analytic review. *Psychological Bulletin, 113,* 472–486.

Herbert, T. B., & Cohen, S. (1993b). Stress and immunity in humans: A meta-analytic review. *Psychosomatic Medicine, 55,* 364–379.

House, J. S., Landis, K. R., & Umberson, D. (1988). Social relationships and health. *Science, 241,* 540–545.

Kennedy, S., Kiecolt-Glaser, J. K., & Glaser, R. G. (1990). Social support, stress and the immune system. In I. G. Sarason, B. Sarason, & G. Pierce (Eds.), *Social support: An interactional view.* New York: Wiley.

Kiecolt-Glaser, J. K., Dura, J. R., Speicher, C. E., Trask, O. J., & Glaser, R. G. (1991). Spousal caregivers of dementia victims: Longitudinal changes in immunity and health. *Psychosomatic Medicine, 53,* 345–362.

Kiecolt-Glaser, J. K., Fisher, L., Ogrocki, P., Stout, J. C., Speicher, C. E., & Glaser, R. (1987). Marital quality, marital disruption, and immune function. *Psychosomatic Medicine, 49,* 13–34.

Kiecolt-Glaser, J. K., Garner, W., Speicher, C. E., Penn, G. M., Holliday, J., & Glaser, R. (1984). Psychosocial modifiers of immunocompetence in medical students. *Psychosomatic Medicine, 46,* 7–14.

Kiecolt-Glaser, J. K., Glaser, R., Gravenstein, S., Malarkey, W. B., & Sheridan, J. (1996). Chronic stress alters the immune response to influenza virus vaccine in older adults. *Proceedings of the National Academy of Sciences, 93,* 3043–3047.

Kiecolt-Glaser, J. K., Marucha, P. T., Malarkey, W. B., Mercado, A. M., & Glaser, R. (1995). Slowing of wound healing by psychological stress. *Lancet, 346,* 1194–1196.

Kimble, G. A. (1990). Mother nature's bag of tricks is small. *Psychological Science, 1,* 36–41.

Lazarus, R. S., & Folkman, S. (1984). *Stress appraisal and coping.* New York: Springer-Verlag.

Lithgow, G. J., & Kirkwood, T. B. L. (1996). Mechanisms and evolution of aging. *Science, 273,* 80–81.

Lovallo, W. R., Pincomb, G. A., Brackett, D. J., & Wilson, M. F. (1990). Heart rate reactivity as a predictor of neuroendocrine responses to aversive and appetitive challenges. *Psychosomatic Medicine, 52,* 17–26.

Malarkey, W. B., Lipkus, I. M., & Cacioppo, J. T. (1995). The dissociation of catecholamine and hypothalamic-pituitary-adrenal responses to daily stressors using dexamethasone. *Journal of Clinical Endocrinology & Metabolism, 80,* 2458–2463.

McGlone, F. B., & Arden, N. H. (1987). Impact of influenza in geriatrics and an action plan for prevention and treatment. *American Journal of Medicine, 82,* 55–57.

McKinnon, W., Weisse, C. S., Reynolds, C. P., Bowles, C. A., & Baum, A. (1989). Chronic stress, leukocyte subpopulations, and humoral response to latent viruses. *Health Psychology, 8,* 389–402.

Munck, A., Guyre, P. M., & Holbrook, N. J. (1984). Physiological functions of glucocorticoids in stress and their relation to pharmacological actions. *Endocrine Reviews, 5,* 25–44.

Ottaway, C. A., & Husband, A. J. (1992). Central nervous influences in lymphocyte migration. *Brain, Behavior, and Immunity, 6,* 97–116.

Rabin, B. S., Cohen, S., Ganguli, R., Lyle, D. T., & Cunnick, J. E. (1989). Bidirectional interaction between the central nervous system and immune system. *CRC Critical Reviews in Immunology, 9,* 279–312.

Saab, P. G., Matthews, K. A., Stoney, C. M., & McDonald, R. J. (1989). Premenopausal and postmenopausal women differ in their cardiovascular and neuroendocrine responses to behavioral stressors. *Psychophysiology, 26,* 270–280.

Sgoutas-Emch, S. A., Cacioppo, J. T., Uchino, B. N., Malarkey, W., Pearl, D., Kiecolt-Glaser, J. K., & Glaser, R. (1994). The effects of an acute psychological stressor on cardiovascular, endocrine, and cellular immune response: A prospective study of individuals high and low in heart rate reactivity. *Psychophysiology, 31,* 264–271.

Turner, R. J. (1989). Individual differences in heart rate response during behavioral challenge. *Psychophysiology*, *26*, 497–505.

Uchino, B. N., Cacioppo, J. T., Malarkey, W. B., & Glaser, R. (1995). Individual differences in cardiac sympathetic control predict endocrine and immune responses to acute psychological stress. *Journal of Personality and Social Psychology*, *69*, 736–741.

Uchino, B. N., Kiecolt-Glaser, J. K., & Cacioppo, J. T. (1992). Age-related changes in cardiovascular response as a function of chronic stressor and social support. *Journal of Personality and Social Psychology*, *63*, 839–846.

U.S. Department of Health and Human Services. (1991). *Healthy people 2000: National health promotion and disease prevention objectives*. DHHS Publication No. (PHS) 91-50212. Washington, DC: US Government Printing Office.

PART TWO

Brain mechanisms

CHAPTER FIVE

Brain plasticity and behavioral change

Bryan Kolb
University of Lethbridge, Lethbridge, Alberta, Canada

This chapter summarizes current knowledge regarding the effects of experience on the structure and synaptic organization of the brain. It is now clear that experience produces multiple, dissociable changes in the brain including: increases in dendritic length, increases (or decreases) in spine density, synapse formation, increased glial activity, and altered metabolic activity. These anatomical changes are correlated with behavioral differences between subjects with and without the changes. Such changes can be observed in species as diverse as insects and humans and thus represent an important mechanism for behavioral change. Experience-dependent changes in neurons are affected by various factors including age, gonadal hormones, trophic factors, stress, and brain pathology.

Sont ici résumées les connaissances actuelles concernant les effets de l'expérience sur la structure et l'organisation synaptique du cerveau. Elles permettent clairement de conclure que l'expérience produit de multiples modifications distinctes dans le cerveau, y compris une augmentation de la longueur des dendrites, une augmentation (ou une diminution) de la densité des épines, la formation de synapses, une augmentation de l'activité des cellules gliales et des changements dans l'activité métabolique. Ces modifications anatomiques sont corrélées à des différences comportementales selon que les individus les manifestent ou non. Puisqu'elles sont observables chez des espèces aussi différentes que les insectes et les humains, elles constituent un important mécanisme de changement comportemental. Les modifications des neurones en fonction de l'expérience sont influencées par divers facteurs dont l'âge, les hormones gonadiques, les facteurs trophiques, le stress et les pathologies cérébrales.

INTRODUCTION

In thinking about the relationship between brain and behavior, there is a tendency to focus on constancy, rather than on change, and on similarities, rather than on differences. Thus, as we try to map the regions of the cerebral hemispheres that are involved in processes like language, we focus on the constancies and similarities in the localization of functions across individuals. Indeed, it could be argued that one of the reasons we now know so much about human brain function is because there are so many constancies in brain organization. But it can also be argued that change and variability are as basic to brain function as uniformity. Indeed, it is only through changes in the brain that the child develops or that we are able to learn new concepts in adulthood. The recognition of the importance of change and variability in brain function has led to the study of the role of environmental events in shaping brain structure and function, a field that is often referred to as the study of brain plasticity.

In principle, there are three ways that experience could alter the brain: By modifying the ontogenetic unfolding of brain structure, or by modifying existing brain circuitry, or by creating novel circuitry. It is reasonable to suppose that the environment influences the brain in all three ways, although it is likely that a particular type of change will vary with the developmental stage of the animal. The goal of this chapter is not to review all of the literature on environmentally induced changes in brain structure and function so much as it is both to demonstrate the power of the environment in sculpting the brain during development and through adulthood and to document a large range of examples, running from insects to people.

Assumptions

I must first admit to making several assumptions First, I assume that the structural properties of the brain are important in understanding its function. Although such an assumption is self-evident to most neuroscientists, it is not as ubiquitously assumed by psychologists who do not study the brain (e.g. Pylyshyn, 1980; Skinner, 1938). An important corollary of this assumption is that changes in the structural properties of the brain reflect changes in the function of neural circuits.

Second, specific mechanisms of neural plasticity are likely to underlie more than one form of behavioral change. The nervous system is likely to be conservative in its mechanisms for change. Thus, general mechanisms that are used for one type of behavioral change, such as in development, may also form the basis of other types of behavioral change, such as in learning and memory, aging, or recovery from injury. This preconception does not exclude the possibility of specific mechanisms for different types of plasticity, but it has the advantage that it allows studies of one form of plasticity to provide insights into mechanisms involved in others. Indeed, it has become clear in recent years that the structural changes underlying experientially induced plasticity, such as in perceptual development, are remarkably similar to those underlying recovery from some types of brain injury. There is a corollary to this assumption: Similar mechanisms of plasticity are likely to be used across a broad range of species. I must admit parenthetically at this point that I am an unabashed vertebrate chauvinist, so my emphasis will be on vertebrates and especially on mammals.

I do not exclude the possibility that animals such as *Aplysia* may use mechanisms similar to those in mammals, but my suspicion is that we will learn more about forebrain function in humans by studying animals whose brains, and thus perceptual processes, are more similar to ours than is the case for most invertebrates.

Third, I assume both that the mechanisms of cortical plasticity are most likely to be found at the synapse and that synaptic changes can be measured by analysis of either pre- or postsynaptic structure. Traditionally, the emphasis in the literature on synaptic plasticity has been upon the presynaptic, or axonal terminal, side. Although this may be a practical site to study if one is interested in reparative processes after injury to peripheral nerves (e.g. Diamond, 1988), it is not so practical for studies of cortical structure. In particular, one difficulty with studying presynaptic changes is that they are very difficult to locate unless one knows *a priori* where to look. In addition, once found, they are difficult to quantify. The ability to quantify specific morphological features is critical if one is to correlate structural change with behavior.

An alternate way to look at synaptic change is to study the postsynaptic, or dendritic, side. This requires that the complete cell body and dendritic tree be stained, such as in a Golgi-type stain. As the dendritic surface receives more than 95% of the synapses on a neuron, it is therefore possible to infer changes in synapse number from measurements of dendritic extent and spine density. One clear advantage of this measure is that one need not know *a priori* where to look because it is possible to stain, and to examine, the structure of cells throughout the entire brain. In addition, analysis requires only a light microscope (and a lot of time!). A strong bias of this review, therefore, will be towards studies that have utilized Golgi-type analyses of postsynaptic structure.

Fourth, although the emphasis in most studies of structure-function relationships falls on the analysis of neurons, there are solid grounds for looking at changes in the structure and number of glial cells. Glial cells play an important role in synaptic modification and thus can be a clue to the location and nature of experience-dependent changes in neurons and their synapses.

Fifth, it is implicit in the foregoing discussion that changes in the postsynaptic structure will be visible in the light microscope. Although the final verification of the nature of structural modification must be at the ultrastructural, and thus electron microscopic (EM) level, EM studies are impractical on a large scale as they are time (and money) consuming, even if one knows where to look. Practically, therefore, most studies are carried out in tissue that is stained with a Golgi-type stain (for neurons) or with other specialized histochemical procedures that identify specific proteins, such as glial fibrillary acidic protein (GFAP), in glial cells.

Sixth, the emphasis of this review will be on the cerebral cortex. As psychologists, our primary interest is in cognitive function and it is our assumption that the changes in the cerebral cortex form the principal mechanism for cognitive change. This assumption comes from several lines of evidence. For instance, it is generally agreed that the relative increase in cortical volume across mammalian evolution is associated with increased cognitive capacity. It follows that changes in cognitive functions in a particular mammal are likely to involve changes in cortical structure or organization. Furthermore, studies of decorticated rats show that although they are capable of a remarkable behavioral repertoire (e.g. Whishaw, 1990), there is limited functional flexibility under conditions that would normally lead to marked functional and/or structural change in intact animals (e.g. Kolb, Whishaw, & van der Kooy, 1986). Finally, there are marked interspecies differences in the details of cortical organization, such as in Old World and New World monkeys, and it has been assumed that these differences reflect the clear differences in perceptual and cognitive abilities (Kaas, 1987).

Finally, I assume that experience-dependent effects are studied most easily by: (a) placing animals in special environments; (b) training animals in specific tasks; or (c) considering ecological pressures that shape the nervous system in the daily lives of animals. I shall therefore emphasize these types of analyses.

Measuring brain plasticity: Analysis of Golgi-stained material

Once the cells are stained with a Golgi-type procedure, the dendritic length can be measured in several ways. Cells are drawn using a microscope, which is typically set at 250–400× magnification. The drawing can be done using some type of computerized imaging system or a camera-lucida procedure (Fig. 5.1) in

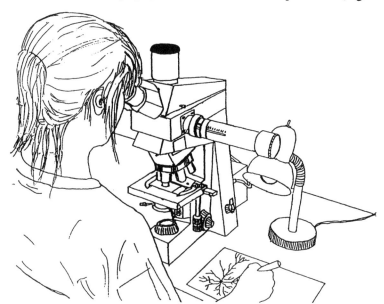

FIG. 5.1   Illustration of the camera lucida method for tracing neurons. Mirrors in the drawing tube allow the drawer to visualize both the cell through the microscope as well as on the tracing page. Cells, therefore, can be traced.

which cells are drawn with pen and ink. The advantage of the computerized systems is that the precise length of all dendritic segments can be calculated and various statistical measurements can be made (e.g. Capowski, 1989). The disadvantage is that these semi-automated procedures are very slow and, somewhat paradoxically, labor-intensive. Although only 1% of the neurons are stained in Golgi-type stains, the cells are still close together and dendritic branches from different cells overlap. The human eye can easily distinguish which branches belong to which cells, but computers cannot yet do so. This means that an operator must guide all of the computer drawing. If cells are drawn by pen and ink, then the analysis is normally done by using a procedure that estimates dendritic length. One way is to count the total number of dendritic branches, whereas another way is to place some sort of grid over the drawing and to count the number of intersections of the dendrites with the grid lines (Fig. 5.2).

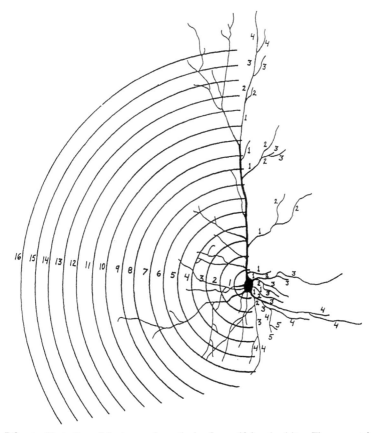

FIG. 5.2   An illustration of the two main methods of quantifying dendrites. The concentric rings on the left form the grid for the Sholl analysis. The number of ring-crossings of each branch gives an estimate of length of dendrite. The numbers on the branches on the right indicate the branch order, which offers a different estimate of dendrite length.

Although the two procedures give very different statistical views of dendritic arborization, both measures lead to the same conclusions (e.g. Stewart & Kolb, 1994).

EXPERIENCE AND THE CHANGING BRAIN

History

Although the idea that experience can modify brain structure can probably be traced back at least to Ramon y Cajal (e.g. 1928), it was Hebb who made this a central feature of his neuropsychological theory (Hebb, 1949). Hebb did the first experiments on the consequences of enriched rearing on the behavior of the rat (Hebb, 1947), but it was not until the group at Berkeley began to demonstrate changes in brain weight, cortical thickness, acetylcholine levels, and dendritic structure that there was any structural correlate of the behavioral changes related to experience (e.g. Diamond, Dowling & Johnson, 1981; Diamond, Lindner & Raymond, 1967; Globus, Rosenzweig, Bennett, & Diamond, 1973; Rosenzweig & Bennett, 1978; Rosenzweig, Krech, Bennett, & Diamond, 1962). Later, beginning in the 1970s and continuing still, William Greenough and his colleagues initiated a multidisciplinary investigation of the effects of rearing animals in visually or motorically enriched environments (see later). Other important lines of work were also instigated by Austin Riesen in his studies of environmental impoverishment in primates (e.g. Riesen, 1982), Richard Tees in his studies of experience and perceptual development in rodents and children (e.g. Tees, 1986; Werker & Tees, 1992), and of course many others whose contributions I am forced to ignore in this short space.

Overview

In the 50 years since Hebb's initial experiments, we can now identify a large range of neural changes associated with experience (Table 5.1). The magnitude of these changes should not be underestimated. For example, in my own studies of the effects of housing rats in enriched environments (Fig. 5.3), we consistently see changes in overall brain weight in the order of 7–10% after 60 days in young animals, even though the body weight is reduced relative to cage-reared littermates (e.g. Kolb, 1995). This general effect in brain size is clearly shown in a stunning photograph published by Beaulieu and Colonnier (1987) (Fig. 5.4).

The most extensive, and successful, line of experiments has been conducted over the past two decades by Greenough and his colleagues at the University of Illinois. Perhaps the fundamental point that this group has made over the past decades is that synapses can form and dendrites can grow well beyond the period of brain development. Although this point is certainly not unique

TABLE 5.1
Principal cellular differences in the occipital cortex between rats raised in enriched condition (EC) and impoverished condition (IC)

Cellular variable	Environmental effect
Neuron size	EC>IC
Neuron density	IC>EC
Dendritic branching	EC>IC
Dendritic spine density	EC>IC
Number of unmyelinated axons in splenium of corpus callosum	EC>IC
Size of unmyelinated axons in splenium of corpus callosum	EC>IC
Number of synapses per neuron	EC>IC
Size of synaptic contact	EC>IC
Synaptic plate perforations	EC>IC
Percentage of total tissue volume	
Capillary vessels	EC>IC
Astrocytic nuclei	EC>IC
Oligodendrocytic nuclei	EC>IC
Mitochondria	EC>IC

From "The structure of the cerebral cortex: Effects of gender and the environment", by J. Juraska, 1990. In B. Kolb & R. Tees (Eds.), *The cerebral cortex of the rat* (p. 486). Cambridge, MA: MIT Press. Copyright 1990 by MIT Press. Reprinted with permission.

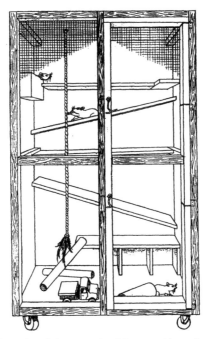

FIG. 5.3   Schematic illustration of the rat condominiums used in studies of the effects of enriched experience.

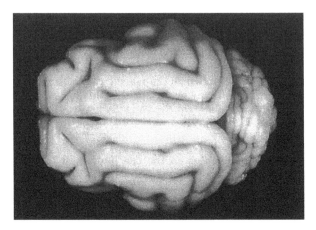

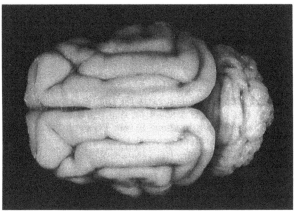

FIG. 5.4   Dorsal view of the brains of two cats, from the same litter, maintained in enriched (top) and impoverished (bottom) conditions from the time of weaning to the age of 8 months. From "Richness of environment affects the number of contacts formed by boutons containing flat vescicles but does not alter the number of these boutons per neuron," by C. Beaulieu and M. Colonnier, 1988, *Journal of Comparative Neurology, 274,* p. 483. Copyright 1988 by Alan R. Liss, Inc. Adapted with permission.

to Greenough, he and his colleagues have shown most forcefully that the adult mammalian brain (and presumably other vertebrate brains as well) can add not only dendrites and synapses in response to behavioral demands but also support-ive tissue elements such as astrocytes and blood vessels.

There are two different lines of work on brain plasticity, behavior, and experi-ence: (1) studies of the neurons and glia in brains of animals housed in enriched environments; and (2) studies of the brains of animals trained in specific tasks. I shall consider each separately.

Environmental enrichment

As mentioned, it was Hebb who first used this paradigm but it was the group of Bennett, Krech, Rosenzweig, Diamond and their colleagues at Berkeley (see earlier) that first showed large changes in various measures of cortical morphology. As important and seminal as the Berkeley experiments were, they had the weakness that they did not demonstrate changes in brain organization so much as in brain size. Thus, in the early 1970s, several groups, including the Berkeley group, began to look at dendritic fields (e.g. Globus et al., 1973; Uylings, Kuypers, Diamond, & Veltman, 1978). The most thorough studies of this sort were carried out, however, by Greenough. Greenough's early experiments focused on the changes in the dendritic fields of neurons in the visual cortex in response to enriched environments. Typical experiments showed that the dendritic fields of these neurons increased by about 20% relative to cage-reared animals (e.g. Greenough & Volkmar, 1973; Volkmar & Greenough, 1972). These effects were not restricted to the visual cortex, although other regions tended to show lesser effects and some cell types were relatively unaffected (e.g. Greenough, Volkmar, & Juraska, 1973). A parallel set of studies has examined changes in the cerebellum of animals in complex environments and, as might be anticipated, there are parallel changes in the Purkinje cells. Furthermore, like in the studies of neocortical regions, there is evidence that these changes are not inevitable consequences of experience as cerebellar granule cells do not show the same changes (e.g. Floeter & Greenough, 1979).

Although most studies of environment-dependent changes in the cortex have been carried out on rodents, there are several studies using monkeys. In general, these studies have found similar results (e.g. Floeter & Greenough, 1979; Stell & Riesen, 1987). One curious difference between the rodent and primate studies appears to be the effects on the visual system. Because monkeys are highly visual relative to rats, one might predict greater effects on the visual cortex of monkeys; yet the opposite appears to be true. In fact, it appears that the effects on the primary visual cortex of monkeys reared in enriched environments is negligible (e.g. Riesen, Dickerson, & Struble, 1977; Struble & Riesen, 1978). It is not immediately clear why this difference should be present but I can think of two explanations. First, much of the exploration of the visual world of monkeys is done without movement and as monkeys in relatively impoverished housing can still visually explore their environment, this stimulation may be sufficient to ensure the development of visual cortical synapses. In contrast, the visual system of the rat has relative poor acuity and is not designed for pattern vision so much as for spatial navigation. The gathering of spatial information is likely to require movement in space. Second, it may be that as the visual areas of the primate have expanded dramatically and as primary visual cortex is multifunctional, it is "higher" visual areas that show greater experience-dependent

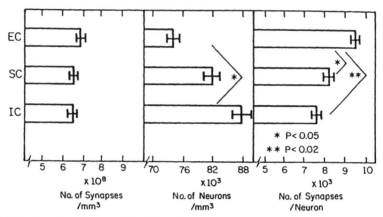

FIG. 5.5 Synaptic and neuronal density and synapses per neuron in upper visual cortex of rats reared for 30 days after weaning in environmental complexity (EC), social cages (SC), or individual cages (IC). Lower density of neurons is assumed to reflect an increase in neuropil and/or associated tissue elements such as glia and blood vessels. The greater number of synapses per neuron in the EC group reflects the increased dendritic field complexity seen in the Golgi results. From "Differential rearing effects on rat visual cortex synapses" by A. M. Turner and W. T. Greenough, 1985, *Brain Research, 329*, p. 200. Copyright 1985 by Elsevier. Adapted with permission.

changes. In this case, one might predict that visual experiences that emphasized object exploration and recognition would lead to growth in the ventral visual pathway, whereas visual experiences that emphasized visuomotor guidance, such as in climbing or object manipulation, would lead to growth in the dorsal visual pathway.

Most studies of dendritic change have utilized a Golgi-type technique to measure dendritic space and from this there is an assumption that dendritic space is correlated tightly with synaptic numbers. Turner and Greenough (1983, 1985) examined this hypothesis directly by calculating the number of synapses per neuron in the cortex of animals housed in enriched environments. (Similar studies were also conducted in rats by Bhide and Bedi [1984] and in cats by Beaulieu and Colonnier [1987]). All of these studies have found an increase of about 20% in the number of synapses per neuron in the brains of enriched versus cage-reared animals (Fig. 5.5). Thus, although the density of synapses in a section of cortical tissue is relatively constant in enriched and cage-reared animals, there is more dendritic space in the enriched animals and, as a result, there are more synapses per neuron. It follows from this that the neurons must be less dense in the enriched brains, as shown in Fig. 5.5.

It is reasonable to expect that if there are increases in the size of the dendritic fields of neurons, and correspondingly in the number of synapses per neuron, then these neurons will require more support both from glial cells, especially astrocytes, as well as blood vessels. In one exceptional series of studies, Sirevaag and Greenough (e.g. 1987, 1988, 1991) used light and electron microscope techniques to analyze 36 different aspects of cortical synaptic, cellular, and vascular morphology in rats raised in complex or caged-housing environments. The simple conclusion was that there is a coordinated change not only in neuronal morphology but also in glial, vascular, and metabolic processes in response to differential experiences. Thus, not only are there more synapses per neuron in animals with enriched experience, there are also more astrocytic material, more blood capillaries, and a higher mitochondria volume. (Mitochondrial volume is used as a measure of metabolic activity.) It is therefore clear that when the brain changes in response to experience there are the expected neural changes but there are also adjustments in metabolic requirements of the larger neurons. One interesting implication of this conclusion is that things that influence the maintenance and adjustment of the metabolic components of the aging brain can be expected to influence the brain's capacity for neural change as well (e.g. Black, Greenough, Anderson, & Isaacs, 1987; Black, Polinsky, & Greenough, 1989). This addresses the importance of examining the effects of exercise and nutrition on the brain's capacity for change, especially in senescence. It is important to note in this context, however, that merely having exercise is not sufficient to induce neuronal changes. Black, Isaacs, Anderson, Alcantara, and Greenough (1990) trained animals to negotiate a complex obstacle course ("acrobat rats") or placed rats in running wheels where they obtained forced exercise. The animals in the wheels showed increased capillary formation but no change in cerebellar Purkinje cell synapses, whereas the acrobat rats showed a 30% increase in Purkinje synapses. Thus, merely increasing neuronal support does not change the neurons. The critical feature for neuronal change is presumably increased neuronal processing, which would be facilitated by a complementary increase in metabolic support. Unfortunately, Black et al. did not conduct what is probably a critical experiment. The animals trained in running wheels and which showed large increases in capillary growth would be expected to acquire motor tasks faster than animals without this training. This is an important issue because it addresses the importance of exercise and the facilitation of brain plasticity in adulthood, and especially in old age.

Training in specific tasks

Although it is tempting to conclude that the synaptic changes observed in animals housed in complex environments reflect changes in the functioning of the brain, there is little direct evidence for this. Thus, there are numerous studies showing behavioral differences between animals raised in complex versus simpler environments, but this need not be a direct result of increased synaptic space (for a review, see Greenough, 1976). One way of approaching this problem is to train animals in specific tasks and then to demonstrate specific changes in dendritic fields of neurons in regions suspected of being involved in the performance of such tasks. For example, it has been known since the time of Karl Lashley that removal of the visual cortex of rats leads to deficits in visual problem learning (e.g. Lashley, 1929). It is reasonable, therefore, to expect that training animals in such problems would lead to changes in the dendritic arborization of cells in visual cortex. Perhaps the most convincing studies of this sort were done by Chang and Greenough (1982). These studies took advantage of the fact that the visual pathways of the laboratory rat are about 90% crossed. That is, about 90% of the cortical projections from the left eye project via the right lateral geniculate nucleus to the right hemisphere. Chang and Greenough placed occluders on one eye of rats and then trained the animals in a visual maze. Comparison of the neurons in the two hemispheres revealed that those in the trained hemisphere had larger dendritic fields. This experiment is compelling because the rest of the two hemispheres (e.g. auditory, somatosensory, or olfactory regions) would still have interacted with the maze and both hemispheres would be required for the motor demands. It was only the visual cortex contralateral to the open eye that could process and/or store the task-specific visual information, however, and this was reflected by the specific dendritic changes in that hemisphere.

A second set of experiments has taken advantage of the fact that rats are very talented at using their forepaws to retrieve food from tubes, through bars, and so on. As the cortical control of the forelimbs is largely crossed, it is possible to train one limb to reach for food and to compare the layer V neurons in the forelimb region of motor cortex, many of which form the cortical spinal tract, in the trained and untrained hemispheres. Two studies have shown dendritic changes in the expected neurons (Greenough, Larson, & Withers, 1985; Withers & Greenough, 1989). The changes in dendritic fields seen in the Greenough studies of visual and motor learning are strikingly reminiscent of the changes seen in studies of enriched rearing, which have been taken as evidence that the observed changes in synaptic connectivity in animals in enriched environments are somehow involved in memory and learning (Greenough & Chang, 1989). Although this is a reasonable conclusion, recent studies by my own group suggest that there may be important differences in details of dendritic change in the enrichment and learning studies. For example, in one study, animals were trained on either a unimanual task (reaching through bars with one forepaw) or a bimanual task (pulling up a string with food attached to the end) (Fig. 5.6). Like Greenough and his colleagues, we found increased dendritic fields in cells contralateral to the reaching hemisphere as well as in both hemispheres in the animals performing the bimanual task (Kolb, Gibb, Gorny, & Ouellette, 1996). We also measured dendritic spines, however, and in contrast to increases in spine density observed in animals housed in enriched environments in adulthood (see later), we found no changes in dendritic spine density when animals were trained to reach. This general enrichment versus specific training difference is probably not related specifically to motor learning as we recently have trained animals in a visual maze and found increased dendritic arbor and an unchanged spine

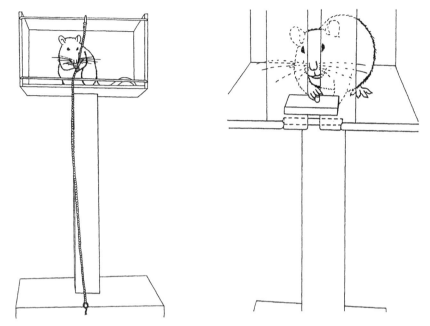

FIG. 5.6   Illustration of the manual reaching task (right) and the string pulling task (left) in the Kolb et al. (1996) study. Rats that used a single limb to reach for food showed an increase in dendritic fields contralateral to the active limb. Rats that used both paws (string pullers) showed an increase, relative to controls, in both hemispheres.

density. Thus, it appears that although there are marked similarities between the effects of enriched rearing and specific training on dendritic fields, there may be differences in other measures of dendritic morphology, especially spine density. This difference is intriguing. It could be that there were initial increases in spine density in the forelimb-trained rats but this was followed by a deletion of some subset of the spines. I return to this idea later.

Age and experience

It has long been assumed in the psychological literature that experiences in early childhood have greater effects on later behavior than do similar experiences in adulthood. The analysis of dendritic changes following exposure to enriched environments suggests that there is a structural basis to this differential effect of early experience on behavior (e.g. Kolb, Forgie, Gibb, Gorny, & Rowntree, in press). My colleagues and I placed rats in enriched environments for 3 months, beginning at weaning (21 days of age), or at young adulthood (4 months of age), or in senescence (2 years or older). The principal finding was that the age at

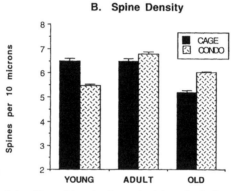

FIG. 5.7 Summary of the effects of housing in condominiums beginning at weaning (young), in young adulthood (adult) or in old age (old). Enriched housing led to an increase in dendritic branching in all groups. In contrast, spine density was decreased in the young group and increased in the adult and old groups.

which animals were placed in the enriched environments has qualitatively different effects on dendritic structure. Rats placed into the condominiums in young adulthood showed effects similar to those reported by others: There was a large increase in dendritic length relative to cage-housed control animals (Fig. 5.7). In addition, there was a small increase in spine density. Parallel results were seen in senescent animals, as they showed significant increases in dendritic length and spine density relative to age-matched control rats. In contrast, when we analyzed the changes in animals who were placed in the condominiums as juveniles, we saw an increase in dendritic branching but a consistent *decrease* in spine density; that is, in comparison to older animals, the young animals showed a qualitatively different change in the distribution of synapses on pyramidal neurons.

The differential effect of enrichment in the young versus older animals led us to look at the effects of environmental manipulation even earlier in the animals' lives. It has been shown that tactile stimulation of premature human babies with a brush leads to faster growth and earlier hospital discharge (e.g. Field et al., 1986; Schanberg & Field, 1987; Solkoff & Matuszak, 1975). In addition, studies on infant rats have shown that similar treatment alters the structure of olfactory bulb neurons and has effects on later behavior (e.g. Coopersmith & Leon, 1984; Leon, 1992a; Sullivan & Leon, 1986; Woo & Leon, 1987). We therefore stroked infant rats with a camel hair paintbrush three times daily from day 7 to day 21 of life. Animals were subsequently raised in standard lab cages and were sacrificed in adulthood. Golgi analysis revealed that the early experience had no effect on dendritic length in adulthood but there was a significant drop in spine density (Kolb & Gibb, submitted). These results surprised us and led us to consider other changes in cortical morphology in the tactile-stroking paradigm. For example, in one experiment infant rats were given tactile stimulation and then were sacrificed at different ages. At sacrifice we measured: (1) the density of acetylcholinesterase staining, which allowed an indirect measure of acetylcholine innervation in the cortex; (2) the density of immunohistochemical staining for OX-42, which is a marker of microglia; and (3) the density of staining for GFAP, which is a marker for astrocytes. The results showed that acetylcholinesterase levels were significantly increased after only 7 days of stimulation and that this increase was still present 6 weeks after the stimulation was ended. Similarly, the number of microglia was significantly decreased after only 7 days of stimulation and remained lower than in controls 6 weeks later. Surprisingly, GFAP-positive astrocytes were virtually unchanged by the experience.

These results lead us to several conclusions. First, "enriched" experience can have very different effects on the brain at different ages. Second, experience not only leads to "more" but can also lead to "less". That is, although there is a temptation to presume that experiences lead to increased numbers of synapses and probably to increases in glia, it appears that there may be either increases or decreases, the details varying with age at experience. Third, changes in dendritic length and dendritic spine density are clearly dissociable. It is not immediately clear what the differences mean in terms of neuronal function but it is clear that experience can alter these two measures independently and in different ways at different ages.

The studies on age-dependent effects of experience in rats are supported by two studies carried out on chicks. In the first study, Patel and Stewart (1988) took advantage of the observation that one-day-old chicks peck spontaneously at a small bright chrome bead. They coated the bead with either an aversively tasting substance or nonaversive water. Chicks presented with the aversive taste learn in one trial to avoid the bead, whereas those presented with the nonaversive bead continue to peck (for a review, see Rose, 1985). Various regions of the chick brain, such as the hyperstriatum, show enhanced activity following training as revealed by both electrophysiological investigations and studies of glucose accumulation. Patel and Stewart used a Golgi technique to impregnate chick brains 25 hours after training and found a twofold increase in spine density in the neurons in a region of the hyperstriatum (intermediate medial hyperstriatum ventrale). They found that there was an *increase* in spine density in the "trained" chicks. Initially, this would seem to be at odds with our studies of infant rats because we had found *decreased* spine density. The second study of chicks addresses this, however. Wallhausser and Scheich (1987) presented newly hatched chicks with a hen or an acoustic stimulus with the goal of imprinting the chicks to the visual or auditory stimulus. The neurons in different regions of the hyperstriatum of the imprinted chicks were compared to those of isolated chicks: There was a *decrease* in spine density. Thus, in the first study, there was an increase 25 hours after training, whereas in the latter study there was a decrease 7 days after training. The earliest we have looked in our infant rats is after 7 days of daily stimulation. The simplest conclusion from the chick and infant rat studies is that the novel stimulation may cause an initial rapid increase in spine density, followed by a pruning. If true, this conclusion may have implications for the difference between enriched experience and specific training that I reviewed earlier. Recall that whereas animals housed in enriched environments showed increased dendritic length and spine density in cortical pyramidal cells, animals trained to make specific limb movements or to learn a visual maze showed only an increase in dendritic length but not in spine density. It is possible, however, that early in the motor and/or maze training the animals had an increase in spine density that was subsequently pruned back. The critical experiment here would be to examine the neurons in the brains of animals killed at different times in the training.

Although the studies correlating learning and changes in spine density in the chick are suggestive of a causal relationship between experience, behavior, and neuronal change, they do not provide proof. One additional experiment is suggestive in this regard. Patel, Rose, and Stewart (1988) trained chicks on the passive avoidance task described earlier but, in their experiment, half of the trained chicks were given a subconvulsive transcranial electroshock 5 minutes after training. This procedure rendered about half of the trained animals amnesic for the experience. The spine density was found to be higher in the chicks that remembered the aversive nature of the training stimulus compared to chicks rendered amnesic. This finding argues strongly in favour of a specific role for dendritic spines in experience-dependent memory formation in the chick.

Visual system of cats

The visual system of kittens has been one of the major systems for the study of experience-dependent changes ever since the now classic studies of Wiesel and Hubel in the early 1960s (e.g. Hubel & Wiesel, 1965; Wiesel & Hubel, 1963,

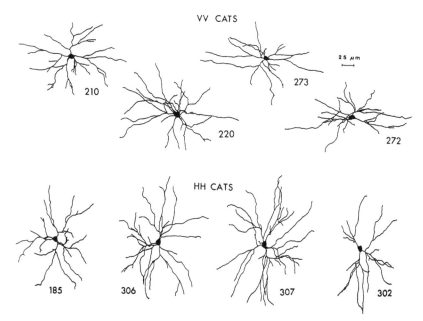

FIG. 5.8 Camera lucida drawings of individual layer III pyramidal cells from cats raised in a vertical visual environment (VV cats) versus a horizontal visual environment (HH cats). Cells in the VV condition have dendritic fields that are oriented horizontally as compared to cells in the HH condition that have fields oriented more vertically.

1965). There are, however, surprisingly few studies on the morphological changes in the brains of the kittens because most studies have been electrophysiological (for a review, see Rauschecker, 1995). One intriguing exception is a study by Tieman and Hirsch (1982). Cats were raised with lenses that restricted visual exposure to lines oriented vertically or horizontally. Many previous studies had shown that cells in the visual cortex of cats with such restricted experience show a marked change in their tuning characteristics. Hence, neurons in cats with selective exposure to lines of vertical orientation are most excitable when presented with lines of the same orientation. The new approach in the Tieman and Hirsch study was that they examined the morphology of visual cortical neurons from cats with selective horizontal or vertical visual experience. Cats raised in a normal environment showed a random distribution of orientation of dendritic fields, but cats raised with selective experiences showed a change in the orientation of the dendritic fields (Fig. 5.8). These changes were specific, however, as they occurred in pyramidal cells in visual cortex and not in the adjacent stellate cells.

One other set of studies deserves mention. I noted earlier that Beaulieu and Colonnier (1987) showed a clear increase in the size of the brains of cats raised in enriched versus impoverished environments (see Fig. 5.4). These authors also found that the density of neurons is lower in the enriched animals, much as

Greenough and Chang (1989) had found in rats, and presumably reflects the increased dendritic material per neuron. In addition, they analyzed the number and type of synapses in an electron microscopic study (Beaulieu & Colonnier, 1988). One important finding was that experience increased the number of excitatory synapses per neuron and decreased the number of inhibitory ones in the visual cortex. Thus, enrichment had modified the excitatory-inhibitory equilibrium of the visual cortex. One prediction from this observation is that neurons in the cortex of enriched animals would be more reactive to visual stimulation than those in impoverished animals. One prediction from this would be that enriched animals would be able to learn to solve visually guided problems more quickly than impoverished animals, and that is the case.

Olfaction in rodents

Rodents have a keen sense of smell so it is reasonable to suppose that experience would have significant effects on the structure of the olfactory system. Two general models of investigation have been used: (1) sensory deprivation and experience; and (2) ecologically relevant olfactorily guided behavior. I will consider each separately.

   Olfactory deprivation and experience.   The general prediction of such studies is that olfactory deprivation should lead to restricted morphological development of the olfactory system, whereas olfactory training or olfactory "enrichment" should lead to enhanced development. In fact, this is the general finding (e.g. Doving & Pinching, 1973; Pinching & Doving, 1974; Rehn & Breipohl, 1986; Rehn, Breipohl, Mendoza, & Apfelbach, 1986) (see also the extensive studies by Leon and colleagues, e.g. Leon, 1992a,b). One surprising finding in olfactory studies is that olfactory experience not only changes the morphology of existing neurons but it also alters the *number* of neurons. For example, odor deprivation results in reductions in neuronal number (e.g. Brunjes & Frazier, 1986; Meisami & Safari, 1981; Skeen, Due, & Douglas, 1986), whereas enriched odor exposure leads to increased neuron numbers (Rosselli-Austin & Williams, 1990). This neuronal increase is not trivial, being in the order of 35–40%! Evidence of increased neuron numbers in the olfactory system is especially intriguing because it has not been seen in analyses of neocortical or cerebellar cortex. One important difference between the olfactory system and neocortical and cerebellar regions is that olfactory neurons are generated throughout the lifetime of rodents (e.g. Lois & Alvarez-Buylla, 1994). Thus, it is likely that enhanced olfactory experience influences neuronal growth in the olfactory bulb throughout life. One possible reason for this could be that the addition and deletion of olfactory neurons throughout life allow a mechanism for the nervous system to form new olfactory memories and to modify existing ones. It is noteworthy that the other forebrain structure that generates neurons throughout adulthood is the dentate gyrus of the hippocampus and this area has been implicated in certain types of learning and memory.

A series of studies by various authors has examined changes in spine density with experience. These changes are germane to those discussed earlier, occurring in rodents and chickens. In the olfactory system, spine loss on granule cells in the bulb has been reported in both rodents and ferrets with restricted olfactory experience (Apfelbach & Weiler, 1985; Rehn, Panhuber, Laing, & Breipohl, 1988). This decreased spine density appears to result from a reduction in the number of spines generated during development, rather than a pruning of spines as in the rodent studies. It is possible that changes in spine density follow different rules in the olfactory bulb and neocortex. It is equally probable, however, that an *absence* of sensory stimulation may lead to a retarded development of spines, whereas the *addition* of sensory stimulation may lead to a selective pruning of spines. It would be worthwhile to test these different hypotheses directly by measuring spine density in the olfactory bulb and olfactory cortex in the same brains.

Ecologically-relevant olfactory behavior.   Although many studies have looked at synaptic plasticity in a variety of learning contexts, few have considered situations that are biologically relevant to species survival. Perhaps the most thorough set of such studies has been conducted by Kaverne and his colleagues on olfactory learning in female mice (e.g. Brennan, Kaba, & Kaverne, 1990; Brennan & Kaverne, 1989; Kaba, Rossier, & Kaverne, 1989). Female mice show an unusual behavior when they copulate with a male: They form an olfactory memory of the male's odors (pheromones). This olfactory memory is of critical biological importance because it prevents subsequent exposure to this male's pheromones from initiating neuroendocrine mechanisms that would terminate pregnancy. Thus, when a female mouse copulates with a male, she learns the odor of the male. If she encounters a different male odor in the hours after mating, the pregnancy is blocked. This memory is formed in the olfactory bulb during a critical period lasting about 4 hours immediately after mating and it lasts about 40 days, after which it fades. Kaverne and his colleagues subsequently have used this model to demonstrate the role of different transmitter systems in the memory formation. For example, they have shown that it is dependent on noradrenergic innervation of the olfactory bulb and involves changes in the efficacy of dendrodendritic synapses in the accessory olfactory bulb.

More recent studies by Kaverne's group have looked at the development of infant-mother bond in sheep (e.g. Kendrick, Levy, & Kaverne, 1992). After having given birth, female sheep form a selective bond with their offspring based on the odor of the lamb. These studies have shown that selective recognition of lambs is accompanied by increased activity of a subset of neurons in the olfactory bulb (mitral cells) that respond to lamb odors. As in the mouse olfactory learning already discussed, this learning is rapid and is dependent on changes in the dendrodendritic synapses between mitral and granule cells.

In sum, the studies of Kaverne's group are unique in that they show not only that animals can form olfactory memories quickly, but they have also found the location of the synaptic changes underlying the memory. I am unaware, however, of any studies of dendritic fields or spine density in this research, but it certainly would be worth pursuing. In particular, the changes in spine density might be particularly illuminating of general mechanisms of memory trace formation.

Dendrites and behavior in humans

There are few studies that have tried to correlate changes in neuronal structure with behavior. One way to approach this would be to look for a relationship between neuronal structure and education. (This is an admittedly loose analogy to enriched versus caged rearing in rats but bear with me!) Jacobs, Schall, and Scheibel (1993) did, in fact, consider this question and found a relationship between extent of dendritic arborization in a cortical language area (Wernicke's area) and amount of education. Hence, the cortical neurons from the brains of deceased people with university education had more dendritic arbor than those from people with high school education who, in turn, had more dendritic material than those with less than high school education. Of course, it may have been that people with larger dendritic fields were more likely to go to university but that is not easy to test.

Another way to look at the relationship between human brain structure and behavior is to consider the functional abilities of people and to correlate this with neuronal structure. For example, one might expect to find differences in language-related areas between people with high and low verbal abilities. This experiment is difficult to conduct, however, because it presupposes behavioral measures prior to death and this is not normally done. However, Jacobs et al. (1993) considered this possibility by taking advantage of the now well-documented observation that females have verbal abilities that are superior to those of males (for a review, see Kolb & Whishaw, 1996). Thus, when they examined the structure of neurons in Wernicke's area, they found that females have more extensive dendritic arbors than males. Furthermore, in a subsequent study, Jacobs et al. (1993) found that this sex difference was present as early as age 9, suggesting that such sex differences emerge within the first decade. These sex differences in cortical architecture in humans are parallel to those reported in other studies showing sex differences in cerebral blood flow and glucose metabolism, with females having a level about 15% higher than that of males (e.g. Baxter et al., 1987).

Scheibel, Conrad, Perdue, Tomiyasu, and Wechsler (1990) approached the matter in a slightly different way. They began with two hypotheses. First, they suggested that there is a relationship between the complexity of dendritic arbor and the nature of the computational tasks performed by a brain area. To test this hypothesis they examined the dendritic structure of neurons in different cortical regions that they proposed to have functions that varied in computational complexity. For example, when they compared the structure of neurons corresponding to the somatosensory representation of the trunk versus those for the fingers, they found the latter to have more complex cells. They reasoned that the somesthetic inputs from receptive fields on the chest wall would constitute less of an integrative and interpretive challenge to cortical neurons than those from the fingers and thus the neurons representing the chest were less complex. Similarly, when they compared the cells in the finger area to those in the supramarginal gyrus (SMG), a region that is associated with higher cognitive processes, they found the SMG neurons to be more complex. The second hypothesis was that dendritic trees in all regions are subject to experience-dependent change. As a result, they hypothesized that predominant life experiences (e.g. occupation) should be reflected in the structure of dendritic trees. Although they did not test this hypothesis directly, they did make an interesting observation. In their study comparing cells in the trunk area, finger area, and the SMG, they found curious individual differences. For example, especially large differences in trunk and finger neurons were found in the brains of people who were a typist, machine operator, and appliance repairmen. In each of these, a high level of finger dexterity maintained over long periods of time may be assumed. In contrast, one case with no trunk-finger difference was a salesman in whom one would not expect a good deal of specialized finger use. These results are suggestive although I would agree with Scheibel et al.'s caution that "a larger sample size and far more detailed life, occupation, leisure, and retirement histories are necessary" (p. 101). The preliminary findings in this study do suggest that such an investigation would be fruitful.

Finally, one can look at pathological development and see if there is a neural correlate of abnormal behavior. In one such study, Purpura (1974) examined the dendritic structure of neurons from the brains of retarded versus average intelligence children. He did not quantify the dendritic length but he did show marked differences in dendritic structure. The retarded children had spindly dendrites that had a very much reduced spine density (Fig. 5.9). This abnormal spine density is intriguing because it is reminiscent of the low spine density that we have consistently observed in rats with cortical injury in what would be equivalent to the third trimester of human development. Like retarded children, these rats have severe behavioral deficits that render them unable to learn cognitive tasks that are solved easily by animals with similar brain injuries later in life (e.g. Kolb & Gibb, 1991a). More recently, there have been several studies of children with trisomic chromosomal states, such as Down's syndrome and trisomy 13 (e.g. Becker, Armstrong, & Chan, 1986; Jay, Chan, & Becker, 1990; Marin-Padilla, 1974), the general observation being that there is anomalous spine morphology, decreased spine density, and small dendritic fields in many types of retardation.

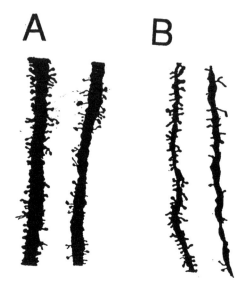

FIG. 5.9   Representative examples of dendritic branches from cortical neurons of children (A) and rats (B). A. The left branch is from a child of normal intelligence whereas the right branch is from a child with mental retardation. B. The left branch is from an adult rat that sustained a frontal lesion at 10 days of age whereas the right branch is from an adult rat that sustained a frontal lesion at 1 day of age. The latter rat performed very badly on all behavioral tests administered. Thus, the animals with severely compromised cognitive skills had dendritic branches with few spines.

Invertebrate plasticity

I would be remiss if I did not at least consider briefly the effects of experience on the nervous system of invertebrates. Two studies on *Drosophila* are especially intriguing. In one, Technau (1984) showed that the complexity of neurons in *Drosophila melanogaster* depends on the flies' living conditions. Flies were housed for 3 weeks either singly in small plastic vials or in groups of 200 in larger enclosures with colored visual patterns on the walls, various odor sources and plants. Analysis of the Kenyon cell fibers in the mushroom bodies (cells in the "brain" of the fly) showed about 15% more fibers in the enriched versus impoverished flies. A subsequent study by Heisenberg, Heusipp, and Wanke (1995) showed that most regions of the *Drosophila* brain were continuously reorganized throughout life in response to specific living conditions. In particular, social and sexual activity was associated with increased brain size, as was the volume of space available. These experience-dependent changes in *Drosophila* are remarkable and leave little doubt that experience is a major force in shaping the nervous system of all animals. Furthermore, these changes in insect brains are not only seen in artificial lab experiments but can also be seen in ecologically valid settings. For example, Withers, Fahrbach, and Robinson (1993) examined the changes in the brain of the honey bee in relation to the division of labor in adult worker bees. Adult worker bees spend about the first 3 weeks of their 4–7 week life performing a variety of tasks within the hive, including caring for the queen and brood ("nursing"). They then make a dramatic transition in behavior and begin to forage outside for food. Food foraging is a complex behavior that requires that the animal learn the location of both the hive and the food, the nature of different foods, as well as learn to recognize and use species-typical signals about food sources from other bees. Withers et al. (1993) not only found that the behavioral change is associated with striking changes in brain structure, but that these changes are dependent not on the age of the animal but on its foraging experience. This honey bee model offers a new entry into the cellular mechanisms of neural and behavioral plasticity.

MODULATION OF EXPERIENCE-DEPENDENT CHANGE

The effects of experience on the brain vary with many factors including sex, neurotrophins, stress, and injury. For example, there is accumulating evidence that the male brain and the female brain differ in their structure and respond differently to environmental events. Specifically, Juraska and her colleagues (e.g. Juraska, 1984, 1986, 1990; Juraska, Fitch, Henderson, & Rivers, 1985; Juraska, Fitch, & Washburne, 1989) were the first to report that the neocortex is more sensitive to experience in males than it is in females. This is not a general increased sensitivity of males, however, as they have also reported that the hippocampus is more sensitive to experience in females than in males. These differences are related to the circulating gonadal hormone, and therefore can be manipulated with hormone injections.

Neurotrophins, which are chemicals known to have growth enhancing properties in the nervous system, also interact with experience. It is known, for instance, that experience differentially modulates the levels of different neurotrophins such as nerve growth factor, which, in turn, stimulates growth (e.g. Schoups, Elliott, Friedman, & Black, 1995). Thus, it is possible that one route of action of experience on the brain is to stimulate (or inhibit?) the production of neurotrophins and these, in turn, alter neuronal structure.

Stress has effects on the neuroendocrine system and this, in turn, has been shown to affect cell morphology (e.g. Sapolsky, 1987; Sirevaag, Black, & Greenough, 1991; Stewart & Kolb, 1988). Most studies to date have focused on the hippocampal formation, but there is reason to suspect that cortical neurons are also vulnerable (Stewart & Kolb, 1988). This promises to be a region of increased interest over the next decade.

Finally, we have already seen that pathological states such as retardation alter the normal dendritic structure of the brain. Similarly, injuries to the brain alter normal dendritic morphology, the details depending on the precise age at injury, sex, and region damaged (e.g. Kolb, 1995). Indeed, I have argued elsewhere that one mechanism for supporting recovery from cortical injury is dendritic growth (e.g. Kolb & Gibb, 1991a). There is now an extensive literature on the modulation of lesion effects by manipulating pre- or postinjury experience (e.g. Schulkin, 1989; Will & Kelche, 1992). In my own studies we have placed rats with cortical injuries in our condominiums and have shown changes in dendritic fields, spine density, and functional recovery (e.g. Kolb et al., in press; Kolb & Gibb, 1991b). Perhaps the simplest, and most important, finding of these studies is that the animal with the most miserable functional outcome after cortical injury is especially helped by environmental therapy.

In sum, the experience-dependent effects on neural morphology and behavior reviewed in this chapter vary with several factors including sex, neurotrophins, and injury.

CONCLUSIONS

One of the most intriguing questions in behavioral neuroscience concerns the manner in which the brain, and especially the neocortex, can modify its structure and ultimately its function throughout one's lifetime. As this review has suggested, the cortex can be changed dramatically by experience and this change is modulated by various factors. Several basic conclusions can be extracted regarding the nature of the relationship between experience, brain plasticity, and behavior.

First, experience alters the synaptic organization of the brain in species as diverse as fruit flies and humans.

Second, changes in synaptic organization are correlated with changes in behavior. Thus, animals with extensive dendritic growth, relative to untreated animals, show facilitated performance on many types of behavioral measures, especially measures of cognitive activity.

Third, there are multiple, dissociable changes in response to environmental experiences. These include increases in dendritic length, dendritic branching pattern, spine density, synapse number, synapse size, glial size and number, and metabolic activity.

Fourth, experience-dependent changes in neurons are affected by various factors including age, gonadal hormones, stress, trophic factors, and brain pathology.

Fifth, the analysis of behavior/anatomy correlations provides important insight into the relationship between brain activity and cognitive functions.

REFERENCES

Apfelbach, R., & Weiler, E. (1985). Olfactory deprivation enhances normal spine loss in the olfactory bulb of developing ferrets. *Neuroscience Letters, 62*, 169–173.

Baxter, L. R., Jr., Mazziotta, J. C., Phelps, M. E., Selin, C. E., Guze, G. H., & Fairbanks, L. (1987). Cerebral glucose metabolic rates in normal human females versus normal males. *Psychiatry Research, 21*, 237–245.

Beaulieu, C., & Colonnier, M. (1987). Effect of the richness of the environment on the cat visual cortex. *Journal of Comparative Neurology, 266*, 478–494.

Beaulieu, C., & Colonnier, M. (1988). Richness of environment affects the number of contacts formed by boutons containing flat vescicles but does not alter the number of these boutons per neuron. *Journal of Comparative Neurology, 274,* 347–356.

Becker, L. E., Armstrong, D. L., & Chan, F. (1986). Dendritic atrophy in children with Down's syndrome. *Annals of Neurology, 20,* 520–526.

Bhide, P. G., & Bedi, K. S. (1984). The effects of a lengthy period of environmental diversity on well-fed and previously undernourished rats. II. Synapse to neuron rations. *Journal of Comparative Neurology, 227,* 305–310.

Black, J. E., Greenough, W. T., Anderson, B. J., & Isaacs, K. R. (1987). Environment and the aging brain. *Canadian Journal of Psychology, 41,* 111–130.

Black, J. E., Isaacs, K. R., Anderson, B. J., Alcantara, A. A., & Greenough, W. T. (1990). Learning causes synaptogenesis, whereas motor activity causes angiogenesis, in cerebellar cortex of adult rats. *Proceedings of the National Academy of Science, USA, 87,* 5568–5572.

Black, J. E., Polinsky, M., & Greenough, W. T. (1989). Progressive failure of cerebral angiogenesis supporting neural plasticity in aging rats. *Neurobiology of Aging, 10,* 353–358.

Brennan, P., Kaba, H., & Kaverne, E. B. (1990). Olfactory recognition: A simple memory system. *Science, 250,* 1223–1226.

Brennan, P. A., & Kaverne, E. B. (1989). Impairment of olfactory memory by local infusions of non-selective excitatory amino acid receptor antagonists into the accessory olfactory bulb. *Neuroscience, 33,* 657–662.

Brunjes, P. C., & Frazier, L. L. (1986). Maturation and plasticity in the olfactory system of vertebrates. *Brain Research Reviews, 11,* 1–45.

Capowski, J. (1989). *Computer techniques in neuroanatomy.* New York: Plenum.

Chang, F.-L. F., & Greenough, W. T. (1982). Lateralized effects of monocular training on dendritic branching in adult split-brain rats. *Brain Research, 232,* 283–292.

Coopersmith, R., & Leon, M. (1984). Enhanced neural response to familiar olfactory cues. *Science, 225,* 849–851.

Diamond, J. (1988). Nerve growth factor and the reinnervation of skin after peripheral nerve lesions. In H. Flohr (Ed.), *Post-lesion neural plasticity* (pp. 35–48). Berlin: Springer-Verlag.

Diamond, M. C., Dowling, G. A., & Johnson, R. E. (1981). Morphologic cerebral cortical asymmetry in male and female rats. *Experimental Neurology, 71,* 261–268.

Diamond, M. C., Lindner, B., & Raymond, A. (1967). Extensive cortical depth measurements and neuron size increases in the cortex of environmentally enriched rats. *Journal of Comparative Neurology, 131,* 357–364.

Doving, K. B., & Pinching, A. J. (1973). Selective degeneration of neurones in the olfactory bulb following prolonged odour exposure. *Brain Research, 52,* 115–129.

Field, T., Schanberg, S. M., Scafidi, F., Bauer, C. R., Vega-Lahr, N., Garcia, R., Nystrom, J., & Kuhn, C. M. (1986). Tactile/kinesthetic stimulation effects on preterm neonates. *Pediatrics, 77,* 654–658.

Floeter, M. K., & Greenough, W. T. (1979). Cerebellar plasticity: Modification of Purkinje cell structure by differential rearing in monkeys. *Science, 206,* 227–229.

Globus, A., Rosenzweig, M. R., Bennett, E. L., & Diamond, M. C. (1973). Effects of differential experience on dendritic spine counts in rat cerebral cortex. *Journal of Comparative and Physiological Psychology, 82,* 175–181.

Greenough, W. T. (1976). Enduring brain effects of differential experience and training. In M. R. Rosenzweig & E. L. Bennett (Eds.), *Mechanisms of learning and memory* (pp. 255–278). Cambridge, MA: MIT Press.

Greenough, W. T., & Chang, F. F. (1989). Plasticity of synapse structure and pattern in the cerebral cortex. In A. Peters & E. G. Jones (Eds.), *Cerebral cortex* (Vol. 7, pp. 391–440). New York: Plenum.

Greenough, W. T., Larson, J. R., & Withers, G. S. (1985). Effects of unilateral and bilateral training in a reaching task on dendritic branching of neurons in the rat motor-sensory forelimb cortex. *Behavioral and Neural Biology, 44,* 301–314.

Greenough, W. T., & Volkmar, F. R. (1973). Pattern of dendritic branching in occipital cortex of rats reared in complex environments. *Experimental Neurology, 40,* 491–504.

Greenough, W. T., Volkmar, F. R., & Juraska, J. (1973). Effects of rearing complexity on dendritic branching in frontolateral and temporal cortex of the rat. *Experimental Neurology, 40,* 371–378.

Hebb, D. O. (1947). The effects of early experience on problem solving at maturity. *American Psychologist, 2,* 737–745.

Hebb, D. O. (1949). *The organization of behavior.* New York: Wiley.

Heisenberg, M., Heusipp, M., & Wanke, C. (1995). Structural plasticity in the *Drosophila* brain. *Journal of Neuroscience, 15,* 1951–1960.

Hubel, D. H., & Wiesel, T. N. (1965). Binocular interaction in striate cortex of kittens reared with artificial squint. *Journal of Neurophysiology, 28,* 1041–1059.

Jacobs, B., Schall, M., & Scheibel, A. B. (1993). A quantitative dendritic analysis of Wernicke's area. II. Gender, Hemispheric, and environmental factors. *Journal of Comparative Neurology, 237,* 97–111.

Jay, V., Chan, F.-W., & Becker, L. E. (1990). Dendritic arborization in the human fetus and infant with trisomy 18 syndrome. *Developmental Brain Research, 54,* 291–294.

Juraska, J. M. (1984). Sex differences in dendritic responses to differential experience in the rat visual cortex. *Brain Research, 295,* 27–34.

Juraska, J. M. (1986). Sex differences in developmental plasticity of behavior and the brain. In W. T. Greenough & J. M. Juraska (Eds.), *Developmental neuropsychobiology* (pp. 409–422). New York: Academic Press.

Juraska, J. M. (1990). The structure of the cerebral cortex: Effects of gender and the environment. In B. Kolb & R. Tees (Eds.), *The cerebral cortex of the rat* (pp. 483–506). Cambridge, MA: MIT Press.

Juraska, J. M., Fitch, J., Henderson, C., & Rivers, N. (1985). Sex differences in the dendritic branching of dentate granule cells following differential experience. *Brain Research, 333,* 73–80.

Juraska, J. M., Fitch, J. M., & Washburne, D. L. (1989). The dendritic morphology of pyramidal neurons in the rat hippocampal CA3 area. II. Effects of gender and experience. *Brain Research, 479,* 115–121.

Kaba, H., Rossier, A., & Kaverne, B. (1989). Neural basis of olfactory memory in the context of pregnancy block. *Neuroscience, 32,* 657–662.

Kaas, J. (1987). The organization of neocortex in mammals: Implications for theories of brain function. *Annual Review of Psychology, 38,* 129–151.

Kendrick, L. M., Levy, F., & Kaverne, E. G. (1992). Changes in the sensory processing of olfactory signals induced by birth in sheep. *Science, 256,* 833–836.

Kolb, B. (1995). *Brain plasticity and behavior.* Mahwah, NJ: Lawrence Erlbaum Associates Inc.

Kolb, B., Forgie, M., Gibb, R., Gorny, G., & Rowntree, S. (in press). Age, experience and the changing brain. *Neuroscience and Biobehavioral Reviews.*

Kolb, B., & Gibb, R. (1991a). Sparing of function after neonatal frontal lesions correlates with increased cortical dendritic branching: A possible mechanism for the Kennard effect. *Behavioral Brain Research, 43,* 51–56.

Kolb, B., & Gibb, R. (1991b). Environmental enrichment and cortical injury: Behavioral and anatomical consequences of frontal cortex lesions in rats. *Cerebral Cortex, 1,* 189–198.

Kolb, B., & Gibb, R. (submitted). *Experience and the changing brain. 1. Age-dependent changes in dendritic growth following enriched rearing at different ages.*

Kolb, B., Gibb, R., Gorny, R., & Ouellette, A. (1996). Experience dependent changes in cortical morphology are age dependent. *Society for Neuroscience Abstracts, 22,* 1133.

Kolb, B., & Whishaw, I. Q. (1996). *Fundamentals of human neuropsychology,* (4th ed.) New York: W. H. Freeman.

Kolb, B., Whishaw, I. Q., & van der Kooy, D. (1986). Brain development in the neonatally decorticated rat. *Brain Research, 397,* 315–326.

Lashley, K. S. (1929). *Brain mechanisms and intelligence.* Chicago, IL: University of Chicago Press.

Leon, M. (1992a). Neuroethology of olfactory preference development. *Journal of Neurobiology, 23,* 1557–1573.

Leon, M. (1992b). The neurobiology of filial learning. *Annual Review of Psychology, 43,* 377–398.

Lois, C., & Alvarez-Buylla, A. (1994). Long-distance neuronal migration in the adult mammalian brain. *Science, 264,* 1145–1148.

Marin-Padilla, M. (1974). Structural organization of the cerebral cortex (motor area) in human chromosomal aberrations: A Golgi study. I. D₁ (13–15) trisomy, Patau syndrome. *Brain Research, 66,* 375–391.

Meisami, E., & Safari, L. (1981). A quantitative study of the effects of early unilateral olfactory deprivation on the number and distribution of mitral and tufted cells and of glomeruli in the rat olfactory bulb. *Brain Research, 222,* 81–107.

Patel, S. N., Rose, S. R. R., & Stewart, M. G. (1988). Training induced dendritic spine density changes are specifically related to memory formation processes in the chick, *Gallus domesticus. Brain Research, 463,* 168–173.

Patel, S. N., & Stewart, M. G. (1988). Changes in the number and structure of dendritic spines 25 hours after passive avoidance training in the domestic chick, *Gallus domesticus. Brain Research, 449,* 34–46.

Pinching, A. J., & Doving, K. B. (1974). Selective degeneration in the rat olfactory bulb following exposure to different odours. *Brain Research, 82,* 195–204.

Purpura, D. P. (1974). Dendritic spine "dysgenesis" and mental retardation. *Science, 186,* 1126–1128.

Pylyshyn, Z. W. (1980). Computation and cognition: Issues in the foundations of cognitive science. *Behavior and Brain Science, 3,* 11–69.

Ramon y Cajal, S. (1928). *Degeneration and regeneration of the nervous system.* London: Oxford University Press.

Rauschecker, J. P. (1995). Developmental plasticity and memory. *Behavioral Brain Research, 66,* 7–12.

Rehn, B., & Breipohl, W. (1986). Transient postnatal impacts on the mouse olfactory epithelium proprium affect the granule cell development in the mouse olfactory bulb. In W. Breipohl (Ed.), *Ontogeny of olfaction in vertebrates* (pp. 143–156). Berlin: Springer-Verlag.

Rehn, B., Breipohl, W., Mendoza, A. S., & Apfelbach, A. (1986). Changes in granule cells of the ferret olfactory bulb associated with imprinting on prey odours. *Brain Research, 373,* 114–125.

Rehn, B., Panhuber, H., Laing, D. G., & Breipohl, W. (1988). Spine density on olfactory granule cell dendrites is reduced in rats reared in a restricted olfactory environment. *Developmental Brain Research, 40,* 143–147.

Riesen, A. H. (1982). Effects of environments on development in sensory systems. In W. D. Neff (Ed.), *Contributions to sensory physiology* (Vol. 6, pp. 45–77). New York: Academic Press.

Riesen, A. H., Dickerson, G. P., & Struble, R. G. (1977). Somatosensory restriction and behavioral development in stumptail monkeys. *Annals of the New York Academy of Sciences, 290,* 285–294.

Rose, S. P. R. (1985). The cell biological consequences of passive avoidance training in the chick. *Advances in Behavioral Biology, 28,* 39–49.

Rosenzweig, M. R., & Bennett, E. L. (1978). Experiential influences on brain anatomy and brain chemistry in rodents. In G. Gottlieb (Ed.), *Studies on the development of behavior and the nervous system* (pp. 289–387). New York: Academic Press.

Rosenzweig, M. R., Krech, D., Bennett, E. L., & Diamond, M. (1962). Effects of environmental complexity and training on brain chemistry and anatomy: A replication and extension. *Journal of Comparative and Physiological Psychology, 55,* 429–437.

Rosselli-Austin, L., & Williams, J. (1990). Enriched neonatal odor exposure leads to increased numbers of olfactory bulb mitral and granule cells. *Developmental Brain Research, 51,* 135–137.

Sapolsky, R. M. (1987). Glucocorticoids and hippocampal damage. *Trends in Neuroscience, 10,* 346–349.

Schanberg, S. M., & Field, T. M. (1987). Sensory deprivation stress and supplemental stimulation in the rat pup and preterm human neonate. *Child Development, 58,* 1431–1447.

Scheibel, A. B., Conrad, T., Perdue, S., Tomiyasu, U., & Wechsler, A. (1990). A quantitative study of dendrite complexity in selected areas of the human cerebral cortex. *Brain and Cognition, 12,* 85–101.

Schoups, A. A., Elliott, R. C., Friedman, W. J., & Black, I. B. (1995). NGF and BDNF are differentially modulated by visual experience in the developing geniculocortical pathway. *Developmental Brain Research, 86,* 326–334.

Schulkin, J. (Ed.) (1989). *Preoperative events: Their effects on behavior following brain damage.* Hillsdale, NJ: Lawrence Erlbaum Associates Inc.

Sirevaag, A. M., Black, J. E., & Greenough, W. T. (1991). Astrocyte hypertrophy in the dentate gyrus of young male rats reflects variation of individual stress rather than group environmental complexity manipulations. *Experimental Neurology, 111,* 74–79.

Sirevaag, A. M., & Greenough, W. T. (1987). Differential rearing effects on rat visual cortex synapses. III. Neuronal and glial nuclei, boutons, dendrites, and capillaries. *Brain Research, 424,* 320–332.

Sirevaag, A. M., & Greenough, W. T. (1988). A multivariate statistical summary of synaptic plasticity measures in rats exposed to complex, social and individual environments. *Brain Research, 441,* 386–392.

Sirevaag, A. M., & Greenough, W. T. (1991). Plasticity of GFA-immunoreactive astrocyte size and number in visual cortex of rats reared in complex environments. *Brain Research, 540,* 273–278.

Skeen, L. C., Due, B. R., & Douglas, F. E. (1986). Neonatal sensory deprivation reduces tufted cell number in mouse olfactory bulbs. *Neuroscience Letters, 63,* 5–10.

Skinner, B. F. (1938). *The behavior of organisms.* New York: Appleton-Century-Crofts.

Solkoff, N., & Matuszak, D. (1975). Tactile stimulation and behavioral development among low-birthweight infants. *Child Psychiatry and Human Development, 6,* 33–37.

Stell, M., & Riesen, A. (1987). Effects of early environments on monkey cortex neuroanatomical changes following somatomotor experience: Effects on layer III pyramidal cells in monkey cortex. *Behavioral Neuroscience, 101,* 341–346.

Stewart, J., & Kolb, B. (1988). The effects of neonatal gonadectomy and prenatal stress on cortical thickness and asymmetry in rats. *Behavioral and Neural Biology, 49,* 344–360.

Stewart, J., & Kolb, B. (1994). Dendritic branching in cortical pyramidal cells in response to ovariectomy in adult female rats: Suppression by neonatal exposure to testosterone. *Brain Research, 654,* 149–154.

Struble, R. G., & Riesen, A. H. (1978). Changes in cortical dendritic branching subsequent to partial social isolation in stumptail monkeys. *Developmental Psychobiology, 11,* 479–486.

Sullivan, R. M., & Leon, M. (1986). Early olfactory learning induces an enhanced olfactory bulb response in rats. *Developmental Brain Research, 27,* 278–282.

Technau, G. (1984). Fiber number in the mushroom bodies of adult *Drosophila melanogaster* depends on age, sex and experience. *Journal of Neurogenetics, 1,* 113–126.

Tees, R. C. (1986). Experience and visual development: Behavioral evidence. In W. T. Greenough & J. M. Juraska (Eds.), *Developmental neuropsychology* (pp. 317–363). New York: Academic Press.

Tieman, S. B., & Hirsch, H. V. B. (1982). Exposure to lines of only one orientation modifies dendritic morphology of cells in the visual cortex of the cat. *Journal of Comparative Neurology, 211,* 353–362.

Turner, A. M., & Greenough, W. T. (1983). Synapses per neuron and synaptic dimensions in occipital cortex of rats reared in complex, social, or isolation housing. *Acta Sterologica, 2* (Suppl. 1), 239–244.

Turner, A. M., & Greenough, W. T. (1985). Differential rearing effects on rat visual cortex synapses. I. Synaptic and neuronal density and synapses per neuron. *Brain Research, 329,* 195–203.

Uylings, H. B. M., Kuypers, K., Diamond, M., & Veltman, W. A. M. (1978). Environmental influences on neocortex in later life. *Progress in Brain Research, 48*, 261–274.

Volkmar, R. F., & Greenough, W. T. (1972). Rearing complexity affects branching of dendrites in visual cortex of the rat. *Science, 176*, 1445–1447.

Wallhausser, E., & Scheich, H. (1987). Auditory imprinting leads to differential 2-deoxyglucose uptake and dendritic spine loss in the chick rostral forebrain. *Developmental Brain Research, 31*, 29–44.

Werker, J. F., & Tees, R. C. (1992). The organization and reorganization of human speech perception. *Annual Review of Neuroscience, 15*, 377–402.

Whishaw, I. Q. (1990). The decorticate rat. In B. Kolb & R. C. Tees (Eds.), *Cerebral cortex of the rat* (pp. 239–268). Cambridge, MA: MIT Press.

Wiesel, T. N., & Hubel, D. H. (1963). Single-cell responses in striate cortex of kittens deprived of vision in one eye. *Journal of Neurophysiology, 26*, 1003–1017.

Wiesel, T. N., & Hubel, D. H. (1965). Comparison of the effects of unilateral and bilateral eye closure on cortical unit responses in kittens. *Journal of Neurophysiology, 28*, 1026–1040.

Will, B., & Kelche, C. (1992). Environmental approaches to recovery of function from brain damage: A review of animal studies (1981–1991). In F. D. Rose & D. A. Johnson (Eds.), *Recovery from brain damage: Reflections and directions* (pp. 79–104). New York: Plenum.

Withers, G. S., Fahrbach, S. E., & Robinson, G. E. (1993). Selective neuroanatomical plasticity and division of labor in the honey bee. *Nature, 364*, 238–240.

Withers, G. S., & Greenough, W. T. (1989). Reaching training selectively alters dendritic branching in subpopulations of layer II-III pyramids in rat motor-somatosensory forelimb cortex. *Neuropsychologia, 27*, 61–69.

Woo, C. C., & Leon, M. (1987). Sensitive period for neural and behavioral response development to learned odors. *Developmental Brain Research, 36*, 309–313.

CHAPTER SIX

Auditory information processing as indexed by the mismatch negativity

Risto Näätänen and Hannu Tiitinen
University of Helsinki, Helsinki, Finland

The mismatch negativity (MMN) is a component of the auditory event-related potential (ERP) that is elicited task-independently by an infrequent change in a repetitive stimulus stream. The MMN can be recorded in response to any discriminable change in the stimulus stream. The MMN data imply the existence of cortical sensory-memory traces in which the features of the frequently occurring standard stimuli are represented. One can probe these traces by presenting deviant stimuli of different magnitudes and thus indirectly determine the accuracy of these central sound representations. Several recent studies have shown that these representations govern attentive auditory discrimination ability in humans. The MMN is an objective, easily quantifiable index of the quality of sensory stimulus representations from which auditory percepts are built. The most recent studies have provided evidence that even complex temporal and linguistic stimulus features and long-term learning effects are reflected in MMN responses, thus significantly broadening the theoretical scope of MMN research. The MMN is consequently of great potential interest as a tool in understanding central auditory function, its development, and various forms of its pathology.

Quelle que soit la tâche auditive en jeu, un changement peu fréquent à l'intérieur d'une série répétitive de stimuli déclenche une composante négative désassortie (CND) à l'intérieur du potentiel évoqué obtenu. Cette composante peut être enregistrée en réponse à toute variation perceptible dans une telle série de stimuli. Les données l'illustrant impliquent l'existence de traces corticales de la mémoire sensorielle où sont représentées les caractéristiques des stimuli étalons, soit ceux fréquemment présentés. Il est possible de sonder plus avant la nature de ces traces à l'aide de stimuli désassortis de configurations différentes, et donc de déterminer indirectement l'exactitude de ces représentations sonores centrales. Chez l'humain, plusieurs travaux récents indiquent que ces représentations régissent la capacité d'attention auditive. La CND constitue un indicateur objectif et facilement quantifiable de la qualité des représentations des stimuli sensoriels à partir desquelles les percepts auditifs sont construits. Les études les plus récentes démontrent que même les caractéristiques de stimuli temporels et linguistiques complexes et les effets d'apprentissage à long terme se reflètent dans les CND, d'où la portée théorique élargie que revêt leur étude. Par conséquent, la CND recèle un grand intérêt potentiel à titre d'outil de compréhension de la fonction auditive centrale, de son développement et de diverses de ses pathologies.

INTRODUCTION

Processing of sensory stimulus features is essential for humans in determining their responses and actions. If behaviorally relevant aspects of the environment are not correctly represented in the brain, then the organism's behavior cannot be appropriate. Without correct representations of the auditory environment our ability to understand spoken language, for example, would be seriously impaired. Cognitive neuroscience has consequently emphasized the importance of understanding brain mechanisms of sensory information processing, that is, the sensory prerequisites of cognition. Most of the data obtained, unfortunately, do not allow the objective measurement of the accuracy of stimulus representations (see Näätänen, 1992).

In audition, recent cognitive neuroscience seems to have succeeded in extracting a unique measure of stimulus representations. This is the mismatch negativity (MMN), a component of the event-related potential (ERP), first reported by Näätänen, Gaillard, and Mäntysalo (1978). An in-depth review of MMN research can be found in Näätänen (1992); other recent reviews also provide information on the generator mechanisms of MMN (Alho 1995), its magnetic counterpart, MMNm (Näätänen, Ilmoniemi, & Alho, 1994), and its clinical applicability (Näätänen & Alho, 1995).

In what follows, the early MMN research and its relationship to auditory sensory memory and selective attention in humans are reviewed. Thereafter, we review the more recent MMN findings concerning complex stimulus-feature processing. These findings are related to sensory long-term memory, learning (plasticity), and speech processing in the human brain.

The MMN for basic stimulus features

The search for an objective index of change detection in the human brain can be traced back to 1975, with the proposition that stimulus deviation *per se* (irrespective of, for example, stimulus significance and attentional mechanisms) should produce a measurable brain response (Näätänen, 1975). Experimental evidence for this suggestion was obtained in a study conducted by Näätänen, Gaillard, and Mäntysalo in 1975, subsequently reported in 1978. In this dichotic listening study, the subject's task was to detect occasional deviant stimuli in

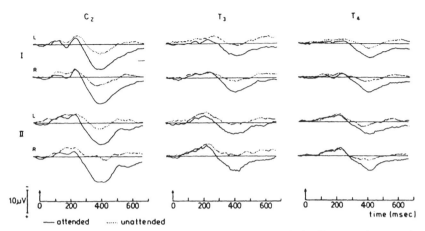

FIG. 6.1 The difference between ERPs to deviant and standard stimuli, averaged across nine subjects, for the three electrode positions separately for the left (L) and right (R) ear when attended and when unattended. These difference curves were obtained by subtracting the corresponding time points of the ERP to standards from the ERP to deviants. I refers to Experiment 1 in which deviants were of higher frequency than standards, II to Experiment 2 where deviants were of higher intensity than standards. Adapted from Näätänen et al., 1978.

the stimulus sequence presented to a designated ear while ignoring the concurrent sequence presented to the opposite ear. The irrelevant stimulus sequence included deviant stimuli that were physically equivalent to the deviant stimuli (targets) of the attended input sequence. The deviant stimuli were either tones of a slightly higher frequency or tones of a slightly greater intensity than the standard tones.

The deviant stimuli both in the attended and unattended stimulus sequence elicited a negativity in the 100–200msec latency range, which could not be seen in response to the standard stimuli (Fig. 6.1). This negativity, termed the MMN, was very similar for the attended and ignored input sequences, suggesting that attention was not required. Näätänen et al. (1978, pp. 324–325) proposed that "it may well be that a physiological mismatch process caused by a sensory input deviating from the memory trace ('template') formed by a frequent 'background' stimulus is such an automatic basic process that it takes place irrespective of the intentions of the experimenter and the subject, perhaps even unmodified by the latter . . .". On the basis of the relatively large MMN amplitudes above the temporal areas, the authors further suggested (pp. 326–328) that "the mismatch negativity reflects specific auditory stimulus discrimination processes taking place in the auditory primary and association areas . . . The latter processes are suggested to be largely automatic, beyond the control of will, instructions, etc. . . .".

This finding, suggesting the existence of an automatic memory mechanism, subsequently paved the way for a series of new experiments where the MMN for changes in basic stimulus features (frequency, intensity, and duration) were addressed in more detail. In these studies, it was established that the MMN is elicited by both increments and decrements in basic stimulus features (for a thorough review, see Näätänen, 1992). The MMN, however, is not elicited when a stimulus sequence begins or, similarly, when stimuli are presented with interstimulus intervals (ISIs) in the order of several seconds (Lounasmaa, Hari, Joutsiniemi, & Hämäläinen, 1989; Näätänen, Paavilainen, Alho, Reinikainen, & Sams, 1987; Sams, Hari, Rif, & Knuutila, 1993). Thus, it was concluded that no stimulus *per se* is an adequate stimulus for the MMN generator mechanism, as the system responds to the *difference* between consecutive stimuli. This response pattern is clearly separable from the behavior of the N1 response; the N1 amplitude is largest in response to the first stimulus of a series, strongly attenuating thereafter, and showing only partial recovery to a subsequent different stimulus (Näätänen & Picton, 1987).

The observations that even decrements in stimulus intensity and, especially, in duration elicited the MMN (Näätänen, Paavilainen, Alho, Reinikainen, & Sams, 1989a; Näätänen, Paavilainen, & Reinikainen, 1989b, respectively) were taken as providing evidence that the MMN is not generated by "fresh" neural activity in topographically organized cortex. According to the "fresh afferent" explanation, neurons responding to a particular frequency, for example, become refractory when a tone of that frequency is repeatedly presented, whereas other neurons remain nonrefractory. An occasional deviant tone therefore activates nonrefractory neurons leading to a larger response than that to the standard tone. Strong evidence against the fresh-afferent explanation was very recently provided by Yabe, Tervaniemi, Reinikainen, and Näätänen (1997) who showed that, with fast stimulus rates, the MMN is elicited even by stimulus omissions.

Generator mechanisms of the MMN

Already in their original article, Näätänen et al. (1978) suggested that the MMN arises from the vicinity of auditory cortex. This issue was left unaddressed for quite some time and was further complicated by Näätänen and Michie (1979) proposing that the MMN actually might consist of two subcomponents: a sensory-specific subcomponent, generated in the auditory cortices, and a frontal subcomponent. Only after considerable advancements in measurement technology (e.g. the development of multichannel-EEG recording apparatus and source localization techniques) and, especially, with the advent of magnetoencephalography (MEG), these problems could be tackled in more detail.

Recent EEG and MEG source-localization studies have revealed that the MMN is, for the most part, generated in supratemporal cortical brain areas (e.g. Alho et al., 1993; Aulanko et al., 1993; Csépe, Pantev, Hoke, Hampson, & Ross, 1992; Giard, Perrin, Pernier, & Bouchet, 1990; Giard et al., 1995; Hari et al.,

1984; Huotilainen et al., 1993; Kaukoranta, Sams, Hari, Hämäläinen, & Näätänen, 1989; Lounasmaa et al., 1989; Sams & Näätänen 1991; Scherg, Vajsar, & Picton, 1989; Tiitinen et al., 1993). Also, the suggestion put forth by Näätänen and Michie (1979) with regard to a possible frontal subcomponent was confirmed in recent studies (Giard et al., 1990).

In humans, the N1 has been localized to the supratemporal plane (Bertrand, Perrin, & Pernier, 1991; Elberling, Bak, Kofoed, Lebech, & Saermark, 1982; Pantev et al., 1988). As opposed to the N1, the MMN source has been found to be located some 7–10mm more anteriorly (Hari, Rif, Tiihonen, & Sams, 1992; Huotilainen et al., 1993; Levänen, Hari, McEvoy, & Sams, 1993; Sams, Kaukoranta, Hämäläinen, & Näätänen, 1991; Scherg et al., 1989; Tiitinen et al., 1993, Woods, Alho, & Algazi, 1993), with the MMN activity having a right-hemispheric preponderance (Paavilainen, Alho, Reinikainen, Sams, & Näätänen, 1991; Levänen, Ahonen, Hari, McEvoy, & Sams, 1996).

Furthermore, direct evidence for the contribution of auditory-cortex activity to MMN was recently provided by intracranial recordings in guinea pig (Kraus

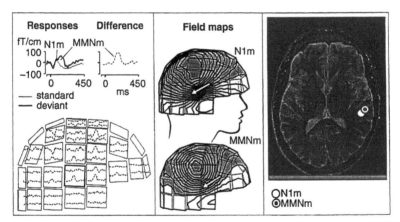

FIG. 6.2 *Left*: Magnetic responses over the right hemisphere of one subject to standard (1000Hz, p = 90%) and deviant (1150Hz, p = 10%) tones delivered to the left ear while the subject was concentrating on a reading task. The responses shown (response to standard is indicated by a thin line; response to deviant is indicated by a thick line) were recorded by one sensor (location indicated by the thick square below). The magnetic counterpart of mismatch negativity (MMNm) to deviant tones is indicated by the difference wave (dashed line) obtained by subtracting the response to standard tones from that to deviant tones. Corresponding difference waves from different recording sites over the right hemisphere are depicted in the bottom-left. *Center*: Field maps for N1m to standard tones (top) and for MMNm to deviant tones (bottom) in the same subject. White arrows indicate the equivalent current dipoles (ECDs). On each isocontour line, the radial component of the magnetic field is constant (the difference in the field amplitude between adjacent lines is 10fT for the N1m and 50fT for the MMNm field). Gray shading indicates magnetic flux out of the head; white, into the head. *Right*: ECD locations in the right hemisphere for N1m and MMNm of the same subject superimposed to the subject's magnetic resonance image. Adapted from Huotilainen et al., 1993.

et al., 1994a; Kraus, McGee, Littman, Nicol, & King, 1994b; Kraus et al., 1995), cat (Csépe, Karmos, & Molnár, 1987; Karmos, Winkler, Molnár, & Csépe, 1993) and monkey (Javitt, Schroeder, Steinschneider, Arezzo, & Vaughan Jr., 1992; Javitt et al., 1995). The MMN has also been successfully recorded directly from the human auditory cortex (Kropotov et al., 1995). Furthermore, indirect evidence for the contribution of auditory-cortex activity to the MMN is provided by the observation that the MMN is attenuated in patients with temporal lobe lesions (Aaltonen, Tuomainen, Laine, & Niemi, 1993).

The question of whether the MMN originates in primary or secondary auditory cortex is still unclear, however. Intracortical recordings of MMN to frequency and intensity changes in the monkey indicate an MMN generator in the primary auditory cortex (Javitt et al., 1992, 1995). Further evidence for the MMN sources being located in this area was provided by recordings of frequency-change MMNs from the cat auditory cortex. These studies showed that the MMN originates from the primary auditory area AI, but also from the secondary area AII (Csépe et al., 1987; Csépe, Karmos, & Molnár, 1989; Karmos et al., 1993). Kraus et al. (1994a,b) further demonstrated that in guinea pigs, even thalamic structures contribute to the MMN.

To summarize, the contribution of supratemporal and frontal brain areas to the MMN is fairly well established. The specific role of primary and secondary auditory cortices and possibly even subcortical brain areas in the generation of the MMN, however, remains to be investigated. This will be partly helped by future measurement methods with better spatial resolution.

The MMN: Interpretation

Relationship to auditory sensory memory. To account for the MMN, Näätänen et al. (1978) proposed that it is generated by a neuronal mismatch between a deviant sensory input and a sensory-memory trace representing a preceding repetitive sound (see also Näätänen, 1984, 1990, 1992). The fact that the MMN could be recorded even without the involvement of attentional processes also suggested that this memory mechanism is able to operate without engaging attention-related, higher-order cognitive processes.

The highly stimulus-specific pattern of the MMN mechanism might be the memory trace of auditory sensory memory (Näätänen et al., 1989a,b), the first memory system storing the acoustic features of auditory stimuli, closely resembling the "echoic" memory described by Neisser (1967). The memory system reflected in the MMN closely resembles echoic memory in that (a) this system contains extensively processed sensory stimulus information, (b) sensory information stored by the MMN system covers all stimulus features, (c) the MMN-trace durations are comparable to the duration of echoic memory (5–10sec; for behavioral results, see Cowan, 1984, 1988; for ERP results, see Böttcher-Gandor

& Ullsperger, 1992; Cowan, Winkler, Teder, & Näätänen, 1993; Mäntysalo & Näätänen, 1987; Näätänen, et al., 1987; for corroborating MEG results, see Sams et al., 1993), and (d) conscious experience and attention are not required for these systems to operate (see, however, Woldorff, Hackley, & Hillyard, 1991).

The inferred memory traces underlying the MMN might also be located where the MMN (i.e. its sensory-specific subcomponent) is generated (see also Näätänen, 1984, 1992). The EEG and MEG measurements cited earlier suggested that this storage mechanism is located on the supratemporal plane, in the auditory cortex. The afore-mentioned studies further suggested that each sound feature is separately processed in different loci of the auditory cortex. The MMN has also been found to be easily separable from other ERP components (most notably, the supratemporal N1) in both behavior and generator location. It follows that the MMN enables easy localization and study of memory traces for separate stimulus features.

Experimental evidence suggests that in measuring the MMN we are dealing with the physiological correlate of auditory sensory memory, however, the correspondence between MMN and memory is not perfect. Even a single stimulus presentation results in a memory trace of the stimulus, whereas the trace underlying the MMN seems to require reinforcement before a deviant stimulus can elicit an MMN (Cowan et al., 1993; see also Ritter, Deacon, Gomes, Javitt, & Vaughan Jr., 1995). This apparent inconsistency will be discussed later.

To summarize, the MMN data appear to provide evidence that stimulus features are separately analyzed and stored in the auditory cortex. The close resemblance of the behavior of the MMN to that of the previously behaviorally observed "echoic" memory system suggests that the MMN provides an objective, task-independently measurable physiological correlate of stimulus-feature representations in auditory sensory memory.

Relationship to attentional processes. Thus far it has been established that the MMN, in essence, indicates an attention-independent, pre-perceptual change detection mechanism that builds up a representation of stimulus events. With the MMN, one can therefore study similarities and differences in auditory processing between current and previous stimuli. Provided that there is a link between the MMN and attentive processing of auditory stimuli, the MMN might turn out to be useful as an objective, physiological measure of attentive auditory discrimination ability.

The early studies showed that the MMN is elicited even by small stimulus changes (frequency deviations ranging from 0.04% to 3.2%, with a 1000Hz standard stimulus; Sams, Paavilainen, Alho, & Näätänen, 1985; see also Näätänen & Gaillard, 1983). It was found that with small deviances the threshold for MMN elicitation coincides approximately with that of attentive discrimination. This seems to suggest that the MMN is involved in attentive processing of changes in the auditory environment.

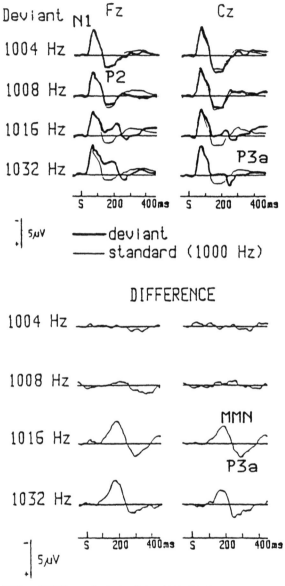

FIG. 6.3 *Top*: ERPs to 1000Hz standard stimuli (p = 80%; thin line) and deviant stimuli (p = 20%; thick line) of 1004, 1008, 1016, and 1032Hz. *Bottom:* The corresponding difference waveforms obtained by subtracting the standard-stimulus ERP from the deviant-stimulus ERP. MMN appears as a negativity that commences at about 100ms from stimulus onset and lasts until about 250ms post-stimulus. Adapted from Sams et al., 1985.

A demonstration that the neural mechanisms underlying the MMN govern the timing of attentive behavior of humans was provided by Tiitinen, May, Reinikainen, and Näätänen (1994) who, using a 1000Hz standard stimulus, mapped the MMN for frequency deviations from 0.05% to 32% in eight steps and, in a separate session, measured the subject's behavioral reaction times (RTs) for deviant stimuli as "targets". Comparison of these measures (depicted in Fig. 6.4) showed that there was a very close correspondence between the MMN peak latency and the RT, with both measures monotonically decreasing

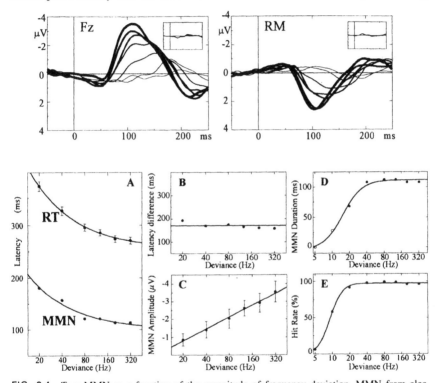

FIG. 6.4   *Top*: MMN as a function of the magnitude of frequency deviation. MMN from electrodes Fz and the right mastoid (RM) for 8 deviance values ranging from 5Hz (0.05%; thin line) to 320Hz (32%; thick line). Stimulus blocks consisting of 1000Hz standard (p = 95%) and deviant stimuli (p = 5%) were presented in random order through earphones to the subject's left ear. The MMN was obtained by subtracting the response to the standard tone from that to the corresponding deviant tone. The MMN amplitude grew and its latency decreased with increasing frequency deviance (see also Fig. 6.3). The invariant responses to the standard tones are depicted in the inserts. *Bottom*: Pre-attentive sensory memory as indexed by the MMN governs attentive processing of changes in auditory stimulation. In (A) both the behavioral RT and the MMN peak latency monotonically decreased as a function of the magnitude of change in tone frequency. In (B) the MMN peak latency has been subtracted from the RT, demonstrating that the difference was constant. The MMN peak amplitude (C) linearly increased as a function of the logarithm of the magnitude of the frequency deviance. With increasing magnitude of deviation, both the MMN duration from Fz (D) and the hit rate (E) increased until they reached a plateau. Adapted from Tiitinen et al., 1994.

as a function of the frequency difference, and with the MMN latency constantly preceding RT by about 180ms. Thus, attentive behavioral latency changes can be explained as originating already from the pre-attentive sensory memory mechanism as indexed by the MMN. In this study, the MMN was reliably elicited at (and above) 2% deviations, the amplitude of the response being directly proportional to the logarithm of the frequency difference. Furthermore, the duration of the MMN stabilized to approximately 100ms at 4% deviations, which was matched with the subject's hit rate (the percentage of target tones found) reaching approximately 100%.

The observations of Sams et al. (1985) and Tiitinen et al. (1994) suggest that the width of stimulus representation for auditory frequency is in the vicinity of 0.05–2%. The representation is very sharply tuned, with even very small deviations being reflected by the MMN mechanism. These studies, however, concentrated on the averaged responses over several subjects and did not account for possible individual variability in discrimination ability.

There is, however, also evidence that individual discrimination ability can be studied with the MMN. Lang et al. (1990) found a strong relationship between the MMN amplitude recorded in passive conditions and individual behavioral pitch-discrimination ability (see also Lang et al., 1995). These authors divided subjects into three groups (good, moderate, and poor) on the basis of the accuracy of behavioral pitch discrimination in a same-different task with paired stimuli, and subsequently measured the MMN responses from these subjects. The standard stimulus was 698Hz and the amount of frequency deviance was varied in different stimulus blocks.

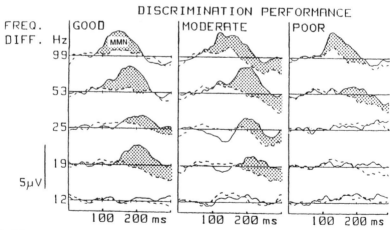

FIG. 6.5 ERPs of good (N = 11), moderate (N = 9), and poor (N = 6) pitch discriminators to 698Hz standard tones (dashed lines), and to deviant tones (solid lines), which were 12, 19, 25, 53, or 99Hz higher frequency than the 698Hz standard tones. Note the differences in the MMN (shaded areas) amplitude as a function of increasing frequency deviation. Adapted from Lang et al., 1990.

The good discriminators produced a measurable MMN with a deviance of 2.7%, some of them with as little as 1.7%. In contrast, for the poor discriminators, the deviance had to be in the range of 7.2–14.3% before an MMN was reliably observed, whereas the moderate discriminator's performance was in the intermediate deviation range.

Converging evidence for a relation between the behavioral discrimination and the MMN can be found from the backward-masking studies of Winkler and Näätänen (1992) and Winkler, Reinikainen, and Näätänen (1993). These authors demonstrated a similar time course for recovery of recognition memory and the MMN amplitude when the time interval between the auditory stimuli and the following masking stimulus was gradually prolonged. When the masking-stimulus onset followed the offset of each standard and deviant stimulus within a short interval, such as 20 or 50msec, no MMN was elicited by deviants nor was the subject able to tell standards and deviants apart. However, when this interval was prolonged to 150msec, both measures recovered considerably.

To conclude, the experimental evidence suggests that the mechanism underlying MMN provides sensory data for attentional processes, and, to an extent, governs attentive information processing. This is evident in the finding that the latency of the MMN determines the timing of behavioral responses to changes in the auditory environment (Tiitinen et al., 1994; see also Novak, Ritter, & Vaughan, 1992). Furthermore, even individual differences in discrimination ability can be probed with the MMN (Lang et al., 1990). The MMN is also a likely component of the chain of brain events causing attention switches to changes in the environment (Näätänen, 1992; Schröger, 1994). In the light of these observations, it seems that the MMN, being temporally the first discriminative response to stimulus deviation, provides the best available physiological measure of automatic, pre-perceptual central auditory processing (see also Näätänen & Alho, 1995).

THE MMN FOR COMPLEX STIMULI

At the early stages of MMN research it was found that, besides being elicited by changes in basic stimulus features such as frequency, intensity, and duration, the MMN could also be obtained in response to more complex changes. Some of these early findings include, for example, MMN to changes in the spatial locus of origin (Paavilainen, Karlsson, Reinikainen, & Näätänen, 1989), ISI decrements (Ford & Hillyard, 1981; Nordby, Roth, & Pfefferbaum, 1988), and the partial omission of aspects of a compound stimulus (Nordby, Hammerborg, Roth, & Hugdahl, 1991).

Subsequently, MMN research proceeded from studies applying sinusoidal stimuli (seldom heard in natural environments) to more complex stimuli (e.g. sinewave complexes, phonemes, and natural speech). The results of these experiments have turned out to be potentially very interesting in that they broaden the theoretical scope from the previously discussed auditory sensory memory and attentional mechanisms to issues such as sensory long-term memory, learning (plasticity), and processing of linguistic stimuli.

Complex stimuli: Recent MMN-results

Changes in phonetic features also elicit an MMN (Aaltonen, Niemi, Nyrke, & Tuhkanen, 1987; Aaltonen, Paavilainen, Sams, & Näätänen, 1992; Aulanko et al., 1993; Kraus, McGee, Sharma, Carrell, & Nicol, 1992; Kraus et al., 1993; Sams, Aulanko, Aaltonen, & Näätänen, 1990; Sharma, Kraus, McGee, Carrell, & Nicol, 1993). Complex sounds are presumably processed or represented by different neural populations from those representing simple sounds. Evidence for this was found in a study in which the MMN elicited by a change in one frequency element of complex sounds (a chord or a sound pattern) was found to be generated in a region of the supratemporal auditory cortex different from that for the MMN to an identical stimulus change in a simple tone (Alho et al., 1996). Further evidence for the separability of the generator locations of the MMN for simple and complex stimulus features was obtained in aphasic patients with left-hemispheric temporo-parietal brain lesions. In these subjects, the MMN to phoneme change was abolished whereas a prominent MMN was elicited in the same patients by frequency change of a simple tone (Aaltonen et al., 1993).

Furthermore, changes in elements of tone pairs (Saarinen, Paavilainen, Schröger, Tervaniemi, & Näätänen, 1992; Tervaniemi, Saarinen, Paavilainen, Danilova, & Näätänen, 1994) or serial tone patterns (Alho et al., 1993; Schröger, Näätänen, & Paavilainen, 1992; Näätänen, Schröger, Tervaniemi, Karakas, & Paavilainen, 1993a) also give rise to an MMN. Consistently with these findings, the MMN can be obtained with different kinds of merely temporal stimulus changes such as changes in stimulus duration (Näätänen et al., 1989b; for corresponding MEG data, see Kaukoranta et al., 1989), stimulus order (Nordby et al., 1988; Tervaniemi et al., 1994), the order of segments in a spectrotemporal stimulus pattern (Schröger et al., 1992; Schröger, 1994), ISI (Ford & Hillyard, 1981; Näätänen, Jiang, Lavikainen, Reinikainen, & Paavilainen, 1993b; Nordby et al., 1988), the direction of a frequency glide (Sams & Näätänen, 1991; Pardo & Sams, 1993), or in a rhythmic stimulus pattern formed by several tones (Imada et al., 1995).

These latter observations are important because they imply that the traces of the memory system involved in MMN generation do not represent static stimuli and their sensory attributes only. Rather, stimuli are represented as events in time, that is, in their temporal frame of reference.

The previously discussed relationship between the behavioral discrimination ability and the presence/absence of the MMN has also been found for complex stimulus-feature processing. An example of this is provided by studies with consonant-vowel (CV) syllables presented to cochlear-implant users with and without hearing problems: "good" implant users, as defined by subjective reports, exhibited an MMN that was very similar in morphology, amplitude and latency to that obtained from normal-hearing subjects, whereas "poor" implant users were unable to behaviorally discriminate differences in stimulation and exhibited no distintinctive MMN (see Kraus et al., 1993; for a review, see Kraus et al., 1995). Evidence for the link between the behavioral discrimination ability and the MMN is also provided by the parallel emergence of the MMN to slight changes in a complex spectro-temporal pattern and the subject's behavioral ability to discriminate these changes as a function of discrimination training during an experimental session (Näätänen et al., 1993a).

In conjunction with these findings, experimental evidence is cumulating to suggest that the MMN elicited by complex stimuli is applicable to the objective measurement of the development of auditory discrimination abilities. Cheour-Luhtanen et al. (1996), presented preterm infants (whose conceptional age at the time of recordings was 30–35 weeks) with stimulus sequences consisting of a repetitive vowel that was occasionally replaced by a different vowel, and found that these speech sounds elicited MMN-like responses. Thus, it seems that very early in life, the human brain is already able to discriminate complex sounds from one another and, furthermore, that this discrimination process can be objectively studied using the MMN.

Finally, using the MMN, Näätänen et al. (1997) very recently succeeded in demonstrating the presence of language-specific memory (phoneme) traces in the left auditory cortex of the human brain. In this study, native speakers of two closely related languages (Finnish and Estonian) were presented with phoneme prototypes common to the two languages. When, in a sequence containing a

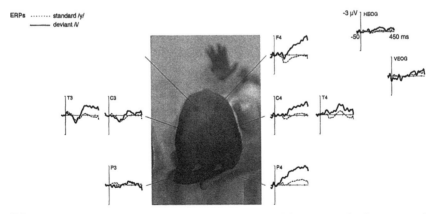

FIG. 6.6   ERPs elicited by vowels averaged across 11 preterm infants (conceptional age at recording time 30–35 weeks), with the Finnish /y/ as a standard (p = 90%) and /i/ as a deviant (p = 10%). Standard and deviant responses are depicted by dashed and solid lines, respectively (HEOG and VEOG are horizontal and vertical electro-oculogram, respectively). The negative displacement of deviance-related responses resembles the MMN both in morphology and scalp topography. Adapted from Cheour-Luhtanen et al., 1996.

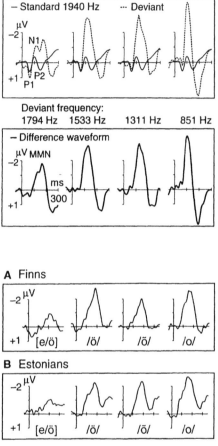

FIG 6.7   *Top*: ERPs from electrode Fz to a standard sinusoidal tone of 1940Hz (solid line, equal to second formants of /e/ used as the standard stimulus in the phoneme experiment) and to deviant sinusoidal tones of 1794, 1533, 1311, and 851Hz (dashed line, equal to second formants of the deviant stimuli of [e/o], /ö/, /õ/, and /o/, respectively). The standard-stimulus response shows small P1, N1, and P2 deflections. The negative displacement is caused by the MMN, better visible by subtracting the standard stimulus response from that of the deviant stimulus response. MMN steadily increases in amplitude with increasing magnitude of frequency change (see also Fig. 6.4). *Bottom*: The amplitude of the MMN at Fz reflects the language-specific phoneme categories of the Finnish and Estonian languages. The MMN amplitude for the deviant /õ/, a nonprototype in Finnish, was clearly smaller than that for the adjacent prototype deviants with Finnish subjects (A) whereas this attenuation did not occur with Estonian (B) subjects (for whom /õ/ was a prototype of their language). Adapted from Näätänen et al., 1997.

repetitive prototype, another prototype was occasionally presented as a deviant stimulus, it elicited a considerably larger MMN response than when this deviant stimulus was an equally complex phoneme nonprototype. With a deviant stimulus that was a phoneme prototype in Estonian but not in Finnish, the enhancement occurred in Estonian subjects but not in Finns. Thus, it seems that with the

MMN, one is able to unravel the experience-dependent traces of the phoneme prototypes belonging to any given language. The authors suggested that the traces might serve as recognition patterns for speech sounds of a language.

Theoretical considerations

Previously, a possible inconsistency between MMN data and echoic memory was mentioned. A single presentation of a stimulus is sufficient for the formation of a representation in echoic memory, whereas the MMN requires two or three preceding standards before it can be elicited (at an amplitude large enough to extract the MMN from noise; Ritter et al., 1995; see also Näätänen, 1992). This inconsistency may be explained by Cowan et al.'s (1993) results, which suggest that a sensory-memory trace can be either in an active or inactive state with regard to possible MMN elicitation. Their data show that a deviant stimulus elicits the MMN only when a previously formed trace is first activated by a stimulus identical to the one represented by the trace.

Interestingly, these "dormant" traces imply the existence of a much longer-lasting form of memory than auditory sensory, or "echoic" memory. The development of these sensory long-term memory traces was demonstrated in a study in which subjects tried to detect a slight change in a complex spectro-temporal sound pattern in the course of a long experimental session (Näätänen et al., 1993a). Discrimination training was given in three parts (early, middle, or late in the session), each of which was preceded by a MMN recording in passive condition. In a number of subjects, no MMN was initially elicited by this change. Later in the session, however, in certain subjects, the MMN began to appear (Fig. 6.8) and, in parallel with the MMN emergence, the subject began to hear the difference. Kraus et al. (1995) describe a similar long-term learning effect in discriminating changes in a consonant-vowel (CV) syllable (/da/) after behavioral discrimination training.

Importantly, these long-term neural traces could serve as recognition patterns in the analysis of the auditory environment (see Näätänen, 1992). For an organism to recognize a complex sound as the same as some previously heard sound, a sensory representation of that previous sound must be activated by the current input. The development of a network of such neural traces for initially difficult or new sounds (from phonemes to words and short sentences) is likely to be essential in learning to hear correctly the acoustic properties of a (foreign) language. The development of those neural traces, or recognition patterns, would be a prequalification for the successful semantic analysis and understanding of a new language.

Such traces apparently can be developed only when subjects attend to auditory stimuli, that is, passive long-duration exposure *per se* is not sufficient (Näätänen et al., 1993a). After such a trace has developed, however, it functions automatically in the service of auditory analysis, judging from the fact that the MMN could be recorded in passive conditions following discrimination training (Näätänen et al., 1993a; see also Kraus et al., 1995).

PHASE:

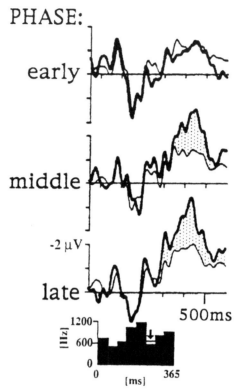

FIG. 6.8 ERPs of 7 subjects at electrode Cz to standard sound patterns (p = 90%; thin line) and to deviant sound patterns (p = 10%; thick line). The standard and deviant sound patterns, illustrated at the bottom, consisted of 8 sinusoidal segments of different frequencies, their only difference being that in the deviant patterns, the frequency of the sixth segment (indicated by the arrow) was higher than in the standard patterns. ERPs were recorded during early, middle, and late phases of a session in which sound patterns were presented to subjects concentrating on a reading task. The behavioral discrimination performance of the subjects belonging to this group ("improvers") considerably improved during the session in a sound-pattern discrimination test applied after each phase. The MMN, which in these subjects first emerged and then increased in amplitude during the session, is indicated by the shaded area. Adapted from Näätänen et al., 1993a.

These MMN findings clarify one of the central issues of the nature of sensory memory, namely, whether this memory is a precategorical, raw (hardwired) replica of acoustic stimulation (Crowder & Morton, 1969; Kallman & Massaro, 1979; Neisser, 1967), or whether there are adaptive changes in this memory system (see Port, 1988). The MMN data reviewed earlier clearly indicate plastic changes in the neurophysiological basis of sensory memory such that long-duration, probably permanent, traces are formed for new complex stimuli when they start to occur relatively frequently, for example, when we have moved to a foreign-language environment. This new stimulation gradually forms a large set of new traces corresponding to phonemes, syllables, perhaps even words and short sentences, which then serve as recognition patterns in our acoustic analysis of the sounds of the new language.

APPLICATIONS OF THE MMN

Attempts to find applications of the MMN can be broadly divided into the measurement of the development of auditory functions and the use of the MMN as a tool in various clinical conditions. The MMN provides us with an easily accessible, objective index of cortical representations and their accuracy for any given auditory stimulus event, even on a single-subject level (Joutsiniemi et al., in press). Because the MMN can be recorded even without the subject's active participation (task-independently) it can be used, for example, in monitoring the development of auditory functions in new-borns and patients. Furthermore, the research on basic and complex stimulus features with regard to the generator mechanism of the MMN has revealed that each stimulus feature is presumably represented in a separate brain area, or at least processed by different neuronal populations, thus enabling the assessment of deficits in feature-specific auditory processing.

In the next section, we will briefly summarize developmental and clinical issues on a general level. More detailed accounts are to be found elsewhere (e.g. Kraus et al., 1995; Kurtzberg, Vaughan Jr., Kreuzer, & Fliegler, 1995; Lang et al., 1995; Ponton & Don, 1995).

Developmental issues

The MMN might be used for investigating the correct development of the auditory system. An MMN-like response to frequency change (Alho, Sainio, Sajaniemi, Reinikainen, & Näätänen, 1990) as well as to phonetic change (Cheour-Luhtanen et al., 1996) has been demonstrated in newborn infants. MMNs to changes in pure tones and phonemes have also been recorded in older children (Kraus et al., 1992, 1993; Leppänen, Laukkonen, & Lyytinen, 1992). Interestingly, Korpilahti and Lang (1994) found that in dysphasic children, the MMN to a frequency change in a simple sinusoidal tone is reduced in amplitude in relation to the MMN in normal children. This finding suggests that a deficit in processing sound frequency contributed to the dysphasia. The study also indicates that the MMN might be used for testing the development of auditory mechanisms needed in speech perception.

The MMN appears to be suitable, for example, for feature-specific testing of auditory functions in different kinds of disorders in hearing and speech perception. This is evident in the previously mentioned study of Aaltonen et al. (1993) on aphasic patients with anterior (frontal) or posterior (temporo-parietal) lesions of the left hemisphere. The patients with anterior lesions showed MMNs to deviations in the frequency of a pure tone as well as to phonetic deviations in a vowel; in patients with posterior lesions no MMN to vowel change could be observed, whereas a frequency change in a pure tone produced an MMN. This suggests that the auditory cortex of patients with posterior lesions could perform simple frequency discrimination but was incapable of phonetic discrimination.

Furthermore, the MMN allows us to estimate individual perceptual capabilities. As already discussed, Lang et al. (1990) found a strong relationship between the individual behavioral pitch-discrimination accuracy and the MMN amplitude for changes in tonal frequency recorded in passive conditions. Tervaniemi, Alho, Paavilainen, Sams, and Näätänen (1993), however, found no differences in the MMN to pitch changes between musicians with or without absolute pitch (an ability to identify or to produce a tone on the Western musical scale without hearing a reference tone). Both pure and piano tones were used as well as tones on and off the musical scale. This finding suggests that absolute pitch is based on some other auditory-memory mechanism than the one revealed by the MMN.

The MMN is also suitable for studying long-term plastic changes in the neural network of auditory stimulus analysis and sensory memory (Recanzone, Schreiner, & Merzenich, 1993), as is evident from the aforementioned results of Näätänen et al. (1993a; see also Fig. 6.8). These results demonstrating long-term learning effects on the MMN with a continued presentation of a complex, unfamiliar stimulus pattern suggest adaptive plastic changes in the auditory functions underlying the MMN. Thus the MMN might, for example, provide a means for testing the development of an individual's ability to discriminate initially unfamiliar sound patterns during learning a foreign language.

Besides linguistic processing, the MMN appears to be suitable for the measurement of individual perceptual capabilities such as components of musical talent (e.g. pitch, interval, duration, rhythm perception; Tervaniemi, Ilvonen, Karma, Alho, & Näätänen, 1997) and training effects in these capabilities.

Clinical issues

The MMN has potential applications in the diagnosis of neurological disorders other than those affecting hearing and speech perception. This is most dramatically documented in the recent results of Kane, Curry, Butler, and Cummins (1993) and Kane et al. (1996) who demonstrated the emergence of MMN in coma patients one to two days before regaining consciousness, and a continuous absence of the MMN in the majority of those patients who later died.

Certain clinical groups have now been studied using the MMN. The MMN amplitude is reportedly reduced in patients with schizophrenia (Javitt, Doneshka, Zyberman, Ritter, & Vaughan Jr., 1993; Oades, 1991; Schrodt, Cohen, Berg, & Hopmann, 1992; Shelley et al., 1991) when compared with the MMN obtained from healthy subjects. Also, in their recent study on patients with Parkinson's disease, Pekkonen, Jousmäki, Reinikainen, and Partanen (1995) found that the MMN amplitude was attenuated, which might point to an impairment of sensory-memory functions in Parkinson's disease.

Other clinical uses of the MMN are, for example, the assessment of the effects of aging (an age-related attenuation of MMN; Pekkonen, Jousmäki, Partanen, & Karhu, 1993), of unilateral lesions of dorsolateral frontal cortex (resulting in an attenuated MMN response; Alho, Woods, Algazi, Knight, & Näätänen, 1994), and of blindness (the MMN in blind subjects to a change in the apparent location of the sound source being larger in amplitude than that of the sighted controls; Kujala et al., 1995). In auditory pathology, the MMN might be used for the objective evaluation of cochlear-implant function (Kraus et al., 1995; Ponton & Don, 1995).

Further, the MMN appears to be useful in the objective diagnosis of aphasic patients (Aaltonen et al., 1993), dysphasic children (Korpilahti & Lang, 1994; Lang et al., 1995), and children with learning problems (Kraus & McGee, 1994; Kraus et al., 1995). Recently, in studying children with and without learning problems, Kraus et al. (1996) demonstrated that impaired behavioral discrimination of a rapid speech change (/da/ vs. /ga/) was correlated with a diminished magnitude in the MMN, thus suggesting that some children's discrimination deficits originate in the auditory pathway even before conscious perception. It seems that the MMN does indeed provide a useful diagnostic tool that has implications for differential diagnosis and targeted therapeutic strategies.

CONCLUSIONS

The experimental evidence reviewed here suggests that the brain has a mechanism that automatically responds to any change in a repetitive sound stimulus. This mechanism generates the MMN, observable both in electric and magnetic recordings.

The MMN can be recorded and studied separately for each basic stimulus feature (e.g. frequency, intensity, duration). Because attention is not required for the MMN to be elicited, it provides a unique window to cortical auditory stimulus representations in the brain, enabling one to measure the accuracy of sensory representations without requiring the subject's attention and response (Näätänen, 1992).

The MMN probably enables one to study the neural basis of sensory memory in audition. The representation reflected in the MMN decays gradually, lasting for several seconds (Böttcher-Gandor & Ullsperger, 1992; Cowan et al., 1993; Näätänen, 1985, 1990, 1992; Winkler & Näätänen, 1992). This representation can be associated with sensory memory, which closely corresponds to echoic memory (Neisser, 1967).

The experimental findings reviewed also demonstrate that the MMN probably has a central role in triggering attention to sound change and, to an extent, governing attentional processes (Sams et al., 1985; Tiitinen et al., 1994). In addition, the MMN enables one to understand brain processes underlying conscious auditory percepts, suggesting that the auditory stimulus representation inferred from the

MMN data provides the stimulus-specific contents of percepts but is not sufficient for conscious auditory perception (see Näätänen, 1990).

Recent research efforts are accumulating evidence that with the MMN we are also able to study processes underlying more complex stimulus representations. The experimental MMN data using complex sine-wave tones, phonemes, and consonant-vowel syllables seem to indicate that issues related to the neurophysiology of plastic changes in the neural mechanisms processing auditory information are now open for experimental investigation. The demonstration that the formation of auditory representations depends on attention (Näätänen et al., 1993a; see also Fig. 6.8) essentially implies that we can now noninvasively study the mechanisms of learning in the human brain.

These learning effects are evident in studies of Cheour-Luhtanen et al. (1996) and Näätänen et al. (1993a, 1997) the results of which reveal how the human brain develops and adapts to the requirements of complex auditory environments, as is the case in the processing of language, for example. The research on these topics has only recently started and we expect that several fundamental findings are yet to come.

Finally, these studies have provided a platform for a multitude of experiments on the applicability of the MMN to various developmental and clinical issues. The MMN seems to be applicable for monitoring, for example, the progress of a patient during different stages of recovery of central auditory function. Furthermore, the complete noninvasiveness of the MMN measurement technique allows one to study objectively, for example, the development of central auditory processes in newborns and cochlear-implant users. We expect that eventually the MMN might be incorporated as a routinely used tool in hospitals as a part of monitoring the effects of development and degeneration.

ACKNOWLEDGEMENTS

Supported by the Academy of Finland and the University of Helsinki. The authors wish to thank Juha Lavikainen and Patrick May for their assistance in the preparation stages of the manuscript.

REFERENCES

Aaltonen, O., Niemi, P., Nyrke, T., & Tuhkanen, M. (1987). Event-related brain potentials and the perception of a phonetic continuum. *Biological Psychology, 24,* 197–207.

Aaltonen, O., Paavilainen, P., Sams, M., & Näätänen, R. (1992). Event-related potentials and discrimination of steady-state vowels within and between phoneme categories: A preliminary study. *Scandinavian Journal of Logopedics and Phonetics, 17,* 107–112.

Aaltonen, O., Tuomainen, J., Laine, M., & Niemi, P. (1993). Cortical differences in tonal frequency versus vowel processing as revealed by an ERP component called the mismatch negativity (MMN). *Brain and Language, 44,* 139–152.

Alho, K. (1995). Cerebral generators of mismatch negativity (MMN) and its magnetic counterpart (MMNm) elicited by sound changes. *Ear and Hearing, 16,* 38–50.

Alho, K., Huotilainen, M., Tiitinen, H., Ilmoniemi, R. J., Knuutila, J., & Näätänen, R. (1993). Memory-related processing of complex sound patterns in human auditory cortex: An MEG study. *NeuroReport, 4,* 391–394.

Alho, K., Sainio, K., Sajaniemi, N., Reinikainen, K., & Näätänen, R. (1990). Event-related brain potential of human newborns to pitch change of an acoustic stimulus. *Electroencephalography and Clinical Neurophysiology, 77,* 151–155.

Alho, K., Tervaniemi, M., Huotilainen, M., Lavikainen, J., Tiitinen, H., Ilmoniemi, R. J., Knuutila, J., & Näätänen, R. (1996). Processing of complex sounds in the human auditory cortex as revealed by magnetic brain responses. *Psychophysiology, 33,* 369–375.

Alho, K., Woods, D. L., Algazi, A., Knight, R. T., & Näätänen, R. (1994). Lesions of frontal cortex diminish the auditory mismatch negativity. *Electroencephalography and Clinical Neurophysiology, 91,* 353–362.

Aulanko, R., Hari, R., Lounasmaa, O. V., Näätänen, R., & Sams, M. (1993). Phonetic invariance in the human auditory cortex. *NeuroReport, 4,* 1356–1358.

Bertrand, O., Perrin, F., & Pernier, J. (1991). Evidence for a tonotopic organization of the auditory cortex observed with auditory evoked potentials. *Acta Otolaryngology Suppl., 491,* 116–123.

Böttcher-Gandor, C., & Ullsperger, P. (1992). Mismatch negativity in event-related potentials to auditory stimuli as a function of varying interstimulus interval. *Psychophysiology, 29,* 546–550.

Cheour-Luhtanen, M., Alho, K., Sainio, K., Rinne, T., Reinikainen, K., Pohjavuori, M., Renlund, M., Aaltonen, O., Eerola, O., & Näätänen, R. (1996). The ontogenetically earliest discriminative response of the human brain. *Psychophysiology, 33,* 478–481.

Cowan, N. (1984). On short and long auditory stores. *Psychological Bulletin, 96,* 341–370.

Cowan, N. (1988). Evolving conceptions of memory storage, selective attention, and their mutual constraints within the human information-processing system. *Psychological Bulletin, 104,* 163–191.

Cowan, N., Winkler, I., Teder, W., & Näätänen, R. (1993). Memory prerequisites of mismatch negativity in the auditory event-related potential (ERP). *Journal of Experimental Psychology: Learning. Memory, and Cognition, 19,* 909–921.

Crowder, R. G., & Morton, J. (1969). Precategorical acoustic storage (PAS). *Perception and Psychophysics, 5,* 365–373.

Csépe, V., Karmos, G., & Molnár, M. (1987). Evoked potential correlates of stimulus deviance during wakefulness and sleep in cat: Animal model of mismatch negativity. *Electroencephalography and Clinical Neurophysiology, 66,* 571–578.

Csépe, V., Karmos, G., & Molnár, M. (1989). Subcortical evoked potential correlates of early information processing: Mismatch negativity in cats. In E. Basar & T. H. Bullock (Eds.), *Dynamics of sensory and cognitive processing by the brain* (pp. 279–289). Berlin: Springer-Verlag.

Csépe, V., Pantev, C., Hoke, M., Hampson, S., & Ross, B. (1992). Evoked magnetic responses to minor pitch changes: localization of the mismatch field. *Electroencephalography and Clinical Neurophysiology, 84,* 538–548.

Elberling, C., Bak, C., Kofoed, B., Lebech, J., & Saermark, K. (1982). Auditory magnetic fields. Source location and "tonotopic organization" in the right hemisphere of the human brain. *Scandinavian Audiology, 11,* 61–65.

Ford, J. M., & Hillyard, S. A. (1981). Event related potentials (ERPs) to interruptions of steady rhythm. *Psychophysiology, 18,* 322–330.

Giard, M. H., Lavikainen, J., Reinikainen, K., Perrin, F., Bertrand, O., & Näätänen, R. (1995). Separate representation of stimulus frequency, intensity, and duration in auditory sensory memory: An event-related potential and dipole-model analysis. *Journal of Cognitive Neuroscience, 7,* 133–143.

Giard, M. H., Perrin, F., Pernier, J., & Bouchet, P. (1990). Brain generators implicated in the processing of auditory stimulus deviance: A topographic ERP study. *Psychophysiology, 27,* 627–640.

Hari, R., Hämäläinen, M., Ilmoniemi, R., Kaukoranta, E., Reinikainen, K., Salminen, J., Alho, K., Näätänen, R., & Sams, M. (1984). Responses of the primary auditory cortex to pitch changes in a sequence of tone pips: Neuromagnetic recordings in man. *Neuroscience Letters, 50*, 127–132.

Hari, R., Rif, J., Tiihonen, J., & Sams, M. (1992). Neuromagnetic mismatch fields to single and paired tones. *Electroencephalography and Clinical Neurophysiology, 82*, 152–154.

Huotilainen, M., Ilmoniemi, R. J., Lavikainen, J., Tiitinen, H., Alho, K., Sinkkonen, J., Knuutila, J., & Näätänen, R. (1993). Interaction between representations of different features of auditory sensory memory. *NeuroReport, 4*, 1279–1281.

Imada, T., Fukuda, K., Kawakatsu, M., Mashiko, T., Okada, K., Hayashi, M., Aihara, K., & Kotani, M. (1995). Mismatch fields evoked by a rhythm passage. In C. Baumgartner, L. Deecke, G. Stroink, & S. J. Williamson (Eds.), *Biomagnetism: Fundamental research and clinical applications* (pp. 249–252). Amsterdam: Elsevier.

Javitt, D. C., Doneshka, P., Zyberman, I., Ritter, W., & Vaughan, H. G., Jr. (1993). Impairment of early cortical processing in schizophrenia: An event-related potential confirmation study. *Biological Psychiatry, 33*, 513–519.

Javitt, D. C., Schroeder, C. E., Steinschneider, M., Arezzo, J. C., Ritter, W., & Vaughan, H. G., Jr. (1995). Cognitive event-related potentials in human and non-human primates: Implications for the PCP/NMDA model of schizophrenia. *Electroencephalography and Clinical Neurophysiology Suppl., 44*, 161–175.

Javitt, D. C., Schroeder, C. E., Steinschneider, M., Arezzo, J. C., & Vaughan, H. G., Jr. (1992). Demonstration of mismatch negativity in the monkey. *Electroencephalography and Clinical Neurophysiology, 83*, 87–90.

Joutsiniemi, S. L., Ilvonen, T., Sinkkonen, J., Huotilainen, M., Terraniemi, M., Lehtokoski, A., Rinne, T., & Näätänen, R. (In press). The mismatch negativity for duration decrement of auditory stimuli in healthy subjects. *Electroencephalography and Clinical Neurophysiology*.

Kallman, H. J. & Massaro, D. W. (1979). Similarity effects in backward recognition masking. *Journal of Experimental Psychology: Human Perception and Performance, 5*, 110–128.

Kane, N. M., Curry, S. H., Butler, S. R., & Cummins, B. H. (1993). Electrophysiological indicator of awakening from coma. *Lancet, 341*, 688.

Kane, N. M., Curry, S. H., Rowlands, C. A., Manara, A. R., Lewis, T., Moss, T., Cummins, B. H., & Butler, S. H. (1996). Event-related potentials—neurophysiological tools for predicting emergence and early outcome for traumatic coma. *Intensive Care Medicine, 22*, 39–46.

Karmos, G., Winkler, I., Molnár, M., & Csépe, V. (1993). Animal model of middle latency auditory evoked responses—Intracortical generators of mismatch negativity. In H.-J. Heinze, T. F. Münte, & G. R. Mangun (Eds.), *New Developments in Event-Related Potentials* (pp. 95–102). Boston, MA: Birkhauser.

Kaukoranta, E., Sams, M., Hari, R., Hämäläinen, M., & Näätänen, R. (1989). Reactions of human auditory cortex to a change in tone duration. *Hearing Research, 41*, 15–21.

Korpilahti, P., & Lang, H. (1994). Auditory ERP components and mismatch negativity in dysphasic children. *Electroencephalography and Clinical Neurophysiology, 91*, 256–264.

Kraus, N., & McGee, T. (1994). Mismatch negativity in the assessment of central auditory function. *American Journal of Audiology, 3*, 139–151.

Kraus, N., McGee, T., Carrell, T., King, C., Littman, T., & Nicol, T. (1994a). Discrimination of speech-like contrasts in the auditory thalamus and cortex. *Journal of the Acoustical Society of America, 96*, 2758–2768.

Kraus, N., McGee, T., Carrell, T., Sharma, A., Koch, D., King, C., Tremblay, K., & Nicol, T. (1995). Neurophysiologic bases of speech discrimination. *Ear and Hearing, 16*, 19–37.

Kraus, N., McGee, T. J., Carrell, T. D., Zecker, S. G., Nicol, T. G., & Koch, D. B. (1996). Auditory neurophysiologic responses and discrimination deficits in children with learning problems. *Science, 273*, 971–973.

Kraus, N., McGee, T., Littman, T., Nicol, T., & King, C. (1994b). Non-primary auditory thalamic representation of acoustic change. *Journal of Neurophysiology, 72*, 1270–1277.

Kraus, N., McGee, T., Micco, A., Sharma, A., Carrell, T., & Nicol, T. (1993). Mismatch negativity in school-age children to speech stimuli that are just perceptibly different. *Electroencephalography and Clinical Neurophysiology*, *88*, 123–130.

Kraus, N., McGee, T., Sharma, A., Carrell, T., & Nicol, T. (1992). Mismatch negativity event-related potential elicited by speech stimuli. *Ear and Hearing*, *13*, 158–164.

Kropotov, J. D., Näätänen, R., Sevostianov, A. V., Alho, K., Reinikainen, K., & Kropotova, O. V. (1995). Mismatch negativity to auditory stimulus change recorded directly from the human temporal cortex. *Psychophysiology*, *32*, 418–422.

Kujala, T., Alho, K., Kekoni, J., Hämäläinen, H., Reinikainen, K., Salonen, O., Standertskjöld-Nordenstam, C.-G., & Näätänen, R. (1995). Auditory and somatosensory event-related brain potentials in early blind humans. *Experimental Brain Research*, *104*, 519–526.

Kurtzberg, D., Vaughan, H. G. Jr., Kreuzer, J. A., & Fliegler, K. Z. (1995). Developmental studies and clinical application of mismatch negativity: Problems and prospects. *Ear and Hearing*, *16*, 104–116.

Lang, H., Eerola, O., Korpilahti, P., Holopainen, I., Salo, S., Uusipaikka, E., & Aaltonen, O. (1995). Clinical applications of the mismatch negativity. *Ear and Hearing*, *16*, 117–129.

Lang, H., Nyrke, T., Ek, M., Aaltonen, O., Raimo, I., & Näätänen, R. (1990). Pitch discrimination performance and auditory event-related potentials. In C. H. M. Brunia, A. W. K. Gaillard, A. Kok, G. Mulder, & M. N. Verbaten (Eds.), *Psychophysiological brain research* (Vol. 1, pp. 294–298). Tilburg: Tilburg University Press.

Leppänen, P., Laukkonen, K., & Lyytinen, H. (1992). Mismatch negativity in children and adults. *Abstracts of the 10th International Conference on the Event-Related Potentials of the Brain* (EPIC X), Eger, Hungary, May 31–June 5 1992, P90.

Levänen, S., Ahonen, A., Hari, R., McEvoy, L., & Sams, M. (1996). Deviant auditory stimuli activate human left and right auditory cortex differently. *Cerebral Cortex*, *6*, 288–296.

Levänen, S., Hari, R., McEvoy, L., & Sams, M. (1993). Responses of the human auditory cortex to changes in one versus two stimulus features. *Experimental Brain Research*, *97*, 177–183.

Lounasmaa, O. V., Hari, R., Joutsiniemi, S. L., & Hämäläinen, M. (1989). Multi SQUID recordings of human cerebral magnetic fields may give information about memory processes in the human brain. *Europhysics Letters*, *9*, 603–608.

Mäntysalo, S., & Näätänen, R. (1987). The duration of a neuronal trace of an auditory stimulus as indicated by event-related potentials. *Biological Psychology*, *24*, 183–195.

Näätänen, R. (1975). Selective attention and evoked potentials in humans—A critical review. *Biological Psychology*, *2*, 237–307.

Näätänen, R. (1984). In search of a short-term memory trace of a stimulus in the human brain. In L. Pulkkinen & P. Lyytinen (Eds.), *Human action and personality. Essays in honor of Martti Takala* (pp. 29–43). Jyväskylä, Finland: University of Jyväskylä.

Näätänen, R. (1985). Selective attention and stimulus processing: reflections in event-related potentials, magnetoencephalogram and regional cerebral blood flow. In M. I. Posner & O. S. M. Marin (Eds.), *Attention and performance XI* (pp. 355–373). Hillsdale, NJ: Lawrence Erlbaum Associates Inc.

Näätänen, R. (1990). The role of attention in auditory information processing as revealed by event-related potentials and other brain measures of cognitive function. *Behavioral and Brain Sciences*, *13*, 201–233.

Näätänen, R. (1992). *Attention and brain function.* Hillsdale, NJ: Lawrence Erlbaum Associates Inc.

Näätänen, R., & Alho, K. (1995). Mismatch negativity—a unique measure of sensory processing in audition. *International Journal of Neuroscience*, *80*, 317–337.

Näätänen, R., & Gaillard, A. W. K. (1983). The orienting reflex and the N2 deflection of the ERP. In A. W. K. Gaillard & W. Ritter (Eds.), *Tutorials in event-related potential research: Endogenous components* (pp. 119–141). Amsterdam: North-Holland.

Näätänen, R., Gaillard, A. W. K., & Mäntysalo, S. (1978). Early selective-attention effect on evoked potential reinterpreted. *Acta Psychologica, 42*, 313–329.

Näätänen, R., Ilmoniemi, R. J., & Alho, K. (1994). Magnetoencephalography in studies of human cognitive brain function. *Trends in Neurosciences, 7*, 389–395.

Näätänen, R., Jiang, D., Lavikainen, J., Reinikainen, K., & Paavilainen, P. (1993b). Event-related potentials reveal a memory trace for temporal features. *NeuroReport, 5*, 310–312.

Näätänen, R., Lehtokoski, A., Lennes, M., Cheour, M., Huotilainen, M., Iivonen, A., Vainio, M., Alku, P., Ilmoniemi, R. J., Luuk, A., Allik, J., Sinkkonen, J., & Alho, K. (1997). Language-specific phoneme representations revealed by electric and magnetic brain responses. *Nature, 385*, 432–434.

Näätänen, R., & Michie, P. T. (1979). Early selective attention effects on the evoked potential. A critical review and reinterpretation. *Biological Psychology, 8*, 81–136.

Näätänen, R., Paavilainen, P., Alho, K., Reinikainen, K., & Sams, K. (1987). Inter-stimulus interval and the mismatch negativity. In C. Barber & T. Blum (Eds.), *Evoked Potentials III* (392–397). London: Butterworth.

Näätänen, R., Paavilainen, P., Alho, K., Reinikainen, K., & Sams, M. (1989a). Do event-related potentials reveal the mechanism of the auditory sensory memory in the human brain? *Neuroscience Letters, 98*, 217–221.

Näätänen, R., Paavilainen, P., & Reinikainen, K. (1989b). Do event-related potentials to infrequent decrements in duration of auditory stimuli demonstrate a memory trace in man? *Neuroscience Letters, 107*, 347–352.

Näätänen, R., & Picton, T. W. (1987). The N1 wave of the human electric and magnetic response to sound: A review and an analysis of the component structure. *Psychophysiology, 24*, 375–425.

Näätänen, R, Schröger, E., Tervaniemi, M., Karakas, S., & Paavilainen, P. (1993a). Development of a memory trace for complex sound patterns in the human brain. *NeuroReport, 4*, 503–506.

Neisser, U. (1967). *Cognitive Psychology*. New York: Appleton-Century-Crofts.

Nordby, H., Hammerborg, D., Roth, W. T., & Hugdahl, K. (1991). ERPs to infrequent omissions and inclusions of stimulus elements. *Psychophysiology Suppl., 28*, S42.

Nordby, H., Roth, W. T., & Pfefferbaum, A. (1988). Event-related potentials to time-deviant and pitch-deviant tones. *Psychophysiology, 25*, 249–261.

Novak, G. P., Ritter, W., & Vaughan, H. C., Jr. (1992). The chronometry of attention-modulated processing and automatic mismatch detection. *Psychophysiology, 29*, 412–430.

Oades, R. D. (1991). Bases for irrelevant information processing in schizophrenia: Room for manoeuvre. *Behavioral and Brain Sciences, 14*, 38–39.

Paavilainen, P., Alho, K., Reinikainen, K., Sams, M., & Näätänen, R. (1991). Right-hemisphere dominance of different mismatch negativities. *Electroencephalography and Clinical Neurophysiology, 78*, 464–479.

Paavilainen, P., Karlsson, M. L., Reinikainen, K., & Näätänen, R. (1989). Mismatch negativity to change in spatial location of an auditory stimulus. *Electroencephalography and Clinical Neurophysiology, 73*, 129–141.

Pantev, C., Hoke, M., Lehnertz, K., Lütkenhöner, B., Anogianakis, G., & Wittkowski, W. (1988). Tonotopic organization of the human auditory cortex revealed by transient auditory evoked magnetic fields. *Electroencephalography and Clinical Neurophysiology, 69*, 160–170.

Pardo, P. J., & Sams, M. (1993). Human auditory cortex responses to rising versus falling glides. *Neuroscience Letters, 159*, 43–45.

Pekkonen, E., Jousmäki, V., Partanen, J., & Karhu, J. (1993). Mismatch negativity area and age-related auditory memory. *Electroencephalography and Clinical Neurophysiology, 87*, 321–325.

Pekkonen, E., Jousmäki, V., Reinikainen, K., & Partanen, J. (1995). Automatic auditory discrimination is impaired in Parkinson's disease. *Electroencephalography and Clinical Neurophysiology, 95*, 47–52.

Ponton, C. W., & Don, M. (1995). The mismatch negativity in cochlear implant users. *Ear and Hearing, 16*, 130–146.

Port, R. F. (1988). Can complex temporal patterns be automatized? *Behavioral and Brain Sciences*, *14*, 762–764.

Recanzone, G. E., Schreiner, C. E., & Merzenich, M. M. (1993). Plasticity in the frequency representation of primary auditory cortex following discrimination training in adult owl monkeys. *The Journal of Neuroscience*, *13*, 47–103.

Ritter, W., Deacon, D., Gomes, H., Javitt, D. C., & Vaughan, H. G., Jr. (1995). The mismatch negativity of event-related potentials as a probe of transient auditory memory: A review. *Ear and Hearing*, *16*, 51–66.

Saarinen, J., Paavilainen, P., Schröger, E., Tervaniemi, M., & Näätänen, R. (1992). Representation of abstract attributes of auditory stimuli in the human brain. *NeuroReport*, *3*, 1149–1151.

Sams, M., Aulanko, R., Aaltonen, O., & Näätänen, R. (1990). Event-related potentials to infrequent changes in synthesized phonetic stimuli. *Journal of Cognitive Neuroscience*, *2*, 344–357.

Sams, M., Hari, R., Rif, J., & Knuutila, J. (1993). The human auditory sensory memory trace persists about 10 s: Neuromagnetic evidence. *Journal of Cognitive Neuroscience*, *5*, 363–370.

Sams, M., Kaukoranta, E., Hämäläinen, M., & Näätänen, R. (1991). Cortical activity elicited by changes in auditory stimuli: Different sources for the magnetic N100m and mismatch responses. *Psychophysiology*, *28*, 21–29.

Sams, M., & Näätänen, R. (1991). Neuromagnetic responses of the human auditory cortex to short frequency glides. *Neuroscience Letters*, *121*, 43–46.

Sams, M., Paavilainen, P., Alho, K., & Näätänen, R. (1985). Auditory frequency discrimination and event-related potentials. *Electroencephalography and Clinical Neurophysiology*, *62*, 437–448.

Scherg, M., Vajsar, J., & Picton, T. (1989). A source analysis of the human auditory evoked potentials. *Journal of Cognitive Neuroscience*, *1*, 336–355.

Schrodt, A., Cohen, R., Berg, P., & Hopmann, G. (1992). Automatic (MMN) vs. controlled (P300) processing deficits in the ERPs of schizophrenic patients. *Abstracts of the 10th International Conference on the Event-Related Potentials of the Brain (EPIC X)*, Eger, Hungary, May 31– June 5 1992, P141.

Schröger, E. (1994). An event-related potential study of sensory representations of unfamiliar tonal patterns. *Psychophysiology*, *31*, 175–181.

Schröger, E., Näätänen, R., & Paavilainen, P. (1992). Event-related potentials reveal how non-attended complex sound patterns are represented by the human brain. *Neuroscience Letters*, *146*, 183–186.

Sharma, A., Kraus, N., McGee, T., Carrell, T., & Nicol, T. (1993). Acoustic versus phonetic representation of speech as reflected by the mismatch negativity event-related potential. *Electroencephalography and Clinical Neurophysiology*, *88*, 64–71.

Shelley, A. M., Ward, P. B., Catts, S. V., Michie, P. T., Andrews, S., & McConaghy, N. (1991). Mismatch negativity: An index of preattentive processing deficit in schizophrenia. *Biological Psychiatry*, *30*, 1059–1062.

Tervaniemi, M., Alho, K., Paavilainen, P., Sams, M., & Näätänen, R. (1993). Absolute pitch and event-related brain potentials. *Music Perception*, *10*, 305–316.

Tervaniemi, M., Ilvonen, T., Karma, K., Alho, K., & Näätänen, R. (1997). The musical brain: Brainwaves reveal the neurocognitive basis of musicality. *Neuroscience Letters*, *226*, 1–4.

Tervaniemi, M., Saarinen, J., Paavilainen, P., Danilova, N., & Näätänen, R. (1994). Temporal integration of auditory information in sensory memory as reflected by the mismatch negativity. *Biological Psychology*, *38*, 157–167.

Tiitinen, H., Alho, K., Huotilainen, M., Ilmoniemi, R. J., Simola, J., & Näätänen, R. (1993). Tonotopic auditory cortex and the magnetoencephalographic (MEG) equivalent of the mismatch negativity. *Psychophysiology*, *30*, 537–540.

Tiitinen, H., May, P., Reinikainen, K., & Näätänen, R. (1994). Attentive novelty detection in humans is governed by pre-attentive sensory memory. *Nature*, *372*, 90–92.

Winkler, I., & Näätänen, R. (1992). Event-related potentials in auditory backward recognition masking: A new way to study the neurophysiological basis of sensory memory in humans. *Neuroscience Letters*, *140*, 239–242.

Winkler, I., Reinikainen, K., & Näätänen, R. (1993). Event-related brain potentials reflect traces of echoic memory in humans. *Perception and Psychophysics*, *53*, 443–449.

Woldorff, M., Hackley, S. A., & Hillyard, S. A. (1991). The effects of channel-selective attention on the mismatch negativity wave elicited by deviant tones. *Psychophysiology*, *28*, 30–42.

Woods, D. L., Alho, K., & Algazi, A. (1993). Intermodal selective attention: Evidence for processing in tonotopic auditory fields. *Psychophysiology*, *30*, 287–295.

Yabe, H., Tervaniemi, M., Reinikainen, K., & Näätänen, R. (1997). Temporal window of integration in the auditory system as revealed by omission MMN. *NeuroReport*, *8*, 1971–1974.

CHAPTER SEVEN

Spatial attention: Mechanisms and theories

Giacomo Rizzolatti and Laila Craighero
Istituto di Fisiologia Umana, Università di Parma, Parma, Italy

Traditionally, attention is conceived as a supramodal mechanism subserved by ana-tomical circuits separated from those involved in data processing. This supramodal mechanism is seen either as unitary or as formed by two or more independent circuits. The necessity for an attentional system anatomically separated from those for sensorimotor integration will be challenged. The view will be proposed that spatial attention results from an activation of the same "pragmatic" circuits that program oculomotion and other motor activities. It will be maintained that spatial attention differs from movement execution in the degree of activation of the same circuits rather than in the activation of separate systems.

Traditionnellement, l'attention est conçue comme un mécanisme supramodal desservi par des circuits anatomiques distincts de ceux impliqués dans le traitement des données. Ce mécanisme supramodal est considéré ou bien comme unitaire ou comme composé de deux ou plusieurs circuits indépendants. La nécessité d'un système attentionnel anatomiquement distinct de celui requis pour l'intégration sensorimotrice est contestée. On propose plutôt que l'attention spatiale résulte d'une activation des mêmes circuits «pragmatiques» qui programment le mouvement oculaire et d'autres activités motrices. On soutient que l'attention spatiale diffère de l'exécution d'un mouvement par le degré d'activation des mêmes circuits plutôt que par l'activation de systèmes distincts.

INTRODUCTION

Scientific concepts frequently derive from a pre-scientific description of natural phenomena. As a consequence, the same word is often employed to indicate the pre-scientific and the scientific concept. Force is a term used in the common language. Its meaning, however, corresponds only approximately to the con-cept of "force" as defined in physics. The same applies to psychological terms.

Everybody knows what attention is. Yet, the intuition of what attention is does not necessarily coincide with "attention" as empirically described in terms of its properties and mechanisms. Similarly, everybody has an intuition of what space is. This, however, is not of great help in understanding what space is in terms of its empirical, psychological, and neural properties.

In this chapter we will review a series of recent psychological and neuro-physiological experiments on space representation and spatial attention. We will conclude that, contrary to common intuition, attention is not a supramodal control mechanism. Attention is modular and embedded in those same circuits that are responsible for sensorimotor transformations. The first part of the chapter will be devoted to space representation, the second to spatial attention.

SPACE REPRESENTATION

Introspectively, space is unitary. It is a kind of a large container where objects are located. Our intuition is that in order to perceive space, the brain should have a center specifically devoted to space. This center is used for all purposes, for walking, for reaching objects, or for describing a scene verbally.

Classically, it has been proposed that this putative multipurpose center is located in the parietal lobe (Critchley, 1953; Hyvärinen, 1982; Ungerleider & Mishkin, 1982). Lesion of this lobe and, in particular, of the inferior parietal lobule produces a series of spatial deficit ranging from space distortions to spatial neglect. Do these findings justify the existence of a space center?

A first argument against this view derives from anatomical considerations. As shown in Fig. 7.1, the parietal lobe is constituted of a large number of independent areas. If one of these areas were the hypothetical space master center, this area should be also the center of a series of convergent and divergent connections. It should receive inputs from the occipital lobe and distribute its output to a variety of centers: to oculomotor centers for looking at the objects, to areas controlling arm movements for reaching, to areas controlling walking for navigating in the environment, and so on. The evidence is exactly the opposite. The connections of parietal lobe with the frontal lobe as well as with subcortical centers are remarkably segregated (Andersen, Asanuma, Essick, & Siegel, 1990a; Cavada & Goldman-Rakic, 1989; Godschalk, Lemon, Kuypers, & Ronday, 1984; Matelli, Camarda, Glickstein, & Rizzolatti, 1986; Pandya & Kuypers, 1969; Petrides & Pandya, 1984). For example, the connections of parietal area LIP, one of the areas in which space is coded, are exclusively or almost exclusively with area 8. Both these areas are related to oculomotion. Area LIP, in contrast, does not send any input to areas related to arm movements.

A second argument derives from the functional properties of the parietal areas and parieto-frontal circuits. For reasons of space we will review here in some detail only the functional properties of two circuits, that formed by area LIP and area 8 (frontal eye field, FEF), and that constituted of parietal area VIP

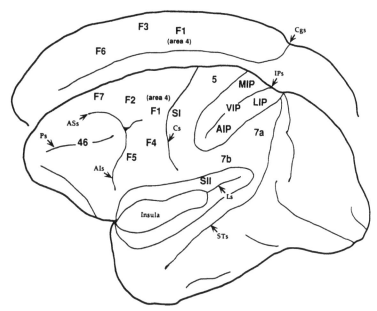

FIG. 7.1   Lateral and mesial views of monkey cerebral cortex. AIP: anterior intraparietal area; LIP: lateral intraparietal area; MIP: medial intraparietal area; VIP: ventral intraparietal area. Frontal agranular cortical areas are classified according to Matelli and colleagues (1985). Abbreviations: AIs: inferior arcuate sulcus; ASs: superior arcuate sulcus; Cs: central sulcus; Cgs: cingulate sulcus; Ips: intraparietal sulcus; Ls: lateral sulcus; Ps: principal sulcus; Sts: superior temporal sulcus. Note that Ips and Ls have been opened to show hidden areas. From "Grasping objects: the cortical mechanisms of visuomotor transformation" by M. Jeannerod, M. A. Arbib, G. Rizzolatti, and H. Sakata, 1995, *Trends in Neurosciences, 18*, p. 317. Copyright 1995 by Elsevier Science Ltd. Adapted with permission.

and frontal area F4 (ventral premotor cortex). The same functional principle is valid, however, also for the other circuits.

The LIP-FEF circuit contains three main classes of neurons: neurons responding to visual stimuli (visual neurons), neurons firing in association with eye movements (movement neurons), and neurons with both visual- and movement-related activity (visuomovement neurons) (Andersen, Bracewell, Barash, Gnadt, & Fogassi, 1990b; Andersen, Essick, & Siegel, 1985; Andersen & Gnadt, 1989; Barash, Bracewell, Fogassi, Gnadt, & Andersen, 1991a,b; Bruce, 1988; Bruce & Goldberg, 1985; Goldberg & Segraves, 1989). Neurons responsive to visual stimuli respond vigorously to stationary light stimuli. Their receptive fields (RFs) are usually large. Complex stimuli or even simply "oriented" stimuli are not necessary to activate them. Movement-related neurons fire in relation to ocular saccades, most of them discharging before the saccade onset. Visuomovement neurons have both visual- and saccade-related activity. Visual RFs and "motor" fields are in register, that is, the visual RF corresponds to the end-point of the effective saccade.

Visual responses in both LIP and FEF neurons are coded in retinotopic co-ordinates (Andersen & Gnadt, 1989; Goldberg & Segraves, 1989). In other words, their RFs have a specific position on the retina in reference to the fovea. When the eyes move, the RF also moves. Most LIP neurons have, however, an important property. The intensity of their discharge is modulated by the position of the eye in the orbit (orbital effect). Now, if the position of the RF on the retina and the position of the eye in the orbit are both known, one can recon-struct the position of the stimulus in spatial (craniocentric) coordinates. Thus, although the firing of a neuron does not specify by itself the position of the triggering stimulus in space, the spatial location of stimulus can be derived from the discharge intensity of different neurons (Andersen & Mountcastle, 1983; Andersen, Essick, & Siegel, 1985; Brotchie, Andersen, Snyder, & Goodman, 1995).

Let us consider now the property of the VIP-F4 circuit. As in the LIP-FEF circuit, neurons in this circuit can be subdivided into three main classes: sensory neurons, movement-related neurons, and sensorimotor neurons. The majority of them belong to the last category. Sensory and sensorimotor neurons respond to tactile or to tactile and visual stimuli. Examples of F4 tactile and visual RFs are shown in Fig. 7.2. Note that for each neuron the RF is restricted to a portion of space adjacent to the tactile RF. Most bimodal F4 neurons have this property.

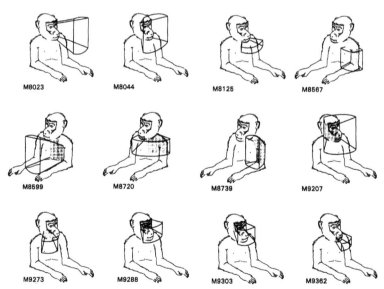

FIG. 7.2   Tactile and visual receptive fields of F4 bimodal neurons. Shadowed areas: tactile recept-ive fields. Solids around different body parts: visual receptive fields. From "Coding of peripersonal space in inferior premotor cortex (Area F4)" by L. Fogassi, V. Gallese, L. Fadiga, G. Luppino, M. Matelli, and G. Rizzolatti, 1996, *Journal of Neurophysiology*, 76, *No. 1*, p. 144. Copyright 1996 by the American Physiological Society. Reprinted with permission.

A few respond also to stimuli far from the body (Colby, Duhamel, & Goldberg, 1993; Fogassi, Gallese, Fadiga, & Rizzolatti, 1996; Gentilucci et al., 1988; Gentilucci, Scandolara, Pigarev, & Rizzolatti, 1983; Graziano & Gross, 1996; Graziano, Yap, & Gross, 1994).

Movement-related neurons and sensorimotor neurons are activated by head movements, face movements, or arm movements. Unfortunately there are no quantitative data on the relation between the effective active movement and the RF location. Informal observations suggest, however, a good correlation between RF position and type of movement coded by the same neuron. For example, neurons with RF near the face are active also during head movements directed toward (or away) the RF.

How is space coded in the VIP-F4 circuit? Some years ago Gentilucci et al. (1983, 1988) provided initial evidence that the visual RFs in F4 do not move with eye movements, but remain anchored to the tactile RF. More recently Fogassi et al. (1992, 1996) addressed the issue of space coding in F4 in a more formal way. Monkeys were trained to fixate a spot of light and detect its dimming. While the monkey performed the detection task a robot arm holding a stimulus was moved toward the animal. The stimulus could be moved inside or outside the neurons' visual RF, previously assessed. At this point the fixation point was moved and the monkey had to perform the task with the gaze deviated to another position. The rationale of the experiment was that if the RF were coded in retinotopic coordinates, its position should change with gaze deviations. In contrast, if the RF were coded in spatial coordinates it should remain in the same spatial location regardless of gaze position. The results showed that in about 90% of the neurons the RF location was independent of eye position, remaining in the same position in the peripersonal space regardless of eye deviation. The space coding in F4 is therefore in body-centered and not in retinal coordinates.

Similar results were obtained by Graziano, Yap, and Gross (1994) in their study of F4 neurons and by Colby et al. (1993) for VIP neurons. Graziano and Gross also studied the coordinate system of F4 neurons with RF around the hand. They found that when they moved the hand, visual RF followed it. The same was true for RF located around the head. The system of coordinates in F4 therefore is multiple and is related to the various effectors controlled by this premotor area.

If we now compare the properties of the VIP-F4 circuit with those of the LIP-FEF circuit, we find there is a common aspect and important differences. The common aspect is that coding of space is not devoted to a multiplicity of purposes but is specifically directed to a particular motor goal: eye movements in the case of the LIP-FEF circuit, body-part movements in the case of the VIP-F4 circuit. The different aspect is the way in which spatial information is obtained. For eye movements it is based on discharge modulation of retinotopic neurons. The visual origin of "eye movement space" is obvious. For head, arm, and hand movements, space is anchored to body-parts. The firing of the neurons signals the location of a stimulus with respect to a specific body-part regardless of the discharge intensity. This "body-parts space" may derive from transformations of retinal information. It may be, however, that given its properties, it is based on internal representations of specific movements on which only subsequently visual information is mapped (motor space).

These differences most likely stem from the different demands that eye movements and body-parts movements pose. Eye movements are rather stereotyped movements executed under the same load conditions. Arm movements (as well as other body movements) are, in contrast, characterized by an extreme variability in terms of load, speed, and degree of freedom. A rather simple system based on retinocentric neurons continuously computing eye position is probably sufficient for programming eye movements. It is not for arm movements. The fact that the frequency of discharge is not involved in signaling the spatial position of the stimulus but is "free" in F4 neurons provides a considerable advantage for this system. It can carry additional information on stimulus properties, thus allowing an appropriate body-part movement preparation.

The difference between the properties of the LIP-FEF circuit on one hand and the VIP-F4 circuit on the other is probably a cue for understanding why there is no multipurpose space map. The various motor effectors need different information and have different sensory requests. These cannot be provided by a unique map. Furthermore, the sensorimotor transformations necessary for organizing different types of movements must obviously have appeared in evolution before conscious space perception. Thus, conscious space perception derived from a conjoint action of the pre-existent spatial maps, rather than from the appearance of a new multipurpose map. The (hypothetical) appearance of a new map specific for conscious space perception would entail an enormous rewiring and a complete reorganization of the whole cerebral cortex. Evolutionary speaking, such a rearrangement is extremely unlikely.

THE CLASSIC THEORY OF SPATIAL ATTENTION

Given this functional scenario for space representation, the problem is how the different sectors of it can increase their efficiency in processing visual stimuli in order to select some of them and discard others. Spatial attention is the mechanism that allows this selection. How does it act and where is it located?

Broadly speaking, there are two main competing hypotheses on how attention works. The first one, which will be referred to as the "classic theory", maintains that attention is a unitary, supramodal system, anatomically separated from the circuits underlying sensorimotor transformation (see Posner & Dehaene, 1994; Posner, Petersen, Fox, & Reichle, 1988). This system acts as a control system, increasing the efficiency of the basic sensorimotor system. Attention is a kind of searchlight that is moved by the individuals and, by "illuminating" some parts of spatial maps, renders the processing of the stimuli falling on those parts more efficient.

Traditionally, as parietal lobe lesion determines attentional deficits, the site of this attentional system has been considered to be the parietal lobe (Bisiach & Vallar, 1988; Brain, 1941; Critchley, 1953). An alternative suggestion has been that of a circuit having its main nodes in the parietal, frontal, and cingulate areas (Mesulam, 1981).

The idea of a controlling system appears to be intuitively true because it corresponds exactly to our introspection on how attention works. We are able to move and allocate our attention on a certain location. Therefore our intuition is that it must be a control system that does the job. In its essence the theory is nothing else but the projection onto the brain of our introspective notion of attention.

To be fair, the hypothesis of a supramodal control system for spatial attention may find an empirical, albeit indirect, support from the way in which intensive attention systems are organized. In the case of arousal and other intensive attentional phenomena, there is indeed a control system that is independent of the basic sensorimotor circuits: the reticular formation (Moruzzi & Magoun, 1949).

The reticular formation (or the various biochemical separate circuits that form it) modifies the neural discharge of the systems processing sensory information (Hubel, 1960). Under the influence of the reticular formation the neural discharge of the sensory and motor system changes from a pattern formed by a sequence of burst of spikes followed by a long pause, to one constituted of a rather regular sequence of action potentials. There is evidence that only this latter pattern of discharge allows a transmission of information, for example, that related to external stimuli. The burst-pause patterns renders them unrecognizable (Maffei, Moruzzi, & Rizzolatti, 1965). Thus, a control system for attention does exist. The problem, however, is whether such a system, that explains global changes as those characterizing arousal with respect to sleep, can be applied also to processes that require stimulus selection.

The original formulation of the classic theory of attention was that there is a global attentional system able to control all functions: from visual attention to motor behavior to language (LaBerge & Brown, 1989; Posner, 1980). This point of view was abandoned with the introduction of modern brain imaging techniques. The results of positron emission tomography (PET) experiments (see, for example, Corbetta, Miezin, Dobmeyer, Shulman, & Petersen, 1990, 1991; Posner et al., 1988) showed that different brain circuits become active according to the task the subjects were required to execute. No evidence was found for a global central attentional system. As Posner wrote in his *Science* paper (1988): "There is no evidence of activation of any parts of the posterior visual spatial attention system (for example, parietal lobe) in any of our PET language studies" (for a more complete discussion of the PET experiments, see Rizzolatti, Riggio, & Sheliga, 1994).

After the demise of a global attentional system, the classic theory of attention was reformulated and adapted to the empirical findings. Recent versions of it suggest the existence of at least two different control systems: a posterior, parietal system subserving spatial attention and an anterior system involved in the attentional recruitment and control of brain areas to perform complex cognitive tasks (see Posner & Dehaene, 1994). Note, however, that the basic tenet of the theory remains unmodified: that attention is a supramodal control system. Now, it is neither global nor completely centralized, but, as before PET experiments, it is conceived as separate from the basic sensorimotor circuits.

MODULAR SENSORIMOTOR ATTENTION THEORIES

The alternative view to the classic theory of attention is that selective attention does not result from nor requires a control system separated from sensorimotor circuits. Attention derives from the activation of the same circuits that, in other conditions, determine perception and motor activity. The first modular theory of attention was the so-called "premotor theory" of attention formulated by Rizzolatti and Camarda (1987) on the basis of neurophysiological data, and by Rizzolatti and Umiltà (Rizzolatti, Riggio, Dascola, & Umiltà, 1987) using as evidence some psychological findings.

The premotor theory of attention addresses specifically spatial attention. According to it, spatial attention derives from an endogenous or exogenous activation of cortical pragmatic maps, that is, of those maps that transform spatial information into movements. When one of these maps becomes active there are two consequences: (a) there is an increase in the motor readiness to respond to some space sectors; (b) there is a facilitation in processing stimuli coming from that space sector toward which the motor program controlled by the pragmatic map was prepared.

The fundamental assumption is that in humans, as well as in higher mammals, there is a stage in which motor programs are set, but not executed. This stage, which occurs either in response to a stimulus or endogenously, is what introspectively is felt as spatial attention. The assumption of the presence of a stage in which the pragmatic areas are active, but action is not executed, aside from its self-evidence (humans and higher animals are not robots driven unconditionally by external stimuli), is supported by a series of physiological data showing that the fronto-parietal circuits, including some premotor areas that are directly connected to the spinal cord, are active in response to visual stimuli in the absence of an overt response. Evidence from single neuron studies of medial motor areas (e.g. pre-SMA) suggests that the motor programs, continuously generated in the lateral cortical circuits, are under inhibitory control of medial areas and are released only when the external contingencies and internal motivations allow their release.

Premotor theory of attention maintains that spatial attention can be produced by any map that codes space (Rizzolatti et al., 1994). In humans and primates, however, as a consequence of the strong development of the foveal vision and the neural mechanisms related to foveation, a central role in selective attention is played by those maps that code space for oculomotion.

More recently, Chelazzi, Miller, Duncan, and Desimone (1993) proposed an attentional mechanism for the selection of visual stimuli among distractors (bidimensional colored patterns) that, like the premotor theory of attention, does not require a control system independent of basic circuits involved in visual pattern analysis. By recording single neurons from monkey inferotemporal cortex, they found that when an animal is cued with a given stimulus the neurons activated by that stimulus increase their background activity. When subsequently the cued stimulus is shown, the response to it is strong, whereas, in contrast, when an uncued stimulus is presented, the response to it is markedly reduced. This "filtering" of uncued stimuli can be explained by postulating that the discharge increase consequent to cue presentation inhibits the neurons coding the uncued stimuli, while it leaves intact or even facilitates those responding to the cue. A control system external to the sensory circuit forming the visual "ventral stream" does not appear to be necessary. The increase in activity of neurons coding the attended stimulus most likely derives from a "memory" circuit involving the frontal lobe. A formal theory based on these and on some psychological data has been recently presented by Duncan (1996).

It is important to note here that the representations of objects and space are differently organized. As discussed earlier, space has a multiple representation in the parietal lobe (visual "dorsal stream"). All these space representations are intimately linked with motor activity. In contrast, objects, in addition of being represented in the visual dorsal stream where their representation is also strictly linked with motor programming, are also represented in the ventral stream (Ungerleider & Mishkin, 1982). This latter representation is responsible for the analysis of object qualities and enables the visual system to categorize objects, regardless of the visual conditions in which the objects are presented. Thus, whereas attention for space necessarily implies a motor program, this is not mandatory in the case of attention for objects.

THE ELUSIVE SELECTIVE ATTENTION CONTROL SYSTEM: LESION EXPERIMENTS

In the case of intensive attention, for which a control system indeed exists, it is also clear where it is located. Its localization in the brain stem was established by stimulation (Moruzzi & Magoun, 1949) and lesion (French & Magoun, 1952; Lindsley, Schreiner, Knowles, & Magoun, 1950) studies since the late 1940s. The same should be true for the putative selective attention control system. Some authors localized it in the inferior parietal lobule because damage to it produces attentional deficits such as neglect or extinction (De Renzi, 1982). However, the situation is more complex. Contrary to what one should expect from a master system for spatial attention, damage to the parietal lobe does not necessarily produce a global bilateral attentional syndrome deficits. Deficits can be limited to specific restricted space sectors (see Rizzolatti & Gallese, 1988).

The initial demonstration of a dissociation between space sectors was provided by some experiments that Rizzolatti, Matelli, and Pavesi (1983) carried out some years ago in monkeys. There were two groups of monkeys. In the first group of monkeys area 8 (frontal eye field) was ablated, whereas in a second group of animals ventral area 6 (the lesion included parts of F4 and F5) was damaged.

It is a classic finding that damage to FEF produces contralateral neglect (Bianchi, 1895; Kennard, 1939). The experiments by Rizzolatti et al. (1983) confirmed these data. However, they also found that neglect was stronger when stimuli were presented far from the monkey than when they were presented near to it. Furthermore, when the stimuli touched the skin the animal reacted normally. "Personal neglect" was therefore absent.

The most interesting results were observed following damage to area 6. Visual stimuli presented outside the monkey's reach (extrapersonal space) were immediately detected. In contrast, they were ignored when presented near the monkey (peripersonal space) and even when they touched its skin. A similar pattern of results, although less dramatic, was obtained following lesion of some sectors of the inferior parietal lobe.

Subsequently, similar dissociations between different space sectors were reported in patients with lesion of parietal and frontal lobe (Cowey, Small, & Ellis, 1994; Marshall & Halligan, 1988; Rapcsak, Cimino, & Heilman, 1988; Shelton, Bowers, & Heilman, 1990). It appears therefore that the neglect as full-fledged syndrome, which includes attentional deficits for personal, peripersonal, and extrapersonal space, is not a consequence of the destruction of an attention control system, but results from lesions of anatomically distinct circuits.

The impossibility to localize anatomically a global attentional system, not only for different psychological functions, but even for attention in space is obviously a strong blow to the classic theory of attention. Even more so if one considers the properties of neurons of the areas ablated in the experiments producing neglect. As described before, the neurons of area 8 and 6 code space for particular motor purposes (eye movements, head movements, reaching). Thus, neglect is not determined by a destruction of a central space control system, or by a series of mini-control systems, but by damage to circuits that program motor actions in space.

THE DIFFICULTY OF "ATTENTION" IN CROSSING THE MERIDIANS OF VISUAL FIELD

Psychological evidence against the classic theory of attention came initially from some experiments performed by Rizzolatti, Umiltà, and their co-workers (Rizzolatti et al., 1987; Umiltà, Mucignat, Riggio, Barbieri, & Rizzolatti, 1994;

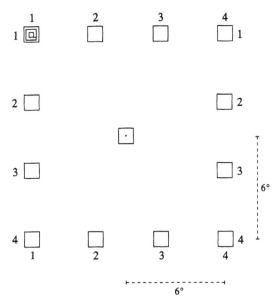

FIG. 7.3 Basic visual display used in "meridian effect" experiments. In all conditions the central (fixation) box and one of the four peripheral rows of boxes were presented. In every condition the cue used for directing attention was a digit (0–4) presented in the fixation box. The command stimulus was a geometrical pattern (see upper left box), which appeared in one of the stimulus boxes. From "Reorienting attention across the horizontal and vertical meridians: Evidence in favor of a premotor theory of attention" by G. Rizzolatti, L. Riggio, I. Dascola, and C. Umiltà, 1987, *Neuropsychologia, 25,* p. 34. Copyright 1987 by Elsevier Science Ltd. Reprinted with permission.

Umiltà, Riggio, Dascola, & Rizzolatti, 1991). The basic visual display used in those experiments is shown in Fig. 7.3. The experimental condition was the following. Subjects were instructed to maintain fixation on the central box, to direct attention to the cued box, and to press as fast as possible a key at the occurrence of the imperative stimulus. There were valid trials, invalid trials, and neutral trials (see Posner, 1980). In valid trials the imperative stimulus appeared in the cued box, in invalid trials it appeared in one of the uncued boxes, and in neutral trials all boxes were cued.

The results showed that: (a) valid trials were faster than invalid trials; (b) invalid trials with the imperative stimulus in the same hemifield as the cued box were faster than invalid trials with the imperative stimulus in the opposite hemifield even if its distance from the cued box was the same; (c) invalid trials in which the imperative stimulus was presented in a box far from the attended one were slower than those with the stimulus presented near to it. This pattern of results was found regardless of whether the stimuli were arranged horizontally, vertically, above, or below the fixation point.

According to the classic theory of attention, the events in the experiment just described should be the following. Attention is directed to the cued box. The reaction times (RTs) to stimuli presented in it are therefore faster than those to stimuli presented in the other boxes ("validity effect"). When the imperative stimulus is shown in an uncued box, attention has to be redirected. This determines a lengthening of RTs. The lengthening is greater when the invalid stimulus is far from the cued box than when it is near to it because the time that attention takes to move from one box to another depends on the distance it has to cover ("distance effect").

The classic theory has, however, serious difficulties in explaining the lengthening of RTs when attention has to cross the visual field meridians. This effect ("meridian effect") is a robust phenomenon of the order of 20–25ms, which has been described by many authors in different experimental conditions (Downing & Pinker, 1985; Gawriszewski et al., 1992; Hughes & Zimba, 1985; Reuter-Lorenz & Fendrich, 1992; Rizzolatti et al., 1987; Shepherd & Muller, 1989; Tassinari, Aglioti, Chelazzi, Marzi, & Berlucchi, 1987; Umiltà et al., 1991). If attention is a control system independent of basic anatomical and physiological circuits, why should its action be delayed by anatomical landmarks such as the principal meridians of the visual field?

Two explanations were offered. The first is that the meridian effect is due to attention crossing the corpus callosum. The second is that the meridian effect is a consequence of the large representation of the fovea in the cortex and the consequent large amount of neural tissue that attention has to traverse when traveling in the visual cortex. However, both these explanations can be ruled out on the basis of the data of Rizzolatti et al. (1987). The display shown in Fig. 7.3 was used. The meridian effect was found when stimuli were presented vertically and, thus, no crossing of the corpus callosum was required. Furthermore, the meridian effect was also present when the stimuli were located away from the fovea in retinal positions with approximately the same cortical magnification factor. It was shown, therefore, that an explanation of the meridian effect based on the amount of nervous tissue that has to be crossed was not tenable.

The situation is quite different if one accepts the premotor theory of attention. Let us examine the sequence of the event according to this theory in the experimental condition of Fig. 7.3. As soon as the cognitive cue is presented, a motor program for a saccade toward the expected location is prepared. This program specifies the direction and the amplitude of the saccade. When the two parameters are set, two events occur. First, the location of the expected stimulus becomes salient with respect to all other locations (Bashinski & Bacharach, 1980; Downing, 1988; Hawkins et al., 1990; Muller & Humphreys, 1991; Riggio & Kirsner, 1997). Second, the readiness to respond to the stimuli at that location increases. When the imperative stimulus occurs in an unexpected location, as suggested by Posner (1980), the manual responses (and other arbitrary responses) can be emitted only when attention is allocated to the new point. Thus, the invalid responses are delayed because a new motor program has to be prepared and the delay will be greater if the changes in the motor program to adjust to the new situation are greater.

Let us come back to the meridian effect. There is agreement that goal-directed saccades are prepared in two steps (Becker & Jurgens, 1979; Findlay, 1982; Komoda, Festinger, Phillips, Duckman, & Young, 1973; Wheeless, Boynton, & Cohen, 1966). First, a decision concerning the direction is taken. Second, when the direction is set, the amplitude is calculated. The consequence of this formulation is that changes in saccade direction require a radical modification in oculomotor program, whereas changes in saccade amplitude imply only a readjustment of a pre-existing program. The premotor theory of attention postulates the same cause for the meridian effect. When the amplitude of the attention movement has to be modified without changing the basic direction parameters (right, left, up, down), only an adjustment of the parameters of saccades is needed, the general program (direction) being already set. In contrast, when the imperative stimulus appears in the hemifield opposite the one containing the cued location, the required changes concern the basic direction parameters. In this case, more time is required because a new program, involving a radically different set of muscles, has to be constructed. This program resetting would be the origin of the meridian effect.

Before reviewing other experiments that provide evidence for the premotor theory of attention, it is important to discuss a crucial point of the theory: The possibility that the preparation of a motor program may facilitate the detection and analysis of visual stimuli.

MOTOR PROGRAMS AND RE-ENTRANT CIRCUITS

What is the evidence that, when a motor program toward a certain space point is prepared, there is a facilitation in responding to stimuli presented to that point? The strongest proof for this comes from some neurophysiological experiments made by Wurtz, Goldberg, and their coworkers (Goldberg & Wurtz, 1972; Mohler & Wurtz, 1976; Wurtz & Mohler, 1976a). They recorded single neurons from the superior colliculus of monkeys trained to fixate a spot of light. While the monkey fixated it, the RF of the recorded collicular neuron was plotted. Then the monkey was tested in two conditions. In the first it had simply to fixate the central point and to detect its dimming. A visual stimulus was presented to the neuron's RF. This stimulus had no meaning for the monkey and did not require any response. In the second condition, the fixation point, after a certain interval, was turned off and, simultaneously, a second stimulus was presented in the neuron's RF. The monkey had to make a saccade to this stimulus and detect its dimming. The stimuli were presented in blocks, in the same spatial position within a block. Thus, after the first trials the monkey could predict the stimulus location.

The experiments showed that a large proportion of collicular neurons responded stronger to the stimulus when this was the subsequent target for the saccade than when it had no meaning for the monkey. Note that physically the stimuli were identical in both conditions. A particularly important finding was that the response enhancement concerned also the neurons of superior colliculus superficial layers. These neurons are typical visual neurons. Thus, the preparation to make a saccade toward a certain space position not only facilitates the motor response toward that point but, most importantly, also increases the responsiveness of visual neurons related to that position.

Subsequent studies by Wurtz, Hikosaka, and their coworkers (Hikosaka & Wurtz, 1983a,b) defined the circuit modulating the excitability of the superior colliculus. This circuit is formed by the cortical oculomotor areas, the caudate, and the pars reticulata of the substantia nigra (SNr). At rest, the SNr neurons are tonically active and inhibit the intermediate layers of the superior colliculus (Hikosaka & Wurtz, 1983a,b). The inhibition is topographically organized. In turn, the SNr is under inhibitory control from the caudate. When a saccade has to be generated, the cortical activity excites the caudate neurons, which, in turn, inhibit the topographically related neurons in the SNr (Hikosaka, Sakamoto, & Usui, 1989a,b). The collicular neurons are therefore disinhibited and ready to generate the appropriate saccade (Hikosaka & Wurtz, 1989).

One can speculate that, during expectancy, a cortical motor program (prepared, but not executed) disinhibits, by means of the caudate nucleus and SNr, the collicular intermediate (motor) neurons related to the cued space position. The increase in firing of these neurons facilitates the collicular superficial neurons through an ascending pathway, allowing a better detection of the stimuli.

The "enhancement" effect was found, subsequently in the pulvinar (Petersen, Robinson, & Keys, 1985), and in cortical oculomotor areas related to eye movements such as the FEF and the posterior parietal cortex (Bushnell, Goldberg, & Robinson, 1981; Goldberg & Bushnell, 1981; Wurtz & Mohler, 1976b). It is likely that the basic mechanism responsible for these enhancement effects is analogous to that described for the superior colliculus. When a cortical motor program is set, the premotor neuron activation increases the excitability of neurons located upstream. If this is so, considering the richness of re-entrant cortical circuits, an interesting possibility arises. A facilitatory effect, that originated in an oculomotor area, for example in the FEF or area LIP, should travel backward, via re-entering fibers, recruiting not only neurons in oculomotor centers, but also neurons located in the mosaic of areas forming the occipital lobe. If at this level there are neurons that send fibers to areas that are part of different circuits (e.g. for arm movements) the attentional facilitation, originally initiating in an oculomotor center, will spread to other circuits. Such a mechanism may give unity and coherence to attentional behavior, without the necessity of postulating the unlikely "response-free" global controller.

A recent series of experiments by Hikosaka, Miyauchi, Takeichi, and Shimojo (1996) strongly suggest that attention indeed "diffuses" to occipital areas. Their basic experimental situation was the following. Subjects were instructed to fixate a point on a screen and to pay attention to one of two peripheral boxes also shown on the screen. In a first series of experiments attention was attracted passively by a peripheral cue. After a random time interval a line was presented connecting the two boxes. A very strong motion illusion was perceived. The line appeared to grow in length over time as if it emanated from the attended box.

In two other series of experiments, attention was allocated to the peripheral boxes by using cognitive cues (Hikosaka et al., 1996) or by preparation of a motor response such as arm-reaching or saccade (Shimojo, Tanaka, Hikosaka, & Miyauchi, 1996). The motion illusion was observed in both cases. The authors argued that in order to obtain motion perception from a stationary stimulus, a facilitation should take place at the level preceding that of motion detectors. As these are present in large number in visual area MT, the site where attention acts should be before this area.

These findings fit well with our interpretation of cortical enhancement effect and the role of re-entrant fibers in attention. They clearly show that a facilitation due to an implicit preparation of a motor program (experiment with cognitive cue) or to an explicit preparation of it (experiment in which this was overtly required) may spread from rostral cortical areas to the occipital lobe until a very early stage of visual processing. This backward diffusion through re-entrant circuits should play an important role in improving the capacity of stimulus processing for responses in the circuit in which the facilitation originally started as well as in other circuits sharing the same visual neurons.

OCULOMOTOR ACTIVATION DURING SPATIAL ATTENTION

The meridian effect is only an indirect evidence in favor of the premotor theory of spatial attention. Recently, a new series of experiments carried out by Sheliga, Riggio, and Rizzolatti (1994, 1995a; Sheliga, Riggio, Craighero, & Rizzolatti 1995b), provided more direct support to this theory.

The basic experimental situation was similar to that used in experiments on meridian effect. As in those experiments, the subjects were instructed to fixate a central cross, and, following the presentation of a cognitive cue, to pay attention to one of the four boxes. The trials could be valid or invalid. The major difference with the previous experiments was that the measured variable was not a manual response, but a vertical saccade directed to a box located below the fixation point.

The logic of the experiment was the following. Studies on oculomotor system in man (Aslin & Shea, 1987; Becker & Jurgens, 1979; Findlay, 1982) and monkeys (Robinson, 1972; Schiller, True, & Conway, 1979; Schiller & Sandel, 1983; Sparks, Mays, & Porter, 1987) demonstrated that when the oculomotor system is activated by two simultaneous or closely consecutive stimuli, there is an effect of one stimulus on the other, resulting in an interference between the responses to them. Now, if spatial attention, as claimed by premotor theory of attention, involves an activation of oculomotor circuits, then this activation should influence an overt oculomotor response. In contrast, if spatial attention is not related to oculomotion, there is no reason why such an influence should occur.

The results showed that when the imperative stimulus appeared on the right of fixation, there was a deviation of the saccade to the left, whereas the opposite was observed when the imperative stimulus appeared on the left of fixation. Furthermore, although the deviation was observed in all trials, its strength was greater when the trials were valid, that is when active attention was on the locus of imperative stimulus presentation. Finally, the saccade deviation depended on the distance from the fixation point. It was smaller when the imperative stimulus was in one of the two boxes close to the fixation point than when it was in the two far boxes (Sheliga et al., 1994).

This experiment demonstrates that the occurrence of the imperative stimulus produces a marked effect on the oculomotor system. It is likely that this occurs because the subjects have a strong natural tendency to look at the new stimulus. However, because they are instructed to maintain fixation, they must counteract this tendency. This counteraction inhibits the superior colliculus and other oculomotor centers. Thus, a deviation occurs in the direction opposite to that where the stimulus was presented. Sheliga et al. (1994) called this interpretation of the saccade deviation the "suppression" hypothesis.

The most interesting finding of the experiment, however, was the influence of endogenous attention on the extent of saccade deviation. As already mentioned, saccade deviation was greater when the location of endogenous attention and that of the imperative stimulus coincided. Is this effect due to the fact that active attention is a consequence of an activation of the oculomotor system?

A possible objection to this interpretation is that in all experimental conditions there was a visual imperative stimulus. It can be argued therefore that the imperative stimulus was the only cause of the deviation, the larger extent of it in valid trials being due to a major salience of the imperative stimulus determined by the recruitment of the putative central "attentional system".

In order to elucidate this point, Sheliga et al. (1995a) carried out a new experiment in which the eye deviation was measured in the absence of passive attention. The display used in the experiment consisted of three filled and two empty boxes. The three filled boxes were arranged horizontally. The two empty boxes were located above and below the central filled box. The central box was the fixation box. The cue was a thin line attached to this box. If the line pointed to the left, the stimulus was going to appear in the left box, if the line pointed to the right, the stimulus was going to appear to the right, and if the line pointed up, the stimulus was presented in the central box. All trials were valid. However, once the subjects had their attention directed to the appropriate box, two different events could occur: either a tiny line appeared in the cued box (visual imperative stimulus) or a computer-generated central sound was presented (acoustic imperative stimulus). Half of the subjects had to make a vertical saccade directed to

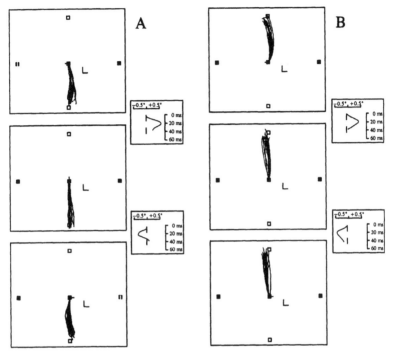

FIG. 7.4   Deviations of ocular saccades when attention is allocated to a peripheral point. A: saccadic responses to presentation of visual imperative stimulus. *Left side*: saccadic trajectories. Upper panel: presentation of the imperative stimulus in the left (cued) box. Middle panel: presentation of the imperative stimulus in the central (cued) box. Lower panel: presentation of the imperative stimulus in the right (cued) box. Calibration marks for all three panels = 1°. *Right side*: Upper panel: mean horizontal deviation of saccades with the imperative stimulus presented in the left box after point-by-point subtraction of the mean horizontal deviation of saccades with the imperative stimulus presented in the central box. Lower panel: mean horizontal deviation of saccades with the imperative stimulus presented in the right box after point-by-point subtraction of the mean horizontal deviation of saccades with the imperative stimulus presented in the central box. In both panels the saccade trajectories in the neutral condition are shown as vertical dashed lines. Abscissa: horizontal deviation, ordinate: time. B: Saccadic responses to presentation of acoustic imperative stimulus. *Left side*: saccadic trajectories. Upper panel: cueing of the left box. Middle panel: cueing of the central box. Lower panel: cueing of the right box. *Right side*: see description in A. The acoustic stimulus was presented centrally. From "Orienting of attention and eye movements" by B. M. Sheliga, L. Riggio, and G. Rizzolatti, 1994, *Experimental Brain Research, 98,* p. 516. Copyright 1994 by Springer-Verlag. Reprinted with permission.

the upper empty box in the case of the acoustic stimulus and to the lower empty box in the case of visual stimulus, the other half had to do the opposite.

Figure 7.4 illustrates the results. All data of one subject are presented. In A the saccades in responses to visual imperative stimuli are shown, in B those in response to acoustic imperative stimuli. The most important results are those in B. They demonstrate that an endogenous allocation of attention is sufficient

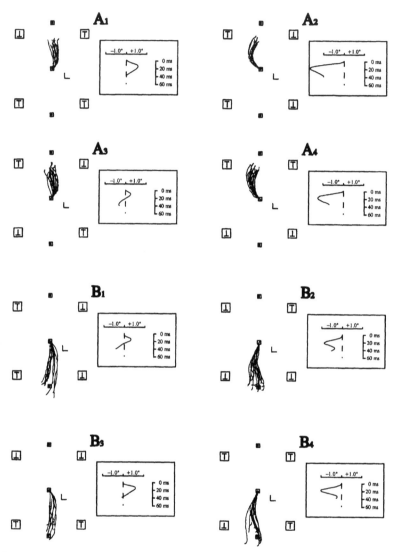

FIG. 7.5 Deviations of ocular saccades when attention is allocated to a peripheral point. Saccadic responses following active (endogenous) orienting to a visual imperative stimulus. The four (upright or inverted) Ts are present in the display before cue presentation. A: Upward saccades following discrimination of inverted Ts inside the cued stimulus box. Four situations are illustrated: imperative stimulus in the left upper box (A1), right upper box (A2), left lower box (A3), and right lower box (A4). Calibration marks = 1°. B: Downward saccades following discrimination of normally oriented Ts inside the cued stimulus box. Imperative stimulus presentation in the left upper box (B1), right upper box (B2), left lower box (B3), and right lower box (B4). For right panels see conventions in Fig. 7.4. From "Spatial attention and eye movements" by B. M. Sheliga, L. Riggio, and G. Rizzolatti, 1995, *Experimental Brain Research*, *105*, p. 268. Copyright 1994 by Springer-Verlag. Reprinted with permission.

to determine a significant deviation of ocular saccades. Similar results were obtained in the other subjects.

An important finding of the experiments was that the extent of the saccade deviation depended on the intensity of attention requirements. For example, the saccade deviations were particularly strong when the subjects were required to discriminate the imperative stimulus, before making the saccade, instead of merely detecting it (Sheliga et al., 1995a). This point is illustrated in the experiment shown in Fig. 7.5.

The displays used in it are shown on the left side of the various panels. The central box was for fixation. The other two small boxes were targets for eye movements. The imperative stimuli were Ts, normally drawn or inverted, presented in the four boxes. The orientation of the imperative stimulus indicated whether the saccade had to be directed upward or downward. The display was presented at the beginning of each trial. The subject, however, did not know which of the four Ts was the imperative stimulus. About one second following display presentation, a tiny line appeared in the central box (see Fig. 7.5) and indicated which of the Ts was the imperative stimulus. The subject had to make, as soon as possible, a vertical saccade upward or downward according to the T-bar direction.

Note that in this paradigm there is no phasic presentation of an imperative stimulus that may cause an orienting reaction—attention is moved endogenously —and that it must be oriented precisely on the required box in order to discriminate the imperative stimulus. Finally, unlike in most endogenous attention paradigms, in this paradigm there is no expectancy. The "attentional" program is made after imperative stimulus presentation, toward it.

Figure 7.5 illustrates the saccades of one subject in all different experimental conditions. The panels in A show the effect of attention to different locations on the trajectory of saccades directed upward. Those in B show the effect of attention on saccades directed downward. In all conditions the saccades deviate contralateral to the location of attention. Note the strength of the effect.

The saccade deviation is present not only with vertical saccades. The same effect was also found when subjects were instructed to pay attention to stimuli located above or below the fixation point and to make horizontal saccades (Sheliga et al., 1995b).

Recent data by Kustov and Robinson (1996) showed that when a monkey pays attention to a given location in space there is a change in the excitability of the superior colliculus. This change was demonstrated by the presence of a saccade shift with respect to their normal trajectory (elicited by the electrical stimulation of the superior colliculus) during allocation of spatial attention. The change was present when attention was allocated as a consequence of both an endogenous and an exogenous cue presentation. Particularly striking was the observation that the collicular excitation also changed when the monkey was instructed to make a manual response and keep the eyes still after imperative stimulus presentation. This last finding clearly shows that a mere shift of attention without any eye movement requirement determines a change in the oculomotor system. This finding is exactly what the premotor theory of attention would predict in that experimental situation. Furthermore, the changes in the collicular excitability shown by Kustov and Robinson (1996) fit perfectly well with saccade deviation described by Sheliga et al. (1994, 1995a,b) and give them a well-proven anatomical and physiological basis.

In conclusion, these data indicate that any time attention is oriented to a certain spatial target, attention orientation is accompanied by an oculomotor programming. Although obviously this does not prove a causal relation between oculomotion and attention, it fully confirms the prediction of premotor theory. In contrast, the account of this phenomenon is not clear if one accepts the tenets of the "classic" theory. If attention is "disembodied" why should it interfere with oculomotor programs? Furthermore, if attention is not related to oculomotion why should the oculomotor program be constantly made and directed to stimuli toward which saccades are not required? A possible tendency to prepare a saccade toward the attended target, even if not required, in parallel to the attentional process, should habituate, if useless, and disappear during the experiment. The fact that, on the contrary, the oculomotor program does not habituate and persists despite the fact that this is never executed (saccades in all the experiments discussed are never directed to the imperative stimulus location) is a further problem for the classic theory of attention.

NONOCULOMOTOR SPATIAL ATTENTION

At the beginning of this chapter we reviewed experiments showing that space is represented in several cortical maps. Some of them control eye movements, others control movements of the head, of the arms, or other body parts. There is nothing unique in the organization of the oculomotor system that may grant it a special status. However, in everyday life most of our actions in space are preceded by foveation. This gives to the oculomotor system a special central position in spatial attention.

There are some conditions, however, in which we do not use, or do not use primarily, eye movements to select stimuli in space. In these cases spatial attention should depend basically on circuits other than those related to eye movements.

An example are head movements in response to stimuli presented in the space around the face. When stimuli are located close to it, foveation is of little help. In this case movement preparation and the relative spatial location selection should depend on neurons that control mostly head movements and with spatial properties as those described for premotor area F4 and parietal area VIP. The peripersonal neglect consequent to lesions of ventral premotor cortex supports this view (Rizzolatti et al., 1983).

Another example is the control of arm movement. Probably the best documented evidence in favor of this type of attention is that deriving from a series of experiments of Tipper, Lortie, and Baylis (1992). They instructed normal subjects to depress one button of a series of nine, located on a board and arranged in three horizontal rows. The subject's hand was located at either the bottom or the top of the board. The arm movement toward a button was triggered by turning on a red light adjacent to the selected button. In most cases a second, yellow, light was also turned on. The effect of this light on arm movements was studied.

The results showed that the interfering effect of the second light depended on the arm starting position. When the hand was at the bottom of the board, the most interfering stimuli were those in the lowest row. In contrast, when the hand was at the top of the board the most interfering stimuli were those in the upper row. These effects cannot depend either on a purely visual representation of the board or on spatial attention related to eye movements, because changing hand location obviously does not modify the visual or oculomotor representation of the board. It is the organization of the hand movement that changes when the hand is placed above or below the board and, as a consequence, changes also the attentional relevance of stimuli close to the hand or far from it.

The fact that stimulus relevance depended on hand position and not on other factors was confirmed by a further experiment in which the subjects performed the task using their left hand. The results showed that the attentional field changed according to the hand used. When the subject used the right hand, the stimuli presented in the right part of the board produced a stronger interference than those presented in the left part. In contrast, when the subject used the left hand, the opposite was observed. These data fit well with previous observations that each arm acts better in its ipsilateral field (Fisk & Goodale, 1985; Prablanc, Echallier, Komilis, & Jeannerod, 1979).

The arm-related attentional effects are probably mediated by premotor (F4) neurons with RF around the hand and around the arm (Graziano et al., 1994; Rizzolatti, Scandolara, Matelli, & Gentilucci, 1981). When arm movements are prepared, there is an activation of the peripersonal space and, given the organization of premotor RFs, the space close to the body is particularly activated. This activation gives relevance to stimuli close to the hand, favoring their detection. When stimuli near the hand are distractors, as in the Tipper experiment, the interference caused by them should therefore be greater than that caused by similar stimuli located at a greater distance.

Pointing is a relatively simple action. Much more complex in term of visuomotor transformations are the actions that allow individuals to grasp objects. These actions consist of two distinct components: Arm transport, a schema in which the space location of the object is transformed into proximal arm movements, and hand shaping, in which the intrinsic properties of the object are transformed into the appropriate hand movements. Is the attention to these two components of the action unitary or can it be dissociated?

Chieffi, Gentilucci, Allport, Sasso, and Rizzolatti (1993) examined this issue by recording the kinematics of hand and arm movements in a woman who suffered a right hemisphere stroke. Immediately after the stroke she developed a left hemiparesis and a left hemineglect. When tested (15 months after the stroke), the neglect had recovered and the motor deficit had markedly improved. Mild attentional deficits were still present at the neuropsychological testing.

The arm movement-related attention was tested as follows. The patient sat in front of a table with her right (normal) hand resting on it in a fixed position. Her task was to grasp a horizontally located red cylinder with her normal hand. The cylinder was located in the ipsilesional, normal hemispace. The length of it varied in different trials. In the control condition only the cylinder, target of the movement, was presented. In the experimental conditions there was also a second cylinder, of a color different from the first one, which served as a distractor. It could be congruent in size with the first one or incongruent with it, and it was presented on the right or on the left of the first cylinder. The trial started by turning on a LED and inviting the patient to fixate it, while the objects were in dark. Then, after a warning signal, the objects were illuminated and the patient was instructed to grasp the red cylinder. A group of normal subjects were also tested in the same experimental conditions.

The patient reached and grasped the objects correctly. The analysis of the kinematics of reaching movements showed, however, that, unlike in normals, the presence of a distractor on the right of the target caused a deviation of the arm toward the distractor. A distractor on the left of the target did not produce any significant trajectory change. The analysis of grasping movements showed that the hand aperture was normally modulated by the size of the target. The presentation of small or large distractors, on the right or on the left of the target, did not change the size of the hand aperture, which remained the same as without distractors.

These results are, at first glance, rather paradoxical, especially if one considers that the transport and hand shaping start simultaneously and not sequentially. The correct hand shaping (and the normal grasping velocity profiles) indicates that attention was from the very beginning on the target. Yet, as shown by the arm deviation toward the distractor, attention was also on the distractor. This is hard to understand if attention were unitary. If one accepts, however, a modular theory of attention, the finding are not surprising. The patient had a lesion of some spatial maps. Thus, as previously described by several authors (De Renzi, Gentilini, Faglioni, & Barbieri, 1989; Kinsbourne, 1987; Ladavas, Petronio, & Umiltà, 1990), there was an "hyperattention" (De Renzi et al., 1989) toward the rightmost stimuli. In contrast, the anatomical and functional system transforming size and shape in grasping movement was intact (see Jeannerod, Arbib, Rizzolatti, & Sakata, 1995). Thus, while attention for reaching moved from target to distractor, that for grasping remained anchored to the target and was not influenced by the spatial attention shift. This explanation is counterintuitive yet it is strictly congruent with physiological reality.

In conclusion, although the evidence for attention related to arm movements is not rich, the available data strongly support the view that this mechanism exists. The relative poverty of the data depends on the fact that most psychological (and physiological) paradigms are rather abstract and not adequate to demonstrate attentional effects related to movements other than those of the eyes.

CATEGORY MISTAKES AND REDUCTIONISM

In *The concept of the mind* Ryle (1949) invites us to consider the case of a visitor to Oxford who wants to see the University. He is shown various colleges, libraries, administration buildings, and laboratories. He sees where the teachers and students live. He visits museums and sport facilities. But at the end of tour he asks: "Where is the University?" It is obvious that in asking this question, he is convinced that the essential element had been omitted from his visit. Although he had seen various colleges and offices and laboratories, he had not seen the University itself, as if the University was some extra entity that exists over and above all that he has seen.

The view of those who defend the "classic theory" of attention against the "modular theories" is exactly that of the visitor to Oxford. They are perfectly aware that during various attentional tasks there is activation of premotor cortex, or of oculomotor centers, or of occipital and inferotemporal areas. These findings, however, are considered by them only secondary to the real "attentional" phenomenon. They are either something that occurs in parallel to "attention" or are a consequence of it. In both cases these processes are of little relevance to "real" attention. It might be that this is so. The evidence accumulated in these years and reviewed in this chapter, however, makes it more and more likely that the chance of finding the "real" attentional center or circuits is no greater than that of the visitor to Oxford of finding the University.

It is obvious that to some cognitive psychologists the idea that spatial attention is nothing else but the introspective counterpart of subject's predisposition to move may appear as reductionism. It is indeed so. The understanding, however, of basic biological attention mechanism not only does not impoverish the attention as a phenomenon, but on the contrary enriches it and allows a better understanding of its properties.

ACKNOWLEDGEMENTS

This research was supported by the European Science Foundation (ENP Collaborative Research Projects) and by CNR and MPI grants to G. R. The authors thank L. Chelazzi, V. Gallese, and D. L. Robinson for their comments and suggestions.

REFERENCES

Andersen, R. A., Asanuma, C., Essick, G., & Siegel, R. M. (1990a). Corticocortical connections of anatomically and physiologically defined subdivisions within the inferior parietal lobule. *The Journal of Comparative Neurology, 296,* 65–113.

Andersen, R. A., Bracewell, R. M., Barash, S., Gnadt, J W., & Fogassi, L. (1990b). Eye position effects on visual, memory, and saccade-related activity in areas LIP and 7a of macaque. *Journal of Neuroscience, 10,* 1176–1196.

Andersen, R. A., Essick, G. K., & Siegel, R. M. (1985). Encoding spatial location by posterior parietal neurons. *Science, 230,* 456–458.

Andersen, R. A., & Gnadt, J. W. (1989). Role of posterior parietal cortex in saccadic eye movements. In R. Wurtz & M. Goldberg (Eds.), *The neurobiology of saccadic eye movements.* Reviews of Oculomotor Research series, Vol. 3. Amsterdam: Elsevier.

Andersen, R. A., & Mountcastle, V. B. (1983). The influence of the angle of gaze upon the excitability of the light-sensitivity neurons of the posterior parietal cortex. *The Journal of Neuroscience, 3,* 532–548.

Aslin, R. N., & Shea, S. L. (1987). The amplitude and angle of saccades to double-step target displacements. *Vision Research, 27,* 1925–1942.

Barash, S., Bracewell, R. M., Fogassi, L., Gnadt, J. W., & Andersen, R. A. (1991a). Saccade-related activity in the lateral intraparietal area I. Temporal properties; comparison with area 7a. *Journal of Neurophysiology, 66,* 1095–1108.

Barash, S., Bracewell, R. M., Fogassi, L., Gnadt, J. W., & Andersen, R. A. (1991b). Saccade-related activity in the lateral intraparietal area II. Spatial properties. *Journal of Neurophysiology, 66,* 1109–1124.

Bashinski, H. S., & Bacharach, V. R. (1980). Enhancement of perceptual sensitivity as the result of selectively attending to spatial locations. *Perception and Psychophysics, 28,* 241–248.

Becker, W., & Jurgens, R. (1979). An analysis of the saccadic system by means of double step stimuli. *Vision Research, 19,* 967–983.

Bianchi, L. (1895). The function of the frontal lobes. *Brain, 18,* 497–530.

Bisiach, E., & Vallar, G. (1988). Hemineglect in humans. In F. Boller & J. Grafman (Eds.), *Handbook of neuropsychology* (Vol. 1, pp. 195–222). Amsterdam: Elsevier.

Brain, W. R. (1941). Visual disorientation with special reference to lesions of the right cerebral hemisphere. *Brain, 64,* 244–272.

Brotchie, P. R., Andersen, R. A., Snyder, L. H., & Goodman, S. J. (1995). Head position signals used by parietal neurons to encode locations of visual stimuli. *Nature, 375,* 232–235.

Bruce, C. J. (1988). Single neuron activity in the monkey's prefrontal cortex. In P. Rakic & W. Singer (Eds.), *Neurobiology of neocortex* (pp. 297–329). New York: Wiley.

Bruce, C. J., & Goldberg, M. E. (1985). Primate frontal eye field. I. Single neurons discharging before saccades. *Journal of Neurophysiology, 53,* 603–635.

Bushnell, M. C., Goldberg, M. E., & Robinson, D. L. (1981). Behavioral enhancement of visual responses in monkey cerebral cortex. I. Modulation in posterior parietal cortex related to selective visual attention. *Journal of Neurophysiology, 46,* 755–772.

Cavada, C., & Goldman-Rakic, P. S. (1989). Posterior parietal cortex in rhesus monkey: II. Evidence for segregated corticocortical networks linking sensory and limbic areas with the frontal lobe. *The Journal of Comparative Neurology, 287,* 422–445.

Chelazzi, L., Miller, E. K., Duncan, J., & Desimone, R. (1993). A neural basis for visual search in inferior temporal cortex. *Nature, 363,* 345–347.

Chieffi, S., Gentilucci, M., Allport, A., Sasso, E., & Rizzolatti, G. (1993). Study of selective reaching and grasping in a patient with unilateral parietal lesion. *Brain, 116,* 1119–1137.

Colby, C. L., Duhamel, J.-R., & Goldberg, M. E. (1993). Ventral intraparietal area of the macaque: anatomic location and visual response properties. *Journal of Neurophysiology, 69,* 902–914.

Corbetta, M., Miezin, F. M., Dobmeyer, S., Shulman, G. L., & Petersen, S. E. (1990). Attentional modulation of neural processing of shape, color, and velocity in humans. *Science, 248,* 1556–1559.

Corbetta, M., Miezin, F. M., Dobmeyer, S., Shulman, G. L., & Petersen, S. E. (1991). Selective and divided attention during visual discrimination of shape, color and speed: functional anatomy by positron emission tomography. *Journal of Neuroscience, 11,* 2383–2402.

Cowey, A., Small, M., & Ellis, S. (1994). Left visuo-spatial neglect can be worse in far than in near space. *Neuropsychologia, 32,* 1059–1066.

Critchley, M. (1953). *The parietal lobes.* London: Arnold.

De Renzi, E. (1982). *Disorders of space exploration and cognition.* Chichester: Wiley.

De Renzi, E., Gentilini, M., Faglioni, P., & Barbieri, C. (1989). Attentional shifts towards the rightmost stimuli in patients with left visual neglect. *Cortex, 25,* 231–237.

Downing, C. J. (1988). Expectancy and visual-spatial attention: Effects on perceptual quality. *Journal of Experimental Psychology: Human Perception and Performance, 14,* 188–202.

Downing, C. J., & Pinker S. (1985). The spatial structure of visual attention. In M. I. Posner & O. S. M. Marin (Eds.), *Attention and Performance XI* (pp. 171–187). Hillsdale, NJ: Lawrence Erlbaum Associates Inc.

Duncan, J. (1996). Cooperating brain systems in selective perception and action. In T. Inui & J. L. McClelland (Eds.), *Attention and Performance XVI* (pp. 549–579). Cambridge, MA: MIT Press.

Findley, J. M. (1982). Global visual processing for saccadic eye movements. *Vision Research, 22,* 1033–1045.

Fisk, J. D., & Goodale, M. A. (1985). The organization of eye and limb movements during unrestricted reaching to targets in contralateral and ipsilateral visual space. *Experimental Brain Research, 60,* 159–178.

Fogassi, L., Gallese, V., di Pellegrino, G., Fadiga, L., Gentilucci, M., Luppino, G., Matelli, M., Pedotti, A., & Rizzolatti, G. (1992). Space coding by premotor cortex. *Experimental Brain Research, 89,* 686–690.

Fogassi, L., Gallese, V., Fadiga, L., Luppino, G., Matelli, M., & Rizzolatti, G. (1996). Coding of peripersonal space in inferior premotor cortex (Area F4). *Journal of Neurophysiology, 76(1),* 141–157.

Fogassi, L., Gallese, V., Fadiga, L., & Rizzolatti, G. (1996). Space coding in inferior premotor cortex (area F4): Facts and speculations. In F. Laquaniti & P. Viviani (Eds.), *Multi-sensory control of movement* (pp. 99–120). Kluwer Academic Publishers.

French, J. D., & Magoun, H. W. (1952). Effects of cronic lesions in central cephalic brain stem of monkeys. *Archives of Neurology and Psychiatry, 68,* 591.

Gawryszewski, L., Faria, R. B., Thomaz, T. G., Pinheiro, W. M., Rizzolatti, G., & Umiltà, C. (1992). Reorienting visual spatial attention: Is it based on cartesian coordinates? In R. Lent (Ed.), *The visual system from genesis to maturity.* Boston, MA: Birkhauser.

Gentilucci, M., Fogassi, L., Luppino, G., Matelli, M., Camarda, R., & Rizzolatti, G. (1988). Functional organization of inferior area 6 in the macaque monkey: I. Somatotopy and the control of proximal movements. *Experimental Brain Research, 71,* 475–490.

Gentilucci, M., Scandolara, C., Pigarev, I. N., & Rizzolatti, G. (1983). Visual responses in the postarcuate cortex (area 6) of the monkey that are independent of eye position. *Experimental Brain Research, 50,* 464–468.

Godschalk, M., Lemon, R. N., Kuypers, H. G. J. M., & Ronday, H. K. (1984). Cortical afferents and efferents of monkey postarcuate area: an anatomical and electrophysiological study. *Experimental Brain Research, 56,* 410–424.

Goldberg, M. E., & Bushnell, M. C. (1981). Behavioral enhancement of visual responses in monkey cerebral cortex. II. Modulation in frontal eye fields specifically related to saccades. *Journal of Neurophysiology, 46,* 773–787.

Goldberg, M. E., & Segraves, M. A. (1989). The visual and frontal cortices. In R. Wurtz & M. Goldberg (Eds.), *The neurobiology of saccadic eye movements*. Reviews of Oculomotor Research series, Vol. 3. Amsterdam: Elsevier.

Goldberg, M. E., & Wurtz, R. H. (1972). Activity of superior colliculus in behaving monkey: II. The effect of attention on neuronal responses. *Journal of Neurophysiology, 35,* 560–574.

Graziano, M. S. A., & Gross, C. G. (1996). Multiple pathways for processing visual space. In T. Inui & J. L. McClelland (Eds.), *Attention and Performance XVI* (pp. 181–207). Cambridge, MA: MIT Press.

Graziano, M. S. A., Yap, G. S., & Gross, C. G. (1994). Coding of visual space by premotor neurons. *Science, 266,* 1054–1057.

Hawkins, H. L., Hillyard, S. A., Luck, S. J., Mouloua, M., Downing, C. J., & Woodward, D. P. (1990). Visual attention modulates signal detectability. *Journal of Experimental Psychology: Human Perception and Performance, 16,* 802–811.

Hikosaka, O., Miyauchi, S., Takeichi, H., & Shimojo, S. (1996). Multimodal spatial attention visualized by motion illusion. In T. Inui & J. L. McClelland (Eds.), *Attention and Performance XVI* (pp. 237–261). Cambridge, MA: MIT Press.

Hikosaka, O., Sakamoto, M., & Usui, S. (1989a). Functional properties of monkey caudate neurons. I. Activities related to saccadic eye movements. *Journal of Neurophysiology, 61,* 780–798.

Hikosaka, O., Sakamoto, M., & Usui, S. (1989b). Functional properties of monkey caudate neurons. III. Activities related to expectation of target and reward. *Journal of Neurophysiology, 61,* 814–832.

Hikosaka, O., & Wurtz, R. H. (1983a). Visual and oculomotor functions of monkey substantia nigra pars reticulata. I. Relation of visual and auditory responses to saccades. *Journal of Neurophysiology, 49,* 1230–1253.

Hikosaka, O., & Wurtz, R. H. (1983b). Visual and oculomotor functions of monkey substantia nigra pars reticulata. IV. Relation of substantia nigra to superior colliculus. *Journal of Neurophysiology, 49,* 1285–1301.

Hikosaka, O., & Wurtz, R. H. (1989). The basal ganglia. In R. H. Wurtz & M. E. Goldberg (Eds.), *The neurobiology of saccadic eye movement*. Reviews of Oculomotor Research, Vol. 3. Amsterdam: Elsevier.

Hubel, D. H. (1960). Single unit activity in lateral geniculate body and optic tract of unrestrained cats. *Journal of Physiology, 150,* 91–104.

Hughes H. C., & Zimba L. D. (1985). Spatial maps of directed visual attention. *Journal of Experimental Psychology, Human Perception and Performance, 11,* 409–430.

Hyvärinen, J. (1982). Posterior parietal lobe of the primate brain. *Physiological Reviews, 62,* 1060–1129.

Jeannerod, M., Arbib, M. A., Rizzolatti, G., & Sakata, H. (1995). Grasping objects: the cortical mechanisms of visuomotor transformation. *Trends in Neuroscience, 18,* 314–320.

Kennard, M. A. (1939). Alterations in response to visual stimuli following lesions of frontal lobe in monkeys. *Archives of Neurology and Psychiatry, 41,* 1153–1165.

Kinsbourne, M. (1987). Mechanisms of unilateral neglect. In M. Jeannerod (Ed.), *Neurophysiological and neuropsychological aspects of spatial neglect* (pp. 69–86). Amsterdam: North Holland.

Komoda, M. K., Festinger, L., Phillips, L. J., Duckman, R. H., & Young, R. A. (1973). Some observations concerning saccadic eye movements. *Vision Research, 12,* 1009–1020.

Kustov, A. A., & Robinson, D. L. (1996). Shared neural control of attentional shifts and eye movements. *Nature, 384,* 74–77.

LaBerge D., & Brown V. (1989). Theory of attentional operations in shape identification. *Psychological Review, 96,* 101–124.

Ladavas, E., Petronio, A., & Umiltà, C. (1990). The deployment of visual attention in the intact field of hemineglect patients. *Cortex, 26,* 307–317.

Lindsley, D. B., Schreiner, L. H., Knowles, W. B., & Magoun, H. W. (1950). Behavioral and EEG changes following chronic brain stem lesions in the cat. *Electroencephalography and Clinical Neurophysiology, 2,* 483–498.

Maffei, L., Moruzzi, G., & Rizzolatti, G. (1965). Geniculate unit responses to sine-wave photic stimulation during wakefulness and sleep. *Science, 149,* 563–564.

Marshall, J. C., & Halligan, P. W. (1988). Blindsight and insight in visuo-spatial neglect. *Nature, 336,* 766–767.

Matelli, M., Camarda, R., Glickstein, M., & Rizzolatti, G. (1986). Afferent and efferent projections of the inferior area 6 in the macaque monkey. *The Journal of Comparative Neurology, 251,* 281–298.

Mesulam, M. M. (1981). A cortical network for directed attention and unilateral neglect. *Annals of Neurology, 10,* 309–325.

Mohler, C. W., & Wurtz, R. H. (1976). Organization of monkey superior colliculus: Intermediate layer cells discharging before eye movements. *Journal of Neurophysiology, 39,* 722–744.

Moruzzi, G., & Magoun, H. W. (1949). Brain stem reticular formation and activation of the EEG. *Electroencephalography and Clinical Neurophysiology, 1,* 459–473.

Muller, H. J., & Humphreys, G. W. (1991). Luminance-increment detection: Capacity limited or not? *Journal of Experimental Psychology: Human Perception and Performance, 17,* 107–124.

Pandya, D. N., & Kuypers, H. G. J. M. (1969). Cortico-cortical connections in the rhesus monkey. *Brain Research, 13,* 13–36.

Petersen, S. E., Robinson, D. L., & Keys, W. (1985). Pulvinar nuclei of the behaving rhesus monkey: Visual responses and their modulation. *Journal of Neurophysiology, 54,* 867–886.

Petrides, M., & Pandya, D. N. (1984). Projections to the frontal cortex from the posterior parietal region in the rhesus monkey. *The Journal of Comparative Neurology, 228,* 105–116.

Posner, M. I. (1980). Orienting of attention. *Quarterly Journal of Experimental Psychology, 32,* 3–25.

Posner, M. I., & Dehaene, S. (1994). Attentional networks. *Trends in Neurosciences, 17,* 75–79.

Posner, M. I., Petersen, S. E., Fox, P. T., & Reichle, M. E. (1988). Localization of cognitive operations in the human brain. *Science, 240,* 1627–1631.

Prablanc, C., Echallier, J. F., Komilis, E., & Jeannerod, M. (1979). Optimal response of eye and hand motor systems in pointing at a visual target: I. Spatio-temporal characteristics of eye and hand movements and their relationships when varying the amount of visual information. *Biological Cybernetics, 35,* 113–124.

Rapcsak, S. Z., Cimino, C. R., & Heilman, K. M. (1988). Altitudinal neglect. *Neurology, Cleveland, 38,* 277–281.

Reuter-Lorenz, P. A., & Fendrich, R. (1992). Oculomotor readiness and covert orienting: differences between central and peripheral precues. *Perception and Psychophysics, 52,* 336–344.

Riggio, L., & Kirsner, K. (1997). The relationship between central cues and peripheral cues in covert visual orientation. *Perception and Psychophysics, 59*(6), 885–899.

Rizzolatti, G., & Camarda, R. (1987). Neural circuits for spatial attention and unilateral neglect. In M. Jeannerod (Ed.), *Neurophysiological and Neuropsychological Aspects of Spatial Neglect* (pp. 289–313). Amsterdam: North-Holland.

Rizzolatti, G., & Gallese, V. (1988). Mechanisms and theories of spatial neglect. In F. Boller & J. Grafman (Eds.), *Handbook of Neuropsychology* (Vol. 1). Amsterdam: Elsevier.

Rizzolatti, G., Matelli, M., & Pavesi, G. (1983). Deficits in attention and movement following the removal of postarcuate (area 6) and prearcuate (area 8) cortex in macaque monkeys. *Brain, 106,* 655–673.

Rizzolatti, G., Riggio, L., Dascola, I., & Umiltà, C. (1987). Reorienting attention across the horizontal and vertical meridians: evidence in favor of a premotor theory of attention. *Neuropsychologia, 25,* 31–40.

Rizzolatti, G., Riggio, L., & Sheliga, B. M. (1994). Space and selective attention. In C. Umiltà & M. Moscovitch (Eds.), *Attention and Performance XV* (pp. 231–265). Cambridge, MA: MIT Press.

Rizzolatti, G., Scandolara, C., Matelli, M., & Gentilucci, M. (1981). Afferent properties of periarcuate neurons in macaque monkey. II. Visual responses. *Behavioral Brain Research, 2,* 147–163.

Robinson, D. A. (1972). Eye movements evoked by collicular stimulation in the alert monkey. *Vision Researh, 12,* 1795–1808.

Ryle, G. (1949). *The concept of the mind.* Chicago, IL: University of Chicago Press.

Schiller, P. H., & Sandell, J. H. (1983). Interactions between visually and electrically elicited saccades before and after superior colliculus and frontal eye field ablations in the rhesus monkey. *Experimental Brain Research, 49,* 381–392.

Schiller, P. H., True, S. D., & Conway, J. L. (1979). Paired stimulation of the frontal eye fields and the superior colliculus of the rhesus monkey. *Brain Research, 179,* 162–164.

Sheliga, B. M., Riggio, L., & Rizzolatti, G. (1994). Orienting of attention and eye movements. *Experimental Brain Research, 98,* 507–522.

Sheliga, B. M., Riggio, L., & Rizzolatti, G. (1995a). Spatial attention and eye movements. *Experimental Brain Research, 105,* 261–275.

Sheliga, B. M., Riggio, L., Craighero, L., & Rizzolatti, G. (1995b). Spatial attention-determined modifications in saccade trajectories. *Neuroreport, 6,* 585–588.

Shelton, P. A., Bowers, D., & Heilman, K. M. (1990). Peripersonal and personal neglect. *Brain, 113,* 191–205.

Shepherd, M., & Muller, H. J. (1989). Movement versus focusing of visual attention. *Perception and Psychophysics, 46,* 146–154.

Shimojo, S., Tanaka, Y., Hikosaka, O., & Miyauchi, S. (1996). Vision, attention, and action: Inhibition and facilitation in sensory-motor links revealed by the reaction time and the line motion. In T. Inui & J. L. McClelland (Eds.), *Attention and Performance XVI* (pp. 597–631). Cambridge, MA: MIT Press.

Sparks, D. L., Mays, L. E., & Porter, J. D. (1987). Eye movements induced by pontine stimulation: interaction with visually triggered saccades. *Journal of Neurophysiology, 58,* 300–318.

Tassinari, G., Aglioti, S., Chelazzi, L., Marzi, C. A., & Berlucchi, G. (1987). Distribution in the visual field of the costs of voluntarily allocated attention and of the inhibitory after-effects of covert orienting. *Neuropsychologia, 25(1A),* 55–71.

Tipper, S. P., Lortie, C., & Baylis, G. C. (1992). Selective reaching: Evidence for action-centered attention. *Journal of Experimental Psychology: Human Perception and Performance, 18(4),* 891–905.

Umiltà, C., Mucignat, C., Riggio, L., Barbieri, C., & Rizzolatti, G. (1994). Programming shifts of spatial attention. *European Journal of Cognitive Psychology, 6(1),* 23–41.

Umiltà, C., Riggio, L., Dascola, I., & Rizzolatti, G. (1991). Differential effects of central and peripheral cues on the reorienting of spatial attention. *European Journal of Cognitive Psychology, 3,* 247–267.

Ungerleider, L. G., & Mishkin, M. (1982). Two cortical visual systems. In D. J. Ingle, M. A. Goodale, & R. J. W. Mansfield (Eds.), *Analysis of visual behavior* (pp. 549–586). Cambridge, MA: MIT Press.

Wheeless, L. Jr., Boynton, R. E., & Cohen, G. H. (1966). Eye movement responses to step and pulse-step stimuli. *Journal of the Optic Society of America, 56,* 956–960.

Wurtz, R. H., & Mohler, C. W. (1976a). Organization of monkey superior colliculus: Enhanced visual response of superficial layer cells. *Journal of Neurophysiology, 39,* 745–765.

Wurtz, R. H., & Mohler, C. W. (1976b). Enhancement of visual responses in monkey striate cortex and frontal eye fields. *Journal of Neurophysiology, 39,* 766–772.

CHAPTER EIGHT

The modular structure of human visual recognition: Evidence from functional imaging

Nancy Kanwisher
Massachusetts Institute of Technology, Cambridge, MA, USA

This chapter reviews the literature on functional brain imaging of human visual recognition. Distinct extrastriate regions have been identified that appear to be specialized for face perception, visual shape analysis, and perhaps word-reading, suggesting a highly modular structure for visual recognition. The ways are discussed in which functional brain imaging may allow us to transcend mere phrenology to derive important clues about the mental processes underlying high-level vision. In particular, the modular structure of human visual recognition suggests that distinct mechanisms may be involved in the recognition of faces, objects, and words. Furthermore, functional imaging has made experimentally tractable some important hypotheses about modularity itself, and we can now empirically test Fodor's (1983) claims that cortical modules are necessarily innately specified, automatic, and domain-specific.

Le présent chapitre recense la littérature relative à l'exploitation de l'imagerie cérébrale fonctionnelle dans l'étude de la reconnaissance visuelle chez l'humain. Cette technique a conduit à identifier diverses régions extrastriées respectivement spécialisées dans la perception des visages, l'analyse des formes visuelles et, peut-être, la lecture des mots, ce qui suggère que la reconnaissance visuelle repose sur une structure hautement modulaire. Sont examinées les façons selon lesquelles l'imagerie cérébrale fonctionnelle permet de transcender la simple phrénologie et de dégager d'importants indices sur les processus mentaux sous-tendant la vision de haut niveau. Entre autres, la structure modulaire de la reconnaissance visuelle chez l'humain suggère l'intervention de mécanismes particuliers dans la reconnaissance respective des visages, des objets et des mots. De plus, l'imagerie fonctionnelle a ouvert la voie à la vérification expérimentale d'importantes hypothèses sur la modularité elle-même. Ainsi, il est maintenant possible de mettre à l'épreuve les affirmations de Fodor (1983) voulant que, par nécessité, les modules corticaux soient définis de manière innée, de même qu'automatiques et spécifiques à un domaine.

This chapter will discuss functional brain imaging, and what it can tell us about human visual recognition. This is a very young field and only a handful of studies in this area has been reported. I will first review some of this past work, and then try to show why I think it is such a promising area for future research.

First, we need to clarify what is meant by visual recognition, as the phrase is used in many different ways. Visual recognition is a process in which the retinal image of the object is first transformed through a series of computations into a more abstract representation and then matched to one of the thousands of visual representations of objects stored in memory. After this visual match is made, the meaning and the name of the object can be retrieved. Visual recognition, as I will use the term here, refers to everything up to and including the visual matching process, but does not include access to the meaning and name of the object.

We humans are pretty spectacular at visual recognition. We can recognize most of the items in a random sequence of objects presented as fast as 8 items per second (Potter, 1975, 1976), and recent evoked potential data suggests that our visual systems have already completed the key steps of visual recognition within about 155ms of the onset of each object (DiGirolamo & Kanwisher, 1995). Current machine vision algorithms lag far behind. What are the processes that go on in our heads that enable us to recognize objects so quickly?

Of course cognitive psychologists have been working on this problem for decades, using simple behavioral measures like reaction time and accuracy, and they have made a great deal of progress. But understanding visual recognition is a hard problem, so we should take clues from wherever we can find them. One obvious place to look is the functional neuroanatomy of the brain.

The main reason to be hopeful that we might learn something about vision from studying the brain is *modularity*—the idea that the mind is made up of a collection of semi-independent processors, or modules, that carry out different operations. In fact, Fodor (1983) went as far as to say that "it is the condition of a successful science that nature should have joints to carve it at ... [and] ... modules satisfy this condition". So if visual recognition is modularly organized, that is good news for our prospects of coming to understand it some day. But the idea of modularity also encompasses a set of theoretically interesting claims. Fodor argues that modular components of the mind are localized to a particular part of the brain, are genetically determined, run automatically on their inputs, and that each one processes a particular kind of information (i.e. modules are "domain-specific").

Thus one sensible research strategy that might provide help in understanding a complex process like visual recognition is to start by trying to find out what its functional components are, and one strategy for doing this is to look at the functional organization of the brain. Of course this is not a new idea.

Neuropsychologists have been finding functional components of high-level vision for a long time by studying patients with focal brain damage. This is a very powerful technique and I do not think functional imaging can ever replace it. But imaging can *complement* patient studies by providing better isolation and localization of specific functions, and by doing all this in large numbers of normal brains. And with functional imaging, we do not have to wait for "experiments of nature", and an arbitrarily large number of subjects can be studied.

In the last few years functional imaging has had some stunning successes mapping out the early stages of the human visual pathway. In a recent review article, Tootell, Dale, Sereno, and Malach (1996) show the 10 different visual areas that have already been mapped out in human visual cortex; most of this work was done in just the last three years. Dale and others have devised techniques to mathematically unfold the brain into a cortical sheet, in which all of these functional areas can be shown on a "flat map" of cortex (Sereno et al., 1995). The question for those of us who care about higher-level vision is whether this division into discrete functional regions found in "early" visual cortex will also be found at higher levels. I will try to argue that although there is not yet a great deal of data on this question, there is definitely room for optimism.

"WHAT" AND "WHERE" PATHWAYS IN HUMAN CORTEX

Two recent experiments used PET to find evidence that the distinction between what Mishkin and Ungerleider called the "what" and "where" pathways in macaques also characterizes human visual cortex. The first is a study by Haxby et al. (1991, 1994). They compared the areas that were activated when subjects determined which of two faces matched a third face with the areas activated when subjects carried out a location-matching task on the same stimuli. Haxby et al. found a large ventral area in the occipitotemporal region that was more strongly activated in the face-matching task than the location-matching task, and an occipitoparietal region that was more active during the location-matching than the face-matching task. This result confirms that the functional division between dorsal and ventral pathways seen in macaques is also found in human visual cortex.

However, Haxby et al. used only faces in their study. Would the same division be found for an analogous task if objects instead of faces were presented? Köhler, Kapur, Moscovitch, Winocur, and Houle (1995) used a similar design to ask whether the ventral pathway in humans is also involved in the visual recognition of objects. They showed subjects pairs of two sequentially presented displays, each containing three objects. Subjects were asked to judge in one condition whether the objects in the two displays occupied the same locations, and in another condition whether the same three objects were present (independent of location). Areas that were significantly more active in the identity task than the location task included the inferior temporal cortex in the region of the fusiform gyrus in the left hemisphere, extending posteriorly into the lingual gyrus, and in the ventral occipital cortex of the right hemisphere in the region of the fusiform gyrus—suggesting that these areas are involved not only in face recognition (as Haxby et al. had shown) but also in visual object recognition.

It is also interesting to note that there was a greater activation in the left hemisphere for objects in the Köhler et al. study, but in the right hemisphere for faces in the Haxby et al. study. This suggests that there might be some differentiation between the areas involved in face and object recognition. Next I will describe several studies that focus in a more fine-grained way on the division of labor within the ventral pathway.

I will start with a study of visual word recognition reported by Petersen, Fox, Snyder, and Raichle in 1990. Its design is elegant and simple, and this study has become something of a classic. In this experiment subjects simply looked at a fixation cross while various words and word-like stimuli were presented just below it. The key manipulation was the exact nature of the stimuli. In different scans subjects viewed sequences of either real English words such as "HOUSE", pseudowords such as "TWEAL", consonant strings such as "NLPFZ", or what Petersen et al. called "false fonts": strings of unfamiliar letter-like stimuli. The nice thing about these stimuli is that they are all extremely similar in terms of their component visual features, yet they are very different in terms of the higher-level processes that can be carried out on them. Petersen et al. compared the activation that resulted from each of these four conditions with the activation that resulted from just looking at a fixation point alone. They found that a left medial extrastriate area showed a significantly greater activation for words and pseudowords compared to fixation, but not for consonant strings and false fonts compared to fixation.

Petersen et al. argued that because this area responded similarly to real words like HOUSE and pseudowords like TWEAL, it cannot be involved in processing the meanings of words, and it doesn't seem to be a visual lexicon either. Instead, they argued that this area is a "visual word form area"—a part of the brain that is involved in visual word recognition and that apparently holds implicit knowledge of English orthography. This is a very important result, if true, because the mental process that is apparently isolated here is so specific. However, the results can only be taken as suggestive for the moment, because the key statistical comparison—between the words and/or pseudowords versus the consonant strings and/or false fonts—was not reported in the paper. The fact that the first two conditions differ significantly from fixation and the latter two do not does not imply that the two sets of conditions differ significantly from each other. (This is a common error in imaging studies.) However, several researchers are now tackling this problem, so a clear verdict on this question will hopefully emerge soon.

CORTICAL REGIONS INVOLVED IN THE ANALYSIS OF VISUAL SHAPE

Visual word recognition is a very different kind of problem from object recognition, so it is reasonable to hypothesize that different brain areas might be involved. I will describe three experiments that look for a key component of object recognition: the analysis of visual object shape. The first of these is a PET study by Schacter et al. (1995). Their study had a number of different conditions, but the ones that bear directly on the present issue involved a comparison of the responses to line drawings depicting three-dimensionally possible versus impossible novel objects. In this study subjects either performed a task judging whether the stimuli were possible or impossible, or they simply passively viewed a sequence of the stimuli. This task manipulation was crossed with a stimulus manipulation: The stimuli were segregated such that for a given scan all the objects were possible, or they were all impossible. This meant that when subjects were doing the possible-impossible task, the correct response was the same for every item in a scan. However, the stimuli were presented briefly, making the task difficult, and subjects reportedly did not notice.

A region in the ventral right hemisphere was active when subjects caried out the object-decision task on possible (but not impossible) objects. Schacter et al. concluded that these inferotemporal and fusiform regions are specifically involved in the computation of global representations of coherent three-dimensional shapes —representations that could be constructed for the possible objects, but not for the impossible objects. Thus, this study implicates the inferotemporal and fusiform gyri in visual shape analysis. However, the differences between the possible and impossible objects are quite subtle, and the possible-impossible task may therefore recruit processes different from those that go on in "normal" object recognition. The next study to be described was an effort to isolate brain areas involved in visual shape analysis for stimuli whose three-dimensional shape is more typical of the kinds of objects we recognize every day.

My collaborators and I (Kanwisher, Woods, Iacoboni & Mazziotta, 1997) used a variant of the design used by Petersen et al. (1990) with words. We reasoned that when line drawings are presented at the fovea and subjects have no other task, then object recognition is automatic. For example, suppose I were to ask you to look at a figure about to be presented on a screen, and analyze its visual features, but asked you *not* to recognize it. If I would then present a picture of an elephant, you could not help recognizing it. Object recognition is highly automatic, at least for foveally presented objects when subjects do not have a demanding simultaneous task. Thus, if you want to differentially engage different component operations of object recognition you cannot do it by just telling the subjects which of those operations you want them to carry out in each condition. But you can do it by changing the stimuli.

In our experiment, we presented subjects in one condition with line drawings of familiar objects. When subjects look at a sequence of these stimuli, all of the major components of object recognition should occur—visual features are extracted, the shape of the object is discerned, and that shape description is successfully matched to a particular representation in memory. However, a different set of mental processes would be expected to occur when subjects look at our second stimulus set, which was composed of line drawings of unfamiliar three-dimensional objects. For these novel objects, one can extract the features, and one can come up with a clear interpretation of the three-dimensional shape of each object, but one cannot successfully match it to a particular object stored in memory. So matching to memory occurs normally for the familiar but not the novel objects. Finally, the stimuli in the third condition were scrambled line drawings that were created by recombining the components of the familiar-object stimuli in a way that preserved luminance, contour length, and many other visual features. For these stimuli, feature extraction should proceed in a similar fashion, but the stimuli do not support any clear interpretation as a coherent three-dimensional shape. So the idea of this experiment was that any brain areas involved in the analysis of visual shape should be more active when the familiar and novel objects are presented than when the scrambled drawings were presented.

We presented subjects with sequences of images of one kind in each scan, and investigated which parts of the brain were more active in the familiar and novel conditions (i.e. for stimuli that depict shapes) than for the scrambled stimuli, which do not depict clear three-dimensional shapes. We found that a lateral and inferior extrastriate area straddling the anterior occipital sulcus was more active bilaterally when subjects passively viewed familiar or novel compared to scrambled stimuli. Because this area was at least as strongly activated by novel as by familiar objects, the activation is unlikely to reflect processes associated with memory-matching, naming, or accessing semantic information. We therefore proposed that it is involved in the bottom-up construction of shape descriptions from simple visual features.

Although I think we did a reasonable job with this study controlling for everything we could, I am also the first to admit that any comparison of only two or three stimuli like these will always be open to several interpretations. For example, one alternative account of our PET study is that our activation reflects differences in attentional recruitment or interest between the different classes of stimuli. I think the only way around this problem is to run many different converging operations to zero in on the computations that are being carried out in a given area. However, there is a problem. All the studies I have discussed so far were done with PET. One cannot just run more tests on the same subjects because of the radiation dose involved. One can run the new tests on different subjects, but this raises the second problem. PET data are rarely strong enough to reveal significant differences within a subject; all of the studies discussed so far required averaging data over many subjects. However, different people's brains are as physically different from each other as their faces are. Averaging data across subjects is like superimposing photographs of several different faces on top of each other: Despite the best efforts at alignment, one person's mouth is bound to land on another person's nose, and in general a great deal of blurring can result. The same thing happens when PET data are averaged across subjects.

But with the advent of fMRI, we do not have either of these problems. We can usually obtain significant differences in the data from a single subject, so we do not need to average across subjects. Also, we can keep running that same subject on many different converging tests, one by one ruling out alternative accounts of our activation. This means that with fMRI we are in a much better position to isolate, identify, and anatomically map individual mental processes.

One study that used fMRI to investigate visual object recognition was reported recently by Malach et al. (1995); their results converge well with our PET study of shape analysis. They presented subjects with a variety of different kinds of photographs of familiar objects, faces, and unfamiliar three-dimensional objects such as Henry Moore sculptures; all of these stimuli activated a common area in the lateral occipital lobe (area LO) compared to random visual textures. Area LO is lateral to (but near) the regions activated in our PET study of line drawings, and also to the regions activated in the Schacter et al. study. Together these three studies converge nicely in implicating bilateral inferolateral cortex in visual shape analysis. Thus, whereas Petersen et al. implicated a more medial region in the left hemisphere in visual word recognition, we now have evidence that visual shape analysis is carried out in a bilateral region of cortex that extends out onto the lateral surface of the brain.

CORTICAL AREAS INVOLVED IN FACE PERCEPTION

What about faces? Where are they processed with respect to cortical regions specialized for the analysis of words and object shape? Several early PET studies implicated regions of the ventral pathway in face recognition—including the Haxby et al. study mentioned earlier and a study by Sergent, Ohta, and MacDonald (1992). Puce, Allison, Asgari, Gore, and McCarthy (1995) reported an fMRI study showing bilateral activations in the fusiform gyrus when subjects looked at intact versus scrambled faces. Clarke et al. (1996) also reported a corroboration with fMRI of the Haxby et al. (1994) face-matching results, this time showing the loci of activations in individual subjects.

Puce et al. (1996) advanced the story yet further by reporting a direct comparison of the brain regions active when subjects viewed faces compared to letter

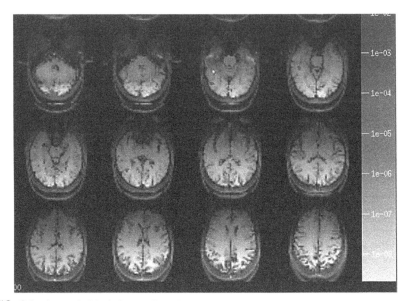

FIG. 8.1   Anatomical brain images for a single subject are shown in grey. Our 12 6mm near-axial slices covered the entire occipital and most of the temporal lobe, starting from the most inferior slice (upper left) showing mostly cerebellum. The left hemisphere is shown on the right in each slice and vice versa. The color-coded overlay shows the significance of the statistical test of whether the activity in each voxel was greater while the subject was viewing faces than while viewing objects.

strings. Using fMRI, they found a region in the fusiform gyrus that was more active during face viewing than during letter-string viewing. They also found a more superior and lateral region to be more active for faces than letter strings. Finally, they found that letter strings activated a primarily left-hemisphere region near but more lateral to the region activated in the Petersen et al. study.

The study by Puce et al. is well designed and the results are clear. But faces and letter strings differ from each other in a large number of different visual features. In any study, the interpretation of any single comparison is bound to be ambiguous, and the only way to really pinpoint the function of a given area is to see how that same area responds to many different tests. Such converging tests should make it possible to arrive at a reasonably precise characterization of the functions of a particular area. This is after all what the physiologists who study face cells have been doing for decades: They compare the response of a given cell to a large number of different stimuli, and argue for selectivity of that cell for faces only if it responds more to faces than to all of these different control stimuli. The kind of approach that functional imagers will have to adopt if they want to provide a compelling argument for functional specificity.

In collaboration with Josh McDermott and Marvin Chun I have been working on how to do functional imaging experiments in a way that allows us to make more precise claims about the functions we are localizing (Kanwisher, Chun, & McDermott, 1996). The main results of one such series of studies of face perception are described next.

We scanned 15 subjects in the MRI scanner at the MGH-NMR Center in Charlestown, MA, while they passively viewed alternating sequences of grey-scale photographs of faces and objects. Each scan lasted five and a half minutes, and included seven 20-second epochs of fixation, and six 30-second epochs during which photographs were presented (at a rate of 1.5 photos/second). Alternating stimulus epochs contained faces or assorted common objects. We wanted to know whether there are regions in the subjects' brains that would respond significantly more strongly during the epochs when the subjects were viewing the faces than during the object epochs, and vice versa. We used twelve near-axial 6mm thick slices covering the entire occipital lobe and the posterior two-thirds of the temporal lobe. Statistics were run separately on each voxel (three-dimensional pixel), testing whether the MR signal in that voxel was significantly higher during face viewing than during object viewing.

We found a region in the fusiform gyrus in 12 out of 15 subjects that responded significantly more strongly during passive viewing of face than object stimuli. The data from one subject are shown in Fig. 8.1, revealing a small region in the fusiform gyrus that responded significantly more strongly to face than object stimuli. Of course we wanted to argue that this area is selectively involved in face perception. But simply showing that the area responds more to faces than objects is not sufficient; it leaves open numerous alternative accounts. The activation for faces that we and others have observed might reflect nothing about faces, but instead (1) the homogeneity of the face set compared to the object set, (2) a response to anything animate or human, (3) a greater engagement of visual attention by faces than other stimuli, or (4) subordinate-level categorization of any class of stimuli. Before we could argue for the selectivity of our area for faces we had to reject all of these alternatives. We tackled this problem as follows.

First we found a face region of interest (ROI) in each of five subjects as before with our old faces versus objects comparison. Then we looked in this same ROI in each subject during several new tests. (There is an added advantage of our technique of running converging tests within specific ROIs defined in advance for each subject: We have no statistical problem of multiple comparisons, because we're doing only one comparison in each test. Thus, no Bonferroni-type corrections are necessary.) To see if the face activation was an artifact of luminance confounds between our face and object set, we created a new set of stimuli by converting all the darker grey-levels in the face photos to black, and all the lighter grey-levels to white to produce two-tone faces (see Fig. 8.3b). Once thresholded, we then scrambled the faces simply by moving the parts around to produce unrecognizable but luminance-matched images. If we still get a specific activation in each subject's face ROI in this intact versus scrambled faces comparison it can not be due to differences in luminance. In fact, the face ROIs in each of five subjects responded more strongly during passive viewing of intact two-tone faces than scrambled versions of the same faces, ruling out luminance differences as an account of the face activation.

Next, what if the face ROI simply responds whenever subjects look at many different exemplars of *any* category of object? To test this we looked again in each subject's face ROI during a new test in which subjects saw alternating sequences of faces and houses. In this test, the average percent signal increase (from the fixation baseline) across the five subjects' face ROIs was over six times greater for passive viewing of faces than for passive viewing of houses, indicating a high degree of stimulus selectivity and demonstrating that the face ROI does not simply respond whenever any set of different exemplars of the same category are presented.

These results allowed us to rule out two accounts of the face activation. However, other alternatives remain to be tested. Perhaps the "face" area responds more generally to any animate or any human forms. To test this idea we asked whether the face ROIs in each of five new subjects would respond to a sequence of three-quarter-view faces with hair concealed, compared to a sequence of different people's hands all in roughly the same position. Indeed, the face ROIs responded more strongly to faces than hands in the passive-viewing condition, ruling out the idea that this area responds to anything animate or human.

Gauthier et al. (1996) have argued that the "face" area is not really a face area, but rather an area that responds whenever subjects must do subordinate-level categorization—that is, distinguish between different exemplars of the same basic visual category. Maybe subjects do this automatically when they look at faces, but they just don't bother to when they look at houses or hands. So in the next test we presented the same faces versus hands stimuli, but we forced subjects to discriminate between the different exemplars by asking them to press a button whenever they saw two consecutive images that were the same. A final alternative account of the face activation is that faces may just recruit attention more automatically than other kinds of stimuli. But the repetition detection task is at least as hard for the hand stimuli as for the faces, so in this case we would expect attention to be at least as strongly engaged during the hands task as the faces task. So if the face ROI responds more strongly for faces than hands in the repetition detection task, then the activation cannot reflect either subordinate-level categorization or general visual attentional mechanisms. The data showed that the face ROIs in all five subjects responded more strongly to faces than hands in the repetition detection task, even though the task is at least as hard for the hands as it is for the faces. So activation in this area does not reflect either general visual effort, or subordinate-level classification of any visual stimuli.

In sum, we can now reject each of the alternative accounts of the face activation raised earlier, to conclude that the fusiform area investigated here is *selectively* involved in face perception.

CONCLUSIONS: BEYOND "MERE" PHRENOLOGY

I have discussed a number of imaging studies that collectively suggest that visual recognition may be composed of a set of separate modular processes localized in different regions of the ventral pathway. Figure 8.2 shows the location of these regions on a ventral view of the brain (superimposed on a drawing adapted from Allison et al., 1994). Although this is a humble beginning, I think that because fMRI allows us to carry out an unlimited number of tests within subjects, we may be able to go far with this project of exploring the modular structure of visual recognition.

I would like to end by considering where we will be if this research program is successful. If we in fact discover a number of new areas in the ventral pathway over the next few years, then what? Are we just doing high-tech phrenology? And if so, are we learning any more than Gall did (Gall & Spurzheim, 1809) with his much maligned faculties of "amativeness" and "veneration"?

Of course, one important difference between the current imaging work and Gall's is that the modules that we are now discovering with fMRI might actually exist. But more importantly, these modules are relevant to cognitive theories about how visual recognition proceeds. My own fMRI data suggest, for example, that there are patches of cortex that are specialized for the perception of faces. This fact further suggests that face recognition may involve algorithms fundamentally different from the recognition of other kinds of visual stimuli. So discovering new modules, new pieces of the puzzle of vision, is not just a project for detail-oriented anatomists, but something that should be of deep interest to cognitive psychologists.

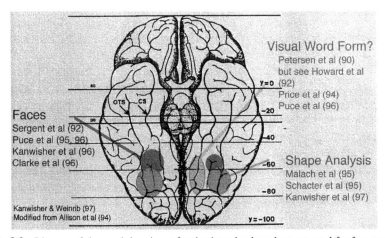

FIG. 8.2   Diagram of the rough locations of activations that have been reported for face perception, visual word reading, and visual shape analysis, overlayed on a ventral view of a brain adapted from Allison et al. (1994).

But I think we can do even better than that. Several of the notions that Fodor posited about the origins and behavior of modules can progress from the status of mere armchair speculations to become experimentally tractable research questions. In closing I will mention three of them.

Innateness. Fodor argued that modules are genetically determined. In the case of face modules, this idea is plausible enough. Face perception has been a critical survival skill throughout much of our evolutionary past, and it is certainly possible that our genes now have specific blueprints for the construction of face modules. However, it is also possible that it is the sheer importance to us and the amount of experience we have with face perception, combined with principles of neural self-organization, that leads to a face module.

One way to approach this question is to ask whether visual expertise in a novel domain with no evolutionary precedent is sufficient to produce a new visual module specialized for this domain. This is a basic and fundamentally important question that we have so far very little data on. Yet there are straightforward fMRI experiments that might answer it. For example, if Petersen et al.'s "visual word form area' is corroborated by future evidence, this would constitute a strong candidate for a module that could not be specified genetically, because people have not been reading long enough for special-purpose hardware for reading to have evolved. In collaboration with Sheng He, Oren Weinrib, and Ken Kwong, I am now approaching this question by scanning students before and after a year's intensive study of Chinese to see if a region of cortex will respond specifically to Chinese characters after, but not before, the acquisition of visual expertise in this domain.

Domain-specificity. A second question is whether modules differ in the classes of stimuli they process, or instead in the general class of computations they carry out. For example, does the fusiform face area really process only faces, and does the "visual word form area" really process only words? Farah (1995) has proposed the alternative hypothesis that the underlying dissociation is not between the classes of stimuli these modules process, but the kinds of computations they carry out. One strong test of this hypothesis will be to ask whether we can activate the "face" area with nonface stimuli (perhaps by inducing a "holistic" processing strategy), or fail to activate the face area when faces are present (perhaps by encouraging a part-based processing strategy). Thus, the question of whether cortical modules are domain specific or whether they instead embody domain-general processes may also become experimentally tractable with brain imaging techniques.

Automaticity. Fodor further speculated that modules function in a mandatory or automatic fashion whenever their relevant inputs are present. With fMRI this idea becomes testable. Ewa Wojciulik, Jon Driver, and I recently ran an

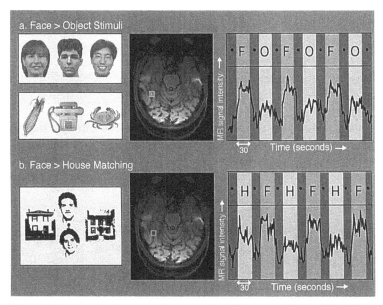

FIG. 8.3   Preliminary results from experiments run in collaboration with Ewa Wojciulik and Jon Driver. (a) Face regions of interest (ROIs) were defined separately for each of three subjects using the face versus object scans as described previously (and shown in Fig. 8.1). The resulting brain slice with statistical overlay for Subject 1 is shown in the center column, and the time course of signal intensity averaged over the three subjects' ROIs is shown at the right. Epochs in which face stimuli were presented are labeled with Fs and epochs in which objects were presented are labeled with Os. (b, left) Sample stimulus used in the attentional test. Retinal stimulation was identical in the two conditions, so any difference between them could only result from effects of covert attention. (b, center) Brain slice showing that voxels in the predefined ROI for Subject 1 also produced a significantly higher MR signal during face matching than house matching; the same was found for the other two subjects. (b, right) The time course of signal intensity averaged across the three subjects' ROI-averages, showing higher MR signal during face-matching epochs (F) than house-matching epochs (H). The stimulus manipulation (a) produced an average 1.2% signal change between face and object epochs, whereas the task manipulation (b) produced an average 0.6% signal change between face- and house-matching epochs.

experiment that shows that face modules do *not* run in a completely automatic way independent of the task the subject is carrying out, but are rather subject to attentional control. In this experiment the retinal stimulation was held constant and only the task varied. The subjects viewed a sequence of brief displays, each containing two houses and two faces (Fig. 8.3b). Subjects fixated on the center dot, and in alternating epochs pressed a button when they detected a match between (1) the faces, or (2) the houses. The face ROI for each of the three subjects was first located on the basis of that subject's faces versus objects comparison as before (Fig. 8.3a). In each subject's face ROI, face matching produced a significantly higher signal intensity than did house matching (Fig. 8.3b). Because the displays were identical in the two tasks and the display timing precluded eye movements, this result demonstrates that face-specific processing can be modulated by covert attention. Similar findings by O'Craven and Savoy (1995) and Corbetta, Miezin, Dobmeyer, Shulman, and Petersen (1990) show that processing in the visual motion area MT is also modulated by covert attention, and collectively these results show that cortical modules do not process their input in a completely mandatory fashion independent of the subject's volition.

In sum, functional imaging can provide valuable insights not just about functional neuroanatomy, but also about cognition. In the case of visual recognition, functional imaging is a powerful technique for discovering the functional components of this complex process. More generally, a number of fundamentally important questions about modularity, once restricted to the domain of armchair speculation, can now be tackled experimentally.

REFERENCES

Allison, T., Ginter, H., McCarthy, G., Nobre, A. C., Puce, A., Luby, M., & Spencer, D. D. (1994). Face recognition in human extrastriate cortex. *Journal of Neurophysiology, 71*, 821–825.

Clarke, V. P., Keil, K., Maisog, J. M., Courtney, S., Ungerleider, S., & Haxby, J. V. (1996). Functional magnetic resonance imaging of human visual cortex during face matching: A comparison with positron emission tomography. *Neuroimage, 4*, 1–15.

Corbetta, M., Miezin, F. M., Dobmeyer, S., Shulman, G. L., & Petersen, S. E. (1990). Attentional modulation of neural processing of shape, color, and velocity in humans. *Science, 248*, 1556–1559.

DiGirolamo, G., & Kanwisher, N. (1995). Accessing stored representations begins within 155ms in object recognition. Paper presented at the Meeting of Psychonomics Society, November 1995.

Farah, M. (1995). Dissociable systems for visual recognition: A cognitive neuropsychology approach. In S. M. Kosslyn & D. S. Osherson (Eds.), *Visual cognition*. Cambridge, MA: MIT Press.

Fodor, J. (1983) *Modularity of Mind*. Cambridge, MA: MIT Press.

Gall, F., & Spurzheim, G. (1809). Research on the nervous system in general and on the brain in particular. [Reprinted in K. Pribram (Ed.) (1969). *Brain and behavior. Vol. 1. Mood states and mind*. Harmondsworth, UK: Penguin Books.]

Gauthier, I., Behrmann, M., Tarr, M. J., Anderson, A. W., Gore, J., & McClelland, J. L. (1996). Subordinate-level categorization in human inferior temporal cortex: Converging evidence from neuropsychology and brain imaging. *Society for Neuroscience Abstracts, 10*, 11.

Haxby, J. V., Grady, C. L., Horwitz, B., Ungerleider, L. G., Mishkin, M., Carson, R. E., Herscovitch, P., Schapiro, M. B., & Rapoport, S. I. (1991). Dissociation of spatial and object visual processing pathways in human extrastriate cortex. *Proceedings of the National Academy of Sciences, USA, 88*, 1621–1625.

Haxby, J. V., Horwitz, B., Ungerleider, L. G., Maisog, J. M., Pietrini, P., & Grady, C. L. (1994). The functional organization of human extrastriate cortex: A PET-rCBF study of selective attention to faces and locations. *Journal of Neuroscience, 14*, 6336–6353.

Kanwisher, N., Chun, M. M., & McDermott, J. (1996). Functional imaging of human visual recognition. *Cognitive Brain Research, 5*, 55–67.

Kanwisher, N., Woods, R., Iacoboni, M., & Mazziotta, J. (1997). A locus in human extrastriate cortex for visual shape analysis. *Journal of Cognitive Neuroscience, 9*, 133–142.

Köhler, S., Kapur, S., Moscovitch, M., Winocur, G., & Houle, S. (1995). Dissociation of pathways for object and spatial vision: A PET study on humans. *Neuroreport, 6*, 1865–1868.

Malach, R., Reppas, J. B., Benson, R. B., Kwong, K. K., Jiang, H., Kennedy, W. A., Ledden, P. J., Brady, T. J., Rosen, B. R., & Tootell, R. B. H. (1995). Object-related activity revealed by functional magnetic resonance imaging in human occipital cortex. *Proceedings of the National Academy of Sciences, USA, 92*, 8135–8138.

O'Craven, K. M., & Savoy, R. L. (1995). Attentional modulation of activation in human MT shown with functional magnetic resonance imaging (fMRI). *Investigative Ophthalmology and Visual Science, 36*, S856.

Petersen, S. E., Fox, P. T., Snyder, A. Z., & Raichle, M. E. (1990). Activation of extrastriate and frontal cortical areas by visual words and word-like stimuli. *Science, 249*, 1041–1044.

Potter, M. C. (1975). Meaning in visual search. *Science, 187*, 965–966.

Potter, M. C. (1976). Short-term conceptual memory for pictures. *Journal of Experimental Psychology: Human Learning and Memory, 2*, 509–522.

Puce, A., Allison, T., Asgari, M., Gore, J. C., & McCarthy, G. (1996). Differential sensitivity of human visual cortex to faces, letterstrings, and textures: A functional magnetic resonance imaging study. *Journal of Neuroscience, 16*, 5205–5215.

Puce, A., Allison, T., Gore, J. C., & McCarthy, G. (1995). Face-sensitive regions in human extrastriate cortex studied by functional MRI. *Journal of Neurophysiology, 74*, 1192–1199.

Schacter, D. L., Reiman, E., Uecker, A., Polster, M. R., Yun, L. S., & Cooper, L. A. (1995). Brain regions associated with retrieval of structurally coherent visual information. *Nature, 376*, 587–590.

Sereno, M. I., Dale, A. M., Reppas, J. B., Kwong, K. K., Belliveau, J., Brady, T. J., Rosen, B. R., & Tootell, R. B. H. (1995). Borders of multiple visual areas in humans revealed by functional magnetic resonance imaging. *Science, 268*, 889–893.

Sergent, J., Ohta, S., & MacDonald, B. (1992). Functional neuroanatomy of face and object processing: a positron emission tomography study. *Brain, 115*, 15–36.

Tootell, R. B. H., Dale, A. M., Sereno, M. I., & Malach, R. (1996). New images from human visual cortex. *Trends in Neurosciences, 19*, 481–489.

CHAPTER NINE

Reciprocal relations between psychology and neuroscience

Mark R. Rosenzweig
University of California, Berkeley, California, USA

Psychology and neuroscience have influenced each other productively for many years, and the pace of interaction is increasing. A major theme in both fields is plasticity of behavior and brain, fostered by Canadian psychologist Donald Hebb, who showed how complex cognitive behavior could be mediated by plastic neural circuits (*The organization of behavior*, 1949).

Some major questions considered are:

What has neuroscience contributed to psychology?

What has psychology contributed to neuroscience?

Is neuroscience draining students away from psychology?

Is biological psychology disappearing into neuroscience?

Each field contributes to the other in four main ways: (1) by devising techniques useful in both fields; (2) by offering models useful in both; (3) by helping to test hypotheses in the other field; (4) members of each field participate in organizations and publications of the other. Examples are given of each kind of contribution. Newer techniques such as noninvasive brain imaging, coupled with appropriate behavioral tests, are helping define the roles of brain regions in perception, learning, language, and emotion. Some international comparisons of research and institutions are made. Prospects for the future are surveyed.

La psychologie et la neuroscience se sont influencées réciproquement et positivement depuis nombre d'années, et ce phénomène s'accentue. Un des thèmes principaux dans les deux domaines est la plasticité du comportement et du cerveau, thème développé par le psychologue canadien Donald Hebb qui a démontré dans son livre, "The organization of behavior" (1949), comment un comportement cognitif complexe peut être produit par des circuits neuronaux plastiques.

Certaines questions importantes à considérer sont les suivantes:

Qu'est-ce que la neuroscience a contribué à la psychologie?

Qu'est-ce que la psychologie a contribué à la neuroscience?

Est-ce que la neuroscience draine des étudiants de la psychologie?

Est-ce que la psychologie biologique (psychophysiologie) est en voie de s'assimiler à la neuroscience?

Chaque champ contribue à l'autre de quatre manières différentes: (1) En inventant des techniques susceptibles d'être utilisées dans les deux disciplines. (2) En présentant des modèles utiles pour les deux disciplines. (3) En aidant à vérifier des hypothèses de l'autre discipline. (4) En favorisant la participation dans les organismes et les publications de l'autre. Des exemples sont donnés pour chaque type de contribution.

De nouvelles techniques, telle l'imagerie cérébrale non invasive, accompagnées de tests appropriés de comportement aident à définir le rôle que jouent les différentes régions du cerveaux dans la perception, l'apprentissage, le langage et l'émotion. Plusieurs comparaisons de recherche et d'institutions internationales sont effectuées. Certaines prévisions pour l'avenir sont examinées.

INTRODUCTION

Biological psychology in relation to psychology and neuroscience

Our topic is the reciprocal relations between psychology and neuroscience, and the area of research and application that spans the two disciplines. In many countries, this area is a major field of instruction and research. As a bridging area, it is sometimes located principally in psychology and sometimes principally in biology. For example, a textbook I co-authored, *Physiological psychology* (Rosenzweig & Leiman, 1989), was translated into French in Montreal and published as *Psychophysiologie* (Rosenzweig & Leiman, 1991), that is, a kind of physiology. In other Latin-language countries, however, such as the Spanish-speaking countries and Italy, the translations are entitled *Psicologia Fisiologica*, keeping the area within psychology. At the Université de Paris V, I gave a course in this field in the Faculty of Biology; most of the students in the course, however, were from the Faculty of Psychology.

In Canada, biological psychology is an integral part of psychology. In the chapter on "Psychology in Canada" in the 1996 *Annual Review of Psychology* (Adair, Paivio, & Ritchie, 1996), the section on "Research contributions" starts with a discussion of "Neuropsychology and neuroscience", and this is the largest part of the section. It begins as follows: "Because of the influence of Donald Hebb at McGill University, Canadian psychologists have been leading developers of neuropsychology, behavioral neuroscience, cognitive neuroscience, and (more generally) biopsychology, areas that were traditionally included under physiological psychology" (p. 349). The account goes on to describe several important contributions of Canadian psychologists to this field and notes Canadian textbooks of biopsychology and neuropsychology.

At the 1996 Montreal International Congress of Psychology, however, the topic category list for papers did not include the terms "Physiological psychology," "Biopsychology", or "Biological psychology." The category list did include

"Neuroscience", and one of the topics under this heading was "Psychophysiology". About three times as many participants chose to classify their papers as Psychophysiology as chose Neuroscience. Whereas participants from the United States favored Neuroscience, Canadians were about equally divided between the two terms, and most participants from the rest of the world chose Psychophysiology.

In China, physiological psychology has been a central part of psychology since the 1920s, and this was reinforced when Chinese psychology came under Pavlovian theory in 1949. In a review chapter on psychology in China, Zhong-Ming Wang (1993, p. 94) notes that when psychology became active again in China in the late 1970s, "both experimental and physiological psychologists took the lead in research ... studies of brain-chemistry and brain functions are popular in physiological psychology ... Many physiological psychologists are involved in areas such as the neurological and neurochemical mechanisms of memory and learning, electrophysiology, and pathology in emotion and sleep." One of the 10 Committees (or Divisions) of the Chinese Psychological Society is the Committee of Physiological Psychology, just as one of the Divisions of the American Psychological Association is Division 6, the Division of Physiological and Comparative Psychology.

In Australia, a report prepared by a working group for the National Committee of Psychology of the Australian Academy of Science (Australian Research Council Discipline Research Strategies, 1996) states that the broad area of neuroscience and physiological psychology, "many parts of which are multidisciplinary, holds particularly high promise of valuable progress in both fundamental understanding and the capacity to solve practical problems, partly because of significant, but expensive, advances in techniques. Australia has a demonstrated capacity for outstanding research in this field, although there are signs that activity has been constrained in recent years ... We believe that funding difficulties have had a particularly adverse impact on research in this area (p. 86)." The report attributes the funding difficulties in part to "The inadequacy of classifying psychology for funding purposes as a social science, and thus not recognising explicitly its essence as a behavioral science, or its crucial biological science aspect ..." (p. 8).

In Sweden, the Council for Research in the Humanities and the Social Sciences, one of the main sources of funding for basic research in psychology, decided in the late 1980s to evaluate research in the most active fields in psychology—biological psychology and cognitive psychology. The evaluation of biological psychology (Everitt, Ursin, Venables, & Weiskrantz, 1992), while acknowledging important accomplishments in this field, stresses some of the difficulties it faces. For example, the classification of psychology as a social science has been an obstacle in obtaining the funding necessary for laboratory research and training. Also, investigators in biological psychology tend to be disregarded by the social sciences because their orientation is too biological, but also disregarded by biologists because their background is in psychology.

This International Congress showed many examples of fruitful interaction between psychologists and neuroscientists. One was the symposium organized by Professor Kurt Pawlik, President of the International Union of Psychological Science (IUPsyS), on "Neuropsychology of Consciousness". It brought together psychologists, neurobiologists, and some who are both. This symposium was organized with the cooperation of the Brain Research Program of the International Council of Scientific Unions, of which IUPsyS is a member.

Some challenging questions

In many ways, it seems to me, the reciprocal relations between psychology, on the one hand, and neuroscience and other biological sciences, on the other, have been stimulating and fruitful. Not only biological psychology but also cognitive psychology interacts positively with neuroscience. But whenever a territory is divided, there are concerns about the claims of the different sides, and worries that one or the other may be losing ground. In considering the reciprocal relations between psychology and neuroscience, here are some challenging questions to be answered:

What has neuroscience contributed to psychology?

What has psychology contributed to neuroscience?

Is neuroscience draining students away from psychology?

Is biological psychology disappearing into neuroscience?

My concern with such questions was heightened when I served from 1971 to 1976 on the Committee for Brain Sciences of the National Academy of Sciences-National Research Council. This Committee, chaired by psychologist-neuroscientist Neal E. Miller, supported the first meeting of the Society for Neuroscience in 1971. I participated in that meeting and in most of the subsequent meetings of the rapidly growing Society for Neuroscience. The worry that neuroscience might drain students away from psychology seemed substantiated by a nationwide survey of graduate students in biological/physiological psychology in which I took part in 1986. It found, among other things, that more students in this area were attending meetings of the Society for Neuroscience (SN) than were attending meetings of the American Psychological Association (APA); similarly, more graduate students in biological/physiological psychology were joining SN than APA (Davis, Elkins, & Rosenzweig, 1987; Davis, Rosenzweig, Becker, & Sather, 1988).

More international information is needed on this topic

As we consider these questions, I hope you will be thinking of their relevance to your countries and regions. My information comes mainly from the United States and Canada and I would welcome information from other places.

THE SCIENCE OF THE NERVOUS SYSTEM AS A PART OF PSYCHOLOGY

The science of the nervous system has been a part of psychology from the start. Even though some pioneer psychologists (such as Wundt and Titchener) excluded the nervous system from their programs, many included it as an integral part. Thus, William James devoted the second chapter of his major textbook, *Principles of Psychology* (1890), to "The functions of the brain", and he offered neural explanations for many phenomena in the later chapters.

Many current textbooks of general or introductory psychology still follow James in devoting an early chapter to biological or neural bases of behavior (e.g. Atkinson, et al., 1996; Morris, 1996; Myers, 1992). They also bring in biological mechanisms and explanations in discussing many aspects of behavior and cognition.

Several presidents of the APA after William James have been biological psychologists or neuroscientists, including at least one in every decade through the 1960s: Robert M. Yerkes (1917); Shepherd Ivory Franz (1920); Karl S. Lashley (1929, president of both APA and the International Congress of Psychology); Edward C. Tolman (1937); Leonard Carmichael (1940); Calvin P. Stone (1943); Harry F. Harlow (1958); Donald O. Hebb (1960); Neal E. Miller (1961); and Gardner Lindzey (1967).

Since the 1960s, however, no biological psychologist has been president of the APA. Does this mean that biological psychology has disappeared from APA? No, many biological psychologists remain active in APA. The situation is similar in Sweden, where the Psychological Association was founded in 1955 as both a trade union and a scientific association. I have been told that no biological psychologist—in fact, no academic psychologist—has been president of the Swedish Psychological Association.

But biological psychologists are far from disappearing from psychology or even from psychological societies. In Sweden, for example, biological psychology is an integral part of psychology, and a biological psychologist heads the program committee for the next International Congress of Psychology.

In the United States, since the academically oriented American Psychological Society (APS) was founded in 1988, two of its seven presidents have been biological psychologists.

CONTRIBUTIONS OF PSYCHOLOGY TO NEUROSCIENCE

Neurophysiologist Charles Sherrington early in the 20th century called for closer relations between physiology and psychology. Noting many suggestively similar and complementary observations between physiology and psychology in regard to sensory and motor functions, he wrote ". . . physiology and psychology, instead of prosecuting their studies, as some recommend, more strictly apart one from another than at present, will find it serviceable for each to give the results achieved by the other even closer heed than has been customary hitherto" (1906, p. 387; 1947, p. 385). This has been taking place, especially in recent decades, with many contributions in both directions. In fact, very often collaborative teams including psychologists and neuroscientists have made important advances.

A report in the May/June 1996 APS *Observer* (Herring, 1996) testified to the contributions of psychologists to research in the field of the National Institute for Neurological Disorders and Stroke (NINDS). It reported that in 1995 over $36 million in NINDS extramural research and research training grants went to labs of over 150 psychologist principal investigators. This represented about 7% of NINDS extramural funding. Hundreds of other psychologists worked as co-investigators on other grants.

Psychology, broadly defined, contributes to neuroscience in four main ways: (1) by devising techniques that can be applied to problems of neuroscience; (2) by offering models that can be applied to areas of neuroscience; (3) by testing hypotheses in neuroscience; (4) psychologists have also participated in neuro-science organizations and publications. Let us look at a few examples of each kind of contribution.

Contributions of psychological techniques to neuroscience

Two important contributions of psychological techniques to neuroscience have been (1) the use of the *subtraction procedure* in studies of brain imaging related to behavior and experience, and (2) the role of properly designed behavioral tests to reveal the special characteristics of split-brain patients.

The subtraction procedure

This section will (a) give a brief history of the subtraction procedure, (b) present some examples of current use of subtraction in studies relating brain imaging to cognitive functions, and (c) note some current concerns and criti-cisms of use or interpretation of subtraction in studies relating brain imaging to cognitive functions.

A brief history.   Psychologists have played major roles in studies of brain imaging related to behavior and experience. Certain subtraction procedures, which are used in many current reports, were introduced to this field by psychologists such as Michael Posner. In fact, the general principle of the subtraction proced-ure has been passed back and forth between physiology and psychology during the last century and a half. This was first used by Helmholtz in 1850 to measure the speed of neural conduction. Helmholtz could not record the nerve impulse, but he could record the onset of a muscle contraction when a nerve was stimu-lated at different distances from the muscle. Subtraction could then be used to calculate the speed over the difference between the two points of stimulation.

The Dutch physiologist F.C. Donders (1862/1969) used the subtraction technique in another way soon after Helmholtz, measuring reaction times in what was called "mental chronometry" to study separate mental processes involved in making judgments. Wundt's laboratory took up the method, but his student Külpe (1895) later criticized it by showing that, in some cases, more complex tasks did not simply add to the processes involved but changed the nature of the task. Külpe's criticism led to abandonment of the method for about 60 years. Then Saul Sternberg (1969) showed that properly chosen tasks are composed of additive factors that can be manipulated separately. Even in tasks where operations are performed in parallel, it is still possible to design the tasks to isolate operations from the overall task (Posner & Raichle, 1994, p. 34). Separable factors are being isolated by the subtraction technique, as we will see shortly, but it is possible that the logic of additive factors may contribute further to brain imaging studies of cognitive functions.

Some examples of current use.   Use of the subtraction procedure is revealing brain regions that are especially active during a particular mental process, as compared with a control process. In the last decade, it has become common to see illustrations of brain activity characteristic of such conditions as attention or alertness with foci of activity in the right frontal and right parietal lobes (e.g. Pardo, Fox, & Raichle, 1991), or depression with increased activity in the frontal lobes and decreases in the parietal and temporal lobes (e.g. Drevets et al., 1992). A frequently reproduced four-part figure shows the brain regions specifically activated when subjects (a) view words, (b) listen to words, (c) speak words, or (d) generate verbs in response to nouns (Petersen, Fox, Posner, Mintun, & Raichle, 1988; Posner & Raichle, 1994, p. 115). Looking at such illustrations, one sometimes forgets that normally the whole brain is active, as shown by a figure from Posner and Raichle (1994, p. 65). In this figure, one positron emission tomography (PET) image was made while a person looked at a flickering visual pattern. Another image was made in the control condition while the person looked at a fixation point. It is hard to see much difference between the two images, but subtraction of the control image from the stimulation image reveals significant differences: In the subtraction image the main activity is in the occipital region, the visual cortex.

Such subtraction images are usually obtained for a few different subjects in an experiment. There are usually individual differences among the subtraction images; for example, in the figure from Posner and Raichle (1994, p. 65) two subjects show greater activity in the left visual regions, two show greater activity in the right visual regions, and one shows about equal activity in the two cerebral hemispheres. For an overall presentation, the subtraction images for different subjects are combined to yield a mean subtraction image, and this is the kind of image most often shown.

Comparisons of subtraction images from individual subjects is sometimes used to advantage, as for example, in a study of conditioning the eye-blink response in human subjects (Logan & Grafton, 1995). In certain brain regions, the relative metabolic change in PET responses was found to correlate significantly with the learning performance.

How have psychologists devised appropriate conditions to find what regions of the brain are activated specifically by a task such as generating a verb in response to a noun? They use a series of tasks: (a) Looking at a fixation point. (b) Seeing or hearing a word. (c) Speaking the word shown on the screen. (d) Generating and speaking a word associated with the noun shown on the screen. When PET brain recordings made under each of these conditions are subtracted from the recordings made under the next condition in the series, one obtains the difference images for seeing a word, hearing a word, speaking a word, and generating a verb, as mentioned a little earlier.

Criticisms of the subtraction procedure. The appearance of Posner and Raichle's *Images of mind* (1994) evoked a multiple book review with commentaries by 27 authors or pairs of authors (Posner & Raichle, 1995). Most commentaries were positive, but seven stated concerns or problems about use or interpretation of the subtraction procedure with regard to PET images. For example, some raised the problem of choice of an appropriate baseline from which to measure effects. Thus, Halgren (1995, p. 358) states that the subtraction procedure is biased against detection of areas that are activated in virtually all cognitive tasks (including control tasks). Horwitz (1995, p. 360) argues that Posner and Raichle put too much emphasis on localization in discrete neural areas and insufficient emphasis on interaction within networks of widely distributed systems. The poor temporal resolution of PET does not permit visualization of such interactions occurring within a few hundred milliseconds. For this reason Posner, Raichle, and associates (Snyder, Abdullaev, Posner, & Raichle, 1995) have begun to combine the evoked-potential method, with its excellent temporal resolution, with PET in order to investigate the succession of processes in generating responses to visually presented nouns.

Dehaene (1996) has extended the subtraction technique to show how the additive-factors method can be employed in an experiment recording event-related potentials. During a task in which subjects responded as rapidly as possible to record their comparisons between numbers presented visually, the potentials indicated six successive processing activations occurring in different brain regions, the whole sequence taking place within 500 milliseconds. I am not aware that the additive-factors method has yet been employed in PET studies.

Studying split-brain patients

Neurosurgeons sectioned the corpus callosum of some epileptic patients in the 1930s to reduce the frequency and severity of their seizures. Studies of such patients, using intelligence tests and other tests of general ability, did not reveal

any apparent changes in brain function. Karl Lashley suggested, with characteristic sardonic humor, that perhaps the only function of the corpus callosum was
to keep the two cerebral hemispheres from floating apart in the cerebrospinal
fluid! But subsequent research with animals in the 1950s, using carefully designed
behavioral tests, revealed that sectioning the corpus callosum produces clear
changes and deficits in behavior (Sperry, Stamm, & Miner, 1956). When a
further set of epileptic patients had the corpus callosum sectioned in the 1960s
to reduce their attacks, psychologists such as Roger Sperry were ready with
revealing tests (Sperry, Gazzaniga, & Bogen, 1969). These tests began to produce much of the basic understanding we now have of the split-brain condition.
This work is continuing and is increasing our knowledge about how the two
hemispheres work, both separately and together.

Contributions of psychological models or concepts to neuroscience

Two important models or concepts contributed by psychologists have been the
concept of *neural plasticity* and the concept of the *cerebral circadian clock.*

Neural plasticity.   One of the main contributions of psychologists has been
the concept of neural plasticity, which was foreshadowed by William James. Canadian psychologist Donald O. Hebb played a major role in the current emphasis
on this topic. Hebb's book of 1949 showed, in principle, how plastic synapses
and the growth of cell assemblies could account for many important phenomena
of behavior and experience. Our research group in Berkeley contributed the first
demonstrations of neural plasticity in adult as well as young animals (Krech,
Rosenzweig, & Bennett, 1960; Rosenzweig, Bennett, & Krech, 1964; Rosenzweig,
Krech, & Bennett, 1961; Rosenzweig, Krech, Bennett, & Diamond, 1962). A technique devised in Hebb's laboratory, which we borrowed from them, is to expose
animals to environments differing in complexity. This was found to lead to significant changes in neural measurements, such as thickness of the cerebral cortex,
size of neural cell bodies, and numbers of dendritic spines (Bennett, Diamond,
Krech, & Rosenzweig, 1964; Diamond, Krech, & Rosenzweig, 1964; Globus,
Rosenzweig, Bennett, & Diamond, 1973). Experience in differential environments
is now used in many laboratories of neuroscience as well as psychology to study
effects on development of the nervous system and also on the endocrine system.

The cerebral circadian clock.   The concept of a cerebral circadian clock was
proposed by a pioneer physiological psychologist, Curt Richter (1967). In 1972
two groups of investigators found evidence for the location of the clock in a
small nucleus in the hypothalamus (the suprachiasmatic nucleus). One group
was composed of psychologists (Stephan & Zucker, 1972) and the other of
neurophysiologists (Moore & Eichler, 1972).

Use of psychological methods to test hypotheses in neuroscience

Psychological methods have been used to test some hypotheses of neuroscience, such as these: (1) Does development of drug dependency (or addiction) require the establishment of physical dependency? (2) Are sensory maps in the cortex fixed after early development?

Drug dependency. Physiologists long believed that people do not become addicted or dependent on a drug such as morphine unless they have become adapted to the drug so that withdrawal, or even reducing the dose, seriously disturbs bodily functioning. Before the 1950s, researchers also believed that animals could not become addicted to drugs. They thought (incorrectly) that animals were not capable of learning an association that spanned the 15–20 minutes between an injection and relief from withdrawal symptoms. Then a few rather simple technological and procedural breakthroughs made it possible for laboratory animals to perform tasks that led to self-administration of drug through a fine flexible tube implanted into a vein. This was an adaptation of B. F. Skinner's operant conditioning procedures that are used in many ways in psychopharmacology. The first investigators to use this technique for drug administration believed that physical dependence was necessary if animals were to administer drugs to themselves. Therefore they first made rats or monkeys dependent on morphine by giving them repeated injections over a period of days before giving them the opportunity to press a lever that caused delivery of morphine through the implanted tube. The animals quickly learned to respond, and it appeared that the drug infusion was acting like a typical experimental reward such as food or water (Thompson & Schuster, 1964).

Further experiments by psychopharmacologist Charles R. Schuster demonstrated that animals that had not been made dependent *would* self-administer doses of morphine so low that no physical dependence ever developed (Schuster, 1970). Colleagues in the same laboratory also showed that monkeys would lever-press in order to administer themselves cocaine and other stimulants that do not produce marked withdrawal symptoms (Pickens & Thompson, 1968).

These and other studies clearly contradicted the assumptions of both the disease model and the physical dependence model of drug addiction. So, although physical dependence may be an important factor in consumption of some drugs, it is not necessary for self-administration and cannot serve as the sole explanation for drug taking. Furthermore, these studies indicated that acquisition of drug self-administration can be interpreted according to operant conditioning theory, that is, according to principles that govern behavior controlled by positive rewards. Therefore there is no need to consider drug self-administration as a disease. Many investigators conclude that the positive reward model accounts much better for drug addiction than does the model of physical plus psychological dependency.

Are cortical maps fixed or plastic in adults? Most neuroscientists long believed in the fixity of cortical maps of sensory and motor regions—until the late 1970s, according to Kandel and O'Dell (1992). Lashley early threw some doubt on this position by showing the variability of maps of the visual cortex among monkeys. Later, psychologists and other neuroscientists used various kinds of training and showed that such experience brought about significant changes in cortical maps and in the receptive fields of cortical cells (see e.g. reviews by Kaas, 1991, and Weinberger, 1995).

Psychologists contribute to neuroscience organizations and publications

Since the Society for Neuroscience was founded in 1970, six of its presidents have been psychologists (including those who earned their doctorates in psychology): Neal E. Miller (1971), David H. Cohen (1981), Mortimer Mishkin (1986), Patricia Goldman-Rakic (1989), Robert H. Wurtz (1990), and Larry R. Squire (1993).

Psychologists are invited regularly to contribute articles to the *Annual Review of Neuroscience*. Thirteen articles by psychologists have appeared there in the last 10 years (about 6% of the total). Mainly these articles have been on neural plasticity and sensory/perceptual processes. Two members of the editorial committee of the *Annual Review of Neuroscience* are psychologists. Psychologist-neuroscientists are also members of the Editorial Board of the *Journal of Neuroscience*.

It may be that the place of psychologists is larger in North American neuroscience than in other parts of the world. For example, in the International Brain Research Organization (IBRO), some psychologists have been officers, but relatively few.

CONTRIBUTIONS OF NEUROSCIENCE TO PSYCHOLOGY

Neuroscience, broadly defined, contributes to psychology in ways that are symmetrical to psychology's contributions to neuroscience: (1) by devising techniques that can be applied to problems of psychology; (2) by offering models that can be applied to areas of psychology (some inappropriate use of models should also be noted); (3) by permitting tests of hypotheses in psychology; (4) neuroscientists also contribute to psychological organizations and publications. Let us look at a few examples of each kind of contribution.

Contributions of neuroscience techniques to psychology

Many neuroscience techniques have been used fruitfully by psychologists. Here are three examples.

Detecting stages of sleep and studying dreams.   Understanding dreaming has been increased by being able to awaken subjects during rapid-eye movement (REM) sleep at various stages of a night's sleep. Aserinsky and Kleitman (1953) found that active dreaming usually occurs only during REM periods, which take place only a few times per night and for relatively short durations. REM periods would be hard to find if not for electrophysiological recordings of the brain's activity.

Noninvasive recording of brain activity during behavior.   This permits recording activity of normal subjects during a variety of tasks, thus helping to reveal the brain regions especially involved. We have already noted such recordings for visual and auditory perception and for generating word responses. Other examples will be given later.

Correlating sizes of brain structures with tests of ability.   Noninvasive recording of brain structure has also permitted correlating sizes of brain structures with tests of ability. Both total brain volume and hippocampal volume show significant correlations with tests of ability and intelligence (Andreasen, et al., 1993; Willerman, Schultz, Rutledge, & Bigler, 1991).

Use of neuroscience concepts or models in psychology

Some neuroscience concepts have been influential in psychology. Two of these are the concept of *localization of function* and the *set-point model of regulation*.

The concept of localization of function.   This concept originated in the physiology of the early 19th century. It was strengthened by Broca's discovery of the speech area in 1861 and by mapping of motor and sensory regions in animal brains by physiologists in the latter part of the 19th century. A major part of research in biological psychology is directed toward uncovering the behavioral specializations of different brain regions.

Strong evidence for separating and localizing the functions of brain systems is provided by evidence of double dissociation, that is, when lesions of brain area A cause impairment on behavioral test X but not on test Y, whereas lesions of area B cause impairment on test Y but not on X. The concept of double dissociation was enunciated by physiological psychologist Hans-Lukas Teuber (1955). Examples of the use of this principle are found in the search for brain regions involved in processing different attributes of memory. For example, psychologist Raymond Kesner has found evidence for a triple dissociation among brain regions involved in different attributes of working memory in the rat: memory for the animal's own responses involves the caudate nucleus; spatial aspects involve particularly the hippocampus and so do temporal aspects, whereas visual aspects involve the extrastriate visual cortex (Kesner, Bolland, & Dakis, 1993). A similar research project in another laboratory found similar results, using three different problems, all run in the radial maze: (1) a neural system that includes the hippocampus acquires information about relationships among stimuli and events (declarative memories); (2) a different system that includes the dorsal striatum (mainly the caudate nucleus) mediates the formation of reinforced stimulus-response associations (habits, or nondeclarative memories); (3) a third system that includes the amygdala mediates rapid acquisition of behaviors based on biologically significant events with affective properties (McDonald & White, 1993).

The set-point model of regulation.   The set-point or set-zone concept came originally from engineering. It has been applied to temperature regulation in the body as well as in thermostatic devices. The concept has also been applied to control of body weight. Normally an adult's body weight fluctuates around a set-point. If a brain lesion in an experimental animal causes a new set-point to be established, this will then be maintained. Subjecting the animal to forced feeding or food deprivation for a few days causes departures from the set-point value, but as soon as these constraints are removed, the animal tends rapidly back to the set-point value (Keesey & Powley, 1986).

Now psychologists have suggested a set-point for happiness (Lykken & Tellegen, 1996). This is based on their findings that a person tends to give a characteristic rating for his or her state of happiness. Good or bad happenings usually cause the ratings to increase or decrease for only relatively brief periods of time, suggesting that a person's happiness tends to revert to its usual level. The availability of the set-point concept may have encouraged the formulation of this hypothesis.

Controversial interpretations of neuroscience findings

When we are pleased to see neuroscience contributions to psychology, we should also admit that interpretations of some findings are doubtful. Here are two examples of controversial interpretations:

1. Does closer packing of neurons in the cortex of women explain their greater proficiency in language?
2. Does size of a nucleus in the hypothalamus account for transsexual orientation?

Does closer packing of neurons in the cortex of women explain their greater proficiency in language?   Witelson, Glezar, and Kigar (1995) reported, based on a small number of cases, that women have a larger number of neurons in a region of the cortex related to language than men, and they speculated that this may account for women's greater proficiency in language. This report received considerable coverage in the news media. Actually the measure was not the total number of neurons in the region but *neurons per unit of volume of cortex*. Thus the results mean closer spacing of neurons. Work on effects of environmental enrichment or training has shown that greater experience increases the spacing of neurons so that there are less per unit of volume of cortex. Thus closer spacing of neurons cannot be taken as presumptive evidence for greater cognitive proficiency.

Does size of a nucleus in the hypothalamus account for transsexual orientation? A recent report (Zhou, Hofman, Gooren, & Swaab, 1995) found that a small nucleus in the brain (the central region of the bed nucleus of the stria terminalis [BSTc]) was about twice as large in men, both heterosexual and homosexual, than in women; in six male-to-female transsexuals, the nucleus was as small as in women. The investigators implied that the small size of the nucleus might account for the female orientation of these individuals. This would conform with a commonly held presumption that brain differences are determined genetically. But it could also be argued that the sexual transformation might account for the small size of the nucleus. For more than 30 years, psychologists and neuroscientists have shown that experience can affect brain measures. At present, small nuclei such as the one in question here can be measured only in post-mortem examinations. As the spatial resolution of noninvasive imaging techniques increases, it will become possible to solve this chicken-and-egg question by measuring the nuclei at different ages.

Neuroscience techniques permit tests of psychological hypotheses

Here are two psychological hypotheses that have been supported by tests using neuroscience techniques:

1. Practiced tasks use different neural circuits than when the same tasks were novel.
2. Encoding and retrieval of information are distinct processes.

Practiced tasks use different neural circuits than when the same tasks were novel. William James proposed this hypothesis, noting that if practice only helped to establish the circuits used while a person was laboriously learning a task, we would be able to accomplish only a few acts during an entire lifetime. Recently it has become possible to examine this question by studying brain activity recorded while subjects practiced a task (Raichle et al., 1994). The task was one we noted earlier—generating verbs to noun stimuli. Subjects responded to the same list of 40 nouns several times in a row. At the start, difference recordings showed activity in the right cerebellum, the left anterior cingulate cortex, and the left frontal and posterior temporal cortex. After the subjects spent 15 minutes practicing this task, they gave responses a little faster and in an automatic manner. Their brain recordings no longer showed the three foci of activity found in the naive subjects, but activity was seen especially in the buried insular cortex in both hemispheres and the midline of the left visual cortex, an area that is responsive to familiar words. When a new list of stimulus words was introduced, the recordings again showed the same areas of activity as seen originally.

Encoding and retrieval of information are distinct processes. Many psychologists have long supposed that processing of information involves distinct stages of encoding, consolidation, and retrieval. But other psychologists (e.g. Bloch & Laroche, 1984) have suggested the opposite hypothesis: That retrieval is essentially reactivation of the sequence of processes that occurred during encoding. Recently PET recordings have helped to decide between the two hypotheses. In one experiment, recordings were made while subjects encoded photographs of unfamiliar faces and tried to memorize them (Grady et al., 1995). Later the same subjects were tested for some of these faces versus new faces. Difference PET responses showed distinct regions activated during encoding and retrieval. Encoding activated especially the *left* prefrontal and inferior temporal cortex, whereas retrieval activated especially *right* prefrontal and parietal cortex. Several groups of investigators have reported either that encoding is processed mainly by the left prefrontal cortex or that retrieval is processed mainly in the right prefrontal cortex, but the study by Grady and colleagues is one of the few to demonstrate a double dissociation between encoding and retrieval and brain regions involved in them. Endel Tulving considered such findings in his Keynote Address at this Congress and discussed the hemispheric encoding/retrieval asymmetry (HERA) hypothesis (Tulving, Kapur, Craik, Moskovitch, & Houle, 1994; Nyberg, Cabeza, & Tulving, 1996).

Grady et al. (1995) also compared the results they obtained with young subjects (mean age 25 years) with those of older subjects (mean age 69) tested in the same way. The older subjects showed patterns of brain activity generally similar to those of the young subjects but much weaker; that is, their brain activation during memory tasks did not differ as far from control levels as in the young subjects. Corresponding to the brain findings, the older subjects were significantly poorer than the young in face recognition, but only slightly poorer in the face matching task.

Neuroscientists participate in psychological meetings and publications

A few examples will suffice here. Many nonpsychologist neuroscientists participated in the program of this International Congress of Psychology. An example is the symposium organized by L. Tauc on "Plastic changes in identified synapses".

Neuroscientists who are not also psychologists contribute chapters regularly to the *Annual Review of Psychology*.

TRENDS AND PREDICTIONS

At this time, when important advances are being made in biological psychology and neuroscience, there are also signs of unease and concern in biological psychology. As well as celebrating the advances, we should state and evaluate some of the concerns.

Problems, difficulties, and challenges in biological psychology

Problems related to difficulties of funding.   Paradoxically, many of the new techniques that increase the power and scope of research are also expensive and so tend to limit the number of investigators who can participate. The reports prepared for the Australian Academy of Science and the Swedish Council for Research in Humanities and Social Sciences mentioned this, and it is undoubtedly true of most, if not all, countries.

Related to this is the concern that modern biological psychology will be limited to industrialized countries and will not be possible in developing countries. Most of the studies reported at this Congress using PET or FMRI techniques were conducted in the United States or Canada. To obtain access to modern facilities and instruments, it will be important for psychologists in developing countries to establish collaborative relationships with neuroscientists and medical investigators, as has occurred in North America. Accomplishing this will require that the psychologists attain recognition as scientists who can contribute to such research.

Most of those who spoke to me at the end of the oral presentation of this lecture were psychologists from developing countries who reported difficulties in engaging in up-to-date research in this area. A survey of resources for psychological science around the world conducted in 1991–92 (Rosenzweig, 1992) confirmed the generality of such problems. It revealed that in most developing countries a much smaller percentage of psychologists engage in research than in industrialized countries; also, physiological psychology, and academic/research areas in general, show lower levels of activity in developing countries than in industrialized countries, whereas health provider fields of psychology show relatively greater activity in developing countries than in industrialized countries.

Obstacles and opposition to animal research.   In the United States and some other countries, psychology is the brunt of "animal rights" campaigns. These tend to make research more expensive than in the past and thus limit the amount that can be accomplished.

Reluctance of some biological psychologists to call themselves "psychologists". Because of the public perception of psychologists as clinicians and practitioners, some biological psychologists are reluctant to call themselves "psychologists". (During the Montreal Congress a local newspaper carried an article explaining that the purpose of an International Congress of Psychology is to aid psychologists improve their skills in aiding patients with diverse ethnic and cultural backgrounds!) The reaction of research psychologists to this kind of characterization of psychology tends to have a positive feedback effect; the more research psychologists tend to avoid the designation of "psychologist", the more psychology appears and becomes a field of clinical practice.

Illustrations of some of these problems are seen in China, where heads of some of the main laboratories of physiology were trained as psychologists. What accounts for their shift to physiology and for their success there? According to a Chinese colleague, one reason for them to move into physiology is the greater ease of obtaining research funding there than in psychology. This is probably also true in other countries. As for their success, the Chinese colleague suggests that after having been trained to deal with the difficult problems of research in psychology, it was easy for them to deal with the simpler problems of physiology. Perhaps so, but many of the problems of neuroscience in which we are interested are the same as those biological psychologists are studying.

Positive factors

At the same time, there are several positive factors that balance and perhaps outweigh the problems.

Increases in the numbers of graduate programs in biological psychology. There have been strong increases in the numbers of graduate programs in biological psychology and in the number of applicants for these programs.

Popularity of courses in biological psychology.   There is encouraging popularity of undergraduate and graduate courses in biological psychology (also titled psychobiology, physiology and behavior, etc.). It is estimated that about 60,000 students in the United States take a basic course in biological psychology each year. A colleague reports that in Sweden, biological psychology and cognitive psychology are the two strongest research areas and are about equally strong.

The number of doctoral programs in physiological or biopsychology in the United States and Canada increased from 40 in 1973 to 76 in 1992; there has also been an increase in total applications for graduate study in this field from 1328 in 1973 to 1520 in 1992 (Norcross, Hanych, & Terranova, 1996).

It is not clear exactly how many doctoral programs in neuroscience there are in the United States and Canada. Nor are figures are available for the growth of neuroscience programs. The latest edition of *Neuroscience training programs in North America* (Association of Neuroscience Departments and Programs, 1994) lists about 130 doctoral programs in the United States, 11 in Canada, and one in Mexico, but these figures may be underestimations because for this edition programs had to pay a fee to be listed. On the other hand, the National Research Council publication *Research-doctorate programs in the United States* (Goldberger, Maher, & Flattau, 1995) lists only 102 research-doctorate programs in neuroscience in the United States. Some of the programs listed in the neuroscience publication are located in departments of psychology (e.g. Baylor University, Boston University, Cornell University, Georgia State University, University of Iowa, University of North Carolina at Chapel Hill), or departments of psychobiology (e.g. University of California at Irvine). In fact, psychology was mentioned as a site of neuroscience programs more frequently than any other specific department. A plurality of the neuroscience programs were listed as interdisciplinary or multidisciplinary, and many of these mentioned psychology as one of the disciplines involved. Overall it appears that psychology is participating in the growth of neuroscience rather than being overshadowed by it. If some students are being drained from doctoral programs in biological psychology by doctoral programs in neuroscience, nevertheless progress in the overall field is stimulating increased numbers of programs in biological psychology and increased numbers of applicants to them.

Biological psychologists are being recognized in several ways. Ways in which biological psychologists are being recognized included the APA Distinguished Scientific Contribution Awards; election to the National Academy of Sciences, USA; election as President of the Society for Neuroscience, and of the American Psychological Society. In the last 25 years about 13 out of 83 APA Awards for Distinguished Scientific contributions, or 16%, have gone to biological psychologists.

Progress is occurring in developing countries. The international survey of resources for psychological science (Rosenzweig, 1992, pp. 44–45) noted some rays of light in the generally gloomy picture in this area:

> It should be noted that, in spite of financial obstacles and insufficient numbers of trained psychologists, many developing countries have at least a few outstanding psychological investigators who overcome barriers and produce research of high theoretical and practical value. International congresses of psychology have featured the contributions of some of these investigators, and some of them have been elected to the national academies of science in their countries. These investigators pave the way for their compatriots. The IUPsyS has made it a high priority to find ways to promote psychological research in developing countries and is seeking ways to expand these efforts.

In keeping with this, several psychologists from developing countries reported research in biological psychology at the International Congress of Psychology in Montreal.

Neuroscientists and funding agencies recognize the contributions of biological psychologists. This recognition is reflected in a guest column by Dr Zach Hall, Director of the National Institute of Neurological Disorders and Stroke (NINDS) in the May/June 1996 *APS Observer*. Hall wrote that at NINDS "We view behavioral science as a key component of the broad effort of neuroscientists to understand how the brain works" (p. 2).

He continued (pp. 2, 42):

> One exciting consequence of the new advances in technology is that behavior and biology are being brought closer together. Because our methods of biological analysis are increasingly able to deal with complex biological systems, we can now make correlations between behavioral and biological changes with a sophistication that was only imagined a few years ago. Imagine being able to see parts of the brain that become activated when one thinks of nouns or verbs, or to trace the neurophysiological circuits that underlie a young bird learning to sing.
>
> On the other side, we are also learning that discrete molecular defects can have such subtle effects on behavior that sophisticated methods of behavioral analysis are required to tease them out. In fact one of the major challenges for neuroscience is to tie together our understanding at various levels of organization. The idea that we can now make a defined genetic alteration in a mouse and examine the consequences of that alteration in terms of function at the molecular, cellular, systems, and behavioral levels is truly exciting. Because studies of biology and behavior have often evolved along separate pathways and belonged to separate traditions, special efforts must be made to train future researchers who will be expert in both fields.

Overall, I am inclined to be optimistic about the progress of biological psychology and cognitive psychology and their continued fruitful interactions with neuroscience. I look forward to the reports in this field at the XXVII Congress of Psychology in Stockholm.

ACKNOWLEDGEMENTS

I thank S. Marc Breedlove and Géry d'Ydewalle for comments and suggestions made on drafts of this paper.

REFERENCES

Adair, J. G., Paivio, A., & Ritchie, P. (1996). Psychology in Canada. *Annual Review of Psychology*, *47*, 341–370.

Andreasen, N. C., Flaum, M., Swayze, V. O., O'Leary, D. S., Alliger, R., Cohen, G., Ehrhardt, J., & Yuh, W. T. (1993). Intelligence and brain structure in normal individuals. *American Journal of Psychiatry*, *150*, 130–134.

Aserinsky, E., & Kleitman, N. (1953). Regularly occurring periods of eye motility, and concomitant phenomena during sleep. *Science*, *118*, 273–274.

Association of Neuroscience Departments and Programs (1994). *Neuroscience training programs in North America*. Washington, D.C.: Association of Neuroscience Departments and Programs.

Atkinson, R. L., Atkinson, R. C., et al. (1996). *Introduction to psychology* (12th ed.). Fort Worth, TX: Harcourt Brace.

Australian Research Council Discipline Research Strategies (1996). *Psychological science in Australia*. Canberra, Australia: National Board of Employment, Education and Training.

Bennett, E. L., Diamond, M. C., Krech, D., & Rosenzweig, M. R. (1964). Chemical and anatomical plasticity of brain. *Science, 146*, 610–619.

Bloch, V., & Laroche, S. (1984). Facts and hypotheses related to the search for the engram. In G. Lynch, J. L. McGaugh, & N. M. Weinberger (Eds.), *Neurobiology of learning and memory* (pp. 249–260). New York: Guilford Press.

Davis, H. P., Elkins, C., & Rosenzweig, M. R. (1987). The role of physiological psychology in neuroscience. *Neuroscience Newsletter, 18*, 6–7.

Davis, H. P., Rosenzweig, M. R., Becker, L. A., & Sather, K. J. (1988). Biological psychology's relationships to psychology and neuroscience. *American Psychologist, 43*, 359–371.

Dehaene, S. (1996). The organization of brain activations in number comparison: Event-related potentials and the additive-factors method. *Journal of Cognitive Neuroscience, 8*, 47–68.

Diamond, M. C., Krech, D., & Rosenzweig, M. R. (1964). The effects of an enriched environment on the histology of the rat cerebral cortex. *Journal of Comparative Neurology, 123*, 111–119.

Donders, F. C. (1969). On the speed of mental processes. *Acta Psychologica, 30*, 412–431. (Translation of 1862 article.)

Drevets, W. C., Videen, T. O., Price, J. L., Preskorn, S. H., Carmichael, S. T., & Raichle, M. E. (1992). A functional anatomical study of unipolar depression. *Journal of Neuroscience, 12*, 3628–3641.

Everitt, B., Ursin, H., Venables, P., & Weiskrantz, L. (1992). *Two faces of Swedish psychology. 2. Frontiers in biological psychology*. Uppsala, Sweden: Swedish Science Press.

Globus, A., Rosenzweig, M. R., Bennett, E. L., & Diamond, M. C. (1973). Effects of differential experience on dendritic spine counts in rat cerebral cortex. *Journal of Comparative and Physiological Psychology, 82*, 175–181.

Goldberger, M. L., Maher, B. A., & Flattau, P. E. (1995). *Research-doctoral programs in the United States: Continuity and change*. Washington, DC: National Academy Press.

Grady, C. L., McIntosh, A. R., Horowitz, B., Maisog, J. M., Ungerleider, L. G., Mentis, M. J., Pietrini, P., Schapiro, M. B., & Haxby, J. V. (1995). Age-related reductions in human recognition memory due to impaired encoding. *Science, 269*, 218–221.

Halgren, E. (1995). PET may image the gates of awareness, not its center. *Behavioral and Brain Sciences, 18*, 358–359.

Hall, Z. (1996). NINDS and behavioral science. *APS Observer, 9*, 42.

Hebb, D. O. (1949). *The organization of behavior: A neuropsychological theory*. New York: Wiley.

Herring, K. L. (1996). NINDS and psychologists share in promise of neuroscience. *APS Observer, 9*, 1, 3, 40–41.

Horwitz, B. (1995). Regions, networks: Interpreting functional neuroimaging data. *Behavioral and Brain Sciences, 18*, 360.

James, W. (1890). *Principles of psychology*. New York: Henry Holt.

Kaas, J. H. (1991). Plasticity of sensory and motor maps in adult animals. *Annual Review of Neuroscience, 14*, 137–167.

Kandel, E. R., & O'Dell, T. J. (1992). Are adult learning mechanisms also used for development? *Science, 258*, 243–245.

Keesey, R. E., & Powley, T. L. (1986). The regulation of body weight. *Annual Review of Psychology, 37*, 109–133.

Kesner, R. P., Bolland, B. L., & Dakis, M. (1993). Memory for spatial locations, motor responses, and objects: Triple dissociation among the hippocampus, caudate nucleus, and extrastriate visual cortex. *Experimental Brain Research, 93*, 462–470.

Krech, D., Rosenzweig, M. R., & Bennett, E. L. (1960). Effects of environmental complexity and training on brain chemistry. *Journal of Comparative and Physiological Psychology, 53*, 509–519.

Külpe, O. (1895). *Outlines of psychology*. New York: Macmillan.

Logan, C. G., & Grafton, S. T. (1995). Functional anatomy of human eye-blink conditioning determined with regional cerebral glucose metabolism and positron emission tomography, *Proceedings of the National Academy of Sciences, USA, 92*, 7500–7504.

Lykken, D., & Tellegen, A. (1996). Happiness is a stochastic phenomenon. *Psychological Science, 7*, 186–189.

McDonald, R. J., & White, N. M. (1993). A triple dissociation of memory systems: Hippocampus, amygdala, and dorsal striatum. *Behavioral Neuroscience, 107*, 3–22.

Moore, R. Y., & Eichler, V. B. (1972). Loss of circadian adrenal corticosterone rhythm following suprachiasmatic lesions in the rat. *Brain Research, 42*, 201–206.

Morris, C. G. (1996). *Psychology* (9th ed.). Upper Saddle River, NJ: Prentice Hall.

Myers, D. G. (1992). *Psychology* (3rd ed.). New York: Worth.

Norcross, J. C., Hanych, J. M., & Terranova, R. D. (1996). Graduate study in psychology: 1992–1993. *American Psychologist, 51*, 631–643.

Nyberg, L., Cabeza, R., & Tulving, E. (1996). PET studies of encoding and retrieval: The HERA model. *Psychonomic Bulletin and Review, 3*, 135–148.

Pardo, J. V., Fox, P. T., & Raichle (1991). PET localization of a human system for sustained attention. *Nature, 349*, 61–64.

Petersen, S. E., Fox, P. T., Posner, M. I., Mintun, M., & Raichle, M. E. (1988). Positron emission tomographic studies of the cortical anatomy of single-word processing. *Nature, 331*, 585–589.

Pickens, R., & Thompson, T. (1968). Drug use by U.S. Army enlisted men in Vietnam: A followup on their return home. *Journal of Pharmacology and Experimental Therapeutics, 161*, 122–129.

Posner, M. I., & Raichle, M. E. (1994). *Images of mind.* New York: Scientific American Library.

Posner, M. I., & Raichle, M. E. (1995). Précis of *Images of mind*, and commentaries. *Behavioral and Brain Sciences, 18*, 327–383.

Raichle, M. E., Fiez, J. A., Videen, T. O., MacLeod, A. M., Pardo, J., Fox, P. T., & Petersen, S. E. (1994). Practice-related changes in human brain functional anatomy during nonmotor learning. *Cerebral Cortex, 4*, 8–26.

Richter, C. (1967). Sleep and activity: Their relation to the 24-hour clock. *Proceedings of the Association for Research in Nervous and Mental Diseases, 45*, 8–27.

Rosenzweig, M. R. (1992). Resources for psychological science around the world. In M. R. Rosenzweig (Ed.), *International psychological science: Progress, problems, and prospects* (pp. 17–74). Washington, DC: American Psychological Association.

Rosenzweig, M. R., Bennett, E. L., & Krech, D. (1964). Cerebral effects of environmental complexity and training among adult rats. *Journal of Comparative and Physiological Psychology, 57*, 438–439.

Rosenzweig, M. R., Krech, D., & Bennett, E. L. (1961). Heredity, environment, brain biochemistry, and learning. In *Current trends in psychological theory* (pp. 87–110). Pittsburgh: University of Pittsburgh Press.

Rosenzweig, M. R., Krech, D., Bennett, E. L., & Diamond, M. C. (1962). Effects of environmental complexity and training on brain chemistry and anatomy: A replication and extension. *Journal of Comparative and Physiological Psychology, 55*, 429–437.

Rosenzweig, M. R., & Leiman, A. L. (1989). *Physiological psychology* (2nd ed.). New York: Random House.

Rosenzweig, M. R., & Leiman, A. L. (1991). *Psychophysiologie*. Montreal, Canada: Décarie; Paris, France: InterEditions.

Schuster, C. R. (1970). Psychological approaches to opiate dependence and self-administration by laboratory animals. *Federation Proceedings, 29*, 1–5.

Sherrington, C. S. (1906). *Integrative action of the nervous system.* New York: Charles Scribner's Sons.

Sherrington, C. S. (1947). *Integrative action of the nervous system.* New Haven, CT: Yale University Press. [Reprint of 1906 edition.]

Snyder, A. Z., Abdullaev, Y. G., Posner, M. I., & Raichle, M. E. (1995). Scalp electrical potentials reflect regional cerebral blood flow responses during processing of written words. *Proceedings of the National Academy of Sciences, USA, 92*, 1689–1693.

Sperry, R. W., Gazzaniga, M. S., & Bogen, J. E. (1969). Interhemispheric relations: The neocortical commissures; syndromes of hemisphere disconnection. In P. J. Vinken & G. W. Bruyn (Eds.), *Handbook of clinical neurology* (Vol. 4, pp. 273–290). Amsterdam: North Holland.

Sperry, R. W., Stamm, J., & Miner, N. (1956). Relearning tests for interocular transfer following division of optic chiasma and corpus callosum in cats. *Journal of Comparative and Physiological Psychology, 49*, 529–533.

Stephan, F. K., & Zucker, I. (1972). Circadian rhythms in drinking behavior and locomotor activity in rats are eliminated by hypothalamic lesions. *Proceedings of the National Academy of Sciences, USA, 69*, 1583–1586.

Sternberg, S. (1969). The discovery of processing stages: Extensions of Donders' method. *Acta Psychologica, 30*, 276–315.

Teuber, H.-L. (1955). Physiological psychology. *Annual Review of Psychology, 6*, 267–296.

Thompson, T., & Schuster, C. R. (1964). Morphine self-administration, food reinforced and avoidance behavior in rhesus monkeys. *Psychopharmacologia, 5*, 87–94.

Tulving, E., Kapur, S., Craik, F. I. M., Moskovitch, M., & Houle, S. (1994). Hemispheric encoding/retrieval asymmetry in episodic memory: Positron emission tomography findings. *Proceedings of the National Academy of Science, USA, 91*, 2012–2015.

Wang, Z.-M. (1993). Psychology in China: A review dedicated to Li Chen. *Annual Review of Psychology, 44*, 87–116.

Weinberger, N. M. (1995). Dynamic regulation of receptive fields and maps in the adult sensory cortex. *Annual Review of Neuroscience, 18*, 129–158.

Willerman, L., Schultz, R., Rutledge, J. N., & Bigler, E. D. (1991). In vivo brain size and intelligence. *Intelligence, 15*, 223–228.

Witelson, S. F., Glezar, I. I., & Kigar, D. L. (1995). Women have greater density of neurons in posterior temporal cortex. *Journal of Neuroscience, 15*, 3418–3428.

Zhou, J. N., Hofman, M. A., Gooren, L. J. G., & Swaab, D. F. (1995). A sex difference in the human brain and its relation to transsexuality. *Nature, 378*, 68–70.

PART THREE

Learning processes

CHAPTER TEN

Instrumental learning: Nature and persistence

Robert A. Rescorla
University of Pennsylvania, Philadelphia, PA, USA

In instrumental learning situations, association relations are learned among the major stimuli, responses, and outcomes. These associations are both binary and hierarchical in character. Their presence can be detected by such procedures as devaluation of outcomes and transfer of stimuli to new responses based on their shared outcome relations. When experimental contingencies are changed so as to extinguish the original learning, these associations remain very well preserved. Apparently, extinction is produced by the superimposition of some new inhibitory process. One possibility is the development of an inhibitory association between stimulus and response. This possibility has implications not only for extinction but also for the manner in which other changes in contingencies have their action.

En situation d'apprentissage instrumental, des relations associatives se constituent entre les principaux stimuli, les réponses et leurs conséquences. Ces associations sont à la fois binaires et de nature hiérarchique. Leur existence peut entre autres être détectée en annulant la valeur des conséquences ou en transférant les stimuli à de nouvelles réponses dont les conséquences sont identiques à celles des réponses originales. Lorsqu'il y a modification des contingences expérimentales en vue d'obtenir l'extinction de l'apprentissage initial, de telles associations se préservent très bien. Il semble que l'extinction résulte de la superposition d'un nouveau processus inhibiteur. Par exemple, une association inhibitrice pourrait se développer entre stimulus et réponse. Cette possibilité comporte des implications non seulement en regard de l'extinction, mais également en ce qui a trait à la manière dont agissent d'autres modifications apportées aux contingences.

INTRODUCTION

Despite dramatic changes in our conceptualizations about learning processes, the notion of an association had remained fundamental to our thinking for thousands of years. The learning of relations among events in the world is essential for the survival of any sophisticated organism. The concept of association has continued to be central to describing how organisms learn those relations.

Our laboratory has pursued the understanding of associations for about three decades. We have attempted to address three fundamental questions: What are the circumstances under which associations are formed? What is the content of that learning? How does that learning exhibit itself in the behavior of the organism? Along the way, we have tried to develop new techniques for the detection and analysis of the nature of associations.

Some of the more recent work we have done will be discussed in this chapter. In doing so, I have three goals: To describe some techniques with broad usefulness in the study of associations, to characterize what we know about the associations underlying one simple situation using those techniques, and then to consider the question of what happens to those learned associations when the relations that led to their formation change and new relations apply.

In our laboratory, we have typically studied two examples of associative learning, both of which involve the learning of relations among events. One example is Pavlovian conditioning in which one stimulus signals the occurrence of another, typically more important, stimulus (an outcome). The second example is instrumental training in which the organism has the opportunity to learn the relation between its own behavior and an important outcome. We commonly use hungry laboratory rats for whom food is a positive outcome; they are eager to learn both what external events signal food and what behaviors of their own produce that food.

I will concentrate on instrumental learning, with only passing reference to Pavlovian conditioning. We have followed others in conceptualizing instrumental learning situations as containing three primary events: a response on the part of the animal, a goal (or outcome) of that behavior, and a stimulus environment. Most instrumental learning situations can be thought of as arranging for some outcome (O) to be contingent on some response (R) in the presence of some stimulus (S). The instrumental learning situation we use is the most frequently studied—laboratory rats in standard operant chambers. In that situation, the behavior is some response such as pressing a lever, pulling a chain, or poking the nose into a hole; the goal is an attractive substance such as a solid pellet or liquid sucrose; and contingencies are typically arranged so that the response can earn the outcome during some stimulus such as a light or noise.

The phenomenon of initial interest is that the animal learns to make the response vigorously during the stimulus, thereby earning the outcome. Consequently, the first question to be addressed is what is the nature of the learning underlying that performance? What associations are learned? Classical accounts of instrumental behavior emphasized one particular association, that between the stimulus and the response; the role of the outcome was to serve as a reinforcer for that S-R association. However, it is now clear, based on work in a variety of laboratories, that this conception fails to capture fully the nature of the learning.

It turns out that three other associations importantly govern instrumental performance, all involving the outcome. We have previously reported substantial evidence for the presence of both R-O and S-O associations. In addition, we have shown results implying the development of a more hierarchical S-(R-O) association. I begin by reviewing some sample experiments demonstrating the role of those associations. This allows me not only to expose some important facts about the associations underlying instrumental performance, but also to introduce two important techniques for assessing those associations. I will then turn to the topic of what happens to those associations when the conditions in the world change.

ASSOCIATIONS UNDERLYING INSTRUMENTAL LEARNING

Response-outcome associations

Probably the best-demonstrated association underlying instrumental learning is that between the response and the outcome. It is now clear that animals learn what outcomes follow what responses. The contribution of this R-O association can be shown in various ways, but one of the most compelling uses an outcome-devaluation technique. The idea behind that technique is that if instrumental training results in an association between a response and an outcome, then if that outcome should subsequently change in value, the response should change in likelihood. That presumption turns out to be correct—the devaluation of an outcome has a highly specific depressive effect on responses that had earned that outcome.

One good illustration of this is an experiment we published about a decade ago (Colwill & Rescorla, 1985), the design of which is shown in the upper portion of Fig. 10.1. In this experiment, rats were trained to make two responses, R1 and R2 (counterbalanced as lever and chain), each earning a particular outcome, O1 and O2 (counterbalanced as solid pellet or liquid sucrose), on a variable-interval schedule. Then we removed the manipulanda from the chambers and paired either the pellets or the sucrose with the toxin LiCl. Such pairings are well known to produce rapid rejection of the associated food substance, thereby resulting in marked devaluation of one outcome. In a subsequent test, the animals were given a choice between lever pressing and chain pulling, but with no outcomes ensuing. The lower portion of Fig. 10.1 shows the animal's likelihood of making the responses during a baseline session at the end of training before devaluation and then after the outcome for one response had been devalued. Although the response levels were comparable at the end of training, devaluation resulted in a strong preference for the response alternative whose outcome had not been paired with LiCl. This result has now repeatedly been observed under a wide variety of circumstances. Certainly R-O associations are formed and contribute importantly to the performance in instrumental learning situations.

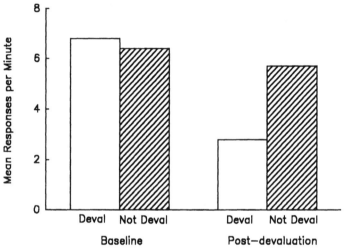

Training	Devaluation	Test
R1--)O1	O1--)LiCl	
		R1 v. R2
R2--)O2	O2--)LiCl	

FIG. 10.1   Design and results of an experiment showing response-outcome associations. Two responses, R1 and R2, each earned a different outcome, O1 and O2. Then one outcome was devalued by pairing with LiCl and the animal was given a choice between the two responses. During the base-line training, prior to devaluation, the responses were made with similar frequencies. After devalu-ation, the response that previously earned the now devalued outcome was made less frequently.

It is worth noting in passing that even the response whose outcome had been devalued continued to occur with substantial frequency. This is a common res-ult in such experiments. Despite the animal's complete rejection of an outcome, the response that formerly produced that outcome is not completely eliminated. Although that result has various interpretations, a common one is that some por-tion of the behavior is under the control of an association that does not import-antly involve the outcome. The most frequently suggested candidate is the classical S-R association.

Stimulus-outcome associations

In instrumental learning, the animal associates the outcome not only with the response but also with the antecedent stimulus. One technique for demonstrating the development of this S-O association involves a transfer design that exploits the fact that the animal forms R-O associations. The idea behind this technique

Discrimination	Target Training	Transfer Test
L: Rc—->O1	R1—->O1	L: R1 v. R2
N: Rc—->O2	R2—->O2	N: R1 v. R2

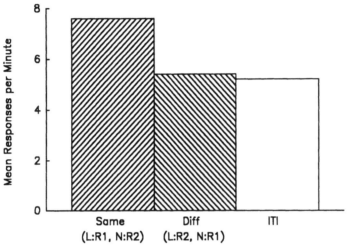

FIG. 10.2 Design and results of an experiment showing stimulus-outcome associations. Initially a common response, Rc, earned different outcomes during a light (L) and noise (N). Then two new responses, R1 and R2, were trained with those different outcomes. During a transfer test L and N were presented while R1 and R2 were available. Responding is shown for the test during the intertrial interval (ITI) when no stimulus was presented and then during the presentation of a stimulus that signaled the same or a different outcome from that which the response had earned.

is to identify that a stimulus is associated with an outcome by asking what kind of new responses it will control in a transfer test. It turns out that a stimulus will be particularly successful at producing responses that have elsewhere been trained with the same outcome, compared with those trained with other outcomes.

The design of a typical transfer experiment (Colwill & Rescorla, 1988) is shown in the upper portion of Fig. 10.2. Rats were first trained to make a common response (nose poking) in the presence of a light and a noise, but not to respond in their absence. During the light, the response led to one outcome (O1, either pellet or sucrose), whereas during the noise it led to the other (O2). Then two other responses, R1 and R2 (lever and chain), were trained to earn those same outcomes. Finally, the light and noise were presented while the animal had the opportunity to lever press and chain pull.

The results of interest are shown in the lower portion of Fig. 10.2. That figure displays responding in the intertrial interval (ITI), when no stimulus was present, and then during the light and noise. The data have been shown separately for those instances in which the stimuli signaled the availability of the same outcome as the response had earned (L:R1 and N:R2) and when they signaled the availability of a different outcome (L:R2, N:R1). It is clear that a stimulus elevated the likelihood only of the response with which it shared an outcome. It left unaffected the other response. This could only occur if the stimuli had associations with particular outcomes; otherwise they could not have selectively elevated responses with a particular outcome. So this selective transfer demonstrates the development of S-O associations. Of course, it also confirms the earlier conclusion, based on devaluation data, that the animal develops R-O associations. The selective transfer also depends on the lever and chain having developed associations with particular outcomes.

Hierarchical associations

The previous results provide evidence for R-O and S-O associations. If one takes seriously classical views of instrumental learning (as well as some evidence we have reported elsewhere), then the animal also develops an S-R association. We can then conclude that the animal learns all of the binary associations among the elements in an instrumental learning situation. But many students of learning have felt uncomfortable with the view that instrumental learning is just an amalgam of these binary associations. Several have suggested instead that there is a hierarchical structure simultaneously involving all three terms. After all, as experimenters we have arranged a three-term contingency such that the R-O association is in effect in the presence of the stimulus. It is not simply that the response produces an outcome or that the stimulus signals that outcome, but rather that the stimulus signals the relation between the response and outcome. In effect, our arrangements have offered the animal the opportunity to learn an association of the form S-(R-O).

This arrangement by the experimenter suggests the possibility that the organism represents the situation in the form of a hierarchical associative structure. It turns out to require rather complex experiments to assess this possibility. But perhaps the simplest is an adaptation of the devaluation technique, as shown in the upper portion of Fig. 10.3. The idea of this experiment (Rescorla, 1991) was to train animals in such a way that if they indeed had learned hierarchical structures of the form S-(R-O), then we would be able to reveal it by the outcome-devaluation procedures we had successfully employed to reveal binary associations.

The training procedure involved what is sometimes called a "switching" design. In such a design, the R-O relations switch as a function of what stimulus is present. In this particular experiment, one stimulus, S1, signaled that making R1 would lead to O1 and making R2 would lead to O2; however, another stimulus,

Discrimination Training	Devaluation	Test
S1: R1 —)O1, R2 —)O2		S1: R1) R2
	O2 —)LiCl	
S2: R1 —)O2, R2 —)O1		S2: R1 (R2

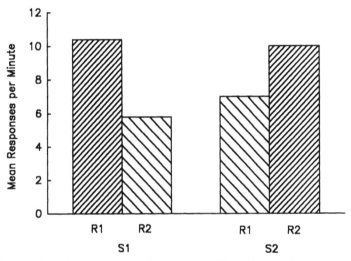

FIG. 10.3   Design and results of an experiment showing a hierarchical associative structure. During discrimination training, R1 and R2 were reinforced with different outcomes during the presentation of two stimuli, S1 and S2. Then one outcome was devalued and the stimuli tested with both responses. The results showed a lower response likelihood when a stimulus signaled that a particular response would earn the now-devalued outcome. From "Association relations in instrumental learning: The Eighteenth Bartlett memorial lecture", by R. A. Rescorla, 1991, *Quarterly Journal of Experimental Psychology, 43B*, pp. 13 and 15. Copyright 1991 by the Experimental Psychology Society. Reprinted with permission.

S2, signaled that the reverse R-O relations obtained. Of course, under these circumstances the animals respond well. After all, the making of either response leads to a positive outcome in the presence of each stimulus. Such a simple result could be accomplished in a variety of ways, including that suggested by the classical S-R reinforcement theories: The establishment of four S-R associations based on the reinforcing action of the outcomes. Although there is a hierarchical structure here, there is nothing inherent in the situation that forces the animal to use it. In order to reveal any possible hierarchical learning, we devaluated one of the outcomes by repeated pairing with LiCl. Then we tested the animal with a choice between the two responses in the presence of each stimulus.

Note that the animal has had all of the individual pairwise associations. Both Rs have been reinforced by both outcomes; both responses have been reinforced in the presence of both stimuli; and both stimuli have had both outcomes in their presence. If the animal only had encoded the binary associations, there is no reason why it should show any differential performance in the test. However, if the animal had encoded the hierarchical structure, then one should anticipate a particular set of outcomes. Because O2 has been devalued, the animals should choose R1 in S1 and R2 in S2, as indicated by the inequalities shown in the design.

The lower portion of Fig. 10.3 shows the results of the test, collapsed across all of the individual elements but separated according to the responses for which the stimuli lead the animal to expect a devalued or not devalued outcome. It is clear that the animal had in fact encoded something of the structure of the situation. Responding was especially low to R2 during S1 and to R1 during S2, those situations in which the devalued outcome would have been earned. So simple devaluation of the O can reveal a hierarchical structure, in much the same manner as it reveals a simple R-O association.

These results lead us to two conclusions: First, the animal richly encodes the outcome in instrumental learning, both in terms of its binary associations with the response and the stimulus and in terms of a more complex hierarchical structure. We have made substantial progress in the analysis of the associations underlying instrumental learning. Second, we now have at hand two techniques that provide powerful leverage for the measurement of associations. They allow one to carry out the kind of analysis that goes well beyond the fact of conditioning to the assessment of its nature. We are then in a position to use those techniques to address any number of other questions about instrumental learning. I will illustrate this by describing how one can exploit these techniques to examine one particularly interesting question: What happens to these associations, once learned, if the world changes so that they are no longer appropriate?

ASSOCIATIONS IN EXTINCTION

One important way in which contingecies might change would be for the outcome that follows a particular stimulus or response to be deleted. Of course, when such an extinction procedure is introduced, responding deteriorates dramatically. The question is then, what happens to the S-O, R-O, and hierarchical S-(R-O) associations when O stops occurring during extinction? In fact, there is strong evidence to suggest that each of these associations persists, perhaps fully intact, through extinction. Some sample experiments will illustrate the point.

Response-outcome associations

Just as one can use the devaluation technique to show the development of an R-O association during learning, one can use it to assess the persistence of the R-O association through extinction. One design is shown in Fig. 10.4 (Rescorla,

Training	Extinction	Retraining	Devaluation	Test
R1→O1	R1−	R1→O3		
R2→O2	R2−	R2→O3		R1 v R2
R3→O1		R3→O3	O1→LiCl	
R4→O2		R4→O3		R3 v R4

FIG. 10.4 Design of an experiment assessing the preservation of R-O associations through extinction. Initially two pairs of responses were trained, with one member of each pair earning O1 and the other earning O2. Then one pair of responses was extinguished. All responses were then trained with a third outcome, O3. This was followed by devaluation of O1 and a choice between the extinguished responses and between the nonextinguished responses.

1993b). This design may seem very elaborate at first, but conceptually it is quite simple. The idea was to train two pairs of responses, provide extinction experience with one pair, and then to test the state of the various R-O associations using the devaluation procedure.

For this purpose, all animals received response training with two pairs of responses, lever and chain as well as nosepoke and handle pull. Within each pair, one response earned pellets and one earned sucrose. Then one pair of responses was extinguished and the other was spared that extinction. Extinction was carried out for 5 sessions, long enough so that behavior had long ago dropped to very low levels. But note that although this ensures adequate extinction experience, it raises another problem that requires a solution. We would like to compare the impact of devaluation on two pairs of responses, but because one pair has been extinguished, those pairs will surely differ considerably in their base rates, making comparisons very difficult. Consequently, in order to ensure similar base rates from which to do a devaluation test, all animals received separate training of each response with a third reinforcer, 5% polycose liquid. This is a polysaccharide that rats find attractive but discriminate from both pellets and sucrose. We knew from many other experiments, including some reported later, that such training with a common outcome would not, in and of itself, affect the R-O associations. But it should raise the response levels to permit a meaningful comparison between responses that have and have not experienced extinction. After this common training, the animals received devaluation of one outcome. Finally, all animals received a test in which they chose between either the extinguished R1 and R2 or the nonextinguished R3 and R4. The question was to what degree we would observe the selective devaluation effect in the extinguished and nonextinguished responses.

Figure 10.5 shows the results of the test session, conducted after devaluation of one outcome. The results are plotted separately for the nonextinguished and extinguished responses. The results for the nonextinguished responses, shown on the left, are like those of previous experiments: There was selective depression

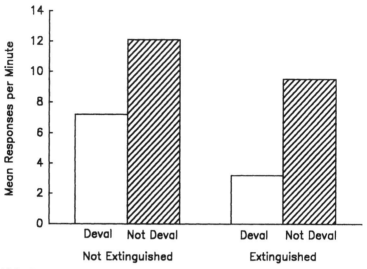

FIG. 10.5   Results of the post-devaluation test of two pairs of responses, one of which had been extinguished. Responding is shown separately for the extinguished and nonextinguished responses when their outcomes had been devalued or not. From "Preservation of response-outcome associations through extinction", by R. A. Rescorla, 1993b, *Animal Learning and Behavior*, *21*, p. 242. Copyright 1993 by the Psychonomic Society. Reprinted with permission.

of the response whose outcome had been devalued. The right-hand side of the figure shows the comparable data from the extinguished response. It is clear that our attempt to match the levels of responding by retraining with O3 was not entirely successful. The overall levels of performance with the extinguished responses are somewhat lower during the test, but the pattern of responding is remarkably similar to that for the nonextinguished responses. Extinguished responses also showed a selective depression when the previously earned outcome was devalued. Comparison between extinguished and nonextinguished responses is complicated by the small differences in overall levels of performance. However, comparison of difference scores or ratios did not give any indication that the differences should be taken seriously. So, this experiment suggests that despite substantial extinction experience, the animal retains a remarkably strong R-O association. It suggests that whatever is responsible for the decrement observed during extinction, it is relatively independent of the state of the R-O association.

Stimulus-outcome associations

The S-O associations are similarly well preserved through extinction. A recent transfer experiment, the design of which is shown in Fig. 10.6, will illustrate the point (Rescorla, 1992). In this experiment, the animals were initially trained with two target responses, R1 and R2 (counterbalanced as lever and chain), each earning a particular outcome, O1 and O2. They then received discrimination

Target Training	Discrimination	Extinction	Test
R1–O1	L: Rc–O1	L: Rc–	L, N: R1
R2–O2	N: Rc–O2	N: Rc–	L, N: R2

FIG. 10.6   Design of an experiment assessing the preservation of S-O associations through extinction. Two responses, R1 and R2, were trained with different outcomes. Then L and N signaled that a common response, Rc, would produce each of those outcomes. Then Rc was extinguished in the presence of either L or N. This was followed by a transfer test that presented L and N while R1 and R2 were available.

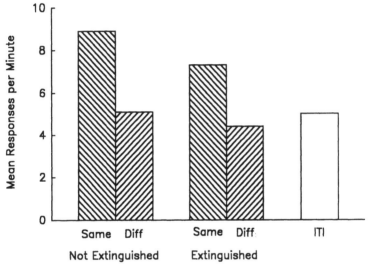

FIG. 10.7   Results of the transfer test with two stimuli, one of which had been extinguished. Responding is shown in the ITI and during the presentation of a stimulus that signaled the same outcome as the response, when that stimulus had or had not been extinguished with its original response. From "Associations between an instrumental discriminative stimulus and multiple outcomes", by R. A. Rescorla, 1992. *Journal of Experimental Psychology: Animal Behavior Processes*, *18*, p. 101. Copyright 1992 by the American Psychological Association. Reprinted with permission.

training in which a nosepoke, Rc, earned O1 during a light and O2 during a noise. We have previously described how this treatment results in L-O1 and N-O2 associations, which would allow those stimuli to selectively transfer to R1 and R2 based on the shared outcomes. However, prior to that transfer, half the animals received extinction with the light and half with the noise. The question of interest was the degree to which the S-O associations, as indexed by selective transfer, would be preserved through extinction.

Figure 10.7 shows the results of this experiment. That figure displays responding to the lever and chain during the ITI and during the extinguished and nonextinguished stimuli separated for responses that shared a same or different outcome with the stimuli. The results for the nonextinguished stimulus are similar to those shown in Fig. 10.2: selective transfer based on a shared outcome. Of more interest, the pattern of results for the extinguished stimulus is virtually identical, suggesting preservation of the S-O association through extinction. Again, the results suggest that something other than an O-specific decremental process has undermined performance. Although as a result of the extinction procedures there was little responding to Rc during the extinguished stimulus, that stimulus retained its ability to transfer to other responses trained with the same outcome.

Hierarchical associations

Finally, there is evidence for the preservation of the hierarchical S-(R-O) associations through extinction. In one recent experiment, we repeated the switching and devaluation experiment illustrated in Fig. 10.3. However, after discrimination training we extinguished one of the stimuli, leaving the other unextinguished. We then carried out the devaluation as before. We can then compare the degree to which we get the devaluation result documenting the presence of the hierarchical associations with and without extinction.

Figure 10.8 shows the results of the test session. We have shown the responding to the extinguished and nonextinguished stimulus separately. In each case, the stimulus retained its ability to differentially control responses that had earned devalued and nondevalued outcomes, as signaled by the hierarchical stimulus.

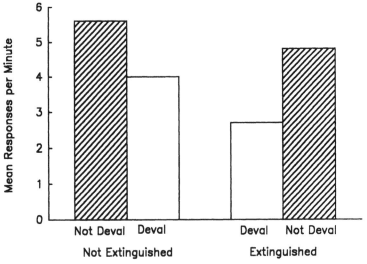

FIG. 10.8   Results of an experiment showing the preservation of a hierarchical association through extinction. Responding is shown during an extinguished and a nonextinguished stimulus when it signaled that the outcome a response had produced had been devalued or not.

Inhibitory S-R associations

These results suggest that all of the associations we have identified as established during original training are preserved through extinction. Apparently, extinction does not involve the removal of the original learning but rather entails the superimposition of some new learning. But what might the character of that new learning be? It does not seem to be specific to the outcomes, because if it were, we would have expected to detect that in one of our procedures.

One possibility we have been exploring is that extinction involves the superimposition of an inhibitory S-R association (Rescorla, 1993a). That is, it may be that during extinction the animal learns specifically not to make a response during a stimulus. Extinction might lead to the development of an inhibitory association between a particular response and a particular stimulus. That association might be superimposed on the original S-O and R-O associations acquired during learning, countermanding their exhibition in performance but leaving them intact.

There is good historical reason to believe that the response is involved in extinction. There are many circumstances that affect the likelihood of a response when a stimulus is nonreinforced; those in turn affect the extinguishing impact of that nonreinforcement. For instance, if the motivational conditions relevant to the outcome are enhanced or decreased, this enhances or decreases the likelihood of the response during extinction. That in turn results in more or less depression of behavior as measured later under common levels of motivation.

However, such results typically allow many alternative interpretations. Consequently, we sought some more specific data that point to the development of an inhibitory S-R association. One recent strategy we have used is to bias the animal artificially towards the making of one of a variety of possible responses during a stimulus (Rescorla, 1993a). Figure 10.9 shows the design of one experiment using this logic. The idea of this experiment was to manipulate the response that occurs in extinction so as to examine the degree to which extinction is response-specific. If extinction of a stimulus intimately involves the establishment of an inhibitory S-R association, then manipulating which R occurs during extinction should influence which R develops an inhibitory relation. With proper

Discrim	Train	Extinction	Test
N: Rc−P	R1−P	L: R1−, N: R2−	N
L: Rc−P	R2−P	L: R2−, N: R1−	L R1, R2

FIG. 10.9   Design of an experiment intended to detect the presence of inhibitory S-R associations. Two stimuli, L and N, each signaled that a common response would produce pellets, P. Then R1 and R2 were each reinforced with pellets. Extinction of L and N was carried out with either R1 or R2 present, and then all four stimulus/response combinations were tested. From "Inhibitory associations between S and R in extinction", by R. A. Rescorla, 1993a, *Animal Learning and Behavior*, *21*, p. 332. Copyright 1993 by the Psychonomic Society. Reprinted with permission.

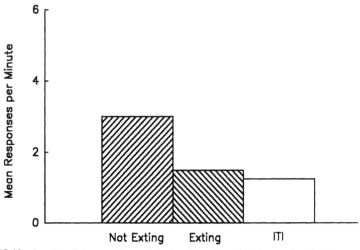

FIG. 10.10   Results of the experimental design from Fig. 10.9. Responding is shown when no stimulus was present (ITI) and in the presence of a stimulus during which the response had been extinguished or not. From "Inhibitory associations between S and R in extinction", by R. A. Rescorla, 1993a, *Animal Learning and Behavior*, 21, p. 333. Copyright 1993 by the Psychonomic Society. Reprinted with permission.

manipulation, one should be able to produce extinction of a stimulus that is relatively specific to that R.

For this purpose, we exploited the transfer procedure that we have used to identify S-O associations. The rats first were given instrumental training with light and noise, each signaling that a common response (Rc), nose poking, would be reinforced with pellets. The intention of this training was to set up L-P and N-P associations. Then the animals were trained with two instrumental responses, R1 and R2, both earning pellets. We know from previous results (e.g. Fig. 10.2) that after this training, presenting either L or N would increase the occurrence of both R1 and R2, because of the associations they all have with P. But instead of conducting transfer immediately, we first extinguished L at a time when R1 was present and we extinguished N at a time when R2 was present. That manipulation should guarantee the higher likelihood of R1 during L and R2 during N. If that results in inhibitory S-R associations, then L should inhibit R1 and N should inhibit R2. But if the associations with the outcomes remain intact, then that extinction should be specific to those cases. That is, the ability of L to provoke R1 should be inhibited by the L-R1 association, but the ability of L to provoke R2 should remain intact. Similarly for N.

Figure 10.10 shows the results of that experiment. The figure displays the rate of making the responses in a final test after each stimulus had been extinguished while allowing the occurrence of one response, but not the other, in its presence. The figure shows the base rate of making a response in the absence of any stimulus, the rate of responding during the stimulus extinguished with that response present, and the rate of responding during the stimulus extinguished with the other response. Obviously, the second stimulus augmented responding, as expected, but the first did not. The continued augmentation in the second case depends on the shared outcomes, thus evidencing retention of the S-O and R-O associations. The lower responding in the first case suggests the development of inhibitory S-R associations. Despite the fact that both stimuli had been extinguished, as had both responses, the effects of the extinction were relatively specific to particular S/R combinations. That is consistent with the view that extinction involves the superimposition of inhibitory S-R associations.

IMPLICATIONS FOR OTHER CHANGES IN OUTCOME RELATIONS

A view according to which extinction involves an outcome-independent depressive process should have implications for other situations in which the contingencies change after initial learning. One particularly interesting case is that in which the consequence of responding changes from one outcome to another. When O1 is replaced by an equivalently valued O2, one might expect behavior to persist, but then the question is what happens to the original association with O1. One way to think about such a situation is that the animal concurrently receives extinction with the first outcome but reinforcement with the second. From this viewpoint, the results described earlier suggest that the original associations would persist but have superimposed on them the new associations. Two recent findings from our lab suggest that in fact this analysis has merit.

The first result suggests that when a response is followed first by one outcome and then by another, not only is the original R-O association preserved, but it continues to contribute to behavior as fully as does the new replacement outcome (Rescorla, 1995). The basic conception of that experiment is simple, although its detailed design was rather complicated. The idea was to allow a response to first earn one outcome, then earn another outcome, and then to devalue either the first-earned outcome, the second-earned outcome, or neither outcome. By asking about the consequences of devaluing each of the outcomes, one can assess the degree to which each contributes to current performance.

The results of that experiment are shown in Fig. 10.11. When neither outcome associated with the response was devalued, substantial responding was observed. However, when either the first- or the second-earned outcomes was devalued, there was a depression of performance. That suggests that the organism preserved information about both of those outcomes, as devaluation of either undermined performance. Moreover, the effects of devaluing the two outcomes were remarkably similar. That suggests that the two R-O associations were of similar strength. Despite the fact that the response had just earned the second outcome, the first-earned outcome was equally important, suggesting the possibility that there is full preservation of the original R-O association through

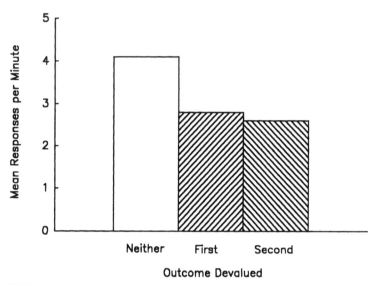

FIG. 10.11 Results of an experiment in which a response was successively reinforced with O1 and then O2. Either the first-earned or the second-earned, or neither of these outcomes had been devalued prior to the test.

training with a second outcome. Current performance seems to depend on the full history of outcomes that responding has earned.

A second implication of this outcome-independent view of extinction is that it predicts the occurrence of a variety of extinction-like phenomena for the case of training with two outcomes. One case we have recently explored is that of spontaneous recovery. When a previously trained response is extinguished, it is well known that with the passage of time there will be spontaneous recovery of a portion of the depressed response. One might then ask whether a similar phenomenon is observed when a response is first followed by one outcome and then by another. As noted earlier, when one outcome is replaced by another of equal value, there is little impact on responding. Yet, we know from the experiments described earlier that this treatment results in an association with the second outcome, without loss of that with the first. But that raises the question of why, when the R is associated with both O1 and O2, it does not show a greater performance than when it is associated with only one outcome. If both associations are present and contributing, why is performance not substantially augmented? One possible reason is that the same inhibitory S-R association occurs here as in extinction, allowing information about both outcomes to be preserved without an augmentation in performance. It may be that the adding of an R-O2 association on top of an existing R-O1 association would in fact lead to a level of performance that is inappropriately high, given that the total value of the outcomes occurring (O2) has not increased. However, that

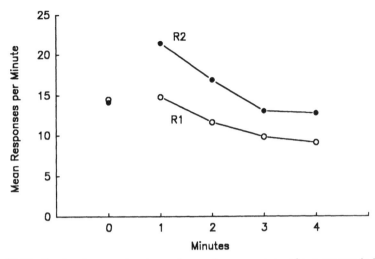

FIG. 10.12   Results of an experiment assessing spontaneous recovery after a response had been successively trained with two outcomes. Responding is shown at the end of training and then for a response tested immediately after training with the second outcome (R1) and for a response tested with a delay after such training (R2). From "Spontaneous recovery after training with multiple outcomes", by R. A. Rescorla, 1996, *Animal Learning and Behavior*, *24*, p. 14. Copyright 1996 by the Psychonomic Society. Adapted with permission.

"overexpectation" led to the development of an inhibitory S-R association that keeps performance down despite the presence of associations with both outcomes. If so, then there is an interesting implication. We know that with the passage of time after extinction there is spontaneous recovery; if our account is correct, then this arises from fading of the inhibitory S-R association. If that S-R association also occurs when two different outcomes are used, then it should fade with the passage of time in that case too. That means that we should expect to see spontaneous improvement in performance to a doubly trained stimulus or response, despite the absence of any observable decrement when the outcomes were changed.

Figure 10.12 shows an example of just such a phenomenon in the case of a response trained with two outcomes (Rescorla, 1996). The figure displays the rate of making two responses, both of which had earned the two outcomes in succession. The pairing with the second outcome occurred in the distant past for R1 but in the recent past for R2. At the end of training with the second outcome, the responses were made with similar frequency. But responding to R1 grew with the passage of time, whereas that for R2 was like that at the end of training.

These results are typical of a large number of Pavlovian and instrumental experiments we have done. They suggest that the inhibitory S-R association may be very pervasive and important in determining performance. They may participate in many procedures in which the contingencies change.

CONCLUSION

These results bring some good news, some bad news, and some advice. The good news comes in two parts. First, the encoding of associations in the instrumental learning situation richly involves the outcomes. Such situations result in the formation of R-O, S-O, and hierarchical associations. Clearly animals learn about many relations in instrumental situations. Second, we have powerful techniques for the detection of these associations, techniques that yield information beyond that inferable from overall response levels. These techniques allow us to learn much more about what is preserved in extinction. They allow us to go beyond the standard claim that extinction does not fully wipe out training to address the more subtle questions of whether the learning is fully preserved and what the nature is of the superimposed process that produces response decrement.

The bad news is that these important associations with outcomes do not seem to account for extinction, one of the basic phenomena in learning. Moreover, we are just beginning to make inroads into the question of what does produce decrement despite the preservation of the S-O and R-O associations. A promising possibility may be inhibitory S-R associations. One may think of S-R theory as the bobo doll of psychological theory: As each new generation comes along, it takes its turn at knocking S-R theory down, perhaps with temporary success. But S-R theory keeps bobbing back up, often turning slightly to offer a somewhat different face for subsequent attacks. This time it seems to have bounced back showing its inhibitory side. Despite the fact that our results suggest that a simple S-R association cannot fully account for the acquisition of instrumental behavior, they also suggest the possibility that they are an important contributor to the depression of responding that comes when contingencies change.

The advice is that if one wants to modify performance following learning, one should concentrate on particular S-R combinations. Our results suggest that once learned, the outcome-based associations that generate initial performance are unlikely to be easily changed. They seem in place to stay. Consequently, if one wants to eliminate a behavior pattern, it may be best to accept the persistence of the underlying learning and try to superimpose on it some other basis for performance change. It may be fruitless to try to erase original learning. We may instead have to live with its presence and think of ways of masking it by training in alternative behaviors or learning.

ACKNOWLEDGEMENTS

This research was supported by National Science Foundation grants BNS-88-03514 and IBN94-04676.

REFERENCES

Colwill, R. M., & Rescorla, R. A. (1985). Post-conditioning devaluation of a reinforcer affects instrumental responding. *Journal of Experimental Psychology: Animal Behavior Processes, 11,* 120–132.

Colwill, R. M., & Rescorla, R. A. (1988). Associations between the discriminative stimulus and the reinforcer in instrumental learning. *Journal of Experimental Psychology: Animal Behavior Processes, 14,* 155–164.

Rescorla, R. A. (1991). Association relations in instrumental learning: The Eighteenth Bartlett memorial lecture. *Quarterly Journal of Experimental Psychology, 43B,* 1–23.

Rescorla, R. A. (1992). Associations between an instrumental discriminative stimulus and multiple outcomes. *Journal of Experimental Psychology: Animal Behavior Processes, 18,* 95–104.

Rescorla, R. A. (1993a). Inhibitory associations between S and R in extinction. *Animal Learning and Behavior, 21,* 327–336.

Rescorla, R. A. (1993b). Preservation of response-outcome associations through extinction. *Animal Learning and Behavior, 21,* 238–245.

Rescorla, R. A. (1995). Full preservation of a response-outcome association through training with a second outcome. *Quarterly Journal of Experimental Psychology, 48B,* 252–261.

Rescorla, R. A. (1996). Spontaneous recovery after training with multiple outcomes. *Animal Learning and Behavior, 24,* 11–18.

CHAPTER ELEVEN

The dynamics of memory in animal learning

John E. R. Staddon
Duke University, Durham, North Carolina, USA

Memory dynamics, the effects on recall of the temporal spacing of to-be-remembered stimuli, reflect three processes: learning, forgetting (trace decay), and interference. A process for trace decay can be derived from a cascaded-integrator model for rate-sensitive habituation. The model predicts nonexponential forgetting functions that are compatible with Jost's law (old memories decay more slowly than new) as well as the 2-parameter summary functions recently derived from a massive dataset on human retention. The same process seems to be involved in other learning phenomena such as the partial reinforcement extinction effect and reinforcement successive-contrast effects.

La dynamique mnémonique, soit les effets qu'exerce sur le rappel l'espacement temporel des stimuli à mémoriser, repose sur trois processus: l'apprentissage, l'oubli (affaiblissement de la trace) et l'interférence. Un processus d'affaiblissement de la trace peut être inféré à partir d'un modèle qui, basé sur une intégration en cascades, rend compte de la sensibilité de l'habituation à l'endroit de l'intervalle de temps entre stimuli successifs. Ce modèle prédit des fonctions non exponentielles de l'oubli qui sont compatibles avec la loi de Jost (les souvenirs anciens s'affaiblissent plus lentement que ceux récents), de même qu'avec les fonctions récapitulatives à deux paramètres qui ont été récemment dérivées d'abondantes données de rétention chez l'humain. Le même processus semble intervenir dans d'autres phénomènes d'apprentissage, tels l'effet du renforcement intermittent sur l'extinction et les effets du renforcement administré en séries contrastées.

It is a curious fact that the major category labels in psychology have no real basis. Cognition and motivation, learning, and memory are not scientific terms. That is to say, they do not emerge from, nor for the most part have they been well justified by, a systematic or theoretical understanding of behavior. It is as if *force* and *energy* in physics were still defined in terms of muscular effort, and the definition of *species* in biology were taken from the *Historia animalium*. Cognition, motivation and the rest are still Aristotelian categories.

Physics and biology have moved on. Force and energy now derive their meanings from Newtonian physics. The term "species" derives its scientific basis from common descent according to the principles of Darwinian evolution (although there are still arguments about this: as Richard Dawkins has commented somewhere, taxonomy is a contentious discipline). But psychology still begins (and ends) with Aristotle.

Sometimes vernacular terms turn out to be valid and useful. Some diseases that have always had common names—smallpox, consumption—have turned out to be coherent entities with an identifiable cause. But a host of others—dropsy, nerve fever, ague, St. Vitus' dance, all the various humors—turned out to be either labels for nothing at all, or for several things, for bouillabaisse or an empty pot. They have vanished from the medical lexicon.[1]

The point is that in the history of science, theory and system have always trumped intuition and tradition. Memory, motivation and the other folk-label categories of psychology still await scientific justification—or replacement by more firmly grounded terms.

We need a theory, but most memory theories tend to assume what is to be proved: Aristotelian categories, cognitive representations, information processes, and the like. Is there another approach? Here is one possibility. There is one property of memory that is objective, universal, and noncontroversial: the effects on recall of the *temporal arrangement* of stimuli to be remembered. If the effects of temporal spacing can be understood in some exact way, we will have made undeniable progress. Moreover, this aspect of memory is something that also lends itself to study in animals and can therefore make a bridge between animals and humans.

I am making a distinction between memory properties that are *structural* and those that are *dynamic*. Structural properties relate to what the to-be-remembered stimuli are and how they resemble or differ from others—how they are encoded, in cognitive jargon. Dynamic properties relate to the spacing of stimuli in time and how this affects the magnitude and timing of a recall (response) measure. Structural properties are very difficult to understand and undoubtedly differ between species and possibly even between individuals. Dynamics should be easier. This chapter is devoted entirely to dynamics.

Because the main part of the chapter may seem to have little to do with memory as it is usually studied, I will begin with a familiar memory example, one of the oldest and best-established phenomena in human and animal memory: the *serial-position effect*. A simple explanation for this effect implicates three

---

[1] It would be tactless to point out that it is only in the realm of mental illness that folk-disease labels with little more justification than dropsy and ague still figure prominently, sanctioned not by science but by vote of the DSM committee of the day. Of course, the "folk" here are psychiatrists and clinical psychologists, not "silly old tribespeople".

processes: learning, memory decay, and interference between memories. I go on to argue that memory decay can be understood through the dynamics of habituation, a ubiquitous form of nonassociative learning that is triggered by exposure to any stimulus. I conclude by showing that a theory of habituation dynamics implies a form of memory-decay function that is compatible with Jost's Law (a general principle of memory), and with summary retention functions.

SERIAL-POSITION EFFECT

The serial-position effect is just the fact that when a list of items is learned, the items in the middle of the list are recalled less well than the items at the beginning (this is known as *primacy*) or the end (*recency*). Many experiments have been devoted to this effect and I make no attempt to summarize them here. I want to use it only to illustrate my theoretical method and show how our work on habituation relates to memory, which, at first sight, may seem an unrelated phenomenon. The theoretical method is to find the simplest dynamic account for the maximum number of experimental facts (cf. Staddon & Zanutto, in press). Our slogan might be "give parsimony a chance"!

Thus regarded, the basic serial-position effect can be derived from just three assumptions: (a) that presenting a stimulus has a positive effect on the recallability of that stimulus (learning), but (b) a negative effect on the recallability of other stimuli that occur close to it in time (interference), and (c) that the recallability of a stimulus decreases with time (forgetting). Once these assumptions are precisely expressed, many of the dynamics can be explained without assumptions about stores, rehearsal buffers, etc.

Figure 11.1 shows the basic idea, for a 3-item list. The shaded arrows show the inhibitory effect of each item on all other items. The positive effect of each stimulus (item presentation) is not shown. Time is not shown either, but our first assumption is that these inhibitory effects depend on proximity in time. To see how this might work, we need an equation:

$$V_i(t + 1) = aV_i(t) + (1 - a)F[\Sigma V_j(t)]S_i(t), \; 0 < a < 1, \qquad (1)$$

where $F[\Sigma V_j(t)]$ is a nonlinear inverse function of $\Sigma V_j(t)$, i.e. as $\Sigma V_j(t)$ increases, F decreases (in the simulations, I used the function $[1 - \Sigma V_j(t)]^2$, but doubtless

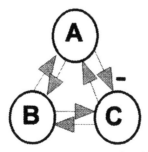

FIG. 11.1   Mutual inhibition (competition) among remembered items of a 3-term list.

many other inverse functions would do as well). This equation just says that from one time step to the next, the recallability, V_i, of an item (response strength in operant jargon) decreases through forgetting and increases through learning; t refers to the fact that this is a discrete-time model: the equation gives V_i in the next time step, $V_i(t + 1)$, as a function of its value in the previous time step, the stimulus value, $S_i(t)$, and the effects of all other stimuli, $F[\Sigma V_j(t)]$. S_i is 1 if stimulus i is present during a time step, but zero otherwise.

To see how this process works, look first at what happens when no stimulus is present. The last term on the right-hand side of the equation is zero, because $S_i(t) = 0$; thus, $V_i(t + 1) = aV_i(t)$. Because parameter a (the memory-decay rate) is < 1, the recallability of stimulus i decreases with each time step, in the absence of any stimulus. The decrease is exponential, because a is constant and, as we will see, this is in fact incorrect. But the form of the decay (forgetting) function could be changed without changing the general structure of Equation 1. The point is that the first term in the equation is a memory-decay term.

The second term in the equation, $(1 - a)F[\Sigma V_j(t)]S_i(t)$, incorporates both learning and interference. It incorporates learning, because the term is positive so long as S_i is positive (the stimulus is present). The term also includes interference, because the positive effect of S_i (the amount of learning in a given time step) is inversely dependent on the strengths (recallabilities), V_j, of *all* the stimuli in the list (because of the multiplier $F[\Sigma V_j(t)]$). The larger the sum of these values, the smaller the positive effect of S_i: the stronger the traces from other stimuli, the smaller the learning increment given to the trace of the stimulus that is present. On the basis of some trial functions, I suspect that the interference term must be nonlinear to produce the serial-position effect with this model structure, but this is not proved and is not essential to my main argument.[2]

The way the process works is illustrated in Fig. 11.2. The large graph shows V_i values for each stimulus in a 4-stimulus list that has been presented repeatedly. Two list presentations late in training are shown in the figure: ABCD . . . intertrial interval . . . ABCD. Each stimulus presentation is denoted by a peak in its V-value curve, which shows the increment in strength caused by stimulus presentation. The heavy line is the trace for Stimulus A, etc. Look at the vertical line marked recall. It indicates the strengths (V-values) for each stimulus some little time after the second list presentation (also shown in the inset graph). The points to note are that (a) each stimulus is less recallable than it was immediately after presentation, (b) the recallability is highest for the last stimulus (recency) and next highest for the first stimulus (primacy); and (c) this order is maintained

---

[2] Alert readers will note that this model incorporates proactive interference (PI: the effect of previous stimuli on the recallability of the current stimulus) but not retroactive interference (RI: the effect of the current stimulus on the recallability of earlier stimuli). RI could be included via a normalizing response rule, or by a competitive effect on decay rates, or by some more selective process limited to certain time scales. It is also possible that PI and RI are not in fact separable processes. As this model is illustrative, not definitive, I only present the simplest version that matches the data.

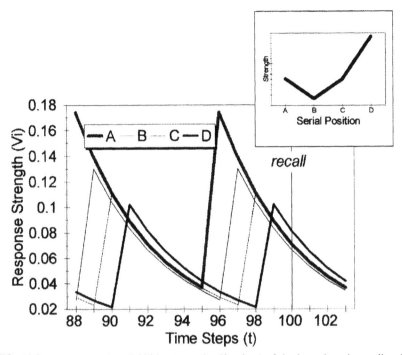

FIG. 11.2   Main graph: Recallabilities (strengths, V_i values) of the items in a 4-term list after extended training according to the process in Equation 1 ($a = 0.8$). Inset: Response strengths for the four stimuli at the time of recall (100 time steps).

indefinitely. Note that the primacy effect is relatively small and that property (c), the fact that the relative recallability of the four items remains the same as time passes, is incompatible with Jost's law, which I will discuss in a moment.

Thus, this simple process reproduces the serial-position effect, but not perfectly. The point of this example is just to show that at least three ingredients are necessary for an account of memory dynamics: learning, interference, and forgetting (decay). The rest of the chapter is concerned with memory decay. It turns out that the dynamics of habituation will lead us to a better, nonexponential memory-decay function. Giving up the assumption of exponential decay improves the primacy prediction of the serial-position-effect model and allows for traces to cross over, as required by Jost's law.

The first-principles question to be asked about memory dynamics is: How does the effect of a stimulus[3] change with time and repeated presentation? Repeated

---

[3] Effect on what? the skeptical reader may ask. Unlike the reflex preparations used for habituation experiments, there is after all no (immediate) response in a memory experiment. However, a stimulus must have some persistent effect if habituation is to occur—or if it is to be recalled later. Thus, the answer to the question is the same for any learning experiment: If learning is to occur, the stimulus must have an effect on the organism's internal state. The job for any model is to suggest what form that effect takes.

presentation of a stimulus, and measurement of its changing effect, is of course the experimental paradigm for the study of habituation, to which I now turn.

HABITUATION

Habituation is the waning in a reflex response to successive presentations of a stimulus.[4] It is widely observed with many different responses and stimuli and across species ranging from protists to humans (Eisenstein & Peretz, 1973; Jennings, 1906; Peeke & Herz, 1973; Peeke & Petrinovich, 1984; Thompson & Spencer, 1966; Wood, 1970). Habituation has two main properties: stimulus specificity and rate sensitivity (Byrne, 1982; Carew, Pinsker, & Kandel, 1972; Davis, 1970; Staddon, 1993). Stimulus specificity means that habituation to one stimulus does not extend to all others. Habituation is more rapid and complete when interstimulus intervals (ISIs) are short than when they are long. Rate sensitivity (Staddon, 1993) means that recovery from habituation is surprisingly also more rapid after short ISIs.

Both stimulus specificity and rate sensitivity seem to be universal properties of habituation. The details of stimulus specificity in primitive animals are not well known, but rate sensitivity has been demonstrated at the cellular level (synaptic depression: Byrne, 1982), in the sea-slug *Aplysia* (Carew et al., 1972), and in the turning behavior of nematodes (Rankin & Broster, 1992), suggesting that the underlying process may be relatively simple.

Staddon (1993) has shown that the basic property of habituation can be duplicated by a process in which response strength is the difference between a constant stimulus effect and a "leaky-integrator" short-term stimulus memory (Fig. 11.3: θ is a threshold, usually 0, X is the stimulus input, V_I, is the inhibitory integrator "charge" and V_o is the response output). This scheme (termed feedforward habituation) is a formalization of a well-known idea of Sokolov (1963). As successive stimuli are presented, the accumulated "charge" of the integrator—the stimulus "memory"—increases. As response output is the difference between

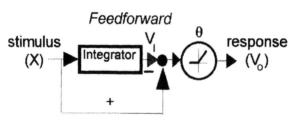

FIG. 11.3   Single-unit feedforward habituation model. Integrated effects of past stimuli, V_I, are subtracted from the direct effects, X, and the above-threshold difference, $\theta - X - V_I$, determines the response strength V_o.

---

[4] This section draws on work reported more extensively in Staddon (1993) and Staddon and Higa (1996).

the integrator charge and the constant stimulus input, output response strength decreases as successive stimuli are presented. If the ISI is too large, however, the integrator "discharges" ("forgets") between stimulus presentations and the system does not habituate. Thus, the degree of habituation in the model, as in nature, is less at longer ISIs.

The single-unit model habituates less at long ISIs than at short, but post-habituation recovery is just as rapid. The main point of the 1993 paper was that a series of at least two cascaded habituation units (the output of the first being the input to the second) is necessary to reproduce the rate-sensitive property (see Fig. 11.4). It is noteworthy that Gingrich and Byrne (1985) proposed a two-stage cascade model for the cellular processes underlying rate-sensitive synaptic depression in *Aplysia*, and Treisman's (1984) response-selector habituation model also used processes with two time scales to account for rate sensitivity.

First, it will be helpful to define four key terms: response strength, reflex, reflex strength, and reflex state. Although these four terms derive from experiments on reflexes, I will argue that the same scheme can easily be adapted to the study of memory dynamics.

Response strength is the level of the actual response (startle, reversal [nematodes], blink) to a reflex stimulus (a touch, a tap, an air puff), usually measured in physical units, such as stabilimeter force reading, turning angle, or eye-blink excursion. In the context of memory experiments, response strength corresponds to a recall measure at the time recall is required.

Reflex is the process that intervenes between a stimulus and the response that the stimulus typically produces. A reflex may be actual (i.e. the actual physiological mechanisms involved—which are imperfectly known, in most cases), or theoretical (i.e. a dynamic model). If the reflex is theoretical, then we can specify exactly its strength and its state at any time. In the case of memory, there may be no immediate response to the stimulus, but the rest of the process can be assumed to proceed.

Reflex strength, V_R, is the *potential* response strength at any time, given a standard response (set by convention at unity). Reflex strength is the response strength that *would have been measured*, had a stimulus been given at time t. Thus, when a stimulus *is* given, response strength equals reflex strength. Note that this definition of reflex strength is strictly empirical and does not depend on any particular model of habituation. Of course, any dynamic model must predict reflex strength, but theoretical values that are below threshold or negative will have no direct behavioral counterpart. I will explain the memory counterpart of reflex strength in a later section.

Reflex state is a theoretical concept. It is simply the values of all the variables that define the underlying dynamic process. In the models we have studied, reflex state is defined by up to 10 variables. Note that "strength" is necessarily unidimensional, whereas "state" is almost always multidimensional. In the habituation model, reflex state is also the *memory* state.

Reflex strength for the single-unit leaky-integrator habituation model with zero threshold is just $V_R = 1 - V_I$, where V_I is the state of the single integrator and 1 is the value of the "standard" stimulus. When the stimulus presented is the standard, unit stimulus, response strength is equal to the suprathreshold part of reflex strength at the instant of stimulus presentation.

Equations. Formally, in discrete-time notation, the single unit feedforward model is:

$$V_O(t) = X(t) - V_I(t), \text{ if } V_O > \theta \tag{2}$$
$$= 0 \text{ otherwise.}$$

(Equivalently, $V_o = \theta(X - V_I)$, where θ denotes a threshold function).

$$V_I(t + 1) = aV_I(t) + bX(t), \quad 0 < a < 1, b > 0 \tag{3}$$

where V_I is the integrated inhibitory effect of past stimuli, V_O is response strength, θ is a threshold (zero in all our simulations), a is a time constant that reflects the period over which past stimuli contribute to habituation, $X(t)$ is the effect of a stimulus at time t, and b is the weighting of the stimulus effect. If a is small, only recent stimuli contribute, and habituation is rapid if the stimulus spacing is short enough. If a is large, even stimuli that occurred a while ago contribute: Habituation will occur even if stimuli are widely spaced, but habituation is slow. Parameter b affects habituation rate but not recovery rate, which is determined entirely by a. This single-unit system does *not* show rate sensitivity, however.

Note that V_I is both reflex state and the state of the memory of the system.

Habituation units can be cascaded, with the output of the jth unit, V_{Oj}, being the stimulus input to unit $j + 1$. The final output is just the output of the last integrator in the chain. Any number of units can be cascaded, depending on the number of different time scales implied by data. In a cascade with unit input and zero thresholds, it is easy to show that the net reflex strength at the last integrator (N) in the cascade is just

$$V_R = 1 - \sum_{j=1}^{N} V_{Ij}. \tag{4}$$

Memory-trace strength. Spontaneous recovery is the change in reflex strength as a function of time in the absence of further stimulation. For a habituated reflex, response strength recovers with time as memory for the stimulus fades. For a memory, strength decreases with time. In the cascaded-integrator model, memory-trace[5] strength—recallability of a stimulus—is thus the complement of reflex response strength:

---

[5] We are dealing with single reflexes here, so the interference term in Equation 1 is assumed to be zero. V_{MT} is therefore the memory-trace term.

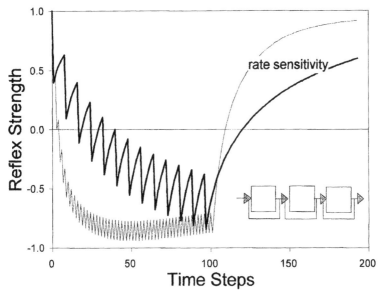

FIG. 11.4   Rate sensitivity in a 3-stage system. *Light line*: reflex strength during and after a 2-time-step stimulus series; *heavy line*: reflex strength after an 8-time-step series. Parameters $a_1 = 0.8$; $a_2 = 0.95$; $a_3 = 0.99.$; thresholds, $\theta_i = 0$. Note the slower recovery after the 8-time-step training series.

$$V_{MT} = \sum_{j=1}^{N} V_{lj}, \tag{5}$$

where V_{MT} is memory-trace strength.

Figure 11.4 shows reflex strength as a function of time for a 3-unit cascaded-integrator model. The light line is reflex strength during and after 50 stimuli at 2 time-step intervals (interstimulus interval, ISI, = 2). The heavy line is reflex strength following a stimulus series at 8 time-step intervals (ISI = 8). Stimuli cease after about time step 100. In Fig. 11.4, spikes in each record indicate stimulus presentations. *Recovery* is defined as *reflex strength in the absence of stimulation*. Thus, the curves after the last stimulus presentation (around time step 100) in the graph in Fig. 11.4 show the recovery curves for a 3-unit feed-forward habituation model. Habituation is complete after 3 time steps when the ISI is 2 and after 17 after training at ISI 8. Nevertheless, recovery from habituation is much more rapid after the shorter ISI. This is *rate sensitivity*.

Parameter constraints.   The cascade model predicts rate sensitivity because we chose time constants (a_j) that increase along the series: smaller (hence faster) on the periphery (i.e. on the input side) than centrally (on the output side). We followed this rule because of informal physiological evidence that peripheral —sensory—processes seem to act faster than central ones, and because it is necessary for rate sensitivity. The ordered a_j values control the behavior of the integrator cascade in the following way. When stimuli are far apart in time (long ISIs), earlier (faster) units in the cascade discharge more or less completely between stimulus presentations. Thus, the *state* of the system (i.e. the vector of V values for the N integrators in the cascade—recall that reflex strength is just $1 - \Sigma V_{Ij}$) during the recovery period is dominated by the V values of "slow" integrators late in the chain. Recovery is therefore slow, because these integrators discharge slowly. Conversely, when stimuli are closely spaced (short ISIs), "fast" integrators early in the chain remain charged between stimulus presentations, consequently block the signal to the slow, later integrators. Recovery is therefore rapid, because the system state is dominated by the V values of fast integrators early in the chain.

A cascaded-integrator model can obviously account for the qualitative properties of rate-sensitive habituation. But we have also shown in some detail that it can match the quantitative properties, where appropriate data are available (Staddon & Higa, 1996). An extensive dataset has been published in a series of papers by Catherine Rankin and her associates on habituation and recovery in *Caenorhabditis elegans*. *C. elegans* is a nematode worm, much studied by molecular and developmental biologists. Every cell lineage during development, from fertilized egg to adult animal, has been perfectly charted. Each of its 302 neurons and 56 glial cells has been separately identified. Despite its simplicity, *C. elegans* shows many of the basic phenomena of nonassociative learning, including habituation. Catherine Rankin and her collaborators have studied turning by this animal in response to taps on the petri dish in which it is swimming. A dish containing a single *C. elegans* is tapped at fixed interstimulus intervals (ISIs). The amount each worm swims backward within 1 second of a tap (termed a *reversal*) on each trial is recorded, and scored as a proportion of its response to the initial tap. The group response is the average of these individual proportional responses. The recovery function was estimated by presenting stimuli at progressively longer ISIs after the training series had ceased.

Staddon and Higa employed a variety of strategies to reduce the parameter space for N-stage cascade models to manageable proportions (2 parameters). They concluded that a 2-stage feedback (rather than feedforward) model gave the best fit. Figure 11.5 shows a typical fit between simulation and data from Broster and Rankin (1994). The left half of the figure shows response strength (for a group of nematodes) during 30 stimulus presentations with different mixes of interstimulus interval (ISI): 15 intervals at 10 seconds ISI followed by 15 at 60 seconds, or the reverse. The right half of the figure shows recovery following the stimulus series. The data are quite variable, but the 2-stage model does a reasonable job of describing them, and this was true for all the data from two studies (Broster & Rankin, 1994; Rankin & Broster, 1992). Figure 11.6 shows that a 5-stage model gives a reasonable fit to more complex habituation data from an old experiment by Carew, Pinsker, and Kandel (1972). In this experiment, *Aplysia* were given 10 trials per day for 5 days. Habituation occurred both within each day and across days and this pattern is readily duplicated by the cascade model.

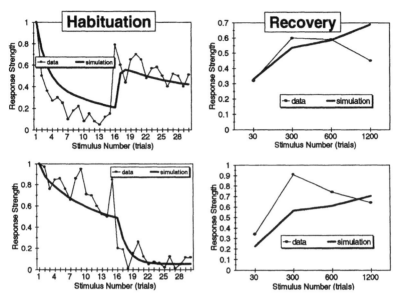

FIG. 11.5 Data (filled circles) and predictions (lines) for a *C. elegans* habituation experiment of Broster and Rankin (1994). The animal received either 15 10-ISI trials followed by 15 60 seconds (top) or the reverse (bottom). Note that habituation during the 10-ISI series is faster in the 60 → 10 condition than the 10 → 60 condition in both data and model.

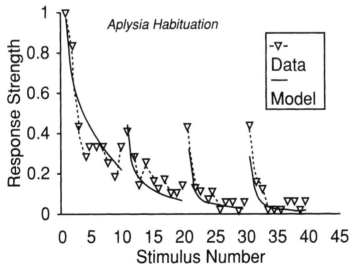

FIG. 11.6 *Aplysia* habituation data from Carew, Pinsker, and Kandel (1972, Figure 1), fit by a 5-stage feedback model with ordered parameters. The data (open triangles), group-average response during 4 groups of 10 daily trials at 30-second ISI, have been normalized as proportions of the maximum response. The model (heavy solid line) captures both the within- and between-session effects. Parameter values: $a_1 - a_5$: 0.001, 0.01, 0.1, 0.97, 0.999999; $b_1 - b_5$: 0.999999, 0.8, 0.6, 0.4, 0.125.

IMPLICATIONS FOR MEMORY

What does the cascaded-integrator habituation model imply for memory? Equation 5 says that memory-trace strength is the sum of several exponentials, as each V_{1j} value declines exponentially in the absence of stimulation and $V_{MT} = \sum_{j=1}^{N} V_{1j}$. This is convenient, because Simon (1966) showed many years ago that simple exponential decay is incompatible with a venerable and well-established memory principle: Jost's (second) law (e.g. Hovland, 1951), which is: *Of two associations of equal strength at time t, the older will gain strength with respect to the newer with lapse of time (t' > t).*

Simon's argument is illustrated graphically in Fig. 11.7. The light line shows a "strong" memory, laid down at $t = 1$. The heavy line shows a "weak" memory laid down later, at time $t = 5$. At $t' = 6$, the strengths of both are equal, but because both traces are exponential, with the same time constant, they decay at the same rate and remain equal for ever. Thus, simple exponential decay is incompatible with Jost's law.

Figure 11.8 shows that Jost's law *is* compatible with the cascade model. As in Fig. 11.7, the figure shows a "strong" memory trace laid down at time $t = 10$ and a "weak" trace laid down later at $t = 26$. The two traces are equal at $t' = 43$, but thereafter, the older trace (light line) remains above the newer (heavy line). The reason the cascade model obeys Jost's law is that trace decay is not exponential (the sum of several exponentials is not itself exponential[6]). Because of the

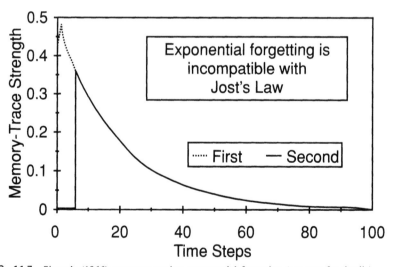

FIG. 11.7   Simon's (1966) argument against exponential forgetting (see text for details).

---

[6] Simon (1966) pointed out that the sum of two exponentials with appropriate time constants is consistent with Jost's law. The cascade habituation model is not limited to two stages, however.

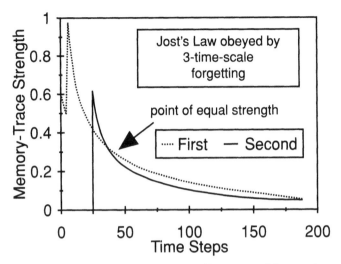

FIG. 11.8   Memory predictions of a multistage cascaded-integrator model are consistent with Jost's law (see text and caption to FIG. 11.4 for details).

rate-sensitive property, decay at long times occurs at a slower rate than at short times: Older memories decay more slowly than newer ones. Hence, given two memories of equal strength, the older one will gain on the newer with lapse of time.

There is now abundant evidence that human and animal retention (forgetting) functions are not exponential (e.g. Hovland, 1951; Staddon, 1984). Rubin and Wenzel (1996) have gathered data from 210 human experiments and fitted them with 105 different of 2-parameter functions (not including the sum of exponentials, unfortunately). The best-fitting functions (which fit most of the data very well indeed) all have the general form of the functions in Fig. 11.8, declining rapidly at first, but then more slowly.

Note that nonexponential, rate-sensitive forgetting will tend to increase the recallability of "old" stimuli at the expense of recent stimuli. Replacing exponential with nonexponential forgetting in the model discussed earlier (Equation 1, Fig. 11.2) will therefore increase the primacy effect, which was small in the original version.

CONCLUSION

The dynamics of habituation in a wide range of species provide a clue to the process of memory-trace decay in humans. Rate-sensitive habituation implies nonexponential memory decay of precisely the right form to accommodate Jost's law: That old memories gain in strength relative to newer ones. The general implication is that any stimulus, whether it is the stimulus for an overt reflex or a neutral stimulus that has no obvious behavioral effect, is processed by the same kind of rate-sensitive mechanism. This mechanism determines the properties both of spontaneous recovery (for reflexes) and of recall (for stimuli that elicit no measurable response).

The same dynamic process may be involved in other learning phenomena. The partial-reinforcement extinction effect (PREE) is observed under many experimental conditions (but not all: see Nevin, 1988) and has two main aspects: (1) Animals trained to respond for infrequent reinforcement stabilize at a performance level that is generally lower than animals trained with more frequent reinforcement. This finding is not paradoxical and fits in with all standard reinforcement theories. (2) However, when reinforcement is discontinued (extinction), partially reinforced animals often persist longer in responding than animals that have been reinforced more frequently. This result is paradoxical both because the partially reinforced animals are responding at a lower level at the beginning of extinction, and because classical reinforcement theories assume that more frequent reinforcement builds more response "strength," hence more persistence.

The PREE is consistent with rate-sensitive habituation in the following sense. The "stimuli" for the system are just the occurrences of reinforcement during training. In a cascaded-integrator system, memory-trace strength is the sum of the V_i values associated with each integrator. This trace strength corresponds to what in cognitive jargon would be called an "expectancy". The larger this sum (the greater the expectancy), the greater the tendency to respond. "Expectancy" in this sense behaves in a sensible way: It will be higher when reinforcers occur frequently than when they are infrequent, and zero after a long time with no reinforcement ($V_{li} = 0$ for all i). Expectancy will also decay more slowly after partial than continuous reinforcement, providing a basis for the PREE.

To understand the process, let us just took at a 2-stage cascaded-integrator model. Consider how ΣV_{li} (i.e. $V_{l1} + V_{l2}$) will change with time when reinforcement is no longer delivered. If reinforcements (stimuli) occurred frequently during the preceding training series (a short ISI), then the level of V_{l1} will be high and the level of V_{l2} will be low, for reasons described earlier. The sum, $V_{l1} + V_{l2}$, will be high. But when reinforcement ceases, V_{l1} will decline rapidly, because a_1 is small, hence the sum—and therefore responding—will decline quite rapidly in extinction. The opposite will occur if the training ISI is long: At the end of training V_{i1} will be small and V_{i2} relatively large, although the sum will be less than with a short ISI. But in extinction, V_{i2} declines slowly (because a_2 is large), hence the sum also declines slowly and responding is more persistent. This difference is the PREE. There are other ways to apply the rate-sensitivity idea to PREE—and the effect is not universal (it is not often found in Pavlovian conditioning, for example, and Nevin (1988) has reported operant experiments that fail to find it). But it is clear that in principle rate sensitivity provides a basis for the effect.

The successive negative-contrast effect (SNCE) is slower responding under low-frequency reinforcement by animals first trained with high-frequency reinforcement (call this group High-Low: HL) compared to animals trained all along with low-frequency reinforcement (Group LL). The effect is usually transient: After sufficient low-frequency training, the performance of both groups eventually converges. The argument of the previous two paragraphs applies here also. For the HL animals, a drop in reinforcement frequency will lead at first to a drop in the sum of $V_{I1} + V_{I2}$, because V_{I2} will be low and most of the sum will be contributed by fast-decaying V_{I1}. With continued experience, the drop in V_{I1} will be compensated by growth in V_{I2}. For the LL animals, on the other hand, V_{I2} will already be high because of the initial training. Thus, in a comparison, at the beginning of the second L period, the HL group will at first respond slower than the LL group.

My conclusion is that the phenomenon of rate sensitivity underlies a broad range of learning and memory effects: habituation, spontaneous recovery, the partial-reinforcement effect, reinforcement-contrast effects, and Jost's memory law. Rate sensitivity implies the existence of processes with multiple time scales. We have shown that a simple cascaded-integrator system with 2–5 stages can model the dynamics of habituation and spontaneous recovery in a wide range of species. The same model may apply to human memory results.

ACKNOWLEDGEMENTS

Research supported by grants from NIMH and NSF to Duke University.

REFERENCES

Broster, B. S., & Rankin, C. H. (1994). Effects of changing interstimulus interval during habituation in *Caenorhabditis elegans*. *Behavioral Neuroscience, 108*, 1019–1029.

Byrne, J. H. (1982). Analysis of synaptic depression contributing to habituation of gill-withdrawal reflex in *Aplysia californica*. *Journal of Neurophysiology, 48*, 431–438.

Carew, T. J., Pinsker, H. M., & Kandel, E. R. (1972). Long-term habituation of a defensive withdrawal reflex in *Aplysia*. *Science, 175*, 451–454.

Davis, M. (1970). Effects of interstimulus interval length and variability on startle-response habituation in the rat. *Journal of Comparative and Physiological Psychology, 72*, 177–192.

Eisenstein, E. M., & Peretz, B. (1973). Comparative aspects of habituation in invertebrates. In H. V. S. Peeke & M. J. Herz (Eds.), *Habituation* (Vol. 1, pp. 1–34). New York: Harcourt Brace Jovanovich.

Gingrich, K. J., & Byrne, J. H. (1985). Simulation of synaptic depression, posttetanic potentiation and presynaptic facilitation of synaptic potentials from sensory neurons mediating gill-withdrawal reflex in *Aplysia*. *Journal of Neurophysiology, 53*, 652–669.

Hovland, C. I. (1951). Human learning and retention. In S. S. Stevens (Ed.), *Handbook of experimental psychology* (pp. 613–689). New York: Wiley.

Jennings, H. S. (1906/1976). *Behavior of the lower organisms*. Bloomington: Indiana University Press. (1906 edn. published by Columbia University Press, New York.)

Nevin, J. A. (1988). Behavioral momentum and the partial reinforcement effect. *Psychological Bulletin, 103*, 44–56.

Peeke, H. V. S., & Herz, M. J. (1973). *Habituation* (Vols. I & II). New York: Harcourt Brace Jovanovich.

Peeke, H. V. S., & Petrinovich, L. (Eds.) (1984). *Habituation, sensitization and behavior*. New York: Academic Press.

Rankin, C. H., & Broster, B. S. (1992). Factors affecting habituation and recovery from habituation in the nematode *Caenorhabditis elegans. Behavioral Neuroscience, 106*, 239–249.

Rubin, D. C., & Wenzel, A. E. (1996). One hundred years of forgetting: a quantitative description of retention. *Psychological Review, 103*, 736–760.

Simon, H. A. (1966). A note on Jost's law and exponential forgetting. *Psychometrika, 31*, 505–506.

Sokolov, Y. N. (1963). *Perception and the conditioned reflex.* Oxford: Pergamon Press.

Staddon, J. E. R. (1984). Time and memory. *Annals of the New York Academy of Sciences, 423*, 322–334.

Staddon, J. E. R. (1993). On rate-sensitive habituation. *Adaptive Behavior, 1*, 421–436.

Staddon, J. E. R., & Zanutto, B. S. (in press). In praise of parsimony. In C. D. L. Wynne & J. E. R. Staddon (Eds.), *Models for Action: Mechanisms for Adaptive Behavior.* New York: Erlbaum.

Staddon, J. E. R., & Higa, J. J. (1996). Multiple time scales in simple habituation. *Psychological Review, 103*, 720–733.

Thompson, R. F., & Spencer, W. A. (1966). Habituation: A model phenomenon for the study of neuronal substrates of behavior. *Psychological Review, 173*, 16–43.

Treisman, M. (1984). A theory of the mechanism of habituation: the assignment of responses to stimuli. In H. V. S. Peeke & L. Petrinovich (Eds.), *Habituation, sensitization and behavior* (pp. 57–101). New York: Academic Press.

Wood, D. C. (1970). Parametric studies of the response decrement produced by mechanical stimuli in the protozoan, *Stentor coeruleus. Journal of Neurobiology, 3*, 345–360.

CHAPTER TWELVE

Recent progress in studies of imitation and social learning in animals

Bennett G. Galef, Jr.
McMaster University, Hamilton, Ontario, Canada

The last two decades have seen remarkable progress in the study of social learning and imitation in animals. Emergence of the field as a dynamic interdisciplinary area of inquiry has been the result of three separate developments: (1) Behavioral ecologists and experimental psychologists have found both in one vertebrate species after another and in one biologically important situation after another that information acquired from conspecifics facilitates development of adaptive patterns of behavior. (2) After nearly a century of effort, primatologist and comparative psychologists have finally succeeded in providing compelling evidence that nonhuman animals can learn by imitation, and (3) population biologists and behavioral ecologists have developed quantitative models that permit exploration of the selective pressures that result in animals depending on social learning in developing responses to environmental demands. Here I review, albeit briefly, the three research streams that have contributed to the recent metamorphosis of the field.

L'étude de l'apprentissage social et de l'imitation chez l'animal a connu un essor remarquable au cours des deux dernières décennies. L'émergence du domaine en tant que champ de recherche interdisciplinaire repose sur trois axes d'évolution. (1) Chez plusieurs espèces de vertébrés et dans plusieurs situations importantes sur le plan biologique, les écologistes comportementaux et les psychologues expérimentalistes ont constaté à répétition que l'information obtenue à partir des congénères facilite l'apparition de patrons comportementaux adaptatifs. (2) Après près d'un siècle d'effort, les primatologues et les chercheurs en psychologie comparée ont finalement réussi à dégager des indices convaincants de la capacité qu'ont les animaux non humains d'apprendre par imitation. (3) Les biologistes spécialistes des populations et les écologistes comportementaux ont élaboré des modèles quantitatifs permettant d'examiner les pressions sélectives qui font que les animaux dépendent de l'apprentissage social dans la production de réponses aux exigences de l'environnement. Bien que ce soit de manière brève, les trois courants de recherche ayant participé à la récente métamorphose du domaine sont ici analysés.

These are exciting times for those of us interested in the study of animal social learning. During the past 20 years, the field has changed remarkably. It has metamorphosed from a rather sluggish subarea of animal learning into a fast-moving, independent, often disputatious area of inquiry that has captured the attention of empiricists and theoreticians working in a range of disciplines from anthropology, through experimental psychology and behavioral ecology to theoretical biology.

Formal evidence of the current high level of activity in the study of social learning in animals is plentiful: Review chapters (Galef, 1988, 1996b; Fragaszy & Visalberghi, 1996; Heyes, 1994; Mitchell, 1989; Whiten & Ham, 1992), edited volumes (Heyes & Galef, 1996; Wrangham, McGrew, de Waal, & Heltne, 1994; Zentall & Galef, 1988), theoretical articles (Coussi-Korbel & Fragaszy, 1995; Galef, 1995; Heyes, 1994), and even book-length monographs (Bonner, 1980; King, 1994; McGrew, 1992; Wyrwicka, 1996) are now appearing at a steady clip; symposia and conferences on the topic are convened almost annually on both sides of the Atlantic.

Informal indications of a marked increase in activity in the field are, perhaps, even more convincing than is the formal evidence; my stack of reprints published during the 1970s and concerned with social learning in animals measures but 5.2cm in height, comparable materials from the 1990s (with four years still remaining in the decade) already stands 27.6cm tall!

The dramatic change in activity in the field is the result of three distinct developments: First, behavioral ecologists and experimental animal psychologists have been able to show, in one vertebrate species after another, that social interactions can facilitate the development of adaptive patterns of behavior. Second, after nearly a century of effort, primatologists and comparative psychologists have finally provided compelling laboratory evidence consistent with the view that nonhuman animals can learn by imitation. Third, and finally, population biologists and behavioral ecologists have developed quantitative models that permit exploration of the selective forces driving the evolution of social learning.

In sum, in the last two decades, the field of animal social learning has gained a momentum, excitement and energy that were not always characteristic of the area.

A LITTLE HISTORY

During the late 1960s, when I first became interested in problems in social learning and imitation, the area was very much a part of experimental psychology. Almost all experimental work in the area was concerned with demonstrating, in standard laboratory apparatus (Skinner box, T maze, etc.), the existence of general learning processes in animals (e.g. social facilitation, local enhancement, contagious behavior, imitation, etc.) that allowed social interactions to influence the course of individual learning. For example, in a well-known study representative of some of the better psychological research on social learning carried out during the 1960s, Chesler (1969) demonstrated that kittens that had observed their respective mothers press a lever to obtain food subsequently learned to press the lever for food more rapidly than did either kittens that had observed a strange female cat press the same lever for food or kittens that learned to press the lever without the opportunity to watch others do so. In Chesler's view (and apparently that of the editors of *Science* as well) this finding demonstrated that kittens could learn to press a lever by observation, though it is hard to see why the result was so interpreted.

Zajonc (1965) was making much of observations indicating that (1) when racing, two human cyclists moved faster than did either cyclist when riding alone (Triplett, 1897) and (2) ants dug more vigorously when in pairs than when in isolation (Chen, 1937). Zajonc interpreted such diverse findings as examples of a single underlying process, social facilitation (the energizing of dominant behaviors by the presence of others), though even the most naive social scientist must have realized that the processes responsible for social enhancement of human performance are likely to be rather different from those producing a similar result in ants.

Richard Solomon (Solomon & Coles, 1954), Russell Church (1957a,b) and Vaughn Stimbert (1970a,b) had conducted (or were conducting) studies demonstrating that the activities of one animal could serve as discriminative stimuli for another, indicating to the observing animal those occasions on which a particular behavior would be rewarded.

In brief, interesting work was underway, but clearly social influence on animal learning was a side issue, generating relatively few experiments and relatively little excitement.

The late 1960s were a time of unprecedented change in the study of behavior. Within psychology, the influence of behaviorism was on the wane. Concurrently, various biological approaches to behavior were gaining adherents, first in Europe, then in North America. Even within psychology, evolutionary perspectives on animal plasticity were coming to the fore (Rozin & Kalat, 1971) and investigations of processes supporting the development of behaviors that affected survival and reproduction in natural normal habitat (rather than behaviors unique to the laboratory) were becoming increasingly common (Garcia & Koelling, 1966; Marler & Tamura, 1964). Such changes gave new life to the study of imitation and social learning and produced the acceleration of research in the area that is still underway today.

NON-IMITATIVE SOCIAL LEARNING

Indeed so much work on social learning is underway in the 1990s that the best one can do in a brief review is to provide a sample of research reflecting the current diversity of investigations in the area. I begin with description of portions of an ongoing, but quarter-century-old line of research underway in my own laboratory.

Learning what to eat: Food selection and poison avoidance by Norway rats

Some years ago, Fritz Steiniger, an applied ecologist who worked on problems of rodent control, discovered that if he used the same poison bait repeatedly in an attempt to control a pest population of Norway rats (*Rattus norvegicus*), he failed to produce a lasting reduction in the size of the target population (Steiniger, 1950). Despite an initial die-off when poison was first introduced into a colony's territory, the colony soon regained the size it had before Steiniger started his campaign of extermination.

Steiniger's failure (and the rats' success) had two causes: First, despite Steiniger's best efforts, a few colony members almost always managed to survive their initial intake of the poison bait and would eat no more of it (Garcia & Koelling, 1966). Second, and even more unfortunately for Steiniger's efforts at pest control, young rats raised by these survivors refused to eat the bait that the survivors had learned to avoid and never even sampled it for themselves.

This socially induced avoidance of a poison bait is a robust phenomenon, easily captured in the laboratory (Galef & Clark, 1971a). Consequently, it has proved possible to explore in depth several social learning processes (Galef, 1996c, in press), each of which has the potential to contribute to the social transmission of both food preferences and poison avoidance (Galef, 1985) from adult rats to their young.

Physical presence of adults at a feeding site.   Galef and Clark (1971b) used a time-lapse video-tape recorder to watch pups born to wild-caught Norway rats take their very first meals of solid food. Each ate: (1) while an adult rat was eating and (2) at the same site where that adult was eating, not at a nearby site where no rats were present. It appeared that the simple physical presence of an adult rat at a feeding site markedly increased the probability that pups would wean to whatever food was to be found there (Galef & Clark, 1971b). And, in fact, we found that simply anesthetizing an adult rat and placing it near a feeding site made that site far more attractive to weaning rat pups than an alternative feeding site that had no rat near it (Galef, 1981).

Further, because wild Norway rats are exceptionally hesitant to eat any foods that they have not previously eaten (Barnett, 1958; Galef, 1970), once a young wild rat had weaned to one food, it was very reluctant to ingest other potential foods that it encountered. Indeed, a young wild rat might wait as long as 5 days before eating, if it had only unfamiliar foods available (Galef, 1970; Galef & Clark, 1971a). Consequently, anything causing rats to wean to a safe food also caused them to avoid eating any poisonous substances present in their environment (Galef, 1985).

Flavor cues on the breath of rats.   Galef and his students have also found that after a naive young rat (an observer rat) interacts with a recently fed conspecific (a demonstrator rat), the observer exhibits considerable enhancement of its preference for whatever food its demonstrator ate (Galef & Wigmore, 1983). Exposing observer rats to either olfactory cues escaping from the digestive tract of demonstrator rats or to the smell of bits of food that cling to their fur and vibrissae causes observers to exhibit a marked enhancement of their preferences for the food that their respective demonstrators ate (Galef, Kennett, & Stein, 1985). On the other hand, exposing observer rats to the smell of a food presented on a piece of cotton wool fails to cause young rats to increase their preference for it (Galef & Stein, 1985). Obviously, there is something about smelling a food odor in the presence of a live, breathing rat that causes an observer rat to change its food preferences (Galef & Stein, 1985).

Mass-spectrographic analysis of rat breath revealed the presence of carbon disulfide in the exhalations of rats (Galef, Mason, Pretti, & Bean, 1988), and exposing rats to pieces of cotton wool both dusted with a food and moistened with a few drops of dilute carbon disulfide solution caused them to exhibit an enhanced preference for the food that they smelled on the cotton wool. On the other hand, exposing rats to pieces of cotton wool dusted with food and moistened with water did not affect their preferences for that food (Galef et al., 1988). Apparently, sulfur compounds carried on rat breath can mediate the social enhancement of food preference that we observed in rats.

Research in laboratories around the world has shown that, like the food choices of Norway rats, food choices of blackbirds (Mason & Reidinger, 1981, 1982), sheep and goats (Provenza, Lynch, & Nolan, 1993), cats (Wyrwicka, 1978, 1981), hyenas (Yoerg, 1991), pigs (Nicol & Pope, 1994), rabbits (Hudson & Altbacker, 1993), gerbils and mice (Valsecchi, Choleris, Moles, Cong, & Mainardi, 1996; Valsecchi & Galef, 1989; Valsecchi, Moles, & Mainardi, 1993) can be influenced by interaction with conspecifics. Such research has also revealed that food selection is not the only aspect of feeding behavior open to influence by social interactions.

Learning how to eat: Roof rats in pine forests

Ron Aisner discovered some years ago that the pine forests of Israel are inhabited by roof rats (*Rattus rattus*) subsisting on a diet of pine seeds and water (Aisner & Terkel, 1992). Extraction of pine seeds has been a stable tradition in these forest-dwelling rodents for many generations, enabling them to survive in evergreen forests where pine seeds are the only food available in sufficient quantity to support a population of mammals.

Laboratory studies have revealed that to gain more energy from eating pine seeds than is expended in securing them, rats must take advantage of the structure of pine cones when removing seeds from beneath the tough scales that conceal and protect them. To show a net energy gain from eating pine seeds, a rat must start by chewing through the scales at the base of a cone and then remove, one after another, the spiral of scales running about a cone's shaft to its apex.

Investigations into the way in which this spiral pattern of scale removal is learned by rats have shown that only 2–3% of adult rats could learn by trial and error to use the spiral pattern of scale removal to gain access seeds. The vast majority of hungry rats either ignored pine cones in their cages or gnawed at them in a way that did not permit extraction of more energy from ingesting pine seeds than was expended in gaining access to them.

On the other hand, essentially all young rats developed the efficient technique if they were reared by an adult rat that stripped scales from pine cones efficiently. Clearly, some aspect of the interaction between adult rats that strip pine cones efficiently and the young they rear is important for transmission of the efficient method of cone stripping from one generation of rats to the next (Aisner & Terkel, 1992; Zohar & Terkel, 1992).

Further experiments by Terkel and his colleagues at the University of Tel Aviv demonstrated that more than 70% of young rats developed the efficient method of attacking cones, if they had opportunity to finish stripping cones started and then abandoned either by efficient adult rats or by an experimenter using a pair of pliers to imitate the pattern of scale removal that is used by efficient rats (Aisner & Terkel, 1992).

Even though the tradition of pine-cone opening is not transmitted by imitation or by any other complex social-learning process, it is particularly interesting, because it demonstrates that social learning can open new ecological niches to social learners thus exposing them to new selective pressures.

Learning what to fear: Predator avoidance in birds and monkeys

The development of predator recognition and patterns of predator avoidance have been of interest to comparative psychologists for many decades. However, attempts to understand the phenomena of predator identification and avoidance on the basis either of individual trial-and-error learning (Hull, 1929) or species-typical defensive reactions to sudden stimuli (Bolles, 1970) have been less than totally successful: Predators do not often provide opportunities for members of prey species to learn from their mistakes, and problems of discriminating harmless from predatory species using unlearned perceptual mechanisms seem insurmountable.

Predator avoidance by blackbirds.   The first indication that social learning might play a role in development of responses of prey species to their predators was provided by the elegant experiments of Curio and his colleagues in Bochum,

Germany (Curio, 1988; Curio, Ernst, & Vieth, 1978) in studies of the effects on conspecifics of species-typical vocalizations that European blackbirds (*Turdus merula*) make when harassing potential predators (mobbing). Using a simple, but ingenious apparatus (see Fig. 12.1), Curio et al. simultaneously presented an owl (a natural predator of blackbirds) to a knowledgeable, wild-caught European blackbird that mobbed the owl and a harmless object (for example, a stuffed song bird or plastic bottle) to a naive, laboratory-reared blackbird.

In Curio's apparatus, the mobbing blackbird seemed to the naive blackbird to be directing its vocalizations toward the harmless object, and in subsequent tests, the naive blackbird responded to the harmless object as though it were a predator, attacking it while emitting mobbing vocalizations.

Curio went on to analyze this socially transmitted behavior as an instance of Pavlovian conditioning. He found that any novel stimulus, whether a stuffed songbird or stuffed owl, elicited mild, unconditioned avoidance responses in naive blackbirds that increased dramatically in intensity once that novel stimulus was experienced together with tape recordings of mobbing vocalizations (Curio et al., 1978). Thus, social learning directed anti-predator responses of naive blackbirds toward those unfamiliar objects that more experienced individuals treated as potential predators. And, as we shall see later, blackbirds are not the only animals that can learn from others of their species what elements in their environment to treat as potentially dangerous.

Fear of snakes in monkeys.   It has been known for more than 40 years that although most wild-caught monkeys and apes vigorously avoid contact with snakes, captive-reared primates are relatively indifferent to snakes and snake-like objects. Possibly conditions of life in captivity are so aberrant that captive-reared individuals fail either to develop or to maintain a species-typical, congenital tendency to avoid snakes. On the other hand, captive monkeys may lack some specific experience that they require to develop snake avoidance.

Sue Mineka and her co-workers at the University of Wisconsin (Cook, Mineka, Wolkenstein, & Laitsch, 1985; Mineka & Cook, 1988) have shown that monkeys reared in captivity and, therefore, without fear of snakes, are terrified of snakes after they see wild-born conspecifics respond to a snake. After laboratory-reared rhesus monkeys (*Macaca mulatta*) watched a wild-reared monkey respond vigorously to the sight of a snake, the laboratory-reared rhesus responded to the appearance of a snake or snake-like object by cowering on the far side of their respective cages and appeared extremely upset, vocalizing and grimacing.

Mineka et al.'s studies contribute substantially to an understanding of how predator recognition and avoidance might develop in free-ranging primates, just as Curio's findings provide a plausible mechanism for understanding the possibly homologous process in birds.

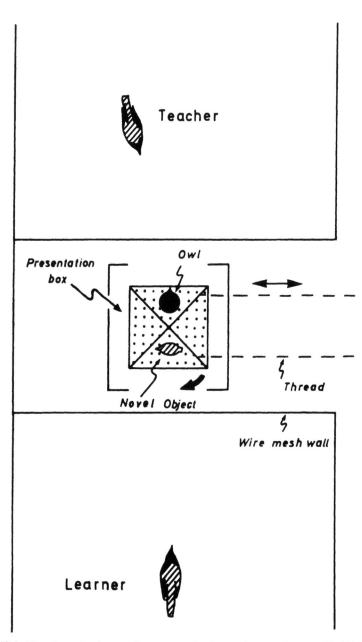

FIG. 12.1 Experimental aviary used to present simultaneously an owl to one blackbird and a harmless songbird or object to another. From "The adaptive significance of avian mobbing. III. Cultural transmission of enemy recognition in blackbirds: Cross-species tutoring and properties of learning", by W. Vieth, E. Curio, and U. Ernst, 1980, *Animal Behavior*, *28*, p. 1218. Copyright 1980 by Ballière Tindall. Reprinted with permission.

Choosing a mate: Social effects on choice of partner in guppies

Although evidence of a role for social learning in development of adaptive patterns of response to potential foods and potential predators is now more than 20 years old, comparable evidence of a role of social interaction in mate selection is considerably more recent.

Dugatkin and his co-workers have investigated the role of social learning in mate choice by wild ancestors of a common aquarium fish, the guppy (*Poecilia reticulata*). Guppies were selected for study both because the behavior of members of the species in their natural environment (the streams of Trinidad) would allow social influences on mate selection to occur and because of the ease with which guppies can be bred, maintained, and observed in the laboratory.

In Dugatkin's studies (Dugatkin, 1992; Dugatkin & Godin, 1992, 1993), female guppies serving as subjects first observed two male guppies, one with a female confined nearby and the other without a female companion. The subject females were then given the opportunity to chose between the two males they had just observed when the males were alone. Dugatkin found that females joined the male they had seen courting a female significantly more often than they joined the male they had seen swimming by himself.

Control experiments showed that females were not going to a location where they had seen two fishes in preference to a location where they had seen only a single fish. Nor were females simply approaching a male they had seen engage in courtship; subject females had to see a male actually courting a female (a male courting with no female visible would not do) before they developed a preference for that male.

And, as one might expect, female guppies are not unique in allowing the behavior of other females to influence their choice of a mate. Indeed, copying of the mate choice of others may provide an explanation for some previously unexplained and rather curious phenomena observed in natural settings. For example, in species such as sage grouse (*Centrocerus urophasianus*), in which males compete directly for females on communal breeding grounds (leks), each day a very small number of males enjoy almost all of the access to females. The temporal pattern of copulatory success of different male grouse competing on a lek are consistent with the hypothesis that females observe and copy the mate choice of others, thus producing near unanimity in mate selection on any day (Gibson, Bradbury, & Vehrencamp, 1991).

Perhaps more puzzling has been the observation that male sailfin mollies (*Poecilia latipinna*) regularly mate with female Amazon mollies (*Poecilia formosa*), a gynogenetic species whose members must obtain sperm from male sailfin mollies to produce young, but do not incorporate that sperm into their offspring. Schlupp, Marler, and Ryan (1994) have found that male sailfin mollies that mate with female Amazon mollies gain a reproductive advantage because of the tendency of female sailfin mollies to copy mate choices of Amazon mollies. There are other ways in which social learning can affect mate choice.

Learning what to sing

It is, of course, impossible to do justice to the immense literature on bird-song learning in a brief review such as the present one. There are, however, several programs of research within that large field that provide evidence that social interactions can direct vocal expression by birds in adaptive directions. I shall review two of the more surprising cases below.

Song learning in cowbirds. It was long thought that song development in males of brood-parasitic species (i.e. species in which females deposit their eggs in the nests of birds of other species and abandon their young for foster parents to rear) was not affected by interaction with conspecifics. However, it is now clear that, like males of other species of song bird, male brown-headed cowbirds (*Molothrus ater*), a brood-parasitic species, learn the fine detail of their songs by interaction with others of their species.

Maintenance of song variants in the repertoires of male cowbirds is determined by responses of females to the songs that males produce. Male songs that, during the breeding season, are most likely to cause female cowbirds to assume the species-typical copulatory posture are responded to by females outside the breeding season with a "wing-stroke" display. After a female responds to a male's song with a wing stroke, the male will repeat the song that elicited the wing stroke several times in succession, thus violating a rule of song production by isolated male cowbirds who normally sing their various song types one after another without repetition.

Those songs that are rewarded by females with wing strokes outside the breeding season are produced by males with greater frequency during the breeding season and increase the probability that the males that sing them will secure copulations (King & West, 1983; West & King, 1988).

The particular form of the songs that male cowbirds sing is further influenced by interactions with conspecific males. Songs that are most effective in eliciting copulatory postures from female cowbirds are also most effective in eliciting attack by cowbird males (West, King, & Eastzer, 1981). Consequently, only dominant male cowbirds can continue to sing the song types most effective in eliciting copulation postures in females (West et al., 1981).

Clearly, social interactions between singers and both male and female members of their audiences determine which elements in the song repertoire of a brow-headed cowbird are most frequently expressed and guide song production in adaptive directions relative to each individual's status within its social group.

Such social shaping of song is particularly interesting because it is one of very few instances in which it is has been convincingly demonstrated that animals actively shape the behavior of conspecifics (for a different view, see Caro & Hauser, 1992).

Tutor tapes, live tutors and song learning in male white-crowned sparrows. Classic studies by Marler (1970) demonstrated that male white-crowned sparrows (*Zenotrichia leucophrys*) readily learn tape-recorded songs. However, such learning from tutor tapes was restricted both to the songs of other white-crowned sparrows and to the first 50 days of life.

Baptista and Petrinovich (1984, 1986) hand reared male white-crowned sparrows for 50 days and then presented them with live (rather than with taped) tutors. Almost all Baptista and Petrinovich's subjects acquired and sang their respective tutors' songs, even though exposure to tutors occurred after the classic, 50-day "sensitive period" for song learning had terminated. Furthermore, songs of live (but not of taped) tutor finches were learned by male white-crowned sparrows, violating the rule, derived from study of responses of male white-crowned sparrows to tutor tapes, that male sparrows will learn to sing only the songs of their own species.

Relatively little is yet known about the aspects of social interaction with live tutors that effect song learning, but in some species, it has been shown that the developing individual will use social cues to select a song model (Payne, 1981). For example, captive Zebra finches (*Taeniopygia guttata*) selectively learned song from the male of a pair that behaved more aggressively towards them (Clayton, 1987).

Conclusion

Exploration of the many ways in which social interaction facilitates acquisition of adaptive patterns of behavior has just begun. We can anticipate further discoveries both of important influences of social learning on the development of behaviors from migration to territoriality and of novel ways in which social interaction shapes and facilitates the acquisition of adaptive patterns of behavior.

IMITATIVE SOCIAL LEARNING

Starting in the late 1890s, and for more than 80 years thereafter, comparative psychologists could not produce convincing experimental evidence that animals could learn by imitation. Consequently, many scientists (myself included) who were interested in whether animals might imitate concluded that they probably could not. The many informal observations suggesting that primates and other animals with relatively large and complex brains spontaneously imitated their keepers (for a review, see Moore, 1992) appeared to be inaccurate, the result of overinterpretation of behavior by scientists observing animals in uncontrolled conditions. However, the last decade has seen a dramatic change in the weight of laboratory evidence concerning the ability of animals to imitate. Indeed today, it is not unreasonable to argue that pigeons, Norway rats and African Grey parrots, as well as chimpanzees and bonobos, can learn by imitation.

During the last decade, there has also been substantial improvement in the quality of observations of imitative behavior in uncontrolled environments that may help to explain earlier failures to demonstrate learning by imitation under controlled conditions as well as some of the recent successes.

Turning anecdotes into observations: Field studies of orangutans

During the 19th century, the study of animal behavior failed as a scientific enterprise, at least in part, because of the willingness of early animal behaviorists to accept at face value anecdotal reports of human-like behaviors of animals (Galef, 1996a). Devastating attacks by Thorndike (1898) and Washburn (1908) on the reliability of informal observation were a necessary first step in the development of a science of animal behavior (Galef, 1996a). Consequently, it is not surprising that the scientific community of the 20th century viewed anecdotal reports of apparent learning by imitation in animals with some skepticism. Only recently has anyone working outside the laboratory attempted to record systematically instances of apparent imitation in a free-living population of animals.

Russon and Galdikas (1993, 1995) used Earthwatch volunteers to observe and record all apparently imitative behaviors spontaneously exhibited by free-ranging orangutans (*Pongo pygmaeus*) at a rehabilitation camp in Borneo where illegally captured animals recovered by the Indonesian government are prepared for life in the wild. Russon and Galdikas (1993) described and recorded on videotape dozens of complex human behaviors that the apes appeared to copy. For example, a worker using a hoe to chop weeds from along the edges of a path placed piles of cut weeds down the center of the path for later collection and disposal. A female orangutan was seen following behind the worker using a foot-long stick and her hands to chop off weeds the worker had missed and piling the weeds she cut in a row down the center of the path.

Although it is, of course, impossible to know just how the apes acquired such behaviors in uncontrolled circumstances, the many instances of copying of complex motor patterns that Russon and Galdikas describe surely suggest that orangutans may be able to imitate under appropriate circumstances. (One must be a little careful here because Russon and Galdikas use the term "imitative behavior" to refer to socially learned behavior sequences, regardless of the behavioral process—e.g. stimulus enhancement, social facilitation, etc.—that may have facilitated their acquisition.) Indeed, Russon and Galdikas's (1995) observations provide some insight into the circumstances that increase the probability of spontaneous imitation by great apes.

Post-hoc analyses of the field observations made in Borneo showed, for example, that a close social relationship between model and mimic increased the probability of spontaneous "imitative behavior". In view of this result, it is, perhaps, not too surprising to find that some of the greatest progress in laboratory studies of imitation of humans by apes have been made using as subjects apes raised in intimate contact with humans.

Affects of "enculturation": Gestural and instrumental imitation by chimpanzees and bonobos

Tomasello, Kruger, and Rutner (1993a) allowed three groups of subjects—(1) human-reared chimpanzees (*Pan troglodytes*) and bonobos (*Pan paniscus*) that had been exposed to "language-like" systems of communication (what Tomasello, Savage-Rumbaugh, and Kruger [1993b, p. 1699] called "enculturated chimpanzees"), (2) chimps and bonobos reared by their natural mothers and (3) two-year-old human children—to observe a human model demonstrate 24 different, novel actions performed on objects (for example, placing an object on one's head or using a lever to pry open a paint can). The children were told to *do this*, and the apes had been pretrained to reproduce modeled actions.

The results were clear-cut; apes reared by their natural mothers failed almost totally to imitate the novel actions modeled by an experimenter, whereas two-year-old children and enculturated apes imitated such actions both frequently and equally often.

Custance, Whiten, and Bard (1995) studied development in two nursery-reared chimpanzees of an ability to imitate novel gestures (e.g. lip smacking, finger wiggling, thumb grabbing) demonstrated by human models. Independent observers scoring videotapes of the chimps' behavior were able to identify which of the 48 modeled behaviors the animals were attempting to imitate far more frequently than would be expected by chance.

Last, Whiten and his collaborators (Whiten & Custance, 1996; Whiten, Custance, Gomez, Teixidor, & Bard, 1996) examined imitative behavior in both chimpanzees raised by humans (though not thoroughly "enculturated" in Tomasello et al.'s [1993b] sense of the word) and human infants. All subjects were presented with a transparent plastic box that was held shut by mechanical contrivances that could be opened to obtain a food reward by using either of two techniques, one of which had been demonstrated by a human experimenter. For example, a box could be opened either by pushing or by twisting and pulling on a bolt passing through a pair of rings that held the box closed. After watching a human demonstrator push the bolt to open the box, the chimps were more likely to push than to pull the bolt; after watching a demonstration of pulling and twisting of the bolt, the chimps were more likely to pull than to push it.

In sum, in the last few years, evidence consistent with the view that chimpanzees raised by humans do imitate has been found in one laboratory situation after another. Whether the increased probability of imitation exhibited by apes reared by humans reflects a difference in the attachment of the apes to humans or a more fundamental change in the apes' cognitive abilities remains to be determined.

Imitation in animals other than apes: Norway rats, pigeons and an African Grey parrot

Recent evidence suggests that not only apes, but also other less likely animals are able to reproduce motor acts after observing them. In a series of studies Heyes and colleagues (Heyes & Dawson, 1990; Heyes, Dawson, & Noakes, 1992) allowed observer Norway rats to watch through a wire-mesh partition while a rat demonstrator pushed a joy stick 50 times either to the left or to the right and received a food reward each time that it did so. Once the observer had watched the demonstrator complete 50 displacements of the joy stick in one direction, the observer was placed alone with the joystick and permitted to push the joy stick 50 times, receiving food reward for displacements in either direction. For some groups of observers, the joystick remained in the same position for both demonstration and testing; for other groups of observers, the joystick was moved before testing from near the screen partition that separated demonstrator and observer to the front wall of the chamber (see Fig. 12.2). Under both conditions, the observer showed a reliable tendency to push the joystick in the same direction, relative to its own body axis, as had its demonstrator.

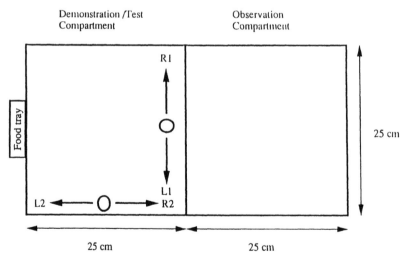

FIG. 12.2   Plan of experimental apparatus showing the position and plane of movement of the joystick during training and testing when the joystick remained in the same position during training and testing (L1, R1) and when it was moved before testing (L2, R2). From "Imitation in rats: Initial responding and transfer evidence", by C. Heyes, G. R. Dawson, and T. Noakes, 1992, *Quarterly Journal of Experimental Psychology, 45B*, p. 83. Copyright 1980 by the Experimental Psychology Society and Lawrence Erlbaum. Reprinted with permission.

Similarly, Zentall, Sutton, and Sherburne (1996) and Akins and Zentall (1996) have reported imitation by pigeons (*Columbia livia*) and Japanese quail (*Coturnix japonica*) of two different motor patterns (pecking and stepping) directed towards a treadle for food reward.

Last, and perhaps most unexpectedly, Moore (1992) has provided evidence of spontaneous imitation by an African Grey parrot (*Psittacus erithacus*). Moore housed the parrot in isolation in a room containing a microphone and video camera that permitted observation of the bird's behavior when it was alone.

Moore visited the bird's aviary several times a day over a period of 5 years. During each visit, he performed repeatedly a small number of movements, each accompanied by a specific word or phrase. For example, as Moore left the parrot's room each day he waved good-bye and repeated the word *ciao*. The bird soon learned to say *ciao* and, by the end of the first year, was observed while alone in its room to say *ciao* and, at the same time, to wave its foot. When in the room with the parrot, Moore would also say *look at my tongue*, open his mouth and stick out his tongue. Some time after it started to wave and say *ciao*, the parrot was observed on television to follow the vocalization *look at my tongue* with mouth opening and tongue raising. The parrot rarely opened its mouth and showed its tongue after saying *ciao* or waved its foot after saying *look at my tongue*.

In all, Moore's parrot was observed to copy 14 different reactions involving six different body parts, associating each with its appropriate verbal label for tens to hundreds of times.

Why the arguing has not ended

An outsider to the field of imitation would probably conclude that, in the face of so much evidence, those interested in imitation learning would have announced the successful demonstration of imitation learning by nonhuman animals and the consequent resolution of a scientific question of long standing. In fact, the announcement has not yet been made. Unfortunately, although almost everyone studying imitation learning in animals now agrees that animal imitation has been demonstrated, there is little agreement as to which experiments demonstrate imitation or even as to which species have been shown to imitate (Byrne & Tomasello, 1995; Heyes, 1995, 1996; Moore, 1996; Tomasello, 1996).

Causes of controversy

Researchers working in different traditions seek evidence of imitation learning in animals for different reasons. Consequently, they use different criteria to identify imitative behavior. Although the criteria researchers use may be appropriate for their respective purposes, without explicit statement of those purposes, disagreement about who has found satisfactory evidence of what is inevitable.

Consider a simple historical example. Edward Thorndike (1898) wanted to know whether, as George Romanes (1884) had proposed, for animals the idea of an act is sufficient instigation to performance of that act. Thorndike (1898) argued if one can from an act witnessed learn to do that act, then clearly the idea of the act is sufficient cause for its execution. Consequently, Thorndike tried to get the cats, monkeys and chickens that he used as subjects in his experiments to imitate very simple actions—in cats, stepping on a treadle or pulling on a string—that are part of their normal behavioral repertoires. Thorndike's repeated failure to find that animals would copy even these very simple acts was one of several pieces of evidence that led him to reject the hypothesis that, in animals at least, the idea of an act suffices for its production.

It should come as no surprise that those working in the tradition of Thorndike (for example, Heyes, 1996, or Zentall et al., 1996) tend to be satisfied with demonstrations that Thorndike was wrong, that animals can, in fact, copy simple actions, and, consequently, that in animals the idea of an act is sufficient to instigate its performance. Such demonstrations of imitation learning are for such researchers, a means to an end, not an end in itself, a starting point for analyses of cognitive processes in the imitating animal.

On the other hand, many contemporary students of imitation learning have adopted Thorpe's (1963) definition of "true imitation" as "the copying of a novel or otherwise improbable act . . ." (p. 135). Thorpe required that the term *imitation* be used to refer only to the copying of unusual actions in order to distinguish imitation from another form of social learning, "local enhancement" ("apparent imitation resulting from directing the animal's attention to a particular object or to a particular part of the environment" [p. 134]) that did not involve the higher mental processes Thorpe felt were involved in true imitation.

Thorpe's reason for requiring that imitation involve copying of complex unusual acts is no longer particularly compelling because in a number of contemporary studies of imitation in animals (e.g. Galef, Manzig, & Field, 1986; Heyes & Dawson, 1990; Whiten et al., 1996; Zentall et al., 1996), discrimination of imitation from local enhancement, social facilitation or other processes has been achieved by requiring not that subjects exhibit a novel behavior, but that they direct two different behaviors towards the same object (Galef, 1988).

On the other hand, those who study imitation in animals because of an interest in the possibility that animals possess human-like cognitive abilities (e.g. Byrne, 1995; Moore, 1996; Russon & Galdikas, 1993; Tomasello et al., 1993a; Whiten, 1996) are, for good reasons, interested in the degree of novelty and complexity of the behavior imitated. If you are interested in similarities in the mental powers of humans and apes (for example, the ability of animals to represent mental states or to understand what others intend [Byrne, 1995]), there is little reason to be interested in studies of the social elicitation of simple skills (like pushing a pole to left or right or pulling vs. pushing a bolt) that are already in an animal's repertoire.

Furthermore, the cumulative culture that supports the biological success of humankind requires an ability to learn complex novel behaviors as a result of observing others exhibit them (Boyd & Richerson, 1996; Tomasello et al., 1993a). Consequently, evidence of an ability to copy faithfully complex, novel behaviors is important to those interested in animal traditions as homologs of human culture (Galef, 1992).

Unfortunately, debating what should or should not be labeled imitation and who has demonstrated imitation in animals has not proved useful. Perhaps attention should be focused instead on the implications of demonstrations of an animal's ability to imitate either novel or familiar acts.

Further difficulties

There is one further problem in using as the sole criterion in studies of imitation either the copying of a novel motor pattern or the directing of two actions toward the same manipulandum. Those interested in behavioral ecology (and I count myself among them) often study imitation in animals not because they wish to understand animal mind or to compare cognitive processes in humans and animals, but because they are interested in how animals acquire patterns of behavior that promote survival and reproduction in natural habitat. For those with an ecological perspective, imitation of meaningless gestures is not nearly so interesting as is imitation of acts that might be instrumental in securing resources that contribute to fitness.

The anecdotal literature has, for decades, provided examples of instances in which captive animals spontaneously reproduce what must be meaningless acts to the animal: Putting on lipstick, blowing smoke rings, limping like a deformed comrade, etc. (for a review, see Moore, 1992). We also now have several laboratory demonstrations of primates or birds (really one bird) copying meaningless gestures they saw demonstrated by humans. What is missing in such examples is any evidence that animals can use their ability to copy motor sequences to learn to solve problems that they might face in the natural world.

Possibility of a solution

Clearly, a demonstration of imitation learning that will satisfy everyone is going to be hard to arrange. It will have to involve comparison of the behavior of observers watching models using one of two different complex, novel motor acts to manipulate the same object in order to secure a reward. The particular motor act used by each observer the first time it manipulates the object will have to match closely that used by its model. Recent work carried out by Whiten and his collaborators (Whiten & Custance, 1996; Whiten et al., 1996) and described earlier, in which "artificial fruits" were opened by chimpanzees using one of two different motor patterns, comes close to satisfying simultaneously all these criteria. There has, however, been some question as to whether the chimpanzees in

Whiten and Custance's (1996) study learned by observation to imitate the specific motor pattern used by their respective models, or simply to either push or to pull the bolt to earn rewards (Tomasello, 1996; Whiten & Custance, 1996; Whiten et al., 1996). Presumably, pushing and pulling were in the chimps' behavioral repertoires before they observed human models opening artificial fruit. Consequently, the imitation may not have been of a novel motor pattern after all.

Still, further development of the technology initiated by Whiten and his coworkers offers hope of demonstration of imitation learning in chimpanzees (or other animals with well-developed manipulative abilities) that all will find satisfactory. Of course, it is always possible that even chimpanzees will lack the ability to imitate when the requirements for imitation are made so severe.

THEORETICAL ANALYSES

The third aspect of the study of social learning that has undergone substantial development during the last decade involves the use of mathematical models similar to those used in population biology, behavioral ecology, and the study of neural networks to explore either the circumstances when it would be advantageous for animals to learn from others or the processes supporting such learning.

The most influential models of social learning in animals build on previous analyses of human culture (Boyd & Richerson, 1985; Cavalli-Sforza & Feldman, 1981) and extend these earlier models to animal populations (Boyd & Richerson, 1988; Laland, Richerson, & Boyd, 1993, 1996; Rogers, 1988). In general, it is assumed in such models that (1) there are different patterns of costs and benefits associated with individual learning, social learning, and the genetic transmission of information, and (2) natural selection acts on this complex of processes supporting behavioral development to optimize net benefits.

Individual learning is hypothesized to involve potentially costly trial-and-error learning and expensive mental machinery, but to permit rapid response to environmental change. Social learning is considered less expensive to carry out than individual learning, but to involve the risk that the individual one learns from might have acquired its behavior when the environment was in a state different from its current one so that social learning leads to error. Genetically transmitted behavioral propensities are considered cheapest to acquire, but most likely to be maladaptive in changing environments.

Obviously, in such models, the rate of environmental change to which a species is exposed should affect the mix of individual learning, social learning, and genetically transmitted information that species members have evolved to use in developing their individual behavioral repertoires: When environments are essentially constant, all information regarding behavioral development should be transmitted genetically; when environmental change is very rapid, pure individual learning should be favored, and at intermediate rates of environmental change, social learning has the advantage.

In the most widely employed of the current models, the guided-variation model of Boyd and Richerson (1985), it is assumed that individuals acquire behaviors socially by interacting with members of the preceding generation and then modify those socially acquired behaviors on the basis of their personal experience. The social learning part of the process of behavior acquisition can be biased in several ways. For example, naive individuals might have evolved to copy either the most common or rarest behavioral variant exhibited by members of the preceding generation (frequency-dependent bias); naive individuals might copy the behavior of healthy rather than ill elders (indirect bias). Also, transmission of behavior might not be from one generation to the next (vertical transmission) but, instead, proceed from one member of a generation to another (horizontal transmission; Laland et al., 1996). The various models that have been developed to date permit exploration of the conditions under which proclivities for different types of social learning are most likely to evolve.

Because current models of social learning and gene-culture interaction address questions at the population level, they have not told us much about social learning within the individual. Indeed, they were not intended to do so (Laland et al., 1996). The models' creators assume quite simple models of processing at the individual level to make the mathematics of higher-level interactions tractable. Consequently, to date, the impact of theoretical models on experimental work in animal social learning has been somewhat limited. In the longer term, examination at the individual level, of features of social learning important to modeling at the population level (for example, copying fidelity, or probability of copying) should result in empirical work on social learning useful at all levels of analysis.

Attempts are underway to develop models that describe social learning at the individual level. For example, Laland and Bateson are currently using an unsupervised neural-network model to explore the processes needed to support various types of social learning. They have reached the counterintuitive conclusion that imitation learning need not depend on processes fundamentally different from those supporting either individual learning or nonimitative forms of social learning. At the same time, others are developing experimental paradigms that permit direct test of predictions derived from population level theories (Chou & Richerson, 1992; Galef & Allen, 1995; Galef & Whiskin, 1997; Laland & Plotkin, 1990) and analyzing pre-existing data in ways that permit discrimination among different models of the social transmission of behavior through populations (Lefebvre, 1995a,b).

Yet other formal treatments directly reflect the concerns of behavioral ecologists. Giraldeau and his co-workers (Giraldeau, Caraco, & Valone, 1994; Giraldeau & Lefebvre, 1987; Giraldeau & Templeton, 1991) have examined the impact of "scrounging" (exploitation of a resource produced by another), foraging group size, and the complexity of the skills required for food acquisition on the probability of social learning. Barta and Szep (1992, 1995) have examined effects of patterns of food distribution on individual and socal strategies of finding food. Again, the impact of such models on the design and conduct of empirical investigations has been limited (though see Templeton & Giraldeau, 1995). Indeed, one of the more important developments to be anticipated in the study of social learning during the next decade is further integration of experimental and mathematical approaches to the study of social learning.

CONCLUSION

Study of both imitative and nonimitative forms of social learning by animals has made immense strides during the last two decades: (1) The importance of social learning in the development of numerous behaviors affecting survival and reproduction has been clearly demonstrated, (2) there are now a sufficient number of reasonably solid laboratory demonstrations of learning by imitation in animals to convince all but the most skeptical that the phenomenon is real, and (3) theoretical analyses of the role of social learning in the acquisition and propagation of behavior are beginning to influence the design of experiments.

These are exciting times for students of imitation and animal social learning. We are now, after nearly 100 years of effort, in a position to begin to explore the cognitive processes that support imitation learning in various animals and to compare them with similar processes in humans. We have in hand numerous examples of an important role for social learning in the development of biologically important patterns of behavior in animals and analyses of the behavioral processes supporting such social learning. We now have models that permit us to explore the relationships among social learning, individual learning, and environmental factors in the evolution of adaptive response to environmental challenge. A great deal of hard work by scientists in many fields has started to pay off. The next decade of research in the area promises to be at least as productive as the last.

ACKNOWLEDGEMENTS

Preparation of this manuscript was greatly facilitated by a grant from the Natural Science and Engineering Research Council of Canada. I thank participants in the soclearn bulletin board, particularly Peter Richerson, Irene Pepperberg, Doree Fragaszy, and Andrew Whiten for stimulating discussion. Errors of omission and commission remain the responsibility of the author.

REFERENCES

Aisner, R., & Terkel, J. (1992). Ontogeny of pine cone opening behavior in the black rat (*Rattus rattus*). *Animal Behavior, 44*, 327–336.
Akins, C. K., & Zentall, T. R. (1996). Imitative learning in Japanese quail (*Corturnix japonica*) involving the two-action method. *Journal of Comparative Psychology, 110*, 316–320.
Baptista, L. F., & Petrinovich, L. (1984). Social interaction, sensitive phases and the song template hypothesis in the white-crowned sparrow. *Animal behavior, 32*, 172–181.

Baptista, L. F., & Petrinovich, L. (1986). Song development in the white-crowned sparrow: Social factors and sex differences. *Animal Behavior, 34*, 1359–1371.

Barnett, S. A. (1958). Experiments on "neophobia" in wild and laboratory rats. *British Journal of Psychology, 49*, 195–201.

Barta, Z., & Szep, T. (1992). The role of information transfer under different food patterns: A simulation study. *Behavioral Ecology, 3*, 318–324.

Barta, Z., & Szep, T. (1995). Frequency-dependent selection on information-transfer strategies at breeding colonies: A simulation study. *Behavioral Ecology, 6*, 308–310.

Bolles, R. C. (1970). Species-specific defense reactions and avoidance learning. *Psychological Review, 77*, 32–48.

Bonner, J. T. (1980). *The evolution of culture in animals.* Princeton, NJ: Princeton University Press.

Boyd, R., & Richerson, P. J. (1985). *Culture and the evolutionary process.* Chicago: University of Chicago Press.

Boyd, R., & Richerson, P. J. (1988). An evolutionary model of social learning: The effects of spatial and temporal variation. In T. R. Zentall & B. G. Galef, Jr. (Eds.), *Social learning: Psychological and biological perspectives* (pp. 29–48). Hillsdale, NJ: Lawrence Erlbaum Associates Inc.

Boyd, R., & Richerson, P. J. (1996). Why culture is common but cultural evolution is rare. *Proceedings of the British Academy, 88*, 77–93.

Byrne, R. (1995). *The thinking ape: Evolutionary origins of intelligence.* Oxford: Oxford University Press.

Byrne, R. W., & Tomasello, M. (1995). Do rats ape? *Animal Behavior, 50*, 1417–1420.

Caro, T. M., & Hauser, M. D. (1992). Is there teaching in nonhuman animals? *Quarterly Review of Biology, 67*, 151–174.

Cavalli-Sforza, L. L., & Feldman, M. W. (1981). *Cultural transmission and evolution: A quantitative approach.* Princeton, NJ: Princeton University Press.

Chen, S. C. (1937). Social modification of the activity of ants in nest building. *Physiological Zoology, 10*, 420–436.

Chesler, P. (1969). Maternal influence in learning by observation in kittens. *Science, 166*, 901–903.

Chou, L., & Richerson, P. J. (1992). Multiple models in social transmission among Norway rats (*Rattus norvegicus*). *Animal Behavior, 44*, 337–344.

Church, R. M. (1957a). Transmission of learned behavior between rats. *Journal of Abnormal and Social Psychology, 34*, 163–165.

Church, R. M. (1957b). Two procedures for the establishment of "imitative behavior". *Journal of Comparative and Physiological Psychology, 50*, 315–318.

Clayton, N. S. (1987). Song tutor choice in zebra finches. *Animal Behavior, 35*, 714–721.

Cook, M., Mineka, S., Wolkenstein, B., & Laitsch, K. (1985). Observational conditioning of snake fear in unrelated rhesus monkeys. *Journal of Abnormal Psychology, 94*, 591–610.

Coussi-Korbel, S., & Fragaszy, D. M. (1995). On the relation between social dynamics and social learning. *Animal Behavior, 50*, 1441–1453.

Curio, E. (1988). Cultural transmission of enemy recognition by birds. In T. R. Zentall & B. G. Galef, Jr. (Eds.), *Social learning: Psychological and biological perspectives* (pp. 75–98). Hillsdale, NJ: Lawrence Erlbaum Associates Inc.

Curio, E., Ernst, U., & Vieth, W. (1978). Cultural transmission of enemy recognition: One function of mobbing. *Science, 202*, 899–901.

Custance, D. M., Whiten, A., & Bard, K. A. (1995). Can young chimpanzees imitate arbitrary actions? Hayes and Hayes (1952) revisited. *Behavior, 132*, 839–858.

Dugatkin, L. A. (1992). Sexual selection and imitation: Females copy the mate choices of others. *American Naturalist, 139*, 1384–1389.

Dugatkin, L. A., & Godin, J.-G. J. (1992). Reversal of female mate choice by copying. *Proceedings of the Royal Society of London, 249*, 179–184.

Dugatkin, L. A., & Godin, J.-G. J. (1993). Female mate copying in the guppy, *Poecilia reticulata*: Age dependent effects. *Behavioral Ecology, 4*, 289–292.

Fragaszy, D. M., & Visalberghi, E. (1996). Social learning in monkeys: Primate "primacy" reconsidered. In C. M. Heyes & B. G. Galef, Jr. (Eds.), *Social learning in animals: The roots of culture* (pp. 65–84). New York: Academic Press.

Galef, B. G., Jr. (1970). Aggression and timidity: Responses to novelty in feral Norway rats. *Journal of Comparative and Physiological Psychology, 70*, 370–381.

Galef, B. G., Jr. (1981). The development of olfactory control of feeding site selection in rat pups. *Journal of Comparative Psychology, 95*, 615–662.

Galef, B. G., Jr. (1985). Direct and indirect behavioral pathways to the social transmission of food avoidance. In P. Bronstein & N. S. Braveman (Eds.), *Experimental assessments and clinical applications of conditioned food aversions* (pp. 203–215). New York: New York Academy of Sciences.

Galef, B. G., Jr. (1988). Imitation in animals: History, definition and interpretation of data from the psychological laboratory. In T. R. Zentall & B. G. Galef, Jr. (Eds.), *Social learning: Psychological and biological perspectives* (pp. 3–28). Hillsdale, NJ: Lawrence Erlbaum Associates Inc.

Galef, B. G., Jr. (1992). The question of animal culture. *Human Nature, 3*, 157–178.

Galef, B. G., Jr. (1995). Why behavior patterns that animals learn socially are locally adaptive. *Animal Behavior, 49*, 1325–1334.

Galef, B. G., Jr. (1996a). Introduction to Part I: Historical origins: The making of a science. In L. D. Houck & L. C. Drickamer (Eds.), *Foundations of animal behavior: Classic papers with commentaries* (pp. 5–12). Chicago: University of Chicago Press.

Galef, B. G., Jr. (1996b). Social learning and imitation. In C. M. Heyes & B. G. Galef, Jr. (Eds.). *Social learning in animals: The roots of culture* (pp. 49–64). New York: Academic Press.

Galef, B. G., Jr. (1996c). Social influences on food preferences and feeding behaviors of vertebrates. In B. Capaldi (Ed.), *Why we eat what we eat* (pp. 207–230). Washington, DC: American Psychological Association.

Galef, B. G., Jr. (in press). Tradition and imitation in animals. In G. Greenberg & M. Haraway (Eds.), *Encyclopedia of comparative psychology*. New York: Garland Press.

Galef, B. G., Jr., & Allen, C. (1995). A new model system for studying animal traditions. *Animal Behavior, 50*, 705–717.

Galef, B. G., Jr., & Clark, M. M. (1971a). Social factors in the poison avoidance and feeding behavior of wild and domesticated rat pups. *Journal of Comparative and Physiological Psychology, 25*, 341–357.

Galef, B. G., Jr., & Clark, M. M. (1971b). Parent-offspring interactions determine time and place of first ingestion of solid food by wild rat pups. *Psychonomic Science, 25*, 15–16.

Galef, B. G., Jr., Kennett, D. J., & Stein, M. (1985). Demonstrator influence on observer diet preference: Effects of simple exposure and the presence of a demonstrator. *Animal Learning and Behavior, 13*, 25–30.

Galef, B. G., Jr., Manzig, L. A., & Field, R. M. (1986). Observational learning in budgerigars: Dawson and Foss (1965) revisited. *Behavioral Processes, 13*, 191–202.

Galef, B. G., Jr., Mason, J. R., Pretti, G., & Bean, N. J. (1988). Carbon disulfide: A semiochemical mediating socially-induced diet choice in rats. *Physiology and Behavior, 42*, 119–124.

Galef, B. G., Jr., & Stein, M. (1985). Demonstrator influence on observer diet preference: Analyses of critical social interactions and olfactory signals. *Animal Learning and Behavior, 13*, 31–38.

Galef, B. G., Jr., & Whiskin, E. E. (1997). Effects of social and asocial learning on longevity of food-preference traditions. *Animal Behavior, 53*, 1313–1322.

Galef, B. G., Jr., & Wigmore, S. W. (1983). Transfer of information concerning distant foods: A laboratory investigation of the "information-center" hypothesis. *Animal Behavior, 31*, 748–758.

Garcia, J., & Koelling, R. A. (1966). Relation of cue to consequence in avoidance learning. *Psychonomic Science, 4*, 123–124.

Gibson, R. M., Bradbury, J. W., & Vehrencamp, S. L. (1991). Mate choice in lekking sagegrouse: The role of vocal display, female site fidelity and copying. *Behavioral Ecology, 2,* 165–180.

Giraldeau, L.-A., Caraco, T. & Valone, T. J. (1994). Social foraging: Individual learning and cultural transmission of innovations. *Behavioral Ecology, 5,* 35–43.

Giraldeau, L.-A, & Lefebvre, L. (1987). Scrounging prevents cultural transmission of food-finding behavior in pigeons. *Animal Behavior, 35,* 387–394.

Giraldeau, L.-A., & Templeton, J. J. (1991). Food scrounging and diffusion of foraging skills in pigeons (*Columbia livia*): The importance of tutor and observer rewards. *Ethology, 89,* 63–72.

Heyes, C. M. (1994). Social learning in animals: Categories and mechanisms. *Biological Reviews, 69,* 207–231.

Heyes, C. M. (1995). Imitation and flattery. *Animal Behavior, 50,* 1421–1424.

Heyes, C. M. (1996). Genuine imitation? In C. M. Heyes & B. G. Galef, Jr. (Eds.), *Social learning in animals: The roots of culture* (pp. 371–390). New York: Academic Press.

Heyes, C. M., & Dawson, G. R. (1990). A demonstration of observational learning in rats using a bidirectional control. *Quarterly Journal of Experimental Psychology, 42B,* 59–71.

Heyes, C. M., Dawson, G. R., & Noakes, T. (1992). Imitation in rats: Initial responding and transfer evidence. *Quarterly Journal of Experimental Psychology, 45B,* 81–92.

Heyes, C. M., & Galef, B. G., Jr. (Eds.) (1996). *Social learning in animals: The roots of culture.* New York: Academic Press.

Hudson, R., & Altbacker, V. (1993). Development of feeding and food preference in the European rabbit. In B. G. Galef, Jr., M. Mainardi, & P. Valsecchi (Eds.), *Behavioral aspects of feeding* (pp. 125–146). Chur, Switzerland: Harwood Academic.

Hull, C. L. (1929). A functional interpretation of the conditioned reflex. *Psychological Review, 36,* 498–511.

King, A. P., & West, M. J. (1983). Epigenisis of cowbird song: A joint endeavor of males and females. *Nature, 305,* 704–706.

King, A. P., West, M. J., & Eastzer, D. H. (1981). Song structure and song development as potential contributors to reproductive isolation in cowbirds (*Molothrus ater*). *Journal of Comparative and Physiological Psychology, 94,* 1028–1039.

King, B. (1994). *The information continuum.* Santa Fé, NM: SAR Press.

Laland, K. R., & Plotkin, H. C. (1990). Social learning and social transmission of digging for buried food in Norway rats. *Animal Learning and Behavior, 18,* 246–251.

Laland, K. R., Richerson, P. J., & Boyd, R. (1993). Animal social learning: Toward a new theoretical approach. *Perspectives in Ethology, 10,* 249–277.

Laland, K. R., Richerson, P. J., & Boyd, R. (1996). Developing a theory of animal social learning. In C. M. Heyes & B. G. Galef, Jr. (Eds.), *Social learning: The roots of culture* (pp. 129–154). New York: Academic Press.

Lefebvre, L. (1995a). Culturally-transmitted feeding behavior in Primates: Evidence for accelerating learning rates. *Primates, 36,* 227–239.

Lefebvre, L. (1995b). The opening of milk bottles by birds: Evidence for accelerating learning rates, but against the wave-of-advance model of cultural transmission. *Behavioral Processes, 34,* 43–54.

Marler, P. (1970). A comparative approach to vocal learning: Song development in white-crowned sparrows. *Journal of Comparative and Physiological Psychology, 71,* 1–25.

Marler, P., & Tamura, M. (1964). Culturally transmitted patterns of vocal behavior in sparrows. *Science, 146,* 1483–1486.

Mason, J. R., & Reidinger, R. F., Jr. (1981). Effects of social facilitation and observational learning on feeding behavior of the red-winged blackbird (*Agelaius phoeniceus*). *Auk, 98,* 778–784.

Mason, J. R., & Reidinger, R. F. (1982). Observational learning of food aversions in red-winged blackbirds (*Agelaius phoeniceus*). *Auk, 99,* 548–554.

McGrew, M. C. (1992). *Chimpanzee material culture: Implications for human evolution.* Cambridge, UK: Cambridge University Press.

Mineka, S., & Cook, M. (1988). Social learning and the acquisition of snake fear in monkeys. In T. R. Zentall & B. G. Galef, Jr. (Eds.), *Social learning: Psychological and biological perspectives* (pp. 51–97). Hillsdale, NJ: Lawrence Erlbaum Associates Inc.

Mitchell, R. W. (1989). A comparative developmental approach to understanding imitation. *Perspectives in Ethology, 7*, 183–215.

Moore, B. R. (1992). Avian movement imitation and a new form of mimicry: Tracing the evolution of a new form of learning. *Behavior, 122*, 231–263.

Moore, B. R. (1996). Avian movement imitation and a new form of mimicry: Tracing the evolution of complex learning. In C. M. Heyes & B. G. Galef, Jr. (Eds.), *Social learning in animals: The roots of culture* (pp. 245–266). New York: Academic Press.

Nicol, C. J., & Pope, S. J. (1994). Social learning in sibling pigs. *Applied Animal Behavior Science, 40*, 31–43.

Payne, R. B. (1981). Song learning and social interaction in indigo buntings. *Animal Behavior, 29*, 688–697.

Provenza, F. D., Lynch, J. J., & Nolan, J. V. (1993). The relative importance of mother and toxicosis in the selection of foods by lambs. *Journal of Chemical Ecology, 19*, 313–323.

Rogers, A. (1988). Does biology constrain culture? *American Anthropologist, 90*, 819–831.

Romanes, G. J. (1884). *Mental evolution in animals*. New York: D. Appleton.

Rozin, P., & Kalat, J. W. (1971). Specific hungers and poison avoidance as adaptive specializations of learning. *Psychological Review, 78*, 459–486.

Russon, A. E., & Galdikas, B. M. F. (1993). Imitation in free-ranging rehabilitant orangutans. *Journal of Comparative Psychology, 107*, 147–161.

Russon, A. E., & Galdikas, B. M. F. (1995). Constraints on great apes' imitation: Model and action selectivity in rehabilitant orangutan (*Pongo pygmeaus*) imitation. *Journal of Comparative Psychology, 109*, 5–17.

Schlupp, I., Marler, C., & Ryan, M. J. (1994). Benefit to male sailfin mollies of mating with heterospecific females. *Science, 263*, 373–374.

Solomon, R. L., & Coles, M. R. (1954). A case of failure of generalization of imitation across drives and across situations. *Journal of Abnormal Psychology, 49*, 7–13.

Steiniger, F. (1950). Beiträge zur Soziologie und sonstigen Biologie der Wanderratte. *Zeitschrift für Tierpsychologie, 7*, 356–379.

Stimbert, V. E. (1970a). Partial reinforcement of social behavior in rats. *Psychological Reports, 26*, 723–726.

Stimbert, V. E. (1970b). A comparison of learning based on social or nonsocial discriminative stimuli. *Psychonomic Science, 20*, 185–186.

Templeton, J. J., & Giraldeau, L.-A. (1995). Patch assessment in foraging flocks of European starlings: Evidence for use of public information. *Behavioral Ecology, 6*, 65–72.

Thorndike, E. L. (1898). Animals intelligence: An experimental study of the associative processes in animals. *Psychological Review Monograph Supplements, 2*, Whole No. 4.

Thorpe, W. H. (1963). *Learning and instinct in animals*. London: Methuen.

Tomasello, M. (1996). Do apes ape? In C. M. Heyes & B. G. Galef, Jr. (Eds.), *Social learning in animals: The roots of culture* (pp. 319–343). New York: Academic Press.

Tomasello, M., Kruger, A. C., & Rutner, H. H. (1993a). Cultural learning. *Behavioral and Brain Sciences, 16*, 495–552.

Tomasello, M., Savage-Rumbaugh, S., & Kruger, A. (1993b). Imitative learning of actions on objects by children, chimpanzees and enculturated chimpanzees. *Child Development, 64*, 1699–1705.

Triplett, R. (1897). The dynamogenic factors in peacemaking and competition. *American Journal of Psychology, 9*, 507–533.

Valsecchi, P., Choleris, E., Moles, A., Cong, G., & Mainardi, M. (1996). Kinship and familiarity as factors affecting social transfer of food preferences in adult Mongolian gerbils (*Meriones unguiculatus*). *Journal of Comparative Psychology, 110*, 243–251.

Valsecchi, P., & Galef, B. G., Jr. (1989). Social influences on the food preferences of house mice (*Mus musculus*): A comparative analysis of behavioral processes. *International Journal of Comparative Psychology, 2*, 245–256.

Valsecchi, P., Moles, A., & Mainardi, M. (1993). Does mother's diet affect food selection of weanling wild mice? *Animal Behavior, 46*, 827–828.

Washburn, M. F. (1908). *The animal mind.* New York: Macmillan.

West, M. J., & King, A. P. (1988). Female visual displays affect the development of male song in the cowbird. *Nature, 334*, 244–246.

West, M. J., King, A. P., & Eastzer, D. H. (1981). The cowbird: reflections on development from an unlikly source. *American Scientist, 29*, 57–66.

Whiten, A. (1996). Imitation, pretence and mindreading: Secondary representation in comparative primatology and developmental psychology? In A. E. Russon, S. T. Parker, & K. A. Bard (Eds.), *Reaching into thought* (pp. 300–324). Cambridge, UK: Cambridge University Press.

Whiten, A., & Custance, D. (1996). Studies of imitation in chimpanzees and children. In C. M. Heyes & B. G. Galef, Jr. (Eds.), *Social learning in animals: The roots of culture* (pp. 291–318). New York: Academic Press.

Whiten, A., Custance, D. M., Gomez, J.-C., Teixidor, P., & Bard, K. (1996). Imitative learning of artificial fruit processing in children (*Homo sapiens*) and chimpanzees (*Pan troglodytes*). *Journal of Comparative Psychology, 110*, 3–14.

Whiten, A., & Ham, R. (1992). On the nature and evolution of imitation in the animal kingdom: Reappraisal of a century of research. In P. J. B. Slater, J. S. Rosenblatt, & C. Beer (Eds.), *Advances in the study of behavior* (Vol. 21, pp. 239–283). New York: Academic Press.

Wrangham, R. W., McGrew, W. C., de Waal, F. B., & Heltne, P. G. (1994). *Chimpanzee cultures.* Cambridge, MA: Harvard University Press.

Wyrwicka, W. (1978). Imitation of mother's inappropriate food preference in weanling kittens. *Pavlovian Journal of Biological Science, 13*, 55–72.

Wyrwicka, W. (1981). *The development of food preferences: Parental influences and the primacy effect.* Springfield, MA: Charles S. Thomas.

Wyrwicka, W. (1996). *Imitation in human and animal behavior.* New Brunswick, NJ: Transaction Publishers.

Yoerg, S. I. (1991). Social feeding reverses learned flavor aversions in spotted hyena (*Crocuta crocuta*). *Journal of Comparative Psychology, 105*, 185–189.

Zajonc, R. B. (1965). Social facilitation. *Science, 149*, 269–274.

Zentall, T. R., & Galef, B. G., Jr. (Eds.) (1988). *Social learning: Psychological and biological perspectives.* Hillsdale, NJ: Lawrence Erlbaum Associates Inc.

Zentall, T., Sutton, J. E., & Sherburne, L. M. (1996). True imitative learning in pigeons. *Psychological Science, 7*, 343–346.

Zohar, O., & Terkel, J. (1992). Acquisition of pine cone stripping behavior in black rats (*Rattus rattus*). *International Journal of Comparative Psychology, 5*, 1–6.

CHAPTER THIRTEEN

Learned helplessness: State or stasis of the art?

J. Bruce Overmier
Center for Research in Learning, Perception, & Cognition,
University of Minnesota, Minneapolis, USA

This chapter is a critical review of the development of the construct of learned helplessness as an abnormal debilitation, its extension by Seligman as a model of reactive depression, and its role in illuminating a number of psychobiological consequences of stress. Selected problems with learned helplessness theory and interpretation of results from the triadic design underlying the construct are considered. An alternative strategy for the study of stress, viewing its consequences as "normal", is presented. Emphasis is on the anagenesis of psychological-behavioral modulation of stressors. It is argued that for some purposes, this alternative opens new research avenues.

Cet article examine d'une façon critique le développment du concept d'impuissance acquise en tant qu'état débilitant anormal, l'extension que lui apporte Seligman comme modèle de dépression réactionnelle et son rôle dans l'éclaircissement d'un certain nombre de conséquences psychobiologiques du stress. On y considère un certain nombre de problèmes concernant la théorie du resignation apprise et l'interprétation des résultats issus du modèle triadique qui sous-tend ce concept. On présente une stratégie alternative pour l'étude du stress, laquelle considère ses conséquences comme étant «normales». L'accent est placé sur l'anagénèse de la modulation psychologique-comportementale des stresseurs. On postule que, pour certains objectifs, cette alternative ouvre de nouvelles avenues de recherche.

My long involvement with the research on learned helplessness has given me a deep appreciation of what we have learned from this phenomenon—but it is an appreciation that also recognizes emergent problems. Hence the title of this chapter. Let me review briefly what we have learned as a context for developing my concerns about the state of learned helplessness research.

Independent of the theoretical origins of the line of research (Overmier, 1996), research on "learned helplessness" is essentially research on the proactive effects

TABLE 13.1
Some parallels between learned helplessness and depression

	Helplessness	Depression
Causal factors	Uncontrollable trauma	Uncontrollable negative life events
Symptoms		
Behavioral	Response initiation deficit	Unresponsiveness, psychomotor retardation
Cognitive	Associative deficit	Disrupted thinking
	Reinforcement ineffective	Negative expectations
	Attentional shifts	Sadness
	Emotional passivity	Emotionally flat
	Augmented recall of aversive	Ruminations
	Reduced aggression	
	Reduced food intake	Anorexia
Physiological	NE depletions	Monoamine dysfunction
	Dexamethasone nonsuppression	Dexamethasone nonsuppression
Treatments	Antidepressants	Antidepressants
	ECT	ECT
	Forced escape	Behavioral efficacy training
	Time	Time

of "stress". In the initial experiments, an experimental group of restrained subjects were exposed to a series of unpredictable and uncontrollable traumatic aversive events. Compared to control groups that had either received no traumatic events (Overmier & Seligman, 1967), or received the identical aversive events but ones that were controllable (Seligman & Maier, 1967), the experimental group was later dramatically impaired in learning new behaviors. Indeed, the experimental group simply failed to respond, and in addition showed both cognitive and emotional debilitations (Overmier & Seligman, 1967). The phenomenon has been shown to be general across a range of species, across a range of physical challenges, and across environments (Maier & Seligman, 1976). An animal showing learned helplessness is a clear instance of a distressed organism.

Although the initial subjects were dogs, Seligman and others soon began theorizing about how this phenomena could generate insights into the consequences of uncontrollable stress on humans, perhaps causing dysphoria and even depression (Seligman, 1974, 1975). Soon, many parallels between learned helplessness and depression were being identified; Table 13.1 lists some of these.

This generated considerable excitement and a vast amount of research (Peterson, Maier, & Seligman, 1993). This body of research can be organized into four major lines. These four lines are shown in Table 13.2.

One line tests for the full range of symptoms unique to the experimental group. Several important ones have been identified, including anorexia, hypoalgesia, gastric ulcer, reduced immune function, and depleted neurochemicals. Another line explores the causal role of fear in learned helplessness. These studies have yielded new insights into the causes of fear itself. Yet another line

TABLE 13.2
Learned helplessness phenomenon: Continuing lines of research

Additional consequences	Modulators of fear	Modeling	Reconceptualization and extension
Anorexia	Prediction	Causes	Perceptual biases
Psychosomatic	of onset	Physiology	Attributions
Finickiness	of offset	Treatments	causes of
Analgesia	of intensity	drugs	measurement of
Amine loss	Control	behavioral	consequences of
Immune fail	of onset	Bidirectional	Explanatory style
CNS activity	of offset		influences on
	of intensity		measurement of
	of duration		consequences of
	Genetics		
	Cellular		

Citations for the individual entries can be found in Overmier (1996).

of research has applied the logic of formal modeling to test for empirical parallels between the animal phenomena and human phenomena. Among the products of this research is the establishment of the learned helplessness model as an effective screening device for therapeutic drugs for depression. The final line addresses limitations of the learned helplessness theory of depression and reformulations of it. This research now focuses on measuring potential cognitive antecedents to helplessness and depression. Illustrative citations for each of these lines of research can be found elsewhere (Overmier, 1996; Overmier & LoLordo, in press).

LEARNED HELPLESSNESS AS (DIS)STRESS

The richness of the contemporary research is impressive. So why raise a cautionary flag? Well, because the research domain of learned helplessness has in general proceeded independently from that on "stress" and uninformed by the research on stress. And that is the problem, given that at its base, the phenomenon of learned helplessness *is* a stress phenomenon—perhaps *the* classic one, Selye's claims aside.

Now of course, the domain of "stress research" has its own set of problems—some contributed by Selye himself and his dual constructs of "distress" and "eustress". Others include "what is stress". I shall not try to define stress here because such a definition is not really critical to the strategic issues I wish to call to your attention.

The job for psychologists is answering the questions (1) "When do potential stressors stress?", (2) "What are the manifestations of stress?", and (3) "What determines which specific 'symptomatology'—physiological, behavioral, or cognitive —will be manifest?"

I wish I had answers to each of these questions. But I do not. The saving grace for me is that nobody else does either. Lacking the answers, however, we can discuss *strategic issues* in the scientific process in hopes of gaining some new insights and possibly new experimental leverage.

Let us begin with the issue of the definition of stress. One strategy many have adopted in defining stressors is to define situations *unitarily*, that is incorporating into the definition the physical events, contextual factors, and psychological factors interfused (e.g. Lazarus & Folkman, 1984). The argument is that the context and psychological state are integral and taken together with the physical event define a unique stressor in that they convey "meaning" to the physical event—and it is this "meaning" that causes the stress.

The psychological factors invoked have been many, diverse, nonsystematic, and sometimes even inconsistent with one another. Included in them have been available social contexts, competitive challenges, perceptions, biases, expectancies —and in humans, attributions about the reasons for the stressor, attributions about the self and/or others, personality traits (e.g. "introvert" vs. "extrovert"), imaginal style, and many others. This strategy might be characterized as treating the psychological contextual factors as primary causes.

To my view, an unfortunate feature of this strategy is that it converts some potential *consequences* of experiences with stressors into *antecedents* of that stress. For example, is it possible that negative attributions about self-efficacy are a consequence of prior stressor challenges? If some of these psychological states are manifestations of stress, then treating them as antecedents induces a circularity that prevents us from answering the first question "When do stressors stress?"

Alternatively, I (along with some others) would suggest an analytical approach, wherein we treat such psychological contextual factors as (potentially) separable features that interact to modulate the stressfulness of the fundamental psycho-biological challenges, rather than as integral components of the stressor *per se*. This analytical approach can be successful even if we initially misidentify which factor is the stressor and which is the modulator! This is because each is varied orthogonally as if it were an independent variable. This strategy might be charac-terized as treating psychological contextual factors as *moderators* (Minor, Dess, & Overmier, 1991; Overmier, 1988). To illustrate the idea, consider a physical treatment like restraint. We can sensibly ask what psychological contextual factors ameliorate or augment the stress of restraint. Does the presence of one or more conspecifics modulate the effect of the physical challenge? Does it matter how many conspecifics there are? Or, does it matter whether the conspecifics are from the individual's social group or not? We need not necessarily define a new, unique stressor for each possible variant on a psychological contextual manipulation.

The strategy proposed here for the analysis of when stressors stress is to attempt to obtain a separation for analytic purposes between the physical-biological challenge event impacting on the organism and the psychological context in which it occurs. This then allows us to attribute separately specific properties to the psychological contextual factors themselves.

Whether we ought to treat psychological contextual factors as primary (the first strategy) or as moderator variables (the second strategy) is an issue of continuing debate. I am arguing for the latter as a matter of productive experimental strategy rather than as a matter of received truth.

I want to consider two versions of the implementation of this "separable factors" definitional approach, both of which I have used in research on learned helplessness, but one of which I think is problematic. These two metatheories are the *medical disease model* and the *anagenesis evolutionary advances model*. We shall consider each in turn.

MEDICAL MODEL AS STATE AND STASIS

We psychologists tend to first look at organisms functioning in the world in their "normal adaptive" ways. Then, after studying this normal functioning, we may shift to study deviations from the normal functioning, seeking to identify the causal variables for these deviations. This metatheoretic orientation is a direct analogue to the physician's disease model. This specific approach to the analysis of biobehavioral phenomena of maladaptive behavior may be exemplified by most research on learned helplessness. Let us review the learned helplessness phenomenon and its symptomatology.

The deficits constituting the learned helplessness syndrome and the originating empirical observations underlying the inferred symptom are shown in Table 13.3. The phenomenon of learned helplessness in animals was initially characterized as including failures to initiate coping behaviors, associative-learning deficits, and reduced expressed emotion. As observed earlier: a clear example of a distressed organism.

Now what is the "cause" of this distress? I have already argued that we do not want to begin by defining the stressor as unitary but rather as a concatenation

TABLE 13.3
Learned helplessness symptomatology and inferred deficits

Symptoms	Inferred deficits
1. Failure to respond to challenges	Response-initiation/motivation
2. Failure to learn from successes	Associative-cognitive
Highly selective attention	
3. Passivity in face of threat/pain	Emotional
Hyper-pituitary/adrenal output	
Vulnerability to neurochemical	
depletions in limbic system	

Learned helplessness theory implies that these 3 features are necessarily co-occurring.

of several separable factors. However, even accepting conceptualization, there still are various possible strategies one might adopt within the medical model. One possibility is theory-based; another is operation-based. There are merits and costs associated with each.

The popular theory suggests that learned helplessness results from the animal learning that responding in the face of aversive events is ineffective, which in turn generates a cognition of "uncontrollability" and "helplessness", which in turn later impairs coping (Maier & Seligman, 1976; Maier, Seligman, & Solomon, 1969). This theory is attractive and enables a broad range of psychologists to integrate it into their own work.

The unpopular operations account is that helplessness symptoms are caused by extended exposure to uncontrollable aversive events.

These theoretical and the operational accounts are similar but far from identical because the theory invokes a hypothetical construct which is *not tied in any absolute way to the inducing operations*. (This is especially clear in the reformulated theory of learned helplessness elaborated on later [Abramson, Seligman, & Teasdale, 1978].) Thus, under the theoretical approach, one must first find an independent assessment of the cognition, then determine the contingencies and conditions under which the cognition is established, and, finally, one must determine conditions under which the cognition produces the symptom set. These are no small tasks.

With respect to the development of the cognition, for example, one is led to the study of how organisms weight various event dependencies that constitute a contingency, how these weightings themselves may vary as a function of various other experiences, and so on (e.g. Alloy & Tabachnik, 1984).

The point to be noted here is that to the extent that we are interested in the psychobiological phenomenon of stress rather than the cognitive ones, the theory inevitably leads one to first answer the cognitive ones. The answers to these questions may only be relevant if the theory is substantially correct in the first place!

In point of fact, careful analysis of the existing data suggest that the initial theory of learned helplessness is at least inadequate because it, as Selye did, poses a single intervening construct in the causal chain of the symptom set. This implies, thresholds aside for the moment, that the individual symptoms of helplessness should be almost perfectly correlated with one another. They are not.

The lack of perfect correlation itself may be addressed through theory or by operational analysis.

To address this lack of perfect correlation, a reformulated theoretical approach was developed that invoked additional hypothetical constructs in the causal chain. The essence of the structure of the reformulation is shown in Fig. 13.1. Because this reformulation introduces additional cognitive processes of perceptual and associative biases and multiple attributions as antecedents to the critical mediating cognition of learned helplessness, it increases exponentially the demands on the cognitive analyses, thus leading us even further from our basic stress phenomenon.

"CAUSAL CHAIN" for Learned Helplessness in Reformulated Theory

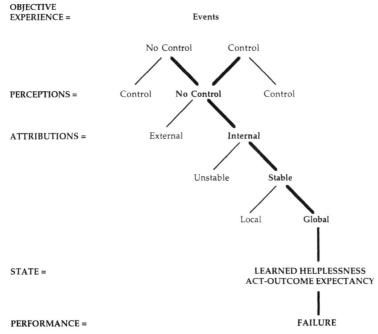

OBJECTIVE
EXPERIENCE =   Events

                    No Control   Control

PERCEPTIONS =   Control   No Control   Control

ATTRIBUTIONS =   External   Internal

                        Unstable   Stable

                           Local   Global

STATE =   LEARNED HELPLESSNESS
                                    ACT-OUTCOME EXPECTANCY

PERFORMANCE =   FAILURE

FIG. 13.1 A representation of the psychological path connecting experience to performance according to the reformulated theory of learned helplessness that includes the hypothesized mediators of biases and attributions.

The theoretical approach has another inherent problem. The specific identification and "naming" of the cognitive state constrains the experimental research. Because the key state in the theory was a cognitive state of "helplessness" arising from perceived "uncontrollability", the degree of control afforded the organism became the only operational factor to receive general attention. This is despite the fact that the inducing aversive events were typically unpredictable as well as uncontrollable.

The operational approach to the lack of perfect correlation immediately obviates this last problem. It leads the experimenter to vary independently and systematically each feature that was a part of the complex of inducing operations. Such an operational approach leads to the discovery that experiencing unpredictable aversive events itself induces an associative or learning impairment. This has been called general learned irrelevance (Dess & Overmier, 1989; Linden, Savage, & Overmier, 1997).

Operational detection of this additional phenomenon suggests that the two features of unpredictability and uncontrollability may operate as separable—and possibly orthogonal—causal factors in producing separable components of the

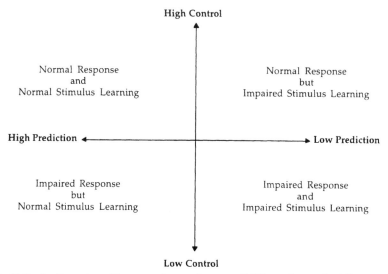

FIG. 13.2   An illustration of how experiences of uncontrollability and unpredictability could be independent factors in contributing to the learned helplessness phenomenon.

observed symptomatology. This idea is illustrated in Fig. 13.2 based on an idea initially proposed by Overmier, Patterson, and Wielkiewicz (1980).

But, to this point, both the theoretical and the operational approaches were constrained by that metatheoretical "disease model" orientation of seeking the causes of the abnormal behavior. The efforts were to study the deleterious effects of *taking away* the control or prediction that is normally afforded to organisms. This orientation is readily evidenced in which of the treatments the researcher chooses to call the control or reference condition. Let us consider the key experimental design features of learned helplessness experiments as illustrated in Fig. 13.3.

The traditional learned helplessness procedures rely on the "triadic design", so-called because it involves a contrast among three groups: (1) one group called Normal is naive with respect to traumatic events, for example foot-shocks, (2) one group called Master receives shocks that it can terminate and which hence are controllable, and (3) one group called Yoked receives shocks matched to those of the Master group but over which the Yoked group has no control. This triadic design uses the coping behavior and psychobiology of a naive animal as the reference condition. In addition, this triadic design also requires virtually identical performances and biological markers during the final test from both the naive animal and from the animal previously exposed to the potential stressor but over which it had control.

According to the theory of helplessness, only if this equality obtains between Normal and Masters and only if the Yoked animal stressed without any control

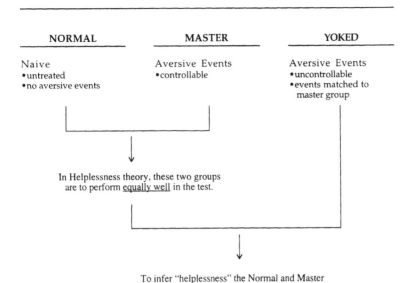

FIG. 13.3   An illustration of the experimental design central to learned helplessness experiments. The three groups receive the treatment described at the top in the experiment's first phase. The outcome expectations based on learned helplessness theory are shown at the foot.

shows impaired function on the test can the stress-induced "helplessness" state be inferred.

But by what rationale would a stress researcher routinely expect such a pattern? Fig. 13.4, top, illustrates the data pattern required by traditional helplessness theory as couched within the medical model. There are many other potential patterns of results as shown in Fig. 13.4; indeed, some of these are commonly reported outcomes. Are not some of these at least as understandable and "expected" as that definitionally required by learned helplessness theory? After all, even the Master organism is severely challenged by both by the physical events and the demands of the learning and behavior that leads to control. These challenges ought to differentiate the Master subject from the Naive subject. And, once having learned something, virtually anything, there is usually some form of transfer of that learning to future tasks; here that is the test task. That the "helplessness" relation three-way pattern did sometimes obtain is extraordinarily interesting. However, it directs attention *only* to the animal that had lacked control. And its behavior is designated as "aberrant", even though it is the reliable, lawful consequent.

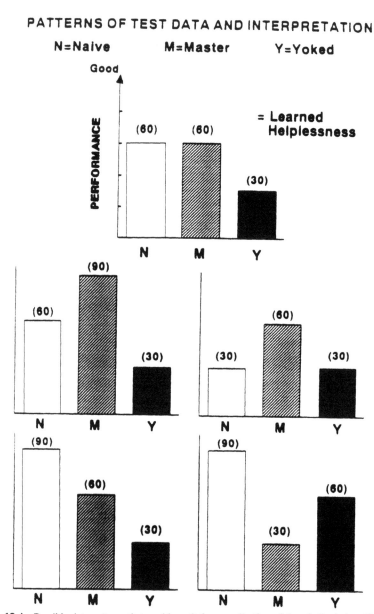

FIG. 13.4 Possible data patterns that could result from application of the triadic design. The top center pattern represents that required by learned helplessness theory. But other patterns have been obtained, and could well be expected according to other perspectives (e.g. Brady et al., 1958).

ANAGENESIS MODEL

The preceding considerations lead me to suggest another strategic shift—a strategic shift that also is a metatheoretic shift. I suggest that it may be especially useful to refocus on the distress-modulating effects of making recognized stressors controllable, and/or predictable, and/or subject to other psychologically relevant manipulations (e.g. habituation, etc.). The shift in view here is subtle but important. That is, whereas the traditional learned helplessness experiments focus on the deleterious consequences of not having control (or whatever), the newly proposed strategy focuses on the advantages of being given control (or whatever). According to this shift in view, the reference condition now becomes the behavioral and psychobiological effects of the physical stressor events themselves *unmodulated* by other organism-environment transactions.

That is, the treatment reference condition becomes the reactions of the "psychologically naked" organism—the so-called helpless organism, the distressed organism. Then, either within subjects or between subjects, the psychological context and "meaning" factors that are the necessary product of organism-environment transactions are then introduced independently as the experimental additions. The changes conveyed to the organism by virtue of these experimental contextual additions—the improvements or even additional debilitations observed—then define the "coping"—or the additional "distress"—afforded by the possible organism-environment transactions. The strategy could be characterized as a functional recapitulation of anagenesis (Huxley, 1958).

Let us pursue the important logic consequences of this shift to the anagenesis model for scientists. There is a logical asymmetry between the learned helplessness theory based on a medical disease model and its inferred causal states, and the operational approach based on an anagenesis model and its inferred states.

Importantly, a virtue of this new operational, anagenesis strategy is that we gain a better basis—an empirical basis—for inferring what psychological factors are operating. To be able to infer that an organism might "know" an event to be controllable requires that indeed the animal exercises control. If it does not, then the *experimenter-defined* controllability is without effect for the animal. (Instructions, of course, may afford other possibilities with humans, see Geer, Davison, & Gatchel, 1970.) That is, an organism's psychological sensitivity to the experimenter operationally defined and arranged controllability and/or predictability can be directly measured—measured through observing the increasing frequency of the defined controlling response (i.e. instrumental learning) and through increasing anticipatory responses during the predicting signal (i.e. classic conditioning).

In contrast, the problem facing those who advocate the learned helplessness theory-based disease model and who wish to infer the psychological causes or bases for the debilitation seen in learned helplessness is that one cannot infer from lack of responses the opposite states: Absence of responses does not insure an underlying cognitive state of "uncontrollability". Imagine a "Pet Rock" that is first exposed to a series of fixed shocks and then tested for its ability to escape further aversive events (Brewster & Wilson, 1976); it will not, of course, but do we want to infer this is because it is manifesting an underlying cognitive state of uncontrollability or helplessness? The criticism posed here applies equally well to theoretical constructs such as "protective inhibition", "conservation-withdrawal", "hopelessness", which are central to a number of other theories of debilitation (e.g. Engel & Schmale, 1972).

This logical asymmetry reinforces the suggestion to adopt the strategy of operationally "adding" to the context the opportunities for potentially psychologically meaningful organism-environment transactions—many of which might have hypothesized stress-reducing consequences for the organism. It may be obvious to note, then, that whereas the learned helplessness model views the manifest "helplessness" and psychobiological disturbances as some special debilitation resulting from distorted behavioral and cognitive processes, the proposed alternative operational anagenesis approach recharacterizes the "learned helplessness" phenomenon as the normal consequence of exposures to stressors in the absence of any adaptive commerce with the environment. (See Engel & Schmale, 1972, on conservation-withdrawal and Pavlov, 1927, on protective inhibition, as lawful adaptive reactions.)

The clever evolutionary biologist could, I suspect, readily construct a sound basis for this shift in strategy to the "anagenesis" adaptive abilities model. It would probably begin by noting that for the early primitive organisms, environmental assaults impacted directly on them, and they were without behavioral or psychological capacity for utilizing the environment's regularities, dependencies, and contingencies. Under these conditions, biological success was limited. But as evolution provided adaptive mechanisms, biological success dramatically improved. This continued process ultimately yielded animals that could predict the environment's regularities and could operate on the environment to take advantage of dependencies and contingencies. To see the adaptive value these abilities have for a contemporary animal, we must first assess its function without these opportunities—a "procedural ablation", if you like, of its psychological abilities—and then add each one back, alone or in combinations.

To summarize, the rejection of a theory of causes driven by a disease model and the adoption of an "anagenic" operational approach of focusing on the change in psychobiological status that results from allowing the organism to "operate" either behaviorally or cognitively on the environment should be especially useful for those who are interested in the study of "coping" with stress.

This operational approach uniquely allows for finding that some coping opportunities may in fact cause further distress rather than less (Brady, Porter, Conrad, & Mason, 1958)—a possibility that is at least inferentially awkward, if not impossible, within the triadic design analysis dictated by traditional learned helplessness theory.

Under the proposed strategic revisions one does not need to infer whether the observed changes are attributable to particular associative, cognitive, or other processes *per se*. One is free to determine empirically which coping opportunities affect the organism and what the effects are on the organism's various psychobiobehavioral systems. Are they for better or worse? It might well be that adaptation or coping at either the physiological, behavioral, or psychological level carries with it increased burden at the other levels. Indeed, Brady's "executive monkey" experiments (Brady et al., 1958), despite their purported flaws, did show that subjects that showed good behavioral adaptation to a shock schedule suffered severe physiological symptoms, whereas those that did not adapt behaviorally in the initial sessions also showed few physiological symptoms. Such reciprocal interdependencies are virtually not imaginable—much less experimentally detectable—within learned helplessness and the learned helplessness theory-based application of the triadic design.

Detecting either such negative, or even positive, interdependencies requires considerable systematic data (Overmier, 1988). We dare not assume that stress-induced changes in all systems will be parallel, nor dare we assume that the effects of affording, say, prediction (or control or other factor) will be parallel for all behavioral and psychobiological functions. Indeed, it is likely that there are many trade-offs to be discovered.

Over time, this operational anagenesis strategy will enable us to determine, over a wide range of conditions, the answer to our opening set of questions of "When do potential stressors stress?", "Which are the symptoms of stress?", and "What factors determine the specific symptomatology manifest?"

CONCLUSION

The presentation here has been substantially different from the usual state-of-the-art review. Rather, it has been more of a sharing of a personal intellectual odyssey in which I have noted not only progress but some perceived scientific limitations imposed by the accepted theory-based research strategies. It is my thesis that the basic and reformulated theories of learned helplessness had their roots in a negativistic disease orientation. This metatheoretic orientation and strategy has led us to limit research to a single pattern of results and foreclosed noticing that some forms of coping may in themselves contribute additional stress or at least burden other organismic systems. Moreover, the evolving learned helplessness theory's hypothesized cognitive states are forcing us away from research on effects of stress *per se* and into efforts to validate cognitive, attributional constructs.

I have suggested that we shift to a more operational approach guided by a positive anagenesis view emphasizing the adaptive psychological capacities of organisms. On this anagenic view, the search begins with the psychologically naked organism's responses to challenge and then determines operationally how the availability of various organism-environment interactions and dependencies can modulate those original raw responses. Those that we can confidently identify as "psychological" will be the grist for our scientific mill and the focus of our future theorizing.

I have also tried to suggest that our efforts may need to be more structured —or at least that we need to try to capture the systematicities that do exist if we are to appreciate fully the contributions of various coping mechanisms to the fullest range of psychobiological adjustments (Murison & Overmier, 1993). On the other hand, as we seek these systematic patterns, we must be sure that we do not take the patterns at face value, but instead also probe the mediating processes involved.

Although we have many years of research behind us, we are still just at the beginning of systematic analyses of stress and coping phenomena. Adoption now of appropriate strategies should yield a future richer in new data sets and in clinically useful new understandings.

REFERENCES

Abramson, L. Y., Seligman, M. E. P., & Teasdale, J. (1978). Learned helplessness in humans: Critique and reformulation. *Journal of Abnormal Psychology, 87,* 49–74.

Alloy, L. B., & Tabachnik, N. (1984). Assessment of covariation by humans and animals: The joint influence of prior expectations and current situational information. *Psychological Review, 91,* 112–149.

Brady, J. V., Porter, R. W., Conrad, D. G., & Mason, J. W. (1958). Avoidance behavior and the development of gastroduodenal ulcers. *Journal of Experimental Analysis of Behavior, 1,* 69–72.

Brewster, R. G., & Wilson, H. E. (1976). Learned helplessness in pet rocks (*roccus pettus*). *Worm Runner's Digest, 18*(2), 111–113.

Dess, N. K., & Overmier, J. B. (1989). General learned irrelevance: Proactive effects on Pavlovian conditioning in dogs. *Learning & Motivation, 20,* 1–14.

Engel, G. L., & Schmale, A. H. (1972). Conservation-withdrawal: A primary regulatory process for organismic homeostasis. In *Ciba Foundation Symposium No. 8* (pp. 57–85). Amsterdam: Elsevier.

Geer, J., Davison, G. C., & Gatchel, R. J. (1970). Reduction of stress in humans through nonveridical perceived control of aversive stimulation. *Journal of Personality and Social Psychology, 16,* 731–738.

Huxley, J. S. (1958). Evolutionary processes and taxonomy with special reference to grades. *University of Uppsalla Aarskrift* (pp. 21–39). Uppsalla, Sweden: University of Uppsalla.

Lazarus, R. S., & Folkman, S. (1984). *Stress, Appraisal, and Coping.* New York: Springer-Verlag.

Linden, D. R., Savage, L. M., & Overmier, J. B. (1997). Pavlovian analog to learned helplessness: General learned irrelevance across stimuli and contexts. *Learning and Motivation, 28,* 230–248.

Maier, S. F., & Seligman, M. E. P. (1976). Learned helplessness: Theory and evidence. *Journal of Experimental Psychology: General, 105,* 3–46.

Maier, S. F., Seligman, R. L., & Solomon, R. L. (1969). Pavlovian fear conditioning and learned helplessness: Effects on escape and avoidance behavior of (a) the CS-US contingency and (b) the independence of US and voluntary responding. In B. A. Campbell & R. M. Church (Eds.), *Punishment and Aversive Behavior* (pp. 299–342). New York: Appleton Century Crofts.

Minor, T. R., Dess, N. K., & Overmier, J. B. (1991). Inverting the traditional view of "learned helplessness". In M. R. Denny (Ed.), *Fear, avoidance, and phobias* (pp. 87–134). Hillsdale, NJ: Lawrence Erlbaum Associates Inc.

Murison, R., & Overmier, J. B. (1993). Parallelism among stress effects on ulcer, immunosuppression, and analgesia: Commonality of mechanisms? *Journal of Physiology* (Paris), *87*, 253–259.

Overmier, J. B. (1988). Psychological determinants of when stressors stress. In D. Hellhammer, I. Florin, & H. Weiner (Eds.), *Neurobiological approaches to human disease* (pp. 236–259). Toronto: Hans Huber.

Overmier, J. B. (1996). Richard L. Solomon and learned helplessness. *Integrative Physiological and Behavioral Science, 31*, 331–337.

Overmier, J. B., & LoLordo, V. M. (in press). Learned helplessness. In W. O'Donohue (Ed.), *Learning and behavior therapy*. Needham, MA: Allyn & Bacon.

Overmier, J. B., Patterson, J., & Wielkiewicz, R. M. (1980). Environmental contingencies as sources of stress in animals. In S. Levine & H. Ursin (Eds.), *Coping and health* (pp. 1–38). New York: Plenum.

Overmier, J. B., & Seligman, M. E. P. (1967). Effects of inescapable shock upon subsequent escape and avoidance learning. *Journal of Comparative & Physiological Psychology, 63*, 28–33.

Pavlov, I. P. (1927). *Conditioned reflexes*. Oxford: Oxford University Press.

Peterson, C., Maier, S. F., & Seligman, M. E. P. (1993). *Learned helplessness: A theory for the age of personal control*. Oxford: Oxford University Press.

Seligman, M. E. P. (1974). Depression and learned helplessness. In R. J. Friedman & M. M. Katz (Eds.), *The psychology of depression: Contemporary theory and research* (pp. 83–126). Washington, DC: Winston-Riley.

Seligman, M. E. P. (1975). *Helplessness: On Depression, Dying, and Death*. San Francisco: Freeman.

Seligman, M. E. P., & Maier, S. F. (1967). Failure to escape traumatic shock. *Journal of Experimental Psychology, 74*, 1–9.

CHAPTER FOURTEEN

Perceptual learning in animals and humans

N. J. Mackintosh and C. H. Bennett
Department of Experimental Psychology,
University of Cambridge, UK

With sufficient practice, we become able to discriminate reliably between initially indistinguishable stimuli. Although many instances of such perceptual learning effects no doubt reflect deliberate and intentional learning, many probably occur incidentally or unintentionally, as a result of simple exposure to the stimuli. Such a conclusion is reinforced by the results of experiments with animals, where mere exposure to two or more confusable stimuli, in the absence of any semblance of differential reinforcement, is sufficient to enhance their discriminability. Associative learning theory, derived from animal conditioning experiments, also suggests a simple explanation of such perceptual learning, based on three processes: differential latent inhibition of common and unique elements; the establishment of unified representations of complex stimuli by associations between their elements; and the establishment of inhibitory associations between the unique elements of stimuli that occur apart.

Avec suffisamment d'entraînement, nous parvenons à établir une discrimination fiable entre deux stimuli au départ indifférenciables. Même si bon nombre d'exemples de tels effets d'apprentissage perceptif reflètent sans conteste un apprentissage délibéré et intentionnel, plusieurs autres se produisent probablement de façon incidente ou non intentionnelle, à la suite de la seule présentation des stimuli. Cette conclusion est corroborée par les résultats d'expériences menées chez l'animal et où la seule présentation de deux ou de plus de deux stimuli susceptibles d'être confondus suffit, en l'absence de tout renforcement différentiel apparent, à accroître la possibilité de leur discrimination. Dérivée d'expériences de conditionnement chez l'animal, la théorie de l'apprentissage associatif suggère également trois explications simples d'un tel apprentissage perceptif: il y aurait inhibition latente et différentielle d'éléments communs et uniques aux stimuli, constitution de représentations détaillées de stimuli complexes à l'aide des associations entre leurs éléments et, enfin, établissement d'associations inhibitrices entre les éléments uniques présents dans des stimuli présentés séparément.

INTRODUCTION

Over 100 years ago, William James noted:

That "practice makes perfect" is notorious in the field of motor accomplishments. But motor accomplishments depend in part on sensory discrimination. In the purely sensorial field we have the well-known virtuosity displayed by the professional buyers and testers of various kinds of goods. (James, 1890, p. 509)

And he proceeded to give examples of the amazing feats of such experts. One man could tell whether a glass of Madeira had been drawn from the upper or lower half of the original bottle. Another could run newly ground flour through his fingers, and tell you whether it was ground from wheat grown in Iowa or Tennessee. Over the years, other commentators have provided numerous other examples. Experts can sex day-old chicks, by brief inspection of their external genitalia, with an error rate of less than 1%, although they are hard pressed to state explicitly the criteria they use for making this discrimination, and novices, explicitly told what relevant, distinguishing features to look for, can do no better than about 70% correct (Biederman & Shiffar, 1987). The photomicrograph of the stained section of brain and the X-ray revealing a lesioned disc that are readily interpreted by the expert neuroscientist or radiographer, mean nothing to the untrained observer.

However, although familiar enough to common experience, the phenomena of perceptual learning have, until very recently, received surprisingly little attention from experimental psychologists and, what is less excusable, even less from learning theorists. For similar perceptual learning effects are readily demonstrated in the laboratory—even in the animal laboratory. In a now classic experiment, Gibson and Walk (1956) trained rats to discriminate between a circle and a triangle, rewarding them for choice of one rather than the other in a standard simultaneous discrimination paradigm. For one group, the stimuli were entirely novel, whereas the second group had lived in cages with circles and triangles hanging on the walls for the past month or so. As can be seen in Fig. 14.1, this pre-exposed group learned the discrimination quite readily, whereas the control group was still performing at chance after 10 days of discrimination training. In a procedure more commonly used today, thirsty rats are given a distinctively flavored solution to drink and then receive an injection of lithium chloride. The lithium injection conditions an aversion to the solution the rats have just drunk, which will generalize to another, similarly flavored solution. But such generalization can be markedly reduced, that is the discrimination enhanced, if the rats have been previously exposed to the two flavors by being allowed to drink measured amounts of each over the past 10 days or so (e.g. Honey & Hall, 1989; Mackintosh, Kaye, & Bennett, 1991).

Students of human learning may well wonder why they should pay any attention to the results of animal experiments, when the phenomena they are

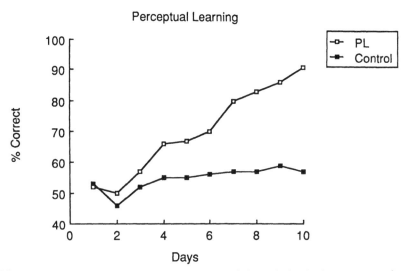

FIG. 14.1   The learning of a discrimination between circles and triangles in two groups of rats, one pre-exposed to the stimuli (PL), the other (Control) for whom the stimuli were novel (after Gibson & Walk, 1956).

interested in studying are just as readily observed in people. One answer is this: Animal experiments may provide a better model of those instances of perceptual learning in people, where proficient discrimination appears to arise incidentally, as a result simply of prolonged exposure to a set of stimuli, without any deliberate effort or intention on the part of the observer to profit from this exposure. For example, we are all experts at recognizing faces: We can identify dozens or hundreds of relatives, friends or acquaintances, often after not having seen them for months or years, and despite dramatic changes in their superficial appearance. Laboratory experiments establish that people can recognize hundreds of faces seen briefly and only once each, and as they are better at recognizing faces from their own ethnic group than those of other groups, it seems clear that such proficiency is partly a consequence of greater familiarity with, or exposure to, some types of face than others (see Chiroro & Valentine, 1995, for a clear demonstration of this). No doubt, we do occasionally make a deliberate effort to remember a particular face, and it would be foolish to suppose that there is no role for reinforcement in the way that infants learn to identify their parents or other caretakers. But this hardly seems sufficient to explain our proficiency with such a wide variety of briefly seen faces.

It is not necessarily a simple matter to model such learning in the laboratory with human participants. Although the techniques of some implicit learning experiments could well be adapted to good effect, if people are specifically asked to look at, or study, a set of stimuli, it seems singularly unsurprising that they should end up discriminating between them more accurately than when they began. Even if the experimenter provides no explicit feedback in the exposure phase, the social psychology of most experimental interactions will be sufficient to persuade many participants that they had better study the stimuli carefully, look for differences between them, or try to memorize them, because these stimuli are bound to be part of the experimenter's attempts to test them or trick them into looking stupid. Consider, as an example, another set of experiments that have attracted recent attention, those on "hyperacuity", where, with sufficient practice, observers can make reliable vernier acuity judgments (i.e. determine whether the upper of two vertical lines is displaced to the right or left of the lower line), when the displacement or offset between the two lines is no more than 5–10 seconds of arc—although the diameter of foveal photoreceptors is about 30 seconds of arc (McKee & Westheimer, 1978; Poggio, Fahle, & Edelman, 1992).[1]

Much is made of the fact that in experiments such as these performance often improves in the absence of any feedback. But such psychophysical experiments explicitly require observers to discriminate between stimuli in a particular way. Even if there is no explicit feedback to inform them whether their judgments are correct or not, they have been told that they will be shown a series of stimuli that differ in some specified way, and that their task is to decide whether, say, one line is to the left or right of another. In other words, they are explicitly told that this is a discrimination task, and are explicitly told about the way in which the stimuli they are about to see differ from one another. The fact that the experimenter does not tell them, on each trial, whether they are right or wrong does relatively little to alter the nature of the task, and it still seems unlikely that such experiments will tell us a great deal about more everyday examples of incidental perceptual learning. Contrast this with the situation of the animal experiments described earlier. Gibson and Walk's (1956) rats were not required (either explicitly or implicitly) to discriminate between the circle and triangle during the pre-exposure phase of the experiment. The stimuli signaled nothing of

---

[1] As with William James's (1890) examples, it is hard to resist the idea that the main point of such demonstrations is to astonish us, by documenting the amazing degree of precision of which the human sensory apparatus is capable. No doubt it is good for us to be occasionally astonished. But we venture to suggest that demonstrations such as these do relatively little to illuminate the nature of the *learning* processes involved in perceptual learning. It is true that the remarkable specificity of the effects seen in such experiments rules out certain rather global explanations. It turns out that the increasing precision of vernier acuity judgments that occurs when observers view two misaligned vertical lines is completely disrupted when they are tested with two misaligned horizontal lines side by side, and asked to say whether one is displaced above or below the other. This implies that the earlier improvement on the vertical lines cannot have been due to a better understanding of the experimenter's instructions, general adaptation to the task, increased attentiveness or concentration. But it certainly does not justify the assertion sometimes made (e.g. by Sagi & Tanne, 1994) that the learning must be located at a relatively peripheral level of the visual system. As Morgan (1992) and, more explicitly, Mollon and Danilova (1996) have noted, the learning processes may be located centrally, and the specificity may lie simply in what is learned (for example, that apparent random noise in a horizontal plane may indicate left or right displacement of one line relative to another).

consequence, and it seems most likely that the rats would have come to ignore them. Similarly, if thirsty rats are simply given one or other of two equally palatable, very dilute solutions to drink, they do not need to discriminate between them during this phase of the experiment: The only thing that matters for the moment is that these solutions quench their thirst. Nevertheless, such exposure dramatically increases rats' subsequent ability to discriminate between those hard-to-discriminate stimuli. Why?

AN ASSOCIATIVE THEORY OF PERCEPTUAL LEARNING

To answer this question, we need to answer an earlier one. Why are some stimuli difficult to discriminate in the first place? It is hardly enough to say that they are confusable or similar. Most conditioning theorists accept the answer suggested by stimulus sampling theory (Neimark & Estes, 1967) that stimuli may be conceptualized as sets of elements, and that the similarity of any two stimuli is measured by the proportion of elements they share in common. Thus two similar stimuli, A and B, should be regarded as each comprising a set of unique elements, A and B, and a set of elements, X, which they have in common. The greater the ratio of X to A and B elements, the more similar the two stimuli are and the greater the generalization, or harder the discrimination, between them.

Pearce and Redhead (1993; see also Redhead & Pearce, 1995) have formally demonstrated, in a variety of experiments, that the explicit addition of a common element to two discriminative stimuli makes the discrimination between them harder to learn. We have shown the same in flavor aversion conditioning. An aversion conditioned to a weak saline solution will generalize only slightly to a weak sucrose solution, or vice-versa. But if a third flavor, dilute lemon juice, is added to the two solutions, the aversion conditioned to saline-lemon generalizes almost completely to sucrose-lemon (Mackintosh et al., 1991; see Table 14.1 and Fig. 14.2). More to the point, in several of our experiments, it is only when we have deliberately added common elements or features to two stimuli that prior exposure to those stimuli will enhance their discriminability, that is, pro-duce evidence of perceptual learning (Mackintosh et al., 1991; similar results are

TABLE 14.1

Design of experiment on the role of common elements in generalization and perceptual learning

Groups	Pre-exposure	Condition	Test
Control	–	A+	A vs. B
	–	AX+	AX vs. BX
Pre-exposed	A/B	A+	A vs. B
	AX/BX	AX+	AX vs. BX

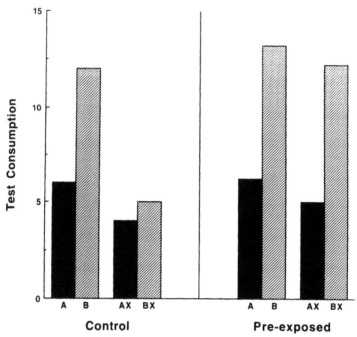

FIG. 14.2   Results of the experiment whose design is shown in Table 14.1. Test consumption (in ml) of two elementary flavors, A and B, or two compound flavors, AX and BX, after an aversion has been conditioned to A or to AX. For control animals, all flavors were novel; pre-exposed groups had drunk their two test solutions over a series of pre-exposure sessions (after Mackintosh et al., 1991).

readily obtained in an entirely different preparation, spatial discrimination learning in mazes: see Chamizo & Mackintosh, 1989; Trobalon, Sansa, Chamizo, & Mackintosh, 1991). For example, prior exposure to simple saline and sucrose solutions did not reduce the generalization of an aversion from one to the other, but prior exposure to saline-lemon and sucrose-lemon solutions substantially reduced generalization between them.

Latent inhibition of common elements

This account of generalization, and these demonstrations of the role of common elements, have not, of course, provided us with a theoretical explanation of perceptual learning. But they do suggest certain theoretical lines that should be pursued and, as will become apparent, our own explanations all rely on this prior analysis.

Eleanor Gibson (1969) proposed one explanation of perceptual learning that also relied on such an analysis. She suggested that, when first exposed to two complex stimuli, AX and BX, people would initially attend equally to their common (X) and unique (A, B) elements; but that with sufficient exposure they would come to attend preferentially to the unique elements and ignore the common elements. It is obvious enough that such a change in attention would result in more rapid learning of a discrimination between AX and BX, but the question that has to be asked is *why* any such change in attention should occur. It is one thing to say that observers in psychophysical experiments, instructed to judge whether one line is above or below another, will try to look for the very subtle features that differentiate these two situations and, even in the absence of any explicit feedback, will end up attending to them and ignoring the background noise (i.e. features common to both). But why should Gibson and Walk's (1956) rats have learned to attend to the features differentiating circles and triangles when these stimuli were simply hanging from the walls of their cages? Why, during initial, unreinforced exposure, should our rats have learned to attend to the salt and sucrose flavors that differentiated the two compound solutions they drank every day? No obvious differential reinforcement depended, at *this* stage of the experiment, on successful discrimination between the two.

A theory should not be dismissed on grounds of implausibility alone. But there is an alternative account, which appeals to nothing more than principles well established in conditioning experiments, and which achieves much the same effect as that postulated by Gibson (McLaren, Kaye, & Mackintosh, 1989). What we want to say is that during the conditioning or discriminative training phase of these experiments, animals pre-exposed to the discriminative stimuli are more likely than control animals to associate the outcome of each trial with the unique, differentiating features of each stimulus rather than with their common features. This is readily predicted by assuming that such pre-exposure results in differential latent inhibition of common and unique elements. The term "latent inhibition" refers to the finding that in simple conditioning experiments unreinforced pre-exposure to the stimulus that later serves as the conditioned stimulus (CS) significantly retards conditioning (Lubow, 1989). The most common interpretation of latent inhibition has been to say that pre-exposure reduces the associability of a stimulus, or decreases the probability that it will enter into any new associations, for example with the outcome of a conditioning trial (Hall, 1991; Mackintosh, 1983). But pre-exposure to two stimuli, AX and BX, sharing a common feature, will necessarily result in twice as much exposure to their common feature, X, as to their unique features, A and B. We should therefore expect that pre-exposure to two stimuli will ensure a greater decline in the associability of the elements they share than of the elements unique to each. It should thus make it easier to discriminate between them.

A variety of experiments have provided evidence consistent with this analysis. In flavor aversion experiments, we have shown that prior exposure to the common X element alone is just about as effective as exposure to AX or BX in enhancing discrimination between them (Bennett, Wills, Wells, & Mackintosh, 1994; Mackintosh et al., 1991). Experiments on spatial discrimination learning in mazes have shown that prior exposure to the landmarks in the experimental room that define the spatial location of different goal arms will facilitate subsequent discrimination learning only if it involves exposure to the landmarks visible from, and therefore common to, the two goal arms; exposure only to the landmarks unique to each arm actually retards subsequent discrimination learning (Rodrigo, Chamizo, McLaren, & Mackintosh, 1994; see also Sansa, Chamizo, & Mackintosh, 1996).

Experiments on categorization learning by both people and pigeons have also yielded results consistent with this analysis (Aitken, Bennett, McLaren, & Mackintosh, 1996; McLaren, Leevers, & Mackintosh, 1994). In his discussion of perceptual learning, William James (1890) used the example of a person learning to discriminate claret from burgundy. The mechanism he proposed involved the person learning to associate slight differences in the taste of the two types of wine with other extraneous features, such as the names *claret* and *burgundy, that wine I drank at so-and-so's table*, etc. The outcome of all this, James argued, would be to produce two stimulus compounds more discriminable than the original flavors themselves. But the trouble with this account, now usually referred to as the "acquired distinctiveness of cues", is that it seems to predict that the experience of placing two classes of stimuli, here clarets and burgundies, into two distinct categories, might make it harder to make discriminations *within* each category. If associating clarets and burgundies with two distinct labels makes them easier to discriminate, by the same token it might be expected to make all clarets, associated with the same label, harder to discriminate. Common experience suggests otherwise: The expert wine taster becomes ever more proficient at making finer and finer discriminations.

Our experiments confirm this expectation. For both people and pigeons, the experience of categorizing two sets of variable exemplars of two different classes of stimuli into their appropriate categories facilitates the learning of a subsequent discrimination between two new instances of one of the categories. What is the explanation? The exemplars are generated as random distortions of two prototype patterns (one for each category). This means that each exemplar will share elements in common with all other exemplars of its category, that is those that it shares with the category prototype, but will also contain elements unique to it alone. Experience with a large number of exemplars of a particular category, therefore, will cause strong latent inhibition of the elements they all share in common, but leave their unique elements, and those of any new exemplars of that category, relatively novel. It will thus make the discrimination between any new exemplars of that category easier than it would otherwise have been.

Establishment of representations of stimuli

Differential latent inhibition of common and unique elements may provide one mechanism of perceptual learning, but it is surely not the only one. It does not capture the intuitive idea that, with practice, we become more adept at identifying a complex stimulus from a brief glimpse, or that experience refines and sharpens our perceptions. And it is not difficult to provide more formal evidence of perceptual learning effects that seem to require a quite different explanation.

Although successful Pavlovian conditioning usually requires a number of trials, there are some preparations where reliable conditioning can be obtained in a single trial. Flavor aversion conditioning provides one example. Another is the conditioning of fear to a novel place. If a rat is placed in a conditioning chamber for a few minutes and then receives a single shock to its feet, it will show evidence of conditioned fear (indexed by crouching and freezing) when replaced in the chamber the next day (Blanchard & Blanchard, 1969). In this latter case, however, rats show no evidence of conditioning if they are shocked within a few seconds of first being placed in the chamber (Blanchard, Fukunaga, & Blanchard, 1976; Fanselow, 1986). The problem, it seems, is that they have had too little time to learn to identify the chamber, and thus fail to recognize it again when replaced there the next day. If placed in the chamber for a few minutes, with no further consequence, the day before the conditioning trial, they show perfectly good conditioning even with a very brief exposure to the chamber on the conditioning trial itself (Fanselow, 1990).

Fanselow's (1990) results have been confirmed and extended by Kiernan and Westbrook (1993). They too found that moderate, prior exposure to the conditioning context enhanced the level of conditioning produced by a single brief conditioning trial. Not surprisingly, they also found that prolonged prior exposure to the context alone reversed this effect by interfering with conditioning. We know that the magnitude of a latent inhibition effect is a function of the amount of prior exposure to a CS, so it is reasonable to expect facilitation to turn into retardation with sufficient pre-exposure. Perhaps their most interesting and striking finding, however, was that a moderate amount of pre-exposure not only enhanced the level of conditioning to the context in which shock occurred, but also reduced the generalization of this conditioning to another context. This is exactly what we should expect on the assumption that the establishment of a more accurate representation of a complex CS will not only enhance the conditioning that accrues to that CS, but also ensure that such conditioning does not generalize to other stimuli.

We have also established that there are circumstances under which brief prior exposure to the CS may enhance, rather than retard, the conditioning that occurs in flavor aversion conditioning (Bennett, Tremain, & Mackintosh, 1996). The two conditions that must be satisfied are that the CS must be a relatively complex flavor, rather than an elementary one, and that it must be presented only very briefly on a single conditioning trial. In one experiment, we used three distinct flavors as our CSs, two of which were elementary, that is dilute solutions of sucrose or of hydrochloric acid, whereas the third could reasonably be regarded as complex, being a mixture of monosodium glutamate, sucrose, and quinine (MSG). Rats received either 4ml or only 1ml of their target solution to drink on a single conditioning trial (followed by a lithium injection), but one of

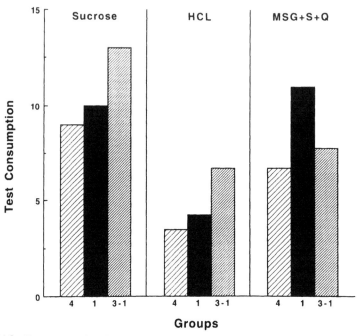

FIG. 14.3   Test consumption (in ml) of each of three solutions, sucrose, HCL (acid), or a mixture of monosodium glutamate, sucrose and quinine, after a single conditioning trial on which the consumption of the solution had been paired with a lithium injection. For each solution, one group had drunk 4ml on their conditioning trial, whereas the other two had drunk only 1ml. But Group 3-1 had previously been exposed to 3ml of the solution (after Bennett et al., 1996).

the two groups that drank only 1ml of the solution on the conditioning trial had been given 3ml to drink in an earlier session. The results of the experiment are shown in Fig. 14.3. Although there were large differences in the overall level of consumption of the two single solutions, sucrose and acid, the pattern of results for each was much the same. Conditioning was not much affected by whether animals drank 4ml or only 1ml on their single conditioning trial, but in those drinking only 1ml, prior exposure to this solution (Groups 3-1) interfered with conditioning. For animals given the MSG solution as their CS, however, there was a quite different pattern of results. Those given only 1ml to drink showed a weaker aversion, that is less conditioning, than those given 4ml, but this weak level of conditioning was *enhanced* by prior exposure to the solution. In other experiments, we found that prior exposure to the MSG solution did *not* enhance conditioning if animals were allowed to drink 4ml of the solution on their conditioning trial. Thus, although prior, unreinforced exposure to a CS will normally retard conditioning to that CS, there are certain restricted circumstances where it may not: These appear to be that the CS should be a complex one, and that it be presented only briefly for a single conditioning trial. Under these circumstances, brief prior exposure may not only enhance conditioning to the CS, it will also reduce generalization to other, similar stimuli.

But how does exposure to a relatively complex stimulus result in the establishment of an increasingly accurate and precise representation of it? McLaren et al. (1989) appealed to a process they referred to as "unitization", but their account adds only one new assumption to stimulus-sampling theory's account of stimuli as sets of elements, only a subset of which is sampled on any one trial. Let us assume that the standard laws of association, which say that events that occur together become associated with one another, apply not only to the events we call stimuli—conditioned (CS) and unconditioned (US)—but also to the elements that comprise those stimuli. Empirical demonstrations of something very like this, where the elements are components of a compound stimulus manipulable by the experimenter, have been provided by Rescorla and Durlach (1981). We need to assume only that all stimuli should be conceptualized as sets of elementary components or features. Where the stimulus is itself an "elementary" one, a pure tone, a single wavelength of light, or an elementary flavor, there will be relatively few distinct hypothetical elements. But complex stimuli, such as an entire experimental chamber, a visual scene, a bird's song, or a complex flavor, will comprise a large number of quite distinct elements, not all of which will be sampled at any given moment. It would follow that the elements of such a stimulus sampled together on a single trial would become associated with one another in accordance with standard laws of association, with the standard consequence that activation of one element of the set will activate all its associated elements. Repeated sampling from the same complex stimulus set over a prolonged series of trials will mean that eventually all elements in the set will become associated with one another, with the consequence that whatever the subset actually sampled on a given trial, these sampled elements will activate all other elements in the set, allowing the retrieval of a complete, veridical representation of a complex whole from a brief glimpse of some of its parts.

Formation of inhibitory associations between unique elements

This, then, is a second mechanism of perceptual learning. But we shall need a third. The formation of associations between the elements of a stimulus may help to establish a complete and accurate representation of a complex stimulus, not all of whose elements can be sampled at once, but a moment's reflection suggests that such associations will not *necessarily* enhance the discriminability of that stimulus from others sharing common elements. Consider our two schematic stimuli, AX and BX, each comprising unique elements A and B, and X elements they share. The formation of associations between the A elements may underlie the establishment of a representation of AX, and may also help to discriminate AX from BX, but the formation of associations between A and X elements can only increase generalization from AX to BX. If A and B are both associated with X, the activation of A elements will also result in activation of B elements. If A elements become associated with a US, so also, by this circuitous route, may B elements. Even more certainly, after conditioning to AX, presentation of BX will retrieve not only X's conditioned reflex (CR), but also any conditioning that accrued to A.

But with sufficient prior exposure to AX and BX, this associative effect will be counteracted by another: the formation of inhibitory associations between the unique A and B elements. Once positive associations have been formed between A and X, and between B and X, the presentation of AX will directly activate both A and X elements, and the latter, by association, will also activate B elements. But the fact remains that the presence of A signals the absence of B, and these are the conditions responsible, in a Pavlovian conditioning experiment, for the establishment of inhibitory associations. If a CS signals a US, but the addition of a second CS to the first signals the absence of the US, this second CS becomes a conditioned inhibitor for that US (Mackintosh, 1983). In exactly the same way, if B and X occur together on some trials, but the addition of A to X means the absence of B, then inhibitory associations should be formed between A and B (and vice versa). As a consequence of such inhibitory associations, the presence of B on a BX trial will suppress any tendency for X to activate A. When animals are conditioned to AX and generalization is tested to BX, B will now suppress the activation of A, reducing the *mediated* generalization that would otherwise arise from X's ability to retrieve a representation of A and hence elicit any CRs conditioned to A.

Two sets of results have provided indirect evidence to suggest that some such mechanism may be operating. Both involve the use of relatively simple compound flavors, where the process of unitization just discussed is unlikely to play an important role. Both reveal a perceptual learning effect that cannot be attributed to differential latent inhibition of common and unique elements. And both establish that such effects occur under conditions that ought to favor the establishment of inhibitory associations between the unique elements of AX and BX compounds. In the first experiment, Mackintosh et al. (1991) showed that enhanced discrimination between AX and BX depended on prior exposure to A and B in the presence of a third common element, which did not even have to be X. The design of this experiment is shown in Table 14.2. As can be seen, two experimental groups were pre-exposed either to AX and BX, or to AY and BY, that is to A and B in the presence of a third, common element; the groups also received additional exposure to Y or X alone to ensure that all animals received equal amounts of exposure to each individual solution. The two control groups were exposed to AX and BY, or to AY and BX, that is to A and B in the presence of distinctively different other flavors. The results of these different pre-exposure treatments were clear: The two experimental groups learned to discriminate between AX and BX significantly more rapidly than the two

TABLE 14.2

Design of experiment on the role of common
elements in perceptual learning with latent
inhibition controlled

Groups	Pre-exposure	Discrimination
Experimental	AX/BX/Y	
	AY/BY/X	
		AX vs. BX
Control	AX/BY/X/Y	
	AY/BX/X/Y	

controls, and it made little difference whether they had been exposed to AX
and BX, or to AY and BY. It is worth noting that this is the exact opposite
of the outcome predicted by William James's (1890) acquired distinctiveness
theory. But as the development of inhibitory associations between A and B should
depend on their occurring in compound with a third, common element, this finding is entirely consistent with our analysis.

A second observation was reported by Symonds and Hall (1995). They found
that alternating exposure to AX and BX resulted in less subsequent generalization of an aversion from one to the other than did a regime in which all exposure
trials to AX occurred before those to BX (or vice versa). We have confirmed this
finding, and also found that these different patterns of pre-exposure do not result
in any difference in the level of conditioning to the common element X. This
latter finding implies that the difference in generalization from AX to BX cannot
be attributed to unsuspected differences in latent inhibition to X. The result is,
however, once again exactly what one would expect from an appeal to mutual
inhibition between A and B. If all AX trials precede BX trials during pre-
exposure, there can be no way that A could signal the absence of B, because the
development of such an inhibitory association must depend on the prior establishment of an excitatory association between X and B. And although B might
come to signal the absence of A, the X-A association would presumably weaken
of its own accord during a block of BX trials. Pavlovian conditioned inhibition
is best achieved by scheduling conditioning trials to CS1 *interspersed* with trials
on which CS1 is accompanied by CS2 but without the US.

Symonds and Hall (1995), although acknowledging this possibility, suggested
another possible explanation, derived from Eleanor Gibson's (1969) analysis,
namely that intermixed presentations of AX and BX would allow better comparison between them, and such comparison would draw attention to their unique
features and lead to the ignoring of their common features. Although it is far too
early to rule this possibility out, it does face one problem: It seems to imply that
the basis for the reduced generalization from AX to BX would be that conditioning had occurred preferentially to A rather than to X. In this respect, Gibson's

attentional account bears a close resemblance to one that appeals to differential latent inhibition of common and unique elements. But as we have seen, there is no evidence that alternating pre-exposure to AX and BX results in less conditioning to X than does blocked pre-exposure.

It remains true that we have no direct evidence of the formation of inhibitory associations between A and B during the course of pre-exposure. We have, however, observed a rather striking, related effect (Espinet, Iraola, Bennett, & Mackintosh, 1995). If rats are pre-exposed to two compound flavors, AX and BX, and an aversion is then conditioned to A alone (not in compound with X) by pairing it with a lithium US, this is sufficient to establish B as a conditioned inhibitor of that US—by both retardation and summation tests of inhibition. We have not yet shown that this effect depends on alternating exposure to AX and BX, as we expect it should, but we do know that it depends on reasonably lengthy exposure to A and B in the presence of a third, common flavor. It thus appears to depend on the establishment of an inhibitory association between A and B, although further theoretical assumptions are required to explain the ability of B to inhibit the representation of a US associated with A (see Espinet et al., 1995, for one suggestion).

CONCLUSIONS

The account of perceptual learning and identification outlined here may seem loose and informal, but it can be stated in more precise and formal, connectionist terms (see McLaren et al., 1989). There is a real sense, however, in which there is little new in the theory we are advancing. The explanation of perceptual learning and of the establishment of accurate representations of stimuli derives naturally and inevitably from some plausible and widely shared assumptions, common to most standard associative learning theories. We have borrowed from stimulus-sampling (or connectionist) theory the idea of stimuli as sets of elements, and added some new assumptions about latent inhibition and the establishment of excitatory and inhibitory associations between elements sampled together or apart. Through simply spelling out the consequences of these assumptions, we end up with an account of perceptual learning that stresses three rather different processes.

First, in certain cases, people and animals may learn, by differential reinforcement or instruction, to attend to the unique, differentiating features of two or more stimuli, rather than to the features they share—just as Gibson (1969) has argued. But where the conditions of exposure to a set of stimuli are not likely to direct subjects' attention to some aspects of them rather than others, a simple associative process, latent inhibition, will produce much the same end result: Differential latent inhibition of common and unique elements will ensure that the elements common to a set of stimuli will suffer a greater decline in associability during the course of exposure to those stimuli than will the elements unique to each.

If this sounds an unduly technical explanation, redolent of the jargon of the conditioning laboratory, for a phenomenon which we have claimed is one of everyday occurrence in the real world, then it may help to rephrase it in a more accessible form. The difficulty of learning to discriminate between members of a novel class of stimuli, whether they be Chinese faces or red wines from France, is that all members of the class share certain common features, which precisely serve to mark them off from other classes. When we first drank red wine, what we were likely to notice were the novel features that distinguished it from other drinks—water, milk, lemonade, beer, or even white wine. But these are, by and large, the features that all red wines have in common. It is only by prolonged exposure to a variety of members of this class that these salient common features start to lose their salience, and we start to notice the subtler, unique features that distinguish claret from burgundy, one claret from another, and so on.

Second, sufficient exposure to a complex stimulus will establish, by association between the elements sampled together on any one occasion, a complete representation of the stimulus, which can then be retrieved even from a brief and necessarily incomplete glimpse of it. This idea is certainly not new. Hall (1991) has written in similar terms, and its origins can be traced at least back to Hebb (1949) and his account of perceptual learning in terms of the building up of cell assemblies. In effect, we are suggesting that the establishment of veridical and detailed representations of complex stimuli can be understood in simple associative terms. It is, of course, far too soon to claim that this account is comprehensive enough, and we do not necessarily wish to rule out the contribution of additional processes, but it is worth starting with a simple idea, and seeing how far it will take us.

Finally, although exposure to two or more stimuli sharing common elements will initially lead to the formation of associations between the elements unique to each and those they share with others, thus possibly increasing generalization between them, this effect will be counteracted by the formation of inhibitory associations between their unique elements, thus driving the representations of the stimuli further apart. Here, we acknowledge that we have little direct evidence, although a reasonable amount of indirect evidence, to support our conjecture. And once again, we should not rule out the possible contribution of something like the processes of contrast and comparison suggested by Gibson (1969), and earlier by William James (1890).

But the virtue of the account we are offering, it seems to us, is that it yields novel and testable predictions, and thus actually offers something new to a set of phenomena so familiar that, in a curious way, experimental psychologists have largely ignored them. And it promises one final benefit. Although virtually all the experiments described here have employed rats, mostly in one conditioning paradigm, and the theory we have advanced derives directly from the animal conditioning laboratory, there seems every reason to believe that it will apply equally to humans. There is no doubt that people learn to distinguish between initially indistinguishable stimuli, and as often as not this learning seems to proceed in just the sort of incidental, unintentional, implicit, unreflective, and automatic way that encourages the application of a simple, associative theory. Perceptual learning seems to be a plausible area to look for parallels between learning by people and learning by animals.

REFERENCES

Aitken, M. R. F., Bennett, C. H., McLaren, I. P. L., & Mackintosh, N. J. (1996). Perceptual differentiation during categorization learning by pigeons. *Journal of Experimental Psychology: Animal Behavior Processes, 22*, 43–50.

Bennett, C. H., Tremain, M., & Mackintosh, N. J. (1996). Facilitation and retardation of flavour aversion conditioning following prior exposure to the CS. *Quarterly Journal of Experimental Psychology, 49B*, 220–230.

Bennett, C. H., Wills, S. J., Wells, J. O., & Mackintosh, N. J. (1994). Reduced generalization following preexposure: Latent inhibition of common elements or a difference in familiarity? *Journal of Experimental Psychology: Animal Behavior Processes, 20*, 232–239.

Biederman, I., & Shiffrar, M. M. (1987). Sexing day-old chicks: A case study and expert systems analysis of a difficult perceptual-learning task. *Journal of Experimental Psychology: Learning, Memory, and Cognition, 13*, 640–645.

Blanchard, R. J., & Blanchard, D. C. (1969). Passive and active avoidance reactions to fear-eliciting stimuli. *Journal of Comparative and Physiological Psychology, 68*, 129–135.

Blanchard, R. J., Fukunaga, K. K., & Blanchard, D. C. (1976). Environmental control of defensive reactions to footshock. *Bulletin of the Psychonomic Society, 8*, 129–130.

Chamizo, V. D., & Mackintosh, N. J. (1989). Latent learning and latent inhibition in maze discriminations. *Quarterly Journal of Experimental Psychology, 41B*, 21–31.

Chiroro, P., & Valentine, T. (1995). An investigation of the contact hypothesis of the own-race bias in face recognition. *Quarterly Journal of Experimental Psychology, 48A*, 879–894.

Espinet, A., Iraola, J. A., Bennett, C. H., & Mackintosh, N. J. (1995). Inhibitory associations between neutral stimuli in flavor-aversion conditioning. *Animal Learning and Behavior, 23*, 361–368.

Fanselow, M. S. (1986). Associative vs. topographical accounts of the immediate shock freezing deficit in rats: Implications for the response selection rules governing species specific defensive reactions. *Learning and Motivation, 17*, 16–39.

Fanselow, M. S. (1990). Factors governing one-trial contextual conditioning. *Animal Learning and Behavior, 18*, 264–270.

Gibson, E. J. (1969). *Principles of perceptual learning and development.* New York: Appleton-Century-Crofts.

Gibson, E. J., & Walk, R. D. (1956). The effect of prolonged exposure to visually presented patterns on learning to discriminate them. *Journal of Comparative Physiology and Psychology, 49*, 239–242.

Hall, G. (1991). *Perceptual and associative learning.* Oxford Psychology Series No. 18. Oxford: Clarendon Press.

Hebb, D. O. (1949). *The organization of behavior.* New York: Wiley.

Honey, R. C., & Hall, G. (1989). Enhanced discriminability and reduced associability following flavor preexposure. *Learning and Motivation, 20*, 262–277.

James, W. (1890). *The principles of psychology.* New York: Holt.

Kiernan, M. J., & Westbrook, R. F. (1993). Effects of exposure to a to-be-shocked environment upon the rat's freezing response: Evidence for facilitation, latent inhibition, and perceptual learning. *Quarterly Journal of Experimental Psychology, 46B*, 271–288.

Lubow, R. E. (1989). *Latent inhibition and conditioned attention theory.* Cambridge: Cambridge University Press.

Mackintosh, N. J. (1983). *Conditioning and associative learning.* Oxford: Clarendon Press.

Mackintosh, N. J., Kaye, H., & Bennett, C. H. (1991). Perceptual learning in flavour aversion conditioning. *Quarterly Journal of Experimental Psychology, 43B*, 297–322.

McKee, S. P., & Westheimer, G. (1978). Improvement in Vernier acuity with practice. *Perception and Psychophysics, 24*, 258–262.

McLaren, I. P. L., Kaye, H., & Mackintosh, N. J. (1989). An associative theory of the representation of stimuli: Applications to perceptual learning and latent inhibition. In R. G. M. Morris (Ed.), *Parallel distributed processing: Implications for psychology and neurobiology* (pp. 102–30). Oxford: Clarendon Press.

McLaren, I. P. L., Leevers, H. L., & Mackintosh, N. J. (1994). Recognition, categorisation and perceptual learning. In C. Umilta & M. Moscovitch (Eds.), *Attention and performance XV: Conscious and nonconscious information processing* (pp. 889–909). Cambridge, MA: MIT Press.

Mollon, J. D., & Danilova, M. V. (1996). Three remarks on perceptual learning. *Spatial Vision, 10*, 51–58.

Morgan, M. J. (1992). Hyperacuity of those in the know. *Current Biology*, 481–482.

Neimark, E. D., & Estes, W. K. (1967). *Stimulus sampling theory.* San Francisco, CA: Holden Day.

Pearce, J. M., & Redhead, E. S. (1993). The influence of an irrelevant stimulus on two discriminations. *Journal of Experimental Psychology: Animal Behavior Processes, 19*, 180–190.

Poggio, T., Fahle, M., & Edelman, S. (1992). Fast perceptual learning in visual hyperacuity. *Science, 256*, 1018–1021.

Redhead, E. S., & Pearce, J. M. (1995). Similarity and discrimination learning. *Quarterly Journal of Experimental Psychology, 48B*, 46–66.

Rescorla, R. A., & Durlach, P. (1981). Within-event learning in Pavlovian conditioning. In N. E. Spear & R. M. Miller (Eds.), *Information processing in animals: Memory mechanisms* (pp. 81–111). Hillsdale, NJ: Lawrence Erlbaum Associates Inc.

Rodrigo, T., Chamizo, V. D., McLaren, I. P. L., & Mackintosh, N. J. (1994). Effects of preexposure to the same or different pattern of extra-maze cues on subsequent extra-maze discrimination. *Quarterly Journal of Experimental Psychology, 47B*, 15–26.

Sagi, D., & Tanne, D. (1994). Perceptual learning: Learning to see. *Current Opinion in Neurobiology, 4*, 195–199.

Sansa, J., Chamizo, V. D., & Mackintosh, N. J. (1996). Apprendizaje perceptivo en discriminaciones espaciales. *Psicologia, 17*, 279–295.

Symonds, M., & Hall, G. (1995). Perceptual learning in flavor aversion conditioning: Roles of stimulus comparison and latent inhibition of common elements. *Learning and Motivation, 26*, 203–219.

Trobalon, J. B., Sansa, J., Chamizo, V. D., & Mackintosh, N. J. (1991). Perceptual learning in maze discriminations. *Quarterly Journal of Experimental Psychology, 44B*, 57–73.

PART FOUR

Cognition, perception and memory

CHAPTER FIFTEEN

Representations for actions

Marc Jeannerod
Institut des Sciences Cognitives, CNRS, Lyon, France

Comparison of brain activation patterns in conditions where actions are mentally simulated, observed in other people, or performed reveals both similarities and differences. PET and fMRI data obtained during these experimental conditions reveal the existence of a network common to all conditions, which includes the inferior parietal lobule (area 40), the ventral premotor area (ventral area 6), and part of the supplementary motor area. Activation of other areas does not overlap between conditions. Area 4 is activated during motor execution and motor imagination, not during observation. Prefrontal areas in the middle and inferior frontal gyri (areas 45 and 46) are activated during simulation and observation, but not during execution. The frontal operculum, at the junction between the precentral (ventral area 6) and the inferior frontal gyrus (areas 44 and 45), seems to play a critical role for recognition of a motor action by matching it with a similar action motorically coded in the same neuronal structures. This mechanism would represent a basis for common motor representations for recognizing, simulating, and executing various sorts of actions, including those related to verbal communication.

La comparaison des zones cérébrales activées lors de la simulation mentale d'une action, de l'observation de cette action réalisée par quelqu'un d'autre, ou de son exécution révèle à la fois des similitudes et des différences. Des données obtenues par les techniques de TEP ou d'IRMf montrent l'existence d'un réseau cortical commun à l'ensemble de ces conditions, qui inclut le lobule pariétal inférieur (aire 40), la région prémotrice ventrale (aire 6 ventrale) et une partie de l'aire motrice supplémentaire. Pour d'autres régions, l'activation est spécifique d'une condition: c'est le cas de l'aire 4 qui est activée pendant l'exécution et la simulation d'une action, mais pas pendant son observation, ou du gyrus frontal inférieur qui est activé pendant la simulation et l'observation, mais pas lors de l'exécution. L'opercule frontal, à la jonction entre la région prémotrice ventrale et le gyrus frontal inférieur, pourrait jouer un rôle important dans la reconnaissance d'une action: comme cela a été postulé pour la compréhension de la parole, comprendre la signification d'une action exécutée par quelqu'un d'autre serait possible dès lors que cette action serait traduite en une disposition à agir chez l'observateur.

INTRODUCTION

Physiological theories of action have long been influenced by the idea that actions are responses to stimuli. This idea spread in a specific context, where the organism was mostly considered as a reactive system dominated by constraints of adaptation to the external milieu. Following the so-called cognitive revolution of the 1950s, other metaphors have been used to account for the production of actions. It became possible to conceive of devices that operate on the basis of *representations* that simulate not only the external environment, but also the internal state of the device, the effects of an action of the device on the external environment, the effects of external changes on the machine itself, etc. These internal models can legitimately be considered as intentional states, in so far as they represent an action and its effects prior to its manifestations (see Wolpert, Ghahramani, & Jordan 1995). Motor representation, as it is understood here, is thus the process by which an action is intended, prepared, and eventually executed. According to the earlier computer metaphor, this process should be involved in many behavioral situations, such as imitating, learning by observation, or mentally simulating an action. The existence of these different motor states raises the question of whether they relate to functional modalities of the same phenomenon or to activation of different mechanisms.

Motor representations can be studied in several ways. One possible approach is that of cognitive psychology, which postulates in the representation the existence of distinct processes, like planning or programming, which are thought to unfold over time. Assuming that their durations add to each other, the time taken to start executing an action reflects the number of informational steps that must be taken into account before the response can be given. This hypothesis (the memory scanning hypothesis, see Sternberg, 1966) is supported by the fact that the time needed to start executing a given sequence increases linearly with the number of sequences in the program. Thus the whole utterance influences the execution of each of its elements, which suggests that the whole program must exist before production of the utterance begins (e.g. Sternberg, Knoll, Monsell, & Wright, 1988). Other experimenters also came to the conclusion of a hierarchical organization of motor representations by studying discrete movements. By manipulating the advance information provided to the subject, and by measuring the temporal costs or benefits of these manipulations, one can infer the structure of the preparation mechanism. Rosenbaum (1980) found that cueing certain aspects of the response to be given (e.g. the direction in which the target will appear) produces a greater benefit than cueing other aspects (e.g. the target distance). Hence the logical conclusion that direction should be represented at a higher level than distance.

An alternative approach attempts to match motor representations with changes in neural activity. Detecting and describing these changes would thus provide insight into the structure and the functioning of the representations (Jeannerod, 1994, 1995). This approach will be developed here by using several modalities of motor representation, including motor imagery and action observation.

MOTOR IMAGERY, A WINDOW ON THE REPRESENTATION OF ACTION

Motor representations are usually nonconscious. Yet, they can be accessed consciously under certain conditions: A normal subject is able to represent an action to himself without executing it, that is, to form a motor image. It will be posited here that motor images are conscious motor representations. According to this definition, motor images should be endowed with some of the properties of the corresponding (covert) motor representation, that is, they should have a similar functional relationship to the represented action and the same causal role in the generation of that action. A study of motor imagery can thus be considered a valid approach for describing the content and the structure of motor representations (for a recent review, see Crammond, 1997).

The hypothesis that motor imagery and motor preparation are both assigned to the same motor representation system is supported by several experiments using the mental chronometry paradigm. Decety and Michel (1989), for example, in comparing actual and mental movement times in a graphic task, found that the time taken to write a short sentence was the same whether the task was executed actually or mentally. Another interesting finding was that it took the subjects the same time, both actually and mentally, whether they wrote the text in large letters or in small letters. Further results suggest that the similarity of duration for actually and mentally performed actions can be generalized beyond the category of learned skills. Decety, Jeannerod, and Prablanc (1989) compared the duration of actually walking toward targets placed at different distances with that of mental simulation of walking toward the same targets. In the actual walking condition, walking times were found to increase with the distance covered. The same effect was observed in the mental walking condition. Moreover, and most importantly, mental walking times were found to be closely similar to those measured in the actual walking condition for the same subjects and for corresponding distances.

These results suggest that, besides duration, other parameters of movement execution, which are coded centrally, should also be expressed during mental simulation. One might expect, for example, that task difficulty should be a factor influencing movement duration in both the actual and the mental conditions. An experiment was undertaken to verify this point (Decety & Jeannerod, 1996). Normal subjects were instructed to walk mentally through gates of different widths positioned at different distances. The gates were presented to the subject with a 3-D visual display (a virtual reality helmet) that had no calibration with external cues and no possibility for the subject to refer to a known environment. Subjects had to indicate the time they started walking and the time they "passed through" the gate. The results showed that the time needed to imagine walking toward a given gate was affected both by its distance and its width. In accordance with Fitts law, the increase in movement time was a linear function of task difficulty.

Other experiments reveal that the representation of an action also takes into account the biomechanical constraints of the represented movement. Parsons (1994) examined the time it takes subjects to mentally rotate their hand from a starting position to a target position displayed on a photograph. The main result was that mental rotation times were very close to the corresponding real rotation times. For the less awkward postures, mental and real rotation times were equal, whereas for the most awkward ones, mental times were shorter than, but still correlated with, the real rotation times. Accordingly, when the picture of a hand at a given orientation was presented, the time it took the subject to determine its side (right or left) was close to the time for the real movement into its orientation. These results have interesting implications. First, they show that mentally rotating one's hand into a target position follows the same rules as mentally rotating other visual objects, where mental rotation time is a function of the angle (Shepard & Metzler, 1971). Second, the fact that mental times were the same as real times suggests that mental rotation of one's hand is constrained by the biomechanics of the hand as a body part. Indeed, in a previous study, Parsons (1987) had found that the times for mentally rotating one's hand or foot into awkward target postures were consistent with the duration of movements along biomechanically plausible trajectories.

PHYSIOLOGICAL CORRELATES OF MENTAL SIMULATION OF ACTION

The assumption that simulating a movement relies on the same mechanisms as actually performing it, except that execution is blocked, generates one specific prediction, namely, that one should find in motor imagery physiological correlates similar to those measured during real action.

First, mental simulation of movement should activate motor pathways. This prediction was confirmed by a recent study of spinal excitability during motor imagery. Bonnet, Decety, Requin, and Jeannerod (1997) instructed subjects either to press isometrically on a pedal, or to simulate mentally the same action. Two levels of strength (weak and strong) were used. The main result of this experiment was that motoneuron excitability, as tested by the amplitude of spinal monosynaptic reflexes, was increased during mental simulation. This increase was only slightly less than the reflex facilitation associated with the current performance of the same movement. Tendinous reflex (T-reflex) amplitude was more increased than H-reflex amplitude. In addition, the change of reflexes in the leg imagined to be involved in the movement was larger for a strong than for a weak simulated pressure. The fact that the T-reflexes were more facilitated than H-reflexes deserves discussion. A first explanation for this phenomenon is that the H-reflex is a test for the excitability of all motoneurons controlling the stimulated leg, including those not involved in the simulated action. T-reflex, by contrast, specifically tests the excitability of the motoneurons involved in simulating the foot pressure. It is thus likely that the change in excitability should be more visible using T-reflex than using H-reflex. Another explanation is that, whereas both reflexes are conveyed via the same monosynaptic neuronal pathways, the effect of the stimulus is, by far, not equivalent: The H-reflex, which is triggered by the electrical stimulation of Ia fibers, short-cuts neuromuscular spindles, whereas the T-reflex, which is triggered by a tendon tap, is a response to stretching these spindles. Insofar as the sensitivity of neuromuscular spindles to muscular stretch is under the control of gamma motoneurons, an increase in excitability of the T-reflex, but not of the H-reflex, would result from a selective increase in gamma motoneuron activity. This possibility of a spindle activation during mental simulation of a movement is an interesting one. Spindle afferents are known to play a role not only during movement execution, but also for organizing the motor output during self-generated actions (Porter & Lemon, 1993). For example, passively executed movements or vibrations of the corresponding tendon strongly facilitate, via spindle activation, the initiation of voluntary movements when such an initiation has become difficult, or even impossible, for example after a lasting immobilization or a cerebral lesion.

Increased excitability of motor pathways is a plausible explanation for the fact that electromyographic activity (EMG) was frequently found to increase with respect to rest during motor simulation (Hale, 1982; Harris & Robinson, 1986; Jacobson, 1930; Shaw, 1940; Wehner, Vogt, & Stadler, 1984). The fact that muscular activity is sometimes only partially blocked during motor simulation (as shown by residual EMG) emphasizes the delicate equilibrium between excitatory and inhibitory influences at the motoneuron level and suggests that motoneurons are close to threshold during motor imagery.

Other effectors normally not submitted to voluntary control, such as the autonomic effectors, are also likely to be activated during motor imagery. This possibility was tested by Decety, Jeannerod, Durozard, and Baverel (1993). In this experiment, subjects were requested to either actually perform or mentally simulate a leg exercise at two levels of effort. Heart rate, respiration rate, and end-tidal P_{CO_2} were measured in both conditions. After only a few seconds of actual exercise, heart rate began to increase up to about 50% over the resting value. In the mental condition, where no work was produced, this increase was about 32%. Respiration rate also increased almost without delay during actual effort and during mental simulation. The average respiration rate was even higher during mental simulation than during actual effort (see also Wuyam et al., 1995). These results confirm earlier findings of Adams, Guz, Innes, and Murphy (1987) who showed that heart rate and cardiac output already increased notably within about five beats after exercise was started and that respiration changed within one breathing cycle. A large fraction of this fast increase in heart and respiration rates at the onset of exercise (both real and mental) is thus likely to be due to the effect of motor preparation, not to metabolic changes. Vegetative activation during preparation to effort would be timed to begin when motor activity starts (for a review, see Requin, Brenner, & Ring, 1991). Autonomic activation during imagined action would pertain to the same phenomenon of preparation to action. An additional argument for this is provided by an experiment by Gandevia et al. (1993). They observed graded cardiovascular changes in artificially paralyzed subjects attempting muscular contractions, a situation close to mental simulation. As paralysis was complete, these changes could not be due to residual muscular activity and had to be of a central origin (see also Vissing & Hjortso, 1996). The possibility that these autonomic changes were a consequence of muscular activity can be ruled out. The spectroscopic analysis performed by Decety et al. (1993), showing no change in muscular metabolism during mental simulation, is against this possibility. In fact, the combination of increased respiration rate and unchanged muscular metabolism during mental simulation resulted in a progressive drop of P_{CO_2} in this condition: This never happens during physical effort, where ventilation eliminates CO_2 at about the same rate as it is produced, and where P_{CO_2} remains constant.

BRAIN ACTIVITY DURING MENTAL SIMULATION

The physiological correlates of mental imagery referred to earlier ultimately reflect the activity of central neurons coding for simulated action. Brain activity during motor simulation has been investigated using the mapping of brain metabolism. Following pioneering studies by Ingvar and Philipsson (1977), Roland, Skinhoj, Lassen, and Larsen (1980) monitored rCBF with single photon tomography in normal subjects during mental simulation of sequential digit movements. They found a significant and localized rCBF change mainly in the supplementary motor area (SMA). A recent series of PET studies (Decety et al., 1994; Grafton, Arbib, Fadiga, & Rizzolatti, 1996; Stephan et al., 1995) confirmed and expanded these early results. In the Decety et al. (1994) study, three-dimensional graspable objects were presented to subjects with the instruction to imagine themselves grasping the objects with their right hand. rCBF was found to be increased in several areas concerned with motor behavior. At the cortical level, area 6 in the inferior part of the frontal gyrus was strongly activated on both sides, as was area 40 in the left inferior parietal lobule. Subcortically, the caudate nucleus was found to be activated on both sides and the cerebellum only on the left side. Another focus of activity was observed in left prefrontal areas, extending to the dorsolateral frontal cortex (areas 9 and 46). Finally, the anterior cingulate cortex (areas 24 and 32) was bilaterally activated. Stephan et al. (1995)

compared the effects of sequential joystick movements on brain activation in three conditions: execution, mental simulation, and preparation to move. During imagined movements, a specific part of SMA (the rostral part) was preferentially activated. This localization was different from that observed during executed movements, where activation was more caudal. This finding reinforces the notion of a partition of SMA into areas with different hierarchical status and different functional implications: The posterior zone would be purely executive (the SMA proper of Matelli et al., 1993), whereas the more anterior zone would be more related to cognitive activity. Stephan et al. also found a bilateral activation of the ventrolateral part of area 6 and of the superior and caudal parts of the parietal lobes (areas 7 and 40). Finally, Grafton et al. (1996) confirmed the results from the earlier two studies (see also Parsons et al., 1995).

Consciously representing an action thus involves a pattern of cortical activation that resembles that of an intentionally executed action (e.g. Frith, Friston, Liddle, & Frackowiak, 1991). An important point remains to be determined, however: It is whether or not primary motor cortex is silent when no execution occurs. Activation of primary motor cortex during mental simulation of movement should in fact not be a surprising finding, as it was already suggested by the monkey experiments conducted by Georgopoulos, Lurito, Petrides, Schwartz, and Massey (1989), where the directional activity of cortical cells was found to be modified during mental rotation of the movement direction by the animal. Experiments using PET first provided negative results (Decety et al., 1994; Roland et al., 1980; Stephan et al., 1995). In contrast, Leonardo et al. (1995) and Kim, Jennings, Strupp, Andersen, and Ugurbil (1995), using fMRI, reported sensorimotor cortex activation in this condition in two out of five subjects (see also Grafton et al., 1996). This was confirmed by Roth et al. (1996), who found an unambiguous contralateral activation of area M1 in four out of six tested subjects during motor imagery of a repetitive finger/thumb opposition movement. The activated zone overlapped that activated during execution of the same movement, although it was smaller. Premotor cortex also was activated, on both sides. Finally, SMA was activated bilaterally: In this structure, however, the area involved during motor imagery was located more rostral than that activated during execution (see also Tyszka, Grafton, Chew, Woods, & Colletti, 1994).

Activation of primary motor cortex during mental simulation of movement or related processes is also suggested by experiments measuring cortical responsiveness to transcranial magnetic stimulation. Pascual-Leone et al. (1995) reported that the size of the excitable area devoted to finger movements (as determined by transcranial stimulation) was increased as movements were repeated over training periods. The important point is that a similar increase in the size of the excitable area was produced by imaginal training. Relevant observations were also made by Gandevia and Rothwell (1987), who showed that concentrating on one hand muscle without activating it increased the effect of subthreshold magnetic stimulation of the cortical area corresponding to that muscle (and not of other muscles). Thus, there is a selective enhancement of responsiveness of motor cortical areas during motor imagery.

The strong relationships of motor imagery to the neural substrate lead to the logical expectation that the central changes produced in the motor system during imagery will affect subsequent motor performance. Conversely, the observed changes might represent an explanation for those effects known to arise as a result of mental training. The sport psychology literature in the early 1960s offers a large number of studies reporting measurable effects of mental imagery on subsequent motor performance (for a review, see Driskell, Cooper, & Moran, 1994, and Feltz & Landers, 1983). Mental training has been shown to affect several aspects of motor performance normally thought to be specific outcomes of training, such as muscular strength (Yue & Cole, 1992), movement speed (Pascual-Leone et al., 1995), reduction of variability, and increase in temporal consistency (Vogt, 1995). The efferent discharges generated during the imagining process might represent the substrate for subsequent facilitation of motor performance through priming of the motor pathways by descending volleys. The possibility that these effects would relate to rehearsal of nonmotor (e.g. visual, visuo-spatial) aspects of the task seems to be excluded by the fact that congenitally blind children show mental practice effects (Millar & Ittyerah, 1991).

The close relationships observed between mental simulation of movement and changes in activity of the motor system suggest that motor imagery should be affected by pathological conditions affecting the central motor structures. The finding that, in normal subjects, mental and real movement times are equal, or at least correlated, provides a means for verifying this prediction. Accordingly, a pathological condition producing a slowness of movements, for example, should also produce an increase in the time taken for simulating the same movements. Results confirming this prediction were obtained in Parkinson patients (Dominey, Decety, Broussolle, Chazot, & Jeannerod, 1995) and in a patient with a left arm progressive hemiparesis due to a right rolandic lesion (Sirigu et al., 1995).

ACTIVATING MOTOR REPRESENTATIONS BY OBSERVATION

Because understanding the meaning of a gesture is an essential aspect of human social communication, a large amount of our daily life is spent watching and interpreting the actions of others. Each individual builds up from this observation his or her own theory of the mind of others. In addition, observation of action is the first step of imitation, a powerful means of establishing contact with other individuals and acquiring new skills from them, which starts at birth and continues throughout life. Many arguments indicate that recognition of actions of conspecifics is a genuine ability, which seems to be highly developed in humans and nonhuman primates (Premack & Woodruff, 1978). Humans can easily distinguish biological motion from impulsions produced by mechanical devices, even when only a limited number of cues are available (Dasser, Ulbaek, & Premack, 1989; Johansson, 1977). The problem is to know what is actually recognized and eventually imitated. Can one conceive of a direct mapping of the perceptual scene into motor commands? Imitation studies in six-week-old infants suggest that this is not the case: These children are able to produce imitative mouth movements after a relatively long delay. In other words, they can produce a movement of a part of their body that they cannot see to match a target-action that is no longer visible (Meltzoff, 1995). It has been postulated that an observed action can be understood and imitated whenever it becomes the source of a representation of the same action within the observer. Perception of actions is constrained by the implicit knowledge that the central nervous system has concerning the movements that it is capable of producing (Viviani & Stucchi, 1992). This interpretation recalls the influential motor theory of perception initially used to account for the perception of speech (see Liberman & Mattingly, 1985).

Results obtained in monkey experiments reinforce this idea. Perrett and his co-workers have disclosed, within the superior temporal sulcus, neuronal populations that appear to be involved, not only in the recognition of body postures (some neurons are more active when the animal is shown the hand or the head of another monkey in a given posture, see Perrett et al., 1989), but also in the recognition of action. Neurons are selective for movements in a particular direction when they are produced by another monkey, whereas they remain silent if these movements are the consequence of the animal's own action (see Carey, Perrett, & Oram, 1997). Goal-directed actions also are coded by neurons selective for the observation of specific hand-object interactions, such as reaching, manipulating, or holding (Perrett et al., 1989). Another group of neurons located in the region of the premotor cortex also have interesting properties in this respect. In striking contrast with the temporal neurons, however, they are selective both for the monkey's active performance of a particular type of hand movements and for the monkey's observation of the same hand movement made by an experimenter or by another animal (mirror neurons, see di Pellegrino, Fadiga, Fogassi, Gallese, & Rizzolatti, 1992; Rizzolatti, Fadiga, Gallese, & Fogassi, 1996a). There are indications that a similar mechanism for matching observation and execution of actions might also exist in man. These arguments suggest that actions (and perhaps also intentions) to be imitated are stored in terms of an action code, not a perceptual code: The observed action is transformed into a potential action. This strengthens the idea that such processes as intending, imagining, observing/imitating, and performing an action share common structural and functional mechanisms.

A recent experiment by Fadiga, Fogassi, Pavesi, and Rizzolatti (1995) in human subjects supports this notion. These subjects were requested to observe for a short period of time (3 seconds) grasping movements performed by an experimenter. At the end of the observation period, a transcranial magnetic stimulus was applied to their motor cortex. The pattern of muscular response to this stimulus was found to be selectively increased in respect to control conditions. In addition, the set of muscles activated by the stimulus was the same as that recorded while the subject himself actually performed the movement. This result demonstrates an increased excitability of the motor system during the observation of actions. It is likely that the same effect would also be obtained during mental simulation, as indicated by the increased spinal excitability observed in this condition. These mechanisms might represent the neural basis for imitation, observational learning, and motor imagery.

A series of PET experiments were recently performed in order to explore this possibility. In the Grafton et al.'s (1996) experiment, subjects were instructed to observe carefully simple meaningful actions (prehension movements performed by the experimenter's right hand). Brain activation in this condition was compared with a control condition where the subjects merely looked at visual objects. The activated areas were mostly located in the frontal and the parietal lobes. On the motor side, the SMA and the lateral area 6 in the precentral gyrus were involved, as well as area 45 in the inferior frontal gyrus. In the parietal lobe, area 40 in the inferior parietal lobule was also involved. This study, however, did not take into consideration the precise nature of the instruction given to subjects during observation. Actions can be observed without being understood, because their meaning is not accessible to the observer. Yet, actions that are not understood can still be imitated. This raises the question of the relationship between perceptual recognition of an action as a spatio-temporal pattern and motoric recognition which will enable the observer to repeat this same action later on. These remarks suggest that observed actions should activate different brain areas whether they are unknown or familiar to the observer; and in addition, that the activation of these different areas should depend on the subject's strategy during observation.

A new PET experiment was designed to evaluate these possibilities (Decety et al., 1997). The cognitive strategy of the subjects was manipulated by giving them instructions to prepare for later imitation, or later recognition of the observed action. The semantic content was manipulated by presenting two types of actions: Meaningful actions that referred to a recognizable goal, or meaningless sequences of movements with a similar content in terms of kinematics and degree of complexity. When the aim of observation was to memorize actions with the purpose of imitation, the SMA, the dorsolateral prefrontal cortex on both sides, and premotor cortex were activated. The bilateral involvement of dorsolateral prefrontal cortex in this condition is in agreement with previous studies concerning the planning of voluntary actions (Frith et al., 1991) and the mental simulation of actions, as already mentioned. This same area, specially on the left side, was also frequently found to be activated during semantic tasks, such as word generation (Frith et al., 1991; Wise et al., 1991) or verbal encoding (Shallice et al., 1994). Thus, it could well be the case that the left prefrontal region would be specialized for generating responses in relation to semantic cues, a hypothesis that is congruent with our findings: Our imitation tasks implied both access to meaning of the movements and memorization for subsequent reproduction.

The pattern of activation also differed according to whether the observed action was meaningful or meaningless. Observing a meaningful action activated areas that were mainly confined to the left hemisphere. The main structures involved were the inferior frontal (area 45), middle temporal (area 21), and parahippocampal regions. Activation of area 45 replicates the Grafton et al. (1996) finding. These authors conjectured that this region might correspond to a system for representation of grasping movements, functionally similar to the monkey ventral area 6 where mirror neurons were recorded. Indeed, the same region is activated during the recognition of man-made tools (Perani et al., 1995) and during mental simulation of hand actions (Decety et al., 1994; Grafton et al., 1996). Activation of the inferior frontal gyrus also raises the problem of the involvement of language during the observation of meaningful actions. Several authors have reported activation of this area in situations related to language for action, such as generation of action words (Martin, Haxby, Lalonde, Wiggs, & Ungerleider, 1995) or naming tools (Martin, Wiggs, Ungerleider, & Haxby, 1996). It is indeed a possibility that during our observation condition the subjects recognized the actions and automatically associated them with action verbs or with the name of the objects evoked by the actions. In fact, activation of area 45 (in conjunction with area 44) was observed in many verbal situations such as verb retrieval (Warbuton et al., 1996), silent word generation (McGuire et al., 1996; Wise et al., 1991), and lexico-semantic tasks (Demonet et al., 1992).

In contrast with observation of meaningful actions, which involved structures mostly located in the left hemisphere, observation of meaningless actions primarily engaged the right hemisphere. This activation involved areas in the occipito-parietal region, including the cuneus and the precuneus, the middle occipital gyrus and the inferior parietal lobule. This pattern of activation fits the role of the occipito-parietal visual pathway for processing the spatial properties of visual scenes (Haxby et al., 1994) and for generating visuo-motor transformation (Faillenot, Toni, Decety, Grégoire, & Jeannerod, 1997). Accordingly, right posterior parietal lesions in man are known to produce visuo-spatial deficits such as spatial disorientation, spatial neglect, or constructional apraxia (see De Renzi, 1982). In addition, lesions on either side can produce deficits in visuo-motor transformation, such as misreaching and lack of finger preshaping during the action of grasping objects (Jeannerod, 1986; Perenin & Vighetto, 1988). Finally, the activation of the right inferior temporal gyrus, also present during observation of meaningless actions, confirms previous results obtained in several experiments. Decety et al. (1994) found activation of left areas 19–37 during observation of a hand moving toward and grasping objects. A similar finding is reported by Rizzolatti et al. (1996b) and Bonda, Petrides, Ostry, and Evans (1996). By homology with its function in monkeys, this cortical region might be involved in processing complex visual motion signals during body movements and intraction with objects.

Thus, the pattern of cortical activation during observation of these two types of actions differs both in terms of hemispheric asymmetry and repartition of the involved areas. The cortical network activated during observation of meaningful actions in the left hemisphere corresponds to the ventral visual pathway, which includes inferotemporal areas as well as part of the hippocampus, and terminates in the ventral part of prefrontal cortex. On the other hand, the network associated with meaningless actions in the right hemisphere corresponds to the dorsal pathway, which includes occipito-parietal areas and is connected with premotor cortex (for a review of literature on cortical visual pathways, see Jeannerod, 1997).

CONCLUSION

Comparison of brain activation patterns in conditions where actions are mentally simulated, observed in other people, or performed reveals both similarities and differences. PET data from several groups have been listed in Table 15.1. These data include experimental conditions such as movement execution (Faillenot et al., 1997; Rizzolatti et al., 1996b; Roth et al., 1996; Stephan et al., 1995), mental simulation (Decety et al., 1994; Grafton et al., 1996; Roth et al., 1996; Stephan et al., 1995), observation of actions (Decety et al., 1997; Grafton et al., 1996), and observation of tools (Perani et al., 1995). The first outcome of this comparison is the existence of a network common to all conditions, in which the inferior parietal lobule (area 40), the ventral premotor area (ventral area 6), and part of SMA participate. The specificity of motor representations for each individual condition should therefore be looked for in those areas, the activation of which does not overlap between conditions. Area 4 is one of those: It is activated during motor execution and motor imagination, not during observation. Similarly, prefrontal areas in the middle and inferior frontal gyri (areas 45 and 46) are strongly activated during simulation and observation, but not during execution. In addition, even within overlapping zones, there are indications that both the extent and the precise topography of the activated areas may differ between conditions: This seems to be the case at least for SMA, where the activation during imagination is more rostral than during execution.

The second interesting point shown in Table 15.1 is the particular status of the imagination condition, which seems to involve both the neural network for execution and that for internal generation of action. This finding is in agreement with many of the results reported earlier in this chapter, showing the influence of mental simulation of action on excitability of the motor pathways or activity of the autonomic system, for example (see Jeannerod, 1994, 1995, 1997). In

TABLE 15.1
Activated areas found in different experiments testing motor representations

Brain regions and Brodman areas	Execute	Imagine	Conditions Observe to imitate	Observe: meaningful	Observe: meaningless
Precentral gyrus Ba 4	2, 6	4, 7			
Precentral gyrus Ba 6	8	1, 4, 8	2	4	2
Ventral premotor area (Ba 6)	8	1, 8	2		2
SMA (rostral) Ba 6	3, 7	4	2	4	
Cingular gyrus Ba 24	6, 8	1, 8			
Superior frontal gyrus Ba 10		1			
Middle frontal gyrus Ba 46,9		1, 4	2		
Inferior frontal gyrus Ba 44,45		4		2, 4, 5, 6	
Inferior parietal lobule Ba 40	3, 6, 8	1, 4, 8	2	4	2

Experiments are listed and numbered by name of authors. Execute: Subjects perform the real movements (grasping or moving a joystick). Imagine: Mental simulation of the same actions. Observe: Observation of meaningless or meaningful actions. Observe to imitate: Observation with the specific instruction to reproduce the observed action.

(1) Decety et al. (1994)   (2) Decety et al. (1997)   (3) Faillenot et al. (1997)
(4) Grafton et al. (1996)   (5) Perani et al. (1995)   (6) Rizzolatti et al. (1996b)
(7) Roth et al. (1996)   (8) Stephan et al. (1995)

fact, motor imagery appears to result from a massive activation of motor representations, with the consequence that the motoneurons would be, at the same time, very close to firing and held under partial inhibition. For this reason, motor imagery should be a valid condition for studying the neural correlates of mechanisms of action generation, which are normally covert and poorly accessible to experimentation.

Finally, Table 15.1 stresses the importance of a cortical zone located in the posterior and inferior part of the frontal lobe, at the junction between the precentral and the inferior frontal gyri (the frontal operculum). This area has a critical location that corresponds to a carrefour between the ventral part of area 6 and areas 44 and 45. According to Rizzolatti et al. (1996a,b), homologous areas in the monkey are involved in a particular form of movement representation, whereby neurons are activated whether the monkey executes a given hand movement or watches the same movement performed by another monkey. Hence Rizzolatti's hypothesis that monkeys recognize a motor action by matching it with a similar action motorically coded in the same neuron. In humans, a similar mechanism might operate for recognizing speech gestures in area 44 (the Broca area) and could account for speech perception. This hypothesis would represent a rationale for common motor representations for recognizing, simulating, and executing various sorts of actions, including those related to verbal communication.

REFERENCES

Adams, L., Guz, A., Innes, J. A., & Murphy, K. (1987). The early circulatory and ventilatory response to voluntary and electrically induced exercise in man. *Journal of Physiology, 383,* 19–30.

Bonda, E., Petrides, M., Ostry, D., & Evans, A. (1996). Specific involvement of human parietal systems and the amygdala in the perception of biological motion. *Journal of Neuroscience, 16,* 3737–3744.

Bonnet, M., Decety, J., Requin, J., & Jeannerod, M. (1997). Mental simulation of an action modulates the excitability of spinal reflex pathways in man. *Cognitive Brain Research, 5,* 221–228.

Carey, D. P., Perrett, D. I., & Oram, M. W. (1997). Recognizing, understanding and reproducing action. In F. Boller & J. Grafman (Series Eds.), M. Jeannerod (Vol. Ed.), *Handbook of neuropsychology. Vol 11: Action and Cognition* (pp. 111–129). Amsterdam: Elsevier.

Crammond, D. J. (1997). Motor imagery: Never in your wildest dream. *Trends in Neurosciences, 20,* 54–57.

Dasser, V., Ulbaek, I., & Premack, D. (1989). The perception of intention. *Science, 243,* 365–367.

Decety, J., Grezes, J., Costes, N., Perani, D., Jeannerod, M., Procyk, E., Grassi, F., & Fazio, F. (1997). Brain activity during observation of action: Influence of action content and subject's strategy. *Brain, 120,* 1763–1777.

Decety, J., & Jeannerod, M. (1996). Fitts' law in mentally simulated movements. *Behavioral Brain Research, 72,* 127–134.

Decety, J., Jeannerod, M., Durozard, D., & Baverel, G. (1993). Central activation of autonomic effectors during mental simulation of motor actions. *Journal of Physiology, 461,* 549–563.

Decety, J., Jeannerod, M., & Prablanc, C. (1989). The timing of mentally represented actions. *Behavioral Brain Research, 34,* 35–42 .

Decety, J., & Michel, F. (1989). Comparative analysis of actual and mental movement times in two graphic tasks. *Brain and Cognition, 11,* 87–97.

Decety, J., Perani, D., Jeannerod, M., Bettinardi, V., Tadary, B., Woods, R., Mazziotta, J. C., & Fazio, F. (1994). Mapping motor representations with PET. *Nature, 371,* 600–602.

Demonet, J. F., Chollet, F., Ramsay, S., Cardebat, D., Nespoulous, J. L., Wise, R., Rascol, A., & Frackowiak, R. S. J. (1992). The anatomy of phonological processing and semantic processing in normal subjects. *Brain, 115,* 1753–1768.

De Renzi, E. (1982). *Disorders of space exploration and cognition.* New York: Wiley.

di Pellegrino, G., Fadiga, L., Fogassi, L., Gallese, V., & Rizzolatti, G. (1992). Understanding motor events: A neurophysiological study. *Experimental Brain Research, 91,* 176–180.

Dominey, P., Decety, J., Broussolle, E., Chazot, G., & Jeannerod, M. (1995). Motor imagery of a lateralized sequential task is asymmetrically slowed in hemi-Parkinson patients. *Neuropsychologia, 33,* 727–741.

Driskell, J. E., Cooper, C., & Moran, A. (1994). Does mental practice enhance performance? *Journal of Applied Psychology, 79,* 481–492.

Fadiga, L., Fogassi, L., Pavesi, G., & Rizzolatti, G. (1995). Motor facilitation during action observation: A magnetic stimulation study. *Journal of Neurophysiology, 73,* 2608–2611.

Faillenot, I., Toni, I., Decety, J., Grégoire, M. C., & Jeannerod, M. (1997). Visual pathways for object-oriented action and object recognition: Functional anatomy with PET. *Cerebral Cortex, 7,* 77–85.

Feltz, D.L., & Landers, D. M. (1983). The effects of mental practice on motor skill learning and performance: A meta-analysis. *Journal of Sport Psychology, 5,* 25–57.

Frith, C. D., Friston, K. Liddle, P. F., & Frackowiak, R. S. J. (1991). Willed action and the prefrontal cortex in man: A study with PET. *Proceedings of the Royal Society, 244,* 241–246.

Gandevia, S. C., Killian, K., McKenzie, D. K., Crawford, M., Allen, G. M., Gorman, R. B., & Hales, J. P. (1993). Respiratory sensations, cardiovascular control, kinesthesia and transcranial stimulation during paralysis in humans. *Journal of Physiology, 470,* 85–107.

Gandevia, S. C., & Rothwell, J. (1987). Knowledge of motor commands and the recruitment of human motoneurons. *Brain, 110,* 1117–1130.

Georgopoulos, A. P., Lurito, J. T., Petrides, M., Schwartz, A. B., & Massey, J. T. (1989). Mental rotation of the neuronal population vector. *Science, 243,* 234–236.

Grafton, S. T., Arbib, M. A., Fadiga, L., & Rizzolatti, G. (1996). Localization of grasp representations in humans by positron emission tomography. 2. Observation compared with imagination. *Experimental Brain Research, 112,* 103–111.

Hale, B. D. (1982). The effects of internal and external imagery on muscular and ocular concomitants. *Journal of Sport Psychology, 4,* 379–387.

Harris, D. V., & Robinson, W. J. (1986). The effect of skill level on EMG activity during internal and external imagery. *Journal of Sport Psychology, 8,* 105–111.

Haxby, J. V., Horwitz, B., Ungerleider, L. G., Maisog, J. M., Pietrini, P., & Grady, C. L. (1994). The functional organization of human extrastriate cortex. A PET-rCBF study of selective attention to faces and locations. *Journal of Neuroscience, 14,* 6336–6353.

Ingvar, D., & Philipsson, L. (1977). Distribution of the cerebral blood flow in the dominant hemisphere during motor ideation and motor performance. *Annals of Neurology, 2,* 230–237.

Jacobson, E. (1930). Electrical measurements of neuro-muscular states during mental activities. III. Visual imagination and recollection. *American Journal of Physiology, 95,* 694–702.

Jeannerod, M. (1986). The formation of finger grip during prehension: A cortically mediated visuomotor pattern. *Behavioral Brain Research, 19,* 99–116.

Jeannerod, M. (1994). The representing brain: Neural correlates of motor intention and imagery. *Behavioral and Brain Sciences, 17,* 187–245.

Jeannerod, M. (1995). Mental imagery in the motor context. *Neuropsychologia, 33,* 1419–1432.

Jeannerod, M. (1997). *The cognitive neuroscience of action.* Oxford: Blackwell.

Johansson, G. (1977). Studies on visual perception of locomotion. *Perception, 6,* 365–376.

Kim, S-G., Jennings, J. E., Strupp, J. P., Andersen, P., & Ugurbil, K. (1995). Functional MRI of human motor cortices during overt and imagined finger movements. *International Journal of Imaging Systems and Technology, 6,* 271–279.

Leonardo, M., Fieldman, J., Sadato, N., Campbell, G., Ibanez, V., Cohen, L., Deiber, M-P., Jezzard, P., Pons, T., Turner, R., Le Bihan, D., & Hallett, M. (1995). A functional magnetic resonance imaging study of cortical regions associated with motor task execution and motor ideation in humans. *Human Brain Mapping, 3,* 83–92.

Liberman, A. M., & Mattingly, I. G. (1985). The motor theory of perception of speech revisited. *Cognition, 21,* 1–36.

Martin, A., Haxby, J. V., Lalonde, F. M., Wiggs, C. L., & Ungerleider, L. G. (1995). Discrete cortical regions associated with knowledge of color and knowledge of action. *Science, 270,* 102–105.

Martin, A., Wiggs, C. L., Ungerleider, L. G., & Haxby, J. V. (1996). Neural correlates of category-specific knowledge. *Nature, 379,* 649–652.

Matelli, M., Rizzolatti, G., Bettinardi, V., Gilardi, M. C., Perani, D., Rizzo, G., & Fazio, F. (1993). Activation of precentral and mesial motor areas during the execution of elementary proximal and distal arm movements: A PET study. *NeuroReport, 4,* 1295–1298.

McGuire, P. K., Silbersweig, D. A., Murray, R. M., David, A. S., Frackowiak, R. S. J., & Frith, C. D. (1996). Functional anatomy of inner speech and auditory verbal imagery. *Psychological Medicine, 26,* 29–38.

Meltzoff, A. N. (1995). Understanding the intentions of others. Re-enactment of intended acts by 18-month-old children. *Developmental Psychology, 31,* 838–850.

Millar, S., & Ittyerah, M. (1991). Movement imagery in young and congenitally blind children. Mental practice without visuo-spatial information. *International Journal of Behavioral Development, 15,* 125–146.

Parsons, L. M. (1987). Imagined spatial transformations of one's hands and feet. *Cognitive Psychology, 19,* 178–241.

Parsons, L. M. (1994). Temporal and kinematic properties of motor behavior reflected in mentally simulated action. *Journal of Experimental Psychology. Human Perception and Performance, 20,* 709–730.

Parsons, L. M., Fox, P. T., Downs, J. H., Glass, T., Hirsch, T. B., Martin, C. C., Jerabek, P. A., & Lancaster, J. L. (1995). Use of implicit motor imagery for visual shape discrimination as revealed by PET. *Nature, 375,* 54–58.

Pascual-Leone, A., Dang, N., Cohen, L. G., Brasil-Neto, J., Cammarota, A., & Hallett, M. (1995). Modulation of motor responses evoked by transcranial magnetic stimulation during the acquisition of new fine motor skills. *Journal of Neurophysiology, 74,* 1037–1045.

Perani, D., Cappa, S. F., Bettinardi, V., Bressi, S., Gorno-Tempini, M., Matarrese, M., & Fazio, F. (1995). Different neural systems for the recognition of animals and man-made tools. *NeuroReport, 6,* 1637–1641.

Perenin, M.-T., & Vighetto, A. (1988). Optic ataxia: a specific disruption in visuomotor mechanisms. I. Different aspects of the deficit in reaching for objects. *Brain, 111,* 643–674.

Perrett, D. I., Harris, M. H., Bevan, R., Thomas, S., Benson, P. J., Mistlin, A. J., Citty, A. J., Hietanen, J. K. &, Ortega, J. E. (1989). Framework of analysis for the neural representation of animate objects and actions. *Journal of Experimental Biology, 146,* 87–113.

Porter, R., & Lemon, R. (1993). *Corticospinal function and voluntary movement.* Oxford: Clarendon Press.

Premack, D., & Woodruff, G. (1978). Does the chimpanzee have a theory of mind? *Behavioral and Brain Sciences, 4,* 515–526.

Requin, J., Brener, J., & Ring, C. (1991). Preparation for action. In J. R. Jennings & M. G. H. Coles (Eds.), *Handbook of cognitive psychophysiology: Central and autonomic nervous system approaches.* New York: Wiley.

Rizzolatti, G., Fadiga, L., Gallese, V., & Fogassi, L. (1996a). Premotor cortex and the recognition of motor actions. *Cognitive Brain Research, 3,* 131–141.

Rizzolatti, G., Fadiga, L., Matelli, M., Bettinardi, V., Paulesu, E., Perani, D., & Fazio, F. (1996b). Localization of grasp representations in humans by PET. 1. Observation versus execution. *Experimental Brain Research, 111,* 246–252.

Roland, P. E., Skinhoj, E., Lassen, N. A., & Larsen, B. (1980). Different cortical areas in man in organization of voluntary movements in extrapersonal space. *Journal of Neurophysiology, 43,* 137–150.

Rosenbaum, D. A. (1980). Human movement initiation: Specification of arm, direction and extent. *Journal of Experimental Psychology: General, 109,* 444–474.

Roth, M., Decety, J., Raybaudi, M., Massarelli, R., Delon-Martin, C., Segebarth, C., Morand, S., Gemignani, A., Décorps, M., & Jeannerod, M. (1996). Possible involvement of primary motor cortex in mentally simulated movement: A functional magnetic resonance imaging study. *Neuroreport, 7,* 1280–1284.

Shallice, T., Fletcher, P. Frith, C. D., Grasby P., Frackowiak, R. S. J., & Dolan, R. J. (1994). Brain regions associated with acquisition and retrieval of episodic memory. *Nature, 368,* 633–635.

Shaw, W. A. (1940). The relation of muscular action potentials to imaginal weight lifting. *Archives of Psychology, 35,* 5–50.

Shepard, R. N., & Metzler, J. (1971). Mental rotation of three-dimensional objects. *Science, 171,* 701–703.

Sirigu, A., Cohen, L., Duhamel, J.-R., Pillon, B., Dubois, B., Agid, Y., & Pierrot-Deseiligny, C. (1995). Congruent unilateral impairments for real and imagined hand movements. *NeuroReport, 6,* 997–1001.

Stephan, K. M., Fink, G. R., Passingham, R. E., Silbersweig, D., Ceballos-Baumann, A. O., Frith, C. D., & FrackowiaK, R. S. J. (1995). Functional anatomy of the mental representation of upper extremity movements in healthy subjects. *Journal of Neurophysiology, 73,* 373–386.

Sternberg, S. (1966). High speed scanning in human memory. *Science, 153,* 652–654.

Sternberg, S., Knoll, R. L., Monsell, S., & Wright, C. E. (1988). Motor programs and hierarchical organization in the control of rapid speech. *Phonetica, 45,* 175–197.

Tyszka, J. M., Grafton, S. T., Chew, W., Woods, R. P., & Colletti, P. M. (1994). Parceling of mesial frontal motor areas during ideation and movement using functional magnetic resonance imaging at 1.5 Tesla. *Annals of Neurology, 35,* 746–749.

Vissing, S. F., & Hjortso, E. (1996). Central motor command activates sympathetic outflow to the cutaneous circulation in humans. *Journal of Physiology, 492,* 931–939.

Viviani, P., & Stucchi, N. (1992). Biological movements look uniform: Evidence of motor-perceptual interactions. *Journal of Experimental Psychology: Human Perception and Performance, 18,* 603–623.

Vogt, S. (1995). On relations between perceiving, imagining, and performing in the learning of cyclical movement sequences. *British Journal of Psychology, 86,* 191–216.

Warburton, E., Wise, R. J. S., Price, C., Weiller, C., Hadar, U., Ramsay, S., & Frackowiak, R. S. J. (1996). Noun and verb retrieval by normal subjects: Studies with PET. *Brain, 119,* 159–179.

Wehner, T., Vogt, S., & Stadler, M. (1984). Task-specific EMG characteristics during mental training, *Psychological Research, 46,* 389–401.

Wise, R., Chollet, F., Hadar, U., Friston, K., Hoffner, E. & Frackowiak, R. S. J. (1991). Distribution of cortical neural networks involved in word comprehension and word retrieval. *Brain, 114,* 1803–1817.

Wolpert, D. M., Ghahramani, Z., & Jordan, M. I. (1995). An internal model for sensorimotor integration. *Science, 269,* 1880–1882.

Wuyam, B., Moosavi, S. H., Decety, J., Adams, L., Lansing, R. W., & Guz, A. (1995). Imagination of dynamic exercise produced ventilatory responses which were more apparent in competitive sportsmen. *Journal of Physiology, 482,* 713–724.

Yue, G., & Cole, K. J. (1992). Strength increases from the motor program: Comparison of training with maximal voluntary and imagined muscle contractions. *Journal of Neurophysiology, 67,* 1114–1123.

CHAPTER SIXTEEN

Model of cognitive processes

Evgeny N. Sokolov
University of Wuppertal, Germany

A geometric model relevant to color perception, color memory, color learning and color semantics is suggested. Colors of different hue, lightness, and saturation are located on a hypersphere in four-dimensional space, so that Euclidean distances between color points closely correlate with perceptual color differences. The Cartesian coordinates of color stimuli correspond to excitations of color-coding neurons: red-green, blue-yellow, lightness, and darkness. The spherical coordinates (three angles of the hypersphere) correspond to subjective aspects of color perception: hue, lightness, and saturation. Short-term and long-term (declarative) color memory constitutes color-coding maps isomorphic with the perceptual color hypersphere. The instrumental conditioned reflexes elaborated in monkeys and fish demonstrate analogous four-dimensional structure of color space, indicating that procedural color learning obeys the same principles. The networks build up from neuron-like elements that simulate the suggested vectorial coding. It is assumed that the suggested geometric cognitive model revealed in color coding is relevant for other cognitive modalities.

Nous suggérons un modèle rendant compte de la perception des couleurs, ainsi que de leur mémorisation, de leur dénomination et de leur sémantique. Ce modèle situe les couleurs variant en tonalité, en luminosité et en saturation sur une hypersphère à l'intérieur d'un espace à quatre dimensions, de manière telle que les distances euclidiennes entre les points correspondant aux diverses couleurs sont étroitement corrélées aux différences perceptives entre ces couleurs. Les coordonnées cartésiennes des stimuli colorés correspondent aux excitations des neurones encodant la couleur: rouge-vert, bleu-jaune et luminosité et obscurité. Les coordonnées sphériques (trois angles de l'hypersphère) correspondent aux dimensions subjectives de la perception des couleurs: tonalité, luminosité et saturation. À court et à long termes, la mémoire (déclarative) des couleurs élabore des cartes d'encodage des couleurs; ces cartes et l'hypersphère perceptive des couleurs sont isomorphes. Les réflexes conditionnés de type opérant mis en place chez les singes et les poissons manifestent une structure à quatre dimensions de l'espace des couleurs qui est analogue, ceci indiquant que l'apprentissage procédural des couleurs est régi par les mêmes principes. Les réseaux se construisent à partir d'éléments qui, semblables à des neurones, simulent l'encodage vectoriel suggéré. Nous postulons la pertinence, en regard d'autres modalités *cognitives*, de ce modèle géométrique valable pour l'encodage des couleurs.

INTRODUCTION

Basic cognitive processes are represented by perception, memory, and semantics. The latter two are continuously modified by learning. To compare these cognitive processes one has to study them using common stimuli. In the present research such common input was based on color-related stimuli: real colors and color names. Real colors were used to study the principal characteristics of perception and memory. Color names were studied to clarify symbolic representation of colors. Systematic study of cognitive processes using color-related stimuli was directed to elucidate their encoding principles. The study of color cognition was supplemented by elaboration of instrumental conditioned reflexes to color stimuli in monkey and fish to bridge the gap between human cognition and animal cognitive functions.

All current theories of color vision suggest a three-dimensional space for representation of colors. The multidimensional scaling of large subjective differences between monochromatic colors of different intensities has shown that all color stimuli can be represented by points on a hypersphere in four-dimensional metric space (Izmailov & Sokolov, 1991). The Euclidean distances between points representing respective colors closely correlate with subjective color differences. Cartesian coordinates of monochromatic colors obtained by multidimensional scaling from the matrix of subjective differences correspond to spectral characteristics of four types of color-coding neurons in monkey's lateral geniculate body: red-green, blue-yellow, brightness, and darkness. Three angles of the hypersphere correspond to three characteristics of color perception: hue, lightness (value), and saturation (chroma). The four-dimensional spherical color space suggests that different colors are coded by four-dimensional excitation vectors equal in their lengths. The achromatic colors are coded by two-dimensional excitation vectors composed of excitations of brightness and darkness neurons. The reduction of color space for achromatic colors results from the elimination of responses of opponent neurons, red-green and blue-yellow, due to mutual cancellation of their excitatory and inhibitory phases. Single achromatic colors occupy the first quadrant corresponding to their lightness from 0 degrees to 90 degrees. The simplest pattern of a circular patch of color surrounded by a colored ring (disc-ring configuration) results in the appearance of blackish shades and extension of the achromatic sphere onto the fourth quadrant from 0 degrees to 270 degrees. This extension of achromatic space under the disc-ring condition is due to brightness contrast (Izmailov & Sokolov, 1991).

Four basic problems arise:

1. Is a four-dimensional spherical structure adequate for representation of chromatic colors under the disc-ring configuration?
2. Is a four-dimensional vector code applicable for memory processing?
3. Can four-dimensional color space be extended to symbolic representation (color names)?
4. Is vector coding adequate to represent learning?

The hypothesis concerning a common vector code for all these cognitive processes was suggested and tested. The color stimuli or color names were presented sequentially pairwise in a series of computer-assisted experiments. The subjects were instructed to estimate the subjective differences between members of pairs of stimuli using numbers from 0 (no difference) to 9 (maximal difference). The data were averaged and represented in the form of a matrix of subjective differences. Multidimensional analysis was used to reveal the coordinates of respective stimuli within a metric space. In learning experiments a matrix of response probabilities to color stimuli was estimated by factor analysis to uncover the dimensionality of color space. The coordinates of the color space found from the matrix were used to calculate inner products between respective vectors. The matrix of inner products was compared with the initial response probability matrix using the correlation procedure.

COLOR VISION IN HUMANS

Color perception

In the case of color perception, 25 colors of different hue, lightness, and saturation were sequentially presented utilizing a test area surrounded by one induction field to the subject. They were required to evaluate color differences between sequential 4 × 4cm test-fields (Izmailov & Sokolov, 1991). The multidimensional scaling of the matrix of subjective differences revealed four basic axes corresponding to red-green, blue-yellow, lightness, and darkness neurons. On the hue plane constructed from red-green and blue-yellow axes, mostly saturated colors located at some distance from the center are positioned anti-clockwise in the following order: red (1) towards yellow (4), green (9), blue (14), purple (16) (Fig. 16.1). The Cartesian coordinates of the color points closely correspond to excitations of red-green, blue-yellow, darkness, and brightness neurons. The Euclidean distances between color points are similar to subjective differences between real colors.

The specific hue of each color was characterized by an angular measure. Saturation refers to the degree of deviation from the center. The less saturated colors and achromatic colors are concentrated close to the center. The distance

HUE PLANE

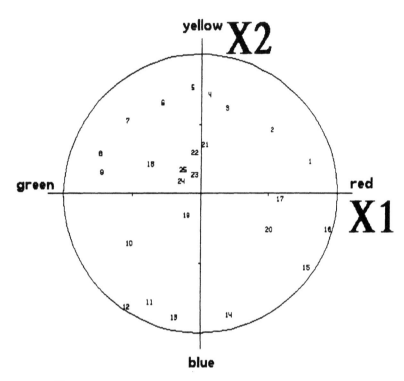

perception

FIG. 16.1   Projection of color stimuli on the hue plane for perception in humans.
X1, red-green axis; X2, yellow-blue axis. Numbers correspond to 25 respective colors specified in
L, X, Y coordinates. Background: L, 5; X, .296; Y, .279 (gray). Numbers refer to color stimuli.

Number	L	X	Y	Name	Number	L	X	Y	Name
1	12	.629	.336	red	14	13	.209	.107	violet
2	17	.568	.386	orange	15	13	.311	.161	purple
3	28	.501	.446	or.yellow	16	11	.455	.237	pr-red
4	41	.463	.471	y.orange	17	37	.346	.333	pale-red
5	55	.418	.518	yellow	18	55	.300	.367	pale-green
6	43	.396	.525	y-green	19	45	.231	.250	pale-blue
7	40	.364	.549	g-yellow	20	35	.287	.234	pale-purple
8	31	.323	.582	green	21	59	.348	.345	pale-yellow
9	29	.251	.375	g-blue	22	80	.282	.280	white
10	31	.219	.275	b-green	23	38	.296	.319	white-gray
11	13	.168	.118	navy-blue	24	18	.282	.290	black-gray
12	7	.153	.069	blue	25	0	.484	.141	black
13	9	.189	.096	b-violet					

LIGHTNESS PLANE

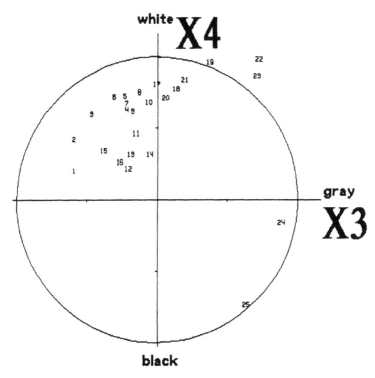

FIG. 16.2   Projection of color stimuli on the lightness plane for perception in humans. X3, gray axis; X4, white-black axis. For key to color stimuli see Fig. 16.1.

from the center corresponds to the saturation of a given color. On the lightness plane constructed from brightness and darkness axes, the achromatic colors deviated from the center are located according their lightness along the circumference in the upper and in the lower quadrants. The dark colors generated by high intensity of the inducing field and low intensity of test field were positioned in the lower right hand quadrant between 0 degrees and 270 degrees (Fig. 16.2). The saturated colors are located close to the center and along the vertical axis in accordance with their degree of lightness. The third angle of the hypersphere corresponds to saturation. The saturation plane was built up from chromatic $SQR(X1^2 + X2^2)$ and achromatic $SQR(X3^2 + X4^2)$ axes. All color stimuli were located in the upper quadrant in accordance with their saturation (Fig. 16.3). Thus, red, blue, green are close to the chromatic axes and black, gray, white are close to the achromatic one.

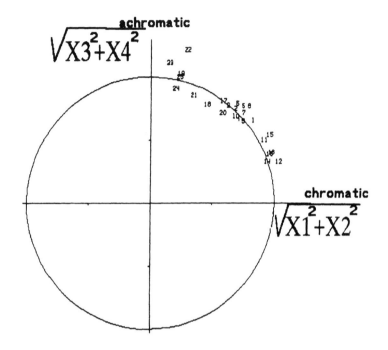

perception

FIG. 16.3   Projection of color stimuli on the saturation plane for perception in humans. SQR($X1^2 + X2^2$), chromatic axis; SQR($X3^2 + X4^2$), achromatic axis.

Conclusion. A variety of perceived colors under test-inducing field conditions are coded by four-dimensional vectors of equal lengths. The subjective differences between colors are coded by absolute values of their vectorial differences. The spherical structure of color space enables one to integrate Cartesian coordinates as excitations of neuronal channels with spherical coordinates (angles) as subjective aspects of color perception within a common structure.

Achromatic perception

The four-dimensional structure of color space suggests that achromatic colors are characterized by two coordinates constituting two-dimensional space (Izmailov & Sokolov, 1991). This conclusion was tested in experiments using a combination of a test-field and inducing field configuration by different intensities of achromatic test-field against a constant achromatic background. To check locations of saturated colors, four colors of different hues were incorporated into the set as test stimuli. The matrix of subjective differences shows that four saturated colors (16th–19th) are separated from all achromatic colors. The distances between neighbouring achromatic colors are of smallest magnitude. The eigen values of the matrix reveal two main axes that contribute to the correlation between experimental subjective differences and calculated differences between respective points. The coordinates found from the matrix of subjective differences correspond to four-dimensional space with constant radii for color points. In accordance with the prediction, all achromatic stimuli are characterized by two main coordinates related to brightness (Br) and darkness (Da) neurons. However, the weak achromatic test stimuli against the strong inducing field were characterized by negative values of Br-neurons, suggesting that the inducing field is activating an opponent—black (Bl)—neuron. Thus, the set of achromatic colors are coded by a two-dimensional vector given by opponent bright (Br) and black (Bl) neurons in combination with a darkness (Da) neuron that can be designated as a gray system and a gray (Gr) neuron. The chromatic colors are characterized by slight contributions of Br, Gr, or Bl neurons. Instead, they show maximal activation of chromatic RG and BY neurons. On the hue plane achromatic stimuli were concentrated around the center and chromatic ones located closer to the periphery. On the lightness plane achromatic stimuli are distributed on the semicircle in upper and lower quadrants close to the periphery, with chromatic ones close to the center. The saturation plane demonstrated all colors on a circumference in the upper quadrant in the order of their saturation. Chromatic colors are close to the chromatic axis and achromatic colors are near to the achromatic one.

Conclusion.   Thus, control experiments with increased number of achromatic colors support the two-dimensional structure of lightness space in the framework of a common four-dimensional color space. The experiments also support the conclusion that lightness as the subjective aspect of light intensity can be characterized by an angular measure.

Short-term color memory

Short-term color memory was studied using different time delays (up to 60sec) between the 20 color stimuli differing in hue, lightness, and saturation presented for evaluation of their subjective differences (Vartanov, Manukyan, Sokolov, & Tsakonas, 1996). The comparison of matrices of subjective differences for zero delay and 60s show close correspondence. The zero delay is relevant to color perception and the matrix of color differences demonstrates the effects shown earlier. The eigen values and coefficients of correlation between initial subjective differences and calculated Euclidean distances between respective color

HUE PLANE

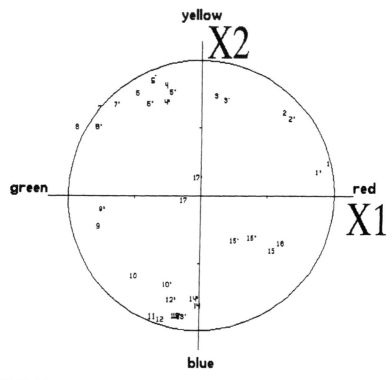

memory

FIG. **16.4**   Projection of color stimuli on the hue plane for perception and short-term memory task in humans.

X1, red-green axis; X2, yellow-blue axis. Numbers refer to color stimuli. Prime refers to 60sec delay in short-term memory. Background: L, 5; X, .296; Y, .279 (gray).

Number	L	X	Y	Name
1	12	.629	.333	red
2	17	.568	.386	orange
3	28	.501	.446	or-yellow
4	41	.463	.471	y-orange
5	55	.418	.508	yellow
6	43	.396	.525	y-green
7	40	.364	.549	g-yellow
8	31	.323	.582	green
9	29	.251	.375	g-blue
10	31	.219	.275	b-green
11	13	.168	.118	navy-blue
12	7	.153	.069	blue
13	9	.189	.096	b-violet
14	13	.209	.107	violet
15	13	.311	.161	purple
16	11	.455	.237	pr-red
17	18	.282	.290	white

LIGHTNESS PLANE

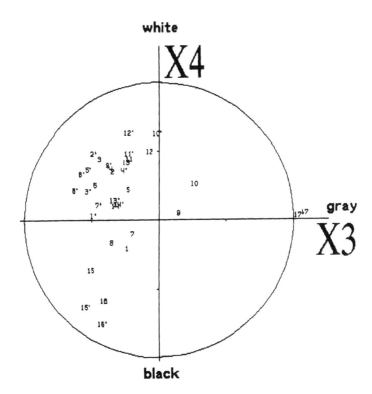

FIG. 16.5   Projection of color stimuli on the lightness plane for perception and short-term memory task in humans.
X3, gray axis; X4, white-black axis. For key to color stimuli see Fig. 16.4.

points suggest a four-dimensional space, where color points were located on the surface of the color hypersphere. On the hue plane, color points for zero delay and 60sec interval are located close to each other in accordance with hue (Fig. 16.4).

Similar close correspondence of color points was demonstrated on the lightness and saturation planes (Figs. 16.5 and 16.6). The only difference between zero and 60sec delays refers to a slight increase of noise for 60sec delay, indicating that memory matches are more difficult.

Conclusion.   The coincidence of color spaces for perception when colors are presented sequentially and for 60sec delay implies that vector coding of color stimuli can be extended to the color memory domain.

SATURATION PLANE

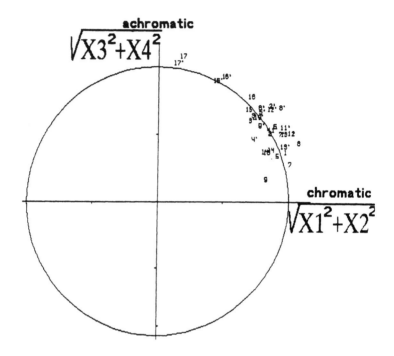

memory

FIG. 16.6   Projection of color stimuli on the saturation plane for perception and short-term memory task in humans.
SQR($X1^2 + X2^2$), chromatic axis; SQR($X3^2 + X4^2$), achromatic axis. For key to color stimuli see Fig. 16.4.

Color semantics

The applicability of a vector code to short-term memory suggests that it might operate also in long-term declarative memory. One can assume that the color hypersphere generated at a perceptual level and revealed in short-term memory is used to keep traces of color perception in long-term memory. The long-term memory traces of declarative memory are linked with their symbolic representations—color names. Thus, it might be expected that by asking a subject about differences between colors indicated by particular color names, one would obtain information on long-term color memory. In experiments with 20 Russian color names subjects were presented with a pair of names and asked to rate the difference between the designated colors (Vartanov & Sokolov, 1995). The matrix of subjective differences between the meanings of color names was treated by a multidimensional scaling procedure. The matrix demonstrates that color names close to each other in meaning are close to each other with respect to subjective differences of colors. The matrix revealed four basic axes corresponding to red-green, blue-yellow, dark, and light neurons, as was shown for perception and short-term memory. The color names were located on a hypersphere so that Euclidean distances between points were closely related to the subjective differences between color names.

The semantic structure reflects the association between symbols (written, spoken, or articulated words) and elements of declarative memory. It was shown with arbitrary color names composed of three-letter patterns associated with elements of long-term color memory. The memory color space is isomorphic with perceptual color space. The elements of the memory map replicate elements of the perceptual map. When the symbolic representation of color (color name) is given, it activates in different degrees a subset of elements of the memory map with divergent excitations. The center of gravity of the excitations determines the relevant color symbolized by a given color name. The second color name activates another subset of units on the color memory map. The subjective difference between the respective color names is equal to the distance separating excitation maxima evoked by these color names. The evaluation of subjective differences is performed in a way similar to the calculation of perceptual color differences.

Conclusion.   The study of color names demonstrates that vector code and mapping are relevant to perception, short-term memory, long-term memory, and semantics.

COLOR LEARNING IN MONKEY AND IN FISH

Color learning in monkey

The study of human color vision has shown that color perception, color memory, and color semantics are based on vector coding realized as superimposed hyperspheres in four-dimensional space. The spheres are represented by different neurons: color-selective detectors for perception, color-selective memory units for memory, and color-dependent semantic units for color terms.

The arbitrary color names acquired via learning suggest that the process of associative learning also operates with a vector code. It was assumed that instrumental learning is due to the modification of plastic synapses on a command neuron that sums up products of multiplication of presynaptic inputs and postsynaptic weights. The results of such an operation are equal to the inner (scalar) product of two vectors: an input excitation vector and a synaptic weight vector. In the process of positive reinforcement the synaptic weight vector of the command neuron becomes coincident in orientation with the input excitation vector, and their inner product reaches a maximum parallel with the excitation maximum of the command neuron. The excitation of the command neuon in turn determines the probability of a conditioned reflex. Thus, response probability is directly proportional to the inner product of the excitation vector generated by a given stimulus and synaptic weight vector elaborated during conditioning. Taking into account the spherical structure of color space in humans, one can assume constant lengths of both the excitation vector and the synaptic weight vector. It suggests that the response probability matrix implicitly contains information concerning excitation and weight vectors. To test the hypothesis concerning vectorial mechanisms of learning, color associative learning was studied in rhesus monkey and carp (Latanov, Polyanskii, & Sokolov, 1991). For instrumental learning in monkey the animals were presented with a set of eight colors. One color was used as a conditional stimulus being positively reinforced by juice for correct responding. The other seven colors were differential stimuli. The process of elaboration of the instrumental conditioned reflex was characterized by a gradual increase of the probability of hits (correct responses) to the conditional stimulus and the reduction of probability of false alarms (erroneous responses) to differential stimuli. When conditioned response probabilities reached a plateau level (about 80–90%), the probabilities of responses to differential stimuli were measured and entered as a column into a matrix. After that, another color was used as a reinforced conditional stimulus, and after reaching plateau level the probabilities of responses were entered as the next column into the probability matrix. Step by step all eight colors were sequentially used as conditional stimuli. The matrix of response probabilities of all combinations of colors used as conditional and differential stimuli was constructed (Table 16.1).

TABLE 16.1
Monkey: The matrix of response probabilities (in percent) taken at the stage of reflex stabilization

Presented colors (nm)	Reinforced colors (nm)						
	605	545	572	470	555*	490	White
605	82	9	26	21	27	23	13
545	12	78	37	14	23	38	20
572	18	14	91	11	25	43	14
470	21	31	24	86	32	39	33
555*	24	18	32	24	86	42	19
490	20	23	33	28	25	82	29
White	12	16	31	21	29	41	72

Each column score corresponds to a probability vector characteristic for a specific conditional stimulus. The probabilities are smaller the more distinct the conditional and differential stimuli are.
* Wavelength of opposite color.

TABLE 16.2
Monkey: Cartesian coordinates of color points in the four-dimensional perceptual color space based on the four factors characterizing color stimuli

Colors (nm)	Cartesian coordinates				Length of radii
	X1	X2	X3	X4	
605	0.742	0.318	−0.487	−0.064	0.945
545	−0.925	0.242	−0.177	−0.141	0.983
572	−0.161	0.674	0.179	0.356	0.800
470	−0.046	−0.912	0.058	0.097	0.920
555*	0.143	0.039	−0.076	0.868	0.884
490	−0.224	0.113	0.547	0.457	0.756
White	0.086	0.034	0.944	−0.133	0.958

* Wavelength of opposite color.
Mean of radii, 0.892 ± 0.032; variance, 0.095.

The matrix was treated by factor analysis to reveal its eigen vectors and factor loads. It revealed four factors corresponding to contributions of red-green, blue-yellow, lightness, and darkness neurons. Thus, each color stimulus was characterized by a four-dimensional excitation vector. The lengths of the excitation vectors were close to a constant, so that color stimuli can be represented in a thin spherical layer about 10% of the mean radius (Table 16.2). The coordinates of excitation vectors found from the matrix were used to calculate inner products of the excitation vectors and weight vectors. The weight vectors were found as vectors equal to excitation vectors of conditional stimuli. It is possible that the reinforcement of the conditional stimulus modifies synaptic weights until the synaptic contacts become directly proportional to synaptic inputs, resulting in equality of excitation vector generated by the conditional stimulus and synaptic weight vector of the command neuron. Under these conditions the inner product of excitation and weight vector, and the response probability, reach maximal magnitude. In this way a calculated matrix of inner products of excitation vectors and weight vectors was constructed (Table 16.3). It was matched against the original matrix of inner products obtained in the experiments. We found that the original and calculated inner products are highly correlated. To visualize locations of color points on a hypersphere in four-dimensional space they were projected on three planes, as was done for humans. On the hue plane composed of red-green and blue-yellow orthogonal axes, chromatic saturated colors (as seen for human observers) were located close to a circumference in accordance with equivalent (dominating) wavelengths of computer-generated colors, with purple positioned between violet and red. The white color was located close to the center and less saturated colors are found around the center (Fig. 16.7).

TABLE 16.3
Monkey: The matrix of scalar products between vectors representing used colors

| Colors (nm) | Colors (nm) | | | | | | |
	605	545	572	470	555*	490	White
605	0.945						
545	−0.514	0.983					
572	−0.010	0.230	0.799				
470	−0.350	−0.200	−0.562	0.920			
555*	0.100	−0.230	0.299	0.038	0.884		
490	−0.420	0.073	0.373	−0.010	0.327	0.756	
White	−0.370	−0.220	0.131	0.007	−0.170	0.440	0.958

* Wavelength of opposite color.
Correlation with lower part of probability matrix .888.
Correlation with upper part of probability matrix .917.

HUE PLANE

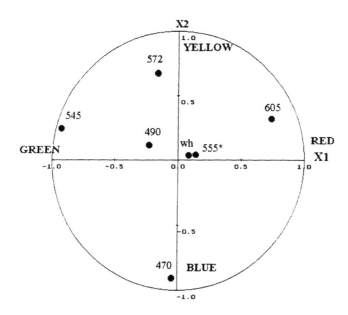

MONKEY

FIG. 16.7   Projection of color stimuli on the hue plane for monkey.
X1, red-green axis; X2, yellow-blue axis; wh, white color. Numbers correspond to equivalent wavelengths in nm. 555*, wave length of color stimulus opponent to purple color.

LIGHTNESS PLANE

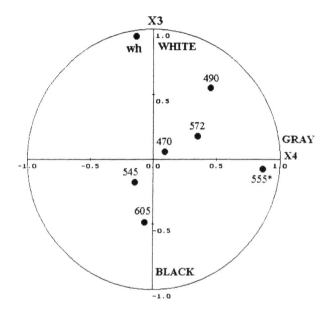

MONKEY

FIG. 16.8 Projection of color stimuli on the lightness plane for monkey. X3, white-black axis; X4, gray axis. For key to color stimuli see Fig. 16.7.

On the lightness plane, composed of brightness and darkness orthogonal axes, the achromatic colors are located on a circumference of the first quadrant according to their lightness, whereas saturated colors are distributed around the center (Fig. 16.8). The saturation plane was constituted from complex axes representing achromatic and chromatic coordinates, respectively.

All colors now are located on the circumference within the first quadrant in accordance with their saturation (Fig. 16.9). Thus, monkey color vision is organized in the same way as in humans. The Cartesian coordinates correspond to neuronal excitations and spherical coordinates (three angles of the hypersphere) correspond to hue, lightness, and saturation.

Conclusion.   The color space of monkeys is similar to that observed in humans.

SATURATION PLANE

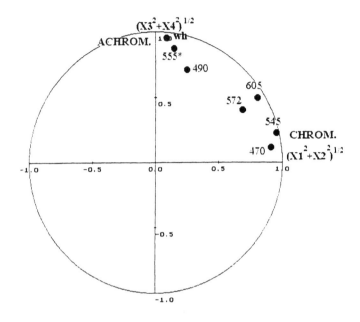

MONKEY

FIG. 16.9 Projections of color stimuli on the saturation plane for monkey.
SQR(X3² + X4²), achromatic axis; SQR(X1² + X2²), chromatic axis. For key to color stimuli see Fig. 16.7.

Color learning in fish

To study the universal character of color coding, conditioned reflexes to colors were elaborated in fish (carp). The animals had to make a choice between two color stimuli presented on the monitor and push a small ball. Correct responses were reinforced by food. The matrix of response probabilities was constructed from data obtained by sequentially reinforced conditional stimuli (Table 16.4). The matrix was reduced by factor analysis. We found four principal components corresponding to red-green, blue-yellow, brightness, and darkness neurons. The radii are close to a constant value with variance 0.094 (Table 16.5). The co-ordinates found from the probability matrix can be used to calculate inner products of excitation and synaptic weight vectors, assuming that coordinates of conditional stimuli are equivalents of synaptic weights. The calculated inner products correspond to response probabilities found in the experiments (Table 16.6). To visualize the distribution of color points within four-dimensional space, their projections on three orthogonal planes were used. On the hue plane red-green

TABLE 16.4
Fish: The matrix of response probabilities (in %)

Presented colors (nm)	Reinforced colors (nm)							
	467	496	533	566	575	610	552*	White
467	90.9	5.3	3.7	0	0	0	4.8	12.0
479	15.4	21.1	3.6	0	0	10.5	0	20.0
496	24.0	90.4	11.1	4.8	8.0	10.0	0	38.5
533	3.8	15.8	90.0	25.0	8.0	0	0	8.0
566	0	11.1	25.0	91.1	24.0	5.0	0	24.0
575	0	0	0	36.4	92.7	15.0	0	20.0
593	4	0	3.6	0	4.3	26.3	5.3	8.0
610	3.8	5.6	3.6	0	8.7	88.2	0	4.0
552*	4.0	5.3	3.4	0	0	15.0	97.2	23.1
White	3.8	10.5	3.7	4.5	0	10.0	15.8	80.2

Each column score corresponds to a probability vector characteristic for a specific conditional stimulus. The probabilities are smaller the more distinct the conditional and differential stimuli are.

TABLE 16.5
Fish: Cartesian coordinates of color points in the four-dimensional perceptual color space based on the four factors characterizing color stimuli

Colors (nm)	Cartesian coordinates				Length of radii
	X1	X2	X3	X4	
467	−0.119	−0.785	−0.01	0.392	0.886
496	−0.130	−0.365	0.518	0.497	0.816
533	−0.991	−0.081	−0.178	0.024	1.000
566	−0.557	0.621	0.014	0.191	0.856
575	0.011	0.687	−0.102	0.274	0.747
610	0.521	−0.059	−0.597	−0.093	0.800
552*	−0.036	−0.258	0.221	−0.859	0.924
White	0.093	0.004	0.872	−0.075	0.880

Mean of radii, 0.865 ± 0.029; variance, 0.094.

and blue-yellow axes color stimuli of high saturation constitute a circle with equivalent wavelengths from 610nm anti-clockwise to 575, 566, 533, 467nm. Less saturated colors, white and purple (with opponent wavelength equal to 552nm and 496nm) are located around the center (Fig. 16.10). On the lightness plane, slightly saturated colors are close to the circumference of the upper and lower quadrants in the range 180 degrees. The darkest stimulus (610nm) is opponent to the white stimulus, and pale purple (with 552nm opponent

TABLE 16.6
Fish: The matrix of scalar products between vectors representing used colors

Colors (nm)	Colors (nm)							
	467	496	533	566	575	610	552*	White
467	0.886							
496	0.492	0.816						
533	0.193	0.078	1.010					
566	−0.340	−0.050	0.504	0.856				
575	−0.430	−0.160	−0.040	0.471	0.747			
610	−0.040	−0.400	−0.400	−0.350	0.001	0.800		
552*	−0.130	−0.210	0.000	−0.300	−0.430	−0.056	0.924	
White	−0.050	0.401	−0.250	−0.050	−0.100	−0.460	0.253	0.880

* Wavelength of opposite color.
Correlation with lower part of probability matrix .905.
Correlation with upper part of probability matrix .895.

HUE PLANE

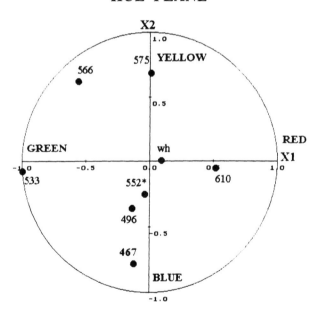

FISH

FIG. 16.10 Projection of color stimuli on the hue plane for fish.
X1, red-green axis; X2, yellow-blue axis. Numbers correspond to equivalent wave lengths in nm. Wh, white color. 552*, wave length of color stimulus opponent to purple color.

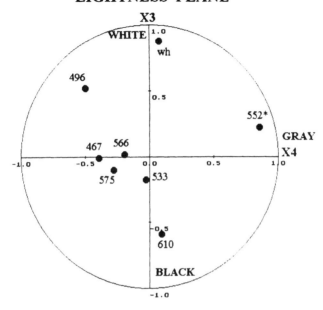

LIGHTNESS PLANE

FISH

Fig. 16.11   Projection of color stimuli on the lightness plane for fish.
X3, white-black axis; X4, gray axis. For key to color stimuli see Fig. 16.10.

wavelength) is close to the gray axis (Fig. 16.11). The extension of colors on the
1st and 4th quadrants is due to the contrast effect, which resulted from the
simultaneous presentation of two stimuli on the monitor for discrimination.
A similar contrast effect was found in humans when the disc-ring configuration
was presented. When single colors were given sequentially, all stimuli were concentrated only in the 1st quadrant. When monkeys were given single sequentially
presented colors, all stimuli on the lightness plane were also located within
the 1st quadrant. On the saturation plane the color stimuli are located in the
1st quadrant close to the circumference (Fig. 16.12). White and pale purple are
close to the achromatic axis, whereas saturated colors (533nm, 566nm) are close
to the chromatic axis.

Conclusion.   The experiments with instrumental conditioned reflexes to
color stimuli in monkey and fish have revealed identical color spaces: a hypersphere in four-dimensional space that closely corresponds to the color space in
humans.

SATURATION

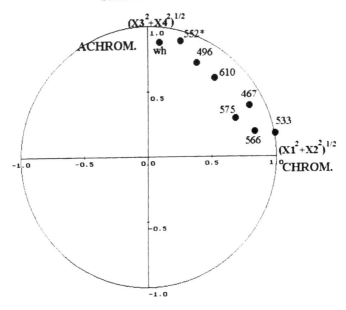

FISH

FIG. 16.12   Projection of color stimuli on the saturation plane for fish.
SQR (X1² + X2²), chromatic axis; SQR(X3² + X4²), achromatic axis. For key to color stimuli see Fig. 16.10.

COLOR CODING NETWORK

Simulation of color learning

Blue, green, and red cones are specified by overlapping characteristics along the wavelength number (frequency) axis, constituting a receptor ensemble in a local patch of retina. The color stimulus generates in the receptor ensemble a receptor excitation vector. The overlapping characteristics of cones suggest that they constitute a nonorthogonal basis. The orthogonalization is achieved in local circuits of ribbon synapses in photopic horizontal cells: monophasic (luminous L-cell), biphasic, and triphasic opponent cells (Izmailov, Sokolov, & Chernorizov, 1989). Thus, each color stimulus at the horizontal cell level is represented by a three-dimensional excitation vector in an orthogonal coordinate system. The orientation of that excitation vector codes color. The length of this vector codes stimulus intensity. The next stage of information processing is related to normalization of the excitation vector. It might be assumed that normalization is done with respect to the sum of excitations. The normalization procedure involves a reduction of independent parameters. To keep initial dimensionality, an additional channel noisy in darkness is added. To enable spiking at inhibitory phases of the opponent cell, each opponent cell is doubled. Thus, at the level of bipolar cells R+ G, R− G+, B+ Y−, B− Y+, brightness (Br) and darkness (Da) neurons are present. The opponent and two nonopponent cells are stimulated. The normalized excitations activate plastic synapses of a command neuron taking part in response generation. In the case where the neuron is reinforced via a nonplastic input (unconditional stimulus), synapses are modified according to the Hebbian rule: the larger the increase of their weights on plastic synapses, the stronger is its afferent input. The plastic synaptic weights approach the magnitudes of inputs reaching these synapses. In this way the synaptic weight vector achieves the same orientation as the input excitation vector of the reinforced conditional stimulus, and the inner product of the weight vector and the excitation vector reaches its maximum value. The smaller the inner products of the established weight vector and excitation vectors of differential stimuli are, the more differential stimuli deviate from the conditional one. The magnitude of the inner product determines command neuron excitation. The fluctuating spiking threshold command neuron triggers a behavioral response with a probability directly proportional to the respective inner product. Thus, response probabilities implicitly contain information concerning inner products, and concerning the vectors producing these inner products. The weight vectors established by reinforced conditional stimuli are equal to excitation vectors generated by these conditional stimuli. Thus, the matrix of probabilities is a matrix of inner products of the total set of excitation vectors. Factor analysis reveals the four-dimensional basis of this set of excitation vectors. The Cartesian coordinates of these excitation vectors can be used to calculate inner products and compare them with their respective response probabilities. The high correlation between these matrixes supports the vector code as the main principle, and the inner product as the main operation, in the command neuron under learning conditions (Sokolov 1995a,b). The model also explains the phenomenon of latent inhibition. Conditioning proceeds more rapidly to a novel conditional stimulus (CS) than to an already familiar one. This phenomenon is due to Hebbian depression of synaptic weights relevant to nonreinforced stimuli. The nonreinforced excitation vector induces an orthogonal synaptic weight vector so that familiar stimui are neglected. Novel stimuli acting on synapses that are not depressed augment their weights more efficiently. The model also provides an account of generalization. Stimuli closely located in perceptual space are characterized by similar excitation vectors. In the command neuron with synaptic weights adjusted to the conditional stimulus, such differential stimuli evoke stronger responses when the stimuli are similar to the conditional stimulus.

Simulation of color differences

The receptor ensemble, and its orthogonalization and normalization on the basis of excitation vectors, was described earlier. New elements refer to the color detector map (Sokolov, 1994). The normalized excitation vectors together with command neurons operate as inputs to color detectors. Each color detector is characterized by a specific combination of stable synaptic weights—weight vectors of equal lengths. The four-dimensional excitation vector acts on all color detectors. A color detector summing up the paired product of input and synaptic weights calculates an inner product of the input excitation vector and weight vector of a given detector. Because color detectors possess different synaptic weights, their inner products are also different. Maximal inner products will be obtained in such detectors that have a weight vector coinciding in orientation with the excitation vector. A change of stimulus resulting in a change of excitation vector will activate another color detector. The set of color detectors constitutes a detector map on which different color stimuli are represented by specific locations of excited color detectors. The detector map makes it possible to compare color stimuli with respect to their differences. The difference is given as the distance between locations of excitation maxima evoked by color stimuli on the color detector map. It is equal to the absolute magnitude of vectorial difference between respective excitation vectors. Thus, the matrix of subjective differences implicitly contains information concerning excitation vectors. The multidimensional scaling procedure extracts this information from the matrix of subjective differences between color stimuli. The coefficient of correlation between experimental subjective differences and calculated Euclidean distances provides a measure of correspondence between the postulated vector code and experimental data.

Simulation of color semantics

To understand color semantics one has to postulate a long-term color memory map (Vartanov & Sokolov, 1995). The memory neurons are recruited by color detectors in the process of color perception from a reserve of memory neurons. The recruitment of a color memory neuron can be explained by one-trial learning according to the Hebbian rule discussed in the case of conditioning. Thus, the declarative color map is extended due to experience. This map is isomorphic with the color detector map. The color memory neurons can be associated with neurons of color names as symbolic representations of colors (Pavlovian Second Signaling System). Color name neurons are in turn linked with command neurons of articulation. Presentation of a color stimulus triggers a sequence of events in the color-selective detector, color-memory unit and color-name neuron. The instruction given to the subject to name the color stimulus activates links between the symbolic unit and the command neuron generating a verbal response. The presentation of a color name activates a set of color units from the declarative memory map connected in different degrees with that color name. Thus, on the declarative color map an excitation vector is generated. This activation pattern of memory units enables the system to compare color name meanings in a way similar to estimation of perceived color differences. The subjective difference between color names is equal to the distance between excitation maxima of excitation patterns generated by the respective color names. Because the long-term color map is isomorphic with the color detector map, the distances between color names correspond to respective color perceptions.

SUMMARY

This chapter integrates behavioral and neuronal data in the framework of a vector model of information processing. The model deals with perception, memory, and learning. It suggests the participation of neuronal ensembles in the generation of excitation vectors representing input stimuli. The excitation vectors due to the normalization procedure performed within neuronal networks are of constant lengths, representing stimuli on the surface of a sphere in the space determined by elements of the neuronal ensemble. The input excitation vector acts in parallel on a set of detectors selectively tuned to specific input stimuli. Such selective tuning of detectors is accomplished by the unique composition of their synaptic weights, constituting link vectors connecting each detector with all elements of the neuronal ensemble. Each synapse of a detector multiplies input excitation by its synaptic weight. The detector sums up these paired products, generating a response equal to the inner product of the input excitation vector and its respective link vector. The link vectors in the set of detectors are equal in length. Thus, the inner product reaches maximum if the input excitation vector and the link vector of a particular detector coincide in orientation, resulting in detector-selective tuning to the stimulus that generates such an excitation vector. The selective detectors occupy local patches of the sphere, constituting a detector map on which input stimuli are represented. When the input stimulus is modified, the excitation vector changes accordingly and the excitation maximum is moved along the detector map. Vector code and neuronal maps contribute to procedural, declarative, and working memory. Procedural memory refers to classic and instrumental conditioning. To elucidate the neuronal basis of conditioning, the concept of command neuron has to be considered. A command neuron triggers a behavioral act or its fragment via divergent pathways directed to premotor and motor neurons. The excitations of these neurons constitute an output excitation vector representing a specific behavioral pattern. A set of command neurons constitutes a neuronal map on which different behavioral acts are represented. The excitation vector generated by a neuronal ensemble reaches all command neurons via plastic synapses (Hebbian synapses). The weights of plastic synapses increase if the command neuron is reinforced by an unconditional stimulus acting via nonplastic synapses. The synaptic weights increase with the amount of their excitation. If the stimulus is not reinforced, the synaptic weights decrease according to their excitations. In the process of conditioning, a command neuron for a specific behavior becomes selectively tuned to the reinforced stimulus. The selective tuning is achieved by modification of the weights of plastic synapses. The link vector of the command neuron in the process of conditioning becomes normalized and colinear with the input excitation vector, and the response of the command neuron to the conditional stimulus reaches maximum. Thus, selectivity of the conditioned reflex with respect to a behavioral act is due to the command neuron and selectivity with respect to the stimulus is due to plastic adjustment of its link vector. If the conditional stimulus is not reinforced, the decrease of synaptic weights results in a deviation of the link vector from the generated input excitation vector and gradually the command neuron stops responding. Procedural memory is incorporated into the synaptic contacts used for transfer of input signals. It means that synaptic weights are re-adjusted in each learning session. Declarative memory is, in turn, characterized by an establishment of long-term fixation of input events and objects by creation of selectively tuned gnostic units. To understand the creation of color gnostic units, one has to follow the ontogenetic process of detector formation. Detectors are tuned to specific input stimuli during the sensitive period, remaining constant afterwards. It can be assumed that declarative memory is an analogue of detector formation. A novel stimulus recruits a reserve neuron, inducing in it a short sensitive period during which synaptic contacts of the recruited neuron become plastic and modified in accordance with Hebbian rule. After the termination of the sensitive period the plastic synapses are transformed into nonplastic ones and the established color gnostic unit operates within the framework of declarative memory. The activation of a gnostic unit is achieved by an input excitation vector composed of a set of excitations of neurons closely related to neurons activated by the development of a given gnostic unit. The subset of gnostic units involving current behavioral acts constitutes working memory. These gnostic units are pre-excited by the task and can be effectively involved in its expression. The presented vector model of cognitive processes —perception, memory and learning—was tested using the comparative study of color vision, color memory, and color learning in fish, monkey, and humans. It was shown, using instrumental conditioning in animals and color naming in humans, that perceptual, memory, and semantic color spaces are spherical surfaces where color percepts, color memories, and color names are represented by local patches corresponding to color-selective neurons. The information transferred in the color-coding network can be summarized as a sequence of the following steps.

1. At the receptor level the color stimulus generates a three-dimensional receptor excitation vector given in a nonorthogonal basis.
2. At the level of horizontal cells the three-dimensional vector is orthoganalized.
3. At the level of bipolar cells, after addition of a neuron active in darkness, the excitation vector is normalized.

4. At the color detector level the excitation vector is transformed into a location of excitation maximum on the detector map.
5. The color detectors switch on units of the declarative color memory map.
6. Symbolic stimuli are associated with elements of the color memory map.
7. Color names generate specific excitation vectors on the color memory map.
8. The subjective differences between color percepts, color memory traces and color names are found through the absolute values of differences between the excitation vectors under consideration. The vector code as basic information processing constitutes the heart of the geometrical model of cognition (Sokolov, 1994, 1995a, b, 1996).

REFERENCES

Izmailov, Ch. A., & Sokolov, E. N. (1991). Spherical model of color and brightness discrimination. *Psychological Science, 2*, 249–259.

Izmailov, Ch. A., Sokolov, E. N., & Chernorizov, A. M. (1989). Psikhofiziologia tsvetovogo zreniya (Psychophysiology of color vision). Moscow: Izd-vo MGU.

Latanov, A. V., Polynskii, V. B., & Sokolov, E. N. (1991). Chetyirechmernoe zvetovoe prostranstvo obezyany. [The four-dimensional color space of monkey.] *Zhurnal VND, 41(4)*, 636–643.

Paramey, G. V. (1996). Color space of normally sighted and color-deficient observers reconstructed from color naming. *Psychological Science, 7(5)*, 311–317.

Sokolov, E. N. (1994). Vector coding in neuronal nets: color vision. In K. H. Pribram (Ed.), *Origins: brain and self organization* (pp. 463–476). Hillsdale, NJ: Lawrence Erlbaum Associates Inc.

Sokolov, E. N. (1995a). Printsip vektornogo kodirovaniya v psikhofiviologii. [Principle of vector coding in psychophysiology.] *Vestn. Mosk. U-ta, Seria 14. Psykhologiya, 4*, 3–13.

Sokolov, E. N. (1995b). Vektornaya psikhofiziologiya. [Vector psychophysiology.] Moscow: Izd-vo MGU.

Sokolov, E. N. (1996). Vectornoe kodirovanie i neironnye karty. [Vector coding and neuronal maps.] *Zhurnal VND, 46(1)*, 7–14.

Sokolov, E. N., & Vaitkyavicus, G. G. (1989). Neirointellect: ot neurona k neirokompyuteru. [From neuron towards neurocomputer.] Moscow: Izd-vo Nauka.

Vartanov, A. V., & Sokolov, E. N. (1995). Rol pervoi i vtoroi signalnyikh sistern v sootnoshenii semanticheskogo i perzeptivnogo zvetovykh prostranstv. [Role of the first and second signal systems in co-organization of sensory and perceptive color spaces.] *Zhurnal VND, 45(2)*, 343–357.

Vartanov, A. V., Manukyan, N. K., Sokolov, E. N., & Tsakonas, K. G. (1996). Sochranenie zvetovogo obraza v kratkivremennoi pamyati. [Retention of color images in short-term memory.] *Zhurnal VND, 45(6)*, 1085–1093.

CHAPTER SEVENTEEN

Language and cognition

Jacques Mehler
LSCP, EHESS-CNRS, Paris, France

Christophe Pallier
Rutgers University, and LSCP, EHESS-CNRS, Paris, France

Anne Christophe
LSCP, EHESS-CNRS, Paris, France

The 4000 or so human languages display an extraordinary surface diversity, there-fore language learning by the infant requires some plasticity. We present here psycholinguistic data suggesting that there are nevertheless some limits to this plasticity. In the first part, we document a "foreign listening syndrome", that is, the fact that people listen to foreign speech sounds through the filter of the phonology of their own language (a perceptual equivalent to a foreign accent in production). Even very good bilinguals seem to retain a dominant language. It thus seems that the perceptual system is shaped by early linguistic experience and stays rather rigid afterwards. In the second part, we show that very young babies are able to distinguish between languages, which is a prerequisite if they are to learn from more than one language. In the third part, we present data from brain-imaging techniques (PET and fMRI) that investigate the cortical representation of speech in more or less proficient bilinguals. The cortical representations of the second language show more inter-individual variability than the ones for the first lan-guage, all the more so when the second language is less well mastered and/or has been acquired later in life.

Les quelque 4000 langues humaines montrent une extraordinaire variabilité de surface; par conséquent l'apprentissage du langage par l'enfant requiert de la plasticité. Nous présentons des données psycholinguistiques qui suggèrent qu'il y a néanmoins des limites à cette plasticité. Dans la première partie, nous décrivons le phénomène de «l'accent étranger en perception», c'est-à-dire le fait que les gens écoutent les sons de parole étrangers à travers le filtre de leur propre phonologie (un équivalent perceptif à l'accent étranger en production). Même de très bons bilingues semblent garder une langue dominante. Il semble donc que le système perceptif est façonné par l'expérience linguistique précoce, et qu'il reste relativement rigide par la suite. Dans la deuxième partie, nous montrons que des bébés très jeunes sont capables de distinguer entre différentes langues, ce qui est nécessaire pour que leur apprentissage du langage puisse se faire à partir de plus d'une langue. Dans la troisième partie, nous présentons des données d'imagerie cérébrale (TEP et RMN fonctionnelle) qui étudient les représentations corticales de la parole chez des bilingues plus ou moins compétents. Les représentations pour la seconde langue montrent plus de variabilité interindividuelle que celles pour la première langue, et ceci est d'autant plus vrai que la seconde langue est moins bien maîtrisée ou a été acquise plus tardivement.

To gain insight into the way in which a species-specific faculty is biologically determined and then shaped by the environment is essential for anyone who has set out to understand the nature of the mind. After more than 150 years of research, theoretical insights are only just beginning to emerge from the accumulated observations. In this chapter we present some recent developments that may help us glean a much better understanding of the biological foundations of language.

Since Broca's 1861 seminal paper it has been known that the third frontal convolution is the locus of *articulated language*. The contributions of Wernicke, Dejerine, Alajouanine and more recently Geschwind, among many others, have shown that the language function spreads over other regions of the temporal, parietal, and frontal cortex in the left hemisphere (Geschwind & Levitsky, 1968). This view has become standard and is taught to all students in the field of neuropsychology. However, knowing which areas of the cortex, when damaged, are responsible for language disorders does not clarify how such structures come to sustain the language(s) acquired by a speaker.

Chomsky (e.g. 1975) has proposed that the study of a complex cognitive function like language should be conducted in the same way as that of any other complex body organ. The language "organ", however, is rather special in two ways. First, it is productive rather than stereotyped, and speakers can generate an infinitely large number of sentences that other speakers can understand. Second, it depends crucially on early language input: Speakers can learn English, Chinese, French, or any other of the 4000 or so recorded natural languages. This input need not even be speech, as children exposed to a sign language learn it as readily as any oral language, even though it rests on a motor-visual rather than an auditory-vocal loop. These two facts taken together make language a very special mixture of constraints and plasticity. Because all adults from a linguistic community reach the same grammatical competence despite the fact that they have been exposed to different sentences, there must be constraints on what a human language can be. However, there are many differences between languages, and only what is shared by all languages of the world can be an innate constraint (it is the project of the Universal Grammar to discover the set of properties shared by all languages of the world). Anything that differs between languages has to be learned by children from the linguistic input they receive.

Lenneberg (1967) documented an observation that is spontaneously made by many naive observers, namely, that when language is acquired after puberty, only partial proficiency is gained regardless of the efforts made (the extent of the limitations in late-acquired language continues to fuel debate today). Lenneberg, among others, used this observation to argue in favor of a sensitive period or window during which impeccable language acquisition can take place. This notion is congruent with the view that language learning is innately guided. Many innately guided learning mechanisms observed in animals or humans have been found to have a critical period during which input from the environment is allowed to shape the system as it will work in the adult organism (e.g. sound localization in the barn owl, Knudsen & Knudsen, 1986, or the very extreme case of imprinting as described by Lorenz). More recently, Weber-Fox and Neville (1996) have found that "maturational changes significantly constrain the development of the neural systems that are relevant for language" (p. 231), based on data from a population of bilingual subjects varying in age of acquisition of the second language. Similarly, Hickok, Bellugi, and Klima (1996) have shown that in native speakers of American Sign Language, the cortical regions where language is represented correspond to the regions that have been determined in speakers of oral-vocal languages. On this basis, they argue that left-hemisphere specialization for language is a characteristic of language itself, in its abstract shape, rather than a by-product of sensory or motor factors. The evidence suggests that the parts of the cortex that are devoted to the mediation of higher cognitive skills display a rather considerable rigidity and a fixed developmental pattern.

However, recent results from the cognitive neurosciences have raised skepticism about the existence of critical periods. The brain of vertebrates has been shown to have an astonishing plasticity. Indeed, Kaas, Merzenich, and Killackey (1983) and Kaas (1991) have reported that learning can result in processing gains throughout the organisms' life through the alteration of the cortical maps underlying sensory functions. An example of exogenous conditions resulting in the functional reorganization of the brain was provided by Sugita (1996) who has shown that the adult visual cortex can undergo extensive functional reorganization in response to the reversal of the retinal projections by prisms. Sadato et al. (1996) have found that blind individuals who are asked to discriminate Braille dots have a significantly greater blood flow, as compared to sighted controls, in the primary visual cortex. This result suggests that when the primary visual cortex is no longer activated by visual input it can become activated by touch. Rauschecker and Korte (1993) have shown that in blind cats there is compensatory auditory representation, which is believed to have arisen by expansion of auditory areas that invade the visual areas. In a recent review of compensatory plasticity in cortex, Rauschecker (1995) has concluded that plasticity might not "be restricted to developmental periods, but may be available, at least to some extent, throughout life" (p. 42). Of course, most of the research reviewed by Rauschecker is concerned with the representation of spatial cognitive maps and the possibility of remapping these on the basis of sensorimotor feedback. It may be that such plasticity would not apply to a much more complex cognitive function such as language.

But in the domain of language itself, Tallal and her colleagues (1996) have illustrated the brain's plasticity by providing extensive training to language-learning impaired children. They trained the children with rate-modified speech and temporal discrimination tasks and noted great improvement in their performance. Interestingly, these rapid gains were made by children whose age ranged from 5 to 10 years. Even more recently, Vargha-Kahdem and her colleagues (personal communication, November 1996) have reported the case of a child who was able to acquire language after the age of nine, when his damaged left hemisphere was removed. This suggests that language can be learned on the basis of the residual abilities of the right hemisphere if the inhibitory action of the damaged left hemisphere is removed even at a rather advanced age. In this view, then, inadequate language learning after a given age would not be attributed to the existence of a critical period, but rather to other reasons, such as differences in motivation, inhibition from competing cognitive resources, etc.

We have arrived at a point where we can clearly state the controversy. On the one hand, we have this view of almost unlimited cortical plasticity. On the other hand, the view that language learning is very much constrained is based on arguments arising from formal analyses (linguistics and learnability theory), brain-damaged patients, brain imaging, etc. This controversy is anything but insignificant; whether language calls for a specialized learning system that only humans possess is one of the essential questions that students of the biology of language need to answer.

How can psycholinguistic research shed light on this controversy? We will review work aimed at evaluating in more detail how second-language learners are impaired, depending on when they acquired their second language and on the similarities between their first and second languages. We will argue that late learners do not just acquire a foreign accent but that they are also affected by a foreign listening syndrome when confronted with speech stimuli not in their first language. In addition, even highly proficient bilingual subjects, who learned both languages in infancy, seem to be incapable of escaping from the perceptual dominance imposed by their first language. We will then review some infant studies suggesting that babies manage to solve part of the problem of distinguishing their mother tongue from foreign language input, a crucial prerequisite for succesful language acquisition in babies exposed to more than one language. Finally, we will attempt to tackle the issues of early bilinguals and critical periods through imaging work with a variety of bilingual populations. We will present some imaging results, based on both PET and fMRI studies, and argue that there seems to exist a corresponding asymmetry between the brain representations of first and second languages. Whereas a major network in the left hemisphere is consistently dedicated to first-language processing across subjects and languages, the way in which a second language is represented by subjects' brain varies greatly, as does the way in which this second language was acquired. This variability is more salient in less proficient than in more proficient bilinguals.

CONTRASTING LANGUAGE-PROCESSING SCHEMES

Psycholinguistics' default assumption has been that all languages are processed in much the same way up until the lexicon is accessed. It has been known for a long time that the collection of segments varies from one natural language to the next, and that speakers who have to process segments not present in their mother tongue often have trouble hearing them. In addition, research on early infant speech perception has established that babies in their first year of life can process segmental contrasts from all human languages, and that only towards the end of the first year of life do they start performing like adults from their linguistic environment (Best, McRoberts, & Sithole, 1988; Eimas, Siqueland, Jusczyk, & Vigorito, 1971; Werker & Tees, 1984). From these data one can entertain the hypothesis that speech-processing mechanisms are identical from one language to the other, at least as far as access to words is concerned, and that the only differences between languages lie in the inventories of phonemes and words (which have to be learned).

More recent research has established that the syndrome we would like to call the *foreign listening syndrome* cannot be reduced to differences in the inventory of phonemes. Indeed, Mehler, Dommergues, Frauenfelder, and Segui (1981) have shown that the syllable is a pre-lexical unit that plays an important role for speakers of French (this result was later extended to other Romance languages, see Sebastian-Gallès, Dupoux, Segui, & Mehler, 1992). Two years later Cutler, Mehler, Norris, and Segui (1983) reported that native English speakers tend to attach more importance to a metrical unit beginning with a strong syllable than to syllables themselves (this result was later extended to other stress-timed languages, see Vroomen & de Gelder, 1995). Otake, Hatano, Cutler, and Mehler (1993) have more recently noted that in response to the very same acoustic items, Japanese, English, and French subjects behaved differently: Each population analyzed the stimuli in a manner congruent with the properties of its native language. The general conclusion of our Human Frontiers Science Program consortium of psycholinguists was that speakers of French, English, Japanese, Spanish, Catalan, and so forth use processing routines that are ideally tailored to exploit the properties of their native language.

More recently Dupoux, Pallier, Sebastian, and Mehler (1997) observed a striking contrast between the way French and Spanish subjects process accentual information. Whereas accent is contrastive in Spanish (as evidenced by minimal pairs such as *bébe* versus *bebé*, meaning "baby" and "drink!", respectively), it consistently falls on the last syllable of words in French. In an ABX task, in which subjects had to judge whether the last of three nonsense words (pronounced

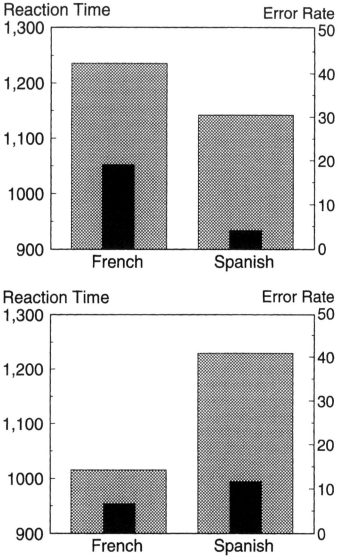

FIG. 17.1 Reaction times (hatched) and error rates (solid) to ABX judgments in French and Spanish subjects. Top panel: ABX on accent only, phonemes fixed (e.g. VAsuma, vaSUma, VAsuma; correct response: first item). Bottom panel: ABX on phonemes only, accent varied orthogonally (e.g. VAsuma, faSUma, vaSUma; correct response: first item). From "A distressing deafness in French", by E. Dupoux et al., 1997, *Journal of Memory and Language*. Copyright 1997 by Academic Press. Adapted with permission.

by native speakers of Dutch) sounded more like the first or the second item heard, Spanish subjects were shown to be fast and accurate when processing stress contrasts (see Fig. 17.1, top panel), but were unable to ignore stress information when it was irrelevant and they had to pay attention to phoneme information only (see Fig. 17.1, bottom panel). In contrast, French subjects experienced considerable difficulty with the stress contrast (see Fig. 17.1, top panel), whereas it was very easy for them to ignore irrelevant stress information (see Fig. 17.1, bottom panel).

Another example of foreign listening can be observed when speakers of Japanese have to process items with consonant clusters (Dupoux et al., submitted). Japanese is a language that does not allow for these clusters (with the exception of VNCV, where the N is a subsyllabic mora). When confronted with a cluster in an imported word, speakers of Japanese report hearing an epenthetic vowel between the consonants. Dupoux et al. (submitted) found that they are not able to distinguish between the nonwords *ebzo* and *ebuzo* in an ABX task: To them, both nonwords are homophonous (see Fig. 17.2). In contrast, they can easily process a vowel-length contrast (*ebuzo* vs. *ebuuzo*), which is linguistically relevant in Japanese. French subjects show exactly the reverse pattern, because consonant clusters are accepted in French but vowel length is not linguistically relevant.

Accent deafness in French and epenthetic vowel insertion in Japanese are both examples of the foreign listening syndrome, a phenomenon equivalent to the well-attested foreign accent observed in speech production. These facts reflect the large extent to which one recodes inputs (and outputs) in order to render them compatible with the structures one has acquired when learning a first language. Indeed, one is tempted to claim that the French do not compute stress at all (they would instead automatically attribute it to the last syllable of any perceived string). Likewise, the native speakers of Japanese will arrange inputs to fit into the CVCV grid that their knowledge of Japanese has led them to take for granted.

There are many other studies that illustrate the foreign listening syndrome. However, our purpose here is not exhaustivity. So, let us accept the conjecture that when one learns a language in infancy, one tends, later on, to use that knowledge to process any string of speech, even if it is in a foreign language. If an item has a badly formed sound structure, one will encode the signal in the way that is nearest to that in one's native language. But what about people who learn more than one language during early childhood? Will bilinguals be able to perform in both of their languages like monolinguals in either language? Will they strike a compromise that places them half way between the two languages? Or will they always be more proficient in one of the languages and try to find ways of coping with their second language in the most efficient way, given that their first and dominant language is there?

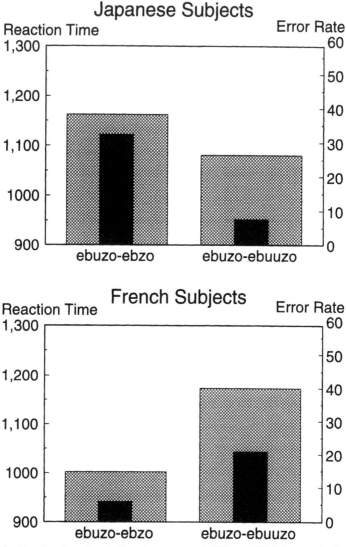

FIG. 17.2   Reaction times (hatched) and error rates (solid) to ABX judgments in French and Japanese subjects on a vowel-length contrast and on an epenthesis contrast. Data from *Epenthetic vowels in Japanese: A perceptual illusion*, by E. Dupoux et al., submitted. Copyright 1997 by E. Dupoux et al. Adapted with permission.

Cutler, Mehler, Norris, and Segui (1989) have reported that even highly proficient French-English bilinguals who learned both languages before the age of four behave as if they had a first language that dominates their second language (even though it is not very easy to determine solely from the subject's history of exposure to both languages which is first and which second).

Likewise, Weber-Fox and Neville (1996) have shown that adult Chinese-English bilinguals exposed to English (their second language) for the first time at between one and three years after their first exposure to Chinese (their first language) displayed some impairment in English because of the time lag (this was especially true of their syntactic processing). This state of affairs obtained despite the fact that these people had lived in the United States from the age of three and had spoken English from then on. Nevertheless, they still were less proficient in their second language than monolingual speakers of English. Another study that shows a similar pattern of results was carried out by Pallier, Bosch, and Sebastian-Gallès (in press) who found that vowel processing differed in bilingual speakers of Spanish and Catalan depending on whether Spanish or Catalan was their dominant language. Their subjects had lived all their lives in Catalunya, in a very bilingual community. Only people who had a clearly established family language (i.e. both parents spoke Catalan, or both spoke Spanish) participated in this study: The family language was therefore their dominant language. Their schooling and daily life were well balanced between the two languages. None the less, their perception of vowels depended clearly on the language first heard in the crib.

These results illustrate a lack of functional plasticity, even for very low-level perceptual capacities, that contrasts with the evidence reported earlier suggesting that the brain has considerable plasticity. What do these contrasting results tell us about language learning and brain plasticity? This is what we wish to examine in the remainder of this paper. We will start by reviewing results about how babies start acquiring the specific properties of their native language during the first year of life. Then we will consider how the baby can cope with more than one language. We will conclude with an examination of the way in which the cortical areas of the brain are organized in monolingual and bilingual people.

THE INFANT'S FIRST ADAPTATIONS TO LANGUAGE

At first, babies cannot know whether the speech they hear represents the output of several speakers, all of whom are speaking one and the same language, or the output of several speakers using different languages, or of one speaker who is switching from one language to another. Babies, none the less, adapt quite rapidly to the relevant properties of the parental language and, so far, nobody has been able to document delays in language acquisition when more than one language is being used in the surrounding environment. A consequence of this is that babies must have a way of distinguishing between languages in the course of acquisition: Otherwise, they would attempt to figure out regularities from a set of sentences coming from more than one language, and would get hopelessly confused.

In the last 10 years or so, a number of studies have clarified this important question. Bahrick and Pickens (1988) have shown that four-month-old infants respond to a change in the language of a sentence more than to a change of sentence without a change of language. Mehler et al. (1988) have observed that four-day-old French infants could discriminate between Russian and French sentences. These infants could also discriminate between Italian and English sentences (i.e. two languages foreign to them). Two-month-olds, unlike newborns, react to a change in language only when their mother tongue is contrasted with a foreign language, but not when two foreign languages are compared. This result suggests that by the time infants are two months old they have already extracted some of the defining properties of their first language, and that from that time on they are interested solely in exploring utterances that belong to their first language, and tend to ignore other utterances as not relevant for them. In that case, they would group all foreign languages into one category, "foreign", regardless of whether they can actually perceive differences between them or not. Much more research will be needed before we can adopt this interpretation. It does none the less seem reasonable to conjecture that by the age of two months, infants have already extracted some of the properties that characterize their mother tongue relative to other languages. We also know that infants discriminate between languages on the basis of their melodic and rhythmic properties (their prosody), because the experiments mentioned replicate when one uses low-pass filtered speech, where segmental information is almost completely disrupted (Mehler et al., 1988; Nazzi, Bertoncini, & Mehler, in press).

If infants rely mostly on prosodic information when discriminating between two languages, it seems likely that they cannot discriminate between any pair of languages. Indeed, it seems rather unlikely that sentences carry enough melodic information to allow for unambiguous identification of the language from which they are drawn. A more reasonable conjecture seems to be that infants sort sentences into classes of languages based on prosody. This conjecture seems to gain some credit from recent work by Nazzi et al. (in press), who have shown that infants tend to ignore changes if languages have similar rhythmic properties. Thus, French infants fail to discriminate filtered English sentences from filtered Dutch sentences (even though they are perfectly able to discriminate between English and Japanese filtered sentences in the same setting). Even more convincing that infants tend to group languages into rhythmic classes, is that infants have no difficulty discriminating between sets of sentences that are drawn from a mixture of languages, as long as all sentences from one set belong to the same rhythmic class, and there is a different rhythmic class for each set. Thus, French newborns react to a change from a mixture of Spanish and Italian sentences to a mixture of Dutch and English sentences (or vice versa). In contrast, they do not react to a change from, say, a mixture of Dutch and Italian sentences to a mixture of English and Spanish sentences (see Fig. 17.3).

To sum up, it appears that babies are born with a capacity to distinguish at least between some pairs of foreign languages, and they seem to do so on the basis of intonation. We suggest that for those languages that are not distinguishable

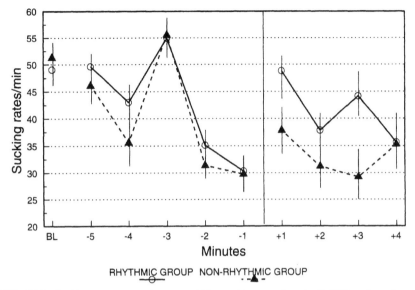

FIG. 17.3 Sucking rate averages in a nonnutritive sucking experiment with 32 French newborns, for the baseline period, 5 minutes before the change in stimulation, and 4 minutes after the change. The rhythmic group was switched from a mixture of sentences taken from two stress-timed languages (Dutch and English) to a mixture of sentences from two syllable-timed languages (Spanish and Italian), or vice versa. The nonrhythmic group also changed languages, but in each phase of the experiment there were sentences from one stress-timed and one syllable-timed language (e.g. Spanish and English, then Italian and Dutch). Infants from the rhythmic group reacted significantly more to the change of stimulation than infants from the non-rhythmic group. From "Language discrimination by newborns: Towards an understanding of the role of rhythm", by T. Nazzi et al., in press, *Journal of Experimental Psychology: Human Perception and Performance*. Copyright 1997 by the American Psychological Association. Reprinted with permission.

on the basis of intonation alone, the very first stages of language acquisition are similar, and that therefore bilingual babies would not suffer from the confusion (Mehler, Dupoux, Nazzi, & Dehaene-Lambertz, 1996). However, what is really needed is direct research on bilingual babies who are exposed to languages that are more or less distinct phonologically. In the next section, we will review some research in which brain-imaging techniques have been used to investigate the end result of the acquisition process in bilingual subjects. How are two different languages processed by the same brain?

BRAIN IMAGING AND SPEECH COMPREHENSION

The cortical representation of language is one of the standard fields explored by traditional neuropsychology through the study of clinical patients who have lost language or parts of it following trauma. Much has been discovered, but it is only in the more recent decades that methods of brain imaging have made it possible to complement such findings by exploring the organization of the cortex in healthy volunteers. Brain-imaging studies were first carried out by using either the printed word or very elementary sounds as stimuli. In our group, we have focused on a more naturalistic system, namely, the speech comprehension system. Most of our studies consist of having subjects listen to spoken sentences that make up a story.

In a first set of studies, Mazoyer et al. (1993) explored how the subjects' brain is activated when they listen to simple stories. This was compared to a control condition where the subjects were exposed to silence. The stories were either in French, the first language of all subjects, or in Tamil, a language that none of the subjects could understand. It was found that when subjects paid attention to the foreign language, the only parts of the cortex that showed a consistent increase in activity were the superior temporal gyrii, without much asymmetry between the right and left hemispheres. In contrast, when subjects listened to French, increased activity was observed in a complex left-hemisphere network that included the superior and medial temporal gyrii, the temporal pole, a frontal cortex area that coincides with what can be called an extended Broca's area, and also a more frontal area, namely, Brodmann's area 8. In the right hemisphere, only the superior temporal gyrus and the temporal pole showed increased activity. It is hardly surprising that this observation coincides with what one might have expected after so many years of classical neuropsychology. Activity was observed in two unexpected areas, however, namely the temporal poles and Brodmann's area 8, and many of us found it surprising that the temporo-parieto-occipital region (often referred to as the carrefour) on the left was not observed while subjects were processing their first language.

This study tells us that the brain does not react in the same way to a story in the subjects' first language as to a story in a language unknown to them. Why is this? Is the observed network actively engaged in processing the first language because it is the subjects' mother tongue, or would this network also participate in the processing of any language that the subjects are capable of understanding?

Neuropsychology has found contrasting results concerning language representation in bilinguals. Paradis (1995) reports that aphasia can affect the first or the second language separately, in ways that seem to be consistent with the view that different languages are represented in different brain areas. Likewise, Albert and Obler (1978) have argued that the second language (L2) is represented more globally than the first language (L1) and that the right hemisphere plays a more important role in its representation. In contrast, using cortical stimulation, Ojemann and Whitaker (1978) have shown that L2 is more broadly represented in the left hemisphere than L1, but have not found much evidence for a right-hemispheric representation of L2, as suggested by Albert and Obler (1978). Recently, Breier et al. (1996) have reported on a single patient tested using the Wada procedure. This patient's L1 was Spanish but he had become equally familiar with English, his L2, a language he claimed he spoke more often. The patient spontaneously counted and named in English. However, following a barbiturate injection into the right carotid, he switched to Spanish. In contrast, after the barbiturate was injected into the left carotid, he was unable to name in either language. Moreover, as the effect of the barbiturate tapered off, both languages were recuperated conjointly. The results from this case study suggest that L1 may be exclusively represented in the left hemisphere, whereas L2 tends to be distributed more broadly over both hemispheres. This hypothesis is consistent with the observations reported by Albert and Obler (1978). Note, however, that it is difficult to decide definitely on this issue on the basis of a single patient. Too many parameters can change from one patient to another and we have no evidence that observations will generalize to the population of bilinguals at large. The database can be expanded, however, using brain-imaging on populations of controlled bilinguals. We collaborated with colleagues in Milan, Italy, who had similar interests and were working on brain imaging. Most of the studies reported as follows have stemmed from this collaboration.

Perani et al. (1996) used the PET scan to study Italian volunteers who also spoke English, a language they had acquired after the age of seven (most of them after the age of 10) and which they spoke with low proficiency. These volunteers listened to stories in Italian, in English, and in Japanese (a language unfamiliar to all of them). Moreover, two control conditions were added, that is, one involving listening to stories in Japanese played backwards and one attentive silence condition. When subjects listened to the stories in Italian, Perani et al. (1996) observed a pattern of activity similar to that noted by Mazoyer et al. (1993) in French subjects listening to French stories.

This replication is welcome, given that the two studies used different languages, different stories, and different equipments, and it strengthens our conviction that the observed pattern of activity uncovers cortical areas that are involved in the representation and processing of L1. What about the network that is devoted to the processing of L2? The cortical areas that are significantly activated in response to L2 are rather modest when compared to the network that responds to L1. The main areas include the left and right superior and middle temporal gyrii. Thus, the activity respectively triggered by L1 and L2 is quite different. Interestingly, the activation in response to Japanese, a language that the subjects did not understand, was rather similar to that observed for English, which they understood. Figure 17.4 shows the activation patterns in all four conditions; the shaded areas correspond to areas where the activation is significantly more important for one condition of stimulation than for the other.

Perani et al. (1996) have reported that a large network of areas are significantly more active in response to L1 than to L2. Indeed, there was more activity in response to L1 in the temporal poles bilaterally, as well as in the left carrefour and also in the left inferior frontal gyrus. In contrast, no area was significantly more active in response to L2 than in response to a language unknown to the subjects. This result is paradoxical as the Italian volunteers were able to respond

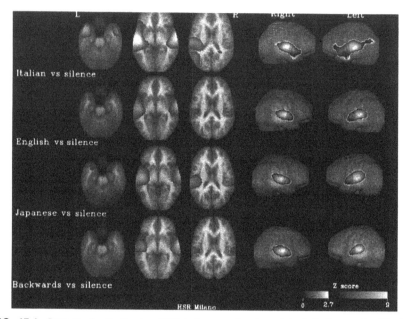

FIG. 17.4   Patterns of activation in a PET study measuring the activity in Italian speakers' brains while listening to Italian (mother tongue), English (second language), Japanese (unknown language), and backward Japanese (not a possible human language). There was a significant activation difference between Italian and English. In contrast, English and Japanese did not differ significantly. Japanese differed significantly from backward Japanese. From "Brain processing of native and foreign languages", by D. Perani et al., 1996, *Neuroreports*, 7, p. 2441. Copyright 1996 by Rapid Science Publishers. Reprinted with permission.

almost as correctly to the questions about the English stories as to those for the Italian stories. If brain-imaging were able to warrant interpretations like those a modern phrenologist would make, one would be tempted to claim that there are no specific areas where the L2 lexicon, syntax, and semantic representations are located. If so, where could our volunteers have looked up the English words, and computed the syntax and semantics of the sentences in order to understand the English stories? Or could it be that they had the atavistic faculty to process the Japanese stories without being aware of this faculty? Obviously none of these possibilities is attractive. We do believe that there are some attractive alternative possibilities to explain the observations Perani et al. (1996) have reported.

One hypothesis we found quite plausible to explain the pattern of results described earlier is that L1 is represented alike in all adults, whereas the representation of L2 varies considerably from person to person. Such a state of affairs might not be unexpected if one considers that all infants acquire their first language under very similar conditions, whereas there is great variation in the way in which L2 is learned. This could have given rise to the pattern of results found by Perani et al. (1996). Indeed, PET results deal only with patterns that arise in all the volunteers under one condition as compared to another. Until recently, methods of analysis made it difficult, even impossible, to evaluate individual results. Thus, Perani et al.'s results could have arisen if all subjects had the same pattern of activity when they were processing Italian but not when they were processing English. To evaluate such a conjecture, Dehaene, Dupoux, Mehler, van de Moortele, and le Bihan (in prep.) carried out an fMRI experiment to study cortical activity in eight native speakers of French. They presented each volunteer with passages of L1 alternating with passages of backward speech; they also presented passages in L2 in alternation with backward speech.

All subjects were low-proficiency speakers of English whose L2 performance was comparable to that of the Italians tested by Perani et al. (1996) The results, as hypothesized, show that whereas L1, by and large, activates the same areas in seven of the subjects, L2 activates cortical areas that differ for each subject. One subject showed a right-hemisphere activation when listening to L1. This is not entirely surprising if one bears in mind that roughly one person in ten has been found to have language localized in his or her right hemisphere (see Bryden, 1982).

These results are instructive because they help us understand the riddle of why previous investigations were unable to determine the cortical representation of L2 on the basis of the aphasiological data. The origin of this difficulty must be in the variability with which L2 is represented in low- or medium-proficiency bilinguals, that is, the most frequent types of bilinguals. Is it possible that in order for L2 to be represented by the same cortical structures as L1, a bilingual has to achieve a very high degree of proficiency? Or, maybe what is critical is the age at which a person masters L2. It is quite possible that if L2 is acquired before the putative critical period comes to a close, its cortical representation will look like that of L1. Certainly, age of acquisition and degree of proficiency are two of the parameters that could influence the way in which L2 is represented. Another one may be the distance between L1 and L2. We cannot at this time rule out the possibility that a bilingual speaker of Japanese and Spanish may have representations for L1 and L2 that are different from those of a bilingual speaker of Spanish and Italian, two close languages. In our own work, we are focusing on the role of proficiency and age of acquisition.

In a preliminary study we asked highly proficient Italian speakers of English who had all learned L2 after the age of ten to undergo a very similar experimental procedure as the one with the low-proficiency volunteers described earlier. Although L1 and L2 seemed to have less distinct representations in these subjects than among low-proficiency bilinguals, significant differences remained. In another study, we examined highly proficient Spanish-Catalan bilinguals who had acquired both languages before the age of four. Again, the representations for L1 and L2 seemed to differ, although conclusive statistical analyses are not yet available. In both of these experiments with proficient bilinguals, the area observed in response to L2 appeared more extended than that for L1 (although this remains to be statistically validated). This result suggests that although L1 and L2 may rely on a similar set of cortical structures, to process the latter the volunteers engage more resources even though their apparent linguistic skill is incredibly good and the two languages extremely close to one another. We see this result as illustrating the same point as the one recently made by Just, Carpenter, Keller, Eddy, and Thulborn (1996). On the basis of a study of the pattern of brain activation that is observed during sentence comprehension, these authors have claimed that the greater the sentence complexity, the more neural tissue will be recruited in areas that are contiguous to those present when processing simple sentences. They have used this result to caution students who argue in favor of a simplistic use of imagery to establish the cartography of the brain.

Our own view is that L1 relies on a definite network that is, by and large, located in the left hemisphere; additional languages acquired by people rely on structures that are associated with the network, as well as on adjacent structures and, in some cases, on areas located elsewhere. In brief, it appears that even if L1 and L2 are similar languages, like Spanish and Catalan, and even if the subjects have attained a high level of bilingual proficiency, one still sees differences in the pattern of activation between L1 and L2, although, it must be granted, these differences have become minor compared to the ones for the low-proficiency bilinguals reported earlier.

There are many supplementary studies that need to be pursued further. Indeed, age of acquisition has been examined but in a way that remains correlated with the distance between L1 and L2. We have not yet studied bilinguals for which L1 and L2 are very distant languages; neither have we studied volunteers who have become less proficient in their L1 than their L2. None the less, on the basis of the results reported so far, we can say that language ability seems to arise because nature has endowed us with structures located in the left hemisphere (a language organ) that are particularly apt to acquire the linguistic system that is used in our environment. Moreover, if more than one language exists in this environment, the language acquisition device remains capable of coping with the multiplicity of inputs. However, in most of the behavioral studies carried out recently, as well as in the brain-imaging studies reported earlier, we have always failed to find a complete identity of L1 and L2. It always looks as if there is an L1 that dominates L2. These results taken as a whole suggest a rather rigid acquisition schedule that does not display as much plasticity as one might expect when people acquire a second language.

ACKNOWLEDGEMENTS

The research was supported by a Human Frontiers Science Program (HFSP) grant entitled "Processing consequences of contrasting language phonologies" (1991–97); a Human Capital and Mobility (HCM) network contract (ERB CHR XCT 920 031); a French-Italian CNRS/CNR joint project grant (3200/1996); a post-doctoral fellowship from the Fyssen Foundation to C. Pallier; and a French-Spanish 1995 Picasso grant. We wish to thank all the members of the HFSP and HCM consortia, as well as Daniela Perani from the Istituto Di Neuroscienze e Bio-Immagini, Milan, for their major contribution to the experimental work reported here.

REFERENCES

Albert, M. L., & Obler, L. K. (1978). *The bilingual brain.* New York: Academic Press.

Bahrick, L. E., & Pickens, J. N. (1988). Classification of bimodal English and Spanish language passages by infants. *Infant Behavior and Development, 11,* 277–296.

Best, C. T., McRoberts, G. W., & Sithole, N. M. (1988). Examination of perceptual reorganization for nonnative speech contrasts: Zulu click discrimination by English-speaking adults and infants. *Journal of Experimental Psychology: Human Perception and Performance, 14,* 345–360.

Breier, J. I., Dede, D., Fiano, K., Fennell, E. B., Leach, L., Uthman, B., & Gilmore, R. (1996). Differential effects of right hemisphere injection during the wada procedure on the primary and secondary languages in a bilingual speaker. *Neurocase, 2,* 341–345.

Broca, P. (1861). Remarques sur le siège de la faculté du langage articulé suivie d'une observation d'aphémie. *Bulletin de la Société d'Anatomie, Paris, 6,* 330.

Bryden, M. P. (1982). *Laterality: Functional asymmetry in the intact brain.* New York: Academic Press.

Chomsky, N. (1975). *Reflexions on language.* New York: Pantheon.

Cutler, A., Mehler, J., Norris, D., & Segui, J. (1983). A language-specific comprehension strategy. *Nature, 304,* 159–160.

Cutler, A., Mehler, J., Norris, D., & Segui, J. (1989). Limits on bilingualism. *Nature, 320,* 229–230.

Dehaene, S., Dupoux, E., Mehler, J., van de Moortele, P.-F., & Bihan, D. L. (in prep.). Functional variability in the cortical representation of first and second languages.

Dupoux, E., Kakehi, K., Hirose, Y., Pallier, C., Fitneva, S., & Mehler, J. (submitted). Epenthetic vowels in Japanese: A perceptual illusion.

Dupoux, E., Pallier, C., Sebastian, N., & Mehler, J. (1997). A destressing "deafness" in French? *Journal of Memory and Language, 36,* 406–421.

Eimas, P. D., Siqueland, E. R., Jusczyk, P. W., & Vigorito, J. (1971). Speech perception in infants. *Science, 171,* 303–306.

Geschwind, N., & Levitsky, W. (1968). Human brain: Left-right asymmetries in temporal speech region. *Science, 161,* 186–187.

Hickok, G., Bellugi, U., & Klima, E. S. (1996). The neurobiology of sign language and its implications for the neural basis of language. *Nature, 381,* 699–702.

Just, M. A., Carpenter, P. A., Keller, T. A., Eddy, W. F., & Thulborn, K. R. (1996). Brain activation modulated by sentence comprehension. *Science, 274,* 114–116.

Kaas, J. H. (1991). Plasticity of sensory and motor maps in adult mammals. *Annual Review of Neuroscience, 14,* 137–167.

Kaas, J. H., Merzenich, M. M., & Killackey, H. P. (1983). The reorganization of somatosensory cortex following peripheral-nerve damage in adult and developing mammals. *Annual Review of Neuroscience, 6,* 325–356.

Knudsen, E. I., & Knudsen, P. F. (1986). The sensitive period for auditory localization in barn owls is limited by age, not by experience. *Journal of Neuroscience, 6,* 1918–1924.

Lenneberg, E. (1967). *Biological foundations of language*: New York: Wiley.

Mazoyer, B. M., Dehaene, S., Tzourio, N., Frak, V., Murayama, N., Cohen, L., Lévrier, O., Salamon, G., Syrota, A., & Mehler, J. (1993). The cortical representation of speech. *Journal of Cognitive Neuroscience, 5,* 467–479.

Mehler, J., Dommergues, J. Y., Frauenfelder, U., & Segui, J. (1981). The syllable's role in speech segmentation. *Journal of Verbal Learning and Verbal Behavior, 20,* 298–305.

Mehler, J., Dupoux, E., Nazzi, T., & Dehaene-Lambertz, G. (1996). Coping with linguistic diversity: The infant's viewpoint. In J. L. Morgan & K. Demuth (Eds.), *Signal to syntax: Bootstrapping from speech to grammar in early acquisition* (pp. 101–116). Mahwah, NJ: Lawrence Erlbaum Associates Inc.

Mehler, J., Jusczyk, P. W., Lambertz, G., Halsted, G., Bertoncini, J., & Amiel-Tison, C. (1988). A precursor of language acquisition in young infants. *Cognition, 29*, 143–178.

Nazzi, T., Bertoncini, J., & Mehler, J. (in press). Language discrimination by newborns: Towards an understanding of the role of rhythm. *Journal of Experimental Psychology: Human Perception and Performance.*

Ojemann, G. A., & Whitaker, H. A. (1978). The bilingual brain. *Archives of Neurology, 35*, 409–412.

Otake, T., Hatano, G., Cutler, A., & Mehler, J. (1993). Mora or syllable? Speech segmentation in Japanese. *Journal of Memory and Language, 32*, 258–278.

Pallier, C., Bosch, L., & Sebastián-Gallés, N. (in press). A limit on behavioral plasticity in vowel acquisition. *Cognition.*

Paradis, M. (1995). *Aspects of bilingual aphasia.* Oxford: Elsevier.

Perani, D., Dehaene, S., Grassi, F., Cohen, L., Cappa, S. F., Dupoux, E., Fazio, F., & Mehler, J. (1996). Brain processing of native and foreign languages. *Neuroreports, 7*, 2349–2444.

Rauschecker, J. P. (1995). Compensatory plasticity and sensory substitution in the cerebral cortex. *Trends in Neurosciences, 18*, 36–43.

Rauschecker, J. P., & Korte, M. (1993). Auditory compensation for early blindness in cat cerebral cortex. *Journal of Neuroscience, 13*, 4538–4548.

Sadato, N., Pascual-Leone, A., Grafman, J., Ibanez, V., Delber, M. P., Dold, G., & Hallett, M. (1996). Activation and the primary visual cortex by Braille reading in blind subjects. *Nature, 380*, 526–528.

Sebastián-Gallés, N., Dupoux, E., Segui, J., & Mehler, J. (1992). Contrasting syllabic effects in Catalan and Spanish. *Journal of Memory and Language, 31*, 18–32.

Sugita, Y. (1996). Global plasticity in adult visual cortex following reversal of visual input. *Nature, 380*, 523–526.

Tallal, P., Miller, S. L., Bedi, G., Byma, G., Wang, X., Nagarajan, S., Schreiner, C., Jenkins, W. M., & Merzenich, M. M. (1996). Language comprehension in language-learning impaired children improved with acoustically modified speech. *Science, 271*, 81–84.

Vroomen, J., & de Gelder, B. (1995). Metrical segmentation and lexical inhibition in spoken word recognition. *Journal of Experimental Psychology: Human Perception and Performance, 21*, 98–108.

Weber-Fox, C. M., & Neville, H. J. (1996). Maturational constraints on functional specializations for language processing: ERP and behavioral evidence in bilingual speakers. *Journal of Cognitive Neuroscience, 8*, 231–256.

Werker, J. F., & Tees, R. C. (1984). Cross-language speech perception: Evidence for perceptual reorganization during the first year of life. *Infant Behavior and Development, 7*, 49–63.

CHAPTER EIGHTEEN

Comprehension activity in individuals and groups

Giyoo Hatano
Keio University, Tokyo, Japan

Comprehension activity, whether individual or collective, includes proposing a possible interpretation, offering evidence for or against the interpretation, deriving a prediction from the interpretation, testing the prediction, evaluating the tested result, proposing another interpretation, etc. I claim that comprehension activity is a high-cost, high-benefit cognitive process, and thus understanding through comprehension activity is in contrast to understanding by schema application, which is almost automatic and needs almost no mental effort. I also claim that understanding through comprehension activity is often more enhanced in groups than in individuals, because seeking a plausible explanation originates in dialogue and is individualized as comprehension activity later. I present some theoretical arguments and empirical findings for these claims, using tasks of interpreting a simple but unusual recipe and of reconstructing a complex but ordinary recipe. I emphasize that the deep understanding achieved by comprehension activity is what best prepares us for the unknown world of the future.

Individuelle ou collective, l'activité de compréhension comporte les étapes suivantes: proposer une interprétation, trouver des éléments de preuve l'appuyant ou l'infirmant, déduire une prédiction de cette interprétation, mettre la prédiction à l'épreuve, évaluer le résultat obtenu, proposer une autre interprétation, et ainsi de suite. L'idée selon laquelle l'activité de compréhension constitue un processus cognitif dont le coût et les bénéfices sont élevés est mise de l'avant, d'où une distinction nette entre l'intelligence d'un problème permise par cette activité et celle qui, résultant de l'applications de schémas, est presque automatique et ne requiert que peu d'effort mental. Est également avancée l'idée selon laquelle l'intelligence d'une question découlant de l'activité de compréhension est souvent plus riche au sein des groupes que chez les individus parce que la recherche d'une explication plausible prend naissance dans le dialogue et ne s'individualise qu'ensuite en activité de compréhension. Des arguments théoriques et des résultats empiriques à l'appui de cette position sont présentés: ces informations proviennent de tâches où une recette simple mais inhabituelle doit être interprétée et où une recette complexe mais usuelle doit être reconstruite. L'insistance est mise sur la suggestion que la profondeur de l'intelligence d'une question atteinte par l'activité de compréhension assure la meilleure préparation possible pour le monde inconnu de demain.

Comprehension activity, I believe, plays a very important role in human cognition, and although the topic has not been completely neglected (see, for example, Bransford & McCarrell, 1975; Collins, Brown, & Larkin, 1980; Dunbar, 1995; Karmiloff-Smith & Inhelder, 1974/5; Klahr & Dunbar, 1988; Miyake, 1986; Stein & Trabasso, 1985), it has not received the intensive investigation it deserves. I would like to emphasize that comprehension activity is a good topic for research by showing that it occurs (and thus can be studied) in everyday cognition as well as in scientific inquiry.

The chapter consists of five sections. First, I propose a distinction between understanding through comprehension activity and understanding by schema application. Second, I will give hypothetical examples of comprehension activity as applied to two recipes. Third, I will discuss experimental studies on individual comprehension activity, and fourth, comprehension activity pursued by pairs of subjects. Finally, I will give a brief conclusion, emphasizing once again the significance of comprehension activity in human cognition.

TWO CLASSES OF UNDERSTANDING

Understanding or comprehension (to be used interchangeably here) can generally be defined as adopting a more or less coherent interpretation with some confidence (Hatano & Inagaki, 1987). It thus may mean to find subjectively satisfactory and intersubjectively plausible explanations for a set of observations, e.g. why a given rule is valid or how a procedure works. Using Piaget's (1978) terminology, it is the solution to the problem of "the 'how' and 'why' of the connections observed and applied in action". We assume that this kind of understanding is usually based on a complex and time-consuming process we call comprehension activity. The term "understanding" can also mean to determine what a unit of observation (e.g. a sentence or an action) means, because this process also fits with the definition of understanding given earlier. We assume this latter process is completed fairly quickly by applying one of the available schemas, not through comprehension activity.

Both understanding through comprehension activity and understanding by schema application serve to make a best guess about what the external world is like, based on observation(s), and thus constitute the core of the function of central systems (Fodor, 1983). In other words, the process of achieving understanding is to solve an ill-posed problem, that is, to find a "reasonable" solution to a problem for which only an incomplete set of information is given, using a variety of constraints. In the case of understanding by schema application, the most salient piece of prior knowledge (i.e. schema) serves as the major constraint. In contrast, in the case of understanding through comprehension activity, interpretations of many related observations can be used as mutual constraints, as in solving a crossword puzzle.

Both kinds of understanding enable us to build enriched, stable, coherent, and usable representations of the world. They often serve as the basis for solving problems, that is, for changing the world as one desires. However, these two kinds of understanding have different features, too. Understanding by schema application, as in understanding a sentence in discourse, is achieved very quickly, and usually offers only one interpretation, which is held until it has proved to be untenable. As elegantly demonstrated by Sperber and Wilson (1986), if someone presents a questioner with a bottle of cold medicine when asked how she is today, her behavior can readily be interpreted as meaning that she is suffering from a cold, although there are many other possible interpretations. In contrast, understanding through comprehension activity may offer multiple interpretations at one time, and requires their plausibility to be monitored carefully. Comprehension activity proceeds by deriving and testing predictions from each of the interpretations being considered, so it is necessarily a time- and effort-consuming process. Scientific inquiry is prototypical of this activity.

Let me present in a schematic fashion how comprehension activity operates (Fig. 18.1). It too involves the process of deriving an interpretation based on prior knowledge including schemas, but it has, in addition, a few characteristic features. First, a number of competing interpretations (or hypotheses) are offered and held simultaneously, and their tenabilities are carefully monitored, by the comprehender, as typically seen among experienced scientists (e.g. Dunbar, 1995). In other words, in comprehension activity it is supposed that the first interpretation coming to mind does not suppress other possible interpretations. Second, the selection of interpretations to be considered is constrained by their consistency with other interpretations and conceptual requirements (e.g. Collins et al., 1980). This is because the goal of comprehension activity is to achieve a coherent set of interpretations that is like a theory. Third, comprehension activity includes active tests of predictions derived from those interpretations. Even a child may engage in such a hypothesis-testing attempt (e.g. Karmiloff-Smith & Inhelder, 1974/5). Fourth and finally, comprehension activity may rely on interpretation-generation heuristics, like modifying a parameter and observing what occurs, when the comprehender does not readily think of interpretations of a given set of observations.

It is my opinion that comprehension activity is a high-cost, high-benefit cognitive process, in contrast to schema application, which is almost automatic and requires very little mental effort. I also like to maintain that understanding through comprehension activity is often more enhanced in groups than in individuals, because, I assume, coordinating various interpretations originates in dialogue and is individualized as comprehension activity only later. In contrast, understanding by schema application is usually not facilitated through social interaction, though the schemas individuals possess usually have a sociocultural origin.

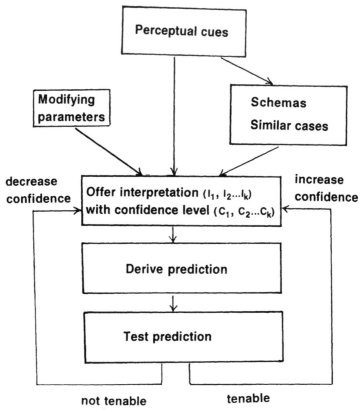

FIG. 18.1   A schematic representation of how comprehension activity operates.

It should be noted that the distinction between these two kinds or classes of understanding is of a conceptual nature. In actuality, there can be many intermediate forms: There is a continuum of types of comprehension, with these two classes of understanding at the extremes. Moreover, understanding by schema application may lead to comprehension activity, for instance, when the initial interpretation obtained by applying the most salient schema clearly contradicts other pieces of information. However, I believe the proposed distinction is useful. Let me discuss four implications of this distinction.

First, the distinction allows us to reconcile two conflicting views of the human tendency to understand. Some cognitive researchers claim that making sense of what they observe is a basic human tendency and that human beings seek understanding that may not be required to solve a given set of problems. In contrast, others assert that understanding is a kind of intellectual luxury and that people often lack comprehension even when they can solve problems. This distinction indicates that humans are prone to understand by schema application, and that they are very good at it, although they are not willing to engage in comprehension activity unless its benefit is obviously greater than its cost. The current view in cognitive psychology that human beings seek pieces of information and try to organize them does not mean that they are always involved in comprehension activity. They may engage in the activity without aversive stimulation or potential danger to their survival, but not always.

Second, the distinction between high-cost and low-cost understanding helps us explain why deep understanding is achieved selectively, and only when strong motivation is operating. Understanding by schema application is achieved automatically, and thus no motivation is involved. However, high-cost comprehension activity is induced highly selectively, not because humans are lazy, but because the activity requires so much time and effort.

This selectivity seems to operate in recognizing the inadequacy of one's comprehension as well as in deciding to pursue more adequate comprehension. Research on metacomprehension has revealed that not only children (Markman, 1977) but also college students (Glenberg, Wilkinson, & Epstein, 1982) tend to have the "illusion of comprehension". College students often believe that they understand a given text, though in fact they do not, at least as assessed by a multiple-choice test. It is probably a general tendency among human beings to fail to recognize their understanding to be inadequate. In a sense, people are guarded by the illusion of comprehension from engaging in prolonged comprehension activity too often, or in too many diverse domains. People promptly recognize their inadequacy of understanding and are willing to engage in comprehension activity only in their own "domains of interest" or "domains of expertise", in which they possess extensive prior knowledge that serves as the basis of understanding, and people also believe in their ability to understand and in the value of understanding in those domains (Hatano & Inagaki, 1987).

Third, this distinction enables us to conceptualize better the relationships between understanding and solving problems. Although correct solutions may reflect understanding, the distinction between being able to solve problems competently using a certain procedure and understanding the procedure has been emphasized, especially in mathematics and science education (e.g. Davis, 1984). It is true that we can solve a great number of mathematical problems using the target procedure at the right time, without understanding why the procedure works. Very few of us, in fact, can explain why a given mathematical procedure works, though we all believe that it is valid and can apply it efficiently. This is similar to the fact that, as will be seen, we can make a nice dish promptly just by following the recipe, without understanding why particular steps in the recipe are needed. Lack of deep understanding becomes a serious deficit only when unusual, novel problems are posed.

However, this does not mean we memorize and apply a procedure in a rote fashion. We often learn and use it meaningfully, but our understanding as achieved by schema application is not deep enough to allow us to use the procedure flexibly in novel situations. Students are sensitive to semantic aspects of problems even when they seem to solve them in an algorithmic way.

Fourth and finally, the distinction between the two kinds of understanding makes us appreciate the cost-benefit correspondence in understanding, more specifically, the high-benefit nature of high-cost understanding through comprehension activity. Prolonged comprehension activity often leads to a plausible, if not the exactly correct, explanation. Achieved understanding may vary, because understanding means to find "subjectively satisfactory" as well as "intersubjectively plausible" explanations, which may differ from individual to individual. However, comprehension activity usually leads to plausible and deep understanding, because humans engaging in comprehension activity check carefully whether generated inferences are harmonious with the given set of information, thus eliminating erroneous explanations that come to mind initially, as will be seen later. Speaking generally, knowing why a given procedure is effective is very different from just knowing that it has been effective. Based on deep understanding, we can modify the known procedure in an adaptive, flexible way.

HYPOTHETICAL EXAMPLES OF COMPREHENSION ACTIVITY

In the remainder of the chapter, I will focus on the understanding of a recipe, as representative of the comprehension of procedures (in terms of changes they produce in the target objects). I have intentionally chosen examples from the domain of cooking, because I want to give wide scope to the term by stressing that comprehension activity may occur in our everyday life as well as in academic pursuit. We may sometimes wonder why a given recipe works so well and engage in a recipe interpretation task. We may also wonder how a given dish has been cooked and become involved in a recipe reconstruction task. Both tasks require understanding a recipe as a sequence of steps in cooking in functional terms.

Let me present two hypothetical examples of comprehension activity directed to recipes, that is, to interpret the recipe indicating how to make *sashimi* of a bonito, and to reconstruct a recipe for the dish known as mousse of perch, to make clear what comprehension activity is like. The former recipe to be interpreted is relatively simple but somewhat unusual, whereas the latter recipe to be reconstructed is a bit complex but more or less ordinary. Both tasks of recipe interpretation and recipe reconstruction may induce an enduring comprehension activity.

The first example concerns the comprehension of a recipe, or more generally, the understanding of why steps in a given procedure are necessary for the final product. The target recipe, starting with a large cut of a bonito, requires us: to roast the skin-covered surface quickly at a high temperature; to put the roasted side into ice-water, and cool it for five minutes; to take it out of the water, and wipe it off; and finally, to cut it into slices 1cm thick. These slices are ready to eat with soy sauce and seasonings (from *Fish and vegetable cooking*, NHK publishers, 1984). The product is unusual for *sashimi* because it is not just sliced raw fish; thus people may wonder why such a recipe is required.

You can follow the recipe without truly comprehending what you are doing and get delicious bonito *sashimi*. However, suppose that you are interested in such questions as why this recipe works or why these steps are necessary, and thus engage in comprehension activity. If you can generate some interpretations relying on your prior knowledge, you might test them. If you cannot, you have to proceed relying on interpretation-generation heuristics; for example, running the procedure with one or more critical steps removed or modified. For example, you might examine how the *sashimi* tastes without roasting, or when roasted at lower temperatures. You will soon find that without roasting, the skin of the *sashimi* is too tough to swallow, even after it has been chewed for a couple of minutes. You will also learn that roasting "quickly at a high temperature" is critical, because otherwise you have well-done bonito steak, instead of *sashimi*. From this experience, you can make an interpretation as to the next step: ice-water is needed to cool the roasted fish very quickly. You can confirm this inference by putting the bonito in water without ice or in a refrigerator. If you have some mental models of the relevant materials and tools, you can run a mental simulation instead of doing the actual experiments.

You may be tempted to go on. You could run more experiments with varying parameters; consult cookbooks or books on ichthyology; ask questions of your family or friends; relate the set of observed facts to similar experiences, for instance, making *sashimi* of other fish (for example, you may note that when *sashimi* is to be served with the skin on, that side is always heated somehow). Because you already know the recipe by which you can make the desired dish, it seems useless to understand why it works. However, understanding is very important for a flexible use of the recipe. Under special conditions, we might omit some step of it. We might think of a good substitute step if the prescribed one could not be executed. In short, if you comprehend the recipe, you can modify it flexibly when you have to meet a different set of constraints, for instance, when you have no ice or no source of searing heat. To achieve comprehension, you have to engage in prolonged comprehension activity, spending much time and effort. It is almost always true that comprehension activity takes time, but this is an investment in an unknown future.

The second example concerns a more challenging task of comprehension, more specifically, understanding how to reconstruct the recipe for a particular dish by analyzing its product. Suppose that you do not know much about French cooking. You are given a piece of "mousse of perch" (MOP), which is rather unfamiliar to you, being told only that this is a kind of hors d'oeuvre, and asked to infer how to make it. What kind of comprehension activity can be induced?

-- Put perch slices and egg white into
a blender and blend until smooth

-- Transfer the mixture into a bowl
and cool it in a refrigerator

-- Add fresh cream to the mixture
while cooling the bowl in ice-water

-- Add salt and pepper; taste and
adjust seasoning; pour into a pan

-- Put the pan into a platter with
boiling water and steam it in an oven

FIG. 18.2   A simplified version of the standard recipe for mousse of perch.

Unlike in the first example, the recipe or cooking procedure is not given but has to be reconstructed, as shown in Fig. 18.2. This reconstruction process is a kind of abduction, but a complete recipe cannot be reconstructed at once. The recipe is reconstructed little by little by coordinating likely constituent steps. In a sense this task is very similar to Miyake's (1986) task of finding how a sewing machine can make stitches.

You can certainly guess some of the MOP ingredients from its taste as well as appearance, particularly in this case, its color of plain white. A kind of white meat fish and milk, cream or another dairy product with salt, pepper, and other seasonings. However, how can you make MOP from these materials? Among others, you have to find how to make fish meat and milk or cream into a smooth mixture, and how to set this mixture for mousse. Suppose two ideas come to your mind regarding the first problem: mincing the fish using a meat grinder, and putting the fish into a blender or food processor. Suppose you know two solutions to the second problem: cooling the mixture after adding gelatin and baking or steaming the mixture in an oven after adding egg white or starch. Now the task of reconstructing the recipe is transformed into a set of subtasks of choosing one each from two or more possible alternatives, so that the chosen alternatives can constitute a runnable sequence.

Even when your knowledge of French cooking is limited, you may know about Japanese cooking, e.g. that *tofu* (bean curd) is made by boiling soy bean puree, and *kamaboko* (boiled fish paste) is made by boiling or steaming fish puree with starch. These products may be recalled easily because of their surface similarity to MOP. Therefore you can test your ideas by examining similarities and differences between MOP and these products. Analogies are often very useful in everyday cognition as well as in scientific reasoning (Dunbar, 1995).

As in the case of comprehending the bonito *sashimi* recipe, it is very unlikely that the correct recipe can be reconstructed from just one slice of MOP, without actually trying various procedures. However, through the initial comprehension activity, we can offer several recipes that might possibly work, which can be examined in the continued comprehension activity.

EXPERIMENTAL STUDIES ON COMPREHENSION ACTIVITY

I present the results of our experiments using these two tasks of recipe comprehension, with college students as subjects. The experiments were conducted in collaboration with Yoko Oura (Niigata University), Aya Sugimura (Keio University), and Kayoko Inagaki (Chiba University). I will discuss whether comprehension activity occurred in these tasks, and how it proceeded and terminated when it did. The students were given one of these tasks either individually or in pairs; the results from individual comprehension activity will be considered first.

Experimental findings on recipe interpretation

Twenty college students were subjects for the individual experiment with the recipe for bonito *sashimi*. They were presented with the recipe, and told that we could make tasty bonito *sashimi* if we followed it. Then they were asked to find out why this recipe worked, in other words, why each step of it was needed. Initially in the pilot experiment we allowed students to ask questions about how the bonito would be affected by using a modified cooking procedure, if they thought it necessary for their understanding. We expected to have questions, such as: If we do not roast the bonito, are people more likely to have diarrhea after eating the *sashimi*? However, because we had almost no questions, we eliminated this opportunity in the main experiment. This lack of questions was probably because the students were simply concentrating on the given recipe.

Most of them said they understood in several minutes. When they did, they were given the following three questions:

1. Is it necessary for us to roast bonito if it is very fresh and is not fishy at all?
2. Can we roast it at low temperatures, taking a longer time, if no strong heat source is available?
3. Can we cool it in a refrigerator after roasting if we have no ice-water?

After answering these questions, the students were asked how they had come to their conclusions.

Three results are important for our discussion (Sugimura, Hatano, & Inagaki, in prep.). First, a large majority of the students answered that we could not modify the original recipe: We could not skip the step of roasting even when the bonito was very fresh, we could not use low temperatures instead of high ones, nor could we cool the fish in a refrigerator instead of using ice-water. This might not be surprising because the original recipe had been given to them as the legitimate one. Some of the students indicated that, although they did not know why, there must be some benefit for roasting the fish at high temperatures quickly, because it was prescribed by the recipe. Second, a few different reasons were offered for their answers to each question. For roasting, for example, better flavor or removal of fishiness was the dominant reason given, but killing bacteria on the bonito was also often referred to. Very few pointed out that the skin of the bonito would be too tough to eat without roasting. Regarding the use of high temperatures, many claimed that roasting slowly might make the bonito less tasty. Third, a small number of the subjects in the pilot experiment who answered that modifying the original recipe would be all right referred to putting the bonito in a freezer, not in a refrigerator. This seemed to reveal their correct functional understanding of the use of ice-water, that is, to cool something very quickly. However, their prediction based on this correct understanding was wrong.

We must conclude that a majority of the students segmented the given recipe into units, and understood each unit by schema application. There was little evidence that they engaged in comprehension activity. This was probably because they thought that comprehension activity, including interpretation- or hypothesis-testing, would take too much effort. From their perspective, it was obvious that roasting was for sterilization and the use of ice-water was for cooling the material down rapidly (correct in this case). There was no reason for them to doubt their initial interpretation.

Our subjects often found the recipe unusual or unexpected. However, this alone failed to induce the specific dissatisfaction that Berlyne (1965) called epistemic curiosity. At least, it was not strong enough to induce comprehension activity.

We asked some of our subjects after they answered the questions about the recipe whether they were confident that they understood the meaning of the steps constituting the recipe. We also asked what else they wanted to know to test their interpretations (whether their answers would be tenable or not). They almost unanimously replied to the first question that they were confident, despite their general modesty. The second question embarrassed them—they had no idea how to examine their interpretations further.

Needless to say, there were several different interpretations, all of which were tenable with the given set of information, in this experimental task. It should be pointed out that in this experimental situation, which did not allow the students to test an interpretation, revising the initial interpretation was hard. However, even when testing, by asking relevant questions, was suggested in the pilot experiment, the students offered almost no competing ideas.

Experimental findings on recipe reconstruction

Twenty female college students participated in this experiment (Oura & Hatano, 1997). Each of the students was given a regular-size slice of the mousse of perch (or scallop, depending on the season), and asked, by tasting it, to guess how it had been made. They were told that this dish is often served as an hors d'oeuvre at a French dinner, but were not given the name of it. They were served wine and salad, and also sauce on the mousse, but their task was to infer what ingredients were in the mousse and how it had been cooked. They were encouraged to verbalize any ideas that came to mind, although not many of them could do so.

A great majority of the students engaged in comprehension activity, spending 5–18 minutes (mean was 10.0). They often proposed ideas that they eventually discarded. They often expressed their feeling of uncertainty (Japanese equivalents to "... well, let me see ...") or puzzlement ("it doesn't make sense"), as well as insight ("oh, I see", "that accounts for it!"). Let me present a few examples:

S12: ... fish is included, probably ... ground fish, what else? ... milk, oh, I see, put white meat fish and milk into a blender, then place it (the mixture) in a pan and cool ... well, it won't set even if it is cooled ... how was this one set? ...
S2: ... if fish is in it, we grind it, strain it, oh, meringue may be in it too, though I'm not sure. If it is included, the mixture will be set ... then put it in a pan and refrigerate.
S1: Fish, ground, kneaded, and congealed. What else is in it? It tastes like *kamaboko*. I do not know.

Most students started their comprehension activity by describing how the target looks or tastes—looks like *kamaboko*, tastes like crumbs dipped in milk, smells strong, looks like *kamaboko* but smells like cheese, must include white meat fish or chicken because it is white, and so on. They also offered possible ingredients but rejected them, based both on the flavor of the dish and on their knowledge of cooking. For example: "vegetables ..., but green vegetables cannot be in it, because it does not have color ... onions or other colorless vegetables may be included after being ground fine; *tofu* or something like that is in it ... it feels like *tofu* ... oh, it cannot be *tofu*, because it is a French dish".

In the comprehension activity, many of the students offered some solution to the two hard problems in the attempt to reconstruct the recipe, that is, how to make fish meat and milk or cream into a smooth mixture, and how to set this mixture for the mousse. Popular solutions to the first problem were to grind the fish in a mortar and to put it into a blender. As to the second problem, a slightly larger number of the students chose cooling the mixture (after adding gelatin) instead of baking or steaming the mixture in an oven after adding egg white or starch. This was probably because there was no discernible evidence that the mousse had been baked. However, a few students pointed out that gelatin could not be in it because it was rather soft and rough.

Another interesting finding was that many of the students relied on inference based on perceptual similarity across cooking domains. They often referred to *kamaboko*, *tofu*, and other Japanese food items. Sometimes they were misled, but in many more other cases, they were helped by this inference, which might be considered a type of analogy.

We scored the students' reconstructed recipe in terms of the following 5 components of the standard recipe: major ingredients (0-3), white meat fish, egg white, and fresh cream; critical steps in cooking (0-2), blend fish and steam the mixture. No student obtained the maximum 5 points, but some got 4, and the mean was 2.95 (SD = 1.07). When we used more lenient scoring criteria (e.g. accepting cooling or baking the mixture as a reasonable solution), the mean was even higher.

Needless to say, even the best-reconstructed recipe was far from perfect. The students' recipes were only qualitative. Furthermore, they were straightforward in their constituent steps. For example, the standard recipe requires us to blend the fish and egg whites, and then to add fresh cream at a low temperature, as shown in Fig. 18.2. No student suggested this order of mixing. The standard recipe was constructed by generations of cooks. It is not realistic to expect that comprehension activity for 15 minutes by a novice cook would be sufficient to reinvent such a recipe. It should also be pointed out that real testing is needed to choose among likely solutions. Therefore, an ideal experiment should allow such testing. I will refer to such an experiment, in which students are provided with materials and devices they think necessary to test their ideas, in the next section.

It is interesting to compare the results of these two experiments on cooking with those of recent experiments by Keiko Kuhara-Kojima and myself on the understanding of detective stories (Kuhara-Kojima & Hatano, 1996). Inspired by Collins, Brown, and Larkin (1980), we wanted to investigate comprehension activity during reading. However, we thought the materials used by Collins et al. were too impoverished and too unnatural as stories. We therefore chose shortened and edited detective stories, expecting that close examination of a variety of hypotheses based on the available set of evidence would be observed. However, contrary to our expectation, but consistent with the model of comprehension activity developed here, most subjects simply made sense of what they read, and did not examine their initial interpretations critically. Moreover, their hypothesis was often induced by applying schemas in the genre, for example, the hero and the heroine never get hurt, the most obvious suspect is never the offender, and so on. Enjoying detective stories is, like learning a given recipe meaningfully, more a schema application process than a comprehension activity.

INDIVIDUAL VERSUS COLLECTIVE
COMPREHENSION ACTIVITY

In this section, I examine whether the presence of a partner enhances comprehension activity, and if it does, when. Before presenting our experimental findings, I would like to summarize potential advantages of collective comprehension activity over the individual one. As indicated in Hatano and Inagaki (1991), I assume that there are both cognitive and social-motivational reasons why comprehension activity in groups tends to be more successful than the corresponding individual attempt. Cognitive reasons include the richer knowledge base of a group and the division of labor that can reduce the cognitive load for each member.

Because a group as a whole has a much richer database than any of its constituent members, it is possible for a group to solve problems that none of its members can solve alone. Similarly, a group can think of a more elaborate explanation than any of its members is likely to think of alone. However, for this to occur, pieces of information distributed among members have to be assembled and coordinated somehow; otherwise, it is unlikely for a group to succeed in achieving understanding. In the worst case, members inhibit the ideas that they might have developed individually, because of social considerations, such as seeking agreement, avoiding standing out, etc., as Levine and Moreland (1991) have indicated.

We assume that collective comprehension activity is often enhanced by the spontaneous division of labor, which enables the members to use their relatively weak knowledge and limited processing capacity effectively. First of all, the exploration of hypothesis space can be distributed among members. This is due to members' varied interests and attitudes toward the target and related entities. Moreover, as pointed out by Miyake (1986), members may take on different roles even when they are examining the same hypothesis: As one member becomes a task-doer, the other tends to become a monitor, in other words, to focus on evaluating a proposed solution rather than offering a solution. When there are three or more members, the entire cognitive enterprise is divided, based on social and motivational factors, between proponents, opponents, and a third party, as well as within each party. Their actual and potential criticisms as well as support and elaboration can make a difference. As shown by Dunbar (1995), interactions with those colleagues who have been less committed to the current hypothesis or interpretation help an investigator to cope aptly with the inconsistent evidence and change the hypothesis accordingly.

Socio-motivational reasons, too, may account for the productivity of collective comprehension activity, especially in everyday life. Peer interaction, or dialogical interaction in general, tends to amplify the cognitive motivation to understand. It invites members to "commit" themselves to some ideas, because they have to state those ideas to others, placing the issue in question in their domain of interest. Furthermore, the social setting makes the enterprise of comprehension more significant. This is especially true when there are different interpretations or hypotheses to which at least one member is committed. Collective comprehension activity is energized by partisan motivation or desire to help one's party win the argument (Hatano & Inagaki, 1991). This motivation serves as a basis for the effective division of labor in the pursuit of comprehension. It enables members to take partial charge of the hard task of collecting and evaluating arguments both for and against each of multiple alternatives. Unless extrinsic motivation (e.g. to win the argument) is so strong that it supersedes the motivation for comprehension, this social aspect will make comprehension activity more enduring.

Let me present our experimental findings. The college students' comprehension activity as individuals versus pairs was compared. As can be seen, the pairs were not necessarily more persistent in the activity or more productive.

Pairs on recipe interpretation

We tested 10 pairs of college students to examine whether they would reveal better comprehension than the students from the same university who were given the bonito *sashimi* task individually. To our surprise, we found that the dyads of female college students rarely spent more than 10 minutes when asked to comprehend jointly why a given series of steps was needed to make bonito *sashimi*.

The pairs agreed very quickly. A number of reasons can be offered for this. First, because both members achieved understanding by schema application, their initial ideas were more or less similar. For example, roasting was accepted as being for removing fishiness or for sterilization. As in the individual experiment, almost none of the students paid attention to the detail of the first step, that is, to roast *its skin-covered surface*. Similarly, using high temperatures was understood to be for roasting it quickly, and the use of ice-water was understood to be for cooling it down quickly. The meaning of these steps all seemed apparent to the students. Moreover, when each member of a pair proposed different reasons, the pair tended to accept both. For example, if A said roasting was for removing fishiness and B for sterilization, they would report to the experimenter that roasting was for removing fishiness and for sterilization. Because both reasons can readily be induced by applying the schema of roasting that includes its salient consequences, neither would object to the partner's reason. In other words, having different initial ideas does not necessarily mean that the members of the pair have to negotiate.

Second, almost no pair was willing to engage in time-consuming comprehension activity. Each student seemed to believe that, as in the individual experiment, though the recipe is somewhat unusual, it makes sense. Some students even guessed that, for unknown reasons, bonito might be more likely to have bacteria than other fish used for *sashimi*. When the step of roasting was justified in this way, it was very easy to justify the next step, because it would have the effect of canceling the effect of the preceding step. In other words, as in the individual experiment, this recipe generally failed to induce strong motivation for understanding among the college students.

Third, the students did not enjoy arguments. They did not seem to take this task as an opportunity to reveal their knowledge or ability, partly because the task of understanding a given recipe was apparently easy. They also wanted to behave politely, by agreeing to what the partner said. Japanese undergraduates usually do not think that to disagree is more fun than to agree. We observed an enduring joint comprehension activity in just a few pairs, with one member insisting that she had yet to figure out why this particular recipe was needed for this particular fish.

The students thought they understood, and that their understanding was shared. Only when asked whether the same procedure should be followed under slightly different conditions was the discrepancy in their interpretations uncovered.

It is interesting to compare the results of this experiment with those from the detective stories experiment involving pairs of subjects (Kuhara-Kojima & Hatano, 1997). Pairs of college students were asked to negotiate and give joint replies after they had given individual replies. For a story describing a series of murders in the latter experiment, college students chose a variety of characters as the suspect at several intermediate points of the story. Good detective stories must induce such distributed predictions. In this case, two ideas were incompatible. As a result, the students could not readily agree with their partners. However, because their understanding was generally by schema application, as mentioned earlier, they had few compelling arguments that they could use to persuade others. Even when they compromised to offer a joint idea at one point, they often returned to their earlier idea at the next point. In other words, they had great difficulty in sharing their understanding until the solution was revealed by the author.

Pairs on recipe reconstruction

Six pairs of female college students participated in this experiment, and we found a quite different picture from the pairs studied on the recipe interpretation task (Oura & Hatano, 1997). First, unlike the pairs trying to understand a given recipe, the paired students on the recipe reconstruction task spent an even longer time (mean, 14.3 minutes; range, 12–18 minutes) than in the corresponding individual experiment. Second, we obtained findings similar to Miyake (1986); that is, that even a less knowledgeable student could contribute to the joint comprehension by serving as a monitor. In other words, the pairs engaged in constructive interactions, producing understanding that would be hard for either member to produce independently. Let me present two examples.

P3A: What can we set it with?
B: Starch, or gelatin.
A: Gelatin? It would be more elastic if gelatin were added.
B: Oh, yeah, then what?

P4A: Can we make such a soft one just by blending?
B: Probably not. Raw eggs, no, egg white.
A: Egg white?
B: Egg white is in it, I am sure.

In the first example, A, while relying on B to get some specific idea, helped B recognize its inadequacy. In the second example, A, who did not know what it was, gave a cue to B to recall another essential ingredient.

Two variables seem critical in inducing different patterns of interaction in these two experimental tasks, pairs on recipe interpretation and reconstruction. First, college students' knowledge about cooking that is not very extensive is sufficient for schema-applicational interpretation for a given recipe, but not for reconstructing a recipe. Therefore, expanding the database by sharing knowledge was needed, and appreciated. This certainly led to a more lively and prolonged interaction between pairs in this experiment.

Second, when given a recipe, following it usually gives a solution. Thus finding the meaning of its constituent steps is in a sense an unnecessary supplement. Moreover, two different interpretations can often be compatible, because one step may have two or more functions. The different interpretations are conflicting only when they suggest different applications of a recipe to different conditions. In contrast, in reconstructing a recipe, any differences could be conflicting, for example, setting the puree by steaming and by cooling it in a refrigerator are not compatible. Thus, the students could not readily agree on different interpretations about the target.

However, this incompatibility sometimes embarrassed the pairs, because each participant had to choose either to agree with the partner to satisfy her or to stick to her original idea. In many cases, our students did not insist on their own idea when their partner hesitated to accept it. As a result, many good ideas, proposed in the middle of the interaction, were not incorporated into the final recipe they reconstructed. For example, the aforementioned second pair proposed only blended fish meat with seasoning as ingredients, though they talked about starch, gelatin, bread crumbs, and flour as possible thickening agents. They eventually dropped all these ideas because no hearty support of one's idea was obtained from the other. The pairs' average score, excluding an uninterested pair, was higher than that in the individual condition ($M = 3.50$, SD = 0.50), but it could have been much higher if the students had been able to coordinate pieces of information distributed between the pairs.

In sum, the dyadic attempt to reconstruct a recipe was enjoyable, but not always productive. The first part of this summary corroborates our earlier studies (Hatano & Inagaki, 1991; 1994) in that social motivation made collective comprehension activity lively, enduring, and cheerful. However, the last part of the summary is inconsistent with the earlier studies. This may be attributed to the fact that students were unable to test their ideas with real materials, nor did they expect to do so in this experiment.

We assert that, because comprehension activity includes seeking further external information, constructive group interaction usually includes seeking information from outside the group. People are not always ready to incorporate information offered by others. Unless the information is persuasive in terms of rationale, or given by someone known to be an authority, people, especially those forming the majority, will not assimilate the information until external feedback proves its plausibility. Miyake's study (1986) showed that empirical confirmation by inspection plays a significant role in facilitating joint comprehension of how a sewing machine makes stitches, even for academically sophisticated subjects.

Can we generalize our findings on comprehension activity by pairs to collective comprehension activity in a larger group? My answer is both Yes and No. I assume that seeking plausible explanations is initially implemented for persuading others, and is interiorized later as comprehension activity. Therefore, the presence of another person is critical for lasting comprehension activity to occur. Moreover, a dyad constitutes a group in the sense that division of labor is possible. However, as we have emphasized elsewhere, the presence of the third party is significant in collective comprehension activity (Hatano & Inagaki, 1991). Although two heads are better than one, Buddha's wisdom can be induced only when three persons collaborate, as a Japanese saying indicates.

Pairs who actually cooked

Six additional pairs of female college students were required to actually reproduce the dish of mousse of perch, after discussing its recipe as in the dyadic condition mentioned earlier (Oura & Hatano, 1997). At the time of cooking, each pair was given a slice of white fish, and all other materials and cooking devices its members wanted to have. In just a few cases the experimenter had to reply that the material or the device requested was not available, indicating that it was unnecessary for the mousse. After the actual attempt to cook, the pairs were asked what changes they would like to make if they had had another chance to cook.

In this dyadic with empirical testing condition, we observed a longer and more heated discussion between the members, probably because they took the attempt to reconstruct the recipe to be real and serious. The pairs' reconstruction score was higher than that in the dyadic condition without actual cooking

(M = 4.00, SD = 0.82 before the cooking; M = 4.50, SD = 0.50 after the cooking). Moreover, the dishes they produced tasted fairly good, even when their taste was not very close to the original mousse.

Interestingly, none of the pairs prescribed the recipe quantitatively before the actual cooking. However, there was almost no conflict within a pair on the amount of each ingredient. The amount of additional materials or seasonings was determined by watching, or even by tasting constituents being cooked. Only after the cooking could participants report quantitative aspects of the recipe (e.g. adding a half cup of cream). The empirical testing also allowed the dyads to eliminate clearly inappropriate ingredients (e.g. onion) or modify a step of cooking in the revised recipe. Its effect was marked both on informational and motivational aspects of the reconstruction process.

CONCLUSION AND IMPLICATIONS

So far I have claimed that comprehension activity is a high-cost, high-benefit cognitive process, and thus understanding through comprehension activity is in contrast to understanding by schema application, which is almost automatic and needs almost no mental effort. I have also claimed that understanding through comprehension activity is often more enhanced in groups than in individuals, because seeking a plausible explanation originates in dialogue and is individualized as comprehension activity later. In contrast, understanding by schema application is usually not facilitated by social interaction. I have presented some theoretical arguments and also some preliminary data that support these claims.

Although I am convinced both classes of understanding are essential for human cognition, my emphasis has been on understanding through comprehension activity. Even among a small number of studies on central systems, comprehension activity has attracted surprisingly little attention. Investigators of comprehension activity can never prosper in the potentially behavioristic intellectual atmosphere in North America. Because research on comprehension activity must include such mentalistic notions as "interpretation" and "plausibility", it is always vulnerable to behavioristic and empiricistic criticisms. To make matters worse, scientific inquiry, the prototype of comprehension activity, is now often unpopular because it is considered too restrictive.

I would like to emphasize that the deep understanding achieved by comprehension activity is what best prepares us for the unknown world of the future, and thus we need highly analytical modes of knowing, such as modern science, if we want to function as more or less rational beings. However, it is also important to note that comprehension activity occurs and can be studied in the everyday world.

Finally, education in science and mathematics might provide students with more opportunities to engage in comprehension activity, and researchers of cognition with more opportunities to study it in quasi-natural contexts. My hope is that psychology will contribute to improving the quality of education so that many more students can appreciate the significance of high-cost, high-benefit comprehension activity in domains in which the learners have not acquired expertise.

REFERENCES

Berlyne, D. E. (1965). Curiosity and education. In J. D. Krumboltz (Ed.), *Learning and the educational process* (pp. 67–89). Chicago: Rand McNally.

Bransford, J. D., & McCarrell, N. S. (1975). A sketch of a cognitive approach to comprehension: Some thoughts about understanding what it means to comprehend. In W. B. Weimar & D. S. Palermo (Eds.), *Cognition and the symbolic processes* (pp. 189–229). Hillsdale, NJ: Lawrence Erlbaum Associates Inc.

Collins, A., Brown, J. S., & Larkin, K. M. (1980). Inference in text understanding. In R. J. Spiro, B. C. Bruce, & W. F. Brewer (Eds.), *Theoretical issues in reading comprehension* (pp. 383–407). Hillsdale, NJ: Lawrence Erlbaum Associates Inc.

Davis, R. B. (1984). *Learning mathematics*. Norwood, NJ: Ablex.

Dunbar, K. (1995). How scientists really reason: Scientific reasoning in real-world laboratories. In R. J. Sternberg & J. E. Davidson (Eds.), *The nature of insight* (pp. 365–395). Cambridge, MA: MIT Press.

Fodor, J. A. (1983). *The modularity of mind*. Cambridge, MA: MIT Press.

Glenberg, A. M., Wilkinson, A. C., & Epstein, W. (1982). The illusion of knowing: Failure in the self-assessment of comprehension. *Memory and Cognition, 10*, 597–602.

Hatano, G., & Inagaki, K. (1987). A theory of motivation for comprehension and its application to mathematics instruction. In T. A. Romberg & D. M. Stewart (Eds.), *The monitoring of school mathematics: Background papers. Vol. 2. Implications from psychology; outcomes of instruction* (Program Report 87–2, pp. 27–46). Madison, WI: Wisconsin Center for Educational Research.

Hatano, G., & Inagaki, K. (1991). Sharing cognition through collective comprehension activity. In L. B. Resnick, J. M. Levine, & S. D. Teasley (Eds.), *Perspectives on socially shared cognition* (pp. 331–348). Washington, DC: American Psychological Association.

Hatano, G., & Inagaki, K. (1994, April). *A two-level analysis of collective comprehension activity*. Paper presented at the symposium, "Integrating the cognitive and social in the construction of mathematical and scientific knowledge", American Educational Research Association Meeting, New Orleans, LA.

Karmiloff-Smith, A., & Inhelder, B. (1974/5). 'If you want to get ahead, get a theory'. *Cognition, 3*, 195–212.

Klahr, D., & Dunbar, K. (1988). Dual space search during scientific reasoning. *Cognitive Science, 12*, 1–48.

Kuhara-Kojima, K., & Hatano, G. (1996, November). *Constructing and revising interpretations during reading a detective story*. Poster presented at the Annual convention of the Japanese Association of Educational Psychology. Tsukuba, Ibaragi. [In Japanese.]

Kuhara-Kojima, K., & Hatano, G. (1997, September). *Joint interpretation of a detective story by pairs of college students*. Poster presented at the Annual convention of the Japanese Association of Educational Psychology. Hiroshima. [In Japanese.]

Levine, J. M., & Moreland, R. L. (1991). Culture and socialization in work groups. In L. B. Resnick, J. M. Levine, & S. D. Teasley (Eds.), *Perspectives on socially shared cognition* (pp. 257–279). Washington, DC: American Psychological Association.

Markman, E. M. (1977). Realizing that you don't understand: A preliminary investigation. *Child Development, 48*, 986–992.

Miyake, N. (1986). Constructive interaction and the iterative process of understanding. *Cognitive Science, 10*, 151–177.

Oura, Y., & Hatano, G. (1997, August). *When can people reconstruct a procedure from its product?: Dyadic comprehension activity with empirical testing.* Paper presented at the 7th European Conference for Research on Learning and Instruction, Athens, Greece.

Piaget, J. (1978). *Success and understanding.* London: Routledge & Kegan Paul.

Sperber, D., & Wilson, D. (1986). *Relevance: Communication and cognition.* Cambridge, MA: Harvard University Press.

Stein, N. L., & Trabasso, T. (1985). The search after meaning: Comprehesion and comprehension monitoring. *Applied Developmental Psychology, 2*, 33–58.

Sugimura, A., Hatano, G., & Inagaki, K. (in prep.). *Interpreting an unusual recipe: Comprehension activity in individuals and groups.*

CHAPTER NINETEEN

Starting from the ventriloquist: The perception of multimodal events

Paul Bertelson
*Université libre de Bruxelles, Brussels, Belgium,
and Tilburg University, Tilburg, The Netherlands*

Studies of perceptual processing have generally been carried out within one particular input modality. But most real-life events produce correlated sensory inputs to several modalities. The research that has dealt specifically with multimodal perception has identified many cases of crossmodal interaction, in which the interpretation of data in one modality is influenced by those from other modalities. These studies have mostly been based on the imposition of experimental conflict between the data available to the involved modalities. The chapter discusses some of the main methodological and conceptual problems of that approach, taking its examples on one hand from the line of research on spatial interactions between audition and vision, often designated by the collective term *ventriloquism*, and on the other from current work on audiovisual speech identification. It focuses successively on the conditions under which conflict reduction processes are triggered (*the pairing problem*), on the degree of automaticity of the interactions, and on the role of the spatial orientation of attention. Finally, the relations between ventriloquism and the integration of visual data from the talker's face with auditory data in speech recognition, as exemplified in the *McGurk illusion*, are considered. New experimental data are presented that are inconsistent with the notion that the two phenomena originate in the same components of the functional architecture.

Les analyses du traitement perceptif ont été menées généralement au sein d'une modalité particulière. Pourtant, la plupart des évènements de la vie réelle produisent des données pour plusieurs modalités à la fois. La recherche portant spécifiquement sur la perception multimodale a identifié de nombreux cas d'interaction intermodale, dans lequels l'interprétation des données d'une modalité est influencée par celles d'une autre modalité. Ces études ont été basées principalement sur l'imposition de conflits expérimentaux entre les données disponibles dans les modalités impliquées.

Le chapitre discute quelques-uns des principaux problèmes méthodologiques et conceptuels de cette approche, en se basant d'une part sur la ligne de recherche consacrée aux interactions spatiales entre la vision et l'audition, souvent désignées par le terme collectif de *ventriloquie*, et d'autre part sur le travail contemporain sur l'identification audiovisuelle de la parole. Il envisage successivement les conditions dans lesquelles les processus de réduction du conflit sont mis en branle (le *problème de l'appariement*), le degré d'automaticité des interactions et le rôle de l'orientation spatiale de l'attention. Finalement, on considère les relations entre la ventriloquie et l'intégration de données visuelles en provenance du visage du locuteur avec les données auditives dans la perception de la parole, mises en évidence dans *l'illusion de McGurk*. De nouvelles données expérimentales sont décrites, qui sont incompatibles avec l'idée que les deux phénomènes trouvent leur origine dans les mêmes composants de l'architecture fonctionelle.

INTRODUCTION

The ventriloquist speaks without visible facial movements and moves a puppet in synchrony with his speech. That creates in the audience a compelling illusion that the speech comes from the mouth of the puppet. A similar illusion occurs in many situations, such as some amateur movie set-ups in which the sound comes from a loudspeaker to one side of the screen and is nevertheless experienced as coming from the mouth of the actor or some other sound-producing object. In older times, ventriloquism was used by priests, deviners, and witches to deliver oracles, and it often played important roles in human affairs.

The example of the ventriloquist is interesting to psychologists because it illustrates the perceptual integration of data from different modalities, here vision and audition. Just as speakers produce streams of changes available to both ear and eye, most real-life events produce correlated inputs to several of our senses. Yet, most research on perception considers one modality at a time. In comparison, the problems of how simultaneous inputs to several modalities are combined has received relatively little attention.

INTERMODAL CONFLICT

The main approach to the psychological analysis of crossmodal interaction has been through experimental conflict. One can disrupt the normal correlation between inputs by displacing or deforming those of one modality, as in the well-known prismatic rearrangement paradigm that Helmholtz (1866) introduced more than 100 years ago. A subject who reaches to a target with the hand seen through a prism initially puts the hand to the side of the target, but if given the opportunity to see where the hand is moving to, the subject rapidly adapts, i.e. the error diminishes. The adaptation is not voluntary, or not completely so, for when the prisms are removed, the subject points to the other side of the target: The adaptation, or recalibration, now manifests itself as an aftereffect.

The extensive work carried out in the 1960s and 1970s (Welch, 1978) has generally been focused on conflicts about the orientation of the body or the location of body parts in relation to each other. Thus, the main questions that were asked concerned the representation of own body—the problems of the so-called *body schema*—and many explanations that were developed were specific to that issue. Charles Harris, for instance, proposed that adaptation involves mostly the proprioceptive system (Harris, 1965). And Richard Held and his collaborators at MIT argued for a central role in prism adaptation of self-produced movement, which presents the system with conflicting *reafferent* proprioceptive and visual inputs (Held & Hein, 1958).

There was little room in those conceptions for conflicts involving only external events. Predictably, the claims triggered falsification attempts, which eventually showed that if active movement could enhance adaptation, it was not a necessary condition. Recalibrations could result from passive movement (Pick & Hay, 1965), from observation of an immobile member through a prism, from visuo-tactile conflict (Howard, Craske, & Templeton, 1965), and also from exposure to spatially discordant auditory and visual inputs. In Brussels we found that exposure to synchronized noise bursts and prismatically displaced light flashes resulted in recalibration of both visual and auditory locations (Radeau & Bertelson, 1969, 1974), and similar findings were reported at about the same time by Canon (1970).

One possible implication of these findings is that the critical condition of adaptation is discrepancy between inputs, whether exafferent or reafferent. Perhaps there is no essential difference between the case of the body schema and the representation of external space. That discordance between exteroceptive inputs could produce recalibration had already been shown by Hans Wallach in his work with conflicting cues to visual depth (e.g. Wallach, Moore, & Davidson, 1963). Starting from there, Wallach went on to develop a general theory of perceptual adaptation based on the notion of "informational discrepancy", which applied equally to situations of intramodal and intermodal conflict (Wallach, 1968; and see Epstein, 1975, for similar views).

Apart from its theoretical implications, audiovisual (AV) conflict is experimentally convenient, for it gives the investigator complete control of inputs from the two modalities, whereas proprioception cannot be switched off when needed. The rest of the chapter will be focused on AV interaction.

MANIFESTATIONS OF VENTRILOQUISM

The experimental situation we used in most of our studies (Bertelson, 1993; Bertelson & Radeau, 1981, 1987; Radeau, 1973, 1974, 1985, 1992; Radeau & Bertelson, 1974, 1976, 1987) involved a pea-lamp and a miniature loudspeaker attached to a target holder that could be moved around a semi-circular track above an horizontal panel. When instructed, the subject indicated the perceived location of inputs by placing a finger under the panel. Discrepancies between visual and auditory locations were created either by having the subject see the lamp through a device with adjustable rotary prisms or by simply separating the lamp and the loudspeaker in actual space. This kind of set-up allows (1) the measurement of auditory and visual apparent locations, through open-loop pointing or other responses like setting the target to straight ahead (Radeau, 1973) or left-right judgments (Radeau & Bertelson, 1987) and (2) the exposure to spatially discordant auditory and visual inputs. Very similar situations have been used by other investigators (Canon, 1970; Choe, Welch, Gilford, & Juola, 1975; Warren, 1979; Warren, Welch, & McCarthy, 1981).

Our early experiments (e.g. Radeau & Bertelson, 1974) dealt with adaptation to the AV conflict, and they were designed just like classic prism adaptation ones. In pre-tests, the accuracy of pointing either to sound bursts or to light flashes was measured. During the exposure period, the subject observed a series of simultaneous bursts and flashes, in this case with a constant 15-degree separation. To force attention to both inputs, the subject was given the task of monitoring them for occasional reductions in intensity. Exposure was followed by post-tests, identical to the pre-tests. In each modality, pointing on post-tests compared to pre-tests was shifted in the direction of the competing modality. The shifts, or aftereffects, were in this case 2.96 degrees in the auditory modality and 1.90 degrees in the visual one, both significant. These results were obviously not consistent with the prevalent notion of a complete dominance of audition by vision at the level of localization. Other studies in which during exposure the subject localized either the sound or the light have shown that forcing attention to one or the other modality influenced the intermodality balance of adaptation (Canon, 1970; Radeau, 1974). Also, Posner, Nissen, and Klein (1976) have proposed that visual dominance results from an attentional adjustment that would compensate for the fact that visual stimuli do not attract attention as automatically as do auditory or tactile ones. In a later study, Radeau and Bertelson (1976) have shown that visual recalibration occurs when the light target appears on a homogeneous dark background, but not if it appears on a structured background.

Adaptation is measured at the level of post-tests, after a period of exposure to the conflict. One can also study immediate reactions to the conflicting data (Welch & Warren, 1980). These have rarely been considered within the prismatic conflict tradition but they have been the main focus of work on AV interaction. Two main tasks have been used. In *discrepancy detection*, the subjects decide after each presentation whether the inputs originated from the same or from different locations, or whether they experienced perceptual fusion (Choe et al., 1975; Jack & Thurlow, 1973; Radeau & Bertelson, 1977, Experiment 3; Witkin, Wapner, & Leventhal, 1952). The typical finding is that subjects fail to detect separations that they would easily detect within either modality. For instance, Choe et al. had their subjects decide whether trains of sounds and light flashes originating in a single location or 11 degrees apart, and were either synchronized or separated by one of several time delays, came from the same place. The percentage of "same place" responses were found to depend on both spatial separation and synchronization.

In *selective unimodal localization*, bimodal pairs are presented and the subject is instructed to localize either the visual or the auditory target (Bertelson & Radeau, 1981; Klemm, 1909; Pick, Warren, & Hay, 1969; Radeau & Bertelson, 1987; Thomas, 1941; Warren, 1979). The typical finding here is *crossmodal bias*: Despite the instructions, the response to the target is displaced in the direction of the distractor. This failure of attentional modality selection has often been compared to the Stroop effect. Most studies have focused on the visual bias of auditory location. When it was measured, the opposite effect, auditory bias of visual location, generally turned out to be smaller, but reached significance in at least two experiments (Bertelson & Radeau, 1981, Experiment 1; Radeau & Bertelson, 1987; but see Radeau, 1985, for a negative result). The failure to follow the pointing instructions is only partial, for the sum of the two biases is generally less than the physical separation: The subjects do not point to the same location when instructed to locate the light or the sound. This finding fits nicely with the effect of pointing instructions on the direction of recalibration that was obtained in adaptation experiments.

Just as with perceptual fusion, bias is strongly influenced by the relative timing of the inputs. Experiments by Thomas (1941) and by Radeau and Bertelson (1987), in which trains of auditory and visual stimuli with different rates of interruption were presented, have shown that synchronization is a powerful determinant, although not the only one. Another factor is saliency. An uninterrupted sound is attracted toward an interrupted light, and on the other hand, Radeau (1985) has shown that the visual biasing of audition depends on the relative intensities of the inputs.

THE PROBLEM OF CROSSMODAL PAIRING

In real life, the stimulation of different senses occurs all the time. Some stimuli originate in the same external events, others in separate ones. How does the system know which data belong together? This is the problem of *pairing*, in the terms of Wallach (1968) and Epstein (1975), or of the *unity assumption*, following Welch and Warren (1980). Obviously, the system must take into account other aspects of the total situation to decide if the registered spatial separation can be overlooked.

Traditional presentations of the problem (Radeau & Bertelson, 1977; Welch & Warren, 1980) have distinguished *cognitive* from *structural* factors. Cognitive factors are those that involve semantic knowledge about the distal situation. The knowledge can be invoked through a context reproducing more or less realistically a situation known to produce correlated visual and auditory data, or can be conveyed directly through instructions informing or deceiving the subject regarding the source of the data. Structural factors are inherent properties of the inputs, like their respective timing or their spatial separation, which might be effective irrespective of the subject's familiarity with the situation.

Many studies of AV interaction have involved more or less realistic situations. Probably the most picturesque was the setup used by Jackson (1953) in which the subject had to localize the noise produced by a hidden steam-kettle whistle while seeing steam emanating (silently) from one of an array of dummy steam kettles. More common examples are a voice and the face of the talker (Warren et al., 1981; Witkin et al., 1952), noises and the sight of a small loudspeaker (Pick et al., 1969), or the moving clapper of a bell and its sound (Canon, 1970).

The resort to such realistic setups was presumably dictated by the assumption that knowledge of the context was an important determinant of crossmodal interaction. However, in most studies, structural factors like synchronized noises and visual changes were also involved, which could by themselves account for the obtained interactions, and there has been little effort to separate the effects of the two kinds of variables. The fact that the different forms of AV interaction have all been obtained in purified situations of the noise-flash kind implies that top-down semantic factors are not necessary to produce them. Whether these nevertheless make a contribution can be examined by comparing the effect of situations involving both cognitive and structural factors, or structural ones only.

Such a comparison has been carried out by Radeau and Bertelson (1977) for the case of recalibration of auditory location. In one of their experiments, the subjects localized the sounds of percussion instruments (bongos) by pointing, before and after monitoring the same sounds while watching on a video screen displaced 20 degrees to one side, either the hands of the performer or light flashes synchronized with the sounds. Well-synchronized homogeneous flashes were obtained by feeding the audio signal into the video input, and blurring the travelling lines that appeared on the screen with layers of tissue paper. Table 19.1 shows that comparable aftereffects occurred in the two conditions. Another experiment involved auditory speech and either the face of the speaker or light flashes produced by the same procedure as in the first experiment. With speech, the result was essentially that one flash accompanied each spoken syllable. There was again no difference between the two conditions in the size of the aftereffects (Table 19.1). On the other hand, delaying the speech by 350ms relative to the corresponding visual inputs reduced the amount of recalibration in both conditions, but to the same degree and without abolishing it. Thus, in the two experiments, realism had no additional effect to that of temporal correlation between low-level components of the two inputs.

AV interactions have sometimes been reported for situations in which only cognitive factors could possibly account for them. In one of their well-known experiments, Pick et al. (1969) had their subjects point to the apparent origin of noise bursts while seeing a prismatically displaced loudspeaker, with no visual changes to correlate with the bursts. The responses were strongly biased toward the

TABLE 19.1
Realism and recalibration of auditory location.
Aftereffects in degrees of angle

Auditory data	Timing	Visual data	
Experiment 1			
		Hands	Flashes
Bongos	Synchronous	3.04	3.49
Experiment 2			
		Face	Flashes
Voice	Synchronous	3.45	2.54
Voice	Voice delayed	1.70	1.87

From Radeau and Bertelson (1977).

apparent location of the loudspeaker. That effect was obviously contingent on the subjects' knowledge of the function of loudspeakers. It is similar to the episode in a strip cartoon by the Belgian author Hergé (1945) in which the hero Tintin and a companion are taken prisoners by some tribesmen and use ventriloquism to give orders to release them, which their guardians take as issued by a nearby fetish. No properly perceptual interaction is involved in their trick. Their success simply exploits the guardians' belief that wooden fetishes can talk, and similarly Pick et al.'s experiment took advantage of the subjects' belief that loudspeakers deliver sounds.

Given that the Pick et al. experiment is often taken as the typical demonstration of visual bias of audition, we found that some replication would be desirable. We had one group of subjects carry out the same task of pointing to the apparent origin of trains of noise bursts while watching a small prismatically displaced loudspeaker, and found no bias (Bertelson & Radeau, 1987; Radeau, 1992). We also measured after-effects, with similarly negative results. Another group of subjects worked in the purified noise bursts and light flashes situation, and produced the usual visual bias and aftereffect.

The negative result regarding bias in the loudspeaker condition indicates that the pure effects of cognitive variables are not obligatory. The reason why they were effective in one study and not in the other is, as for the traditional New Look phenomena, a problem for the social psychologist interested in the phenomena of belief formation rather than for the student of perception.

LEVELS OF PROCESSING AND AV CONFLICT

Separating the effects of genuine perceptual processes from those of post-perceptual or judgmental adjustments is a problem of central importance in any field of study based on subjects' choice of responses. In Fodor's (1983) terms, it concerns the distinction between the contributions of modular input systems and those of nonmodular central processes. These distinctions have received little attention in the literature on crossmodal interaction. The traditional way of asking the pairing question in terms of structural versus cognitive factors has tended to ignore the possibility that these factors simply operate at different levels of the functional architecture. A simple conception of the relevant architecture, which we have put forward in several papers (Bertelson, 1994; Radeau & Bertelson, 1977, 1987), involves a perceptual level sensitive only to structural factors and a post-perceptual level of *belief formation* at which the output of the perceptual level is integrated with semantic influences from cognitive inputs. The performances recorded in the different tasks would reflect in various proportions the outputs from the two levels.

The results from manipulations of realism that we examined in the preceding section suggested that the role of post-perceptual factors in the generation of ventriloquism is rather limited. However, Welch and Warren (1980, 1984; see also Warren et al., 1981, and Welch, 1994) have argued repeatedly that the effects of structural variables, like synchronization and spatial separation, can also be mediated through judgmental processes. The notion was that these effects might result from an explicit application by the subject of the principle that simultaneously occurring events in different modalities probably have a common origin.

The notion received some apparent support from the study by Choe et al. (1975) of the effect of the synchronization of auditory and visual inputs on same-different origin decisions. Application of detection theory to the results indicated that synchronization affected the decision criterion *beta* and not *d'*. The authors concluded that ventriloquism originates in a response bias, not in a perceptual shift.

The Choe et al. paper was probably the first in the literature on crossmodal bias to address the perception versus judgment issue. However, closer examination of their method showed that the particular perceptual process that the detection analysis had discarded (a translation without deformation of the distributions of subjective sound-light separations along the abscissa, in the synchronous condition) was an implausible one, and that a more likely form of perceptual attraction (a proportional reduction of all subjective distances) was consistent with the data (Bertelson & Radeau, 1976). Our own provisional conclusion was that an effect on registered locations of the inputs was still a valid possibility. On the other hand, we insisted that response biases or deliberate judgments could also play a role in some exerimental tasks.

Immediate responses to the bimodal situation are particularly susceptible to voluntary effects, to the extent that the situation is *transparent*, that is, when all the data necessary for explicit deliberation—the spatial separation, the timing, plus eventually the visual context—can be perceived consciously. Moreover, in the case of the selective localization task through which immediate biases are studied, the instructions to respond in terms of one of the modalities unavoidably suggests the possibility of a discrepancy. The adaptation paradigm does not present that danger to the same extent because the critical measures are obtained in a straightforward unimodal localization task that leaves less room for deliberate strategies. That consideration was at the origin of the predominant use of that paradigm in studies of prismatic displacement, as well as in much of our own ventriloquism work. However, whenever the experimental discrepancy is detected during the exposure phase of the experiment, the setting of response criteria during the post-tests can still be influenced.

The preceding discussion suggests that the most convincing arguments for genuine perceptual contributions would be obtained in nontransparent situations, in which the subject has no awareness of the discrepancy.

In the past two years, Gisa Aschersleben of the Max Planck Institute for Psychological Research in Munich and I have been exploring a new way of addressing the problem. Our approach is based on the use of psychophysical staircases (Cornsweet, 1962). The subject sits facing a vertical curtain. On each trial a train of sound bursts is presented and the task is to indicate by pressing one of two keys whether the sounds originated left or right of a vertical bar in the middle of the curtain. The sounds are actually delivered from two loudspeakers hidden respectively to the left and the right of the display, and their apparent azimuthal origin is controlled stereophonically. Locations presented on successive trials are controlled by two randomly mixed staircases, one starting far to the left and the other far to the right. When the "left" key is pressed, the following sound on the same staircase is moved one step to the right, and vice versa after a "right" key press. This procedure normally results in the two staircases progressively converging toward the middle, as shown in Fig. 19.1. The session stops as soon as 10 reversals have occurred on each staircase.

In the first experiment, two conditions were compared. In the experimental condition, flashes were produced in an LED lamp situated in the middle of the median line in exact synchrony with the sound bursts. In the control condition, the lamp stayed on all the time. The idea was that if the sounds were attracted by the simultaneous flashes, response *reversals*, that is, responses different from the immediately preceding one, would begin to occur with the sounds further from center than in the control condition, as in the example presented in Fig. 19.2. Locations of mean successive reversals in the two conditions for a group of nine subjects appear in Fig. 19.3. As predicted, convergence of the staircases is slowed down in the experimental condition in comparison to the control condition, because response reversals begin to occur earlier. The important aspect of the procedure is that the occurrence of reversal also indicates the breakdown of explicit left-right discrimination. Thus, the critical effect was observed when the nontransparency condition necessary to rule out any systematic voluntary influence was met. The result was replicated in a new experiment with a slightly different control condition (LED off instead of continuously on) (Bertelson & Aschersleben, 1996).

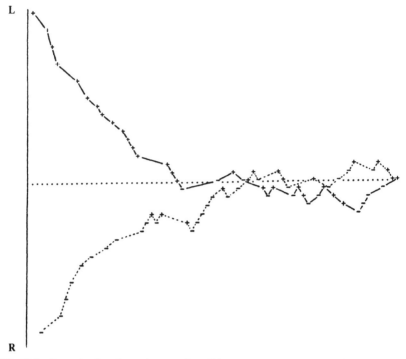

FIG. 19.1 Example of session under control condition with the central LED steadily on. Abscissa, successive trials; ordinate, phase difference between delivery of tone on left and right loudspeaker. Differences are called positive when the left loudspeaker leads.

The results so far supported the notion of an automatic attraction of the apparent locations of the sounds by the flashing light. It remained to check that the attraction is contingent on synchronization of the flashes with the sounds, as found in conventional bias studies (Radeau & Bertelson, 1987; Warren et al., 1981). In a recently completed experiment, the same experimental condition with synchronized sounds and flashes was compared to a new control condition, with unpredictably·variable sound-flash intervals. No effect of the flashes was observed in that condition. The overall results were indistinguishable, in fact, from those of the other experiments in the series.

Evidence of another kind for some automatic biasing of auditory location by visual inputs has been made available recently by a study by Driver (1996) with the traditional "cocktail party" situation. Listeners heard two word sequences recorded by the same speaker and delivered simultaneously from a single loudspeaker. Their task was to shadow one of the two sequences, the one that appeared in a video recording of the speaker's face shown on one of two screens. One screen was situated immediately on top of the loudspeaker, the other one at a distance from the loudspeaker. The interesting finding was that shadowing

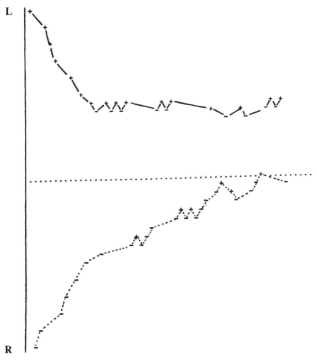

FIG. 19.2 Example of session under experimental condition, with LED flashing in synchrony with the sound. Same subject as in Fig. 19.1.

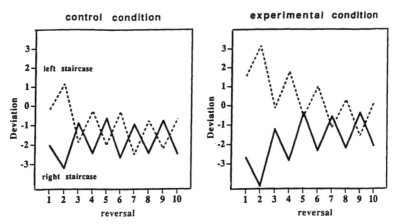

FIG. 19.3 Mean location of successive response reversals on left and right staircase. Left, control condition (LED steadily on); right, experimental condition (LED in synchrony with tones). Deviation units (ordinate) represent 40 microseconds of phase difference, equivalent to 2.4 degrees of angle.

performance was much better with the face on the distant screen than on the close-by one. Presumably, the apparent location of the target auditory items was attracted toward the screen, thus creating a spatial separation between the simultaneous inputs, a condition that has long been known to facilitate selective listening (Broadbent, 1958). The nontarget items were probably not attracted, because they were not synchronized with the movements of the face.

In this elegant experiment, the occurrence of spatial bias could be inferred *indirectly*, from its effect on recognition. It is very unlikely that this reflected any voluntary adjustment. Although the experiment was not designed specifically to make that point, its results converge nicely with those of our study, based on the usual task of having the subject report apparent location *directly*. To exclude the possible influence of conscious volition, we had to measure localization under conditions in which the intermodal discrepancy went undetected.

Because of time and space limitations, our presentation was by and large restricted to the behavioral evidence. At this point, it must be noted that the existence of a genuinely perceptual component in AV bias is consistent with existing physiological knowledge concerning the convergence at the neuronal level of auditory and visual inputs in the superior colliculus of the cat (Stein & Meredith, 1993) or the optical tectum of the owl (Knudsen, 1982). The relevance of these data to the present concerns has been discussed by Radeau (1994).

CROSSMODAL BIAS AND THE ORIENTATION OF VOLUNTARY ATTENTION

So far, the discussion has been focused on two main processes that might produce AV interaction—deliberate response correction and automatic attraction. The results of the staircase experiments have brought strong confirmation to earlier suggestions that crossmodal bias occurs in nontransparent conditions excluding the possibility of voluntary correction. There is, however, another alternative to the automatic attraction view. The notion is that bias occurs when *attention* is focused on different locations in the two modalities. The difference from the automatic attraction hypothesis is that now the critical factor is where attention is oriented rather than where the inputs occur. The hypothesis seemed consistent with evidence presented by Driver and Spence (1994) that it is difficult to orient visual and auditory attention simultaneously to different locations. These authors' findings suggest the existence of an obligatory link between the attention-orienting processes in the two modalities. On the other hand, in an informal survey of students of attention, I found that a clear majority considered the attentional conflict view as the most likely explanation of crossmodal bias.

One result that seemed to support the hypothesis was the finding reported by Weerts and Thurlow (1971) that instructing subjects simply to look at a fixed steady target (a cross) at some distance from a hidden auditory source produced both an immediate bias of auditory localization and an adaptive aftereffect.

However, Radeau and Bertelson (1977) used the steady visual target condition as a control and obtained no after-effect, and a similarly negative result was reported by Warren et al. (1981) for both immediate bias and aftereffects.

An experiment Jean Vroomen, Béatrice de Gelder, and I carried out recently in collaboration with Jon Driver was focused on the attentional conflict hypothesis. We used a classic visual bias situation. The task was to localize trains of tones while monitoring visual events on a computer screen. A bright square appeared to the left or the right of the screen, in exact synchrony with the tones, in a random half of the experimental trials. No square appeared in the other half. The attentional manipulation consisted of having the subject monitor either the center of the display, or the center of the lateral square, for occasional occurrences of a catch stimulus. The study focused therefore on overt voluntary attention. The prediction from the attentional hypothesis was that pointing would shift toward the square by a larger amount with lateral than with central attention. In fact, strong shifts toward the presented square were obtained, but they were of comparable magnitude, wherever attention was focused.

The result suggests that spatial crossmodal interaction, far from being contingent on the orientation of attention, actually occurs before the orienting process, at the level of the pre-attentive segmentation of the scene. The notion that crossmodal interaction operates pre-attentively is of course consistent with the recent demonstration by Driver (1996), already described in the preceding section, that ventriloquism can help the listener focus on the target message in a multiple-listening situation.

AV INTERACTION IN SPEECH IDENTIFICATION

The classic ventriloquist illusion affects the apparent location of events. Could crossmodal interaction also affect the identification of events? If, for instance, the face of the puppet produced recognizable articulatory movements, would that make comprehension of the ventriloquist's speech easier? Present evidence suggests that this might happen.

It has in fact been known for some time that information useful for speech recognition is made available by the sight of a speaker's face. Profoundly deaf people can be taught to some limited extent to use that information. The ability has come to be called "lipreading", or more recently "speechreading". A more impressive use of facial visual information is the improvement in speech recognition that it allows under conditions of poor auditory intelligibility. In a now classic study, Sumby and Pollack (1954) showed that the improvement could reach the equivalent of a 20dB increase in signal to noise ratio, and more recent work has confirmed the reality of this *facial speech advantage* (Campbell & Dodd, 1980; Summerfield, 1987).

An essential step in the understanding of these effects has resulted from the application of the conflict paradigm. In 1976, McGurk and MacDonald reported experiments in which subjects had been presented with short auditory utterances dubbed on to video recordings of different visual ones. For some audio-visual pairs, the reports were definitely influenced by the visual inputs. The best-known case is that of auditory /baba/, which when synchronized to visual /gaga/ led in a large proportion of listeners to the "fusion" response DADA. With the opposite pair, auditory /gaga/ with visual /baba/, the combination BABGA was often reported.

The most spectacular visual interference effects have been obtained with pairings of the bilabial consonants /p/, /b/, and /m/, in whose pronunciation the lips close, with non-labial ones such as /t/, /d/, /k/, /g/, and /n/. As a consequence, a majority of subsequent studies have used bilabial-nonbilabial pairings (e.g. Green, 1996; MacDonald & McGurk, 1978; Massaro & Cohen, 1983). But other visually distinctive consonants like /v/ (which shows the upper teeth) or /th/ (showing the tongue) have allowed interesting effects (Manuel, Repp, Liberman, & Studdert-Kennedy, 1983). The pronunciation of vowels also produces distinctive visible patterns, but except for a study on facial advantage by Summerfield and McGrath (1984) and an interesting program in progress at the Grenoble Institut de la Communication Parlée (Abry, Lallouache, & Cathiard, 1996), the opportunity has been little exploited.

Naive subjects generally have little awareness of the discrepancy, and it has been shown that the interference survives explicit descriptions of the conflict situation (Manuel et al., 1983). Also, instructions to focus attention on the data from one of the two modalities fail to prevent interference from those in the other modality (Massaro, 1987). Thus, the integration of visual and auditory speech data is probably mandatory, not a deliberate strategy resorted to by the listener when confronted with deficient auditory evidence.

Speechreading is, like ventriloquism, a case of integration of auditory and visual data, and the two phenomena exhibit a good degree of perceptual autonomy. Such considerations seem to have led many people to the more or less implicit assumption that the two sets of phenomena have common underlying processes. Since McGurk and MacDonald (1976) reported their original findings, several commentators have pointed to communalities between the two groups of phenomena like perceptual locus, the effect of orienting attention to either modality (Massaro, 1987, pp. 83–84), or the eventual role of assumptions of identity (Welch, 1989). Massaro (1987) in particular felt that such communalities provided arguments against modular views of language processing (Liberman & Mattingly, 1985), and he has proposed that speechreading can be seen as one particular manifestation of a general manner of combining separate pieces of evidence that applies all the way from perception to social relations (Massaro, 1996).

On the other side of the theoretical divide, arguments against the common process view can be derived from neuropsychological evidence that speechreading is associated with language and dissociates from nonlinguistic perceptual performance like face recognition (Campbell, 1994; Campbell, Landis &

Regard, 1988). Radeau (1994) and Bertelson (1994) have proposed somewhat converging interpretations of audio-visual interactions that assume the existence of two separate, although both perceptually autonomous, functional components, one responsible for speech identification and the other for crossmodal spatial integration. The major consideration was that the domains of the two phenomena are not co-existent. Ventriloquism occurs with both speech and nonspeech inputs, whereas crossmodal speech perception concerns speech identity, and presumably requires data with close relations to speech sounds and facial movements, respectively. The dual determination view is on the other hand consistent with neuropsychological and neurophysiological evidence for separate visual channels dealing with "what" versus "where" kinds of questions (Ungerleider & Mishkin, 1982).

A research project we have been carrying out in recent years in Tilburg was designed to test the common process hypothesis. We have developed a setup in which both identity conflict, conducive to McGurk interference, and spatial conflict, conducive to spatial bias, can be manipulated with the same material (Bertelson, Vroomen, Wiegeraad, & De Gelder, 1994). It involves delivery of an auditory utterance from one of several loudspeakers laid out in an array in front of the subject, and presentation, on a centrally located video screen, of a face articulating the same or a different utterance. On each trial, the subject performs two tasks. He repeats what he thought the speaker said and he indicates the location of the auditory source, by pressing with the hidden hand one of several buttons arranged in a semi-circle. Control trials, on which the face remains still, allows the measurement of conflict-free auditory speech identification and localization. McGurk interference is measured by the increased frequency observed in each experimental condition compared to the control condition of responses deviating from the presented auditory utterance. Ventriloquism is measured by comparing for each laterally located loudspeaker the mean pointing response under each experimental condition to the value in the control condition. The predicted bias was a reduction of the distance in the control condition.

A first set of experiments has been devoted to the effect on the two phenomena of the orientation of the face, which was shown either upright or upside-down. In one experiment, the auditory utterances were either /ama/ or /ana/ and the face was seen articulating one of these or staying still. Pronouncing the bilabial consonant /m/ involves closure of the lips, which, as mentioned earlier, is one of the most effective visual features for speechreading. Strong McGurk effects were obtained in the two incongruent conditions. With auditory /ama/, subjects reported /ama/ on more than 90% of both control trials and congruent trials with visual /ama/, but on only 36% with the upright face pronouncing /ana/. With auditory /ana/, there was already a substantial proportion (37%) of the bilabial response /amna/ on control trials. This proportion was increased (to about 84%) with the presentation of the visual /ama/. As shown in Table 19.2, both of these effects are significantly reduced when the face is inverted.

TABLE 19.2
Effect of visual utterance on bimodal item identification
(in per cent bilabial responses)*

Auditory utterance	Visual utterance	Face orientation			
		Up	Down	t	P
/ama/	/ama/	+2	+1	0.29	NS
	/ana/	−51	−33	3.33	0.003
/ana/	/ama/	+49	+43	2.13	0.05
	/ana/	−26	−23	0.79	NS

* The score is the difference between the percentage bilabial responses (/ama/ + /amna/) on trials with the face pronouncing the indicated utterance and on control trials with the face still.

TABLE 19.3
Spatial attraction by talking face (in degrees)*

Auditory utterance	Visual utterance	Face orientation			
		UP	Down	t	P
/ama/	/ama/	2.74	2.37	0.71	NS
	/ana/	1.53	1.34	0.35	NS
/ana/	/ama/	2.59	4.09	−2.66	0.02
	/ana/	2.34	2.17	0.27	NS

* Mean difference over the six lateral loudspeakers (1–3 and 5–7) between mean pointing location on experimental trials with the face seen articulating the indicated utterance and control trials with the face remaining still. Differences are considered as positive when they go in the direction of the midpoint.

Regarding localization (Table 19.3), the mean pointing location to laterally presented auditory inputs was closer to the central screen on the trials on which the face was seen talking than on those on which it remained still. This attraction toward the talking face was as strong with the face upside-down as upright. As a matter of fact, it was significantly stronger with the upside-down face for auditory /ana/ paired with visual /ama/ (a somewhat paradoxical result for which we have no explanation for the time being), and there was no significant effect with the other three pairs.

These results confirm those obtained in an earlier experiment with a single ambiguous synthetic auditory utterance intermediate between /ama/ and /ana/, and the face pronouncing either /ama/ or /ana/ (Bertelson et al., 1994). Inversion had no effect on spatial attraction toward the talking face, but it reduced significantly the amount of McGurk interference produced by visual /ana/. Visual /ama/, on the other hand, brought the proportion of bilabial responses (mainly the combination /amna/) close to 100% with both upside-down and upright faces, and the difference between the two shifts was not significant. That result may have been the reflection of a ceiling effect. However, although the effect of visual /ama/ was in the new experiment significantly reduced by face inversion, the reduction was smaller than for visual /ana/. Thus, there is a possibility that the strength of the inversion effect varies with idiosyncrasies of the different articulatory patterns. Results that further support that notion have been reported by Green (1996).

The fact that the dissociation between spatial bias and phonetic integration was obtained under conditions in which the two processes had access to exactly the same total inputs is important, for it implies that each process responds to a selective subset of the available data.

The independence of spatial bias from face orientation, as well as from phonetic congruence, is consistent with the earlier finding (Radeau & Bertelson, 1977) that exposure to spatially separated auditory speech and visual data produced comparable degrees of adaptation whether the visual data consisted of homogeneous light flashes or of the moving face of the speaker. These results suggested that temporal correlation at the level of low-level visual and auditory data available in the two conditions was sufficient to produce crossmodal pairing, and that the additional information brought by the details of facial movements contributed no additional effect. This view of ventriloquism as depending on temporal correlation of low-level data has received further support from an incidental finding. In both experiments, the attraction toward the talking face was significantly stronger with the visual bilabial /ama/ than with the nonbilabial /ana/. The difference could be due to the fact that with a bilabial consonant the closing of the lips provides a precise temporal cue that is missing in nonbilabial consonants.

Crossmodal phonetic integration on the other hand appears to depend on the fine grain of inputs to the two modalities. The strong effects of inversion obtained in the case of the recognition of personal identity from faces has often been attributed to the role in the identification of upright faces of orientation-specific configural features (Valentine, 1988). One might conjecture that similarly, some attributes of a speaking face important for speechreading are less available under inversion. There is, of course, no implication here that the critical attributes are the same for personal identification and for speechreading.

Going back to the main purpose of the study, one can conclude that the manipulation of face orientation has produced an experimental dissociation between McGurk interference, which is affected, and ventriloquism, which is not. The result is certainly inconsistent with the single-process notion. Another aspect of the results that points in the same direction is that there was no systematic effect of loudspeaker location on the amount of McGurk interference over the roughly 65 degree of angle spanned by our setup. A similar independence of the effect from voice-to-face distance over a full 180 degree angle was reported at the Congress by Jones and Munhall (1996). Spatial attraction of the voice toward the face, on the other hand, was strongly dependent on distance (see Bertelson et al., 1994, Fig. 1). Thus, the effect of AV distance also dissociates ventriloquism and crossmodal speech integration. This dissociation goes in the opposite direction from the one produced by face orientation, thus providing the double dissociation picture, generally considered the most convincing argument for the existence of separate functional components.

One might ask what domains exactly the components which have been dissociated are competent for. That is not a question that can be answered on the sole basis of the present results. For the spatial component subserving ventriloquism, considerations of parsimony would suggest that it does not deal specifically with audiovisual interaction but rather with spatial scene analysis across modalities (Bertelson, 1994). The suggestion should of course be put to empirical test. Regarding identification, the question is whether one should think in terms of a single component dealing indifferently with linguistic and nonlinguistic events, as considered for instance by Rosenblum (1994), or rather with two specialized components. There is a large literature concerning the specificity of speech processing (Liberman & Mattingly, 1985), but on the other hand very few data are available about the functional status of nonspeech event identification. Rosenblum referred to the results of experiments in which identification of cello sounds from a pluck-to-bow continuum were influenced by the sight of a cello being either plucked or bowed (Saldaña & Rosenblum, 1993). However, before the small biases obtained in these experiments can be attributed to the same process as speechreading, further analyses of the conditions under which they occur would be necessary. In particular, the possibility that they originated in some kind of voluntary adjustment should also be given serious consideration.

ACKNOWLEDGEMENTS

Our work on crossmodal interaction was supported by the Belgian National Fund for Scientific Research (F.N.R.S.) and the Belgian Fund for Collective Fundamental Research (F.R.F.C.) and is currently supported by the Ministry of Education and Scientific Research of the French-speaking Community of Belgium (Action de Recherche Concertée 96/01-2037). The collaboration with Gisa Aschersleben was made possible by invitations from the Max Planck Gesellschaft. Thanks are due to Christian Abry, Felice Bedford, Kerry Green, Richard Held, Bernhard Hommel, Alvin Liberman, Tony Marcel, Jacques Paillard, Wolfgang Prinz, Lawrence Rosenblum, Carlo Umiltà, Paolo Viviani, and Bob Welch for stimulating discussions of several of the present issues.

REFERENCES

Abry, C., Lallouache, M. T., & Cathiard, M. A. (1996). How can coarticulation models account for speech sensitivity to audio-visual desynchronization? In D. G. Stork & M. E. Hennecke (Eds.), *Speechreading by humans and machines: Models, systems, and applications* (pp. 247–256). Berlin: Springer.

Bertelson, P. (1993). The time-course of adaptation to auditory-visual spatial discrepancy. In C. Bundesen & A. Larsen (Eds.), *Proceedings of the 6th Conference of the European Society for Cognitive Psychology*, 3–4. Copenhagen: University of Copenhagen.

Bertelson, P. (1994). The cognitive architecture behind auditory-visual interaction in scene analysis and speech identification. *Current Psychology of Cognition, 13*, 69–75.

Bertelson, P., & Aschersleben, G. (1996). Visual bias of auditory location: Evidence for automaticity. *Abstracts of the Psychonomic Society, 1*, 74.

Bertelson, P., & Radeau, M. (1976). Ventriloquism, sensory interaction and response bias: Remarks on the paper by Choe, Welch, Gilford and Juola. *Perception and Psychophysics, 19*, 531–535.

Bertelson, P., & Radeau, M. (1981). Cross-modal bias and perceptual fusion with auditory-visual spatial discordance. *Perception and Psychophysics, 29*, 578–587.

Bertelson, P., & Radeau, M. (1987). Adaptation to auditory-visual conflict: Have top-down influences been overestimated here also? *2nd Meeting of the European Society for Cognitive Psychology*, Madrid, Spain.

Bertelson, P., Vroomen, J., Wiegeraad, G., & De Gelder, B. (1994). Exploring the relation between McGurk interference and ventriloquism. *International Congress on Spoken Language Processing 1994* (Yokohama), pp. 559–562.

Broadbent, D. E. (1958). *Perception and communication*. London: Routledge.

Campbell, R. (1994). Audiovisual speech: Where, what, when, how? *Current Psychology of Cognition, 13*, 76–80.

Campbell, R., & Dodd, B. (1980). Hearing by eye. *The Quarterly Journal of Experimental Psychology, 32*, 85–89.

Campbell, R., Landis, T., & Regard, M. (1986). Face recognition and lipreading: A neurological dissociation. *Brain, 109*, 509–521.

Canon, L. K. (1970). Intermodality inconsistency of input and directed attention as determinants of the nature of adaptation. *Journal of Experimental Psychology, 84*, 141–147.

Choe, C. S., Welch, R. B., Gilford, R. M., & Juola, J. F. (1975). The "ventriloquist effect": Visual dominance or response bias? *Perception and Psychophysics, 18*, 55–60.

Cornsweet, T. N. (1962). The staircase-method in psychophysics. *American Journal of Psychology, 75*, 485–491.

Driver, J. (1996). Enhancement of listening by illusory mislocation of speech sounds due to lipreading. *Nature, 381*, 66–68.

Driver, J., & Spence, C. J. (1994). Cross-modal synergies in attention. In C. Umiltà & M. Moscovitch (Eds.), *Attention and performance XV* (pp. 311–332). Hillsdale, NJ: Lawrence Erlbaum Associates Inc.

Epstein, W. (1975). Recalibration by pairing: A process of perceptual learning. *Perception, 4*, 59–72.

Fodor, J. A. (1983). *The modularity of mind*. Cambridge, MA: Bradford Books.

Green, K. P. (1996). The use of auditory and visual information in phonetic perception. In D. G. Stork & M. E. Hennecke (Eds.), *Speechreading by humans and machines: Models, systems and applications* (pp. 55–78). Berlin: Springer.

Harris, C. S. (1965). Perceptual adaptation to inverted, reversed and displaced vision. *Psychological Review, 72*, 419–444.

Held, R., & Hein, A. (1958). Adaptation of disarranged hand-eye coordination contingent upon reafferent stimulation. *Perceptual and Motor Skills, 8*, 87–90.

Helmholtz, H. von (1866). *Handbuch der physiologischen Optik* (Vol. III). Leipzig: Leopold Voss.

Hergé (1945). *L'oreille cassée*. Tournai: Casterman.

Howard, I. P., Craske, B., & Templeton, W. B. (1965). Visuo-motor adaptation to discordant exafferent stimulation. *Journal of Experimental Psychology, 70,* 189–191.

Jack, C. E., & Thurlow, W. R. (1973). Effects of degree of visual association and angle of displacement on the "ventriloquism" effect. *Perceptual and Motor Skills, 38,* 967–979.

Jackson, C. V. (1953). Visual factors in auditory localization. The *Quarterly Journal of Experimental Psychology, 5,* 52–65.

Jones, J. A., & Munhall, K. G. (1996). Spatial and temporal influences on audiovisual speech perception. Abstracts of the XXVI International Congress of Psychology (Montreal 1996), *International Journal of Psychology, 31,* 473–474.

Klemm, O. (1909). Localisation von Sinneneindrücken bei disparaten Nebenreizen. *Psychologische Studien (Wundt), 5,* 73–161.

Knudsen, E. I. (1982). Auditory and visual maps of space in the optic tectum of the owl. *Journal of Neuroscience, 2,* 1177–1194.

Liberman, A. M., & Mattingly, I. G. (1985). The motor theory of speech perception revised. *Cognition, 21,* 1–36.

MacDonald, J., & McGurk, H. (1978). Visual influences on speech perception processes. *Perception and Psychophysics, 24,* 253–257.

Manuel, S. Y., Repp, B. H., Liberman, A. M., & Studdert-Kennedy, M. (1983). *Exploring the "McGurk effect".* Paper presented at the 24th annual meeting of the Psychonomic Society, San Diego, CA.

Massaro, D. M. (1987). *Speech perception by ear and eye: A paradigm for psychological inquiry.* Hillsdale, NJ: Lawrence Erlbaum Associates Inc.

Massaro, D. M. (1996). Bimodal speech perception: A progress report. In D. G. Stork & M. E. Hennecke (Eds.), *Speechreading by humans and machines: Models, systems and applications* (pp. 79–102). Berlin: Springer.

Massaro, D., & Cohen, M. M. (1983). Evaluation and integration of visual and auditory information in speech perception. *Journal of Experimental Psychology: Human Perception and Performance, 9,* 753–771.

McGurk, H., & MacDonald, J. (1976). Hearing lips and seeing voices. *Nature, 264,* 746–748.

Pick, H. L., & Hay, J. C. (1965). A passive test of the Held reafference hypothesis. *Perceptual and Motor Skills, 20,* 1070–1072.

Pick, H. L., Warren D. H., & Hay, J. C. (1969). Sensory conflict in judgments of spatial direction. *Perception and Psychophysics, 6,* 203–205.

Posner, M. I., Nissen, M. J., & Klein, R. M. (1976). Visual dominance: An information-processing account of its origins and significance *Psychological Review, 83,* 157–171.

Radeau, M. (1973). The locus of adaptation to auditory-visual conflict. *Perception, 2,* 327–332.

Radeau, M. (1974). Adaptation au déplacement prismatique sur la base d'une discordance entre la vision et l'audition. *L'Année Psychologique, 74,* 23–34.

Radeau, M. (1985). Signal intensity, task context, and auditory-visual interaction. *Perception, 14,* 571–577.

Radeau, M. (1992). Cognitive impenetrability in auditory-visual interaction. In J. Alegria, D. Holender, J. Morais, & M. Radeau (Eds.), *Analytic approaches to human cognition* (pp. 41–55). Amsterdam: Elsevier.

Radeau, M. (1994). Auditory-visual interaction and modularity. *Current Psychology of Cognition, 13,* 3–51.

Radeau, M., & Bertelson, P. (1969). Adaptation à un déplacement prismatique sur la base de stimulations exafférentes en conflit. *Psychologica Belgica, 9,* 133–140.

Radeau, M., & Bertelson, P. (1974). The after-effects of ventriloquism. *The Quarterly Journal of Experimental Psychology, 26,* 63–71.

Radeau, M., & Bertelson, P. (1976). The effect of a textured visual field on modality dominance in a ventriloquism situation. *Perception and Psychophysics, 20,* 63–71.

Radeau, M., & Bertelson, P. (1977). Adaptation to auditory-visual discordance and ventriloquism in semi-realistic situations. *Perception and Psychophysics, 22*, 137–146.

Radeau, M., & Bertelson, P. (1987). Auditory-visual interaction and the timing of inputs: Thomas (1941) revisited. *Psychological Research, 49*, 17–22.

Rosenblum, L. D. (1994). How special is audiovisual speech integration? *Current Psychology of Cognition, 13*, 110–117.

Saldaña, H. M., & Rosenblum, L. D. (1993). Visual influences on auditory pluck and bow judgments. *Perception and Psychophysics, 54*, 406–416.

Stein, B. E., & Meredith, M. A. (1993). *The merging of the senses.* Cambridge, MA: Bradford Books.

Sumby, W. H., & Pollack, I. (1954). Visual contribution to speech intelligibility in noise. *Journal of the Acoustical Society of America, 26*, 212–215.

Summerfield, Q. (1987). Some preliminaries to a comprehensive account of audio-visual speech perception. In B. Dodd & R. Campbell (Eds.), *Hearing by eye: The psychology of lip-reading* (pp. 3–51). Hove, UK: Lawrence Erlbaum Associates Ltd.

Summerfield, Q., & McGrath, M. (1984). Detection and resolution of audio-visual incompatibility in the perception of vowels. *The Quarterly Journal of Experimental Psychology, 36*, 51–74.

Thomas, G. J. (1941). Experimental study of the influence of vision on sound localisation. *Journal of Experimental Psychology, 28*, 167–177.

Ungerleider, L. G., & Mishkin, M. (1982). Two cortical visual systems. In D. J. Ingle, M. A. Goodale, & R. J. W. Mansfield (Eds.), *Analysis of visual behavior* (pp. 549–586). Cambridge, MA: MIT Press.

Valentine, T. (1988). Upside-down faces: A review of the effect of inversion upon face recognition. *British Journal of Psychology, 79*, 471–491.

Wallach, H. (1968). Informational discrepancy as a basis of perceptual adaptation. In S. J. Freeman (Ed.), *The neuropsychology of spatially oriented behavior* (pp. 209–230). Homewood, IL: Dorsey Press.

Wallach, H., Moore, M. E., & Davidson, L. (1963). Modification of stereoscopic depth perception. *American Journal of Psychology, 76*, 191–204.

Warren, D. H. (1979). Spatial localization under conflict conditions: Is there a single explanation? *Perception, 8*, 323–337.

Warren, D. H., Welch, R. B., & McCarthy, T. J. (1981). The role of visual-auditory "compellingness" in the ventriloquism effect: Implications for transitivity among the spatial senses. *Perception and Psychophysics, 9, 30*, 557–564.

Welch, R. B. (1978). *Perceptual modification: Adapting to altered sensory environments.* New York: Academic Press.

Welch, R. B. (1989). A comparison of speech perception and spatial localisation. *Behavioral and Brain Science, 12*, 776–777.

Welch, R. B. (1994). The disssection of intersensory bias: Weighting for Radeau. *Contemporary Psychology of Cognition, 13*, 117–123.

Welch, R. B., & Warren, D. H. (1980). Immediate perceptual response to intersensory discrepancy. *Psychological Bulletin, 88*, 638–667.

Welch, R. B., & Warren, D. H. (1984). Intersensory interactions. In K. R. Boff, L. Kaufman, & J. P. Thomas (Eds.), *Handbook of perception and human performance. Vol. 1. Sensory processes and perception* (pp. 25.1–36). New York: Wiley.

Weerts, T. C., & Thurlow, W. R. (1971). The effect of eye position and expectation on sound localisation. *Perception and Psychophysics, 9*, 35–39.

Witkin, H. A., Wapner, S., & Leventhal, T. (1952). Sound localization with conflicting visual and auditory cues. *Journal of Experimental Psychology, 43*, 58–67.

CHAPTER TWENTY

Brain/mind correlates of human memory

Endel Tulving
*Rotman Research Institute of Baycrest Centre,
University of Toronto, Toronto, Ontario, Canada*

The neurocognitive approach to the study of memory has received a good deal of support from brain imaging methods such as positron emission tomography (PET). PET has been used not only to localize memory processes, but also to arbitrate theoretical disputes. On the localization side, PET studies have pointed to the existence of extensive cortical and subcortical memory circuits that are specific to encoding and retrieval processes. With respect to disputes, PET studies have helped to distinguish between episodic and semantic memory. The HERA model holds that episodic memory encoding processes, together with semantic memory retrieval processes, differentially engage the left hemisphere, whereas episodic memory retrieval processes differentially engage the right hemisphere, including the right prefrontal cortex. The function of the frontal lobes includes the establishment, maintenance, and switching the episodic retrieval mode and other kinds of neurocognitive sets.

Les méthodes d'imagerie cérébrale, telle la tomographie par émission de positrons (TEP), ont fourni un bon appui à l'analyse neurocognitive des phénomènes mnémoniques. La TEP a été exploitée non seulement afin de localiser les processus de mémorisation, mais également dans le but de trancher certaines querelles théoriques. En rapport avec les questions de localisation, les études exploitant la TEP ont montré l'existence de larges circuits, aussi bien corticaux que sous-corticaux, qui sont spécifiques aux processus d'encodage et de recouvrement. En ce qui a trait aux querelles, elles ont facilité la distinction entre mémoire épisodique et mémoire sémantique. Le modèle AHER (Asymétrie hémisphérique pour l'encodage et le recouvrement) postule que les processus d'encodage responsables de la mémoire épisodique, de même que les processus de recouvrement en mémoire sémantique, font intervenir l'hémisphère gauche de manière différentielle; par contre, les processus de recouvrement en mémoire épisodique feraient intervenir de manière différentielle l'hémisphère droit, y compris le cortex préfrontal droit. La fonction des lobes frontaux inclut la mise en place, le maintien et le renversement du mode de recouvrement épisodique et d'autres types d'attitudes neurocognitives.

INTRODUCTION

In this chapter I discuss findings from recent positron emission tomography (PET) studies of memory that have contributed to our understanding of memory.

Psychologists have generally shied away from, or at least largely ignored, the connection between brain activity and mental processes in memory, for what have been good reasons. Edwin "Garry" Boring, one of the great historians of psychology, wrote on this topic almost 50 years ago:

> Where or how does the brain store its memories? That is a great mystery . . . The physiology of memory has been so baffling a problem that most psychologists in facing it have gone positivistic, being content with hypothesized intervening variables or with empty correlations. (Boring, 1950, p. 670)

He went on to elaborate on the reasons for such a state of affairs:

> In general it seems safe to say that progress in this field is held back, not by lack of interest, ability or industry, but by the absence of some one of the other essentials for scientific progress. Knowledge of the nature of the nerve impulse waited upon the discovery of electric currents and galvanometers of several kinds. Knowledge in psychoacoustics seemed to get nowhere until electronics developed. *The truth about how the brain functions may eventually yield to a technique that comes from some new field remote from either physiology or psychology.* (Boring, 1950, p. 688, emphasis added)

We now have witnessed the birth and development of several new techniques that have helped to change the situation: EEG and ERP (event-related potentials), MEG (magnetoencephalography), fMRI (functional magnetic resonance imaging), and PET (positron emission tomography). These mutually complementary techniques are being increasingly used by multidisciplinary research teams in which psychologists play an important role (Hari, 1994; Näätänen & Alho, 1995; Picton, 1995; Posner & Raichle, 1994; Raichle, 1994). Although the application of these techniques to the study of memory is still in its very early stages, they have already opened new vistas and yielded valuable information (Buckner & Tulving, 1995; Cabeza & Nyberg, 1997; Fletcher, Dolan, & Frith, 1995a; Fletcher et al., 1995b; Nyberg, Cabeza, & Tulving, 1996a). These initial successes leave no doubt that the potential of the imaging techniques is tremendous. Other newer techniques, such as near-infrared optical imaging (Gratton et al., 1995), and analyses of power spectra in EEG recordings (Klimesch, Schimke, & Schwaiger, 1994), may turn out to be equally or even more exciting. It is safe to predict that all these techniques, and others as yet unknown, will revolutionize the study of the brain/mind very much in the same way in which the telescope changed the study of the heavens and the microscope reformed the investigation of the invisible structure of the world around us.

My purpose here is to illustrate the progress in the understanding of memory that neuroimaging techniques have made possible. I draw my examples from work done with PET, because I am most familiar with it, and have been personally involved in some of it.

The chapter consists of seven sections. The first section concerns memory. The major point I make here is that memory can be and has been studied from several different perspectives. I will distinguish between two approaches to memory: cognitive and neurocognitive. The pursuit of problems of memory guided by the neurocognitive approach has led to ideas about different forms of memory, organized into multiple systems and subsystems. In this chapter I am concerned primarily with episodic memory.

In the second section I summarize how PET is used in cognitive studies of memory, what it can do and what it cannot do. Although the PET method is very useful, like any other technique it has shortcomings, and these have to be kept in mind when using it. I will also make the point that there are two rather independent functions that PET studies serve. The first one is widely known: PET allows us to identify brain regions that are differentially involved in memory; it can be used to *localize* memory processes in the brain. The second is less apparent but equally important: PET helps to *arbitrate* theoretical disputes.

In the third section I illustrate the localization function of PET by presenting some recent findings pertaining to the hippocampus and its adjacent allocortical areas in the medial temporal lobes. The medial temporal lobe (MTL) regions have been widely regarded as an important brain structure of memory; some even think of it as the "seat" of memory in the brain. The hippocampus has been difficult to capture in PET studies, but some data are available, and I will mention them.

In the fourth section I provide another example of how PET localizes processes. There are large regions of the brain that are more involved in processes of episodic-memory encoding than retrieval, and other large areas are more involved in the processes of episodic-memory retrieval than encoding.

In the fifth section, I summarize and discuss PET data that have been classified under the label of HERA: hemispheric encoding/retrieval asymmetry. Left frontal brain regions are more involved in encoding, whereas right frontal regions are more involved in retrieval. This finding illustrates both the localization function and the arbitration function, because it clearly separates semantic and episodic retrieval neuroanatomically.

In the sixth section I review data suggesting that the right-frontal brain activity, which is strongly associated with episodic-memory retrieval, actually signifies a mental retrieval *set* rather than actual retrieval success. The brain sites that are involved in successful retrieval, or ecphory, seem to be situated in more posterior cortical areas.

I conclude with a brief summary of what we have learned from these initial PET studies.

MEMORY

The scientific study of human memory began a little more than a hundred years ago (Ebbinghaus, 1885). The progress we have made since then has been truly remarkable, especially that in the last couple of decades. There has been a literal explosion of new methods, new approaches, new questions, and new ideas, and the pace of activity and discovery is clearly accelerating. Here it is useful to distinguish between two different approaches to the study of memory. I refer to them as cognitive and neurocognitive. Cognitive is historically older and somewhat narrower in its scope than neurocognitive, which encompasses the cognitive approach, but also goes considerably beyond it.

We can draw a thumbnail sketch of the cognitive approach as follows: It is oriented towards psychological issues of memory. It usually works "bottom-up" from phenomena of memory to their more general theoretical explanations. Much of the empirical evidence is derived from controlled experiments with normal human subjects. The explanations of experimental findings rely heavily on concepts such as information processing and cognitive processes. The ultimate objective of the research is thought of as the construction of comprehensive theories and models of memory. Researchers in the cognitive tradition tend not to take much interest in studies of animals or brain-damaged patients, and they seldom try to relate their findings to brain processes, perhaps for the reasons of the kind that Boring speculated about.

The neurocognitive approach adopts the basic cognitive orientation but its domain extends beyond the purely psychological. It takes its inspiration not only from cognitive (experimental) psychology, but also from developmental psychology, neuropsychology, psychopharmacology, biopsychology, evolutionary biology, and brain sciences. It seeks evidence relevant to the understanding of memory from a variety of sources, including work with animals and brain-damaged patients. Its objective is to understand not only memory processes but also the relation between such processes and brain structures and mechanisms that support them. It frequently works "top-down", beginning with broad ideas about the organization and functioning of memory and evaluating those ideas in light of evidence from a wide range of sources, which recently have come to include neuroimaging.

These two working definitions are summarized in Table 20.1 that lists some of the characteristic features of the two approaches in point form.

The top-down neurocognitive orientation is aimed at elucidation of the nature of memory as an important part of the brain/mind. It is concerned with questions such as, What is memory? How many different kinds of memory are there? How did they evolve? For what purpose? How is memory related to (i.e. similar to and different from) other categories of brain/mind, such as perception, thought, and language? How are different kinds of memory related to one another? How are memory systems similar and different in different species? How does memory change with ontogenetic development?

TABLE 20.1
Two approaches to the study of memory

Cognitive	*Cognitive neuroscience*
Psychological	Biological
Bottom-up	Top-down
Epistemological	Ontological
Models; causes	Organization; classification
Explanatory	Descriptive
Predictions	No predictions
Human adults	"Higher" animals
Memory tasks	Memory systems
Mentalistic	Reductionistic
Cognitive processes	Brain/mind correlations
Behavior	Brain lesions; neuroimaging

Most of the traditional psychological research on memory, guided by the cognitive approach, does not throw much light on these kinds of questions. It can be conducted, and largely has been conducted since Ebbinghaus (1885), without raising such questions. Because it has been quite successful in its endeavours, the absence of the neurocognitive concerns from the cognitive agenda has not diminished it.

Although the top-down biological approach is concerned with issues such as the organization of memory as an extensive neurocognitive system, whereas the bottom-up approach is concerned with psychological explanation of memory phenomena, the two approaches are not alternatives. They must not be thought of as seeking rival formulations of memory. They *complement* each other. The students of memory interested in biological organization and those who are interested in psychological explanation are like two teams of engineers digging a tunnel under a mountain, starting at opposite sides with the objective of meeting, end-to-end, in the middle. We need to be aware of their separate starting points and different routes. The failure to do so will create unnecessary conflict and futile debates.

A central issue in memory research today concerns the basic nature of the organization of memory. The traditional assumption for a long time was that of a unitary memory. More recently, under the general direction of the neurocognitive approach, this assumption is gradually being replaced by the assumption of multiple memory systems (Foster & Jelicic, in press; Schacter & Tulving, 1994a). According to one current formulation, it is possible to distinguish among five major human memory systems (Schacter & Tulving, 1994b): procedural, PRS (perceptual representation system), primary (or working), semantic, and episodic. In this chapter I am concerned with episodic memory, especially in relation to semantic memory (Tulving, 1991, 1993).

Episodic memory makes possible the "autonoetic" recollection of person-ally *experienced events as experienced* (Perner & Ruffman, 1995; Wheeler, Stuss, & Tulving, 1997), including "miniature events" such as the presentation of words or other discrete items in the memory laboratory. The appearance of such an item in a particular experiment list is a to-be-remembered event (Tulving, 1983).

Semantic memory, on the other hand, is a brain system that makes possible acquisition, retention, and use of generic knowledge of the world. Whereas the episodic system is concerned with autonoetic recollection of personal experi-ences, the semantic system is concerned with "noetic" knowledge acquired and used in the course of life's happenings. The cognitive operations involved in encoding of information are very similar for episodic and semantic memory, but retrieval of information from one of the two systems can occur independently of the retrieval from the other system (Tulving, 1995).

PET

Let us now turn to PET, positron emission tomography. PET works by measur-ing cerebral blood flow by detecting the distribution of a radioactive isotope, usually ^{15}O, that has been injected with a small amount of water into the general blood flow of the subject. Sophisticated computer algorithms are used to localize the changes in this distribution to specific sites in the three-dimensional brain. Because mental activity that occurs during any cognitive task is tightly correlated with neuronal activity in the brain, and because neuronal activity is correlated with changes in the cerebral blood flow, changes in the blood flow that PET detects reflect the brain correlates of mental activity.

A subject in a typical "activation" PET study usually participates in one scanning session that includes 6 to 10 single scans, spaced about 10 minutes apart. Each scan lasts about 2 minutes during which the subject is engaged in a particular directed mental activity. The cognitive activity begins at the start of the 2-minute period, shortly after the subject receives the injection, the tracer reaches the brain in about 8 seconds, and then the actual scanning begins, lasting between 40 and 60 seconds.

The pattern of the blood flow (functional brain map) is usually derived from the data pooled over a number of scans of a particular kind (involving a fixed mental task) from a sample of subjects. The brain map yielded by such a pro-cedure represents the *average* not only of the subjects but also of all of the mental activity in which the subjects engaged during the 40–60sec duration of the scan. This means that the typical brain map yielded by PET is like a composite photograph: It contains the *cumulated* traces of the total activity of a number of brains over the duration of relevant single scans. Like any single observation made by an experimenter, such a map is not interpretable: It is not possible to attribute any of its details to any aspects of the mental task.

This is why the logic of the most widely used PET procedure is based on a comparison of scans (Buckner & Tulving, 1995; Petersen, Fox, Posner, Mintun, & Raichle, 1988). The simplest comparison involves the subtraction of one brain map obtained during one scan, from a map obtained during another scan. The *difference* between the two brain maps reflects the *difference* between the mental activities in which the subjects engaged during the two scans.

This, then, is what PET can do: Provide data on a rough *correlation* of differences between two mental activities and differences between two brain maps reflecting localized neuronal activity. These data, like all others in science, are informative and potentially useful to the extent that they are reliable. A single finding may at best serve to focus the researcher's interest, and not much more. This is why an important objective of PET studies of memory at the present early stage of the proceedings is the garnering of systematic and reliable data. Eventually these data will guide the construction of meaningful models of the brain/mind relations in memory.

Because of the relatively poor temporal resolution, PET cannot be used to study short-lived processes or to find out what happens to individual items. Thus, if we "pick up" different brain regions in a particular comparison of tasks, we have no way of telling anything about the temporal relations in their activity; we know nothing about the flow of information among the identified regions. For that purpose, EEG and MEG-based techniques are much more suitable.

PET data can be used to *localize processes* to specific brain regions. But it is also important to realize that PET data can equally well help us to *clarify theoretical issues*, quite independently of specific loci of memory processes. An example is the distinction between episodic and semantic memory. Although all students of memory accept and use the distinction at a descriptive level, in the sense of different kinds of information or different tasks, there is as yet no general agreement as to the biological reality of the distinction. Many people still believe that episodic and semantic memory are just two different modes of operation of a large declarative memory system. This attitude is quite unlike that towards, say, vision and audition. Everyone agrees that they represent different brain systems; no one argues that they are just two different ways or modes in which the general "distant sensation" system operates. The reason for the different attitudes is obvious. In the case of two sensory modalities there are clearly visible differences in the anatomy, whereas in the case of memory anatomical differences have, until recently, been mostly a matter of inference.

This is where PET studies can help. As we will see presently, there are prominent differences in the brain maps produced by retrieval of otherwise similar semantic and episodic information. The anatomical differences are particularly striking in the frontal lobes. But the point I want to make here is that the exact localization of these differences does not matter. The hypothesis that episodic and semantic memory represent different brain systems would gain support from any finding of systematic differences in brain activity, regardless of the brain regions involved. Thus, PET can function as an *arbiter* in theoretical disputes, quite independently of specific localization of any particular process in the brain.

LOCALIZATION: HIPPOCAMPUS AND MTL

The long history of research showing that the hippocampal formation in the medial temporal lobes plays a critical role in memory is well known to most psychologists. Much of the relevant evidence is derived from studies of patients with damage to these structures who show impairment in various kinds of memory processes (Markowitsch & Pritzel, 1985; Milner, 1966; Squire, 1993). So, what is the story of PET and the hippocampus? An early study done by Squire and colleagues at Washington University (Squire et al., 1992) did reveal evidence of the involvement of the right parahippocampal region in explicit recall, but many other studies of memory, done subsequently, failed to detect any hippocampal activity (Andreasen et al., 1995; Buckner et al., 1995; Fletcher et al., 1995b). The impression quickly spread therefore that PET is insensitive or inadequate to "pick up" a small structure such as the hippocampus. Actually this is not quite true.

A number of PET memory studies have now identified the involvement of the hippocampus in memory. The difficulty so far has been in detecting any *general pattern* in the data. Activations of MTL regions have been observed unilaterally in the left hemisphere or in the right hemisphere, as well as bilaterally; they have been observed during encoding as well as during retrieval; they have been found with verbal materials and nonverbal materials (Blaxton, 1996; Cabeza & Nyberg, 1997; Tulving & Markowitsch, 1997).

A different kind of a PET finding of the involvement of the MTL regions in memory processes is one of correlation, across individual subjects, between hippocampal activity, as revealed by ratio-adjusted measures of blood flow, and behavioral memory performance. The graph in Fig. 20.1 illustrates this type of finding. The data come from a joint Swedish-Canadian PET project done in Toronto on recognition of previously studied words (Nyberg, McIntosh, Houle, Nilsson, & Tulving, 1996d). The abscissa of the graph in Fig. 20.1 represents the relative amount of blood flow in a region near the left hippocampus in each individual subject's brain. The ordinate represents individual subjects' recognition performance expressed in terms of the hit rate. Thus, each point in the scatterplot represents an individual subject. We see that the higher a subject's blood flow at this hippocampal site, the higher was his or her recognition memory performance. The finding was replicated in two different scans within the study, and replicated, at a slightly different hippocampal site, in another study, done independently of the first one (Nyberg et al., 1996b). Similar individual subjects' correlations have been reported for the amygdala and recall of emotional material by Larry Cahill and colleagues, at the University of California at Irvine

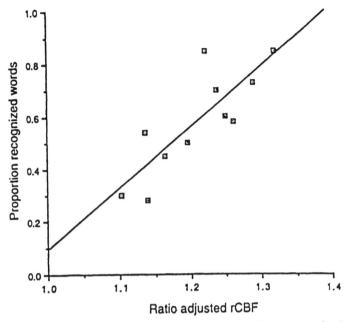

FIG. 20.1   Scatterplot showing a positive relation between episodic memory retrieval (hit rates in recognition) and standardized measures of regional cerebral blood flow at a site in left medial temporal lobe (Talairach & Tournoux, 1988, stereotactic x,y,z coordinates: −24, 2, −16). Each data point represents one of 11 subjects. From Nyberg, McIntosh, Houle, Nilsson, and Tulving (1996), *Nature, 380*, 715–717.

(Cahill et al., 1996), and between response latencies in imagery and activation of occipital regions by Stephen Kosslyn and colleagues at Harvard (Kosslyn, 1996).

In summary of this section, then, we can say that although it has not always been easy to detect "hippocampal" (MTL) activation in PET studies of memory, more recent experiments have produced promising data. Different regions in the medial temporal lobes are involved in various aspects of memory, and some may be directly related to memory performance. Although a clear larger picture is still missing, the PET data have at least in general terms confirmed and elaborated evidence from lesion studies of brain damaged patients (Markowitsch & Pritzel, 1985; Milner, 1966; Squire, 1993).

ARBITRATION: ENCODING AND RETRIEVAL

Let us now proceed to examine encoding and retrieval processes "in the brain". We can think of the psychological issue here as this: Are encoding and retrieval processes basically similar or basically different? It has been traditionally assumed that retrieval is largely a matter of "reactivation" of encoding processes.

Bower and Hilgard attributed the idea to earlier generations of researchers, such as Wolfgang Köhler (1938), and summarized it as follows:

> Recall or remembering involves the reactivation of a given memory trace; in effect, it is a revival of the same perceptual processes that corresponded to the original perception. The trace continues to exist as an active process in the nervous system; but is of too low an intensity to enter consciousness. In recall, a cue selects out and amplifies the intensity of a particular trace to raise it over the threshold of consciousness. (Bower & Hilgard, 1981, p. 311)

Many others, on the basis of different kinds of evidence, have adopted a similar position, assuming that retrieval consists essentially of recapitulation of the same patterns of mental or neural activity that occurred when the original event was perceived and comprehended (Craik, 1983; Köhler et al., in press; Nyberg et al., 1996d; Rosler, Heil, & Hennighausen, 1995). Quite independently of actual findings, it makes sense to imagine that particular processes must run their course in order to store some information in memory, and that the same processes must run the same course again when the stored trace is reactivated at retrieval. The question is, how large is the overlap? Are there differences as well as similarities between encoding and retrieval processes?

As long as we are limited to purely behavioral data, the question of similarities or differences is not easy to handle. However, when we pose the question at the level of brain activity, the issue becomes more tractable. All we need to do is to measure, and then compare, regional blood flow while subjects are (1) encoding some material into memory, and (2) retrieving the same, previously encoded material. When we subtract the retrieval map from the encoding map, we will see those brain regions that were more active during encoding than during retrieval; when we subtract the encoding map from the retrieval map, we will see those brain regions that were more active during retrieval than during encoding.

Figure 20.2 shows "encoding regions" and "retrieval regions". These data were provided by a direct comparison of brain maps associated with study and test of experimental materials. The data here were pooled from four different experiments, and are based on a total of 48 subjects. The four experiments were carried out at Toronto (Cabeza et al., 1997; Kapur et al., 1996; Köhler et al., in press; Nyberg et al., 1996b). The experiments differed with respect to a number of details, including the to-be-remembered materials, but they were identical in that all included scanning of both encoding and retrieval. Thus, in every one of the four experiments, subjects were studying the items during some scans, and taking a recognition or recall test during other scans. In composite comparisons, such as this one, therefore, commonalities related to encoding or retrieval are accentuated, whereas specific activations related to specific features of individual studies are likely to be cancelled out.

The "encoding regions" here (on the left of Fig. 20.1) are brain regions in which regional blood flow was higher during encoding than during retrieval.

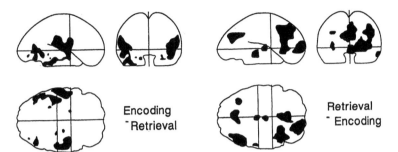

FIG. 20.2   PET results of a direct comparison between encoding and retrieval. Left: brain regions that are more active during encoding than during retrieval (temporal lobes bilaterally, left fusiform gyrus and perirhinal cortex in the medial temporal lobe, right parahippocampal gyrus, and entorhinal cortex bilaterally). Right: brain regions that are more active during retrieval than during encoding (right prefrontal cortex, anterior cingulate cortex, thalamus, brainstem, and midline parietal regions near cuneus and precuneus). Data were pooled from four different PET studies in which a total of 48 young healthy subjects participated. Reprinted from Tulving & Markowitsch, 1997.

They include bilateral temporal lobes, left fusiform gyrus that extends to the perirhinal cortex in the medial temporal lobe, as well as small but statistically highly significant activations in the hippocampal regions bilaterally, namely in the entorhinal cortex, and in the right parahippocampal gyrus. We can think of these regions as representing components of widely distributed neuroanatomical "encoding circuits".

Encoding, of course, is a highly complex process that consists of many subprocesses, and therefore the knowledge we have gained from this analysis is rather gross. But these data put us greatly ahead in our understanding of memory processes in the brain, when we compare where we are now with where we were, say, only five years ago.

Two points are worth noting. First, given that the brain maps shown in Fig. 20.2 represent the *relative* amounts of activations at encoding and retrieval, areas showing greater activation at encoding (as in the left half of Fig. 20.2) may also be interpreted as showing relatively *less* activation at retrieval. This reduced activation has sometimes been attributed to perceptual priming (Demb et al., 1995; Squire et al., 1992; Tulving et al., 1994b). The idea is that primed items require less processing at retrieval, and this reduced processing is reflected in the attenuation of the activation of the regions that subserve the initial encoding. In light of the massive size and multiplicity of the regions that show such "deactivation" it is somewhat unlikely that they all signify priming. Moreover, the regions showing "deactivations" in the medial temporal regions (Fig. 20.2, also Tulving, Markowitsch, Craik, Habib, & Houle, 1996), cannot be critically involved in priming, because patients with lesions in these regions have been shown to perform indistinguishably from normal subjects in perceptual priming studies.

Second, the absence of activation in most regions of the brain in this subtractive comparison does not mean that these regions were not involved with encoding or retrieval. A direct comparison of the kind made here does not reveal any brain regions that are equally active during both encoding and retrieval, nor does it distinguish between equally active and equally inactive regions. It is quite possible that some of the "blank" regions in Fig. 20.2 were equally active in encoding and retrieval, and therefore cancelled out in the subtraction. Indeed, we know from other analyses that there exist many brain regions that are involved in both encoding and retrieval (e.g. Köhler et al., in press; Nyberg et al., 1996b). The present data simply highlight the differences.

The right half of Fig. 20.2 shows "retrieval regions": brain regions that were more active during retrieval than during encoding in the data pooled from the four experiments (Cabeza et al., 1997; Kapur et al., 1996; Köhler et al., in press; Nyberg et al., 1996b). Retrieval activation was especially prominent in the right frontal lobes; this area will be discussed in more detail later. Other regions that were more active in retrieval than in encoding include the anterior cingulate cortex, and midline parietal activations in cuneus and precuneus. There was also a conspicuous activation in the thalamus. Altogether these regions can be thought of as representing the most prominent components of widely distributed neuroanatomical "retrieval circuits".

The "retrieval regions" shown in Fig. 20.2 agree remarkably well with episodic-memory retrieval regions recently identified by Randy Buckner and his colleagues at Washington University (Buckner, Raichle, Miezin, & Petersen, 1996). The right frontal and medial parietal (precuneus-cuneus) activations seen in the right half of Fig. 20.2 also agree well with observations made by Tim Shallice and Paul Fletcher, and their colleagues, in London, England (Shallice et al., 1994; Fletcher et al., 1995a,b).

These data illustrate what is now well known from many other PET studies of memory, namely, that there are distinctive and easy-to-identify differences in locations that are differentially active in encoding versus those that are differentially active in retrieval. Thus, although encoding and retrieval processes do share common brain processes, their substrates in the brain are also quite different.

The "encoding regions" and "retrieval regions" shown in Fig. 20.2 look massive, but the appearance here, as in all other such pictures of PET activations, is deceptive (Roland, Kawashima, Gulyas, & O'Sullivan, 1995). In either case, the "activated" areas shown comprise less than 2 per cent of the volume of the brain. Their extent in the subtraction analysis is determined not only by the cerebral blood flow changes associated with the encoding and retrieval tasks, but also by the threshold selected for the comparison by the experimenter. Here the threshold is conservative: Only those brain regions where the differences between the compared conditions reached the z-score of 4.5 ($P < .0001$) are shown in Fig. 20.2. The adoption of a lower threshold would, of course, have resulted in the expansion of the boundaries of the encoding and retrieval "circuits".

ARBITRATION: HERA

Let us now turn to the so-called HERA model. HERA stands for hemispheric encoding/retrieval asymmetry. Initial PET studies investigating encoding and retrieval processes in episodic memory, done at Toronto (Kapur et al., 1994; Moscovitch, Kapur, Köhler, & Houle, 1995; Tulving et al., 1994a,b), the Hammersmith Hospital in London (Shallice et al., 1994; Fletcher et al., 1995b) and Washington University (Buckner et al., 1995; Squire et al., 1992) suggested a surprising empirical regularity: Left prefrontal cortex is differentially more involved than right in encoding information into episodic memory, whereas right prefrontal cortex is differentially more involved than left in episodic memory retrieval. Because in many cases episodic encoding (for instance, deep encoding judgments) involve semantic memory retrieval, the HERA model assigns semantic-memory retrieval also to the left frontal lobe. We call HERA a model, because we have used two paired concepts from cognitive psychology, namely encoding and retrieval, and episodic and semantic memory, to make sense of the highly regular asymmetry in neuronal activity.

Let me illustrate HERA with an example from a PET study done at Toronto with university students as subjects (Cabeza et al., 1997; Kapur et al., 1996). Subjects were scanned under two conditions. In one, they saw pairs of words, such as PENGUIN—TUXEDO, and they had to think of a meaningful relation between the words of each pair. They were also told that their memory for these pairs would be tested. Two processes occur in this situation. First, subjects make use of their semantic knowledge (general knowledge of the world) in relating the paired words to each other, that is, they engage in semantic-memory retrieval. Second, the presented information is encoded and stored in episodic memory, that is, subjects later on remember that they saw such and such pairs of words. In the other experimental condition, subjects again saw pairs of words, such as PENGUIN—TUXEDO, and they had to decide whether the pair had appeared in the study list. This is an episodic-memory retrieval (recognition) condition.

The left part of Fig. 20.3 shows the results yielded by the subtraction of the retrieval activations from the encoding activations: extensive regions in the left hemisphere, including prefrontal cortex, were more strongly activated during encoding than during retrieval. The right part of Fig. 20.3 shows an asymmetrical pattern of the other kind: activation on the right but not left. This pattern was yielded by the subtraction of the blood flow pattern associated with the encoding condition from that associated with retrieval (recognition). In addition to the right frontal retrieval activation, there are other posterior regions that were more involved in recognition than in initial study. Although in this particular study the HERA pattern extended well beyond the frontal regions, this is not always the case. For the time being at least we speak of HERA mostly in connection with the frontal regions of the brain.

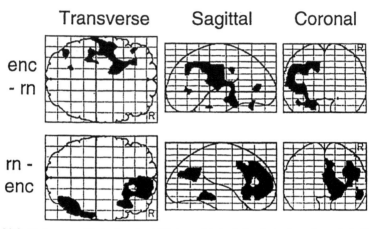

FIG. 20.3 Brain maps illustrating the HERA model. Left hemispheric regions, including the frontal lobe, are more active than right hemispheric regions during intentional study of pairs of words (at the top of the figure), whereas right hemispheric regions, including the frontal lobe, are more active than left hemispheric regions during recognition of the same pairs of words (at the bottom of the figure). Average data for 12 young healthy subjects. From Kapur et al., 1996, and Cabeza et al., in press. Figure reprinted from Nyberg, Cabeza, and Tulving (1996), *Psychonomic Bulletin and Review*, *3*, 135–148.

The HERA Model

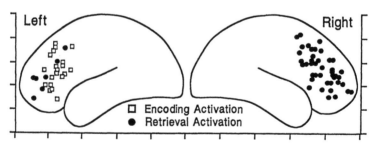

FIG. 20.4   A schematic representation of the HERA model. Data pooled from 25 different PET studies of episodic-memory encoding and retrieval. Each data point represents the outcome of the subtractive analysis of encoding or retrieval against suitable reference conditions. The peaks of activated regions are projected to the left and right lateral surface of the brain. Figure reprinted from Nyberg, Cabeza, and Tulving (1996), *Psychonomic Bulletin and Review*, *3*, 135–148.

Although initially unexpected, the HERA pattern in the frontal lobes is now well established and indeed represents one of the most robust facts of the PET-memory literature. Figure 20.4 presents a schematic summary of the results of 25 relevant PET studies from different laboratories whose results were available in May 1996 (Nyberg et al., 1996a). The distribution of the peaks of activations shown in the graph tell the story of the asymmetry. All encoding activations were located in the left hemisphere, none were on the right, whereas a large majority of retrieval activations were on the right, with a few also appearing on the left. This pattern provides massive support for the HERA model. It holds widely, for different kinds of material (both verbal and nonverbal), for different kinds of encoding and retrieval tasks, and despite a great deal of variability in other experimental conditions. However, as shown in Fig. 20.4, within the general left/right encoding/retrieval regularity there exists considerable variability in localization of function, depending on particular conditions of the studies in the set. This variability invites more detailed analyses of the data, some of which have already been reported (Buckner, 1996; Nyberg et al., 1996b).

The HERA findings illustrate both localization and arbitration functions of PET. Not only do they tell us something about what brain regions are involved in memory processes such as encoding and retrieval, they also help to arbitrate the issue of the biological reality of the distinction between episodic and semantic memory. The fact that semantic retrieval seems to be localized largely to the left, whereas episodic retrieval involves processes subserved by regions in the right hemisphere (Andreasen et al., 1995, 1996; Haxby et al., 1996) points to basic differences in the neuroanatomy of the two memory systems. An especially pleasing feature of the episodic/semantic retrieval asymmetry is that it is consistent with the possibility that the two hemispheres play different roles in subserving *autonoetic and noetic consciousness*, which in theory are associated with episodic and semantic memory (Tulving, 1985; Wheeler et al., 1997).

FRONTAL LOBES AND RETRIEVAL SET

What are we to make of the frontal lobes showing up as prominently as they have in many PET studies of episodic memory? It happens that we have available some data that address this question, with respect to the right frontal (episodic retrieval) activity. When people are tested in an explicit memory test, such as recognition, two things happen: (1) They try to think back to a particular study episode, trying to decide whether the test item before them also appeared in that episode (retrieval attempt), and (2) they succeed in doing so in many cases (retrieval success).

The data from two PET studies (Kapur et al., 1995; Nyberg et al., 1995) suggest that the right frontal activation reflects retrieval attempt rather than, or perhaps in addition to, retrieval success (McIntosh, Nyberg, Bookstein, & Tulving, 1997; Rugg, Fletcher, Frith, Frackowiak, & Dolan, 1996; see also Schacter, Alpert, Savage, & Rauch, 1996). Two independent variables were manipulated in these studies: (1) presence versus absence of retrieval attempt, and (2) successful versus failed retrieval. There were two relevant findings. First, the PET data confirmed the overall HERA pattern, showing prominent right frontal activation in successful retrieval (recognition of previously studied words as "old"). Second, such prominent right frontal activation was also present when subjects attempted to recognize test items but failed to do so, because all the test items were "new", not previously seen in the experiment. Thus, the fact that the right frontal lobe shows activation in both cases suggests that this activation does not depend on retrieval success but rather reflects attempts at retrieval, or the episodic "retrieval mode" (Tulving, 1983).

These studies also revealed other regions, in more posterior brain areas, that were more active in successful remembering than in unsuccessful remembering. These regions presumably reflect the processes involved in actual retrieval ("storage sites") of the information that subjects used in successful recognition.

Although the jury is still out on the issue of the involvement of right frontal lobe regions in episodic retrieval, the available data leave little doubt that the maintenance of the episodic retrieval mode is one of the important roles that the right frontal lobe plays, most likely in close interaction with other regions (Nyberg et al., 1996c).

What is this retrieval mode that we think we have spotted in the frontal lobes? A plausible hypothesis is that is simply a particular instance of the important concept of "set". Set, under various names, has been studied in psychological laboratories from the earliest days, beginning with the Würzburg school. A great deal of evidence suggests that set plays an exceedingly important role in all sorts of mental activity. It does so by determining the kind of processing that is to be performed on incoming stimuli and inhibiting the many other kinds of processing that the brain is capable of performing on the same stimuli.

Thus, neuroimaging findings suggest that one of the main functions of the frontal lobes is the establishment, maintenance, and switching of sets. This idea is in good agreement with a great deal of clinical and neuropsychological evidence that is pointing in the same direction, and that has been discussed under the rubrics of sustained and selective attention, executive functions, supervision, monitoring, organizing, temporal sequencing, and so on. Many of these concepts can be thought of as referring to different kinds of set, that is, readiness for specific action coupled with inhibition of other possible actions.

CONCLUSION

Let me sum up under the title "lessons learned". What is it that we now know about memory that we did not know, or did not quite know, before these early PET studies were carried out? We have learned a number of things.

We have learned that PET can be used both to localize cognitive processes and to arbitrate theoretical disputes.

We have learned that PET is capable of "picking up" the hippocampus, but that there is as yet no simple way of describing exactly what the role of the hippocampus is.

We have learned that memory circuits in the brain are much more extensive than previously thought, clearly going beyond the medial temporal regions that have received a great deal of attention before. They encompass many widely distributed subcortical and cortical regions.

We have learned that memory circuits in the brain, even if extensive, are quite specific, perhaps surprisingly so. Even the separation between encoding circuits and retrieval circuits is quite striking.

We have learned that a curious hemispheric asymmetry exists between encoding and retrieval in episodic memory, as well as between episodic retrieval and semantic retrieval.

Finally, we have reaffirmed the highly specific role of the frontal lobes as the master control center of the cognitive operations of the brain, influencing cognitive processing and mental phenomena through the adoption, maintenance, and switching of sets.

At the start of this chapter, I quoted "Garry" Boring, the historian, and one of my professors when I was a graduate student: "The truth about how the brain functions may eventually yield to a technique that comes from some new field remote from either physiology or psychology." If he came back today, to find out how his prophecy has fared, I am sure he would be as impressed and pleased with what has happened as we all are. He would be even more impressed, I think, to find out how quickly, in just a few years after the introduction of the new technique, our understanding of the brain/mind relations in memory has begun to change. He would call it genuine progress.

ACKNOWLEDGEMENTS

Endel Tulving's research is supported by the Natural Sciences and Engineering Research Council of Canada (Grant A8632), and by an endowment by Anne and Max Tanenbaum in support of research in cognitive neuroscience. I am grateful for help to Reza Habib and Eva McGrath.

REFERENCES

Andreasen, N. C., O'Leary, D. S., Arndt, S., Cizadlo, T., Hurtig, R., Rezai, K., Watkins, G. L., Ponto, L. L., & Hichwa, R. D. (1995). Short-term and long-term verbal memory: a positron emission tomography study. *Proceedings of the National Academy of Sciences USA, 92,* 5111–5115.

Andreasen, N. C., O'Leary, D. S., Arndt, S., Cizadlo, T., Hurtig, R., Rezai, K., Watkins, G. L., Ponto, L. L. B., & Hichwa, R. D. (1996). Neural substrates of facial recognition. *Journal of Neuropsychiatry and Clinical Neuroscience, 8,* 139–149.

Blaxton, T. (1996). Distinguishing false from true in human memory. *Neuron, 17,* 191–194.

Boring, E. G. (1950). *A History of experimental psychology* (2nd ed.). New York: Appleton-Century-Crofts.

Bower, G. H., & Hilgard, E. R. (1981). *Theories of learning* (5th ed.). Englewood Cliffs, NJ: Prentice Hall.

Buckner, R. (1996). Beyond HERA: Contributions of specific prefrontal brain areas to long-term memory. *Psychonomic Bulletin and Review, 3,* 149–158.

Buckner, R. L., Petersen, S. E., Ojemann, J. G., Miezin, F. M., Squire, L. R., & Raichle, M. E. (1995). Functional anatomical studies of explicit and implicit memory retrieval tasks. *Journal of Neuroscience, 15*, 12–29.

Buckner, R., Raichle, M., Miezin, F. M., & Petersen, S. E. (1996). Functional anatomic studies of memory retrieval for auditory words and visual pictures. *Journal of Neuroscience, 16*, 6219–6235.

Buckner, R. L., & Tulving, E. (1995). Neuroimaging studies of memory: Theory and recent PET results. In F. Boller & J. Grafman (Eds.), *Handbook of Neuropsychology* (Vol. 10, pp. 439–466). Amsterdam: Elsevier.

Cabeza, R., Kapur, S., Craik, F. I. M., McIntosh, A. R., Houle, S., & Tulving, E. (1997). Functional neuroanatomy of recall and recognition: A PET study of episodic memory. *Journal of Cognitive Neuroscience, 9*, 254–265.

Cabeza, R., & Nyberg, L. (1997). Imaging cognition: An empirical review of PET studies with normal subjects. *Journal of Cognitive Neuroscience, 9*, 1–26.

Cahill, L., Haier, R. J., Fallon, J., Alkire, M. T., Tang, C., Keator, D., Wu, J., & McGaugh, J. L. (1996). Amygdala activity at encoding correlated with long-term, free recall of emotional information. *Proceedings of the National Academy of Sciences USA, 93*, 8016–8021.

Craik, F. I. M. (1983). On the transfer of information from temporary to permanent memory. *Philosophical Transactions of the Royal Society, London, Series B, 302*, 341–359.

Demb, J. B., Desmond, J. E., Wagner, A. D., Vaidya, C. J., Glover, G. H., & Gabrieli, J. D. (1995). Semantic encoding and retrieval in the left inferior prefrontal cortex: a functional MRI study of task difficulty and process specificity. *Journal of Neuroscience, 15*, 5870–5878.

Ebbinghaus, H. (1885). *Über das Gedächtnis.* Leipzig: Duncker & Humblot.

Fletcher, P. C., Dolan, R. J., & Frith, C. D. (1995a). The functional anatomy of memory. *Experientia, 51*, 1197–1207.

Fletcher, P. C., Frith, C. D., Grasby, P. M., Shallice, T., Frackowiak, R. S. J., & Dolan, R. J. (1995b). Brain systems for encoding and retrieval of auditory-verbal memory: An *in vivo* study in humans. *Brain, 118*, 401–416.

Foster, J. K., & Jelicic, M. (in press). *Unitary versus multiple systems account of memory.* London: Oxford University Press.

Gratton, G., Corballis, P. M., Cho, E., Fabiani, M., & Hood, D. C. (1995). Shades of gray matter: noninvasive optical images of human brain responses during visual stimulation. *Psychophysiology, 32*, 505–509.

Hari, R. (1994). Human cortical functions revealed by magnetoencephalography. *Progress in Brain Research, 100*, 163–168.

Haxby, J. V., Ungerleider, L. G., Horwitz, B., Maisog, J. M., Rapoport, S. L., & Grady, C. L. (1996). Face encoding and recognition in the human brain. *Proceedings of the National Academy of Sciences USA, 93*, 922–927.

Kapur, S., Craik, F. I. M., Jones, C., Brown, G. M., Houle, S., & Tulving, E. (1995). Functional role of the prefrontal cortex in retrieval of memories: a PET study. *NeuroReport, 6*, 1880–1884.

Kapur, S., Craik, F. I. M., Tulving, E., Wilson, A. A., Houle, S., & Brown, G. (1994). Neuroanatomical correlates of encoding in episodic memory: Levels of processing effect. *Proceedings of the National Academy of Sciences USA, 91*, 2008–2011.

Kapur, S., Tulving, E., Cabeza, R., McIntosh, R. A., Houle, S., & Craik, F. I. M. (1996). Neural correlates of intentional learning of verbal materials: a PET study in humans. *Cognitive Brain Research, 4*, 243–249.

Klimesch, W., Schimke, H., & Schwaiger, J. (1994). Episodic and semantic memory: an analysis in the EEG theta and alpha band. *Electroencephalography and Clinical Neurophysiology, 91*, 428–441.

Köhler, S., Moscovitch, M., Winocur, G., Houle, S., & McIntosh, A. R. (in press). Networks of domain-specific and general regions involved in episodic memory for spatial location and object identity. *Neuropsychologia.*

Köhler, W. (1938). *The place of value in a world of facts.* New York: Liveright.

Kosslyn, S. M., Thompson, W. L., Kim, I. J., Rauch, S. L., & Alpert, N. M. (1996). Individual differences in cerebral blood flow in Area 17 predict the time to evaluate visualized letters. *Journal of Cognitive Neuroscience, 8*, 78–82.

Markowitsch, H. J., & Pritzel, M. (1985). The neuropathology of amnesia. *Progress in Neurobiology, 25*, 189–287.

McIntosh, A. R., Nyberg, L., Bookstein, F. L., & Tulving, E. (1997). Differential functional connectivity of prefrontal and medial temporal cortices during episodic memory retrieval. *Human Brain Mapping, 5*, 323–327.

Milner, B. (1966). Amnesia following operation on the temporal lobes. In C. W. M. Whitty & O. L. Zangwill (Eds.), *Amnesia* (pp. 109–133). London: Butterworth.

Moscovitch, M., Kapur, S., Köhler, S., & Houle, S. (1995). Distinct neural correlates of visual long-term memory for spatial location and object identity: A positron emission tomography (PET) study in humans. *Proceedings of the National Academy of Sciences USA, 92*, 3721–3725.

Näätänen, R., & Alho, K. (1995). Mismatch negativity—a unique measure of sensory processing in audition. *International Journal of Neuroscience, 80*, 317–337.

Nyberg, L., Cabeza, R., & Tulving, E. (1996a). PET studies of encoding and retrieval: the HERA model. *Psychonomic Bulletin and Review, 3*, 135–148.

Nyberg, L., McIntosh, A. R., Cabeza, R., Habib, R., Houle, S., & Tulving, E. (1996b). General and specific brain regions involved in retrieval of events: What, where, and when. *Proceedings of the National Academy of Sciences USA, 93*, 11280–11285.

Nyberg, L., McIntosh, A. R., Cabeza, R., Nilsson, L.-G., Houle, S., Habib, R., & Tulving, E. (1996c). Network analysis of positron emission tomography regional cerebral blood flow data: Ensemble inhibition during episodic memory retrieval. *Journal of Neuroscience, 16*, 3753–3759.

Nyberg, L., McIntosh, A. R., Houle, S., Nilsson, L.-G., & Tulving, E. (1996d). Activation of medial temporal structures during episodic memory retrieval. *Nature, 380*, 715–717.

Nyberg, L., Tulving, E., Habib, R., Nilsson, L.-G., Kapur, S., Houle, S., Cabeza, R., & McIntosh, A. R. (1995). Functional brain maps of retrieval mode and recovery of episodic information. *NeuroReport, 7*, 249–252.

Perner, J., & Ruffman, T. (1995). Episodic memory and autonoetic consciousness: Developmental evidence and a theory of childhood amnesia. *Journal of Experimental Child Psychology, 59*, 516–548.

Petersen, S. E., Fox, P. T., Posner, M. I., Mintun, M., & Raichle, M. E. (1988). Positron emission tomographic studies of the cortical anatomy of single-word processing. *Nature, 331*, 585–589.

Picton, T. W. (1995). The neurophysiological evaluation of auditory discrimination. *Ear & Hearing, 16*, 1–5.

Posner, M. I., & Raichle, M. E. (1994). *Images of mind.* New York: Scientific American Books.

Raichle, M. E. (1994). Images of the mind: Studies with modern imaging techniques. *Annual Review of Psychology, 45*, 333–356.

Roland, P. E., Kawashima, R., Gulyas, B., & O'Sullivan, B. (1995). Positron emission tomography in cognitive neuroscience: Methodological constraints, strategies, and examples from learning and memory. In M. S. Gazzaniga (Ed.), *The cognitive neurosciences* (pp. 781–788). Cambridge, MA: MIT Press.

Rosler, F., Heil, M., & Hennighausen, E. (1995). Exploring memory functions by means of brain electrical topography: a review. *Brain Topography, 7*, 301–313.

Rugg, M. D., Fletcher, P. C., Frith, C. D., Frackowiak, R. S. J., & Dolan, R. J. (1996). Differential activation of the prefrontal cortex in successful and unsuccessful memory retrieval. *Brain, 119*, 2073–2083.

Schacter, D. L., Alpert, N. M., Savage, C. R., & Rauch, S. L. (1996). Conscious recollection and the human hippocampal formation: Evidence from positron emission tomography. *Proceedings of the National Academy of Sciences USA, 93*, 321–325.

Schacter, D. L., & Tulving, E. (1994a). *Memory systems 1994.* Cambridge, MA: MIT Press.

Schacter, D. L., & Tulving, E. (1994b). What are the memory systems of 1994? In D. L. Schacter & E. Tulving (Eds.), *Memory systems 1994* (pp. 1–38). Cambridge, MA: MIT Press.

Shallice, T., Fletcher, P., Frith, C. D., Grasby, P., Frackowiak, R. S. J., & Dolan, R. J. (1994). Brain regions associated with acquisition and retrieval of verbal episodic memory. *Nature, 368,* 633–635.

Squire, L. R. (1993). Memory and the hippocampus: A synthesis from findings with rats, monkeys, and humans. *Psychological Review, 99,* 195–231.

Squire, L. R., Ojemann, J. G., Miezin, F. M., Petersen, S. E., Videen, T. O., & Raichle, M. E. (1992). Activation of the hippocampus in normal humans: A functional anatomical study of memory. *Proceedings of the National Academy of Sciences USA, 89,* 1837–1841.

Talairach, J., & Tournoux, P. (1988). *A co-planar stereotactic atlas of the human brain.* Stuttgart, Germany: Thieme.

Tulving, E. (1983). *Elements of episodic memory.* Oxford: Clarendon Press.

Tulving, E. (1985). Memory and consciousness. *Canadian Psychology, 26,* 1–12.

Tulving, E. (1991). Concepts of human memory. In L. Squire, G. Lynch, N. M. Weinberger, & J. L. McGaugh (Eds.), *Memory: Organization and locus of change* (pp. 3–32). New York: Oxford University Press.

Tulving, E. (1993). What is episodic memory? *Current Perspectives in Psychological Science, 2,* 67–70.

Tulving, E. (1995). Organization of memory: Quo vadis? In M. S. Gazzaniga (Ed.), *The Cognitive Neurosciences* (pp. 839–847). Cambridge, MA: MIT Press.

Tulving, E., Kapur, S., Craik, F. I. M., Moscovitch, M., & Houle, S. (1994a). Hemispheric encoding/retrieval asymmetry in episodic memory: Positron emission tomography findings. *Proceedings of the National Academy of Sciences USA, 91,* 2016–2020.

Tulving, E., Kapur, S., Markowitsch, H. J., Craik, F. I. M., Habib, R., & Houle, S. (1994b). Neuroanatomical correlates of retrieval in episodic memory: Auditory sentence recognition. *Proceedings of the National Academy of Sciences USA, 91,* 2012–2015.

Tulving, E., Markowitsch, H. J., Craik, F. I. M., Habib, R., & Houle, S. (1996). Novelty and familiarity activations in PET studies of memory encoding and retrieval. *Cerebral Cortex, 6,* 71–79

Tulving, E., & Markowitsch, H. J. (1997). Memory beyond the hippocampus. *Current Opinion in Neurobiology, 7,* 209–216.

Wheeler, M. A., Stuss, D. T., & Tulving, E. (1997). Towards a theory of episodic memory: The frontal lobes and autonoetic consciousness. *Psychological Bulletin, 121,* 331–354.

CHAPTER TWENTY-ONE

Metamemory: The feeling of knowing and its vagaries

Asher Koriat
Department of Psychology, University of Haifa, Haifa, Israel

The study of the "feeling of knowing" (FOK) provides insights regarding some of the fundamental issues concerning the subjective monitoring of one's own knowledge. How accurate are FOKs? What are the processes underlying their accuracy? Recent work suggests that metacognitive judgments do not reflect direct access to the underlying memory traces, but are mediated by inferential heuristics, which generally work. Sometimes, however, these heuristics result in serious dissociations between knowing and the FOK. These dissociations may have troubling consequences, because people generally trust their subjective feelings, and use them to control their behaviors.

L'étude du "sentiment de savoir" (SdS) éclaire quelques-unes des questions fondamentales portant sur le contrôle continu qu'un individu exerce sur ses connaissances. Dans quelle mesure le SdS est-il exact? Quels sont les processus responsables de cette exactitude? Des travaux récents suggèrent que les jugements métacognitifs ne reflètent pas un accès direct aux traces mnémoniques sous-jacentes; leur servent plutôt d'intermédiaires des heuristiques inférentielles qui fonctionnent habituellement bien. Il arrive parfois que ces heuristiques entraînent cependant de sérieuses dissociations entre le fait de savoir et le SdS. Ces dissociations peuvent avoir des conséquences problématiques parce que les gens ont en général confiance en leurs sentiments et les utilisent pour contrôler leurs comportements.

At any point in time we can retrieve from memory only a small portion of what is stored there. Often we fail to retrieve a piece of information although we may be able to recall it at some later time or recognize it among distractors. Such episodes of recall failures are sometimes accompanied by a strong conviction that the needed information is available in memory. This is what happens, for example, in the of tip-of-the-tongue (TOT) state, when we struggle to retrieve an elusive name or word from memory. The TOT state has attracted attention because it combines two seemingly inconsistent features: On the one hand, the person is unable to retrieve the sought for target. On the other hand, he or she experiences a strong feeling of knowing, and can sometimes monitor the emergence of the elusive target into consciousness.

The discrepancy between subjective and objective indices of knowledge that occurs in the TOT state raises the question of how do I know that I know a name or a word in the face of being unable to produce it? Experimental work on the feeling of knowing (FOK) has addressed this question, and more generally, has attempted to unravel the mechanisms responsible for the FOK and its accuracy. The importance of this work is that it would seem to contribute to our understanding of the interface between subjective and objective knowledge. In particular, it may shed some light on the role of consciousness in information processing, and on the distinction between explicit and implicit memory. After all, the major feature distinguishing between explicit and implicit memory is that in the case of explicit memory not only do I possess some information about the past but I also subjectively know that I know it, whereas in implicit memory I may possess information without knowing that I know it. Perhaps, then, the study of the relationship between knowledge and metaknowledge can provide clues to some of the basic issues about consciousness and subjective experience.

THE TWO FACES OF METACOGNITION

What, then, is the status of metacognition *vis-à-vis* the distinction between explicit and implicit modes of knowing? Several quotes from recent work of leading experts, all taken from Reder (1996), reveal a basic confusion. Thus, Kelley and Jacoby (1996b, p. 287), discussing the relationship between implicit memory and metacognition noted:

> How does [the work on implicit memory] relate to questions about metacognition? After agreeing to write this chapter, we went through a long period thinking the answer was "it doesn't". As the deadline for the chapter drew near, we became more creative (desperate?) in our analysis, and have now arrived at the position that metacognition and implicit memory are so similar as to not be separate topics.

Funnell, Metcalfe, and Tsapkini (1996, p. 172), on the other hand, concluded:

> We understand the feeling-of-knowing judgment to be an explicit task and to rely on *explicit* knowledge. Indeed the judgment of what and how much you know about what you know or will know is a classic, almost definitional, explicit task ... Because feeling-of-knowing judgments are explicit, it is unlikely that subliminal activation could affect these judgments.

A different opinion, still, was expressed by Reder and Schunn (1996, p. 50):

> Given that feeling of knowing, like strategy selection, tends to be thought of as the essence of a metacognitive strategy, it is important to defend our claim that this rapid feeling of knowing is actually an *implicit process* rather than an *explicit process* ... The decision-making process involves rapid and automatic flow of activation rather than slow and controlled decision making about discrete features in the environment.

These quotations imply a fundamental ambivalence about the status of metacognitive judgments. In the conceptual scheme that I would like to propose here, I argue that this ambivalence actually discloses the two faces of metacognition: Metacognitive judgments, such as judgments of learning (Benjamin & Bjork, 1996; Koriat, in press b; Nelson & Dunlosky, 1991), feeling of knowing (Metcalfe, 1996; Schwartz, 1994), subjective confidence (Baranski & Petrusic, in press; Gigerenzer, Hoffrage, & Kleinbölting, 1991), and the variety of subjective monitoring processes that accompany thought and action, occupy a unique position in the distinction between implicit and explicit processes. Generally speaking, we may distinguish between two modes of operation, an explicit mode and an implicit mode. The explicit mode of operation underlies much of our conscious-controlled activities: When we have a clear goal, we evaluate the options, choose the most appropriate course of action, and guide our behavior accordingly.

In the implicit mode of operation, in contrast, various factors registered below full consciousness may influence our behavior directly. Bargh and Gollwitzer (1994, p. 72) stated:

> We argue that goal-directed action can be triggered directly by environmental stimuli, without the need of conscious involvement. Given a specific set of situational features, an individual may behave in ways he or she did not consciously choose or intend or may not be aware of the reasons for that behavior at the time.

Recent work in social psychology supports this statement: For example, in a study by Bornstein, Leone, and Galley (1987) subjects were subliminally presented with a photograph of one of two confederates with whom they later interacted. They were found then to express greater agreement with the primed than with the unprimed confederate. Similarly, in a recent study by Bargh, Chen, and Burrows (1996), the activation of the elderly stereotype through advance priming caused subjects to walk more slowly across the hall when the experiment was over, compared to a control group. These and other findings reviewed by Bargh (1997) indicate that a variety of processes can affect behavior *directly* and *automatically* without the mediation of consciousness.

Where do metacognitive judgments lie in this simplistic scheme? I propose that metacognitive judgments, particularly those that are based on a sheer gut feeling, occupy a unique position in mediating between implicit and explicit modes of operation: They are generally implicit as far as their antecedents are concerned, but explicit as far as their consequences are concerned. Thus, metacognitive judgments like subjective confidence and the feeling of knowing may be influenced and shaped by implicit factors that operate below full consciousness. Once formed, however, these judgments can serve as the basis for controlled, conscious action. It is this crossover function of metacognitive judgments that is responsible for the confusion that I noted about the status of metacognition, and it is also what makes metacognitive judgments interesting and important.

Let me first illustrate the implicit segment of the crossover mode. As I have indicated, unconscious activations may influence behavior directly and automatically. In addition, however, such activations may also shape subjective experience and inform metacognitive judgments. For example, in several studies (e.g. Reder, 1987; Schwartz & Metcalfe, 1992) people were asked to answer general-information questions. FOK judgments about the answer were found to increase when some of the words of the question had been primed in the context of an allegedly unrelated task. Similarly, in a study by Kelley and Lindsay (1993) people expressed stronger confidence in the correctness of their answer if that answer had been primed previously in the context of an unrelated task. This occurred both when the primed answer was correct and when it was wrong.

Let me turn now to the explicit segment of the crossover mode. Metacognitive processes are clearly explicit in terms of the two components of metacognition—monitoring and control (see Nelson & Narens, 1990). Monitoring refers to the subjective feelings that accompanies learning and remembering, whereas control refers to operational decisions that follow from such feelings. As far as monitoring is concerned, the phenomenal quality of metacognitive judgments clearly makes them part of the explicit mode. Thus, although I may not know the reason for my strong feeling of knowing about an elusive name, the feeling itself is part and parcel of conscious, subjective experience.

As far as the control aspect is concerned, a common assumption among students of metacognition is that metacognitive judgments play a causal role in determining and guiding behavior, and constitute an important basis for controled processes (see Nelson, 1996). For example, when studying a list of paired-associates under self-paced conditions, subjects allocate study time to different items in accordance with the judgments of learning associated with each item (e.g. Mazzoni & Cornoldi, 1993; Nelson & Leonesio, 1988). Also, in answering general-information questions, people spend more time searching when they have a strong FOK than when they have a weak FOK (e.g. Costermans, Lories, & Ansay, 1992; Gruneberg & Monks, 1974; Nelson, Gerler, & Narens, 1984).

Some recent findings from our laboratory can help illustrate the causal role played by metacognitive judgments (Koriat & Goldsmith, 1996). We speculated that a person on a witness stand, who is sworn to tell the whole truth and nothing but the truth, must deliberate whether to volunteer a piece of information that comes to mind or not. How does he do that? Possibly on the basis of his feelings about the correctness of the information. To simulate this process, we asked students to answer general-information questions under the instructions that they will win one Israeli Shekel for each correct answer, but will lose one Shekel for each wrong answer they produce. In one condition they were forced to answer all questions, whereas in another they had the option to skip answers. As expected, those who had the option to choose which questions to answer were more accurate, and therefore made more money. How did they do that? Apparently they monitored the correctness of each candidate answer and withheld those answers that were likely to be wrong. Indeed, the within-subject gamma correlation between the confidence associated with an answer, measured in one phase of the experiment, and the tendency to report that answer in a second phase of the experiment was .93 for recognition, and .97 for recall! Thus, people rely heavily on their confidence judgments in deciding which answers to volunteer. This is obviously a good policy because people's confidence judgments are generally accurate. In this manner, metacognitive accuracy can help people enhance the accuracy of what they report.

There are conditions, however, in which people's confidence judgments have little validity in distinguishing between correct and incorrect answers (see e.g. Fischhoff, Slovic, & Lichtenstein, 1977). What happens then? We found that even then subjects rely very heavily on their confidence judgments, volunteering answers that they believe are right and withholding those that they believe are wrong. Of course, now our subjects ended up losing a great deal of money (or at least they would have if we had made them pay their losses). Thus, people are blind followers of their metacognitive judgments and intuitions, and these judgments may have profound effects on behavior. Therefore, the importance of metacognitive judgments for researchers is that they provide an excellent predictor of one's behavior regardless of whether they are right or wrong.

In sum, I propose that metacognitive judgments lie at the interface between implicit and explicit modes of knowing. They sometimes play the role of a go-between, allowing a transition from automatic influences to controlled, reasoned behavior.

THE EXPERIMENTAL INVESTIGATION OF THE FEELING OF KNOWING

In view of the fact that metacognitive judgments play a causal role in controlling information processing and behavior, it is important to examine the accuracy or validity of these judgments. The systematic investigation of the effectiveness of subjective monitoring following recall failure began with the classic studies of Brown and McNeill (1966) on the TOT state, and Hart's studies (1965) on the feeling of knowing. An important contribution of these studies is that they introduced experimental paradigms for examining the relationship between subjective and objective indices of knowing. In both paradigms subjects are presented with a memory pointer (see Koriat & Lieblich, 1977), that is, a cue intended to point to a particular memory entry that the subject must attempt to retrieve. In TOT studies, the focus is on the accuracy of the partial information retrieved when recall of the complete target fails. Thus, in Brown and McNeill's study the pointer consisted of a word definition, and the solicited target was the corresponding word. When subjects signaled that the elusive word was on the tip of their tongue, they were able to retrieve some partial structural information about the word, such as its initial letter, the number of syllables it contained, and so on. Koriat and Lieblich (1974) later established that the partial information provided was more likely to be correct when people signalled a TOT state than when they signalled a "don't know" state. The TOT procedure has been extended to the study of experimentally presented information (Smith, 1994). Also, it was demonstrated that people can access other attributes of a momentarily inaccessible target besides its phonological characteristics, such as whether the solicited word has a positive or negative connotation (see e.g. Lovelace, 1987; Schacter & Worling, 1985; Yarmey, 1973).

In the Recall-Judgment-Recognition paradigm introduced by Hart (1965), in contrast, the focus is on the accuracy of FOK judgments in predicting the subsequent recognition of a nonrecalled target. Subjects are first presented with a memory pointer (e.g. "What Biblical character allegedly lived 969 years?"). When they fail to find the answer, they are asked to judge whether or not they "know" the answer to the extent of being able to recognize it among distractors. Finally, they are tested on that question using a forced-choice recognition memory test. Many studies that used this paradigm have found that FOK judgments following recall failure are predictive of recognition success. The correlations are generally not very high, but they are nevertheless sizable and significant (see Schwartz, 1994; Schwartz & Metcalfe, 1994).

The bulk of the experimental work on the TOT and FOK states has focused on evaluating the accuracy of FOK judgments. FOK was found to predict later performance in a variety of memory tasks such as general information questions, episodic memory of words, paired associates, and memory for nonsense syllables (Blake, 1973; Hart, 1967; Leonesio & Nelson, 1990; Reder, 1987; Ryan, Petty, & Wenzlaff, 1982; Schacter, 1983). Also, it was found to be relatively accurate in predicting several criterion tests, including recognition memory, later recall, cued recall, attribute identification, relearning, and perceptual identification (e.g. Gruneberg & Monks, 1974; Nelson et al., 1984; Shimizu & Kawaguchi, 1993). Work on FOK accuracy has indicated, for example, that the accuracy of the FOK varies with the number of test alternatives in the recognition test (Leonesio & Nelson, 1990; Schwartz & Metcalfe, 1994), and that it is rather low among certain brain-damaged populations. Korsakoff patients, for example, were found to be considerably lower than normals not only in their memory performance but also in their FOK accuracy (Shimamura & Squire, 1986). Janowsky, Shimamura, and Squire (1989) found deficits in FOK accuracy to be associated with frontal lobe damage. On the other hand, FOK accuracy in anomic patients and in elderly people seems to be relatively normal (Bäckman & Karlsson, 1985; Funnell et al., 1996).

In recent years, however, there has been a greater concern with uncovering the mechanisms underlying the feeling of knowing and its accuracy. Several mechanisms have been proposed. These will be classified here into three general categories: (1) trace access, (2) global heuristics, and (3) explicit inferences. I would like to take up explicit inferences first, because they represent the most obvious basis for metacognitive judgments.

FOK judgments based on explicit-analytic inferences

Undoubtedly, FOK judgments are often based on explicit inferences. Thus, I may judge that I should know the name of the leading actress in the movie *Room at the Top* because I can see her face, and can recollect that she has been married to Yves Montand, or else I can judge that there is no chance that I will be able to recognize the name of the winner of the Pulitzer Prize for photography in 1970 because I know nothing about photography or the Pulitzer Prize. Indeed, Nelson et al. (1984) listed six inferential mechanisms that can contribute to the FOK, such as retrieval of specific episodic information, or expertise in the area of the question. Clearly, these inferential mechanisms are not very different from those underlying, for example, the prediction whether I am likely to find a parking place near the office today, or which soccer team is likely to win. Inferential mechanisms often give rise to what might be termed "judgments of knowing" (see Costermans et al., 1992). Possibly metacognitive judgments would not have attracted special attention if they were based entirely on analytic inferences.

Consider, however, the type of intuitive feeling discussed in connection with the creative process: A scientist may experience a strong intuition that he is on the right track, and can sense that the solution to a problem is about to emerge into consciousness (Polanyi, 1962; Policastro, 1995). The phenomenal quality of such intuitive feelings or "hunches" is more like that of direct perception than of analytic reasoning. On a smaller scale, when I am in the TOT state I sometimes feel that I can *directly* detect the presence of an elusive target, and can monitor its emergence into consciousness (see James, 1893). These feelings suggest the operation of a different type of mechanism than that underlying analytic, reasoned inferences.

The trace-access account of the feeling of knowing

The trace-access account of the FOK was first proposed by Hart (1965) and has been implicitly endorsed by many researchers since. Basically the idea is that there must exist some specialized monitoring mechanism that allows one to know that one knows. Thus, when I search for a certain name, there must be some way by which I can recognize that name when I retrieve it from memory, otherwise the search process may continue indefinitely. Perhaps, then, this mechanism can also monitor the presence of the name in my memory even before

I retrieve it. This mechanism was termed memory-monitoring by Hart (1967). According to Hart, the memory-monitoring module has privileged access to memory traces, and can detect the availability of the target in memory when recall fails. Thus, whenever a person is required to recall a target from memory, the monitoring module is first activated to ensure that the target is available in the store before attempting to retrieve it. Consistent with this assumption is the finding that subjects spend more time searching for a target when the initial FOK is high than when it is low (Gruneberg & Monks, 1974). Hart stressed the functional utility of a monitoring module given the fallibility of the memory system.

The trace-access model is appealing for two reasons. First, it is consistent with the phenomenology of FOK and TOT states, namely, the feeling that one directly monitors the presence of the elusive target. Second, it explains why the FOK is accurate: Clearly, if the FOK monitors directly the availability of the target in memory, then it should be predictive of the subsequent recall or recognition of the target. An additional appeal of the idea of a specialized monitoring mechanism is that it can handle observations suggesting selective impairment of the subjective monitoring of knowledge among certain patient populations. For example, it has been proposed that frontal lobe damage may cause selective breakdown of the metacognitive function (see Metcalfe, 1996).

Heuristic-based accounts of the feeling of knowing

An alternative account of the FOK is that it is based on the implicit application of heuristics that rely on global, internal mnemonic cues (Jacoby & Brooks, 1984; Jacoby & Kelley, 1987; Kelley & Jacoby, 1996a; Koriat, 1994). Indeed, recent discussions of metacognition have stressed the role of internal, subjective cues as a source for metacognitive judgments such as FOK, judgment of learning, and retrospective confidence (see Koriat, in press b). Several mnemonic cues have been considered, including the accessibility of pertinent information (Dunlosky & Nelson, 1992; Koriat, 1993; Morris, 1990), the ease with which information comes to mind (Kelley & Lindsay, 1993; Mazzoni & Nelson, 1995), cue familiarity (Metcalfe, 1993; Metcalfe, Schwartz, & Joaquim, 1993; Reder, 1987; Reder & Ritter, 1992), and the ease or fluency of processing of a presented item (Begg, Duft, Lalonde, Melnick, & Sanvito, 1989; Benjamin & Bjork, 1996). Each of these internal cues can support a heuristic for monitoring one's own knowledge. Although such heuristics are also inferential in nature, they differ from analytic inferences in that they are used implicitly or unconsciously, and their effects are relatively automatic (see Jacoby & Brooks, 1984; Kelley & Jacoby, 1996a). This is why their effects are experienced as intuitive feelings rather than as logical deductions. Thus, explanations of metacognitive judgments in terms of nonanalytic heuristics have the advantage that they may be able to account for the direct, unmediated quality of metacognitive judgments without postulating trace access.

I would like to focus here on two candidate heuristics for the FOK that have received experimental attention in recent years, the accessibility heuristic and the cue-familiarity heuristic.

THE ACCESSIBILITY ACCOUNT OF THE FEELING OF KNOWING

One account of the FOK that does not postulate privileged access to memory traces is provided by the accessibility model. This model emerged from some of our early observations concerning the TOT phenomenon (Koriat & Lieblich, 1977). These observations indicated that there are reliable differences between memory pointers (e.g. word definitions) in the tendency to evoke a strong or weak FOK, and that these differences are independent of the likelihood with which the pointer elicits the correct target. In fact, knowing and the feeling of knowing emerged as two orthogonal factors for characterizing memory pointers. It does not seem, then, that the FOK monitors the availability of the target's trace in memory.

Rather, an analysis of the pointers that tend to produce an overly high FOK suggested that the critical factor is the overall amount of partial information they tend to precipitate regardless of whether that information is correct or not. This amount seems to depend both on characteristics of the pointer and as on characteristics of the solicited target. I will mention just two examples: As far as the pointer is concerned, word definitions that contain redundancies and repetitions tend to produce inflated FOKs, presumably because they generate a large amount of activation without enhancing the likelihood of recall. As far as the solicited target is concerned, pointers whose target has many "close neighbors" tend to produce inflated initial FOK even when the person ultimately retrieves the correct target. It would seem that the FOK is based on an unfocused scanning of a broad region of memory in which the target is likely to reside, and that activations from neighboring entries enhance the FOK. It is as if entries in the vicinity of the target are mistaken for the target when they are inspected from a distance, although when one gets closer one can easily reject them and home in on the correct target.

These and other observations gave rise to the accessibility model of the FOK (Koriat, 1993), which will now be examined.

The accessibility model assumes that people have *no* knowledge of their own memory over and above what they can retrieve from it. However, when they try to search for a target, often partial information comes to mind, and the FOK is based on the overall accessibility of such information, that is, on the amount of the partial clues and on the ease with which they come to mind. Essentially the FOK monitors the *accessible* information in *short-term* memory rather than the information available in long-term memory. Therefore, monitoring does not precede retrieval but follows it: It is by attempting to search for the solicited target that one can appreciate whether the target is available in memory.

Some of the clues that come to mind originate from the target and constitute "correct partial information", whereas others stem from many other sources and represent "wrong partial information". It is assumed that people cannot tell these two types of clues apart because they cannot monitor directly the accuracy of what comes to mind. Therefore both correct and wrong partial information contribute equally to the FOK. As a consequence, when memory goes astray as a result of spurious activations, so will the FOK.

The main question, of course, is why FOK judgments are nevertheless accurate in predicting the future recall or recognition of momentarily inaccessible targets. The answer is that the accuracy of metamemory stems directly from the accuracy of memory itself. Memory is by and large accurate in the output-bound sense (see Koriat & Goldsmith, 1994, 1996): Information that comes to mind during retrieval is more likely to be correct than wrong. This is almost part of the definition of memory: If you learn the name of a person, you are more likely to recall that name in the future than to recall another name instead. You may fail to retrieve any name at all, but if some name comes to mind, it is more likely to be right than wrong. Because most of the information that comes to mind is correct, a monitoring mechanism that relies on the accessibility of information, as such, is bound to predict actual recall and recognition performance.

Some support for the model comes from an experiment (Experiment 1, Koriat, 1993) in which subjects memorized a four-letter string (e.g. KBDR) on each trial, and following a filled interval were asked to report the full target or as many letters as they could remember. They then made FOK judgments about the probability of identifying the target among distractors, and their recognition memory for the target was tested. The results indicated the following: Both number of correct letters recalled and number of wrong letters recalled were positively correlated with FOK judgments (the estimated correlations for the grouped data were +.83 and +.76, respectively), suggesting that these judgments were affected by the sheer amount of information accessible regardless of the accuracy of that information. Recognition memory, on the other hand, was positively correlated with the amount of correct partial information (+.61) but negatively correlated with the amount of incorrect partial information (−.52), suggesting that correct partial information contributes to the accuracy of the FOK, whereas incorrect partial information contributes to its inaccuracy.

Nevertheless, despite the conflicting contributions of correct and wrong partial recalls to the validity of FOK judgments, these judgments were quite accurate in predicting recognition performance. The reason is that about 90% of all the letters recalled were correct. Therefore, although subjects did not have access to the accuracy of what they recalled, they could successfully monitor their knowledge on the basis of the sheer amount of information accessible. In fact, the predictive validity of FOK judgments was about the same as that of the sheer number of letters recalled.

DISSOCIATIONS BETWEEN KNOWING AND THE FEELING OF KNOWING

The implication of these results is that there is nothing mysterious about the FOK. The FOK relies on the implicit use of a simple heuristic that generally works: This heuristic is predicated on the assumption that one is more likely to know the answer to a question if that question brings a large number of partial clues to mind than if it brings to mind few clues. However, it is clear that this is not always true. Some questions activate a great deal of information for a variety of irrelevant reasons, and one may still not recognize the correct target among distractors. These questions should produce an illusion of knowing, that is, a strong unjustified FOK. Thus, we may expect a dissociation between knowing and the FOK in those conditions in which the overall amount of information that comes to mind is not diagnostic. This possibility was examined with general-information questions (Koriat, 1995). The procedure required certain assumptions because of the difficulties in measuring the amount and quality of the partial information that is activated by a general-information question when recall fails. Based on earlier results (Koriat & Lieblich, 1977), it was assumed that memory pointers differ reliably in two parameters: (1) the tendency to produce a high or a low FOK, and (2) the validity of the FOK elicited.

According to the accessibility model, the tendency to produce a high or a low FOK depends on the overall amount of partial information elicited by the pointer, whereas the validity of the FOK in predicting subsequent recall or recognition of the target depends on the output-bound accuracy of that information. To examine these predictions a pool of general-information questions was compiled, which were expected to vary greatly in both the amount of information they tend to precipitate and the quality of that information. These were presented to subjects who were asked to answer each question (Experiment 1). The percentage of subjects who produced an answer, regardless of whether that answer was right or wrong, was used as an index of Accessibility (ACC). If we assume that overt responses are diagnostic of covert responses, that is, that pointers that produce many answers across subjects also activate a large number of partial clues among subjects who fail to retrieve the answer, then we should expect high-ACC pointers to elicit higher FOK judgments than low-ACC pointers.

The output-bound accuracy of the information precipitated by a pointer was estimated from the Output-Bound Accuracy of the answers provided, that is, the percentage of correct answers out of all answers produced. On the basis of this index, all pointers were divided into two categories, Consensually-Correct, and Consensually-Wrong. Consensually-Correct pointers were those that produced more correct than incorrect answers across subjects. As noted earlier, most pointers belong to this category. Some of the pointers, however, were Consensually-Wrong or "deceptive" (see Fischhoff et al., 1977): They produced predominantly incorrect answers. It was hypothesized that only for the typical, Consensually-Correct pointers, would FOK judgments be valid in predicting subsequent recognition of the target when recall fails, whereas for Consensually-Wrong pointers FOK accuracy should be very poor.

To examine these hypotheses, the pointers were presented to another group of subjects (Experiment 2) who were asked to give a fast FOK judgment before trying deliberately to search for the answer, but to write down the answer if it came to mind spontaneously. A two-alternative recognition test was used. Subjects did reach an answer in 6% of the trials and these trials were eliminated from the analyses.

The results indicated the following: First, as far as the basis of the FOK is concerned, high-ACC pointers produced significantly higher FOK judgments than low-ACC pointers. This was true for both the Consensually-Correct and the Consensually-Wrong pointers. Thus, FOK judgments following recall failure can be predicted from the mere number of answers elicited by the pointer. These results are consistent with the idea that the FOK monitors the overall accessibility of partial clues regardless of their accuracy.

Second, as far as FOK accuracy is concerned, this was found to vary greatly depending on Output-Bound Accuracy. Thus, the Consensually-Correct and Consensually-Wrong pointers evoked practically identical preliminary FOK judgments, (76.1 and 76.4, respectively), but differed considerably in recognition memory (73.3 and 43.9, respectively). In fact, recognition performance was no better for the Consensually-Wrong pointers than for a set of pointers that had been found to elicit practically no answers across subjects (43.9 and 45.1, respectively), although the former pointers elicited markedly higher FOK judgments (76.4) than the latter pointers (58.7). These results demonstrate a clear double dissociation between knowing and the feeling of knowing.

A similar dissociation was observed in the within-subject correlation between the FOK and recognition performance: The average within-subject correlation was positive and significant (.31) for the Consensually-Correct pointers, indicating that FOK judgments were moderately accurate in predicting recognition memory. For the Consensually-Wrong pointers, in contrast, recognition memory *decreased* significantly as FOK increased, yielding a significantly negative correlation within individuals, −.18! Thus, for these pointers the more one feels that one knows, the less likely that one actually knows.

In sum, these results are consistent with the assumption of the accessibility model that the accuracy of metamemory is a by-product of the accuracy of memory. In general, FOK monitors the overall accessibility of partial clues about the target regardless of whether these clues are correct or not. Because most of the information that comes to mind is correct, FOK judgments tend to be accurate in predicting recognition performance. However, when pointers elicit predominantly incorrect clues, a dissociation will occur between knowing and the feeling of knowing.

THE CUE-FAMILIARITY ACCOUNT OF THE FEELING OF KNOWING

The assumption underlying the accessibility account is that the FOK is not based on the operation of a monitoring mechanism that has direct access to memory traces, but on the implicit use of an inferential heuristic that relies on internal mnemonic cues. An alternative account of the FOK that also shares this assumption is the cue-familiarity account first proposed by Reder (1987; see also Metcalfe, 1993). It assumes that FOK judgments are based on the overall familiarity of the pointer, not on the retrievability of the target. A rapid FOK is routinely and automatically elicited by the parsing of the question. The purpose of this FOK is to regulate the choice of question-answering strategy, and this operates for all questions, not just for those for which the answer is currently inaccessible.

The cue-familiarity account has gained consistent empirical support in a number of studies. In Reder's (1987, 1988) studies, subjects were presented with general-information questions and were asked to decide quickly whether they could retrieve the answer. Some of the words of the question were primed earlier in the context of a frequency judgment task. Advance priming was found to enhance FOK judgments without correspondingly improving recall or recognition of the answer. Schwartz and Metcalfe (1992) replicated these results with FOK judgments elicited following recall failure. They compared the effects of cue priming and target priming and found that whereas cue priming enhanced FOK judgments, the priming of the target itself generally did not. Metcalfe et al. (1993), using a proactive interference paradigm with two lists of paired associates, found that repetition of the cue word across the two lists enhanced FOK judgments, presumably because of increased stimulus familiarity. In contrast, repetition of the response terms did not affect FOK judgments.

Some impressive results in support of the cue-familiarity account have been obtained by Reder and her associates with arithmetic problems. In a study by Reder and Ritter (1992), subjects were presented with arithmetic problems such as 38 + 54, and were asked to determine rapidly whether they know the answer and can retrieve it or whether they have to compute it. FOK judgments, that is, judgments that the answer can be retrieved, increased with increasing frequency of previous exposures to the same parts of the problem, not with the availability of the answer. FOK judgments also increased when the problem changed, for example, from 38 + 54 to 38 × 54, or when only some of the components of the problem were repeated (e.g. 38 + 29). Hence, familiarity with problem parts and not familiarity with the answer contributes to the FOK.

Furthermore, in recent studies (Schunn, Reder, Nhouyvanisvong, Richards, & Stroffolino, 1997) some of the arithmetic problems were presented under conditions in which subjects had little chance to actually solve the problem. Nevertheless, FOK judgments increased with increasing frequency of previous exposures to these problems. Thus, once again, there was a dissociation between knowing and the feeling of knowing: When exposure to the problem and exposure to the answer were decoupled, exposure to the problem predicted the feeling of knowing, whereas exposure to the answer predicted actual knowing. These results clearly indicate that the FOK is affected by the familiarity of the pointer, not by access to the target.

THE JOINT EFFECTS OF FAMILIARITY AND ACCESSIBILITY

We have, then, two nonanalytic heuristics that can serve to drive the FOK, accessibility and cue-familiarity. In the metacognitive literature these are sometimes seen to represent two alternative, competing accounts of the FOK (e.g. Schwartz & Metcalfe, 1992). They share the basic assumption that the FOK does not monitor the presence of the target in memory, but is based on the implicit application of a nonanalytic heuristic. However, whereas in the cue-familiarity account the FOK occurs at a pre-retrieval stage and depends solely on the characteristics of the pointer, in the accessibility account it is assumed to rely on the output of the retrieval attempt. Some of our recent work, however, suggests that both mechanisms may operate in an interactive manner in influencing the FOK.

That work concerns the illusion of knowing (see Koriat, in press a). The question we asked is what makes a pointer deceptive in the sense of evoking an unduly high FOK? An analysis of the Consensually-Wrong pointers in Koriat (1995) suggested that familiarity of the pointer may play a significant role in mediating the potential effects of accessibility on the FOK. In general, a pointer that has a large set of candidate answers stored in memory will tend to evoke a stronger FOK than one that has only a small set. This seems to occur, however, only when the pointer is familiar enough, because only then does the person tend to explore possible answers, and thus enhance accessibility. It would seem that familiarity serves as a gating mechanism for the effects of accessibility: It allows information to be released from long-term to short-term memory. The activated information in short-term memory, then, is what affects the FOK when recall fails. Indeed, some preliminary data from our laboratory indicate that familiarity and potential accessibility interact so that the amount of potentially accessible information affects the FOK when cue familiarity is relatively high, but not when it is low.

THE CASCADED MECHANISMS OF THE FOK

Let me summarize the view that emerges from the recent work on metacognitive monitoring. This work suggests that the FOK is multiply determined (see Nelson et al., 1984). Thus, even if we eliminate the possibility that FOK is based on a specialized monitoring module that has direct access to memory traces, there remain at least three types of mechanisms for the FOK: cue familiarity, accessibility, and explicit-analytic inferences. These mechanisms are arranged in the order in which they seem to be activated. Thus, in the very early stages of inspecting a question, FOK may be based on the sheer familiarity of the pointer. This preliminary FOK may encourage or discourage search for the target: when a pointer is unfamiliar, that is, "does not ring a bell", a fast "don't know" judgment is issued. When the pointer evokes some degree of familiarity, this familiarity drives mental exploration, and then the overall accessibility of partial clues also affects the FOK.

Both cue familiarity and accessibility are nonanalytic heuristics that do not involve reasoned, explicit inferences. As far as the cue-familiarity heuristic is concerned, it is clear from the work of Reder and her associates that cue familiarity affects rapid, preliminary FOK through a process that is basically implicit. This is suggested by the findings that the FOK depends on the familiarity of the pointer rather than on the availability of the answer, and by the results suggesting familiarity-mediated effects of advance priming on the FOK. Thus, the nonanalytic use of cue familiarity as the basis for the FOK should be distinguished from the explicit use of familiarity (e.g. familiarity with a topic, or expertise in the area in question, see Nelson et al., 1984) as a basis for an educated probability judgment about the likelihood of recognizing a currently inaccessible target.

Similarly, the accessibility heuristic too is an implicit heuristic that should be distinguished from analytic inferences: It does not entail an explicit deduction that one ought to know the answer to the question because the question precipitates many partial clues, or because these clues are easily accessed. In fact, some of the effects on the FOK would seem to run counter to those following from a logical deduction. For example, FOK judgments, including those elicited following commission responses, seem to increase as the number of candidate answers that come to mind increases (see Brown & Bradley, 1985; Koriat, 1995). If FOK were to depend on a logical deduction, we might have expected the reverse pattern to occur. Rather, the accessibility heuristic, like the cue-familiarity heuristic, is a nonanalytic heuristic that is applied implicitly, and it is its implicit nature that is responsible for the phenomenology of the FOK—the feeling that we directly sense the presence of the elusive target in memory.

The accessibility heuristic operates on the overall amount of information that comes to mind and its ease of access, without regard to the content of that information. Under some conditions, however, particularly in the later stages of the search process, FOK judgments may be based on an explicit consideration of the content of the clues that come to mind (Koriat, 1993). When the content of the retrieved information is consulted, the monitoring process changes its quality from an automatic, nonanalytic process, to a deliberate, inferential process of probability estimation (see Jacoby & Brooks, 1984). The experience then is more like a judgment of knowing than a *feeling* of knowing. Content-based inferences require more time and more effort than nonanalytic, heuristic-driven FOKs (Kelley & Jacoby, 1996b). In many cases, however, the process underlying the FOK never proceeds beyond a consideration of the mere accessibility of partial clues. This may occur either because the partial clues that come to mind are not articulate enough, and/or because the plausibility of these clues cannot be evaluated. For example, a person in a TOT state is typically unable to determine whether the letters that come to mind are correct or not. Thus, people in the TOT state cannot tell whether these clues originate from the target itself, from related memory entries, or from other sources, and therefore they are often unable to escape the effects of contaminating clues that come to mind by attributing them to their source (see Koriat, 1994). Sometimes only after a TOT state has been resolved does one realize that some of the partial clues initially accessed were actually false.

CONCLUSION

This chapter examined the work on metacognitive judgments in the context of the distinction between implicit and explicit cognitive modes. It was argued that the feeling of knowing (in distinction from the "judgment" of knowing) occupies a unique role in mediating between implicit and explicit processes. As far as its antecedents are concerned, the feeling of knowing (and perhaps other metacognitive feelings) is based on nonanalytic heuristics that operate implicitly. It is the implicit nature of these inferential heuristics that is responsible for the special phenomenal quality of the feeling of knowing, namely, the subjective experience that one actually senses the presence of the elusive target in the memory store, or that one directly monitors its emergence into consciousness. The chapter centered on two main heuristics that have received some experimental support in recent years, cue familiarity and accessibility. However, the feeling of knowing is part and parcel of the explicit mode of operation. This is evident, first, in its "aware" qualities, and second, in the role it plays in the controlled regulation of behavior. The feeling of knowing, then, fulfils an important crossover function in mediating between implicit and explicit modes of operation.

ACKNOWLEDGEMENTS

I wish to thank Ravit Levy for her help in the preparation of this chapter. The writing of this chapter was supported by Grant 40/96 from the Israeli Foundation Trustees.

REFERENCES

Bäckman, L., & Karlsson, T. (1985). The relation between level of general knowledge and feeling-of-knowing: An adult age study. *Scandinavian Journal of Psychology, 26,* 249–258.

Baranski, J. V., & Petrusic, W. M. (in press). Probing the locus of confidence judgments: Experiments on the time to determine confidence. *Journal of Experimental Psychology: Human Perception and Performance.*

Bargh, J. A. (1997). The automaticity of everyday life. In R. S. Wyer (Ed.), *Advances in social cognition* (vol 10, pp. 1–61). Hillsdale, NJ: Lawrence Erlbaum Associates Inc.

Bargh, J. A., Chen, M., & Burrows, L. (1996). Automaticity of social behavior: Direct effects of trait construct and stereotype activation on action. *Journal of Personality and Social Psychology, 71*, 230–244.

Bargh, J. A., & Gollwitzer, P. M. (1994). Environmental control of goal-directed action: Automatic and strategic contingencies between situations and behavior. *Nebraska Symposium on Motivation, 41*, 71–124.

Begg, I., Duft, S., Lalonde, P., Melnick, R., & Sanvito, J. (1989). Memory predictions are based on ease of processing. *Journal of Memory and Language, 28*, 610–632.

Benjamin, A. S., & Bjork, R. A. (1996). Retrieval fluency as a metacognitive index. In L. M. Reder (Ed.), *Implicit memory and metacognition* (pp. 309–338). Hillsdale, NJ: Lawrence Erlbaum Associates Inc.

Blake, M. (1973). Prediction of recognition when recall fails: Exploring the feeling-of-knowing phenomenon. *Journal of Verbal Learning and Verbal Behavior, 12*, 311–319.

Bornstein, R. F., Leone, D. R., & Galley, D. J. (1987). The generalization of subliminal mere exposure effects: Influence of stimuli perceived without awareness on social behavior. *Journal of Personality and Social Psychology, 53*, 1070–1079.

Brown, A. S., & Bradley, C. K. (1985). Semantic prime inhibition and memory monitoring. *Bulletin of the Psychonomic Society, 23*, 98–100.

Brown, R., & McNeill, D. (1966). The "tip of the tongue" phenomenon. *Journal of Verbal Learning and Verbal Behavior, 5*, 325–337.

Costermans, J., Lories, G., & Ansay, C. (1992). Confidence level and feeling of knowing in question answering: The weight of inferential processes. *Journal of Experimental Psychology: Learning, Memory, and Cognition, 18*, 142–150.

Dunlosky, J., & Nelson, T. O. (1992). Importance of the kind of cue for judgments of learning (JOLs) and the delayed-JOL effect. *Memory and Cognition, 20*, 373–380.

Fischhoff, B., Slovic, P., & Lichtenstein, S. (1977). Knowing with certainty: The appropriateness of extreme confidence. *Journal of Experimental Psychology: Human Perception and Performance, 3*, 552–564.

Funnell, M., Metcalfe, J., & Tsapkini, K. (1996). In the mind but not on the tongue: Feeling of knowing in an anomic patient. In L. M. Reder (Ed.), *Implicit memory and metacognition* (pp. 171–194). Hillsdale, NJ: Lawrence Erlbaum Associates Inc.

Gigerenzer, G., Hoffrage, U., & Kleinbölting, H. (1991). Probabilistic mental models: A Brunswikian theory of confidence. *Psychological Review, 98*, 506–528.

Gruneberg, M. M., & Monks, J. (1974). Feeling of knowing and cued recall. *Acta Psychologica, 38*, 257–265.

Hart, J. T. (1965). Memory and the feeling-of-knowing experience. *Journal of Educational Psychology, 56*, 208–216.

Hart, J. T. (1967). Memory and the memory-monitoring process. *Journal of Verbal Learning and Verbal Behavior, 6*, 685–691.

Jacoby, L. L., & Brooks, L. R. (1984). Nonanalytic cognition: Memory, perception and concept learning. In G. H. Bower (Ed.), *The psychology of learning and motivation: Advances in research and theory* (Vol. 18, pp. 1–47). San Diego, CA: Academic Press.

Jacoby, L. L., & Kelley, C. M. (1987). Unconscious influences of memory for a prior event. *Personality and Social Psychology Bulletin, 13*, 314–336.

James, W. (1893). *The principles of psychology* (Vol. 1). New York: Holt.

Janowsky, J. S., Shimamura, A. P., & Squire, R. L. (1989). Memory and metamemory: Comparisons between frontal lobe lesions and amnesic patients. *Psychology, 17*, 3–11.

Kelley, C. M., & Jacoby, L. L. (1996a). Adult egocentrism: Subjective experience versus analytic bases for judgment. *Journal of Memory and Language, 35*, 157–175.

Kelley, C. M., & Jacoby, L. L. (1996b). Memory attributions: Remembering, knowing, and feeling of knowing. In L. M. Reder (Ed.), *Implicit memory and metacognition* (pp. 287–308). Hillsdale, NJ: Lawrence Erlbaum Associates Inc.

Kelley, C. M., & Lindsay, D. S. (1993). Remembering mistaken for knowing: Ease of retrieval as a basis for confidence in answers to general knowledge question. *Journal of Memory and Language, 32*, 1–24.

Koriat, A. (1993). How do we know that we know? The accessibility model of the feeling of knowing. *Psychological Review, 100*, 609–639.

Koriat, A. (1994). Memory's knowledge of its own knowledge: The accessibility account of the feeling of knowing. In J. Metcalfe & P. Shimamura (Eds.), *Metacognition: Knowing about knowing* (pp. 115–135). Cambridge, MA: MIT Press.

Koriat, A. (1995). Dissociating knowing and the feeling of knowing: Further evidence for the accessibility model. *Journal of Experimental Psychology: General, 124*, 311–333.

Koriat, A. (in press a). Illusions of knowing: A window to the link between knowledge and meta-knowledge. In V. Y. Yzerbyt, G. Lories, & B. Dardenne (Eds.), *Metacognition: Cognitive and social dimensions*. London: Sage.

Koriat, A. (in press b). Monitoring one's own knowledge during study: A cue-utilization approach to judgments of learning. *Journal of Experimental Psychology: General.*

Koriat, A., & Goldsmith, M. (1994). Memory in naturalistic and laboratory contexts: Distinguishing the accuracy-oriented and quantity-oriented approaches to memory assessment. *Journal of Experimental Psychology: General, 123*, 297–315.

Koriat, A., & Goldsmith, M. (1996). Monitoring and control processes in the strategic regulation of memory accuracy. *Psychological Review, 103*, 490–517.

Koriat, A. & Lieblich, I. (1974). What does a person in a "TOT" state know that a person in a "don't know" state doesn't know? *Memory and Cognition, 2*, 647–655.

Koriat, A., & Lieblich, I. (1977). A study of memory pointers. *Acta Psychologica, 41*, 151–164.

Leonesio, R. J., & Nelson, T. O. (1990). Do different metamemory judgments tap the same underlying aspects of memory? *Journal of Experimental Psychology: Learning, Memory, and Cognition, 16*, 464–470.

Lovelace, E. A. (1987). Attributes that come to mind in the TOT state. *Bulletin of the Psychonomic Society, 25*, 370–372.

Mazzoni, G., & Cornoldi, C. (1993). Strategies in study time allocation: Why is study time sometimes not effective? *Journal of Experimental Psychology: General, 122*, 47–60.

Mazzoni, G., & Nelson, T. O. (1995). Judgments of learning are affected by the kind of encoding in ways that cannot be attributed to the level of recall. *Journal of Experimental Psychology: Learning, Memory and Cognition, 21*, 1263–1274.

Metcalfe, J. (1993). Novelty monitoring, metacognition and control in a composite holographic associative recall model: Implications for Korsakoff amnesia. *Psychological Review, 100*, 3–22.

Metcalfe, J. (1996). Metacognitive processes. In E. L. Bjork & R. A. Bjork (Eds.), *Handbook of perception and cognition: Memory* (Vol. 10, pp. 381–407). San Diego, CA: Academic Press.

Metcalfe, J., Schwartz, B. L., & Joaquim, S. G. (1993). The cue-familiarity heuristic in metacognition. *Journal of Experimental Psychology: Learning, Memory and Cognition, 19*, 851–861.

Morris, C. C. (1990). Retrieval processes underlying confidence in comprehension judgments. *Journal of Experimental Psychology: Learning, Memory, and Cognition, 16*, 223–232.

Nelson, T. O. (1996). Consciousness and metacognition. *American Psychologist, 51*, 102–116.

Nelson, T. O., & Dunlosky, J. (1991). When people's judgments of learning (JOLs) are extremely accurate at predicting subsequent recall: The "delayed-JOL effect". *Psychological Science, 2*, 267–270.

Nelson, T. O., Gerler, D., & Narens, L. (1984). Accuracy of feeling-of-knowing judgment for predicting perceptual identification and relearning. *Journal of Experimental Psychology: General, 113*, 282–300.

Nelson, T. O., & Leonesio, R. J. (1988). Allocation of self-paced study time and the "Labor-in-vain effect". *Journal of Experimental Psychology: Learning, Memory, and Cognition, 14*, 676–686.

Nelson, T. O., & Narens, L. (1990). Metamemory: A theoretical framework and new findings. In G. H. Bower (Ed.), *The Psychology of learning and motivation: Advances in research and theory* (Vol. 26, pp. 125–173). San Diego, CA: Academic Press.

Polanyi, M. (1962). *Personal Knowledge*. Chicago: University of Chicago Press.

Policastro, E. (1995). Creative intuition: An integrative review. *Creative Research Journal, 8*, 99–113.

Reder, L. M. (1987). Strategy selection in question answering. *Cognitive Psychology, 19*, 90–138.

Reder, L. M. (1988). Strategic control of retrieval strategies. *The Psychology of Learning and Motivation, 22*, 227–259.

Reder, L. M. (Ed.) (1996). *Implicit memory and metacognition*. Hillsdale, NJ: Lawrence Erlbaum Associates Inc.

Reder, L. M., & Ritter, F. E. (1992). What determines initial feeling of knowing? Familiarity with question terms, not with the answer. *Journal of Experimental Psychology: Learning, Memory, and Cognition, 18*, 435–451.

Reder, L. M., & Schunn, C. D. (1996). Metacognition does not imply awareness: Strategy choice is governed by implicit learning and memory. In L. M. Reder (Ed.), *Implicit memory and metacognition* (pp. 45–78). Hillsdale, NJ: Lawrence Erlbaum Associates Inc.

Ryan, M. P., Petty, C. R., & Wenzlaff, R. M. (1982). Motivated remembering efforts during tip-of-the-tongue states. *Acta Psychologica, 51*, 137–147.

Schacter, D. L. (1983). Feeling of knowing in episodic memory. *Journal of Experimental Psychology: Learning, Memory and Cognition, 9*, 39–54.

Schacter, D. L., & Worling, J. R. (1985). Attribute information and the feeling of knowing. *Canadian Journal of Psychology, 39*, 467–475.

Schunn, C. D., Reder, L. M., Nhouyvanisvong, A., Richards, D. R., & Stroffolino, P. J. (1997). To calculate or not to calculate: A source activation confusion (SAC) model of problem-familiarity's role in strategy selection. *Journal of Experimental Psychology: Learning, Memory, and Cognition, 23*, 3–29.

Schwartz, B. L. (1994). Sources of information in metamemory: Judgments of learning and feeling of knowing. *Psychonomic Bulletin and Review, 1*, 357–375.

Schwartz, B. L., & Metcalfe, J. (1992). Cue familiarity but not target retrievability enhances feeling-of-knowing judgments. *Journal of Experimental Psychology: Learning, Memory, and Cognition, 18*, 1074–1083.

Schwartz, B. L., & Metcalfe, J. (1994). Methodological problems and pitfalls in the study of human metacognition. In J. Metcalfe & A. P. Shimamura (Eds.), *Metacognition: Knowing about knowing* (pp. 93–113). Cambridge, MA: MIT Press.

Shimamura, A. P., & Squire, L. R. (1986). Memory and metamemory: A study of the feeling-of-knowing phenomenon in amnesic patients. *Journal of Experimental Psychology: Learning, Memory, and Cognition, 12*, 452–460.

Shimizu, H., & Kawaguchi, J. (1993). The accuracy of feeling-of-knowing judgments for general-information questions using the recall retest method. *Japanese Psychological Research, 35*, 215–220.

Smith, S. M. (1994). Frustrated feelings of imminent recall: On the tip of the tongue. In J. Metcalfe & A. P. Shimamura (Eds.), *Metacognition: Knowing about knowing* (pp. 27–45). Cambridge, MA: MIT Press.

Yarmey, A. D. (1973). I recognize your face but I can't remember your name: Further evidence on the tip-of-the-tongue phenomenon. *Memory and Cognition, 1*, 287–289.

PART FIVE

Cognitive development

The early development of visual perception and its relation to action and cognition

Claes von Hofsten
Umeå University, Umeå, Sweden

The dramatic development of the visual system during the first half year of life is discussed in the context of action and cognition. Already at birth, the visual system is connected to various effector systems in a meaningful way, which makes it possible for experience to enter into the ontogenetic process to shape and to steer it. Two important sensorimotor developments are discussed: gaze control and eye-hand coordination. They turn the visual system into a sophisticated organ for exploration and manipulation, and the chapter outlines how this comes about.

Le développement dramatique du système visuel de l'enfant durant ses premiers six mois d'existence est considéré dans le contexte de l'action et de la cognition. Déjà, à la naissance, le système visuel est relié de façon significative aux différents systèmes effecteurs, ce qui rend possible l'introduction de l'expérience dans le processus ontogénétique pour lui donner forme et le diriger. Deux développements importants au plan sensori-moteur sont discutés: le contrôle du regard et la coordination visuomotrice. Ils transforment le système visuel en un organe sophistiqué d'exploration et de manipulation. Cet article explique comment se réalise cette transformation.

The visual system develops very dramatically during the first half-year of life and several basic abilities are approaching adultlike performance by the end of this period, including acuity (Dobson & Teller, 1977) and binocular function (Birch, Gwiazda, & Held, 1982). Infants can then, for instance, predictively stabilize gaze on a moving target even if it is fast, reach for it, and catch it. In this chapter I present and discuss some aspects of this development.

First of all, the visual system is in itself a sensorimotor system. Its function is to scan the world, focus on objects and events, and track them over the visual field. The development of oculomotor control is as important to vision as the development of the receptor function itself. If a subject cannot control its eye movements, the visual system is useless. For instance, it has been found that multihandicapped patients with severe eye movement disorders who have been diagnosed as cortically blind often have almost normal visual acuity (Jacobsen, Magnussen, & Smith, 1997).

Secondly, the visual system is involved in guiding our actions towards the external world. For example, reaching for objects and manipulating them are crucially dependent on visual functioning. Keeping balance and maintaining a stable orientation to the world are other examples. Blind children are especially delayed in these respects (Fraiberg, 1977). In order to guide actions and interact with objects and events, it is not only necessary to perceive what has just happened but also what is going to happen next. Visual perception is designed to provide that information. To perceive what has not yet happened may sound paradoxical, but events obeying the law of physics clearly tell us not only what has already happened but, more importantly, how they are going to evolve in the near future. For instance, David Lee (1992) has shown that the relative expansion of elements in the optic array supplies information about upcoming encounters with external objects and surfaces, time to contact with them, and whether the encounter is going to be rough or smooth. Much of this learning takes places in early infancy. The development of these sensorimotor links is an important part of an understanding of the development of the visual system.

THE CAPACITY AND FUNCTIONS OF THE NEONATE'S VISUAL SYSTEM

In contrast to the other sensory systems, patterned visual information is not available in the womb and therefore all visual abilities present at birth must be the result of phylogenetic adaptation. The mapping of the visual system is accomplished in two stages. In the first stage, migrating axons from the ganglions at the retina are guided by protein markers to their receiving structures, the lateral geniculate nucleus and the superior colliculus. This process results in a crude mapping at the receiving structures (Retaux & Harris, 1996). The second stage requires the system to be activated. Through a self-organizing process, mainly determined by the Hebbian plasticity rule and the competition for synaptic space, patterned excitation at the retina transforms the crude map into a more precise one (von der Malsburg & Singer, 1988). Patterned excitation may be accomplished by patterned visual input available after birth. Thus, as Shatz (1992) has shown, the lack of patterned input before birth is compensated for by spontaneously elicited patterns of excitations in the retina, which provide the conditions necessary for mapping the system.

Visual acuity depends on both spatial frequency and contrast, and the neonate's performance in both these respects is estimated at only around 3% of the normal adult's performance (Banks & Bennett, 1988). These deficiencies are primarily

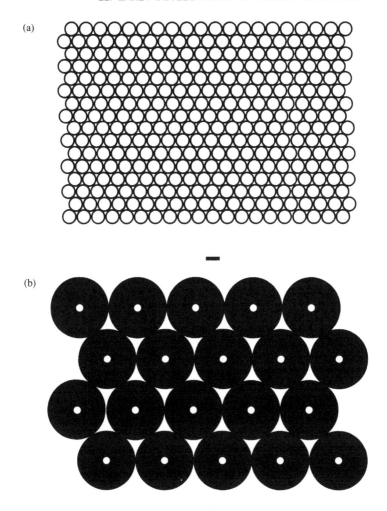

FIG. 22.1   Schematics of the receptor lattices used in (a) adult and (b) neonatal ideal observers. The black bars represent 0.5min arc.; black areas represent the inner segments; white areas represent effective collecting areas. The effective collecting areas cover 65% of the adult central fovea but only 2% of the newborn central fovea. From Banks and Bennett, 1988.

the result of the immaturity of the neonate's retina. The cones are much more shallow and much less densely packed than on the adult retina, as can be seen in Fig. 22.1. Banks and Bennett (1988) calculated the contrast sensitivity function that could be derived from just considering the distribution of receptors and their light-absorbing properties (ideal observer). They found that the ideal observer function predicts a better contrast sensitivity function than the one empirically obtained, which reflects the immaturities of the neonate's visual system beyond the receptors themselves.

Imitation is a neonatal ability that has often been discussed in relation to visual acuity. Meltzoff and Moore (1977) reported that neonates, for example, would imitate mouth opening and tongue protrusion. These observations have been replicated (see e.g. Heimann, Nelson, & Schaller, 1989), but considering the poor visual acuity of the neonate, one might wonder whether these observed behaviors are really a function of the gestures that were supposed to have elicited them. The answer depends on observer distance, facial contrasts, and lighting conditions, and these aspects have typically not been reported on in sufficient detail. Even if the acuity requirements are fulfilled, imitation is only possible if additional advanced processing of facial features is applied to the visual pattern.

Neonates' ability to control their eye movements determines an absolute limit to how usable the visual system is to them. Neonates have some ability to direct gaze towards interesting parts of the optical array, towards parts containing much optical change, and towards certain specific stimuli like faces and moving objects (Johnson & Morton, 1991). Therefore, it can be argued that neonates are prepared to explore their surrounding. They can also coordinate the movements of both eyes to some degree and converge them towards the object on which they are fixating (Haineline, Riddell, Grose-Fifer, & Abramov, 1992). There are, however, important restrictions to the use of the oculomotor system. Kremenitzer, Vaughn, Kurtzberg, and Downing (1979) found that neonates would smoothly track a 12° of visual angle black disc, but only with low relative amplitude and only approximately 15% of the time. Small targets, on the other hand, are followed with discrete saccadic steps. Bloch and Carchon (1992) used a red transparent ball covering 4° of visual angle and found only saccadic tracking in neonates. Similar findings were reported by Aslin (1981) who used a black bar 2° wide and 8° of visual angle high moving sinusoidally in a horizontal path.

Although successful reaching does not appear until around 4 months of age, the link between the eye and the hand is already established in the neonate. Von Hofsten (1982, 1984) studied arm and hand movements of neonates in the presence and absence of a large, colorful, and slowly moving object: a tuft made of yarn. It was found that the newborn infants performed proportionally more forward extended arm movements in the presence of this object. Quantitative analyses of these movements showed that when the object was fixated, the forward extended arm movements of the infants were aimed towards it. The immediate function of this reaching behavior cannot be to manipulate objects, because the infant cannot yet individually control arm and hand. Getting the hand into the visual field and towards the focus of attention, however, opens up optimal conditions for perceptual and sensorimotor learning.

Viewing their hands seems attractive in itself for neonates, and van der Meer, van der Weel, and Lee (1995) recently showed that neonates will make an effort to continue to view their hand if they have it in sight. When both hands of the neonate were gently pulled downwards, he or she counteracted this pulling but only for the hand they could see. This was observed whether the hand was in the direction in which they turned the head or whether it was in the opposite direction and only seen on a TV monitor.

Development of Receptor Function

Several ocular and neural changes occur during infancy and childhood that modify the relationship between proximal and distal stimuli (Banks, 1988). The most important change is the massive migration of receptors towards the fovea during the first year of life, producing the characteristic superb resolution of foveal vision (Yuodelis & Hendrickson, 1986). The consequence of this development is that the patterns of receptor excitation elicited by a specific visual stimulus will change with age. Only topological properties will remain the same. This implies that perceptual learning in early infancy cannot be based on simple template matching, but must rely on some higher-order invariances in the optic array. It also tells us that visual directions and visual distances must be continuously calibrated.

Visual acuity develops rapidly over the first half-year of life. As measured by forced-choice preference looking, it is roughly 3% of the adult acuity at birth, 6% at 1 month, 10% at 2 months, and 25% at six months (Dobson & Teller, 1977). Sensitivity to binocular disparity develops very rapidly between 3 and 5 months of age. Fox, Aslin, Shea and Dumais (1980) found that 3.5-month-old infants would track a moving virtual object, specified by binocular disparity in a dynamic random-dot stereogram, whereas 2.5-month-old infants would not. Using preferential looking, Birch et al. (1982) found a rapid rise in sensitivity to binocular acuity from 3 months, which approached an adult level between 5 and 7 months of age.

DEVELOPMENT OF GAZE CONTROL

The development of functional vision is coupled to the development of gaze control. Two tasks have to be mastered: Stabilizing gaze on a stationary or moving visual target and switching gaze between visual targets. Both tasks rely on the acquisition of head and eye control and are guided by at least three types of information: visual, vestibular, and proprioceptive.

Stabilizing gaze

There are at least two reasons for stabilizing gaze on the target of interest. First, it is important to keep the target of interest within the foveal area of the retina. Secondly, retinal slippages grossly deteriorate acuity. A stable gaze is accomplished by smooth and continuous adjustments of eye direction, which usually involves both eye and head movements. The relationship between these two component movements is very dynamic. In the tracking of a target, the eye and head movements must add up to the target motion. However, to stay on the target, eye movements also have to compensate for head movements unrelated to the tracking. Such head movements may arise as a result of more gross body movements like locomotion, from external perturbations of the head, or from the internal modulations of voluntary head movements. In an everyday situation, eye movements must simultaneously serve both compensatory and pursuit functions to make it possible to move around while fixating on a target.

All these adjustments require predictions. Maintaining a steady gaze on a moving target requires prediction of the target's motion. If the tracking involves both head and eyes, these two component movements must be timed and scaled to each other, which is only possible if the mechanism that controls the eye movements "knows" what the head is going to do ahead of time. Finally, the eye movements must predict the modulations in head movement to be able to compensate for them.

Eye and head tracking.   Kerstin Rosander and I (von Hofsten & Rosander, 1996, 1997) studied the development of gaze stabilization in a situation where the infant could freely move eyes and head. Eye movements were recorded with high-resolution EOG and head movements with an opto-electronic device (Selspot). A 2-month-old subject ready to be recorded is shown in Fig. 22.2. A happy face moving horizontally back and forth was used as the fixation target. In one study (von Hofsten & Rosander, 1996) involving 1-, 2-, and 3-month-old infants, the happy face was situated in front of a large, vertically striped background that covered most of the visual field. The target and the background moved together in a sinusoidal fashion. The patterned background was introduced in order to facilitate smooth following of head and eyes. Some smooth-pursuit eye movement was observed in all infants, including the 1-month-olds. The head was involved and contributed to the tracking. This pattern can be seen in Fig. 22.3.

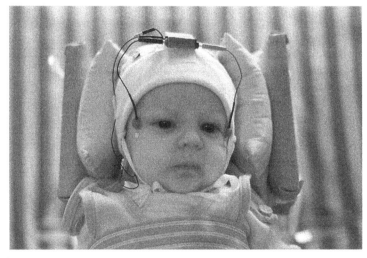

FIG. 22.2   A 2-month-old infant in the experimental situation of von Hofsten and Rosander (1996). Note the EOG pre-amplifier on the head of the infant.

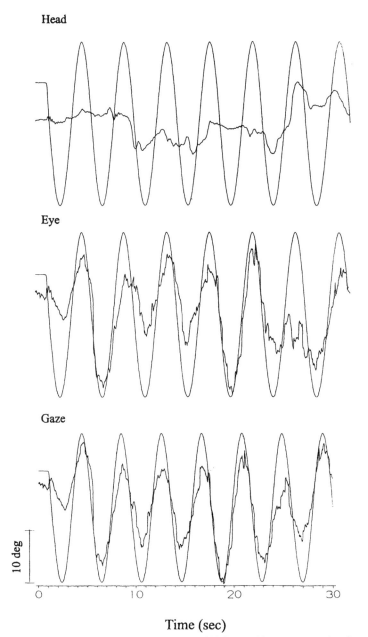

FIG. 22.3 Eye, head, and gaze records of a 1-month-old infant tracking a target moving sinusoidally at 0.3Hz. It can be observed that both head and eyes participate in the tracking and that the gaze record shows a better fit to the target motion than either the eye or head record alone.

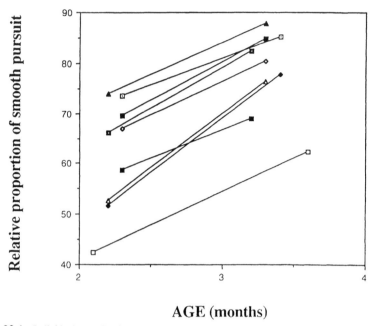

AGE (months)

FIG. 22.4   Individual records of proportion of smooth pursuit for a group of subjects studied at 2-
and 3-months of age. The different symbols denote different subjects. Note how parallel the curves
are. From von Hofsten and Rosander, 1996.

A second study (von Hofsten & Rosander, 1997) involving one group of
infants seen at 2, 3, and 5 months of age, focused on the development of
smooth-pursuit eye tracking. In this study, the background was unpatterned. The
target, which moved back and forth along a horizontal path, either changed its
motion in a smooth and continuous fashion (sinusoidal motion) or moved along
the path with a constant velocity that abruptly reversed at the turning points
(triangular motion). These two types of motion were chosen for an important
reason. Although it is possible to determine when and where an object in sinusoidal
motion is going to turn, this is not possible for an object in triangular motion
because the turn is abrupt. To anticipate the turning of an object in triangular
motion, the periodicity of the motion has to be known.

For the target (10° of visual angle), we found that smooth pursuit was clearly
established at 2-months of age. All the 11 infants studied performed some smooth-
pursuit eye tracking at 2 months of age, but the proportion of it ranged from
40% to almost 80% of the total amount of eye movements. In all infants, the
proportion increased from 2 to 3 months of age and in everyone by almost the
same amount. The correlation between proportion smooth pursuit at 2 and 3
months was found to be 0.89. This can be seen in Fig. 22.4.

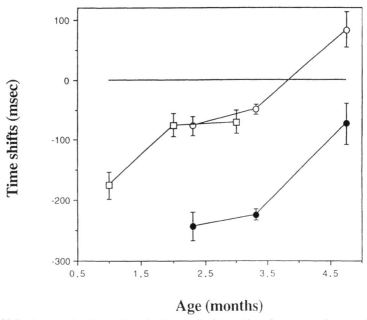

Age (months)

FIG. 22.5   Average time lags and standard errors for the tracking of targets moving according to a sinusoidal (open symbols) or a triangular (solid symbols) motion function. The diagram combines data from von Hofsten and Rosander (1996, squares) and from von Hofsten and Rosander (1997, circles).

The timing of the smooth pursuit for different ages and motion types is depicted in Fig. 22.5. For the sinusoidal motions used by von Hofsten and Rosander (1996), we found that the eyes were lagging the target substantially in the 1-month-olds, but only slightly in the 2- and 3- month-olds. A similar small lag in tracking of a sinusoidal target at 2 and 3 months of age was found by von Hofsten & Rosander (1997).

At 2 and 3 months of age, the lag was much larger, however, for the triangular motion. This indicates that the predictive mechanism functioned at a local but not at a global level. In other words, the infants were able to extrapolate the object's imminent future motions by watching its past motion, but were not able to predict where or when an object in triangular motion would turn. Finally, at 5 months of age, the eyes were leading the sinusoidally moving target and the lag for the triangular motion was much reduced. This shows that at 5 months the child is able to handle prospectively both local and global aspects of a motion. The development is parallel for the two kinds of motions, indicating that a new kind of global prediction is introduced and added to the old one. The data indicated that the infants anticipated where the target was going to turn. That infants of this age form anticipations of where and when discrete events are going to happen

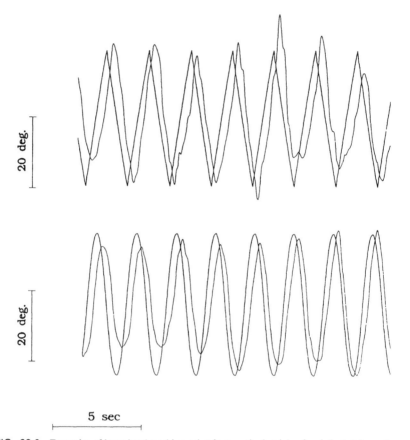

FIG. 22.6   Examples of large head-tracking gains for two single trials of an infant at 4 months and 3 weeks of age. The thicker line in each diagram corresponds to the target motion and the thinner line to the head-tracking record. The mean head-tracking gain was 1.08 for the triangular motion and 0.84 for the sinusoidal motion.

has earlier been found by Marshall Haith and associates (Canfield & Haith, 1991; Haith, Hazan, & Goodman, 1988). They demonstrated that 4-month-old infants will predict where and when the next picture in a left-right sequence is going to be shown. This was proved by the infants moving their eyes there, just before the picture appeared.

Head tracking was found to increase between 3 and 5 months of age. At 5 months, head tracking even dominated in some subjects (see Fig. 22.6). This is in line with observations by Daniel and Lee (1990). They studied tracking in 11- to 28-week-old infants and found that some of their oldest infants used head movements almost exclusively to track moving targets. Von Hofsten, Vishton, Spelke, Feng, and Rosander (submitted) reported that head movements could account for all the tracking of 6-month-old infants presented with an object moving diagonally over a large screen.

Compensatory eye movements.   Head movements unrelated to tracking are generally of higher frequency than the tracking itself, and their compensation is predominantly controlled by vestibular information. These compensations function very early in development. Figure 22.7 shows records of eye and head movements of a 1-month-old and a 3-month-old infant during the tracking of a moving target. Two results should be observed. First, the fit between the gaze and the target records is much better than either the eye-target or head-target alone. Secondly, the eye and the target records are clearly reciprocal. This indicates that the eyes compensate for head movements unrelated to the tracking of the target at the same time as they add to the head movements geared to the motion of the target.

It was found that the compensatory eye movements did not lag the head systematically, not even for the 1-month-olds. The fit was less good for 1-month-olds, however. This can be seen in Fig. 22.7.

Compensatory eye movements in response to head movements have traditionally been conceived of in terms of the vestibulo-ocular reflex (VOR). Reflexes generally show some lag, however. The reason why no lag was found for these compensatory movements is that they were part of ongoing actions. The head movements were self-produced and predictible.

Shifting gaze

The ability to shift gaze is of crucial importance for the development of visual perception, because it turns the visual sense into an instrument for exploring the world. This requires the infant not only to be able to stabilize gaze on a target of interest but also to switch the gaze to a new target, and through a series of fixations, systematically explore the surrounding. Shifting gaze involves a process of disengaging attention to the currently fixated target and moving gaze to the new target. The ability to engage attention on targets of interest improves greatly over the first few months of life, but the ability to disengage attention and control it by internal means comes somewhat later. This means that, whereas infants become better at stabilizing gaze on an attractive target, they become less able to look away from it. This phenomenon has been termed "sticky fixation". By 3–4 months of age, however, infants become very good at willfully disengaging attention and can then excel in looking around. In our studies of gaze tracking, the effect of sticky fixation expressed itself rather dramatically. At 2 and 3 months of age, infants rarely looked away from the moving target during the 20 second trials. At 5 months, however, this was the rule rather than the exception. In most trials, the infant would look away at least once and then quickly return to the moving target. It was as if the infants looked away, not because they were bored, but because they wanted to check whether anything else of importance was happening elsewhere.

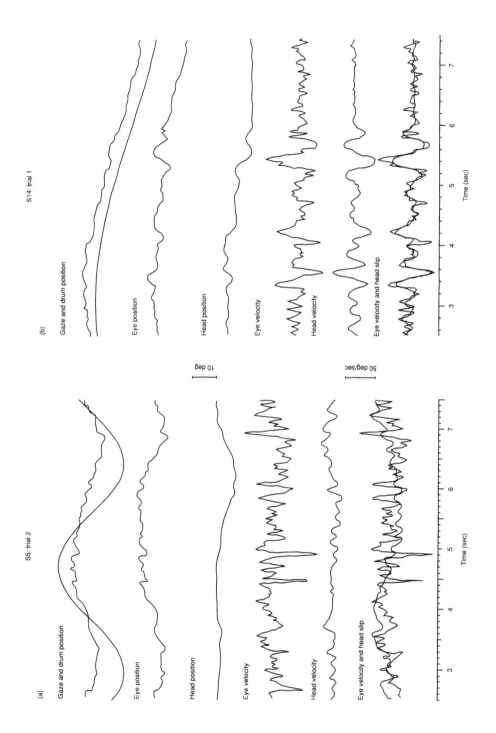

DEVELOPMENT OF EYE-HAND COORDINATION

The visual system is involved in the control of many important actions, including balance and locomotion, but seems most intimately connected to the guidance of manipulatory action. The eye-hand link shows certain primitive functioning already at birth but the hand does not become an instrument for manipulation until the 4th or 5th month of life.

Newborn infants do not grasp objects reached for. One important reason for this is that the movements of their arms and hands are synergistically coupled. As the arm is extended forward, the hand has a tendency to open, and as the arm is flexed toward the body, the hand has a tendency to close (von Hofsten, 1984). This tendency interferes with grasping an object reached for because that requires the hand to close while the arm is extended. The described synergy between arm and hands starts to decouple around 2 months. At 3 months of age, infants were observed to open and close the hand repeatedly at the end of an arm extension, but only as if they were actively trying to grasp the object being reached for.

Functional reaching does not just mature. It requires the infant to be active. At 3–4 months of age, infants spend considerable time watching their hands move in front of them in the visual field (Piaget, 1953). If an attractive object is placed in front of an infant at this age, he or she will try to get to the object and grasp it. Children at this age may try for hours to grasp an object in front of them, despite the fact that they often fail. A simplistic reinforcement model would predict that because of the high rate of failure, infants would give up, but they do not. They really want to be in control. Of course, from a biological point of view, their stubbornness makes sense. Their persistence makes it possible for the eye-hand system to become organized itself through the continued action of the infant.

Once infants are successful enough in contacting and grasping objects, reaching develops very rapidly. Within only a few months, the approach becomes smooth, and the grasping efficient. Through the establishment of the direct cortico-motoneuronal pathway around 9 months of age, infants are able to control individual finger movements, which creates possibilities for more refined manual control. This is reflected in infants' preoccupation with picking up very small artifacts with their thumb and index finger at that age.

When reaching for a stationary object, there are several problems that need to be dealt with in advance to ensure that the encounter with the object will be smooth and efficient. The hand needs to open up during the approach, adjust its

FIG. 22.7 (facing page)   Records of target and gaze position superimposed, eye and head position, eye and head velocity, and eye velocity with head slip superimposed. (a) A 1-month-old infant inspecting a 0.3Hz oscillation of the drum. Peak cross-correlation was 0.42 at a lag of the eyes of 0.004sec. (b) A 3-month-old infant inspecting a 0.1Hz oscillation of the drum. Peak cross-correlation was 0.83 at a lag of the eyes of 0.002sec. From von Hofsten and Rosander, 1996.

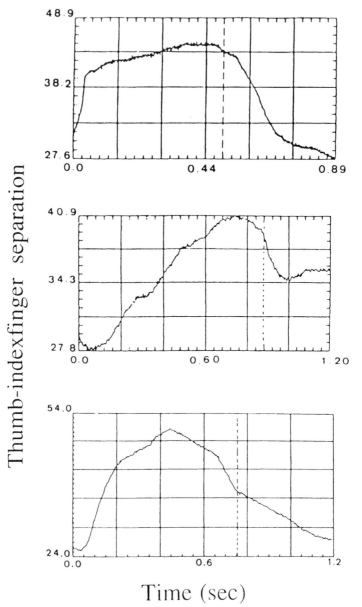

FIG. 22.8 Changes in the distance between thumb and index finger of the reaching hand as it approaches the object to be grasped. Examples from individual reaches at 5 months, 9 months, and 13 months of age are shown. The dashed line represents the time that the object was encountered. From Von Hofsten and Rönnqvist, 1988.

orientation to fit the object, and close around it at the time of the encounter. Grasping must begin in anticipation of the encounter with the target and can only occur under visual control. Tactually controlled grasping initiated after contact will, by necessity, induce an interruption in the reach-and-grasp act. Thus, the emergence of visual control of grasping is crucial for the development of manual skill.

At 5 months of age, infants will crudely adjust the orientation of the hand to the orientation of the object before it is encountered (von Hofsten & Fazel-Zandy, 1984). Such adjustments are necessary, especially for getting an elongated object into the hand in the right way. Adjusting the hand to the size of a target is less crucial. Von Hofsten and Rönnqvist (1988) found that 9-month-olds and 13-month-olds adjusted the opening of the hand to the size of the target reached for, whereas 5- to 6-month-olds did not. These researchers also determined at what point the distance between thumb and index finger started to diminish during the approach. At all three age levels, the hand started to close in anticipation of the encounter with the object. In the two younger groups, the hand first moved to the neighborhood of the target and then started to close around it. For the 13-month-olds, however, the grasping action typically started during the approach, well before touch. In other words, at this age the grasping movement was becoming integrated with the approach movement into one continuous approach-and-grasp act. Figure 22.8 shows examples of how the hand opens and closes around the object for infants at different ages.

Before the reach begins, postural adjustments must be made so that the forward movement of the arm does not upset balance. Von Hofsten and Woollacott (1990) found evidence for such adjustments in 9-month-old infants. This is the age when infants start to control independently the balance of their body. The infants were seated astride on one of the knees of an accompanying parent who supported the child by holding him or her at the hips. Muscle responses were recorded from the abdominal and trunk extensor muscles and from the deltoid muscle of the reaching arm. The results showed that trunk muscles participated in the reaching actions of these 9-month-old infants. Trunk extensors and sometimes abdominal muscles were activated before the arm extended forward.

Catching

Catching constitutes the most striking example of anticipation in infants' manual action. To be able to catch a fast-moving object, infants must not only perceive the position of the object in an instant, but must also determine where the object is going and how fast. Appropriate arm movements must be initiated before the object is within reaching distance. The reach must be aimed towards a future location where the paths of the object and the hand will intersect. When the hand is in the right position, it must close around the object at the right time, to ensure that the object is caught. Obviously, timing must be very precise. Studies of catching skills in infancy show that as infants start to successfully grasp stationary objects, they also catch moving ones. Von Hofsten and Lindhagen (1979) found that 18-week-old infants catch objects moving at 30cm/sec. In another study (von Hofsten, 1983), 8-month-olds were found to catch objects moving at 120cm/sec. The initial aim of these reaches was within a few degrees of the meeting point with the target, and the variable timing error was around 50msec.

Emergence of visual cognition

Prediction of an object's future position can be made by extrapolating the observed motion into the future. Such extrapolations have their limitations, however. They can only be applied to continuous motions and then only over small time windows. When dealing with abruptly changing motions, such as triangular motion, or when placed in situations where the moving object temporarily goes out of sight, the subjects must rely on more rule-based predictions. The most basic ones are the physical constraints that apply to all moving objects. They include the rules of *gravity* (objects accelerate downward in the absence of support), and *inertia* (objects continue their ongoing motion in the absence of forces and change their motion smoothly when forces are present). Such rules and other, more task-dependent ones, may be used by infants to anticipate how an object will move.

In one experiment, we investigated how 6-month-old infants reach for objects that move on discontinuous motion paths (von Hofsten et al., submitted). The object moved along the diagonals of a large vertical screen placed in front of the infant. The motion paths intersected out of reach, straight above the infant. Two kinds of motion were used. The object either moved along the same diagonal all the time and passed within reach on one side of the infant, or it abruptly changed its direction of motion at the intersection of the diagonals and passed within reach on the other side of the infant. To catch the object, the infants had to decide, already before the object had reached the point of intersection, on which side it would pass them.

The reaching observed showed that the infants always acted as if the object would continue to move on a straight path. This was valid even after eight consecutive nonlinear trials. The findings suggest that 6-month-old infants predict that an object moving in a straight line will continue to move in the same way in the near future.

When the area of the screen where the two diagonals intersected was occluded, the subject still tended to predict that the object would continue to move in a straight line. The tracking of the object was disrupted as the object disappeared but after a short delay, the eyes and head moved to the opposite side of the occluder. This behavior is shown in Fig. 22.9.

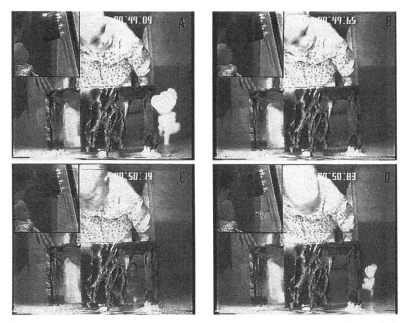

FIG. 22.9   A 6-month-old infant observing an object (teddy bear) moving behind an occluder on a straight oblique path. Behind the occluder, the path of motion is abruptly changed, and instead of appearing at the lower right corner of the occluder, the teddy bear appears at the lower left corner. At A, the object is just disappearing at the upper left corner of the occluder. At B, 0.5sec later, the eyes have moved over to the lower right corner. At C, another 0.5sec later, the head has moved to the lower right corner as well. At this time, the object is appearing at the lower left corner. Finally at D, another 0.7sec later, the subject moves head and eyes over to the left and continues to track the object.

SUMMARY AND CONCLUSIONS

At birth, the visual system is functioning at a level sufficient to allow the infant to start exploring the world. However, most visual abilities still need to be developed. During the first half-year of life, the visual system shows dramatic development into mature performance, incorporating all aspects of visual functioning. Acuity and binocular vision are adultlike by 6 months of age, as is oculomotor functioning. The visual system begins to guide actions in a prospective way before 6 months of age, and to use knowledge of the external world to improve visual functioning.

Visual skills do not just emerge; the participation of an active organism is required. From birth onwards, experience enters into the ontogenetic process with great efficiency to shape and steer it. It is also important to note that experience does not just add to what is genetically determined, but rather works with the genetic factors to guide the system into its final organizational form.

The system is implemented in the tasks to be performed and the problems to be solved. The tasks and problems encountered determine the specific abilities to be developed—whether they are oculomotor, attentional, perceptual, or conceptual. Visual development could not be understood without considering motivation. The infant finds pleasure in exploring, understanding, and mastering the world. This is both extremely basic and crucially important for development. The same principle applies to the sensorimotor system itself. When infants spend hours trying to prehend an object in front of them without succeeding, they are still exercising control of their arm movements and discovering how to accomplish the task better, by getting the hand closer to the object and coordinating arm and hand movements properly. Thus, the infant finds pleasure in just exploring its sensory and motor capabilities, understanding how they fit together, and mastering sensorimotor coordination.

ACKNOWLEDGEMENT

This chapter was made possible by grants to the author from the Swedish Council for Research in the Humanities and Social Sciences.

REFERENCES

Aslin, R. N. (1981). Development of smooth pursuit in human infants. In D. F. Fisher, R. A. Monty, & J. W. Senders (Eds.), *Eye Movements: Cognition and visual perception* (pp. 31–51). Hillsdale NJ: Lawrence Erlbaum Associates Inc.

Banks, M. S. (1988). Visual recalibration and the development of contrast and optic flow perception. In A. Yonas (Ed.), *Perceptual development in infancy: The Minnesota Symposia on Child Psychology* (Vol. 20, pp. 145–196). Hillsdale, NJ: Lawrence Erlbaum Associates Inc.

Banks, M. S., & Bennett, P. J. (1988). Optical and photoreceptor immaturities limit the spatial and chromatic vision of human neonates. *Journal of the Optical Society of America A, 5,* 2059–2079.

Birch, E. E., Gwiazda, J., & Held, R. (1982). Stereoacuity development for crossed and uncrossed disparities in human infants. *Vision Research, 22,* 507–513.

Bloch, H., & Carchon, I. (1992). On the onset of eye-head co-ordination in infants. *Behavioral Brain Research, 49,* 85–90.

Canfield, R. L., & Haith, M. M. (1991). Young infants' visual expectations for symmetric and asymmetric stimulus sequences. *Developmental Psychology, 27,* 198–208.

Daniel, B. M., & Lee, D. (1990). Development of looking with head and eyes. *Journal of Experimental Child Psychology, 50,* 200–216.

Dobson, V., & Teller, D. Y. (1977). Visual acuity in human infants: A review and comparison of behavioral and electrophysiological studies. *Vision Research, 18,* 1469–1483.

Fox, R., Aslin, R., Shea, S., & Dumais, S. (1980). Stereopsis in human infants. *Science, 207,* 323–324.

Fraiberg, S. (1977). *Insights from the blind: Comparative studies of blind and sighted infants.* New York: Basic Books.

Haineline, L., Riddell, P., Grose-Fifer, J., & Abramov, I. (1992). Development of accommodation and convergence in infancy. *Behavioral Brain Research, 49,* 33–50.

Haith, M., Hazan, C., & Goodman, G. S. (1988). Expectation and anticipation of dynamic visual events by 3.5-month-old babies. *Child Development, 59,* 467–479.

Heimann, M., Nelson, K. E., & Schaller, J. (1989). Neonatal imitation of tongue protrusion and mouth opening: Methodological aspects and evidence of early individual differences. *Scandinavian Journal of Psychology, 30*, 90–101.

Jacobsen, K. Magnussens, S., & Smith, L. (1997). Hidden visual capabilities in mentally retarded subjects diagnosed as deaf-blind. *Vision Research, 37*, 2931–2935.

Johnson, M. H., & Morton, J. (1991). *Biology and cognitive development: The case of face recognition.* Oxford: Blackwell.

Kremenitzer, J. P., Vaughan, H. G., Kurtzberg, D. & Dowling, K. (1979). Smooth-pursuit eye movements in the newborn infant. *Child Development, 50*, 442–448.

Lee, D. N. (1992). Body-environment coupling. In U. Neisser (Ed.), *Ecological and interpersonal knowledge of the self.* Cambridge: Cambridge University Press.

Meltzoff, A. N., & Moore, M. K. (1977). Imitation of facial and manual gestures by human neonates. *Science, 198*, 75–78.

Piaget, J. (1953). *The origins of intelligence in the child.* New York: Routledge.

Rétaux, S., & Harris, W. A. (1996). Engrailed and retinotectal topography. *Trends in Neuroscience, 19*, 542–546.

Shatz, C. J. (1992). The developing brain. *Scientific American*, September, 35–41.

van der Meer, A. L. H., van der Weel, F. R., & Lee, D. N. (1995). The functional significance of arm movements in neonates. *Science, 267*, 693–695.

von der Malsburg, C., & Singer, W. (1988). Principles of cortical network organisations. In P. Rakic & W. Singer (Eds.), *Neurobiology of neocortex* (pp. 69–99). London: Wiley.

von Hofsten, C. (1982). Eye-hand coordination in newborns. *Developmental Psychology, 18*, 450–461.

von Hofsten, C. (1983). Catching skills in infancy. *Journal of Experimental Psychology: Human Perception and Performance, 9*, 75–85.

von Hofsten, C. (1984). Developmental changes in the organization of pre-reaching movements. *Developmental Psychology, 20*, 378–388.

von Hofsten, C., & Fazel-Zandy, S. (1984). Development of visually guided hand orientation in reaching. *Journal of Experimental Child Psychology, 38*, 208–219.

von Hofsten, C., & Lindhagen, K. (1979). Observations on the development of reaching for moving objects. *Journal of Experimental Child Psychology, 28*, 158–173.

von Hofsten, C., & Rönnqvist, L. (1988). Preparation for grasping an object: A developmental study. *Journal of Experimental Psychology: Human Perception and Performance, 14*, 610–621.

von Hofsten, C., & Rosander, K. (1996). The development of gaze control and predictive tracking in young infants. *Vision Research, 36*, 81–96.

von Hofsten, C., & Rosander, K. (1997). Development of smooth pursuit tracking in young infants. *Vision Research, 37*, 1799–1810.

von Hofsten, C., Vishton, P., Spelke, E. S., Feng, Q., & Rosander, K. (submitted). Predictive action in infancy: Tracking and reaching for moving objects.

von Hofsten, C., & Woollacott, M. (1990). *Postural preparations for reaching in 9-month-old infants.* Unpublished data.

Yuodelis, C., & Hendrickson, A. (1986). A qualitative and quantitative analysis of the human fovea during development. *Vision Research, 26*, 847–855.

CHAPTER TWENTY-THREE

Infants' understanding of the physical world

Renée Baillargeon
University of Illinois, Champaign, Illinois, USA

Traditionally, researchers believed that infants understand very little about the physical world. With the advent of new methodologies, however, investigators came to realize that even young infants possess a surprising wealth of knowledge about physical events. These findings led researchers to orient their efforts in a new direction and to ask how infants attain their physical knowledge. The account my colleagues and I have proposed holds that infants are born with a specialized learning mechanism that guides their acquisition of physical knowledge. I first present this model and then review some of the evidence supporting it, focusing in particular on findings from investigations of infants' knowledge about collision, occlusion, and support events. Finally, I examine alternative accounts of infants' approach to the physical world and discuss ways in which these different accounts can be reconciled.

Les chercheurs ont longtemps cru que les nourrissons n'avaient qu'une compréhension très limitée de l'univers physique. Cependant, la mise au point de nouvelles méthodologies a permis d'observer que, même tôt, les nourrissons disposaient de connaissances étonnamment riches sur les phénomènes physiques. Ce constat a réorienté les efforts dans une direction consistant à se demander comment les nourrissons accèdent à de telles connaissances. Selon l'explication ici proposée, ces derniers naîtraient dotés d'un mécanisme spécialisé d'apprentissage qui guide leur acquisition. La présentation de ce modèle est suivie de l'examen de certains des éléments de preuve le validant, avec une insistance particulière sur les résultats de travaux mettant en évidence les connaissances des nourrissons sur les phénomènes de collision, de masquage (produit par un écran) et d'appui. Sont enfin présentées d'autres explications de l'accès des nourrissons à l'univers physique et discutées les façons de concilier les diverses explications existantes.

INTRODUCTION

As they look about them, infants routinely observe many different physical events: For example, they may see a parent pour juice into a cup, stack dishes on a table, or store groceries in a cupboard, or they may see a sibling drop a ball, hit a tower of blocks, or send a toy car crashing into a wall. How well do infants understand such events? Traditionally, investigators assumed that infants understand very little about the physical world (e.g. Piaget, 1952, 1954). This conclusion was based primarily on analyses of infants' performance in object-manipulation tasks. For example, young infants were said to be unaware that an object continues to exist when hidden because they consistently failed tasks that required them to search for a toy hidden behind or under a cover (e.g. Piaget, 1952, 1954).

In time, however, researchers came to realize that young infants might perform poorly in object-manipulation tasks, not because they lacked the necessary physical knowledge, but because they had difficulty planning and executing complex action sequences. This concern led investigators to seek alternative methods for assessing infants' physical knowledge, methods that did not depend on the performance of complex actions.

During the 1980s, several new methods were developed that focused on infants' visual attention to events. These methods were inspired by the well-documented finding that infants tend to look longer at novel than at familiar stimuli (e.g. Fagan, 1970, 1971, 1972, 1973; Fantz, 1964; Friedman, 1972). One such method is the *habituation-dishabituation* method (e.g. Kellman & Spelke, 1983; Kotovsky & Baillargeon, 1994; Leslie & Keeble, 1987; Oakes, 1994; Spelke, Kestenbaum, Simons, & Wein, 1995a; Woodward, Phillips, & Spelke, 1993). In a typical experiment, infants are first habituated to an event (i.e. they are shown the event repeatedly until their looking time declines to a pre-selected criterion level). Next, infants are presented with one or two test events. Dishabituation or increased looking at one or both events (with appropriate controls) is taken to indicate that infants' physical knowledge leads them to perceive the event(s) as novel or unexpected relative to the habituation event presented earlier.

Another visual-attention method that is commonly used in investigations of infants' physical knowledge is the *violation-of-expectation* method (e.g. Arterberry, 1993; Baillargeon, 1986; Baillargeon, Spelke, & Wasserman, 1985; Needham & Baillargeon, 1997; Spelke, Breinlinger, Macomber, & Jacobson, 1992; Wilcox, Nadel, & Rosser, 1996). In a typical experiment, infants are presented with a possible and an impossible test event. The possible event is consistent with the knowledge or expectation being examined in the experiment; the impossible event, in contrast, violates this expectation. Longer looking at the impossible than at the possible event (with appropriate controls) is taken to indicate that infants' physical knowledge leads them to view the impossible event as more novel or unexpected than the possible event. Prior to the test trials, infants often

Habituation: Causal Event

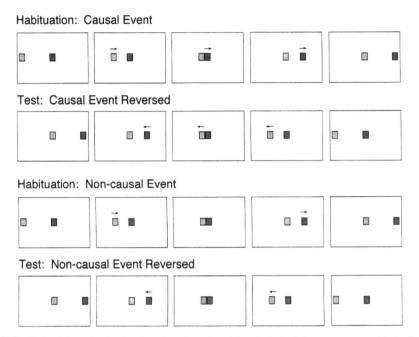

Test: Causal Event Reversed

Habituation: Non-causal Event

Test: Non-causal Event Reversed

FIG. 23.1   Schematic drawing (based on the authors' description) of the test events used in Leslie and Keeble (1987).

receive familiarization or habituation trials designed to acquaint them with various aspects of the test events. However, these trials play a different role in the violation-of-expectation than in the habituation-dishabituation method: They are intended simply to introduce infants to the test situation, not to provide them with an essential basis of comparison for evaluating the novelty of the test events.

Multiple tests of infants' physical knowledge conducted with these new visual-attention methods revealed that, contrary to traditional claims, even young infants possess a surprising wealth of knowledge about the physical world (for recent reviews, see Baillargeon, 1995; Leslie, 1995; Mandler, in press; Needham, Baillargeon, & Kaufman, 1997; Oakes & Cohen, 1995; Spelke, 1994). To illustrate this claim, I will describe two experiments: a habituation-dishabituation experiment conducted by Leslie and Keeble (1987), and a violation-of-expectation experiment conducted by Spelke et al. (1992).

The experiment conducted by Leslie and Keeble (1987) examined whether 6-month-old infants distinguish between causal and non-causal events (see Fig. 23.1). The infants were habituated to one of two filmed events: (a) a causal event in which a red brick approached and contacted a green brick, which immediately moved off; or (b) a noncausal event in which the two bricks' motions were separated by a 0.5sec delay. Following habituation, the infants watched the

Habituation Event

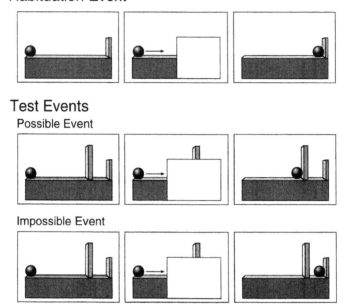

Test Events
Possible Event

Impossible Event

FIG. 23.2   Schematic drawing (based on the authors' description) of the test events used in Spelke et al. (1992). From "Physical reasoning in infancy" (p. 183), by R. Baillargeon, 1995, in M. S. Gazzaniga (Ed.-in-chief), *The cognitive neurosciences* (pp. 181–204). Cambridge, MA: MIT Press. Copyright 1995 by Massachusetts Institute of Technology. Reprinted with permission.

same event in reverse. The authors reasoned that, whereas only spatiotemporal direction was reversed in the noncausal event, both spatiotemporal and causal direction was reversed in the causal event; therefore, if the infants were sensitive to causality, they should dishabituate more to the causal than to the noncausal test event. The infants looked reliably longer when the causal as opposed to the noncausal event was reversed. These and control results suggested that, by 6 months of age, infants are already sensitive to the causal properties of events.

The experiment conducted by Spelke et al. (1992) tested whether 2.5-month-old infants realize that objects exist continuously in time and move along continuous, unobstructed paths (see Fig. 23.2). The infants sat in front of a wide platform; at the right end of the platform was a tall, thin box. The infants were habituated to the following event: First, a screen was lowered in front of the right half of the platform; next, a ball rolled from left to right along the platform and disappeared behind the screen; after a pause, the screen was raised to reveal the ball resting against the box at the end of the platform. Following habituation, the infants saw a possible and an impossible test event similar to the habituation event except that a second box was placed on the platform; this box was taller than the end box and protruded above the screen. At the end of the test events, the screen was removed to reveal the ball resting against either the tall box (possible event) or the end box (impossible event). The infants looked reliably longer at the impossible than at the possible event, suggesting that they (a) understood that the ball continued to exist, and pursued its trajectory, after it moved behind the screen; (b) realized that the ball could not roll through the space occupied by the tall box; and hence (c) expected the ball to stop against the tall box and were surprised when it did not. These and control results suggested that, by 2.5 months of age, infants already conceive of objects as permanent entities that exist and move continuously in time and space.

The discovery that even young infants possess sophisticated intuitions about objects led researchers to focus their efforts in a new direction and to ask not only *what* infants know about the physical world, but also *how* they attain this knowledge. Largely as a result of this new developmental focus, several accounts have been proposed in recent years that attempt to explain infants' rapid mastery of the physical world (e.g. Baillargeon, 1995; Karmiloff-Smith, 1992; Leslie, 1995; Mandler, in press; Spelke, 1994; Thelen & Smith, 1994). In the next section, I describe the account that my colleagues and I have developed over the past few years (e.g. Baillargeon, 1994, 1995; Baillargeon, Kotovsky, & Needham, 1995). Next, I describe a few alternative accounts of infants' approach to the physical world, and discuss ways in which these different accounts can be reconciled.

INFANTS' LEARNING MECHANISM

According to our model, infants are born with a specialized learning mechanism that guides their acquisition of physical knowledge (e.g. Baillargeon, 1994, 1995; Baillargeon et al., 1995). This mechanism is thought to be responsible for at least two closely intertwined learning processes. One is the formation of broad *event and object categories. Event* categories correspond to distinct ways in which objects behave or interact. We believe that infants' early event categories include: collision events (events in which an object approaches and hits another object); arrested-motion events (events in which an object approaches and hits a broad surface such as a wall or floor); occlusion events (events in which an object becomes occluded by another, closer, object or surface); and support events (events in which an object becomes supported by another object or surface). *Object* categories refer to the distinct types of objects that exist in the world. We suspect that infants' early object categories include: animate objects (objects such as people who possess certain facial features, can express emotions, respond contingently, are capable of a wide range of self-motions, and so on); inanimate, self-moving objects (objects such as cars that lack many of the properties of animate objects but are capable of at least limited self-motion); and inanimate, inert objects (objects such as cups that move only when acted on). From an early age, infants take into account the type of object involved in an event when interpreting the outcome of the event. To illustrate, infants respond somewhat differently to collision events involving self-moving and inert objects (e.g. Kotovsky & Baillargeon, in prep., in press a,b; Leslie, 1982, 1984a,b; Leslie & Keeble, 1987; Oakes, 1994; Oakes & Cohen, 1995; Spelke, Phillips, & Woodward, 1995b; Woodward et al., 1993). Ongoing experiments in our laboratory are exploring infants' expectations about the behavior of self-moving objects (e.g. Kaufman, 1997). Due to lack of space, however, the remainder of this chapter will focus exclusively on research conducted with inert objects.

The second process that is controlled by infants' learning mechanism is the identification, for each event category, of an *initial concept* and *variables*. We believe that, when learning about a new event category, infants first form a preliminary, all-or-none concept that captures only the essence of the event. With further experience, this initial concept is progressively elaborated. Infants slowly identify variables that are relevant to the event and incorporate this additional knowledge into their reasoning, resulting in increasingly accurate predictions and interpretations over time.

What is the nature of the learning mechanism that directs infants' formation of event categories and identification of initial concepts and variables? To answer this question, we have been pursuing a dual research strategy. A first strategy has been to investigate distinct event categories (e.g. collision, occlusion, and support events) and trace their respective developmental courses. We believe that specifying and comparing the sequences of variables that emerge for different event categories can yield fundamental insights about the nature of infants' learning mechanism. A second strategy has been to conduct experiments in which we attempt to "teach" infants variables they have not yet identified, by presenting them with pertinent observations. We hope that by discovering precisely what observations, and how many observations, infants require for learning, we can better understand how their learning mechanism processes and stores new information and integrates it with prior information to yield new knowledge. I now describe some of the findings we have obtained in pursuing these two strategies.

Knowledge about different event categories

Collision events. In our first series of experiments on the development of infants' reasoning about collision events (e.g. Kotovsky & Baillargeon, 1994, in press a, in prep.; see Baillargeon, 1995, and Baillargeon et al., 1995, for reviews), infants aged 2.5 to 11 months were presented with collision events involving a moving object (a cylinder rolling down a ramp) and a stationary object (a wheeled toy bug positioned on a track at the bottom of the ramp).

The results of these experiments (summarized in Fig. 23.3) indicate that, by 2.5 months of age, infants have formed an initial concept of collision centered on a simple *impact/no-impact* distinction: They expect a stationary object to be displaced when hit by a moving object, and to remain stationary otherwise. Thus, infants are surprised to see the bug remain stationary when hit by the cylinder, and to see the bug move when not hit.

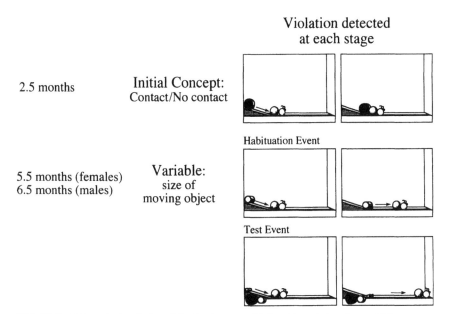

Violation detected
at each stage

2.5 months   Initial Concept:
Contact/No contact

Habituation Event

5.5 months (females)   Variable:
6.5 months (males)   size of
moving object

Test Event

FIG. 23.3   Schematic description of the development of infants' knowledge about collision events: 2.5 to 6.5 months.

At about 5.5 to 6.5 months of age (females precede males by a few weeks in this development), infants add a variable to their initial concept: They begin to appreciate that in a collision between a moving and a stationary object, the *size*[1] of the moving object affects the length of the stationary object's displacement. After seeing a medium cylinder cause the bug to roll to the middle of the track, infants judge that the bug should roll farther when hit by a larger but not a smaller cylinder. Younger infants are not surprised to see the bug roll farther with either the larger or the smaller cylinder, even though (a) all three of the cylinders are simultaneously present in the apparatus, so that their sizes can be readily compared, and (b) infants have no difficulty remembering (as shown in other experiments) that the bug rolled to the middle of the track when hit by the medium cylinder. These results suggest that, prior to 5.5 to 6.5 months of age, infants do not understand the proportional relation between the size of the cylinder and the length of the bug's trajectory.

In a second series of experiments, 8-month-old infants were presented with collision events similar to those in our initial experiments except that the bug was replaced with a box (e.g. Kaufman & Kotovsky, 1997; Kotovsky & Baillargeon, in press b). The results of these experiments (summarized in Fig. 23.4) suggest that, at about 8 months of age, infants begin to distinguish

---

[1] We refer to the moving object's size rather than mass because our data are insufficient to determine which variable guided the infants' responses (Kotovsky & Baillargeon, 1994, in press a).

Variable: Verticality of Stationary Object

Infants expect box:

Not to move   To move

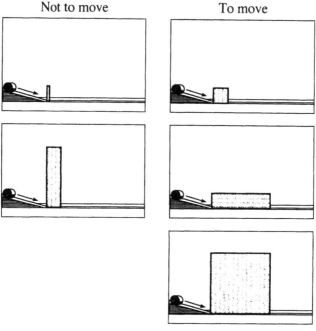

FIG. 23.4 Schematic description of the development of infants' knowledge about collision events: 8 months.

among stationary objects between those that are likely to be displaced when hit, and those that are not. The basis for this distinction appears to be *verticality*: Infants expect objects with a salient vertical dimension to be immovable, and objects lacking such a dimension to be movable. Thus, infants expect boxes that are taller than they are wide, irrespective of their absolute dimensions, to remain stationary when hit by the cylinder; all other boxes are expected to move, again irrespective of their absolute dimensions.

How can we explain the developmental sequence revealed by these experiments? According to our model, infants cannot identify a variable as relevant to an event category unless they have available *contrastive data* from which to abstract it. By contrastive data, we mean observations or manipulations indicating that an outcome occurs when some condition is met (positive data), and does not occur when the condition is not met (negative data). As an illustration, consider the finding that at about 8 months of age infants use verticality or its absence as a basis for predicting whether an object will remain stationary or move when hit. At about 7 to 8 months of age, infants begin to crawl and to pull themselves upright by holding on to surfaces that are often tall and thin:

the legs of tables and chairs, the vertical slats in cribs and banisters, and so on. On the basis of these manipulations, infants may conclude that objects with a salient vertical dimension, unlike other objects, typically remain stationary when acted on. Prior to this stage, infants would typically have been given only light objects to manipulate (e.g. cups, spoons, bowls, rattles, bottles, shoes, toy cars, blocks, keys, stuffed animals, and so on). Hence, infants' experiences with objects (as distinct from broad surfaces such as walls, floors, or tables) would all support the notion that objects typically move when acted on. Infants' observations of their caretakers' actions on objects would be consistent with the same conclusion: After all, infants must have few opportunities to observe their parents act on objects that remain stationary when pushed, pulled, or struck. When infants begin to navigate their environment, and to look for safe handholds to pull themselves upright, they must quickly learn to recognize, among the entire class of objects, a vertical subclass that can be relied on to remain stationary when acted on.

With further experience, infants presumably refine their ideas about verticality, and come to realize that only vertical objects that are rigidly anchored at the top or bottom are likely to provide useful handholds. At the same time, infants must also learn that nonvertical objects that are large or heavy are less likely to move when acted on than are small or light ones. As infants begin to explore their environment on their own, they encounter objects far heavier than those they have previously experienced. Many parents will fondly remember their crawling infants intently pulling heavy books from shelves or dragging heavy saucepans out of cupboards. Such experiences must lead infants to consider objects' size as well as verticality when predicting the outcome of collision events. Experiments are under way in our laboratory to test these speculations.

Occlusion events. In our experiments on the development of infants' knowledge about occlusion events (e.g. Aguiar & Baillargeon, submitted a,b; Baillargeon & DeVos, 1991; Baillargeon & Graber, 1987), infants aged 2.5 to 5.5 months were tested with simple occlusion problems involving a screen and a toy such as a toy mouse. The infants were first habituated to the mouse moving back and forth behind the screen. Following habituation, a portion of the screen was removed, and infants judged whether the mouse should remain continuously hidden or should become temporarily visible when passing behind the screen.

The results of these experiments (summarized in Fig. 23.5) suggest that, by 2.5 months of age, infants have formed an initial concept of occlusion centered on a simple *behind/not-behind* distinction: They expect an object to be hidden when behind an occluder, and to be visible otherwise. This concept leads infants to be surprised when the mouse fails to appear between two separate screens (see Fig. 23.5). Presumably, infants (a) assume that the mouse exists continuously in time and moves continuously through space; (b) expect the mouse to

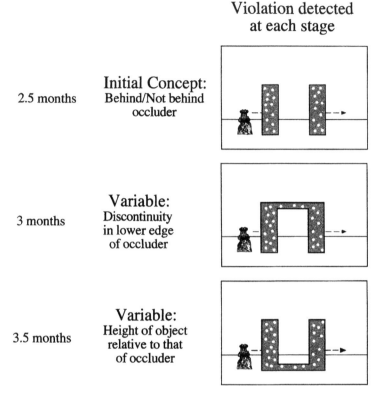

FIG. 23.5   Schematic description of the development of infants' knowledge about occlusion events: 2.5 to 3.5 months.

be hidden behind each screen and to be visible between them; and hence (c) are surprised when this last expectation is violated. However, infants' understanding of occlusion is still extremely primitive: When the two screens are connected by a narrow strip at the top or bottom, infants no longer show surprise when the mouse fails to appear between them. Infants apparently view the connected screens as forming a single object and, consistent with their simple behind/not-behind distinction, they expect the mouse to be hidden when passing behind it. Infants are not able to take into account additional variables to predict whether the mouse should remain hidden or become temporarily visible when passing behind the screen.

By 3 months of age, infants have already progressed beyond their initial concept of occlusion and identified a variable that enables them to better predict the outcome of occlusion events. When an object moves behind an occluder, infants now attend to the lower edge of the occluder; if this lower edge presents a discontinuity, infants expect the object to appear in the opening. As shown in Fig. 23.5, when faced with two screens that are connected at the top, 3-month-olds, unlike 2.5-month-olds, are surprised if the mouse fails to appear between the screens. Infants still show little or no surprise, however, when the mouse fails to appear between two screens that are connected at the bottom: Infants attend to lower but not upper occluder discontinuities.

By 3.5 months of age, infants have added a further variable to their knowledge of occlusion events. When an object moves behind an occluder that has a discontinuity along its upper edge, infants take into account the *height* of the object to predict whether it will remain fully hidden or become partly visible when passing behind the occluder. As shown in Fig. 23.5, when the two screens are connected at the bottom by a strip shorter than the mouse, infants are now surprised when the mouse fails to appear above the strip.

How can we account for the developmental sequence just described? The most likely explanation, we believe, is the same one that was advanced when discussing the development of infants' knowledge about collision events. As they look about them, infants experience countless occlusion events every day. These data (which no doubt steadily improve in quality as infants' visual tracking ability itself improves; see Aslin, 1981, and Banks, 1983) then feed into the infants' learning mechanism. The mechanism in turn produces a sequence of increasingly refined variables that enable infants to predict occlusion outcomes more and more accurately over time. As with collision events, we believe that the primary data infants use to identify occlusion variables are contrastive data: For example, infants identify height as an important variable after noting that, when an object passes behind a screen with an upper window, the object is likely to appear in the window if it is taller (positive data) but not shorter (negative data) than the window's lower edge.

Support events.   In our experiments on the development of infants' knowledge about support events (e.g. Baillargeon, Needham, & DeVos, 1992; Needham & Baillargeon, 1993; see Baillargeon, 1995, and Baillargeon et al., 1995, for reviews), infants aged 3 to 12.5 months were presented with simple support problems involving a box and a platform; the box was released in one of several positions relative to the platform (e.g. off the platform, on top of it, against its side, and so on), and the infants judged whether the box should remain stable when released.

The results (summarized in Fig. 23.6) indicate that, by 3 months of age, infants have formed an initial concept centered on a *contact/no-contact* distinction: They expect an object to fall if it does not contact another object when released, and to be stable if it does. As shown in Fig. 23.6, infants expect the box to fall when released off the platform, but not against its side. Ongoing experiments in our laboratory suggest that infants also show little surprise when the box is released under the top of an open platform and fails to fall. In this initial stage, infants apparently view *any* contact between the box and the platform as sufficient to ensure the box's stability.

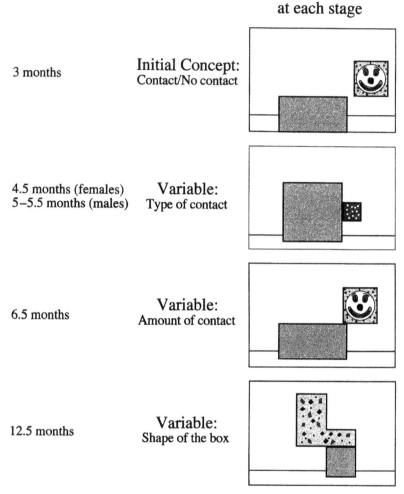

FIG. 23.6 Schematic description of the development of infants' knowledge about support events: 3 to 12.5 months.

By about 4.5 to 5.5 months of age (females precede males by a few weeks in this development),[2] infants have progressed beyond their initial concept of support: They now realize that the *type of contact* between an object and its support must be taken into account when judging the object's stability. Infants

---

[2] The reader may find puzzling the sex differences noted here and earlier in our discussion of the development of infants' knowledge about collision events. We believe that these two sex differences, which are both found in infants aged 4 to 6 months, reflect the slower development of male infants' binocular depth perception. Research by Held, Gwiazda, and their colleagues (e.g. Bauer, Shimojo, Gwiazda, & Held, 1986; Gwiazda, Bauer, & Held, 1989a,b) indicates that, compared to female infants, male infants show slower development of stereopsis during the third through sixth

now expect the box to remain stable when released on but not against or under the platform. Nevertheless, as shown in Fig. 23.6, infants' understanding of support is still very limited: They believe that any amount of contact between the box and the platform can lead to stability.

At about 6.5 months of age, infants overcome this limitation: They begin to appreciate that the *amount of contact* between an object and its support affects the object's stability. Infants now expect the box to fall when a small portion (e.g. the left 15%), but not a large portion (e.g. the left 70%), of its bottom surface rests on the platform (see Fig. 23.6).

Another important development in infants' understanding of support events takes place at about 12.5 months of age. Prior to this stage, infants treat symmetrical and asymmetrical (e.g. L-shaped) objects alike: They expect any object to be stable as long as half or more of its bottom surface lies on a support. At about 12.5 months, however, infants begin to take into account an object's *shape or proportional distribution*[3] when judging its stability. When shown an L-box that has 50% of its bottom surface supported on a platform (see Fig. 23.6), infants attend to the entire box, not just its bottom surface, and they expect the box to be stable only if the proportion of the box that lies on the platform is greater than that off the platform.

How can we explain the developmental sequence just described? As was the case with collision and occlusion events, our model assumes that each successive support variable is identified by infants' learning mechanism through the analysis of pertinent contrastive data. To illustrate, consider the finding that it is not until about 6.5 months of age that infants begin to appreciate how much contact is needed between objects and their supports. Prior to this age, infants must often see their caretakers deposit objects on horizontal surfaces. In most cases, objects will be released with sufficient overlap with their supporting surfaces to remain stable—only in rare accidental cases will infants see an object fall after being deposited on a surface. Because infants cannot learn in the absence of contrastive data, they will not be able to abstract the variable "amount of contact" from seeing only positive instances of the variable (objects remaining stable when in sufficient contact with their supports). The identification of the variable will thus typically be delayed until infants are able to generate the necessary data for themselves. Researchers have pointed out that when infants attain the ability to sit at about 6 months of age, their upper limbs and hands are relieved from the encumbrance of postural maintenance and thus become free to manipulate objects (e.g. Rochat, 1992). For the first time, infants may have the opportunity to deposit objects on horizontal surfaces and to gather contrastive

---

months of life. It seems plausible that infants with a less mature depth perception—be they males or younger females—would be slower at gathering data about objects' spatial arrangements and displacements than infants with a more mature depth perception.

[3] We refer to the object's shape or proportional distribution rather than mass or weight distribution because our data are insufficient to determine which variable guided the infants' responses (see Baillargeon, 1995).

data indicating that objects remain stable when half or more of their bottom surface is supported, and fall otherwise.

According to the model, it is necessary that infants generate contrastive data for the variable "amount of contact" only because in the natural course of events caretakers are unlikely to generate such data for them. Hence, one prediction of the model is that infants might identify this or other variables sooner if they were presented with appropriate contrastive observations. The "teaching" experiments described in the next section were designed to explore this possibility.

Teaching infants new physical variables

As mentioned earlier, our second research strategy to shed light on the nature and operation of infants' learning mechanism has been to teach infants variables they have not yet identified. Our rationale is that by specifying how many observations, and what precise observations, infants require for learning, we can better understand how their learning mechanism processes and stores new information and integrates it with prior information to yield new knowledge.

Jerry DeJong, Julie Sheehan, and I have been attempting to teach infants variables relevant to support events. Two series of experiments are under way, one focusing on the variable "amount of contact", and the other focusing on the variable "shape or proportional distribution". Due to lack of space, only the second series of experiments is described here.

We saw in the previous section that 12.5-month-old infants consider the shape or weight distribution of an asymmetrical box when judging its stability, whereas younger infants do not (e.g. Baillargeon, 1995). Part of the evidence for this conclusion was obtained with a possible and an impossible static display involving an L-shaped box resting on a platform (see Fig. 23.7). In each display, half of the box's bottom surface lay on the platform. In the possible display, the taller, heavier portion of the box rested on the platform; in the impossible display, the shorter, lighter portion of the box was on the platform. Results showed that 12.5-month-old infants looked reliably longer at the impossible than at the possible display; in contrast, younger infants tended to look equally, and equally low, at the two displays. These and other results indicated that infants less than 12.5 months of age expect any box—whether symmetrical or asymmetrical—to be stable as long as 50% or more of its bottom surface is supported.

In our first teaching experiment, 11.5-month-old infants were again shown the possible and impossible L-box test displays. Prior to seeing these displays, however, the infants received two pairs of training trials (see Fig. 23.8). These trials were designed to help the infants realize that a 50%-rule is inadequate for judging the stability of an asymmetrical object. In each pair of trials, the infants saw an asymmetrical box being deposited on a platform; the overlap between the box's bottom surface and the platform was always 50%, as in the L-box displays. In one trial, the heavier portion of the box was placed on the platform and

Possible Display

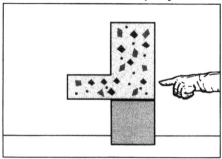

Impossible Display

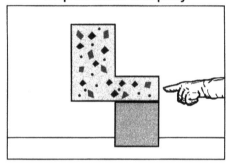

FIG. 23.7   Schematic drawing of the static test displays used in experiments on infants' knowledge of the support variable "shape or proportional distribution of the box". From "A model of physical reasoning in infancy" (p. 332), by R. Baillargeon, 1995, in C. Rovee-Collier and L. Lipsitt (Eds.), *Advances in infancy research* (Vol. 9, pp. 305–371). Norwood, NJ: Ablex. Copyright 1995 by Ablex Publishing Corporation. Reprinted with permission.

the box remained stable when released (box-stays event). In the other trial, the lighter portion of the box was placed on the platform and the box now fell when released (box-falls event). In each training trial, the event was shown repeatedly until the infant either (a) looked away for 2 consecutive seconds or (b) looked 60sec without looking away for 2sec. The infants thus had the opportunity to see the event several times per trial. The two pairs of training trials were identical except that different asymmetrical boxes were used. The box used in the first training pair was shaped like a "B" on its side and was covered with a pink paper decorated with yellow dots; the box used in the second training pair was a right triangle covered with a green paper decorated with white flowers.

After receiving the two pairs of training trials, the infants looked reliably longer at the impossible than at the possible L-box test display. The same posit-ive result was obtained in a second experimental condition in which the B-box was replaced with a right triangle of the same color and pattern as the B-box

Training Events
Box-stays Event

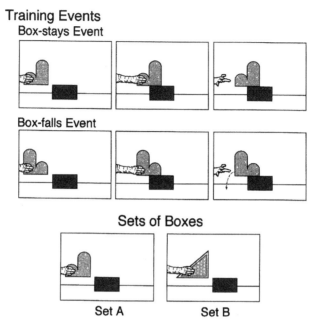

Box-falls Event

Sets of Boxes

Set A   Set B

FIG. 23.8 Schematic drawing of the events shown in the experimental teaching condition (see text). Set A was used in the first pair of training trials, and set B in the second pair.

(pink with yellow dots). Together, these results suggest that the infants were able to use the training observations to acquire new knowledge about support. Instead of focusing only on the L-box's bottom surface, the infants now attended to the entire box: they expected it to remain stable when the proportion of the box resting on the platform was greater but not smaller than that off the platform.

There was, however, an alternative interpretation for our findings. Perhaps the infants preferred the impossible display because they had formed during the training trials a superficial association between the box's orientation and its lack of stability (e.g. "when the taller side of the box is on the left, it falls when released"). To test this interpretation, we conducted two control conditions identical to the first experimental condition just described, with one exception: The box-falls training trials were modified so that the infants could form the same association as before, but could no longer acquire new knowledge about support (see Fig. 23.9). In one condition (box-dropped condition), after depositing the B-box or triangle on the platform in each box-falls event, the hand swiftly lifted and released the box; the infants could thus explain the box's fall in terms of their prior knowledge that an object typically falls when released in midair (see Fig. 23.6). In the other control condition (25% condition), only the right 25% of the box's bottom surface was deposited on the platform in each box-falls event; the box's fall was thus consistent with the infants' prior knowledge that

Control Condition: Box Dropped

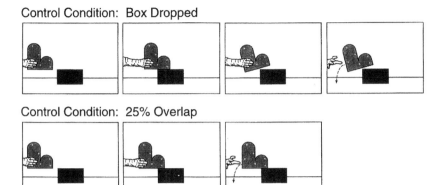

Control Condition: 25% Overlap

FIG. 23.9   Schematic drawing of the box-falls teaching event shown in each of the two control conditions (see text).

an object typically falls when less than half of its bottom surface is supported (see Fig. 23.6). Thus, in both control conditions, the infants could still learn the same superficial association as in the experimental conditions; however, they could acquire no new knowledge about support because they were shown only outcomes consistent with their existing knowledge.

The infants in the two control conditions tended to look equally at the impossible and possible L-box test displays. These results provided evidence that the infants in the experimental conditions preferred the impossible display because they had acquired new support knowledge during the training trials that affected their responses to the L-box displays during the test trials. These findings point to two important conclusions. First, infants can learn from observation alone important facts about support events. Although acting on objects may at times help infants focus more narrowly on the links between actions and their outcomes, the present data make clear that actions are not necessary for learning, at least for infants of this age learning this type of physical knowledge. Second, the present findings are exciting in that they reveal just how efficient is infants' learning mechanism: Our experiments demonstrate that just a few training trials are sufficient to induce a reliable change in infants' interpretation of support displays.

Would infants still show evidence of learning if given even less information during the training trials than was provided in our initial experiments? In one experiment, we asked whether infants would still succeed if the training trials they received involved a single box, as opposed to two distinct boxes. The infants received two pairs of training trials identical to those used in the experimental conditions described earlier, with one exception: Both pairs of trials were conducted with the same box (the B-box or one of the triangle boxes). The results indicated that the infants tended to look equally at the impossible and possible L-box test displays. This negative finding suggests that, at 11.5 months of age, infants must see at least two distinct boxes or exemplars behaving in the same general manner to abstract a variable. Whether the boxes differ in both shape and coloring, or only in coloring, is immaterial (recall that the infants in our experimental conditions succeeded whether they were trained with the B-box and green triangle or with the pink and green triangles). What matters, apparently, is that two perceptually distinct boxes be seen to behave according to the same physical pattern.

In additional experiments, we found that, unlike 11.5-month-old infants, 11-month-old infants showed no evidence of learning when given four training trials involving two distinct boxes. These younger infants did show a reliable preference for the impossible L-box test display, however, after receiving six training trials involving three distinct boxes (a staircase-shaped box was used in a third pair of training trials).

Why do 11-month-olds require three exemplars, and 11.5-month-olds only two exemplars, to demonstrate learning? One possibility is that older infants possess more efficient information processing abilities and hence need less data to identify variables. Another possibility is that older infants bring to the testing situation more relevant prior observations than younger infants. According to this account, infants slowly become aware in the course of their daily object manipulations that a 50%-rule does not fully account for objects' behavior in support situations: Objects sometimes fall even though half or more of their bottom surface is supported. Infants begin storing such observations, thereby building partial knowledge structures that eventually lead to the identification of the variable "shape or proportional distribution". Thus, 11.5-month-old infants require fewer exemplars to show learning because they bring to the test situation more extensive partial structures than younger, 11-month-old infants.

A final experiment suggests that the second of the two possibilities just described is more likely to be correct. This experiment examined whether 11.5-month-old infants would still show evidence of learning if trained with events depicting *reverse* outcomes—outcomes opposite from those that would normally occur in the world (see Fig. 23.10). As in our initial experiment, 11.5-month-old infants were given two pairs of training trials, one with the B-box and one with the green triangle. Each training pair was composed, as before, of a box-stays and a box-falls trial. The only difference was that outcomes were now reversed so that the box fell when released with its heavier portion on the platform (box-falls event), and remained stable when released with its heavier portion off the platform (box-stays event).

We reasoned that if the infants merely abstracted the invariant relation embedded in the training trials, they should expect the L-box to fall when its heavier portion was off the platform and be surprised when this expectation was violated; the infants should therefore look reliably longer at the possible than at the impossible L-box test display. On the other hand, if the infants attempted to integrate the information conveyed in the training trials with their prior knowledge

Training Events
Box-stays Event

Box-falls Event

FIG. 23.10   Schematic drawing of the events shown in the reverse teaching condition (see text).

of support, then they should be puzzled by the training trials and show no preference for either the possible or the impossible L-box display.

The infants tended to look equally at the two test displays, suggesting that they had not abstracted during the training trials a rule which they then readily applied to the test trials. These results underscore the fact that infants' responses to training observations cannot be understood solely in terms of the number and content of these observations. When infants bring to a training situation prior knowledge structures relevant to the situation, the net effect of the training will depend on how readily infants can reconcile what they observe with what they know—or, to borrow well-known Piagetian terms, can assimilate their observations to their existing knowledge structures (e.g. Piaget, 1952, 1954, 1970).

Together, the results of these last experiments indicate that at least two factors affect whether training is likely to produce learning: (a) how many distinct exemplars are involved in the training observations; and (b) whether the observations are consistent or inconsistent with infants' prior knowledge of the event category. Although these findings represent only a first, preliminary step in the investigation of infants' responses to training observations, they already make clear how valuable this approach can be in shedding light on the fundamental processes of infants' learning mechanism.

ADDITIONAL INNATE CONTRIBUTIONS

Our account of infants' approach to the physical world holds that infants are born with a specialized learning mechanism that guides their formation of event categories and their identification for each category of a sequence of increasingly refined variables (e.g. Baillargeon, 1994, 1995; Baillargeon et al., 1995). Is infants' learning mechanism the primary innate structure involved in their acquisition of physical knowledge, or do additional innate structures contribute to this acquisition process? We briefly consider two other types of innate structures that have been proposed by other investigators.

Representational vocabulary

One type of innate structures that has been proposed has to do with the information infants would include from the start in their representations of physical events. Such information might include simple physical categories such as "object" and "surface", with object being defined initially as any collection of adjacent, bounded surfaces (e.g. a cup, a spoon, a toy car), and surface as any broad, unidimensional expanse (e.g. a wall, a floor, a table's surface) (e.g. Craton & Yonas, 1990; Kestenbaum, Termine, & Spelke, 1987; Needham et al., 1997; Spelke, 1982; Spelke, Breinlinger, Jacobson, & Phillips, 1993; Termine, Hrynick, Kestenbaum, Gleitman, & Spelke, 1987). Additional information might involve simple spatiotemporal relations between objects and surfaces. Infants would represent, in at least some situations, whether an object is in front of or behind another object, is adjacent to or spatially distant from another object or surface, moves immediately on being contacted by another object or only after some delay, and so on (e.g. Leslie, 1982; Leslie & Keeble, 1987; Oakes, 1994; Oakes & Cohen, 1995; Slater, Mattock, & Brown, 1990; Slater & Morison, 1985; Yonas & Granrud, 1984; Yonas, Pettersen, & Lockman, 1979).

Leslie (1995) has proposed that, in addition to spatiotemporal information, infants include from the start mechanical information in their representations of physical events. According to Leslie, infants are born with a primitive notion of mechanical force: "The general idea behind the FORCE representation is that (a) when objects move, they possess or bear FORCE, and (b) when objects contact other objects, they transmit, receive, or resist FORCE" (p. 124). In arguing that infants possess an innate notion of force, Leslie does not mean that infants fully understand from the start how forces operate in the world. As infants observe different ways in which objects interact, they would come to understand how forces are implemented in different interactions—how forces are resisted in one context or transmitted in another. A sensitivity to force relations between objects would thus allow infants to "make useful assumptions regarding simple mechanisms . . . and rapidly learn about them" (p. 130).

Leslie's (1995) proposal that infants represent interactions between objects in terms of force reations suggests an intriguing interpretation for our findings on the development of infants' knowledge about collision events, described in an earlier section (e.g. Kotovsky & Baillargeon, 1994, in press a, in prep.). For example, Leslie's view suggests that, as early as 2.5 months of age, infants include in their representation of each collision between the cylinder and the bug a unidirectional force or push exerted by the cylinder onto the bug. Furthermore, the fact that 5.5- to 6.5-month-old infants expect a larger cylinder to displace the bug farther than a smaller cylinder could be taken to mean that infants expect the larger cylinder to exert a greater force onto the bug, thereby producing a greater displacement. Conversely, the finding that younger infants have no expectation that the bug should roll farther after contact with a larger than with a smaller cylinder would suggest that they have not yet learned that larger objects typically exert greater forces than smaller objects, and/or that greater forces typically translate into greater displacements than smaller forces.

Although it is obvious how Leslie's (1995) proposal can be applied to our findings on infants' knowledge of collision events, it is less clear how well the notion of a core force representation can be extended to our findings concerning other event categories, such as occlusion or support events. In the case of occlusion events, forces simply do not come into play; the representation of the relations between objects and their occluders will involve spatiotemporal rather than mechanical information. As occlusion events appear to follow the same developmental pattern as other event categories, one wonders whether Leslie's (1995) assumption that infants' notion of force lies at the core of their "theory of body" may be overstating the case. Similarly, it is not clear at present whether infants represent support events in terms of force relations or more simply in terms of spatiotemporal regularities.

Considerable empirical research needs to be carried out before we can ascertain whether infants include force relations in their representations of physical events, and, if yes, whether all or only some event categories are concerned with such relations. From the perspective of our model of infants' acquisition of physical knowledge, there are at least two reasons why such research is important. First, at a concrete level, the results of these investigations will literally determine how we describe the variables that infants identify as they learn about specific event categories. For example, in the case of collisions between moving and stationary objects, are infants initially learning that the larger the moving objects, the farther the stationary objects are displaced, or are they learning that the larger the moving objects, the greater the force they exert on the stationary objects, leading to longer displacements? What infants learn will depend on what they represent, and what they represent will in turn depend on both their innate vocabulary and their accumulated physical knowledge.

The second reason why considerations of infants' mechanical intuitions can enrich our approach is that they make room within our model for an explicit notion of mechanical causality that was hitherto lacking. Causal reasoning can be defined at a very general level in terms of an ability to detect and reason about regularities in objects' displacements and interactions with other objects. Causal reasoning can also be defined more narrowly in terms of an ability to identify mechanical sequences in which one event brings about another event through the transmission of a physical force. In our work to date, infants' reasoning has been characterized exclusively in terms of the first, more general type of causal reasoning. By admitting that forces may be a part of infants' event representations, however, we can make explicit the place of mechanical causality within our approach. In this new perspective, infants still bring order to their physical world by forming event categories and identifying increasingly refined variables. The main difference is that event categories are now acknowledged to fall into two broad types: those that are defined purely in spatiotemporal terms (e.g. occlusion events), and those that depend on both mechanical and spatiotemporal relations (e.g. collision events). As Leslie (1995) suggested, these rudimentary mechanical intuitions may pave the way for the more complex mechanistic reasoning that is observed in children and adults.

Physical principles

A second type of innate structures that has been posited has to do with physical principles that would from the start constrain objects' displacements and interactions within infants' event representations. Spelke (1994; Spelke et al., 1995b), in particular, has argued that infants are born with a number of core physical principles that guide their interpretation of physical events. One such principle is the continuity principle, which states that objects exist and move continuously. Another, related principle is the solidity principle, which states that objects move on continuous, unobstructed paths, so that two distinct objects can never occupy the same space at the same time (Spelke et al., 1995b).

The claim that infants possess a continuity or a solidity principle is sometimes taken to mean that infants should readily detect *any* violation of the principles (e.g. Spelke, 1991; Spelke et al., 1992). Thus, an infant should be surprised if all or only part of an object fails to become visible when passing behind an occluder with an opening. Similarly, an infant should be surprised if an object moves through all or only part of an object placed behind it.

Existing evidence does not support these predictions. As we saw when discussing the development of infants' knowledge about occlusion events, infants aged 2.5 to 3 months detect some but by no means all continuity violations (e.g. Aguiar & Baillargeon, submitted b; Baillargeon & DeVos, 1991). The range of violations infants detect steadily grows over the first few months of life, as their understanding of occlusion develops. The same is true for solidity violations. For example, when watching a screen rotate through a box placed behind it, 4.5-month-old infants show surprise when the screen stops after rotating through 100% but not 80% of the box (Baillargeon, 1991). Infants understand *that* the screen should stop when it encounters the box, but they are unable to use the box's height to predict *when* the screen should stop; therefore, the only violation they can detect is one in which the screen fails to stop altogether.

In light of this evidence, at least two options are possible. The first is to conclude that infants do not possess core physical principles that guide their interpretation of events. The second option is to assume that infants do possess core principles, but that these principles are only rudimentary notions that facilitate but still leave open considerable room for learning. In this view, infants' notions of continuity and solidity would thus be similar to the primitive notion of force discussed by Leslie (1994, 1995). Infants would progressively learn, in the course of observing and interacting with objects, how continuity and solidity operate in different physical contexts. To illustrate, consider the case of occlusion events. Because of their continuity principle, infants would realize that an object continues to exist and follows its trajectory when passing behind a screen —however, this is all that their continuity principle would tell them. Infants would need to learn what variables can be used to predict whether the object will remain hidden or become temporarily visible when behind the screen, how soon the object will reappear at the far edge of the screen, and so on.

How can we decide which of these two options—no innate principles, or weak innate principles—is correct? There is no firm evidence available today that enables us to select one option rather than the other. Our own intuition is that, in the end, the second option (or some version of this option) will be proved correct. This intuition is derived from a consideration of the type of data infants appear to require to identify physical variables. Earlier we suggested that infants cannot acquire a new variable unless they have *contrastive* data pertinent to the variable: positive data showing that an outcome occurs when a condition is met and negative data showing that an outcome does not occur when the condition is not met. We speculated, for example, that infants less than 5.5 to 6.5 months of age do not learn the variable "amount of contact" in support events because they typically see only positive outcomes—situations in which objects are placed on surfaces with sufficient contact to be adequately supported. At about 5.5 to 6.5 months, however, infants begin to generate their own negative data—they release objects on the edges of surfaces, causing them to fall— and then quickly identify "amount of contact" as an important support variable.

These speculations on infants' need for contrastive inputs suggest a new approach to the issue of innate physical principles. Essentially, we must ask ourselves: What contrastive data could infants use to learn that objects exist continuously in time? Or move continuously in space? Or move only through unoccupied space? We know that infants aged 2.5 months already detect at least some violations of these principles (e.g. Aguiar & Baillargeon, submitted b; Kotovsky & Baillargeon, in prep.; Spelke et al., 1992). If we cannot identify contrastive data that infants could use in the first two months of life to acquire the principles, then we have only two recourses: We must conclude that the principles are, in some fashion, available at birth; or we must assume that infants are born with two distinct learning mechanisms, one that requires contrastive evidence and one that does not.

Before these issues can be resolved, considerable research will need to be carried out on two fronts. One will be to specify more fully the nature and operation of infants' learning mechanism, and to test directly the hypothesis that learning typically occurs only in the presence of contrastive evidence. The other front will be to examine the implications of these findings for infants' early competences. If infants' learning mechanism is shown to learn only under conditions "x", and infants at a very early age reveal physical knowledge for which learnability conditions "x" could not have been met, we may be compelled to agree with Spelke et al. (1995b) that a number of innate physical principles direct from birth infants' approach to the physical world.

CONCLUSION

The research reviewed in this chapter makes clear that a full account of how infants attain their physical knowledge is likely to include many distinct parts: a description of the representational vocabulary infants draw on to represent objects' displacements and interactions, and of how this vocabulary develops over time; a description of the physical principles that guide from birth infants' interpretation of objects' displacements and interactions; a description of the learning mechanism that makes possible infants' formation of event categories and identification of initial concepts and variables; and finally, a discussion of the role that infants' accumulated physical knowledge plays in their representation and interpretation of physical events, and hence in infants' acquisition of new knowledge.

ACKNOWLEDGEMENTS

I would like to thank Andrea Aguiar, Jerry DeJong, Sue Hespos, Lisa Kaufman, Marsha Keeler, Laura Kotovsky, Amy Needham, and Elissa Newport for helpful comments and discussions.

REFERENCES

Aguiar, A., & Baillargeon, R. (submitted a). *Can young infants generate explanations for impossible occlusion events?*

Aguiar, A., & Baillargeon, R. (submitted b). *2.5-month-old infants' reasoning about occlusion events.*

Arterberry, M. E. (1993). Development of spatiotemporal integration in infancy. *Infant Behavior and Development, 16*, 343–363.

Aslin, R. N. (1981). Development of smooth pursuit in human infants. In D. F. Fisher, R. A. Monty, & J. W. Senders (Eds.), *Eye movements: Cognition and visual perception* (pp. 31–51). Hillsdale, NJ: Lawrence Erlbaum Associates Inc.

Baillargeon, R. (1986). Representing the existence and the location of hidden objects: Object permanence in 6- and 8-month-old infants. *Cognition, 23*, 21–41.

Baillargeon, R. (1991). Reasoning about the height and location of a hidden object in 4.5- and 6.5-month-old infants. *Cognition, 38*, 13–42.

Baillargeon, R. (1994). How do infants learn about the physical world? *Current Directions in Psychological Science, 3*, 133–140.

Baillargeon, R. (1995). A model of physical reasoning in infancy. In C. Rovee-Collier & L. P. Lipsitt (Eds.), *Advances in infancy research* (Vol. 9, pp. 305–371). Norwood, NJ: Ablex.

Baillargeon, R., & DeVos, J. (1991). Object permanence in 3.5- and 4.5-month-old infants: Further evidence. *Child Development, 62*, 1227–1246.

Baillargeon, R., & Graber, M. (1987). Where's the rabbit? 5.5-month-old infants' representation of the height of a hidden object. *Cognitive Development, 2*, 375–392.

Baillargeon, R., Kotovsky, L., & Needham, A. (1995). The acquisition of physical knowledge in infancy. In D. Sperber, D. Premack, & A. J. Premack (Eds.), *Causal cognition: A multidisciplinary debate* (pp. 79–116). Oxford: Clarendon Press.

Baillargeon, R., Needham, A., & DeVos, J. (1992). The development of young infants' intuitions about support. *Early Development and Parenting, 1*, 69–78.

Baillargeon, R., Spelke, E. S., & Wasserman, S. (1985). Object permanence in 5–month-old infants. *Cognition, 20*, 191–208.

Banks, M. S. (1983). Infant visual perception. In P. H. Mussen (Series Ed.) & M. M. Haith & J. J. Campos (Vol. Eds.), *Handbook of child psychology: Vol. 2. Infancy and developmental psychobiology* (4th ed., pp. 435–571). New York: Wiley.

Bauer, J., Shimojo, S., Gwiazda, J., & Held, R. (1986). Sex differences in the development of binocularity in human infants. *Investigative Ophtalmology and Visual Science, 27*, (Suppl.), 265.

Craton, L., & Yonas, A. (1990, April). *Infants' figure-ground segregation from kinetic information.* Paper presented at the biennial meeting of the International Conference on Infant Studies, Montreal, Canada.

Fagan, J. F. (1970). Memory in the infant. *Journal of Experimental Child Psychology, 9*, 217–226.

Fagan, J. F. (1971). Infants' recognition memory for a series of visual stimuli. *Journal of Experimental Child Psychology, 11*, 244–250.

Fagan, J. F. (1972). Infants' recognition memory for faces. *Journal of Experimental Child Psychology, 14*, 453–476.

Fagan, J. F. (1973). Infants' delayed recognition memory and forgetting. *Journal of Experimental Child Psychology, 16*, 424–450.

Fantz, R. L. (1964). Visual experience in infants: Decreased attention to familiar patterns relative to novel ones. *Science, 146*, 668–670.

Friedman, S. (1972). Newborn visual attention to repeated exposure of redundant vs. "novel" targets. *Perception & Psychophysics, 12*, 291–294.

Gwiazda, J., Bauer, J., & Held, R. (1989a). Binocular function in human infants: Correlation of stereoptic and fusion-rivalry discriminations. *Journal of Pediatric Ophthalmology and Strabismus, 43*, 109–120.

Gwiazda, J., Bauer, J., & Held, R. (1989b). From visual acuity to hyperacuity: A 10-year update. *Canadian Journal of Psychology, 43*, 109–120.

Karmiloff-Smith, A. (1992). *Beyond modularity: A developmental perspective on cognitive science.* Cambridge, MA: MIT Press.

Kaufman, L. (1997, April). *Infants distinguish between inert and self-moving inanimate objects.* Paper presented at the biennial meeting of the Society for Research in Child Development, Washington, DC.

Kaufman, L., & Kotovsky, L. (1997, April). *9.5-month-old infants' reasoning about collision events: Should all objects be displaced when hit?* Paper presented at the biennial meeting of the Society for Research in Child Development, Washington, DC.

Kellman, P. J., & Spelke, E. S. (1983). Perception of partly occluded objects in infancy. *Cognitive Psychology, 15*, 483–524.

Kestenbaum, R., Termine, N., & Spelke, E. S. (1987). Perception of objects and object boundaries by three-month-old infants. *British Journal of Developmental Psychology, 5*, 367–383.

Kotovsky, L., & Baillargeon, R. (1994). Calibration-based reasoning about collision events in 11-month-old infants. *Cognition, 51*, 107–129.

Kotovsky, L., & Baillargeon, R. (in press a). *The development of calibration-based reasoning about collision events in young infants.*

Kotovsky, L., & Baillargeon, R. (in press b). *Reasoning about collisions involving inert objects in 7.5-month-old infants.*

Kotovsky, L., & Baillargeon, R. (in prep.). *Reasoning about collision events in 2.5-month-old infants.*

Leslie, A. M. (1982). The perception of causality in infants. *Perception, 11,* 173–186.

Leslie, A. M. (1984a). Infant perception of a manual pick-up event. *British Journal of Developmental Psychology, 2,* 19–32.

Leslie A. M. (1984b). Spatiotemporal continuity and the perception of causality in infants. *Perception, 13,* 287–305.

Leslie, A. M. (1994). ToMM, ToBy, and agency: Core architecture and domain specificity. In L. Hirschfeld & S. Gelman (Eds.), *Mapping the mind: Domain specificity in cognition and culture* (pp. 119–148). New York: Cambridge University Press.

Leslie, A. M. (1995). A theory of agency. In D. Sperber, D. Premack, & A. J. Premack (Eds.), *Causal cognition: A multidisciplinary debate* (pp. 121–141). Oxford: Clarendon Press.

Leslie, A. M., & Keeble, S. (1987). Do six-month-old infants perceive causality? *Cognition, 25,* 265–288.

Mandler, J. M. (in press). Representation. In W. Damon (Series Ed.) & D. Kuhn & R. Siegler (Vol. Eds.), *Handbook of child psychology: Vol 2. Cognition, perception, and language* (5th ed.). New York: Wiley.

Needham, A., & Baillargeon, R. (1993). Intuitions about support in 4.5-month-old infants. *Cognition, 47,* 121–148.

Needham, A., & Baillargeon, R. (1997). Object segregation in 8-month-old infants. *Cognition, 62,* 121–149.

Needham, A., Baillargeon, R., & Kaufman, L. (1997). Object segregation in infancy. In C. Rovee-Collier & L. P. Lipsitt (Eds.), *Advances in infancy research* (Vol. 11, pp. 1–44). Greenwich, CT: Ablex.

Oakes, L. M. (1994). The development of infants' use of continuity cues in their perception of causality. *Developmental Psychology, 30,* 869–879.

Oakes, L. M., & Cohen, L. B. (1995). Infant causal perception. In C. Rovee-Collier & L. P. Lipsitt (Eds.), *Advances in infancy research* (Vol. 9, pp. 1–54). Norwood, NJ: Ablex.

Piaget, J. (1952). *The origins of intelligence in children* (M. Cook, Trans.). New York: International Universities Press. (Original work published 1936.)

Piaget, J. (1954). *The construction of reality in the child* (M. Cook, Trans.). New York: Basic Books. (Original work published 1937.)

Piaget, J. (1970). Piaget's theory. In P. H. Mussen (Ed.), *Carmichael's manual of child psychology* (Vol. 1, pp. 103–128). New York: Wiley.

Rochat, P. (1992). Self-sitting and reaching in 5- to 8-month-old infants: The impact of posture and its development on early eye-hand coordination. *Journal of Motor Behavior, 24,* 210–220.

Slater, A. M., Mattock, A., & Brown, E. (1990). Size constancy at birth: Newborn infants' responses to retinal and real size. *Journal of Experimental Child Psychology, 49,* 314–322.

Slater, A. M., & Morison, V. (1985). Shape constancy and slant perception at birth. *Perception, 14,* 337–344.

Spelke, E. S. (1982). Perceptual knowledge of objects in infancy. In J. Mehler, E. Walker, & M. Garrett (Eds.), *Perspectives on mental representation* (pp. 409–430). Hillsdale, NJ: Lawrence Erlbaum Associates Inc.

Spelke, E. S. (1991). Physical knowledge in infancy: Reflections on Piaget's theory. In S. Carey & R. Gelman (Eds.), *The epigenesis of mind: Essays on biology and cognition* (pp. 133–169). Hillsdale, NJ: Lawrence Erlbaum Associates Inc.

Spelke, E. S. (1994). Initial knowledge: Six suggestions. *Cognition, 50,* 431–445.

Spelke, E. S., Breinlinger, K., & Jacobson, K., & Phillips, A. (1993). Gestalt relations and object perception: A developmental study. *Perception, 22,* 1483–1501.

Spelke, E. S., Breinlinger, K., Macomber, J., & Jacobson, K. (1992). Origins of knowledge. *Psychological Review, 99,* 605–632.

Spelke, E. S., Kestenbaum, R., Simons, D. J., & Wein, D. (1995a). Spatiotemporal continuity, smoothness of motion and object identity in infancy. *British Journal of Developmental Psychology, 13,* 1–30.

Spelke, E. S., Phillips, A., & Woodward, A. L. (1995b). Infants' knowledge of object motion and human action. In D. Sperber, D. Premack, & A. J. Premack (Eds.), *Causal cognition: A multidisciplinary debate* (pp. 44–78). Oxford: Clarendon Press.

Termine, N., Hrynick, R., Kestenbaum, R., Gleitman, H., & Spelke, E. S. (1987). Perceptual completion of surfaces in infancy. *Journal of Experimental Psychology: Human Perception and Performance, 13,* 524–532.

Thelen, E., & Smith, L. B. (1994). *A dynamic systems approach to the development of cognition and action.* Cambridge, MA: MIT Press.

Wilcox, T., Nadel, L., & Rosser, R. (1996). Location memory in healthy preterm and fullterm infants. *Infant Behavior and Development, 19,* 309–323.

Woodward, A. L., Phillips, A., & Spelke, E. S. (1993). Infants' expectations about the motion of animate versus inanimate objects. *Proceedings of the Fifteenth Annual Meeting of the Cognitive Science Society, Boulder, CO* (pp. 1087–1091). Hillsdale, NJ: Lawrence Erlbaum Associates Inc.

Yonas, A., & Granrud, C. (1984). The development of sensitivity to kinetic, binocular and pictorial depth information in human infants. In D. Ingle, D. Lee, & M. Jeannerod (Eds.), *Brain mechanisms and spatial vision* (pp. 113–145). Dordrecht: Martinus Nijhoff.

Yonas, A., Pettersen. L., & Lockman, J. (1979). Young infants' sensitivity to optical information for collision. *Canadian Journal of Psychology, 33,* 1285–1290.

CHAPTER TWENTY-FOUR

Développement cognitif et différences individuelles

Anik de Ribaupierre
Université de Genève, Carouge, Suisse

L'objectif de ce chapitre est de démontrer qu'il est important de tenir compte de la variabilité inter- et intra-individuelle dans l'étude du développement cognitif et que la diversité observée est source de renseignements pour les lois générales. Après une brève revue de la façon dont on a tenu compte des différences individuelles en psychologie du développement, cet article se centre sur l'importance de la variabilité intra-individuelle, et en particulier sur l'étude des décalages intra-individuels. Trois illustrations empiriques sont brièvement présentées: l'approche de Longeot (1969, 1978), les recherches de Lautrey, de Ribaupierre et Rieben, et, avec un peu plus de détails, une étude longitudinale conduite à Genève plus récemment à l'aide de quatre épreuves (Pliage de Lignes, deux variantes de l'épreuve de la Balance, et les Iles). La relation entre spécificité et généralité du développement est ensuite discutée, à la lumière du modèle des processus vicariants suggéré par Reuchlin.

The objective of this chapter is to demonstrate that the study of cognitive development must take into account inter- and intra-individual differences, and that the diversity of behavior is informative for general, developmental laws. The ways in which individual differences have been articulated with developmental aspects are first briefly reviewed. The focus is then placed on the issue of intra-individual variability, in particular that of horizontal, intra-individual decalages. Three empirical illustrations are briefly summarized: Longeot's approach (Longeot, 1969, 1978), the studies led by Lautrey, de Ribaupierre, and Rieben, and, somewhat more detailed, a longitudinal study recently conducted by our group in Geneva, using four tasks (Line Folding, two variants of the Balance task, and the Islands task). The relation between the generality and the specificity of development is finally discussed, based on a model of vicarious or equifunctional processes suggested by Reuchlin.

L'objectif de cet article est de plaider pour une meilleure intégration des différences individuelles dans l'étude du développement cognitif. Ce genre de plaidoyer est, bien entendu, très ancien. Cronbach (1957) attirait déjà l'attention sur le fait qu'il y avait deux psychologies bien distinctes, la psychologie expérimentale et la psychologie différentielle ou corrélationnelle et proposait que la communication soit plus soutenue entre ces deux courants. Reuchlin proposait, en 1964 déjà, de mieux articuler psychologie corrélationnelle et psychologie développementale ou génétique (Reuchlin, 1964). Depuis lors, il y a eu plusieurs tentatives de rapprochement; il n'en reste pas moins que l'on s'est le plus souvent contenté de signaler l'ampleur des différences individuelles, sans pour autant qu'elles fassent réellement partie des théories générales du développement (voir aussi Cohen, 1994). Or, non seulement il faut se demander si, et jusqu'à quel point, une théorie générale du développement peut s'accommoder de la diversité individuelle, mais il faut aussi rechercher en quoi cette diversité peut nous renseigner sur les lois générales. En effet, si la diversité est une propriété du développement de tous les individus, alors elle doit représenter une caractéristique importante du développement, et donc une loi générale en elle-même (pour un argument semblable, voir Howe, 1994; Reuchlin & Bacher, 1989).

Après une brève revue de la façon dont on a tenu compte des différences individuelles en psychologie du développement, je me centrerai sur le problème des différences interindividuelles dans la variabilité intra-individuelle; je donnerai un certain nombre d'exemples empiriques, puis j'essaierai de conclure sur l'articulation possible entre processus généraux et différences individuelles.

DÉVELOPPEMENT ET DIFFÉRENCES INDIVIDUELLES

La psychologie du développement a tenu compte des différences individuelles de différentes façons. Une première approche, malheureusement la plus fréquente, a consisté à les *négliger* ou à les *neutraliser*. Les développementalistes n'ont jamais nié l'existence de différences individuelles, mais, à l'instar des psychologues expérimentalistes, les ont considérées comme du bruit, ou, au mieux, comme étant du ressort de la psychologie appliquée. On a étudié le «sujet moyen» ou le «sujet épistémique», c'est-à-dire un sujet défini théoriquement sur la base soit de moyennes statistiques, soit d'une reconstruction de différents sujets étudiés dans différents domaines. Dans ce cadre, les différences individuelles sont considérées comme de simples variations quantitatives autour d'une même norme. Au mieux, elles reviennent à de simples différences de vitesse le long d'un même chemin développemental. C'est dans ce sens que l'on peut considérer la plupart des modèles développementaux comme unitaires ou unidimensionnels: une seule dimension permet de différencier les individus les uns des autres, et ils sont tous censés se développer le long de cette même dimension. Si l'on a considéré le modèle piagétien du développement comme le prototype de ce type d'approche, c'est que l'on a eu tendance à négliger le fait que l'objectif premier de Piaget n'était pas la compréhension du développement cognitif chez l'enfant en soi, mais celui des connaissances (Chapman, 1988; Lourenço & Machado, 1996). Il n'en est pas moins vrai que cette perspective unidimensionnelle a longtemps été dominante, en psychologie du développement comme en psychologie expérimentale, où l'on a cherché à réduire la variance d'erreur. Ce n'est que très récemment que la tendance s'est renversée, avec un nombre croissant de chercheurs qui mettent l'accent sur la variabilité interindividuelle, mais également sur la variabilité intra-individuelle (voir par exemple Siegler, 1995; Siegler & Jenkins, 1989).

Une deuxième perspective a consisté à se centrer sur les différences interindividuelles, ou plus exactement *intergroupes*. On s'est, dans ce contexte, intéressé à l'influence qu'une variable indépendante pouvait avoir sur la variable développementale d'intérêt. On a généralement pris en considération deux types de variables indépendantes: soit des variables externes, telles que la classe sociale, ou le genre des individus, soit d'autres variables de nature psychologique. Au lieu de comparer des groupes constitués a priori sur la base de telle ou telle variable, on a pu chercher à connaître la corrélation entre cette variable et la tâche développementale. Dans le cas de l'approche intergroupes comme dans celui de l'étude corrélationnelle, on s'est essentiellement intéressé à la quantité de variance dont la variable considérée comme indépendante rend compte. A ce propos, une recherche de littérature très sommaire avec les mots clés «Développement cognitif et différences individuelles» montre que la plupart des très nombreux articles qui répondent à ces mots-clé s'intéressent uniquement à la façon dont on peut rendre compte de la variance, et non pas à la forme de ces différences. Les différences individuelles sont donc encore une fois considérées comme de simples variations quantitatives et le modèle développemental reste unidimensionnel. Sur le plan théorique, une telle approche peut bien sûr nous renseigner sur les influences susceptibles de s'exercer sur les processus généraux, mais elle ne nous renseigne pas vraiment sur la nature de ces processus.

Dans une troisième perspective, beaucoup plus rarement adoptée, on a cherché à mieux contrôler les différences individuelles, afin de faire ressortir plus clairement les phénomènes développementaux. C'est dire alors que les différences individuelles sont prises au sérieux, puisqu'il faut les contrôler. Cette approche est, en quelque sorte, la réciproque de la précédente (dans laquelle on s'intéressait à l'influence d'une variable dite modératrice). Ici, la variable modératrice est contrôlée, parce qu'on considère qu'elle peut interférer avec le phénomène développemental qu'on veut mettre en évidence. C'était par exemple l'objectif de Pascual-Leone lorsqu'il a étudié le développement de la puissance M chez un certain type de sujets spécifiquement (Pascual-Leone, 1970, 1987; de Ribaupierre & Pascual-Leone, 1984). Considérant que le développement est généralement codéterminé par un certain nombre de facteurs, mais voulant mettre en évidence le développement d'un seul de ces facteurs, la puissance M, Pascual-Leone a restreint certaines de ses études à des sujets de QI moyen supérieur, et indépendants à l'égard du champ. Une telle sélection restreint bien évidemment la généralisabilité des résultats, mais a l'avantage de permettre d'isoler le facteur développemental. Pour démontrer, ensuite, que les variables modératrices jouent bien un rôle important, il suffit de trouver que le phénomène développemental se comporte différemment lorsque ces variables ne sont plus contrôlées. Ce genre d'approche est rarement utilisé, dans la mesure où elle demande des analyses théoriques préalables approfondies. La méthode de «testing-the-limits» utilisée par Baltes et collaborateurs (Baltes & Kliegl, 1992; Kliegl & Baltes, 1987; Kliegl, Smith, & Baltes, 1986) est un autre exemple de contrôle des différences individuelles permettant de mieux faire ressortir le phénomène développemental. En fournissant aux sujets une pratique extensive de la tâche, et/ou en enseignant des stratégies, on minimise les différences individuelles en termes de base de connaissances (ou répertoire des schèmes) et de stratégies utilisées. Les différences d'âge qui subsistent sont alors plus susceptibles de refléter de vraies différences développementales. A noter que Baltes et collaborateurs ont jusqu'à très récemment, utilisé ce type de méthode avec des personnes âgées uniquement.

La quatrième approche est celle sur laquelle nous allons nous centrer dorénavant. Il s'agit d'une centration sur *l'ampleur et la forme des différences intra- et interindividuelles*. La méthode la plus fréquente est de recourir à des corrélations. C'est d'ailleurs souvent ce qu'on entend par approche différentialiste. Mais, généralement, on n'a pas tiré toutes les conséquences développementales possibles de cette approche. On s'est le plus souvent borné à conclure, en face de corrélations faibles, à l'indépendance ou la spécificité des domaines (tâches) en question et au fait que des processus différents sont en jeu. On a rarement fait le lien entre facteurs au sens psychométrique du terme, et facteurs développementaux, alors que ce passage peut paraître relativement évident à un certain nombre de différentialistes, et devrait au moins donner lieu à des études empiriques (Lautrey, de Ribaupierre, & Rieben, 1990). C'est un signe de plus de la scission qui a existé, et existe encore dans une certaine mesure, entre différentes disciplines de la psychologie. Si, dans une batterie d'épreuves, on trouve un facteur général important, il pourra probablement se traduire en un facteur général développemental, les trajectoires développementales des différents enfants étant relativement semblables. Par contre, lorsqu'on trouve des facteurs de groupe (cas le plus fréquent), il est alors vraisemblable que l'on trouve également des trajectoires développementales différentes. Ce point sera repris plus bas.

Lorsqu'on trouve une variabilité intra-individuelle importante, il est alors intéressant d'examiner les différences interindividuelles quant aux patterns intra-individuels (Buss, 1979). Des épreuves cognitives du type piagétien se prêtent particulièrement bien à une telle étude: les variables étant catégorisables, il est relativement facile de définir des patterns et, sur cette base, des types d'individus. La définition de patterns est bien sûr plus difficile avec des épreuves qui donnent lieu à des scores continus, telles que les épreuves psychométriques; mais on pourrait imaginer, dans ce cas, de subdiviser l'échantillon sur la base de terciles ou quartiles pour chacune des tâches, par exemple, puis de comparer les patterns au travers des tâches.

L'accent va être dorénavant placé, dans la suite de cet article, sur cette quatrième approche qui s'est intéressée à mettre en évidence des différences interindividuelles dans la variabilité intra-individuelle, c'est-à-dire dans les types de *décalages* observés, et à les transcrire sur un plan développemental. Même si, dans ce cas, des études longitudinales sont importantes, on peut déjà tirer des conclusions sur la base d'une étude transversale, en recourant à des méthodes d'analyse hiérarchique permettant de tester les séquences, ou à l'étude des décalages.

Décalages intra-individuels

L'existence de décalages est un phénomène très connu de la plupart des chercheurs qui ont recouru à des épreuves piagétiennes, ou plus généralement à des épreuves cognitives. On s'est par contre limité à en tirer des conclusions quant à la spécificité des situations. Piaget (par exemple Piaget & Inhelder, 1941) avait défini deux types de décalages: des *décalages verticaux*, qui correspondent à la reconstruction d'une même notion sur un plan différent (par exemple de l'invariance de l'objet à la conservation de la quantité), reconstruction qui peut souvent prendre plusieurs années, et des *décalages horizontaux*, qui résultent de l'application d'une structure de même complexité à des contenus différents (par exemple le décalage bien connu entre conservation de la quantité, du poids, et du volume). Longeot (1978) a affiné la notion de décalage horizontal, en distinguant des *décalages collectifs*, c'est-à-dire un décalage de même sens pour tous les sujets (par exemple, de nouveau, le décalage entre substance, poids et volume) et des *décalages dits individuels*, qui sont de sens différent pour différents sujets.

La Figure 24.1 présente un exemple fictif de différents types de relations entre épreuves, l'axe horizontal correspondant au niveau de construction de la notion. Les deux premiers sont classiques: synchronisme (cas a dans la figure), et décalage collectif homogène (cas b), montrant que, pour deux sujets A et B, la conservation de la substance, par exemple, est en avance sur la conservation du poids, cette avance étant de même amplitude pour les deux sujets. Dans ces deux cas, synchronisme et décalage collectif homogène, la corrélation entre les deux épreuves serait élevée. Dans le cas d'un décalage collectif hétérogène (cas c), le décalage est encore de même sens pour les deux sujets A et B. Toutefois, il est plus grand pour A que pour B, ce qui va se traduire par une permutation de l'ordre des sujets dans la conservation du poids par rapport à celle de la substance, et donc par une corrélation faible. Notons que ces deux cas de décalage collectif sont compatibles avec un modèle unidimensionnel du développement, et correspondent simplement à des différences de vitesse pour les différentes épreuves et les différents sujets. Par contre, dans le cas d'un décalage individuel (cas d), le sujet A est en avance dans sa construction de la notion de sériation relativement à celle d'inclusion, alors que le sujet B présente le pattern inverse.

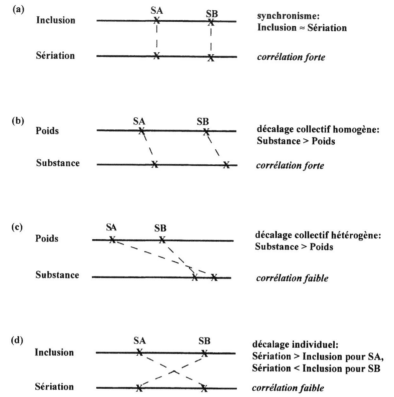

FIG. 24.1 Différents types de décalages horizontaux et différences individuelles. SA et SB correspondent à deux individus différents.

Le décalage est donc de sens différent pour les deux sujets et s'avère incompatible avec un modèle unidimensionnel. Si l'on traduit un tel cas de décalage individuel sur un plan développemental, les chemins des deux sujets seraient différents: le sujet A passerait par un chemin sériation- inclusion, alors que le sujet B passerait par le chemin inclusion- sériation. On peut aussi noter en passant qu'une étude corrélationnelle n'est pas suffisante, puisqu'elle ne permet pas de distinguer entre ces différents cas. Il faut donc également passer par une analyse du sens du décalage, par exemple à l'aide d'analyses de prédiction (voir plus bas).

ILLUSTRATIONS EMPIRIQUES

Les boucles développementales de Longeot

Longeot (1969, 1978) est le premier auteur qui s'est appuyé sur l'approche corrélationnelle aussi bien que sur des méthodes d'analyse hiérarchiques pour étudier si tous les sujets se conformaient aux séquences développementales qui peuvent être dérivées du modèle piagétien. Dans une première étude (Longeot, 1969), il a suggéré, sur la base des résultats d'analyses factorielles, l'existence de chemins d'accès différents au stade des opérations formelles: un certain nombre d'enfants entreraient dans ce stade (quand ils y entrent—voir de Ribaupierre, 1975) par une voie correspondant à l'acquisition de la proportionnalité (structure INRC—Inhelder & Piaget, 1955), alors que d'autres y entreraient par une voie combinatoire. Dans une deuxième série d'études, Longeot (1978) a appliqué ce même raisonnement à des épreuves logico-mathématiques et des épreuves infra-logiques, et s'est servi d'analyses hiérarchiques à la Guttman, ou plus exactement d'une modification de ce type d'analyse, permettant de tester des séquences non linéaires (voir aussi Fischer & Lamborn, 1989, pour l'utilisation d'analyses hiérarchiques dans ce cas).

La logique de ce type d'analyse est assez simple. La Figure 24.2 représente le cas (fictif) de 4 items, dont les deux premiers (A et B) sont censés être réussis au début des opérations concrètes et les deux derniers (C et D) dans la période supérieure des opérations concrètes, cette plus grande difficulté étant attestée par le pourcentage de réussites à chacun des items; ces items sont administrés avec deux autres items, l'item X, de niveau préopératoire et l'item Y de niveau opératoire formel. Les patterns 0, 1, 3, 5 et 6 sont parfaitement conformes à la séquence postulée; les patterns 1 et 4 n'en sont que de légères variations, montrant que les items B et D sont un peu plus difficiles que, respectivement, les items A et C. Par contre, les patterns 3A et 3B sont problématiques pour un modèle unidimensionnel (à condition, bien entendu, qu'ils correspondent à un nombre appréciable de sujets), puisque, dans les deux cas, les sujets réussissent un item supposé difficile alors qu'ils échouent encore un item supposé facile. Dans tous les cas, toutefois, les quatre items s'ordonnent relativement aux items X et Y. Cela peut se traduire sous forme de trois voies développementales différentes, comme représenté dans la dernière partie de la figure. Il s'agit bien sûr d'un cas simple avec peu d'items, les chemins développementaux pouvant se multiplier dès que le nombre d'items augmente.

Sur la base de telles analyses, Longeot a suggéré de modifier le modèle piagétien en introduisant la notion de boucles développementales. En particulier, il a suggéré que l'une des voies corresponde à une progression le long d'une demi-échelle logico-mathématique et l'autre le long d'une demi-échelle infra-logique ou spatiale. Cela l'a donc conduit à faire l'hypothèse de deux voies développementales distinctes, au moins. Une question non résolue est celle de la convergence à la fin d'un stade: pour Longeot, les voies développementales divergentes seraient caractéristiques de la phase de préparation d'un stade, mais devraient converger avant la phase de préparation du stade suivant. La réponse à cette question nécessiterait d'une part de voir des tranches d'âge plus étendues, et d'autre part de conduire une étude longitudinale.

Fischer, Knight et Van Parys (1993) ont récemment utilisé une approche très semblable, en s'intéressant au développement de la lecture. Ils ont, comme

Pattern	Items						N
	X	A	B	C	D	Y	
0	-	-	-	-	-	-	10
1	+	-	-	-	-	-	15
2	+	+	-	-	-	-	5
3	+	+	+	-	-	-	65
3A	+	+	-	+	-	-	5
3B	+	-	-	+	+	-	30
4	+	+	+	+	-	-	5
5	+	+	+	+	+	-	25
6	+	+	+	+	+	+	5
%	97	70	61	45	36	3	

Séquence développementale prédite:

Séquences développementales"observées":

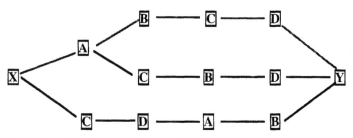

FIG. 24.2   Analyse hiérarchique et séquences développementales

Longeot, pris un certain nombre d'épreuves ou d'items de différente difficulté
(6 tâches qui, dans le cas présent, ont été évaluées comme réussies ou échouées,
pour 16 mots), et montré qu'il existait au moins deux voies développementales
différentes.

Variabilité inter- et intra-individuelle chez l'enfant de 6 à 12 ans

Dans un programme de recherche commun avec Lautrey et Rieben, nous sommes parvenus à des conclusions similaires à celles de Longeot. Dans cette recherche, un ensemble de huit tâches, comprenant une cinquantaine d'items, et représentatives de différents domaines cognitifs (conservations, construction de volumes, logique, espace, image mentale), ont été administrées à des enfants de 6 à 12 ans. La variabilité intra-individuelle a été étudiée de plusieurs façons, tant sur les réussites/échecs (au moyen d'analyses hiérarchiques sur chacune des épreuves et sur quelques épreuves regroupées, et d'analyses de correspondances), que sur les décalages entre niveaux de conduite aux différentes épreuves.

Les résultats de cette recherche ne vont pas être repris en détail, dans la mesure où ils ont déjà donné lieu à un certain nombre de publications (par exemple Lautrey, de Ribaupierre, & Rieben, 1985; de Ribaupierre, Rieben, & Lautrey, 1991; Rieben, de Ribaupierre, & Lautrey, 1983, 1986). La plupart des analyses ont mis en évidence une organisation systématique de la variabilité intra-individuelle, autour de deux grands axes, l'un défini par les tâches ou items de nature logico-mathématique et l'autre par les tâches ou items de nature infra-logique (ou spatiale en l'occurrence).[1] Les résultats nous ont amenés à faire l'hypothèse qu'on pouvait regrouper les sujets en fonction du mode de traitement ou format représentationnel qu'ils semblent privilégier: un mode propositionnel ou symbolique, et un mode analogique. Un traitement de nature propositionnelle est analytique, de nature abstraite dans la mesure où les relations entre unités représentationnelles et objets représentés sont arbitraires, et probablement séquentiel; il semble particulièrement bien adapté pour résoudre des problèmes de nature logico-mathématique. Un traitement analogique est plus global ou holistique; il maintient un certain isomorphisme entre les objets et leurs représentations (le prototype d'un tel traitement est la rotation mentale, dont on a montré qu'elle possédait des caractéristiques structurales similaires à la perception). Ce format semble plus adapté au traitement d'épreuves infra-logiques. Il s'agirait de processus vicariants, au sens de Reuchlin (1978), c'est-à-dire de processus également adaptatifs, présents chez tous, mais différant quant à leur hiérarchie d'évocabilité à la fois selon les situations et selon les sujets; la notion de processus vicariants sera discutée plus en détail plus bas. Sans qu'on puisse établir une

---

[1] Pour Piaget, la distinction entre opérations logico-mathématiques et opérations infra-logiques se référait à une différence d'échelle, et non pas de complexité (Piaget & Inhelder, 1947). Les opérations logico-mathématiques portent sur des relations de ressemblance et de différence entre des objets discrets, alors que les opérations infra-logique, telles qu'elles sont à l'oeuvre dans des épreuves spatiales par exemple, structurent des propriétés continues et des relations de proximité entre parties d'une même objet. Le terme «infra-logique» n'est donc pas équivalent à prélogique, mais indique que c'est l'objet lui-même et ses parties constituantes qui sont structurés (par opposition à un ensemble d'objets distincts dans le cas des opérations infra-logiques). Piaget considérait ces deux types d'opérations comme isomorphes, et non pas comme deux types radicalement différents.

correspondance terme à terme entre type de tâche et mode de traitement, le mode propositionnel semble donc plus efficace pour traiter les tâches de nature logico-mathématique, et le mode analogique plus adapté pour les tâches infra-logiques. Cerains sujets pourraient néanmoins privilégier, au moins de prime abord, un mode sur l'autre, plus ou moins indépendamment des situations. Cette interaction sujets-situations conduirait alors à différents types de décalages (de Ribaupierre, 1993; de Ribaupierre & Rieben, 1995; Rieben et al., 1986). Les sujets préférant un mode analogique à un mode propositionnel pourraient présenter un certain retard dans les épreuves logico-mathématiques relativement aux épreuves infra-logiques où l'utilisation d'un mode de représentation analogique les avantage; à l'inverse, les sujets préférant recourir à un mode propositionnel présenteraient un décalage en faveur des épreuves logico-mathématiques. C'est probablement à ce deuxième type de traitement que Piaget s'est intéressé au premier chef, ce qui l'a conduit à faire l'hypothèse d'un retard des opérations infra-logiques relativement aux opérations logico-mathématiques. Enfin, les sujets synchrones seraient des sujets qui pourraient utiliser relativement indifféremment un mode ou l'autre, la question étant encore de savoir s'ils utilisent le mode le plus adéquat pour chaque situation.

Traduite sur un plan développemental, la variabilité intra-individuelle observée, soit sous forme de décalages soit sous forme de facteurs de groupe, implique à nouveau qu'il y aurait plusieurs voies développementales différentes, certains sujets avançant d'abord sur une voie logico-mathématique, d'autres sur une voie infra-logique, d'autres en parallèle sur ces deux voies, toutes les combinaisons étant ensuite possibles. Lors d'une deuxième évaluation (de Ribaupierre et al., 1991), avec les mêmes épreuves, qui a pris place trois ans plus tard, des résultats identiques ont été obtenus, attestant d'une certaine fidélité (réplicabilité) dans la forme des décalages bien que les âges soient différents. De plus, la forme du décalage s'est avérée relativement stable: les sujets ont eu tendance à conserver le même type de décalage à la deuxième évaluation. Seule une étude longitudinale à plus long terme, avec un plus grand nombre d'évaluations nous permettrait, toutefois, de tirer des conclusions sur la stabilité des trajectoires développementales elles-mêmes, notamment sur la question de savoir si les individus tendent à rester sur la même trajectoire ou s'il y a convergence de ces trajectoires à un moment ou à un autre du développement.

Variabilité inter- et intra-individuelle dans une étude longitudinale (Etude CHANGES)

Lors d'une étude plus récente (par exemple, de Ribaupierre et al., 1993), qui portait principalement sur le développement de la mémoire de travail (MT) et secondairement sur les relations entre MT et fonctionnement cognitif dans des épreuves piagétiennes, on a administré des épreuves piagétiennes à trois reprises, au cours des cinq années de la recherche (Table 24.1). L'épreuve du

TABLE 24.1
Etude longitudinale de la capacité attentionnelle et du
niveau cognitif à l'aide d'épreuves piagétiennes (Etude
CHANGES): plan expérimental

EPREUVE	Année				
	1	2	3	4	5
capacité attentionnelle					
CSVI	X	X	X	X	X
Cacahuète Couleur	X	X	X	X	X
Cacahuète Couleur	X	X	X	X	X
FIT	X		X		
Counting Span		X			
Listening Span				X	
Reading Span					X
Epreuves piagétiennes					
Conservation	X				
Pliages de Lignes	X	X	X		
Iles		X	X		X
Balance		X	X		X
Autres épreuves					
CEFT	X		X		
PM 38 ou PM 47		X			
Vitesse articulatoire				X	
Cacahuète Perceptif					

Pliages de Lignes a été administrée annuellement au cours des trois premières années; les épreuves de la Balance et des Iles ont été données les 2ème, 3ème, et 5ème années. Le Pliages de Lignes est une épreuve d'image mentale (Piaget & Inhelder, 1966; Rieben et al., 1983), dans laquelle il s'agit d'imaginer la transformation d'une figure géométrique après pliage de la feuille. La Balance est une épreuve de proportionnalité, adaptée de Inhelder et Piaget (1955), dans laquelle nous avons adopté deux types de procédures: les items A consistant en jugements seulement (voir aussi Siegler, 1981), et les items B consistant en placement de poids avec lecture de l'expérience. L'épreuve des Iles (Piaget, Inhelder, & Szeminska, 1948) est une tâche de conservation de volumes, dans laquelle il s'agit de construire des volumes équivalents («maisons») sur des surfaces («îles») différentes. Chaque épreuve comportait plusieurs items, de difficulté variable. Il faut toutefois relever que les items ont varié d'une année à l'autre, pour éviter des effets de retest. Quatre groupes d'âges (N = 30 par groupe) ont été suivis, âgés de 5, 6, 8 et 10 ans au début de la recherche. Pour chacune des épreuves, les conduites ont été analysées en termes de dimensions de transformation, système d'analyse repris et généralisé de nos recherches précédentes avec Rieben et Lautrey (de Ribaupierre, 1993; Rieben et al., 1983, 1986, 1990) qui permet d'attribuer un niveau sur une échelle de 1 à 6. Pour les

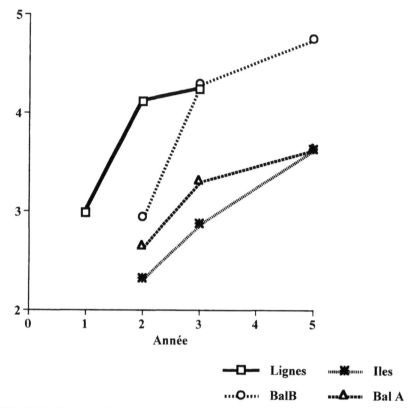

FIG. 24.3   Niveau médian moyen par épreuve et par année (tous âges confondus)

analyses statistiques évoquées ici, on a attribué à chaque enfant un niveau médian par épreuve, sur la base des niveaux observés à chacun des items.

La Figure 24.3 présente les résultats moyens par épreuve et par année, tous groupes d'âge confondus. Lorsque les quatre épreuves ont été administrées la même année (Années 2 et 3), on peut voir que l'épreuve des Lignes semble la plus facile (Année 2), suivie par les items B de la Balance, ces deux épreuves étant à leur tour plus faciles que les items A de la Balance (jugements seulement, sans feed-back) et les Iles. Ces différences attestent bien du rôle du contenu, et des différences dans la procédure expérimentale. Il semble également y avoir une certaine progression au niveau du groupe au cours des années, dans chacune des épreuves, la progression étant la plus marquée pour le Pliage de Lignes et les items B de la Balance. Ces deux dernières épreuves sont encore loin d'être réussies dans la cinquième année, bien que les enfants soient alors âgés de 9 à 14 ans.

On s'est intéressé à deux types de variabilité intra-individuelle, le changement intra-individuel au cours des années et les décalages entre épreuves. Dans les

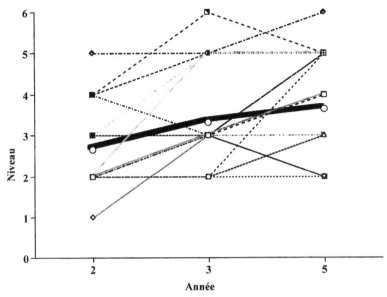

FIG. 24.4   Epreuve de la Balance (Items A): trajectoires développementales observées au cours des trois passations. Note. Seuls les patterns représentés par au moins deux enfants ont été retenus; dans ce cas, il s'agit de 17 patterns, distribués sur 81 enfants. La trajectoire moyenne du groupe est indiquée en gras.

deux cas, des analyses de prédiction ont été effectuées (Hildebrand, Laing, & Rosenthal, 1977). En ce qui concerne le changement développemental, les différences interindividuelles sont fortes, même si la progression du groupe est claire. Cela montre, une fois de plus si nécessaire, qu'il est important de dépasser les analyses de groupes. La Figure 24.4 donne une idée de la diversité; elle présente les trajectoires développementales observées dans les items A de la Balance de la deuxième à la troisième, puis à la cinquième année; la trajectoire moyenne du groupe est indiquée en gras. Seuls les patterns qui se retrouvent chez au moins deux sujets ont été retenus, pour éviter une analyse complètement idiosyncratique; ainsi, dans cette épreuve, 17 patterns différents ont été observés chez 81 sujets (sur 100 sujets examinés à trois reprises avec cette épreuve). La diversité est tout aussi forte dans chacune des autres épreuves.

   Pour dépasser la simple inspection visuelle des trajectoires développementales, deux modèles ont été testés au moyen d'analyses de prédiction, pour chacune des épreuves: un modèle de progression au sens strict, qui exige un changement d'une année à l'autre, et un modèle de progression au sens large, qui admet que les sujets restent au même niveau; la Figure 24.5 présente les modèles testés, et la Table 24.2 les résultats obtenus. Seul le modèle de progression large s'est avéré significatif pour chacune des épreuves; conformément aux résultats du groupe rapportés dans la Figure 3, la progression développementale est plus

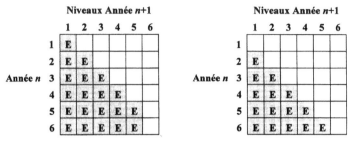

FIG. 24.5   Analyses de prédiction: modèles utilisés pour tester la progression. Les cases erreur (E) sont grisées.

TABLE 24.2
Analyses de prédiction: modèles de progression

	Modèle strict		Modèle large		
	Del	z	Del	z	z (diff)
Lignes 1—Lignes 2	.373	4.420**	.878	13.24**	−5.38**
Lignes 1—Lignes 3	.324	3.700**	.819	9.82**	−4.84**
Lignes 2—Lignes 3	.039	0.650	.414	4.77**	−4.18**
Bal2A—Bal3A	−.013	−0.200	.545	4.40**	−3.95**
Bal2A—Bal 5A	.174	2.740**	.754	6.70**	−4.76**
Bal 3A—Bal 5A	−.063	−1.250	.273	3.05**	−3.23**
Bal 2B- Bal3B	.221	2.610**	.577	4.45**	−2.64*
Bal 2B—Bal 5B	.426	3.540**	.666	4.06**	−1.55
Bal 3B—Bal 5B	.080	0.166	.512	4.49**	−3.86**
Il2—Il3	−.029	−0.440	.531	5.41**	−4.97**
Il2—Il5	.247	2.560*	.837	9.52**	−5.12**
Il3—Il5	.152	1.950	.617	5.96**	−4.10**

* $P < .05$ ** $P < .01$

forte pour le Pliages de Lignes et les items B de la Balance, pour lesquels le modèle de progression au sens strict est significatif de la première à la deuxième passation. Par contre, pour les items A de la Balance et les Iles, il n'y a progression au sens strict que lorsque l'écart entre les passations est de trois ans. Ces résultats démontrent bien qu'un certain nombre de sujets ne progressent pas, ou très peu.

Les décalages entre épreuves sont également nombreux. Les analyses de prédiction ont contrasté un modèle de synchronisme au sens large, avec deux modèles de décalage collectif dans un sens ou dans l'autre. La Figure 24.6 présente les modèles testés et les valeurs des pondérations qui ont été accordées aux cases erreur. La Table 24.3 résume les résultats des analyses et indique quel(s) modèle(s) s'est avéré le meilleur chaque année. Il s'agit donc ici d'analyses transversales. Les résultats sont moins stables d'une année à l'autre que dans nos

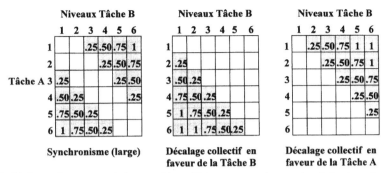

FIG. 24.6   Analyses de prédiction: modèles utilisés pour tester le type de relation inter-épreuve. Les cases erreur (E) sont grisées et contiennent les valeurs des pondérations utilisées.

TABLE 24.3
Etude transversale des décalages: Résumé des résultats des analyses de prédiction

	Année 2	*Année 3*	*Année 5*
Lignes—Bal A	Lignes > Bal A	Lignes ≥ Bal A	
Lignes—Bal B	Lignes > Bal B	synchronisme	
Lignes—Iles	Lignes > Iles	Lignes > Iles	
Bal A—Bal B	synchronisme	Bal B > Bal A	Bal B > Bal A
Bal A—Iles	synchronisme	Bal A ≥ Iles	synchronisme
Bal B—Iles	Bal B ≥ Iles	Bal B > Iles	Bal B > Iles

Le signe > signifie que l'épreuve *x* est plus facile que l'épreuve *y*, le modèle de décalage collectif en faveur de l'épreuve *x* étant significativement supérieur aux deux autres. Le signe ≥ signifie que le modèle de décalage collectif en faveur de l'épreuve *x* et le modèle de synchronisme ne différaient pas significativement l'un de l'autre, tout en étant meilleurs que le modèle de décalage collectif en faveur de l'épreuve *y*.

recherches précédentes (de Ribaupierre et al., 1991; Rieben et al., 1986). Ceci peut tenir au fait que les items ont changé d'une passation à l'autre, même s'ils ont été construits selon les mêmes principes; il peut donc y avoir de légers changements en termes de difficulté globale de chacune des épreuves. Il n'y a cependant pas d'inversion majeure, les seuls changements allant dans le sens du passage d'un cas de synchronisme à un cas de décalage collectif (Pliage de Lignes et items B de la Balance), ou l'inverse. Il faut aussi relever que des cas de décalages individuels clairs n'ont pas été observés (cas dans lesquels aucun modèle ne s'avère meilleur). Il se peut que ces épreuves soient plus semblables en termes des processus auxquels elles font appel, ou que les items soient plus différents les uns des autres au sein d'une même épreuve, si bien que leur regroupement par le calcul d'un niveau médian aurait pour effet de neutraliser ces différences. Des analyses plus détaillées de chacun des items s'avèrent donc nécessaires, tant sur le plan théorique qu'empirique. Il faut enfin relever le fait

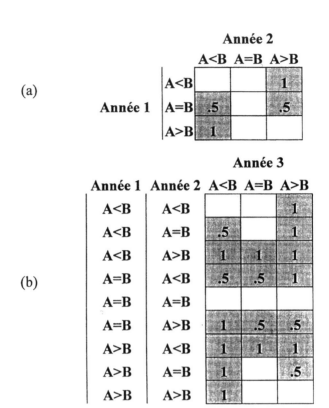

FIG. 24.7 Analyses de prédiction: modèles utilisés pour tester la stabilité longitudinale des décalages sur deux passations (a) et sur trois passations (b). Les cases erreur (E) sont hachurées et contiennent les valeurs des pondérations utilisées.

TABLE 24.4
Etude longitudinale de la stabilité des décalages sur deux passations:
Indices de prédiction

	Année 2—Année 3		Année 3—Année 5		Année 2—Année 5	
	Del	z	Del	z	Del	z
Lignes—Balance A	.56	4.05**				
Lignes—Balance B	.13	1.51				
Lignes-Iles	.14	1.15				
BalA—Bal B	.09	1.31	.10	0.87	−.13	−1.82
Bal A—Iles	.23	2.71*	.18	1.50	.04	0.38
Bal B—Iles	.05	0.77	.25	2.44*	.08	0.13

* P < .05   ** P < .01

Les modèles testés sont indiqués dans la Figure 24.7a.

TABLE 24.5
Etude longitudinale de la stabilité
des décalages sur trois passations:
Indices de prédiction

	Del	z
Bal A—Bal B	−0.01	−0.12
Bal A—Iles	0.02	0.26
Bal B—Iles	0.23	2.16*

* $P < .05$
Les modèles testés sont indiqués dans
la Figure 24.7b.

que nous n'avions pas d'hypothèse précise sur le regroupement de ces épreuves; la relative instabilité observée traduirait alors l'absence de processus généraux responsables du décalage. Il semble en effet difficile ici d'organiser les épreuves autour de deux grands facteurs traduisant un mode de traitement préférentiel. Si un mode de traitement analogique semble bien un avantage dans l'épreuve du Pliage de Lignes, l'appariement entre mode de traitement et type de décalage est plus difficile en ce qui concerne la Balance et les Iles. Ces deux dernières épreuves semblent en effet se prêter à toutes sortes de stratégies différentes, qui pourraient changer d'une année à l'autre, en fonction tant du changement dans les items que de l'avance en âge.

On s'est enfin intéressé à la stabilité des décalages, par exemple à savoir si un enfant qui était en avance à l'épreuve A par rapport à l'épreuve B lors de la 2ème année, gardait cette avance lors de la 3ème ou de la 5ème année. Pour rester compatible avec l'analyse des décalages entre épreuves, et également pour éviter de considérer comme présentant un décalage des enfants qui seraient en pleine transition, on a considéré ici qu'il n'y avait décalage que lorsque l'écart entre deux épreuves étaient de au moins deux niveaux. Des analyses de prédiction ont à nouveau été utilisées, testant un modèle relativement large; un passage d'un décalage à un cas de synchronisme n'a pas été considéré comme erreur, en particulier pour tenir compte des cas où l'enfant réussit aux deux épreuves. La Figure 24.7a présente le modèle utilisé pour tester la stabilité sur 2 ans, et la Figure 24.7b le modèle utilisé pour tester la stabilité sur 3 ans; les indices de prédiction Del correspondants sont rapportés dans les Tables 24.4 et 24.5. Malgré la laxité des modèles utilisés, la plupart des Del se sont avérés non significatifs, même dans le cas des épreuves qui présentent le décalage le plus systématique au niveau du groupe, telles que les Lignes et les Iles. Par exemple, sur 55 enfants qui étaient très clairement en avance au Pliage de Lignes relativement aux Iles lors de la deuxième année de la recherche (cas très clair de décalage collectif, voir Table 24.3), 25 sont devenus synchrones l'année suivante, et un a même présenté un décalage dans l'autre sens. Ceci témoigne donc également d'une forte variabilité dans les changements intra-individuels.

DE LA RELATION ENTRE DIFFÉRENCES INDIVIDUELLES ET MODÈLES GÉNÉRAUX DU DÉVELOPPEMENT: UNE QUESTION DE PERSPECTIVE

Je crois avoir bien démontré l'importance de la variabilité inter- et intra-individuelle, et des différences interindividuelles dans la variabilité intra-individuelle. On pourrait évidemment multiplier les exemples. Le programme de recherche de Siegler (Siegler, 1995; Siegler & Jenkins, 1989) en est un autre, qui montre que non seulement les sujets varient largement quant aux stratégies qu'ils utilisent, mais aussi qu'ils varient d'un moment à l'autre, d'un point de vue micro-génétique et pas seulement macro-génétique comme dans les recherches décrites ci-dessus. Fischer (Bidell & Fischer, 1992; Fischer & Granott, 1995; Fischer et al., 1993) et, plus récemment, Lewis (1994, 1995) ont également insisté sur l'existence de voies développementales multiples. Ils ont proposé de jolies images de cette diversité: Fischer a parlé de «developmental web» alors que Lewis a proposé l'image d'un arbre. S'ils ont tous deux fortement insisté sur la multiplicité des voies développementales, ils n'ont par contre pas toujours clairement explicité si et comment cette diversité est réconciliable avec l'hypothèse de processus généraux et universels tels que ceux que Piaget avait définis, ou ceux d'un certain nombre de modèles néo-piagétiens (par exemple, Case, 1985, 1992a,b; Pascual-Leone, 1987). Par ailleurs, il manque, à mon avis, dans ces métaphores, une indication des contraintes qui pourraient s'exercer sur cette diversité. On a un peu le sentiment que la variabilité augmente avec le temps, dans le sens d'une multiplication des voies développementales et d'une divergence croissante entre elles. Ceci n'a, à ma connaissance, pas été empiriquement montré.

Ceci m'amène à la dernière question que j'aimerais discuter, notamment celle de la relation entre universalité ou généralité et spécificité du développement. Tout d'abord, j'aimerais insister sur le fait qu'il est possible d'adopter plusieurs perspectives pour interpréter les mêmes données. L'accent a été mis ici sur la variabilité individuelle, mais il aurait également pu être placé sur une plus grande généralité. Dans la dernière recherche longitudinale dont il a été question, les corrélations entre les épreuves étaient significatives; elles ne sont donc pas complètement indépendantes l'une de l'autre. Dans cette même recherche, nous avons aussi montré que la capacité en mémoire de travail était un bon prédicteur (tout aussi bon que l'âge) des conduites à l'épreuve de la balance (Thomas, Pons, & de Ribaupierre, 1996) ce qui va bien dans le sens d'un mécanisme général sous-jacent. Il s'agit donc, en partie, d'une question d'accent (voir aussi Case, Okamoto, Henderson, & McKeough, 1993). La variabilité individuelle (et situationnelle) est toutefois trop importante pour qu'on puisse la négliger, ou la considérer seulement comme un épiphénomène, de nature quantitative. Il faut aussi se demander, comme je l'ai mentionné au début, en quoi cette variabilité peut nous informer sur les lois générales.

La seule façon de réconcilier cette apparente contradiction entre processus généraux et variabilité intra-individuelle est de faire l'hypothèse d'une multi-dimensionnalité du développement, ou d'une «pluralité» du développement pour reprendre la terminologie de Lautrey (1990a,b, 1993), c'est-à-dire de faire appel à plusieurs processus sous-jacents, en interaction les uns avec les autres (de Ribaupierre, 1993). D'autres auteurs ont bien sûr déjà fait cette proposition, mais ils sont plus nombreux parmi ceux qui se sont intéressés au développement tout au long de la vie (par ex., Baltes, 1987), ou parmi ceux qui sont issus d'une tradition psychométrique (par ex., Demetriou & Efklidès, 1987, 1994; Sternberg, 1987, 1988).

Le modèle des processus vicariants proposé par Reuchlin (1978) paraît ici particulièrement approprié. La vicariance est une forme de redondance, que Reuchlin considère comme fondamentale d'un point de vue adaptatif. Il s'agit d'un modèle probabiliste du fonctionnement cognitif, qui a été essentiellement proposé pour rendre compte des différences individuelles, mais qui peut être facilement généralisé aux aspects développementaux. Il comporte un certain nombre de principes, dont les suivants me paraissent les plus importants:

1. Chaque individu dispose de plusieurs processus pour élaborer une réponse de nature adaptative dans de nombreuses situations. De plus ce *catalogue* de processus est identique pour tous.
2. Il existe une hiérarchie d'évocabilité de ces processus, qui peut être formalisée en termes de probabilité d'activation.
3. La hiérarchie d'évocabilité peut différer d'un individu à l'autre (variabilité interindividuelle, intra-situation). Dans une même situation, tous les individus ne vont pas nécessairement activer le même processus.
4. La hiérarchie d'évocabilité peut aussi différer selon les situations (variabilité intra-individuelle, inter-situation) et/ou occasions. Différentes situations n'activent pas forcément le même processus chez un individu donné.
5. Dans une situation donnée, tous les processus susceptibles de remplir une même fonction ne sont pas également efficaces, même si, dans l'ensemble, ils sont équivalents. Des principes 3–5, il découle que certains individus peuvent évoquer préférentiellement un processus, même dans les situations dans lesquelles il n'est pas le plus efficace.
6. Les différents processus peuvent se substituer les uns aux autres, mais peuvent également entretenir des relations d'interaction (complémentarité, interférence, etc.).

Ces principes sont très abstraits et généraux, et, même s'ils ont été développés pour rendre compte des différences individuelles, ils sont également applicables au développement. Il est d'ailleurs intéressant de relever à ce propos que c'est à partir de théories sur l'apprentissage que Reuchlin a développé ce modèle. Lautrey (Lautrey, 1996; Lautrey & Caroff, 1996) a montré en quoi ils peuvent être rapprochés d'une approche connexionniste ou des théories neurobiologiques évolutionnistes. J'ai ailleurs aussi montré comment de tels principes peuvent s'appliquer au concept de mémoire de travail, et aux changements en mémoire de travail au cours de la vie (de Ribaupierre, 1995, 1996; de Ribaupierre & Bailleux, 1994). Les modes de traitement dont j'ai parlé plus tôt peuvent être interprétés dans le cadre d'un tel modèle (de Ribaupierre, 1993; de Ribaupierre & Rieben, 1995; de Ribaupierre et al., 1991; Rieben et al., 1990). Je voudrais enfin souligner à quel point la Théorie des Opérateurs Constructifs développée par Pascual-Leone (Pascual-Leone, 1970, 1987; Pascual-Leone & Ijaz, 1989) est proche des propositions de Reuchlin. Elle permet même de leur donner une certaine substance. Pascual-Leone a en effet défini un certain nombre d'opérateurs ou de mécanismes qui fonctionnent tout à fait comme les processus vicariants décrits par Reuchlin. Ils sont présents chez tous les individus, donc universels, et leur fonction est d'activer des schèmes ou des stratégies. Leur efficacité (ou puissance d'activation) varie en fonction des individus ou de l'âge, en particulier en ce qui concerne les opérateurs M, pour puissance mentale, et I, pour inhibition (Pascual-Leone & Baillargeon, 1994). Leur probabilité d'activation diffère également selon les situations (voir à ce sujet la distinction introduite entre situations trompeuses et situations facilitantes-Pascual-Leone, 1969, 1989). Enfin, ils peuvent agir indépendamment l'un de l'autre, se compléter ou au contraire mener à des solutions incompatibles; c'est alors la solution la plus fortement activée qui sera adoptée.

Il n'est sans doute pas nécessaire de faire appel à une multiplicité de processus pour comprendre la diversité du développement. Au moins deux types d'arguments plaident en faveur d'un petit nombre de processus seulement. Tout d'abord, on a pu mettre en évidence des régularités développementales remarquables au travers de différentes situations, régularités qui ne peuvent s'interpréter qu'en recourant à des mécanismes généraux. C'est le cas de Case (Case, 1985, 1992b; Case & Okamoto, 1996), par exemple, qui a montré que le développement prenait une forme très semblable dans des situations très différentes et que les décalages étaient relativement réduits. Ces résultats pourraient d'ailleurs paraître contradictoires avec les nôtres si l'on ne prenait pas en compte le fait que Case a privilégié une perspective générale par opposition à une perspective locale, notamment en développant des scores relativement partiels portant essentiellement sur la forme et non le contenu des conduites; il a d'ailleurs reconnu que ses données, analysées autrement, pourraient démontrer une variabilité tout aussi forte (Case et al., 1993). C'est ici le problème du vase à moitié plein ou à moitié vide! Dans un autre domaine, Kail (1990, 1995) a également montré l'existence de régularités développementales remarquables, en termes de vitesse de traitement. Dans le champ du vieillissement cognitif, on a aussi montré qu'un petit nombre de processus généraux étaient suffisants pour rendre compte d'une bonne partie du changement avec l'âge (Lindenberger & Baltes, 1994; Salthouse, 1992, 1994b).

La deuxième raison pour laquelle il n'est pas nécessaire de multiplier le nombre de mécanismes sous-jacents pour rendre compte de la diversité observée tient aux démonstrations récentes des modélisations en termes de systèmes dynamiques. On a ainsi pu montrer, dans différents domaines, que des petites différences ou fluctuations dans les conditions initiales pouvaient entraîner des divergences importantes par la suite (par ex., Howe, 1994). L'interaction de deux processus serait déjà suffisante pour provoquer des différences considérables. Pour rendre compte de la diversité individuelle, il suffirait donc de considérer que deux ou trois mécanismes seulement sont conjointement responsables du développement. Par contre, un seul mécanisme, comme on l'a souvent proposé en psychologie du développement n'est pas suffisant, pas seulement parce qu'il ne permet pas de rendre compte des phénomènes de variabilité dont j'ai parlé, mais également parce qu'il n'y aurait alors pas de dynamique. Actuellement, quatre mécanismes ou processus semblent en vogue en psychologie du développement, encore que la plupart des chercheurs ne se soient centrés que sur un seul de ces mécanismes à la fois (par ex., de Ribaupierre, 1996). Il s'agit d'un accroissement dans les ressources de traitement ou dans la mémoire de travail, d'une augmentation dans la vitesse de traitement, d'une augmentation des capacités d'inhibition avec l'âge et d'une optimisation des processus de contrôle ou processus exécutifs. Ces mêmes mécanismes sont d'ailleurs aussi invoqués par les chercheurs qui se sont intéressés au vieillissement cognitif, notamment l'inhibition (Hasher, Stoltzfus, Zacks, & Rypma, 1991; Hasher & Zacks, 1988) et la vitesse de traitement (Salthouse, 1992, 1994a). L'augmentation des ressources ou la puissance d'activation et la vitesse de traitement me semblent représenter deux facettes d'un même mécanisme général; en simplifiant à outrance, on peut très bien concevoir qu'une plus grande puissance d'activation, qui permet de tenir compte de plus d'informations en même temps, résulte en une plus grande vitesse de traitement; réciproquement, un traitement plus rapide permet de traiter plus d'informations dans un même laps de temps. Par conséquent, des mécanismes comme l'activation et l'inhibition pourraient être des bons candidats en tant que processus responsables du développement, pour autant qu'on les conçoive comme des processus vicariants, dont les probabilités d'activation varieraient légèrement d'un individu à l'autre, d'un âge à l'autre et bien sûr aussi d'une situation à l'autre. En interaction au sein d'un système dynamique et le plus probablement couplés avec des stratégies de contrôle ou exécutives et le répertoire de connaissances des individus, ils permettraient sans doute de rendre compte d'une bonne partie de la diversité observée, tant quantitative que qualitative.

NOTE D'AUTEUR

La préparation de cet article a été effectuée lorsque l'auteur était chercheur invité au Max-Planck Institut for Human Development and Education à Berlin. Elle aimerait remercier tous les membres du Center for Psychology and Human Development (Director: Paul Baltes) pour l'atmosphère chaleureuse qu'ils offrent à leurs visiteurs et pour les nombreuses possibilités de discussions stimulantes. Ce travail est basé sur des recherches qui ont bénéficié de subsides du Fonds National Suisse de la Recherche Scientifique (requêtes 11-27671.89 et 1114-040465.94).

RÉFÉRENCES

Baltes, P. B. (1987). Theoretical propositions of life-span developmental psychology: on the dynamics between growth and decline. *Developmental Psychology, 23,* 611-626.

Baltes, P. B., & Kliegl, R. (1992). Further testing of limits of cognitive plasticity: negative age differences in a mnemonic skill are robust. *Developmental Psychology, 28,* 121-125.

Bidell, T. R., & Fischer, K. W. (1992). Beyond the stage debate: Action, structure, and variability in Piagetian theory and research. In R. J. Sternberg & C. Berg (Eds.), *Intellectual development* (pp. 100-140). New York: Cambridge University Press.

Buss, A. R. (1979). Toward a unified framework for psychometric concepts in the multivariate developmental situation: intraindividual change and inter- and intra- individual differences. In J. R. Nesselroade & P. B. Baltes (Eds.), *Longitudinal research in the study of behavior and development: design and analysis* (pp. 41-59). New York: Academic Press.

Case, R. (1985). *Intellectual development. Birth to adulthood.* New York: Academic Press.

Case, R. (1992a). Neo-piagetian theories of intellectual development. In H. Beilin & P. B. Pufall (Eds.), *Piaget's theory: prospects and possibilities* (pp. 61-104). Hillsdale, NJ: Lawrence Erlbaum Associates Inc.

Case, R. (1992b). *The mind's staircase: exploring the conceptual underpinnings of children's thought and knowledge.* Hillsdale, NJ: Lawrence Erlbaum Associates Inc.

Case, R., Okamoto, Y. (Eds.) (1996). Modeling the dynamic interplay between general and specific change in children's conceptual understanding. *Monographs of the Society for Research in Child Development. 61* (Serial no 246).

Case, R., Okamoto, Y., Henderson, B., & McKeough, A. (1993). Individual variability and consistency in cognitive development: new evidence for the existence of central conceptual structures. In R. Case & W. Edelstein (Eds.), *The new structuralism in cognitive development: theory and research on individual pathways* (pp. 71-100). Basel: Karger.

Chapman, M. (1988). *Constructive evolution: origins and development of Piaget's thought.* New York: Cambridge University Press.

Cohen, R. L. (1994). Editorial: Some thoughts on individual differences and theory construction. *Intelligence, 18,* 3-13.

Cronbach, L. J. (1957). The two disciplines of scientific psychology. *American Psychologist, 12,* 671-684.

Demetriou, A., & Efklidès, A. (1987). Experiential structuralism and neo-piagetian theories: toward an integrated model. *International Journal of Psychology, 22,* 679-728.

Demetriou, A., & Efklidès, A. (Eds.) (1994). *Intelligence, mind, and reasoning.* Amsterdam: Elsevier.

Fischer, K. W., & Granott, N. (1995). Beyond one-dimensional change: Parallel, concurrent, socially distributed processes in learning and development. *Human Development, 38,* 302-314.

Fischer, K. W., Knight, C. C., & Van Parys, M. (1993). Analyzing diversity in developmental pathways: methods and concepts. In R. Case & W. Edelstein (Eds.), *The new structuralism in cognitive development. Theory and research on individual pathways* (pp. 33-56). Basel: Karger.

Fischer, K. W., & Lamborn, S. D. (1989). Mechanisms of variation in developmental levels: Cognitive and emotional transitions during adolescence. In A. de Ribaupierre (Ed.), *Transition mechanism in child development* (pp. 33-67). Cambridge: Cambridge University Press.

Hasher, L., Stoltzfus, E. R., Zacks, R. T., & Rypma, B. (1991). Age and inhibition. *Journal of Experimental Psychology: Learning, Memory, and Cognition, 17,* 163-169.

Hasher, L., & Zacks, R. T. (1988). Working memory, comprehension, and aging: A review and a new view. In G. H. Bower (Ed.), *The psychology of learning and motivation* (pp. 193-225). San Diego, CA: Academic Press.

Hildebrand, D. K., Laing, J. D., & Rosenthal, H. (1977). *Prediction analysis of cross-classifications*. New York: Wiley.

Howe, M. L. (1994). Dynamics of cognitive development: A unifying approach to universal trends and individual differences. *Learning and Individual Differences*, *6*, 365–377.

Inhelder, B., & Piaget, J. (1955). *De la logique de l'enfant à la logique de l'adolescence: essai sur la construction des structures opératoires formelles*. Paris: Presses Universitaires de France.

Kail, R. (1990). More evidence for a common, central constraint on speed of processing. In J. T. Enns (Ed.), *The development of attention: Research and theory* (pp. 159–173). Amsterdam: North Holland.

Kail, R. (1995). Processing speed, memory, and cognition. In F. E. Weinert & W. Schneider (Eds.), *Memory performance and competencies. Issues in growth and development* (pp. 71–88). Mahwah, NJ: Lawrence Erlbaum Associates Inc.

Kliegl, R., & Baltes, P. B. (1987). Theory guided analysis of mechanisms of development and aging through testing-the-limits and research on expertise. In C. Schooler & K. W. Schaie (Eds.), *Cognitive functioning and social structure over the life course* (pp. 95–119). Norwood, NJ: Ablex.

Kliegl, R., Smith, J., & Baltes, P. B. (1986). Testing-the-limits, expertise, and memory in adulthood and old age. In F. Klix & H. Hagendorf (Eds.), *Human memory and cognitive capabilities. Mechanisms and performances* (pp. 395–407). Amsterdam: Elsevier.

Lautrey, J. (1990a). Esquisse d'un modèle pluraliste du développement cognitif. In M. Reuchlin, J. Lautrey, C. Marendaz, & T. Ohlmann (Eds.), *Cognition: l'universel et l'individuel* (pp. 185–216). Paris: Presses Universitaires de France.

Lautrey, J. (1990b). Unicité ou pluralité dans le développement cognitif: les relations entre image mentale, action et perception. In G. Netchine-Grynberg (Ed.), *Développement et fonctionnement cognitifs chez l'enfant*. Paris: Presses Universitaires de France.

Lautrey, J. (1993). Structure and variability: A plea for a pluralistic approach to cognitive development. In R. Case & W. Edelstein (Eds.), *The new structuralism in cognitive development: Theory and research on individual pathways* (pp. 101–114). Basel: Karger.

Lautrey, J. (1996). *Individual differences and evolution theory: Toward a new phase*. Communication présentée au XXVIth Congrès International de Psychologie, Montréal, 16–21 août.

Lautrey, J., & Caroff, X. (1996). Variability and Cognitive Development. *Polish Quarterly of Developmental Psychology*, *2*, 71–90.

Lautrey, J., de Ribaupierre, A., & Rieben, L. (1985). Intra-individual variability in the development of concrete operations. Relations between logical and infra-logical operations. *Genetic, Social and General Psychology Monographs*, *111*, 167–192.

Lautrey, J., de Ribaupierre, A., & Rieben, L. (1990). L'intégration des aspects génétiques et différentiels du développement cognitif. In M. Reuchlin, J. Lautrey, C. Marendaz, & T. Ohlmann (Eds.), *Connaître différemment* (pp. 181–208). Nancy: Presses Universitaires de Nancy.

Lewis, M. D. (1994). Reconciling stage and specificity in neo-Piagetian theory: Self-organizing conceptual structures. *Human Development*, *37*, 143–169.

Lewis, M. D. (1995). Cognition-emotion feedback and the self-organization of developmental paths. *Human Development*, *38*, 71–102.

Lindenberger, U., & Baltes, P. B. (1994). Sensory functioning and intelligence in old age: A strong connection. *Psychology and Aging*, *9(3)*, 339–355.

Longeot, F. (1969). *Psychologie différentielle et théorie opératoire de l'intelligence*. Paris: Dunod.

Longeot, F. (1978). *Les stades opératoires de Piaget et les facteurs de l'intelligence*. Grenoble: Presses Universitaires de France.

Lourenço, O., & Machado, A. (1996). In defense of Piaget's theory: A reply to 10 common criticisms. *Psychological Review*, *103*, 143–164.

Pascual-Leone, J. (1969). *Cognitive development and cognitive style: A general psychological integration*. Unpublished doctoral dissertation, University of Geneva.

Pascual-Leone, J. (1970). A mathematical model for the transition rule in Piaget's developmental stages. *Acta Psychologica, 32*, 301–345.

Pascual-Leone, J. (1987). Organismic processes for neo-Piagetian theories: A dialectical causal account of cognitive development. *International Journal of Psychology, 22*, 531–570.

Pascual-Leone, J. (1989). An organismic process model of Witkin's field-dependence-independence. In T. Globerson & T. Zelniker (Eds.), *Cognitive style and cognitive development* (pp. 36–70). Norwood, NJ: Ablex.

Pascual-Leone, J., & Baillargeon, R. (1994). Developmental measurement of mental attention. *International Journal of Behavioral Development, 17(1)*, 161–200.

Pascual-Leone, J., & Ijaz, I. (1989). Mental capacity testing as a form of intellectual-developmental assessment. In R. J. Samuda, S. L. Kong, J. Cummins, J. Pascual-Leone, & J. Lewis (Eds.), *Assessment and placement of minority students* (pp. 143–171). Toronto: C. J. Hogrefe.

Piaget, J., & Inhelder, B. (1941). *Le développement des quantités chez l'enfant.* Neuchâtel, Switzerland: Delachaux et Niestlé.

Piaget, J. and Inhelder, B. (1947). *La représentation de l'espace chez l'enfant.* Paris: Presses Universitaires de France.

Piaget, J., & Inhelder, B. (1966). *L'image mentale chez l'enfant.* Paris: Presses Universitaires de France.

Piaget, J., Inhelder, B., & Szeminska, A. (1948). *La géométrie spontanée chez l'enfant.* Paris: Presses Universitaires de France.

Reuchlin, M. (1964). L'intelligence: Conception génétique opératoire et conception factorielle. *Revue Suisse de Psychologie Pure et Appliquée, 23*, 113–134.

Reuchlin, M. (1978). Processus vicariants et différences individuelles. *Journal de Psychologie, 2*, 133–145.

Reuchlin, M., & Bacher, F. (1989). *Les différences individuelles dans le développement cognitif.* Paris: Presses Universitaires de France.

de Ribaupierre, A. (1975). Mental space and formal operations. Unpublished doctoral dissertation, University of Toronto.

de Ribaupierre, A. (1993). Structural and individual differences: On the difficulty of dissociating developmental and differential processes. In R. Case & W. Edelstein (Eds.), *The new structuralism in cognitive development: Theory and research on individual pathways* (pp. 11–32). Basel: Karger.

de Ribaupierre, A. (1995). Working memory and individual differences: A review. *Swiss Journal of Psychology, 54*, 152–168.

de Ribaupierre, A. (1996). *From child development to life-span development.* Communication présentée au XIVème congrès de lISSBD Meetings, Québec, 12–16 août.

de Ribaupierre, A., & Bailleux, C. (1994). Developmental change in a spatial task of attentional capacity: An essay toward an integration of two working memory models. *International Journal of Behavioral Development, 17*, 5–35.

de Ribaupierre, A., Bailleux, C., Garcia, A., Lecerf, T., Pous, O., & Thomas, L. *Etude longitudinale de la capacité d'attention mentale chez l'enfant de 5 à 14 ans: une investigation néo-piagétienne (CHANGES study). Rapport interne no 6.* Manuscrit non publié, Université de Genève.

de Ribaupierre, A., & Pascual-Leone, J. (1984). Pour une intégration des méthodes en psychologie: approches expérimentale, psycho-génétique et différentielle. *L'Année Psychologique, 84*, 227–250.

de Ribaupierre, A., & Rieben, L. (1995). Individual and situational variability in cognitive development. *Educational Psychologist, 30*, 5–14.

de Ribaupierre, A., Rieben, L., & Lautrey, J. (1991). Developmental change and individual differences. A longitudinal study using Piagetian tasks. *Genetic, Social and General Psychology Monographs, 117*, 285–311.

Rieben, L., de Ribaupierre, A., & Lautrey, J. (1983). *Le développement opératoire de l'enfant entre 6 et 12 ans. Elaboration d'un instrument d'évaluation.* Paris: Editions du CNRS.

Rieben, L., de Ribaupierre, A., & Lautrey, J. (1986). Une définition structuraliste des formes du développement cognitif: un projet chimérique. *Archives de Psychologie, 54*, 95–123.

Rieben, L., de Ribaupierre, A., & Lautrey, J. (1990). Structural invariants and individual modes of processing: On the necessity of a minimally structuralist approach of development for education. *Archives de Psychologie, 58*, 29–53.

Salthouse, T. A. (1992). *Mechanisms of age-cognition relations in adulthood.* Hillsdale, NJ: Lawrence Erlbaum Associates Inc.

Salthouse, T. A. (1994a). The nature of the influence of speed on adult age differences in cognition. *Developmental Psychology, 30*, 240–259.

Salthouse, T. A. (1994b). How many causes are there of age-related decrements in cognitive functioning? *Developmental Review, 14*, 413–437.

Siegler, R. S. (1981). Developmental sequences within and between sequences. *Monographs of the Society for Research in Child Development, 46* (6, Serial no 189).

Siegler, R. S. (1995). Children's thinking: How does change occur? In F. E. Weinert & W. Schneider (Eds.), *Memory performance and competencies. Issues in growth and development* (pp. 405–430). Mahwah, NJ: Lawrence Erlbaum Associates Inc.

Siegler, R. S., & Jenkins, E. (1989). *How children discover new strategies.* Hillsdale, NJ: Lawrence Erlbaum Associates Inc.

Sternberg, R. J. (1987). A day at developmental downs: sportscast for race no 2—Neopiagetian theories of cognitive development. *International Journal of Psychology, 22*, 507–529.

Sternberg, R. J. (1988). Lessons from the life-span: what theorists of intellectual development among children can learn from their counterparts studying adults. In E. M. Hetherington, R. Lerner, & M. Perlmutter (Eds.), *Child Development in life-span Perspective* (pp. 259–275). Hillsdale, NJ: Lawrence Erlbaum Associates Inc.

Thomas, L., Pons, F., & de Ribaupierre, A. (1996). Attentional capacity and cognitive level in the balance task. *Cahiers de Psychologie Cognitive, 15*, 137–172.

CHAPTER TWENTY-FIVE

Domain specificity in cognitive development: universals and nonuniversals

Rochel Gelman
University of California, Los Angeles, USA

An account of domain specific theories of cognitive development is presented. One theme is that there is an ongoing change about the meaning of key theoretical terms, including *learning*. The account of learning highlights the role of structure-mapping and other mental learning tools, as opposed to the laws of association. Another theme is that there are core and noncore domains, ones that do and ones that do not benefit from innate skeletal structures. Much of the discussion about domains is organized around a series of questions, including: What is a domain; What is and is not innate; What constitutes learning in a domain; How many domains are there; How can knowledge be innate and yet variably applied; How can a domain be both innate and learned; and How can we distinguish between universal and non-universal domains?

Sont ici exposées les théories du développement cognitif invoquant l'existence de domaines spécifiques. Un des thèmes abordés concerne le changement en cours dans la signification de termes clés sur le plan théorique, y compris celui d'*apprentissage*. La section relative à l'apprentissage met en évidence le rôle de la cartographie des structures et d'autres outils d'apprentissage mental, en les contrastant par rapport aux lois d'association. Un autre thème a trait à l'existence de domaines centraux et d'autres non centraux, selon qu'ils s'appuient ou non sur des structures fondamentales innées. L'essentiel de la discussion relative aux domaines s'articule autour d'une série de questions: par exemple, qu'est-ce qu'un domaine; qu'est-ce qui est inné et qu'est-ce qui ne l'est pas; qu'est-ce qu'apprendre dans un domaine; combien y a-t-il de domaines; comment la connaissance peut-elle être innée tout en étant appliquée de manière variable; comment un domaine peut-il être à la fois inné et appris; et comment distinguer entre des domaines universels et d'autres non universels?

INTRODUCTION

The focus of this chapter is on domain-specific accounts of cognitive development. A question and answer format is used to cover key issues about this class of theories, including what counts as a domain, the nature of domains, and whether domains are innate. Gelman and Williams' (1997) distinction between *core* and *noncore* domains is a leitmotif that appears throughout the discussion. We assume that it is only *core* domains that benefit from innate contributions to their epigenesis, both core and noncore domains are learned. The presence of skeletal structures for core concepts, e.g. objects, and natural number, facilitates early learning about these domains. To master a noncore domain, e.g. chess, literary criticism, or sushi making, one has to acquire both the structure and body of knowledge in that domain.

KEY QUESTIONS ABOUT A DOMAIN-SPECIFIC THEORY OF COGNITIVE DEVELOPMENT

What is a domain?

I define a domain of knowledge in much the same way that formalists do, by appealing to the notion of a set of interrelated principles. A given set of principles, the rules of their application, and the entities to which they apply together constitute a domain. Different structures are defined by different sets of principles. Therefore, we can say that a body of knowledge constitutes a domain of knowledge if we can show that a set of interrelated principles organizes its rules of operation and entities. Sets of principles carve the psychological world at its joints, producing distinctions that guide and organize our differential reasoning about entities in one domain versus another. In this way, available domain-specific structures encourage attention to inputs that have a privileged status because they have the potential to nurture learning about that domain; they help learners find inputs that are relevant for knowledge acquisition and problem solving within that domain.

Counting is a part of a number-specific core domain, because the representatives of numerosity (what I call numerons), generated by counting are operated on by mechanisms informed by, or obedient to arithmetic principles. For counting to provide the input for arithmetic reasoning, the principles governing counting must complement the principles governing arithmetic reasoning. For example, the counting principles must be such that sets assigned the same cardinal numeron are numerically equal and sets assigned different cardinal numerons are either greater than or less than each other in value. However, their engagement does not require attention to the weight or kind of material of the items being counted. In contrast, causal principles encourage attention to variables that bear on how to move the items around, variables like the weight and material of the objects. The analysis of the cause of an object's movements is based on domain-specific causal principles that encourage perceptual processing of information about the movements of biological or inanimate objects as a whole (Gelman, 1990). Of course, if an individual has yet to acquire the principles that organize a given noncore domain, these considerations about selective attention cannot apply. Core domains facilitate learning about the domain because they have innate skeletal structures; the structures of noncore domains have to be learned from scratch (Gelman & Williams, 1997).

General processes like discrimination, or general purpose processing mechanisms like short-term memory, do not constitute domains any more than the process of applying rewrite rules, which is common to all formal systems, constitutes a domain of mathematics. Nor does a script structure constitute a domain. Scripts are analogous to the heuristic prescriptions for solving problems in mathematics, which should not be confused with the mathematical domains themselves (algebra, calculus, theory of functions, and so on). Still, information-processing limits on short-term memory can influence whether a given domain-specific problem is solved correctly. For example, although there is nothing in Gelman and Gallistel's (1978) counting principles that requires children to place items in a row and count from one end to the other, efforts to honor the one-to-one principle favor this kind of solution because one is less likely to make domain-relevant errors like the double-counting or skipping of items. In this case we can say that the principles potentiate some procedures over others, ones that can contribute to the generation of well-formed plans for solving the task at hand. Preschool children know that systematic left to right or right to left counts are conventional as opposed to required counting procedures. They accept skip-around counts as "okay, but silly, for counting" (Gelman, Meck, & Merkin, 1986).

How many domains are there?

Leslie (1994) identified a common objection to the idea that cognitive development benefits from sets of innate, domain-specific, learning-enabling structures: "There could turn out to be too many domains" (Leslie, 1994, p.120). In this regard, it is important to point out that there is nothing in our definition of a domain that requires that a domain-specific knowledge structure be built on an innate foundation. To say that some of the many domains that people can acquire have an innate basis is not to say that all domains are core domains. Core, or innate, domains are universally shared because they are developed from a common set of existing skeletal structures. Given their presence, learners already have the wherewithal to find and assimilate relevant data. If the data are present in the surrounding environments, learning can proceed without the explicit help of others. In this sense, learning can take place "on the fly", as the learner encounters domain-relevant inputs to assimilate to an existing structure. Because learning in a noncore domain must proceed without the benefit of even a skeletal structure, the acquisition of knowledge in the domain must be more difficult. Given the wide variety of noncore domains and the different opportunities for encountering domain-relevant learning inputs, we should expect different people to master different noncore domains. In addition, the number of noncore domains we become expert at will probably be limited in number. It is unlikely that there will be many Leonardo da Vinci's among us.

Our move to answer the question of "how many domains are there" in the context of the distinction between core and noncore domains is akin to the linguistic distinction between closed and open class morphemes. All who acquire their language as young children share knowledge of the small set of closed class of morphemes in their language. These morphemes serve the capacity to generate utterances that honor the combinatorial rules underlying the morphology and syntax of their language. The open class of morphemes includes all learned and to-be-learned nouns, verbs, adjectives and adverbs—a potentially infinitely large class. Different individuals can master different examples and different numbers of entries in the open class. Similarly, the set of noncore domains is potentially very large and can vary from individual to individual. In contrast, the set of core conceptual domains is relatively small, with their underlying structures being shared by all.

What is innate for a core domain?

When I say that core domains benefit from the presence of innate structures, I find it helpful to use the metaphor of a skeleton. Were there no skeletons to dictate the shape and contents of the bodies of the pertinent mental structures, then the acquired representations would not cohere. Just as different skeletons are assembled according to different principles, so too are different coherent bodies of knowledge. Skeletons need not be evident on the surface of a body. Similarly the underlying axiom-like principles that enable the acquisition of coherent knowledge need never be accessible. Most importantly, skeletons lack flesh and some relevant body structures. Therefore, in no way can they be said to represent full-blown knowledge of their domain; instead they are potential structures, ones that can contribute to the epigenesis of their respective flesh and structures as they interact with the kinds of environments that have the potential to nourish such development.

If we postulate core domains, we achieve an account of the fact that infants respond to structured data as opposed to simple punctate sensations. Because application of even skeletal structures means that the class of relevant data will be relational and overlap with the abstract principles that lime the domain. That is, it is not the case that infants will be confronted with William James' blooming buzzing confusion of punctate bits of uninterpretable sensations. Instead, it is an environment with things "out there", things to find and learn about. Different implicit knowledge structures should encourage attention to and exploration of different kinds of structured data and the assimilation of these helps nourish the coherent growth of these nascent structures.

A wide range of findings about very young infants' perceptual and conceptual competencies lend support to this shift in view of what kind of perspective the infant has. For example, 1-month-old infants' sucking behaviors reveal an interest in speech as well as the ability to make categorical speech-sound discriminations (Fernald, 1985; Juscyck, 1996; Mehler & Cristophe, 1995). Seven-month-olds separately categorize replicas of animals and nonanimals, as revealed by their reliable tendency to touch items within one category before switching to explore those in another category (Mandler & McDonough, 1996). In related findings, Leslie (1995) has shown that 6- to 8-month-old infants are surprised when an inanimate object moves without assistance, but not when an animate object does so. Baillargeon (1995) demonstrated that even younger infants look longer at "impossible events" (in which objects appear to violate physical laws) than they do at "possible events". For example, in one of her studies 5-month-old infants respond in ways consistent with the belief that one solid object cannot pass through another (Baillargeon, Spelke, & Wasserman, 1985). Infants were first shown a screen as it rotated towards and away from them through an 180° arc, from flat to upright to flat and back again. When their interest in the moving screen declined, that is, when the infants habituated, they were shown a new display. This consisted of an object that was held to the left side of the screen, and then moved behind the screen once the infant had looked at it. At this point the screen once again rotated toward and away from the infant, either stopping at 110° or continuing all the way through the 180° arc (thanks to the use of trick mirrors and invisible doors). From an adult's perspective, the latter event would look like an impossible event where the screen seems to pass through a known hidden object. Because infants preferred to look at this event, we can infer that they too thought the event was impossible. Otherwise, there is no reason for them to have treated it as a novel event, given that they habituated to demonstrations of the 180° arc.

Infants also develop expectations for the number of things or events they are shown, including heterogeneous objects or drum beats, moving dots on a monitor, or events like a rabbit jumping (Starkey, Spelke, & Gelman, 1990; van Loosbroek & Smitsman, 1990; Wynn, 1995). They look preferentially longer at a 2-item or 3-item heterogeneous visual display depending on whether they hear 2 or 3 drum beats (Starkey et al., 1990), and are surprised when the number of objects they encounter changes as a result of unseen, surreptitious additions and subtractions (Wynn, 1992, 1995). Some authors (e.g. Cooper, 1984; Simon, Hespos, & Rochat, 1995; Xu & Carey, 1996) resist the idea that these findings reveal a number-specific structure at work. Even if we accept their position that infants *only* use a one-for-one category mapping rule, the description of the primary data is still abstract and relational. Infants surely are not responding to bits of sensory input, punctate bits of light, color, and so on; otherwise they would not habituate in experiments where the items change on every trial.

To summarize, the first principles that constitute a skeletal structure feed the epigenesis of the respective structures. They do so by focusing attention on inputs that are relevant for the acquisition of concepts and providing a way to store incoming data in a coherent fashion. In other words, the active use of existing nascent structures enables the search for and zeroing in on domain-relevant learning paths. Relevant inputs, that is, ones that map structurally to existing mental structures, can then feed the coherent development of knowledge within their respective domains, the result being that still further examples of relevant data can be found, and so on. The interaction between structures of the mind and environment is bidirectional from the start.

The aptness of the skeleton metaphor is less than perfect. It carries the implication that all principles are in place before their respective bodies of knowledge are acquired. This is unlikely. In fact, it is possible that only some subset of principles of a domain serve as part of the initial skeleton. Furthermore, initial principles might even be replaced or expanded over the course of learning. An example of how encounters with the world can lead to learning about principles not contained in the skeleton of a domain comes from work on infants' ability to make inferences about an object's continued path. Whereas infants of four months of age or younger know that an object will move if it is struck by another one, they seem not to know how far it will go. It takes experience with the path of particular objects to shift from relying on quantitative expectations about the distance an object will traverse after it is hit. A salient example of the role of experience with moving objects comes from Spelke. She shows that, although infants learn quickly about the effects of gravity, they do not start out with implicit knowledge of its effects on falling objects (see Carey & Spelke, 1994).

Given the human capacity to map symbol systems to existing structures (Lee & Karmiloff-Smith, 1996), we should expect the nature of domain-relevant knowledge to expand, and even change, as a function of the kinds of symbolic experiences young learners encounter on the domain-relevant learning paths their environments offer. We return to this matter after a consideration of a question we are sure that many readers will be asking, namely, how can we use the term "learning" in the same context as the term "innate"?

How can core domains be both "innate" and "learned"?

Those who endorse a variation of the empiricist theory of knowledge acquisition treat the terms "innate" and "learned" as opposites. This is because the theory takes it as given that infants are born with a tabula rasa and that all knowledge is learned from scratch. Learning about the world proceeds as a result of the ability to form associations, initially between sensations and responses that occur closely together in time and/or space. The more frequent these contiguous pairings, the more likely associations about given sources are formed in memory. Clearly, such a definition of the nature of concept development does not fit with ones that assume there are innate sources of some of the knowledge that will be acquired. This is especially so for turn-of-the-century determinist theories of knowledge wherein it was assumed that innate contributions are always in a mature steady state, waiting to generate perfect and nonvariable performance, no matter what the context. In such a theoretical context it is true that the idea that knowledge is learned is incompatible with the idea that it is innate. However, a long time has gone by since the turn of the century. Determinism is a very outdated theory in present-day biology. The explosion of work and theory in developmental biology, ethology, animal cognition, behavioral genetics, and evolutionary psychology has generated new ideas about acquisition, so much so that a new theory of learning has evolved, one in which the concepts of *innate* and *learned* both play critical roles in the account of how species-specific knowledge is acquired as the learner interacts with relevant environments. Gould and Marler (1987; Marler, 1991) even write about the "instinct to learn".

The skeletal principles of an innate domain of conceptual development need not be represented within the system in a symbolic or linguistic form. Most likely they are first represented within the structure of the information processing mechanisms that assimilate experience and direct action (cf. Karmiloff-Smith, 1992). Marr (1982) presents many cases where the algorithms by which the visual system processes visual input incorporate implicitly various principles about the structure of the world. Gallistel (1990; Cheng & Gallistel, 1984) argues that the principles of Euclidean geometry are implicit in the mechanisms by which the rat constructs and uses a map of its environment. Knudsen's (1983) work on the development of the tectal circuitry for representing the angular positions of distal stimuli apprehended by different sensory modalities in the barn owl provides a clear example of how a principle can be implicit in a developmental mechanism. Implicit in the mechanism that controls the development of tectal circuitry is the principle that the spatial matrix for experience is unitary and transcends sensory modality. An object cannot have one location in the space apprehended through the visual modality and a different location in the space apprehended through the auditory modality. Thus, when the mapping of visual locations is experimentally put out of register with the mapping of auditory locations, the maturing circuitry reorganizes so as to bring the mappings back into register.

These theoretical and related empirical developments mean that we no longer can tie the definition of the term *learning* to one class of theories. Instead it is important to recognize that there are competing theories of learning, each with its own assumptions and therefore theoretical primitives. True, a theory that posits innate structures is unlikely to be a variant of an empiricist theory of learning, but this does not rule it out as a theory of learning. It is a theory of learning if it assumes that learners must interact with relevant environments and build knowledge representations as a function of these. The idea that learning in core domains is privileged, owing to the presence of innate, skeletal mental structures, clearly is not a variant of the biological theory of determinism. Nevertheless, many in the field of psychology write as if determinism is the model underlying the work of those who are trying to detail the learning mechanisms that provide enabling constraints for some domains of knowledge. Nelson's (1988) critique of "constraints theory" provides an illustration of this usage within the field of developmental psychology: "A true constraint would be manifested in all or none type responses; ... If the constraint is universal (cognitive or linguistic), all children should follow the pattern ... If they are innate, they should apply from the beginning of the language learning process" (pp. 227–228). Plunkett adopts a similar view when he reviews reasons for rejecting domain-specific origins of knowledge (Plunkett & Marchman, 1991; Plunkett, this volume). Such conclusions are not warranted. This is because the terms "innate" and "learned" are not opposites on a priori grounds. Theoretical terms do not stand alone as regards their meanings; they are imbued with theory-laden assumptions. Whether a pair of terms are opposites is dependent on the theoretical frame of reference in which they are used. Given a rational-constructivist theory of learning, and the related shift in meaning, the terms "innate" and "learned" are no longer opposite in meaning. The shift in meaning of terms goes hand in hand with the shift in the theory about learning. There is no reason to think this is less true for theories in psychology than it is for those in biology, physics, and mathematics, and thus for terms like *learning* as opposed to *energy*, *matter*, and *number*.

Differences in the intended meaning of how a term is used within a discipline can provide clues that there is either an ongoing theory change or that qualitatively different theories are existing side by side. Gelman and Williams (1997) develop this theme with respect to the notion of *learning*. For a large number of psychologists, the term *learning* is embedded in a version of Empiricism and its assumption of a blank slate at birth. Within this theoretical frame of reference, it is true that terms like *biological constraint*, *innate* and *instinct* have meanings that are opposite to *learned*. As the everyday meanings of such terms are commonly paraphrased as *restricted*, *required*, *forced*, and pitted against words like *acquired*, *learned*, *experienced*, *educated*, we are not surprised when we are asked "how can a domain be both learned and innate?" This is a straightforward question, if it is posed within the framework of association theory. But it becomes a nonquestion within a theory that recognizes that innate mental structures include learning requirements. As our account is fundamentally committed to the premise that concept learning is what happens as a function of experience, it is a learning account. It is best classified as a rational-constructivist theory, as opposed to an empiricist or associationist theory, as regards its foundational assumptions. Also, it takes as given that learners must encounter domain-relevant experiences, even for core domains. Without the opportunity to interact with and store relevant data, there cannot be a forward moving construction of the knowledge of a domain, be it core or noncore in kind.

What constitutes learning in a domain— core or otherwise?

Like others we assume that learning leads to the build up of domain-relevant knowledge and relevant characteristics of such knowledge. Gelman and Williams (1997) couch their account of learning in terms of the kinds of mental learning tools that can contribute to the active construction of knowledge. They argue that the mind favors *structure-mapping* as the fundamental learning process (Gelman & Williams, 1997). Given the mind actively applies its existing structures to find examples of structured data in the environments with which it interacts, learning in core domains is privileged. Skeletal structures provide the beginning learner with the wherewithal to find and map inputs that are examples to available structures. Even though initial mental structures are skeletal in form, they nevertheless are available structures. For learning with understanding to occur in a noncore domain, the mind has to acquire both the structure and the domain-relevant data base of the novel domain. Therefore nascent skeletal structures help learners move onto relevant learning paths, ones that have the potential to support the mind's everpresent structure-mapping proclivities.

In sum, our mind's ever-present tendency to find and map inputs to our existing mental structures benefits from structure-mapping as a foundational learning device. This enables the recognition, identification, and assimilation, of relevant inputs with the result that there will be attention to the relevant learning paths in the environment that can nurture the acquisition of a coherent, data-rich, organized body of knowledge. In turn, the acquired knowledge base can foster upgrades in the range of inputs and specification of domain-relevant inputs. In these ways skeletal structures serve as initial, but not determining, domain-specific engines of learning for young minds.

The ability to achieve a structural map is as critical for learning in a noncore as it is in a core domain. However, learning in noncore domains can be handicapped for a straightforward reason: There is no domain-relevant structure, not even a skeletal one, to start the ball rolling. This means that the mental structures have to be acquired de novo for noncore domains like chess, sushi making, computer programming, literary criticism, and so on. In these cases, learners have a twofold task. They have to acquire both domain-relevant structures and a coherent base of domain-relevant knowledge about the content of that domain (see also, Brown, 1990). It is far from easy to assemble truly new conceptual structures (see, for example, Carey, 1991; Chi, 1992; Kuhn, 1970) and it takes a very long time. Something resembling formal instruction is usually required and often this is not effective unless there is extended practice and effort on the part of the learner (Ericsson & Smith, 1996). Efforts to provide domain-relevant instruction in noncore domains must recognize and overcome a crucial challenge: Learners may assimilate inputs to existing conceptual structures even when those inputs are intended to force accommodation and conceptual change (Gelman, 1993, 1994; Slotta, Chi, & Joram, 1995). That is, learners may fail to interpret novel inputs as intended and instead treat the data as further examples of the kinds of understanding they have available. As discussed later, the risk for this happening is especially high in mathematics classes.

As learning can and does take place in noncore domains, it must be that there are learning tools that serve as mental stepping stones. In this regard, it is important to keep in mind the fact that humans learn symbolic and notational systems. I also note that imitation and analogical learning can function as examples of structure creation and structure mapping, respectively, if care is taken to assure that the learner attends to and assimilates the structure of the offered data bases (Brown & Campione, 1996; Gelman & Lee Gattis, 1995; Piaget, 1951). For example, young children know that there are different rules for different notation systems, even though they have much to learn about the details and conventions for these (Brenneman, Massey, Machado, & Gelman, 1996). They are also pretty good at imitating what they see others do and at using basic conversational rules (Siegal, 1991). Together, these structural tools can be viewed as learning tools for identifying what aspects of new information is relevant and what information about different domains should be treated as coming from different categories, events, and so on. They afford the mind ways of identifying relevant novel data sets and setting up new memory drawers in which to collect and keep together in memory the new domain-relevant knowledge. Over time, these memory drawers will start to fill up, most likely in an unorderly way, given the lack of understanding about them. But, with continued interaction with inputs and informal or formal instruction about these, there will come a point where we will, so to speak, look into our messy memory drawers, and organize them in a systematic way (cf. Karmiloff-Smith, 1992). How and when this happens are key research questions that are especially likely to inform understanding about the shift from novice to expert levels of knowledge.

What to do about frequency effects?

We know that young children are sensitive to the frequency with which they encounter examples of a relevant data set, including the frequency of irregular verbs (e.g. Marcus et al., 1992; Plunkett & Marchman, 1991) and relevant attributes of concept exemplars (e.g. Macario, 1991). Indeed, there is good evidence that animals and humans of all ages keep track *automatically* of the frequency of relevant events and objects (Hasher and Zacks, 1979; Gallistel, 1990). For example, Hasher and Zacks (1979) showed 5- to 8-year-old children a series of pictures, in which each picture appeared 0–4 times. Children in all age groups were highly and equally successful at reporting how many times a picture had been shown, even though they did not receive any instructions to keep track of this information. Similarly, robust abilities to pick up frequency information about objects or events abound. Hasher and Zacks (1984) have documented frequency learning across populations (college students, learning-disabled children, depressed and elderly persons), as well as across a wide range of variable-frequency materials (letters of the alphabet, familiar words, surnames, and professions).

Some might conclude that data such as the preceding provide especially strong support for an associationist account of learning, in particular, and domain-general learning mechanisms in general. Neither conclusion is warranted, given that the proposed computational device computes one and only one kind of data, frequency. As regards the status of association theory, it is well to keep in mind that the theory assumes that association strength builds as a function of frequency and contiguity. Within associationism, frequency (as well as contiguity) is a condition for the formation and increase in strength of a given association. The more frequent a given pairing, the greater the strength of the association stored in memory. Certain associations are stronger than others because they had the benefit of more frequent encounters with particular pairings of stimuli, and/or short delays between the CS, UCS, longer or larger rewards, and the like. Note, that there is nothing about the associative strength that represents the values of the conditions that contributed to its growth. The idea is that frequency and contiguity work together to determine associative strength, not create representations of the values of these factors. If associative strengths do not contain information about the frequencies that contributed to them, it follows that frequency information cannot be recovered from them. The fact that the mind does register the frequency with which a class of objects or events occurs is a real problem for association theory. If frequency is not encoded by associative strength, associations cannot be the mental device that keeps track of frequency *per se*. It must be that there is some other way that the mind is able to represent the frequency data it encounters as frequency *per se*.

If we are to argue that the mind does, in fact, keep track of the frequency of relevant learning events, then we need a mechanism to accomplish this. This is what motivated Gelman and Williams (1997) to conclude that the mind has a frequency-computing learning tool that is called in to play by a domain when frequency is relevant information for that domain. Our idea that there is a frequency-computing device allows us to make sense of the data that are used to favor feature and prototpye theories of concepts over theories that include the notions of essences, conceptual coherence, and core domains as explanatory hypotheses. The assumption is that a domain can engage a frequency counter to keep track of how often it encounters domain-relevant exemplars or characteristics.

The fact that more than one domain can make use of frequency data does *not* license the conclusion that a frequency-computing learning tool is domain-general.

Discussions of domain-general learning processes are treated as content neutral. Even if different domains call on a frequency-computing learning tool, the stuff that is counted is given by the principles of the domain. Cheng and her colleagues (Cheng, 1997) refer to domain-specific abilities to compute frequencies that index relevant and irrelevant covariations for particular cases of knowledge. Others appeal to the use of a frequency counter as part of their explanation of how children learn to classify moving objects as animate or inanimate based on the causal conditions of animate versus inanimate motion (Gelman, 1990; Gelman, Durgin, & Kaufman, 1995). Keil (1995) has proposed that learning about the structures of "concepts in theories" is supplemented by feature tabulation processes. Schwartz and Reisberg (1991) suggest that we may need a three-part theory of concepts, in which "concepts are represented by a prototype, some set of specifically remembered cases, and some further abstract information" (p. 391), where the parts all interact to accomplish correct similarity judgments and inferences. In our account, the recorded knowledge of frequencies and contingencies underlies subjects' ability to answer questions in ways that make them look like they learn prototypes and some salient domain-relevant exemplars. More generally, our account provides a way to reconcile these response patterns with the compelling arguments against defining feature and prototype theories (Armstrong, Gleitman, & Gleitman, 1983; Fodor & Lepore, 1996). High-frequency features or exemplars data are more memorable. Because low-frequency encounters are less memorable, they are less likely to be accessed in tasks designed to encourage subjects to provide "defining" features for a given concept. Nevertheless, if the example of the concept yields a structural map to the domain in question, the item or event will be accepted as one that belongs to the concept in question. Frequency computations provide heuristic value, they support reasonable guesses about the identity of novel instances. But, in the end, they do not determine concept identification. This is a job for structural-mapping (see also Holyoak & Thagard, 1997).

How can knowledge be innate and yet variably applied?

Some authors argue that findings of early conceptual competence are obtained under too limited a set of conditions and therefore do not justify the attribution of principled knowledge about objects and numerosity. For example, Fischer and Bidell (1991) take the fact that infants fail to reveal comparable knowledge on Piagetian tasks as compelling reason to reject Baillargeon's and Spelke's attributions of conceptual competence for objects to the very young. Systematic within and across condition variability in the extent to which performance conforms to abstract principles is consistent with traditional learning and developmental theories in which unprincipled "habits" are acquired prior to the induction of principles.

Contrary to widespread assumption, wih rare exception, any genetic program carries with it extensive requirements for interactions with those kinds of environments that can nurture, support, and channel the differentiation of adult structure. In the absence of those environments, the program will almost certainly fail. The same is surely true for skeletal mental structures; the existence of a primordial input-structuring mechanism does not guarantee that related knowledge will spring forth full-blown the moment the individual encounters a single example of the requisite environment. Without opportunities to interact with, learn about, and construct domain-relevant inputs, as well as to practice components of relevant action plans, the contributions of skeletal structures will remain unrealized, or will lead to atypical developments. Learners must encounter opportunities to interact with and assimilate relevant supporting environments (c.f. Scarr, 1993). It also follows that variability is a characteristic of any learning, be it about core domains that benefit from skeletal structures or noncore domains that do not (cf. Siegler & Shipley, 1995). It therefore behooves us to consider more carefully how one understands systematic cross-task variability in different accounts of concept development.

Gelman and Greeno (1989) point out that there are a number of systematic sources of variability that can mask conceptual competence, including limited procedural and interpretative competence. As Gallistel and Gelman's (1992) competence model of preverbal counting makes use of mechanisms whose outputs are inherently variable, it is also necessary to find ways to relate details of variability at this level to choices of models. Gelman and Greeno (1989) expand on their initial proposal (Greeno, Riley, & Gelman, 1984) that competent plans of action require the successful integration of *conceptual, procedural,* and *interpretative* (utilization) competence. A competent plan of action must honor the constraints of conceptual competence. For example, for a plan for counting to be competent, it must incorporate the constraints of the one-to-one counting principle. The plan must not embrace component acts of double tagging, item skipping, or tag repeating. Additionally, the plan has to be responsive to constraints on the interpretations of the task setting, instructions, domain-related terms, conversational rules, and so on. The limited development or misapplication of setting-relevant conversational rules can lead to faulty plans of action in a given setting and therefore variability in success levels across studies or tasks. One example of this is illustrated in Gelman et al.'s (1986) use of the "Doesn't Matter" counting task that asked children to count a row of items in a novel way.

The Doesn't Matter task begins when the experimenter points to an object that is not at an end of a row of items and asks the child to make that object "the one" and count all of the objects. To accomplish this, a child has to skip back and forth over the items while counting, switch the designated item with one that is at an end, or count as if the row of items were in a circle. Interestingly, very young children who were given a chance to count a row of items before they started the Doesn't Matter task did more poorly than children who had no pre-test counting experience. Inspection of their error patterns on the experimental task revealed that the latter group tried to find a way to meet the constraints of the new task while counting from one end of the array to another. It is as if they took their regular counting experience as an instruction to continue to count in the conventional way.

Conversational rule use also contributes a systematic source of variation to performance on the "How Many" task, one where individuals are to indicate how many items are present for different set sizes. This was illustrated in a study we reported in Gelman and Meck (1992). Adults were asked to participate in a control study for a task that is used with preschoolers. We scattered 18 counting blocks on a table and asked "How many blocks are here?". Subjects were encouraged to think out loud while figuring out "How Many" there were but they were not told to count. All subjects counted (sometimes using grouping strategies, e.g. counting by twos); only one repeated the last tag spontaneously. This means that almost no one stated the cardinal value after they had completed counting. This failure of subjects to answer the question we asked led us to use a second version of the procedure in a follow-up experiment. Now we repeated the "How Many" question if subjects had completed counting and did not repeat their last counting tag. Still, only 4 of 10 individuals answered in a straightforward way, that is by stating their last count tag when the question was repeated. The rest behaved as if they thought the question was odd. For example, one person laughed nervously and another said she assumed we were telling her that her initial count was wrong and so she recounted; another person said "Eighteen, I hope".

We expected these results on the grounds that repeating a question is a violation of the conversational rules adults follow, especially ones that converge on the maxim "do not repeat the obvious". Given that young children are likewise sensitive to this stricture (Siegal, 1991), it is reasonable to conclude that similar results reflect a common interpretative competence variable. This is important because much has been made of the variable ways that young children respond on "How Many?" tasks. For example, in one of her tasks Wynn (1990) asked 2- to 4-year-old children to count so as to indicate "How Many" items were in a given display. Children younger than 3-and-a-half tended to simply count or recite as many count words as there are items; they stopped without repeating the last tag, i.e. without stating the cardinal value of the set. When their correct counts led to a repeat of the "How Many" questions young children recounted. Fuson (1988) holds that even older preschoolers—sometimes as old as 5 years of age—are likely to repeat the last tag when asked "How Many", after either a correct or incorrect count.

Wynn (1990) also reports that her younger subjects (especially between 2- and 3-and-a-half years of age) solved her "give X" task by grabbing 2 or 3 items no matter what the set size (other than one). Only "Non-Grabbers" counted out the requested number of items. Wynn concluded that "Grabbers" are especially disinclined to repeat the last tag after they count, doing so on only 26% of their correct count trials. In contrast, the mean percentage of cardinality answers of her "Counters" was 78%. As the tendency for children to give the cardinal answer after their count shifts abruptly at 3-and-a-half years—the same age that separates "Grabbers" from "Counters"—Wynn concludes that the younger children do not have a principled understanding of counting. Her idea is that they do not understand that counting is related in a principled way to the cardinal value of the set. This is unlikely given that adults behave in the same way. As no one would conclude that adults do not have a principled understanding of the count numbers, we should entertain the hypothesis that the seemingly straightforward "How Many" task is not especially good for assessing principled understanding of the principles of counting and their relationship to principles of addition and subtraction. This is why there has been a renewed effort in my lab to develop new counting and arithmetic tasks that are suitable for use with very young children (see Gelman, 1993).

The Gallistel and Gelman (1992) model of nonverbal counting illustrates how there can also be systematic variability that follows from some aspects of the operation of the machinery in whose structure the implicit principles of the conceptual competence resides. In our model, the preverbal counting mechanism generates mental magnitudes to represent numerosities; there is trial-to-trial variability in the magnitudes generated to represent one and the same set size; and this variability obeys Weber's law, that is, the standard deviation of the distribution increases in proportion to its mean. Given an additional systematic source of variability, an increasing tendency to lose track of what has and what remains to be counted as set size increases, it is likely that the spread on the distributions as set size increases is even wider than predicted from the Weber law. This is important in understanding a potent within-task source of systematic variability in children's numerical performance, the effect of the set size. It is especially pertinent to discussion of the systematic effect of set size on the tendency of infants and young children to respond correctly to the numerical information in a display.

To date, demonstrations of infants' ability to use numerical information have been limited to set sizes of 3 to 4. This fact has encouraged many to conclude that infants use perceptual mechanisms in lieu of mechanisms that embody implicit numerical principles. The favored perceptual mechanism is "subitizing", an example of a process that is assumed to allow subjects to make discriminations between set sizes without any implicit or explicit understanding of numerical principles (e.g. Cooper, 1984; Cooper, Campbell, & Blevins, 1983; Sophian, 1994; von Glaserfeld, 1982).

The preference for a subitizing account of how infants respond to variations produced by different set sizes is tied to studies of the reaction time adults require to state the number of dots in an array. Over the entire range of numerosities, the greater the numerosity, the longer the reaction time, but the first few increments in reaction time per additional dot in the display are smaller. (For reviews, see Gallistel & Gelman, 1992; Mandler & Shebo, 1982). As the slope of the reaction times function in the small number range ($N < 5$) is apparently shallower than in the large number range, it is commonly assumed that different processes underlie the responses to the small and large sets, subitizing and counting, respectively. If one yokes infants' failures on larger sets to the assumption that a counting mechanism is needed for larger set sizes, it follows that infants are limited to the use of a subitizing process. This would allow infants to succeed with very small sets but make it impossible for them to succeed on larger sets. On the subitizing model, the ability to discriminate threeness from twoness is akin to the ability to discriminate treeness from cowness; unlike counting processes, it does not depend in any way on numerical principles. There are several problems with this line of reasoning.

Conclusions that infants use a perception-only "subitizing" mechanism are based in large part on a methodological decision to score infants' numerical discriminations as correct (exact) or not, rather than looking at the variance in errors that are produced for larger set sizes. This method is unable to determine whether errors are due to an inability to use a preverbal counting process, or instead to increases in inherent variability. Thus, the claim that infants cannot deal at all with larger numbers is problematic. To distinguish between these alternatives, it will be necessary to find ways to obtain infants' estimates of variability as a function of set size. This has not yet been done, but corresponding studies have already been done with animals that reveal an ability to use set sizes much greater than 3 or 4. Because the infant data that do exist in other areas of numerical reasoning map well onto the animal data, Gallistel and Gelman (1992) have proposed that infants use a mechanism that is like the animal counting model developed by Church and Meck (1984).

Core domains and cultural variation?

Although different cultures use different lists and although older individuals might work with numbers in their head and use larger values, the underlying structure of the reasoning is the same. Different count lists all honor the same counting principles (Gelman & Gallistel, 1978) and different numbers are made by adding, subtracting, composing, and decomposing natural numbers that are thought of in terms of counting sets. The mathematical operations involved are always addition and subtraction, even if the task is stated as a multiplication or division one. In the latter case, people use repeated addition and subtraction to achieve an answer. Those who have learned to count by multiples of one, e.g. by fives, tens, fifties, hundreds, etc., are at an advantage because they can count and add faster than if they had to count by one (Nunes, Schliemann, & Cararaher, 1993; Vergnaud, 1983). This commonality of structure across tasks and settings is an important additional line of evidence for the idea that counting principles and some simple arithmetic principles are universal. So too are the cross-cultural studies of "street" arithmetic.

Variations in performance levels and time to learn the count list are systematically related to schooling, the degree to which numbers are used in the everyday activities of a culture, what functions the count list serves, and the degree to which the base-10 structure is transparent in a given language system (e.g. Miller, Smith, Zhu, & Zhang, 1995; Saxe, 1979; Zaslavsky, 1973). For example, in Chinese, the words for 11, 12, 13, . . . , 20 translate as 10-1, 10-2, 10-3, . . . , 2-10s, 2-10s-1, 2-10s-3 . . . , 3-10s-1 . . . , etc. English count rules are not as transparent in the same range; consider the counting strings twelve, thirteen, fourteen, fifteen, and twenty, thirty, forty, and fifty. Miller et al. (1995) obtained the predicted interactions between age and range of count words on rate of learning. They found no differences for very young children learning to count in Chinese or English. That is, the number of count words learned was comparable. So too was the ability to use them to solve simple numerical problems. In contrast, Chinese-speaking children learned the teens more rapidly than English-speaking children. These are especially important findings for they illustrate the idea that common underlying conceptual structures can exist despite notable differences in how these play out in different cultures.

Those committed to the idea that the ability to learn about the natural numbers is culture specific might point to studies done in Africa and the South-Sea Islands (e.g. Menninger, 1969). The claim is that there are communities who cannot count, mainly because they use a small number of count words or hand-body configurations. However, the presumed limited ability to understand counting could be an artifact of cultural taboos against counting familiar objects, like cattle, houses, and children (Gelman & Gallistel, 1978). Some additional support for this hypothesis was obtained when, during a stay in Israel, my colleagues took me to visit a family who had emigrated from Ethiopia.[1] Rather than start with requests to count familiar objects, we decided to jump in and ask how to say various count words in Ahmaric. Questions about counting were addressed to the eldest male in the household and his answers in Ahmaric were interpreted by his Hebrew-speaking teenage daughter who had emigrated at an earlier date. By simply asking what was the word for a sample of "20, 31 . . ."; "100, 200, 301, . . .", "1000, 1001, . . .", etc., we ascertained that the father knew how to

---

[1] The visit occurred during June 1987 and was arranged by Dr B., a doctor much admired by the Falasha community. Others in the interview group were Professor Iris Levin, Tel Aviv University, and Dr Shaul Levin. Questions were addressed to the eldest male in the household; our interpreter was a teenage daugther who had emigrated ahead of other members of her family and already knew Hebrew. The "interview" was embedded in a conversation over tea that lasted about 45 minutes to an hour. The conversation took place in a combination of Hebrew, Ahmaric, and English. As it was the Sabbath, we did not write or record during the interview. Questions were prepared in advance and we wrote down our joint memories of anwers immediately after we left the family.

count verbally well into the thousands with a base-10 generative counting rule. This line of questioning stopped when we were given the Hebrew word for a million. No comparable word existed in the father's Ahmaric count vocabulary; he explained that this was because there were never that many things to count before he arrived in Israel. This led to discussions about what one counts. It was introduced with an open-ended format and then moved to an inquiry about specific kinds of items. When we asked if one counts children, the teenage daughter interrupted "You never count children. It's not done. . . . Well, except maybe in the hospital—when a doctor asks a pregnant woman".

It is true that some languages only have two or three count words. It does not follow, however, that the people who use these languages cannot count in a principled way, as is often suggested (e.g. Andrews, 1977; Menninger, 1969). The Bushmen of South Africa are a case in point. They indeed have but two separate count words. However, this does not keep them from counting at least to 10. They manage the latter by using the operation of addition to generate terms that represent successive larger cardinal values. For example, the word for eight translates as "two+two+two+two" (Flegg, 1989). Of course, this is the very same addition solution that plays so significant a role in "Street Mathematics". Thus, despite the notable differences in the particular verbal counting solutions that different cultures embrace, there is overlap at the structured, counting principle level.

There is nothing about the structural description of the counting principles that requires counts to be the tags used in the service of counting with understanding. Some cultures use hand configurations and body positions as the tagging entries in their count list (Zaslavsky, 1973). The Oksapmin of New Guinea provide us with an especially compelling case of using sequential positions on the body as counting tags. Their count list is made up of 29 unique entries that starts with the right thumb, which corresponds to "1", moves to the right index finger to "2" and so on (Saxe, 1979). Tagging continues to the right, up through points on the right arm and shoulder, around the outside of the head, down the left shoulder and arm, and ending with the left thumb which corresponds to "29". We cannot claim that these count lists are not "real" count lists because they are "concrete" and not "abstract" (i.e. verbal). Saxe (1981) found that the Oksapmin use their lists in a principled way. He first told the participants in his study about people in a far-away village who started their count on the left side of their bodies instead of the right side. Then he continued with the fact that men from theirs and the far-away village counted sweet potatoes, ending their counts at the same body part (e.g. left shoulder). Finally, he asked who would have counted more potatoes, themselves or those from the other far-away village? If they had said that the men from both villages counted the same number, we could conclude that they were not using body parts as arbitrary symbols in an ordered list. However, the participants did answer appropriately, depending on which villager's system was used. We can conclude that they were able to use both counting and reasoning principles.

Further evidence for the worldwide use of counting and the arithmetic principles of addition and subtraction is presented in Crump (1990). Compelling examples are provided by studies of "Street Arithmetic". Reed and Lave (1979) found that Liberian tailors who had not been to school solved arithmetic problems by laying out a set of familiar objects (e.g. buttons, pebbles), or drawing lines on paper, and then counting them. Nunes et al. (1993) found that 9- to 15-year-old street vendors were able to indicate what a number of coconuts would cost by performing a chain of additions on known numbers. For example, a 9-year-old said "Forty, eighty, one twenty" when asked the cost for 3 coconuts at a price of 40 cruzeiros each. When another child was asked to determine how much a customer would have to pay for 15 of an item costing 50 cruzeiros each, he answered, "Fifty, one hundred, one fifty, two hundred, two fifty. (Pause). Two fifty, five hundred, five fifty, six hundred, six fifty, seven hundred, seven fifty" (p. 43, Nunes et al.).

Thus we see that when the focus is on the abstract level of structure, there are multiple lines of evidence that fit together to support the conclusion that skeletal principles of counting and arithmetic reasoning form a core domain. Similar conclusions are reached by others in their studies of biological classifications (Atran, 1994; Gelman & Wellman, 1991; Simons & Keil, 1995) and the animate-inanimate distinction (Gelman et al., 1995; Premack & Premack, 1995). This makes it possible for cognitive universals to live alongside culturally-specific interpretations (Boyer, 1995; Gelman & Brenneman, 1994; Sperber, 1994) and illustrates how a domain can be both innate and learned.

As skeletal principles give the young constructivist mind a way to attend to and selectively process data, they similarly contribute to the nurturing and development of the concepts that are related to the structure of the domain in question. No matter how skeletal these first principles may be, they still can organize the search for, and assimilation of, inputs that can feed the development of the concepts of the domain. Actively assimilated inputs help flesh out the skeletal structure. The more structured knowledge there is, the more it is possible for the learner to find domain-relevant inputs to attend to and actively assimilate to the existing structure. The positive feedback set up underlies the continual build up of the knowledge structure within the domain.

ACKNOWLEDGEMENTS

Partial Support for the preparation of this paper came from NSF (Grant No. DBS—92009741). Special thanks to Stephanie Reich for her helpful comments on earlier drafts.

REFERENCES

Andrews, F. E. (1977). *Numbers, please*. New York: Teacher's College Press, Columbia University.

Atran, S. (1994). Core domains versus scientific theories: Evidence from systematics and Itza-Maya folkbiology. In S. A. Gelman & L. A. Hirschfeld (Eds.), *Mapping the mind: Domain specificity in cognition and culture* (pp. 316–340). New York: Cambridge University Press.

Armstrong, S. L., Gleitman, L. R., & Gleitman, H. (1983). What some concepts might not be. *Cognition, 13*, 263–308.

Baillargeon, R. (1995). Physical reasoning in infancy. In M. S. Gazzaniga (Ed.), *The cognitive neurosciences* (pp. 181–204). Cambridge, MA: MIT Press.

Baillargeon, R., Spelke, E. S., & Wasserman, S. (1985). Object permanence in five-month-old infants. *Cognition, 20*, 191–208.

Boyer, P. (1995). Causal understandings in cultural representations: Cognitive constraints on inferences from cultural input. In D. Sperber, D. Premack, & A. J. Premack (Eds.), *Causal cognition: A multidisciplinary approach* (pp. 615–644). Oxford: Oxford/Clarendon Press.

Brenneman, K., Massey, C., Machado, S., & Gelman, R. (1996). Notating knowledge about words and objects: preschoolers' plans differ for "writing" and drawing. *Cognitive Development, 11*, 397–419.

Brown, A. L. (1990). Domain-specific principles affect learning and transfer in children. *Cognitive Science, 14*, 107–133.

Brown, A. L., & Campione, C. (1996). Psychological theory and the design of innovative learning environments: On procedures, principles and systems. In L. Schauble & R. Glaser (Eds.), *Contributions of instructional innovation to understanding theory* (pp. 289–325). Hillsdale, NJ: Lawrence Erlbaum Associates Inc.

Carey, S. (1991). Knowledge acquisition: Enrichment or conceptual change? In S. Carey & R. Gelman (Eds.), *Epigenesis of mind: Studies in biology and cognition* (pp. 257–291). Hillsdale, NJ: Lawrence Erlbaum Associates Inc.

Carey, S., & Spelke, E. S. (1994). Domain specific knowledge and conceptual change. In L. A. Hirschberg & S. A. Gelman (Eds.), *Domain specificity in cognition and culture* (pp. 169–200). New York: Cambridge University Press.

Cheng, P. W. (1997). From covariation to causation: A causal power theory. *Psychological Review, 103*, 367–405.

Cheng, K., & Gallistel, C. R. (1984). Testing the geometric power of an animal's spatial representation. In T. G. B. H. Roitblat & H. Terrace (Eds.), *Animal cognition* (pp. 409–423). Hillsdale, NJ: Erlbaum Associates Inc.

Chi, M. T. H. (1992). Conceptual change within and across ontological categories: Examples from learning and discovery in science. In R. Giere (Ed.), *Cognitive models of science: Minnesota studies in the philosophy of science* (pp. 129–186). Minneapolis, MN: University of Minnesota Press.

Church, R. M., & Meck, W. H. (1984). The numerical attribute of stimuli. In H. L. Roitblat, T. G. Bever, & H. S. Terrace (Eds.), *Animal cognition* (pp. 445–464). Hillsdale, NJ: Lawrence Erlbaum Associates Inc.

Cooper, R. G., Jr. (1984). Early number development: Discovering number space with addition and subtraction. In C. Sophian (Ed.), *Origins of cognitive skill* (pp. 147–192). Hillsdale, NJ: Lawrence Erlbaum Associates Inc.

Cooper, R. G., Jr., Campbell, R. L., & Blevins, B. (1983). Numerical representation from infancy to middle childhood: What develops? In D. L. Rogers & J. A. Sloboda (Eds.), *The acquisition of symbolic skills* (pp. 523–533). New York: Plenum.

Crump, T. (1990). *The anthropology of numbers*. Cambridge: Cambridge University Press.

Ericsson, K. A., & Smith, J. (Eds.) (1996). *Toward a general theory of expertise: Prospects and limits*. New York: Cambridge University Press.

Fernald, A. (1985). Four-month-old infants prefer to listen to motherese. *Infant Behavior and Development, 8*, 181–195.

Fischer, K. W., & Bidell, T. (1991). Constraining nativist inferences about cognitive development. In S. Carey & R. Gelman (Eds.), *The epigenesis of mind: Essays on biology and cognition* (pp.199–235). Hillsdale, NJ: Lawrence Erlbaum Associates Inc.

Flegg, G. (Ed.) (1989). *Number through the ages: Reader in the history of mathematics*. London: Macmillan in association with The Open University.

Fodor, J. A., & Lepore, E. (1996). The red herring and the pet fish: Why concepts still can't be prototypes. *Cognition*, *58*, 253–270.

Fuson, K. C. (1988). *Children's counting and concepts of number.* New York: Springer-Verlag.

Gallistel, C. R. (1990). *The organization of learning.* Cambridge, MA: MIT Press.

Gallistel, C. R., & Gelman, R. (1992). Preverbal and verbal counting and computation. Special Issue: Numerical cognition. *Cognition*, *44*, 43–74.

Gelman, R. (1990). First principles organize attention to and learning about relevant data: Number and the animate-inanimate distinction as examples. *Cognitive Science*, *14*, 79–106.

Gelman, R. (1993). A Rational-constructivist account of early learning about numbers and objects. In D. Medin (Ed.), *Learning and motivation* (pp. 61–96). New York: Academic Press.

Gelman, R. (1994). Constructivism and supporting environments. In D. Tirosh (Ed.), *Implicit and explicit knowledge: An educational approach* (pp. 55–82). Norwood, NJ: Ablex.

Gelman, R., & Brenneman, K. (1994). First principles can support both universal and culture-specific learning about number and music. In L. A. Hirschfeld & S. Gelman (Eds.), *Mapping the mind: Culture and domain-specificity* (pp. 369–390). New York: Cambridge University Press.

Gelman, R., Durgin, F., & Kaufman, L. (1995). Distinguishing between animates and inanimates: Not by motion alone. In D. S. Sperber, D. Premack, & A. J. Premack (Eds.), *Causal cognition: A multidisciplinary approach* (pp. 150–184). Oxford: Clarendon Press.

Gelman, R., & Gallistel, C. R. (1978). *The child's understanding of number.* Cambridge, MA: Harvard University Press.

Gelman, R., & Lee Gattis, M. (1995). Trends in educational psychology in the United States. In *Recent trends and developments in educational psychology: Chinese and American perspectives. Educational studies and documents, Vol. 61* (pp. 23–52). Paris, France: UNESCO Publishing.

Gelman, R., & Greeno, J. G. (1989). On the nature of competence: Principles for understanding in a domain. In L. B. Resnick (Ed.), *Knowing and learning: Essays in honor of Robert Glaser* (pp. 125–186). Hillsdale, NJ: Erlbaum Associates Inc.

Gelman, R., & Meck, B. (1992). Early principles aid initial but not later conceptions of number. In J. Bideaud, C. Meljac, & J. Fischer (Eds.), *Pathways to number* (pp. 171–189). Hillsdale, NJ: Lawrence Erlbaum Associates Inc.

Gelman, R., Meck, E., & Merkin, S. (1986). Young children's numerical competence. *Cognitive Development*, *1*, 1–29.

Gelman, S. A., & Wellman, H. M. (1991). Insides and essence: Early understandings of the non-obvious. *Cognition*, *38*, 213–244.

Gelman, R., & Williams, E. (1997). Enabling constraints on cognitive development. In D. Kuhn & R. S. Siegler (Eds.), *Cognition, perception and language. Vol. 2. Handbook of child development.* (5th ed.) (pp. 575–630). (W. Damon, Ed.) New York: Wiley.

Gould, J. L., & Marler, P. (1987). Learning by instinct. *Scientific American*, *256*, 74–85.

Greeno, J. G., Riley, M. S., & Gelman, R. (1984). Conceptual competence and children's counting. *Cognitive Psychology*, *16*, 94–143.

Hasher, L. & Zacks, R. T. (1979). Automatic and effortful processes in memory. *Journal of Experimental Psychology*, *108*, 356–388.

Hasher, L., & Zacks, R. T. (1984). Automatic processing of fundamental information: The case of frequency of occurrence. *American Psychologist*, *39*, 1372–1388.

Holyoak, K., & Thagard, P. (1997). The analogical mind. *American Psychologist*, *52*, 35–44.

Juscyck, P. W. (1996). *The discovery of spoken language.* Cambridge, MA: MIT/Bradford Books.

Karmiloff-Smith, A. (1992). *Beyond modularity: A developmental perspective on cognitive science.* Cambridge, MA: Bradford/MIT Press.

Keil, F. C. (1995). The growth of causal understandings of natural kinds. In D. S. Sperber, D. Premack, & A. J. Premack (Eds.), *Causal cognition: A multidisciplinary approach* (pp. 234–302). Oxford: Clarendon Press/Oxford Press.

Knudsen, E. (1983). Early auditory experience aligns the auditory map of space in the optic tectum of the barn owl. *Science*, *222*, 939–942.

Kuhn, T. S. (1970). *The structure of scientific revolutions* (2nd ed.). Chicago, IL: University of Chicago Press.

Lee, K., & Karmiloff-Smith, A. (1996). The development of external symbol systems: the child as a notator. In R. Gelman & T. Au Kit-fong (Eds.), *Perceptual and cognitive development* (pp. 185–211). San Diego, CA: Academic Press.

Leslie, A. (1995). A theory of agency. In D. S. Sperber, D. Premack, & A. J. Premack (Eds.), *Causal cognition: A multidisciplinary approach* (pp. 121–141). Oxford: Clarendon Press.

Leslie, A. M. (1994). ToMM, ToBy, and Agency: Core architecture and domain specificity. In S. A. G. Lawrence & A. Hirschfeld (Eds.), *Mapping the mind: Domain specificity in cognition and culture* (pp. 119–148). New York: Cambridge University Press.

Macario, J. F. (1991). Young children's use of color and classification: Foods and canonically colored objects. *Cognitive Development, 6*, 17–46.

Mandler, J. M., & McDonough, L. (1996). Drinking and driving don't mix: Inductive generalization in infancy. *Cognition, 59*, 307–335.

Mandler, G., & Shebo, B. J. (1982). Subitizing: An analysis of its component processes. *Journal of Experimental Psychology: General, 11*, 1–22.

Marcus, G. F., Ullman, M., Pinker, S., Hollander, M., Rosen, T. L., & Xu, F. (1992). Overregularization in language acquisition. *Monographs of the Society for Research in Child Development, 57*, Serial No. 228.

Marler, P. (1991). The instinct to learn. In S. Carey & R. Gelman (Eds.), *The epigenesis of mind* (pp. 37–66). Hillsdale, NJ: Lawrence Erlbaum Associates Inc.

Marr, D. (1982). *Vision*. San Francisco, CA: Freeman.

Mehler, J., & Christophe, A. (1995). Maturation and learning of language in the first year of life. In M. S. Gazzaniga (Eds.), *The cognitive neurosciences* (pp. 943–954). Cambridge, MA: MIT Press.

Menninger, K. (1969). *Number words and number symbols*. Cambridge, MA: MIT Press.

Miller, K. F., Smith, C. M., Zhu, J., & Zhang, H. (1995). Preschool origins of cross-national differences in mathematical competence: The role of number-naming systems. *Psychological Science, 1*, 56–60.

Nelson, K. (1988). Constraints on word learning? *Cognitive Development, 3*, 221–246.

Nunes, T., Schliemann, A. D., & Carraher, D. W. (1993). *Street mathematics and school mathematics.* Cambridge: Cambridge University Press.

Piaget, J. (1951). *Play, dreams and imitation in childhood*. New York: Norton.

Plunkett, K., & Marchman, V. (1991). U-shaped learning and frequency effects in a multilayered perception: implications for child language acquisition. *Cognition, 38*, 43–102.

Premack, D., & Premack, A. J. (1995). Intention as psychological cause. In D. Sperber, D. Premack, & A. J. Premack (Eds.), *Causal cognition: A multidisciplinary debate* (pp. 185–199). Oxford: Clarendon Press/Oxford University Press.

Reed, H. J., & Lave, J. (1979). Arithmetic as a tool for investigating relations between culture and cognition. *American Ethnologist, 6*, 568–582.

Saxe, G. B. (1979). Developmental relations between notational counting and number conservation. *Child Development, 50*, 180–187.

Saxe, G. B. (1981). Body parts as numerals: A developmental analysis of numeration among the Oksapmin in Papua, New Guinea. *Child Development, 52*, 306–316.

Scarr, S. (1993). Genes, experience, and development. In D. Magnusson, P. Jules, & M. Casaer (Eds.), *Longitudinal research on individual development: Present status and future perspectives. European network on longitudinal studies on individual development* (pp. 26–50). Cambridge: Cambridge University Press.

Schwartz, B., & Reisberg, D. (1991). *Learning and memory*. New York: Norton.

Siegal, M. (1991). *Knowing children: Experiments in conversations and cognition*. Hove, UK: Lawrence Erlbaum Associates Ltd.

Siegler, R. S., & Shipley, C. (1995). Variation, selection, and cognitive change. In T. Simon & G. Halford (Eds.), *Developing cognitive competence: New approaches to process modeling* (pp. 31–76). Hillsdale, NJ: Lawrence Erlbaum Associates Inc.

Simons, D. J., & Keil, F. C. (1995). An abstract to concrete shift in the development of biological thought: The insides story. *Cognition, 56*, 129–163.

Simon, T. J., Hespos, S. J., & Rochat, P. (1995). Do infants understand simple arithmetic? A replication of Wynn (1992). *Cognitive Development, 10*, 253–269.

Slotta, J. D., Chi, M. T. H., & Joram, E. (1995). Assessing students' misclassifications of physics concepts: An ontological basis for conceptual change. *Cognition and Instruction, 13*, 373–400.

Sophian, C. (1994). *Children's numbers.* Madison, WI: WCB Brown & Benchmark.

Sperber, D. (1994). The modularity of thought and the epidemiology of repesentations. In L. A. Hirschfeld & S. A. Gelman (Eds.), *Mapping the mind: Domain specificity in cognition and culture* (pp. 39–67). New York: Cambridge University Press.

Starkey, P., Spelke, E. S., & Gelman, R. (1990). Numerical abstraction by human infants. *Cognition, 36*(2), 97–127.

van Loosbroek, E., & Smitsman, A. W. (1990). Visual perception of numerosity in infancy. *Developmental Psychology, 26*, 916–922.

Vergnaud, G. (1983). Multiplicative structures. In R. Lesh & M. Landau (Eds.), *Acquisition of mathematics concepts and processes.* New York: Academic Press.

von Glaserfeld, E. (1982). Subitizing: The role of figural patterns in the development of numerical concepts. *Archives de Psychologie, 50*, 191–218.

Wynn, K. (1990). Children's understanding of counting. *Cognition, 36*, 155–193.

Wynn, K. (1992). Addition and subtraction by human infants. *Nature, 358*, 749–750.

Wynn, K. (1995). Infants possess a system of numerical knowledge. *Current Directions in Psychological Science, 4*, 172–177.

Xu, F., & Carey, S. (1996). Infants' metaphysics: the case of numerical identity. *Cognitive Psychology, 30*, 111–153.

Zaslavsky, C. (1973). *Africa counts.* Boston, MA: Prindle, Wever & Schmidt.

CHAPTER TWENTY-SIX

Connectionism and development

Kim Plunkett
University of Oxford, Oxford, UK

What features of brain processing and neural development support linguistic and cognitive development in young children? To what extent are the profile and timing of development in young children determined by a preordained genetic programme. Does the environment play a crucial role in determining the patterns of change observed in children growing up? These questions have been of central concern to developmental psychologists for well over a century. Yet none of them have received answers that are generally accepted by the profession. This chapter reviews some recent computational modeling of developmental change in children that promises to contribute to a deeper understanding of the issues behind these questions. The computational modeling work exploits artificial neural networks that mimic some of the basic properties of neural processing in the brain. These networks involve densely connected webs of simple processing units that propagate and transform complex patterns of activity. When exposed to a training environment, they undergo a process of self-organization, yielding information processing systems that support new forms of behavior. The study of the dynamics of these systems and their learning capabilities promises to provide us with important clues as to the nature of the mechanisms underlying development in infants and young children.

Quels sont les aspects du traitement de l'information par le cerveau et du développement du système nerveux qui appuient le développement linguistique et cognitif chez les jeunes enfants? Dans quelle mesure le profil et la synchronisation du développement chez les jeunes enfants sont-ils établis par une programmation génétique prédéterminée? Est-ce que l'environnement joue un rôle crucial dans la détermination des modalités de changement observées chez les enfants lors de la croissance? Ces questions ont pris une importance capitale pendant plus d'un siècle chez les psychologues intéressés aux questions de développement. Par ailleurs, aucune d'entre elles n'a reçu de réponse généralement acceptable par la profession. Cette étude passe en revue certains modèles informatiques récents du processus de développement chez l'enfant, modèles qui promettent de contribuer à une compréhension en profondeur des problématiques qui sont derrière ces questions. Le travail de modélisation informatique exploite des réseaux nerveux artificiels qui imitent certaines des propriétés de base du traitement de l'information dans le cerveau. Ces réseaux impliquent des systèmes enchevêtrés densément interconnectés d'unités simples de traitement de l'information qui propagent et transforment des modèles complexes d'activité. Lorsqu'ils sont exposés à un environnement éducatif, ils subissent un processus d'auto-réorganisation qui donne des systèmes de traitement de l'information qui appuient les nouvelles formes de comportement. L'etude de la dynamique de ces systèmes et de leurs capacités d'apprentissage promet de nous livrer d'importants indices sur la nature des mécanismes qui sous-tendent le développement chez les nourrissons et les jeunes enfants.

A DEVELOPMENTAL PARADOX

Two findings in developmental psychology stand in apparent conflict. Piaget (1952) has shown that at a certain stage in development, children will cease in their attempts to reach for an object when it is partially or fully covered by an occluder. This finding is observed in children up to the age of about 6 months and is interpreted to indicate that the object concept is not well established in early infancy. The object representations that are necessary to motivate reaching and grasping behavior are absent. In contrast, other studies have shown that young infants will express surprise when a stimulus array is transformed in such a way that the resulting array does not conform to reasonable expectations. For example, change in heart rate, sucking, or GSR is observed when an object, previously visible, fails to block the path of a moving drawbridge or a loco-motive fails to reappear from a tunnel, or has changed color when it reappears (Baillargeon, 1993; Spelke, Katz, Purcell, Ehrlich, & Breinlinger, 1994). These results are interpreted as indicating that important representations of object properties such as form, shape, and the capacity to block the movement of other objects are already in place by 4 months of age. The conflict in these findings can be stated as follows: Why should the infant cease to reach for a partially or fully concealed object when it already controls representational characteristics of objects that confirm the stability of object properties over time, and that predict the interaction of those represented properties with objects that are visible in the perceptual array?

One answer to this conflict is that Piaget grossly underestimated young children's ability to retrieve hidden objects. However, this answer is no resolution to the conflict: Piaget's findings are robust. Alternatively, one might question Piaget's interpretation of his results. Young infants know a lot about the permanent properties of objects but recruiting object representations in the service of a reaching task requires additional sensorimotor skills which have little to do with the infant's understanding of the permanence of objects. Again, this response must be rejected. Young infants who are in full command of the skill to reach and grasp a visible object still fail to retrieve an object which is partially or fully concealed (von Hofsten, 1989). Motor skills are not the culprit here. The capacity to relate object knowledge to other domains seems to be an important part of object knowledge itself. Object knowledge has to be accessed and exercised.

A resolution

A resolution of the conflict can be found in considering some fundamental differences in the nature of the two types of task that infants are required to perform. In experiments that measure "surprise" reactions to unusual object transformations, such as failure to reappear from behind an occluder, the infant is treated as a passive observer (Baillargeon, 1993). In essence, the infant is evaluated for its expectations concerning the future state of a stimulus array. Failure of expectation elicits surprise. In the Piagetian task, the infant is required to actively transform the stimulus array. To achieve this, not only must the infant know where the object is but he/she must be able to coordinate that information with knowledge about the object's identity—typically, the infant reaches for objects he/she wants. We suppose that this coordination is relatively easy for visible objects, because actions are supported by externally available cues. However, when the object is out of sight, the child has to rely on internal representations of the object's identity and position. We assume that the internal representations for object position and identity develop separately. This assumption is motivated by recent neurological evidence that spatial and featural information is processed in separate channels in the human brain—the so-called "what" and "where" channels (Ungerlieder & Mishkin, 1982). In principle, the child could demonstrate knowledge of an object's position without demonstrating knowledge about its identity, or vice versa. Surprise reactions might be triggered by failure of infant expectations within either of these domains. For example, an object may suddenly change its featural properties or fail to appear in a predicted position. Internal representations are particularly important when the object is out of sight. Hence, we might expect infants to have greater difficulty performing tasks that involve the coordination or spatial and featural representations—such as reaching for hidden objects—when these representations are only partially developed.

Building a model

The outlined resolution constitutes a theory about the origins of infants' surprise reactions to objects' properties (spatial or featural) that do not conform to expectations and attempts to explain why these surprise reactions precede the ability to reach for hidden objects even though they possess the motor skills to do so. Mareschal, Plunkett, and Harris (1995) have constructed a computational model that implements the ideas outlined in this theory. The model consist of a complex neural network that processes a visual image of an object that can move across a flat plane. Different types of objects distinguished by a small number of features appear on the plane one at a time. These objects may or may not disappear behind an occluder. All objects move with a constant velocity so that if one disappears behind an occluder, it will eventually reappear on the other side. Object velocities can vary from one presentation to the next.

The network is given two tasks. First, it must learn to predict the next position of the moving object, including its position when hidden behind an occluder. Second, the network must learn to initiate a motor response to reach for an object, both when visible and when hidden. The network is endowed with several information-processing capacities that enable it fulfil these tasks. The image of the object moving across the plane is processed by two separate modules. One module learns to form a spatially invariant representation of the object so that it can recognize its identity irrespective of its position on the plane (Foldiak, 1991). The second module learns to keep track of the object but looses all information about the object's identity (Ungerlieder & Mishkin, 1982). This second module does all the work that is required to predict the position of the moving object. However, in order to reach for an object, the network needs to integrate information about the object's identity and its position. Both modules are required for this task. Therefore, the ability to reach can be impeded either because the representations of identity and position and not sufficiently developed or because the network has not yet managed to integrate these representations properly in the service of reaching.

Given the additional task demands imposed on the network for reaching, it would seem relatively unsurprising to discover that the network learns to track objects before it learns to reach for them. The crucial test of the model is whether

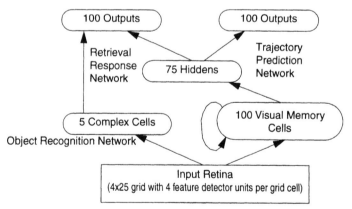

FIG. 26.1   The modular neural network (Mareschal et al., 1995) used to track and initiate reaching responses for visible and hidden objects. An object recognition network and a visual tracking network process information from an input retina. The object recognition network learns spatially invariant representations of the objects that move around the retina. The visual tracking network learns to predict the next position of the object on the retina. The retrieval response network learns to integrate information from the other two modules in order to initiate a reaching response. The complete system succeeds in tracking visible objects before it can predict the reappearance of hidden objects. It also succeeds in initiating a reaching response for visible objects before it learns to reach for hidden objects.

it is able to make the correct predictions about the late onset of reaching for hidden objects relative to visible objects. In fact, the model makes the right predictions for the order of mastery in tracking and reaching for visible and hidden objects. It quickly learns to track and reach for visible objects, tracking being slightly more precocious than retrieval. Next, the network learns to track occluded objects as its internal representations of position are strengthened and it is able to "keep track" of the object in the absence of perceptual input. However, the ability to track hidden objects together with the already mastered ability to reach for visible objects does not guarantee mastery of reaching for hidden objects. The internal representations that control the integration of spatial and featural information require further development before this ability is mastered.

Evaluating the model

Note how this modeling endeavor provides a working implementation of a set of principles that constitute a theory about how infants learn to track and reach for visible and hidden objects. It identifies a set of tasks that the model must perform and the information-processing capacities required to perform those tasks. All these constitute a set of assumptions that are not explained by the model. However, given these assumptions, the model is able to make correct predictions about the order of mastery of the different tasks. The model implements a coherent and accurate (not necessarily true—the assumptions might be wrong) theory. However, this model just like any other has a number of free parameters which the modeler may "tweak" in order to achieve the appropriate predictions. It is necessary to derive some novel predictions that can be tested against new experimental work with infants, in order to evaluate the generality of the solution the model has found. This model makes several interesting predictions, including improved tracking skills at higher velocities and imperviousness to unexpected feature changes while tracking. The first experimental prediction has been confirmed (see Mareschal et al., 1995) and the second prediction is currently being tested. This instance of model building and evaluation thus seems to support the initial insight that children's object representations develop in a fragmentary fashion, and that the development of these fragments of knowledge shape infant performance on various tasks in line with their manner of involvement in the tasks concerned.

CONNECTIONIST INSIGHTS

The model described in the previous section is an example of a computer simulation that uses the learning capabilities of artificial neural networks to construct internal representations of a training environment in the service of several tasks (reaching and tracking). Neural networks are particularly good at extracting the statistical regularities of a training environment and exploiting them in a structured manner to achieve some goal. They consist of a well-specified architecture driven by a learning algorithm. The connections or weights between the simple processing units that make up the network are gradually adapted over time in response to localized messages from the learning algorithm. The final configuration of weights in the network constitutes what it knows about the environment and the tasks it is required to perform.

Connectionist modeling provides a flexible approach to evaluating alternative hypotheses concerning the start state of the organism (or what we may think of as its innate endowment), the effective learning environment that the organism occupies, and the nature of the learning procedure for transforming the organism into its mature state. The start state of the organism is modeled by the choice of network architecture and computational properties of the units in the network. There are a wide range of possibilities that the developmentalist can choose from. The effective learning environment is determined by the manner in which the modeler chooses to define the task for the network, For example, the modeler must decide on a representational format for the pattern of inputs and outputs for the network, and highlight the manner in which the network samples patterns from the environment. These decisions constitute precise hypotheses about the nature of the learning environment. Finally, the modeler must decide how the network will learn. Again, a wide variety of learning algorithms are available to drive weight adaptation in networks. Any particular connectionist model embodies a set of decisions governing all of these factors, which are crucial for specifying clearly one's theory of development. Quite small changes in one of the choices can have dramatic changes for the performance of the model—some of them quite unexpected. Connectionist modeling offers a rich space for exploring a wide range of developmental hypotheses.

In the remainder of this chapter I will briefly review some connectionist modeling work that has explored some important areas in the hypothesis space of developmental theories. I aim to underscore four main lessons or insights that these models have provided:

1. When constructing theories in psychology, we use behavioral data from experiments or naturalistic observation as the objects that our explanations must fit. We attempt to infer underlying mechanisms from overt behavior. Connectionist modeling encourages us to be suspicious of the explanations we propose. Often, networks surprise us with the simplicity of the solution they discover to apparently complex tasks—sometimes leading us to the conclusion that learning may not be as difficult as we thought.
2. When we seen new forms of behavior emerging in development, we are tempted to conclude that come radical change has occurred in the mechanisms governing that behavior. Connectionist modeling has shown us that small and gradual internal changes in an organism can lead to dramatic

nonlinearities in its overt behavior—new behavior need not mean new mechanisms.

3. Theories of development are often domain specific. Behaviors that are discrete and associated with distinguishable modalities promote explanations that do not reach beyond the specifics of those modalities or domains. These encapsulated accounts often emphasize the impoverished character of the learning environment and lead to complex specifications of the organism's start state. Connectionist models provide a framework for investigating the interaction between modalities and a formalism for entertaining distributed as well as domain-specific accounts of developmental change. This approach fosters an appreciation of developing systems in which domain-specific representations emerge from a complex interaction of the organism's domain-general learning capacities with a rich learning environment.

4. Complex problems seem to require complex solutions. Mastery of higher cognitive processes appears to require the application of complex learning devices from the very start of development. Connectionist modeling has shown us that placing limitations on the processing capacity of developing systems during early learning can actually enhance their long-term potential. The ignorance and apparent inadequacies of the immature organism may, in fact, be highly beneficial for learning the solutions to complex problems. Small is beautiful.

INFERRING MECHANISMS FROM BEHAVIORS

Children make mistakes. Developmentalists use these mistakes as clues to discover the nature of the mechanisms that drive correct performance. For example, in learning the past tense forms of irregular verbs or plurals of irregular nouns, English children may sometimes overgeneralize the "-ed" or "s" suffixes to produce incorrect forms like "hitted" or "mans". These errors often occur after the child has already produced the irregular forms correctly, yielding the well-known U-shaped profile of development.

A dual-mechanism account

A natural interpretation of this pattern of performance is to suggest that early in development, the child learns irregular forms by rote, simply storing in memory the forms that occur in the adult language. At a later stage, the child recognizes the regularities inherent in the inflectional system of English and re-organizes his or her representation of the past tense or plural system to include a qualitatively new device that does the work of adding a suffix, obviating the need to memories new forms. During this stage, some of the original irregular forms may get sucked into this new system and suffer inappropriate generalization of the regular suffix. Finally, the child must sort out which forms cannot be generated with the new rule-based device. Children this by strengthening their

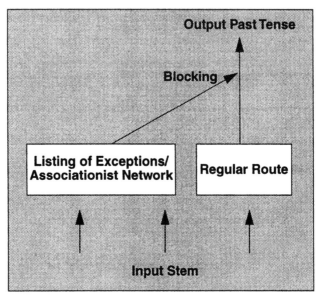

FIG. 26.2   The dual-route model for the English past tense (Pinker & Prince, 1988). The model involves a symbolic regular route that is insensitive to the phonological form of the stem and a route for exceptions that is capable of blocking the output from the regular route. Failure to block the regular route produces the correct output for regular verbs but results in overgeneralization errors for irregular verbs. Children must strengthen their representation of irregular past tense forms to promote correct blocking of the regular route.

memories for the irregular forms which can thereby block the application of the regular rule and eliminate overgeneralization errors (Pinker & Prince, 1988).

This account of the representation and development of past tense and plural inflections in English assumes that two qualitatively different types of mechanism are needed to capture the profile of development in young children—a rote memory system to deal with the irregular forms and a symbolic rule system to deal with the rest. The behavioral dissociation between regular and irregular forms—children make mistakes on irregular forms but not on regular forms—make the idea of two separate mechanisms very appealing. Double dissociations between regular and irregular forms in disordered populations add to the strength of the claim that separate mechanisms are responsible for these different types of forms: In some language disorders children may preserve performance on irregular verbs but not on regulars, whereas in other disorders the opposite pattern is observed.

Although the evidence is consistent with the view that a dual-route mechanism underlies children's acquisition of English inflectional morphology, this is no proof that the theory is correct. There may be other types of mechanistic explanations for these patterns of behavior and development. Connectionist modeling offers a tool for exploring alternative developmental hypotheses.

Single-mechanism account

One of the earliest demonstrations of the learning abilities of neural networks was for English past tense acquisition. Rumelhart and McClelland (1986) suggested that the source of children's errors in learning past tense forms was to be found in their attempts to systematize the underlying relationship that holds between the verb's stem and its past tense form. For most verbs in English, the sound of the stem does not affect the past tense form. You just add "ed" on the end. However, there is a small subset of verbs that exhibit a different relationship between stem and past tense form. For example, there is a set of no change verbs where the stem and past tense forms are identical (*hit→hit*). All these verbs end in an alveolar consonant (/t/ or /d/). Other verbs undergo a particular type of vowel change (*ring→rang, sing→sang*), apparently triggered by the presence of the rhyme *-ing* in the stem. Neural networks are particularly good at picking up on these types of regularities, so Rumelhart and McClelland trained a simple network to produce the past tense forms of verbs when presented with their stems. The details of the learning procedure and network architecture are not important here (see Plunkett, 1995, for a detailed review of this and related models).

What is important is to note that Rumelhart and McClelland were successful in training the network to perform the task and that en route to learning the correct past tense forms of English verbs, the network made mistakes that are similar to the kind of mistakes that children make during the acquisition of inflectional morphology. Furthermore, the network did not partition itself into qualitatively distinct devices during the process of learning—one for regular verbs and one for irregular verbs. The representation of both verb types seemed to be distributed throughout the entire matrix of connections in the network, Nevertheless, a behavioral dissociation between regular and irregular verbs was observed in the network. Most of its errors occurred on irregular verbs.

More recently, Marchman (1993) has shown that damage to a network trained on the past tense problem results in further dissociations between regular and irregular forms: Production of irregular forms remains intact, whereas production of regular verbs deteriorates, mimicking patterns of performance observed in disordered populations. As with the Rumelhart and McClelland model, the representation of regular and irregular verbs was distributed throughout the network, i.e. there was no evidence of dissociable mechanisms.

As it turns out, there were a lot of fundamental design problems with the Rumelhart and McClelland model that made it untenable as a realistic model of children's acquisition of the English past tense (Pinker & Prince, 1988). Some of these problems have been fixed, some have not (MacWhinney & Leinbach, 1991; Plunkett & Marchman, 1991, 1993; Cottrell & Plunkett, 1994). However, the basic insight that the original model offered still remains: The observation of behavioral dissociations in some domain of performance does not necessarily

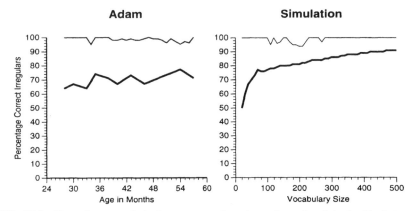

FIG. 26.3 Network overregularization errors on irregular verbs as found in the Plunkett and Marchman (1993) simulation compared to those produced by one of 83 children analyzed by Marcus et al., (1992). The thick line indicates the percentage of regular verbs in the child's/network's vocabulary at various points in learning.

imply the existence of dissociable mechanisms driving those dissociations in behavior. Behavioral dissociations can emerge as the result of subtle differences in the graded representations constructed by these networks for different types of verbs.

Of course, just because one can train a network to mimic children's performance in learning the past tense of English verbs does not mean that children learn them the same way as the network. The relatively simple learning system that Rumelhart and McClelland and other researchers have used to model children's learning may underestimate the complexity of the resources that children bring to bear on this problem. However, the neural network model does show that, in principle, children could use a relatively simple learning system to solve this problem. The modeling work has thereby enriched our understanding of the range and types of mechanism that might drive development in this domain.

DISCONTINUITIES IN DEVELOPMENT

Developmentalists often interpret discontinuities in behavior as manifesting the onset of a new stage or phase of development (Piaget, 1955; Karmiloff-Smith, 1979; Siegler, 1981). The child's transition to a new stage of development is usually construed as the onset of a new mode of operation of the cognitive system, perhaps as the result of the maturation of some cognitively relevant neural system. For example, the vocabulary spurt that often occurs towards the end of the child's second year has been explained as a naming insight (McShane, 1979), in which the child discovers that objects have names. Early in development, the child lacks the necessary conceptual machinery to link object names with their referents. The insight is triggered by a switch that turns on the naming machine. Similar arguments have been offered to explain the developmental stages through which children pass in mastering the object concept, understanding quantity and logical relations.

It is reasonable supposition that new behaviors are caused by new events in the child, just as it is reasonable to hypothesise that dissociable behaviors imply dissociable mechanisms. However, connectionism teaches us that new behaviors can emerge as a result of gradual changes in a simple learning device. It is well known that the behavior of dynamical systems unfolds in a nonlinear and unpredictable fashion (van Geert, 1991). Neural networks are themselves dynamic systems and they exhibit just these nonlinear properties. For example, Plunkett et al., (1992) trained a neural network to associate object labels with distinguishable images. The images formed natural (though overlapping) categories so that images that looked similar tended to have similar labels. The network was constructed so that it was possible to interrogate it about the name of an object when only given its image (call this production) or the type of image when only given its name (call this comprehension).

Network performance during training resembles children's vocabulary development during their second year. During the early stages of training, the network was unable to produce the correct names for objects—it got a few right but improvement was slow. However, with no apparent warning, production of correct names suddenly increased until all the objects in the network's training environment were correctly labeled. In other words, the network went through a vocabulary spurt. The network showed a similar improvement of performance for comprehension, except that the vocabulary spurt for comprehension preceded the productive vocabulary spurt. Last but not least, the network made a series of under- and over-extension errors en route to masterful performance—again, a phenomenon observed in young children using new words (Barrett, 1995).

There are several important issues that this model highlights: First, the pattern of behavior exhibited by the model is highly nonlinear *despite the fact that the network architecture and the training environment remain constant throughout learning.* The only changes that occur in the network are small increments in the connections that strengthen the association between an image and its corresponding label. No new mechanisms are needed to explain the vocabulary spurt. Gradual changes within a single learning device are, in principle, capable of explaining this profile of development. McClelland (1989) has made a similar point in the domain of children's developing understanding of weight/distance relations for solving balance beam problems (Siegler, 1981).

Second, the model predicts that comprehension precedes production. This in itself is not a particularly radical prediction to make. However, it is an emergent property of the network that was not "designed in" before the model was built. More important is the network's prediction that there should be a nonlinearity in the receptive direction, i.e. a vocabulary spurt in comprehension. When the model was first built, there was no indication in the literature as to the precision of this prediction. The prediction has since been shown to be correct (Reznick

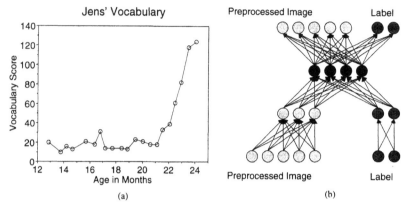

FIG. 26.4   (a) Profile of vocabulary scores typical for many children during their second year—taken from Plunkett (1993). Each data point indicates the number of different words used by the child during a recording session. It is usually assumed that the "bumps" in the curve are due to sampling error, though temporary regressions in vocabulary growth cannot be ruled out. The vocabulary spurt that occurs around 22 months is observed in many children (Bates, Bretherton, & Snyder, 1988). It usually consists of an increased rate of acquisition of nominals—specifically names for objects (McShane, 1979). (b) Simplified version of the network architecture used in Plunkett et al., 1992. The image is filtered through a retinal pre-processor prior to presentation to the network. Labels and images are fed into the networks through distinct "sensory" channels. The network is trained to reproduce the input patterns at the output—a process known as auto-association. Production corresponds to produce a label at the output when an image is presented at the input. Comprehension corresponds to producing an image at the output when a label is presented at the input.

& Goldfield, 1992). This model provides a good example of how a computational model can be used not only to evaluate hypotheses about the nature of the mechanisms underlying some behavior but also to generate predictions about the behavior itself. The ability to generate novel predictions about behavior is important in simulation work as it offers a way to evaluate the generality of the network model for understanding human performance.

The behavioral characteristics of the model are a direct outcome of the interaction of the linguistic and visual representations that are used as inputs to the network. The nonlinear profile of development is a direct consequence of the learning process that sets up the link between the linguistic and visual inputs, and the asymmetries in production and comprehension can be traced back to the types of representation used for the two types of input. The essence of the interactive nature of the learning process is underscored by the finding that the network learns less quickly when only required to perform the production task. Learning to comprehend object labels at the same time as learning to label objects enables the model to learn the labels faster.

It is important to keep in mind that this simulation is a considerable simplification of the task that the child has to learn in acquiring a lexicon. Words are not always presented with their referents and even when they are it is not always obvious (for a child who does not know the meaning of the word) what the word refers to. Nevertheless, within the constraints imposed on the model, its message is clear: New behaviors do not necessarily require new mechanisms and systems integrating information across modalities can reveal surprising emergent properties that would not have been predicted on the basis of exposure to one modality alone.

SMALL IS BEAUTIFUL

The immature state of the developing infant places the child at a decided disadvantage in relation to his or her mature, skilled caregivers. In contrast, the newborn of many other species are endowed with precocious skills at birth. Why is homo sapiens not born with a set of cognitive abilities that match the adult of the species? This state of affairs may seem all the more strange, given that we grow very few new neurons after birth and even synaptic growth has slowed dramatically by the first birthday. In fact, there may be important computational reasons for favoring a relatively immature brain over a cognitively precocious brain.

A complete specification of a complex nervous systems would be expensive in genetic resources. The programming required to determine fully the precise connectivity of any adult human brain far exceeds the information capacity in the human genome. Most current research in brain development and developmental neurobiology points to a dramatic genetic underspecification of the detailed architecture of the neural pathways that characterize the mature human brain— particularly in the neocortex. So how does the brain know how to develop? It appears that evolution has hit on a solution that involves a trade-off between nature and nurture: You do not need to encode in the genes what you can extract from the environment. In other words, use the environment as a depository of information that can be relied on to drive neural development.

The emergence of neural structures in the brain is entirely dependent on a complex interaction of the organism's environment and the genes' capacity to express themselves in the environment. This evolutionary engineering trick allows the emergence of a complex neural system with a limited investment in genetic pre-wiring. Of course, this can have disastrous consequences when the environment fails to present itself. On the other hand, the flexibility introduced by genetic underspecification can also be advantageous when things go wrong, such as brain damage. As information is available in the environment to guide neural development, other brain regions can take over the task of the damaged areas. Underspecification and sensitivity to environmental conditions permit a higher degree of individual specialization and adaptation to changing living conditions. Starting off with a limited amount of built-in knowledge can therefore be an advantage if you are prepared to take the chance that you can find the missing parts elsewhere.

There are, however, other reasons for wanting to start out life with some limits on processing capacity. It turns out that some complex problems are easier to solve if you first tackle them from a over-simplistic point of view. A good example of this is Elman's (1993) simulation of grammar learning in a simple recurrent network. The network's task was to predict the next word in a sequence of words representing a large number of English-like sentences. These sentences included long-distance dependencies, i.e. the sentences included embedded clauses that separated the main noun from the main verb. Because English verbs agree with their subject nouns in number, the network must remember the number of the noun all the way through the embedded clause until it reaches the main verb of the sentence. For example, in a sentence like "The boy with the football that his parents gave him on his birthday chases the dog", the network must remember that "boy" and "chases" agree with each other.

After a considerable amount of training, the network did rather poorly at predicting the next word in the sequence—as do humans (cf. "The boy chased the ???"). However, it did rather well at predicting the grammatical category of the next word. For example, it seemed to know when to expect a verb and when to expect a noun, suggesting that it had learnt some fundamental facts about the grammar of the language to which it had been exposed. On the other hand, it did very badly on long-distance agreement phenomena, i.e. it could not predict correctly which form of the verb should be used after an intervening embedded clause. This is a serious flaw if the simulation is taken as a model of grammar learning in English speakers, as English speakers clearly are able to master long-distance agreement.

Elman discovered two solutions to this problem: The network could learn to master long-distance dependencies if the sentences to which it was initially exposed did not contain any embedded clauses and consisted only of sequences in which the main verb and its subject were close together. Once the network had learnt the principle governing subject-verb agreement under these simplified circumstances, embedded clauses could be included in the sentences in the training environment and the network would eventually master the long-distance dependencies. Exposure to a limited sample of the language helped the network to decipher the fundamental principles of the grammar, which it could then apply to the more complex problem. This demonstration shows how "motherese" might play a facilitatory role in language learning (Snow, 1977).

Elman's second solution was to restrict the memory of the network at the outset of training while keeping the long distance dependencies in the training sentences. The memory constraint made it physically impossible for the network to make predictions about words more than three or four items downstream. This was achieved by resetting what are called context units in recurrent networks and is equivalent to restricting the system's working memory. When the network was constrained in this fashion it was only able to learn the dependencies between words that occurred close together in a sentence. However, this limitation had the advantage of preventing the network from being distracted by the difficult long-distance dependencies. So again, the network was able to learn

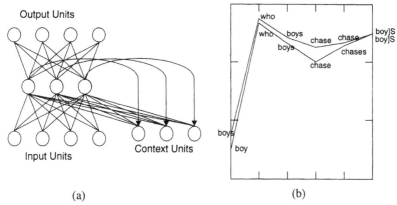

Output Units

Input Units

Context Units

(a)

(b)

FIG. 26.5   (a) A simple recurrent network (Elman, 1993) is good at making predictions. A sequence of items is presented to the network, one at a time. The network makes a prediction about the identity of the next item in the sequence at the output. Context units provide the network with an internal memory that keeps track of its position in the sequence. If it makes a mistake, the connections in the network are adapted slightly to reduce the error. (b) When the input consists of a sequence of words that make up sentences, the network is able to represent the sequences as trajectories through a state space. Small differences in the trajectories enable the network to keep track of long-distance dependencies.

some of the fundamental principles of the grammar. The working memory of the network was then gradually expanded. The network was able to learn the long-distance dependencies. It succeeded in predicting the correct form of verbs after embedded clauses. The initial restriction on the system's working memory turned out to have beneficial effects: Somewhat surprisingly, the network succeeded in learning the grammar underlying word sequences when working memory started off small and was gradually expanded, whereas it failed when a full working memory was made available to the network at the start of training.

The complementary nature of the solutions that Elman discovered to the problem of learning long-distance dependencies highlights the way that nature and nurture can be traded off against one another in the search for solutions to complex problems. In one case, exogenous environmental factors assists the organism in solving the problem. In the other case, endogenous processing factors point the way to an answer. In both cases, though, the solution involved an initial simplification in the service of long-term gain. In development, big does not necessarily mean better.

CURRENT SHORTCOMINGS

One-trial learning

Children and adults learn quickly. For example, a single reference to a novel object as a *wug* may be sufficient for a child to use and understand the term appropriately on all subsequent occasions. The connectionist models described in this paper use learning algorithms that adjust network connections in a gradualistic, continuous fashion. An outcome of this computational strategy is that new learning is slow. To the extent that one-trial learning is an important characteristic of human development, these connectionist models fail to provide a sufficiently broad basis for characterizing the mechanisms involved in development.

There are two types of solution that connectionist modelers might adopt in response to these problems. First, it should be noted that connectionist learning algorithms are not inherently incapable of one-trial learning. The rate of change in the strength of the connections in a network is determined by a parameter called the learning rate. Turning up the learning rate will result in faster learning for a given input pattern. For example, it is quite easy to demonstrate one-trial learning in a network that exploits a Hebbian learning algorithm. However, a side effect of using high learning rates is that individual training patterns can interfere with each other, sometimes resulting in undesirable instabilities in the network. Of course, interference is not always undesirable and may help us explain instabilities in children's performance such as in their acquisition of the English past tense. Generally, though, *catastrophic interference* between training patterns (when training on one pattern completely wipes out the traces of a previously trained pattern) is undesirable. One way to achieve one-trial learning without catastrophic interference is to ensure that the training patterns are orthogonal (or dissimilar) to each other. Many models deliberately choose input representations that fulfil this constraint.

An alternative response to the problem of one-trial learning in networks is to suggest that one-trial learning is illusory, i.e. when individuals demonstrate what is apparently entirely new learning they are really exploiting old knowledge in novel ways. Vygotsky (1962) coined the term the *Zone of Proximal Development* to describe areas of learning where change could occur at a fast pace. Piaget (1952) used the notion of *moderate novelty* in a similar fashion. The performance of networks can change dramatically over just a couple of learning trials. For example, the Plunkett et al. (1992) simulation of vocabulary development exhibited rapid vocabulary growth after a prolonged period of slow lexical learning. The McClelland (1989) balance beam simulation shows similar stage-like performance. In both cases, the networks gradually move towards a state of readiness that then suddenly catapults them into higher levels of behavior. Some one-trial learning may be amenable to this kind of analysis. It seems unlikely, however, that all one-trial learning is of this kind.

Defining the task and the teacher

Some network models are trained to carry out a specific task that involve a teacher. For example, the Rumelhart and McClelland model of past tense acquisition is taught to produce the past tense form of the verb when exposed to the corresponding stem. These are called supervised learning systems. It is not always clear where the teacher signal that drives learning in these networks originates or how the task got to be defined in the way it did. Other models use an unsupervised form of learning such as auto-association (Plunkett et al., 1992) or prediction (Elman, 1993; Mareschal et al., 1995). In these models, the teacher signal is the input to the network itself. These are called unsupervised learning systems. In general, connectionist modelers prefer to use unsupervised learning algorithms. They involve fewer assumptions about the origins of the signal that drive learning. However, some tasks seem to be inherently supervised. For example, learning that a dog is called a *dog* rather than a *chien* involves exposure to appropriate supervision. Nevertheless, it is unclear how the brain goes about conceptualizing the nature of the task to be performed and identifying the appropriate supervisory signal. Clearly, different parts of the brain end up doing different types of things. One of the future challenges facing developmental connectionists is to understand how neural systems are able to define tasks for themselves in a self-supervisory fashion and to orchestrate the functioning of multiple networks in executing complex behavior.

Biological plausibility

Throughout this chapter I have tried to demonstrate how connectionist models can contribute to our understanding of the mechanisms underlying linguistic and cognitive development. Yet the learning algorithms employed in some of the models described here are assumed to be biologically implausible. For example, the learning algorithm called backpropagation (Rumelhart, Hinton, & Williams, 1986) involves propagating error backwards through the layers of nodes in the network. However, there is no evidence indicating that the brain propagates error across layers of neurons in this fashion and some have argued that we are unlikely to find such evidence (Crick, 1989).

There is a considerable literature concerning the appropriate level of interpretation of neural network simulations (see Smolensky, 1988). For example, it is often argued that connectionist models can be given an entirely functionalist interpretation and the question of their relation to biological neural networks left open for further research. In other words, the vocabulary of connectionist models is couched at the level of software rather than hardware, much like the classic symbolic approach to cognition. Many developmental connectionists, however, are concerned to understand the nature of the relationship between cognitive development and changes in brain organization. Connectionist models that admit the use of biologically implausible components appear to undermine this attempt to understand the biological basis of the mechanisms of change.

Given the success of connectionist approaches to modeling development, it would seem wasteful to throw these simulations onto the garbage pile of the biologically implausible. Clearly, the most direct way forward is to implement these models using biologically plausible learning algorithms, such as Hebbian learning. Nevertheless, there are several reasons for tentatively accepting the understanding achieved already through existing models. First, algorithms like backpropagation may not be that implausible. The neurotransmitters that communicate signals across the synaptic gap are still only poorly understood. It is known that they communicate information in both directions. Information may be fed backwards through the layered system of neurons in the cortex—perhaps also exploiting the little-understood back projecting neurons in the process.

A second, less radical proposal assumes that algorithms like backpropagation belong to a family of learning algorithms all of which have similar computational properties and some of which have biologically plausible implementations. The study of networks trained with backpropagation could turn out to yield essentially the same results as networks trained with a biologically plausible counterpart. There is some support for this point of view. For example, Plaut and Shallice (1993) lesioned a connectionist network trained with backpropagation and compared its behavior with a lesioned network originally trained using a contrastive Hebbian learning algorithm. The pattern of results obtained were essentially the same for both networks. This result does not obviate the need to build connectionist models that honor the rapidly expanding body of knowledge relating to brain structure and systems. However, it does suggest that, given the rather large pockets of ignorance concerning brain structure and function, we should be careful about jettisoning our hard-won understanding of computational systems that may yet prove to be closely related to the biological mechanisms underlying development.

SOME LESSONS

A commonly held view has been that connectionism involves a *tabula rasa* approach to human learning and development. It is unlikely that any developmental connectionist has ever taken this position. Indeed, it is difficult to imagine what a *tabula rasa* connectionist network might look like. All the models reviewed in this chapter assume a good deal of built-in architectural and processing constraints to get learning off the ground. In some cases, such as the Rumelhart and McClelland model of the past tense, the initial constraints are relatively minimal. In others, such as the Mareschal et al. model of visual tracking and reaching, the initial architectural and computational assumptions are quite complex. These modeling assumptions, together with the task definition, imply a commitment to the ingredients that are necessary to get learning off the ground.

What is needed to get learning off the ground? We have seen that there are two main sources of constraint:

1. The initial state of the organism embodies a variety of architectural and computational constraints that determine its information processing capabilities.
2. Environmental structure supports the construction of new representational capacities not initially present in the organism itself.

Modeling enables us to determine whether a theory about the initial state of the organism can make the journey to the mature state given a well-defined training environment. Modeling also enables us to investigate the minimal assumptions about the initial state that are needed to make this journey.

A minimalist strategy may not necessarily provide an accurate picture of the actual brain mechanisms that underlie human development. However, it provides an important potential contrast to theories of the initial state that are based on arguments from the poverty of the stimulus. Investigating the richness of the stimulus shifts the burden away from the need to postulate highly complex, hard-wired information-processing structures. A minimalist strategy may also provide valuable insights into alternative solutions that the brain may adopt when richer resources fail.

Theories about the initial state of the organism cannot be dissociated from theories about what constitutes the organism's effective environment. Release two otherwise identical organisms is radically different environments and the representations they learn can be quite disparate. Connectionist modeling offers an invaluable tool for investigating these differences as well as examining the necessary conditions that permit the development of the emergent representations that we all share.

REFERENCES

Baillargeon, R. (1993). The object concept revisited: New directions in the investigation of infant's physical knowledge. In C. E. Granrud (Ed.), *Visual perception and cognition in infancy* (pp. 265–315). Mahwah, NJ: Lawrence Erlbaum Associates Inc.

Barrett, M. D. (1995). Early lexical development. In P. Fletcher & B. MacWhinney (Eds.), *The handbook of child language* (pp. 362–392). Oxford: Blackwell.

Bates, E., Bretherton, I., & Snyder, L. (1988). *From first words to grammar: Individual differences and dissociable mechanisms.* Cambridge, MA: Cambridge University Press.

Cottrell, G. W., & Plunkett, K. (1994). Acquiring the mapping from meanings to sounds. *Connection Science, 6,* 379–412.

Crick, F. H. C. (1989). The real excitement about neural networks. *Nature, 337,* 129–132.

Elman, J. L. (1993). Learning and development in neural networks: the importance of starting small. *Cognition, 48,* 71–99.

Foldiak, P. (1991). Learning invariance in transformational sequences. *Neural Computation, 3,* 194–200

Karmiloff-Smith, A. (1979). Micro- and macrodevelopmental changes in language acquisition and other representational systems. *Cognitive Science, 3,* 91–118.

MacWhinney, B., & Leinbach, A. J. (1991). Implementations are not conceptualizations: Revising the verb learning model. *Cognition, 40,* 121–157.

Marchman, V. A. (1993). Constraints on plasticity in a connectionist model of the English past tense. *Journal of Cognitive Neuroscience, 5,* 215–24.

Marcus, G. F., Ullman, M., Pinker, S., Hollander, M., Rosen, T. J., & Xu, F. (1992). Overregularization in language acquisition. *Monographs of the Society for Research in Child Development, 57,* Serial No. 228.

Mareschal, D., Plunkett, K., & Harris, P. (1995). Developing object permanence: A connectionist model. In J. D. Moore & J. F. Lehman (Eds.), *Proceedings of the Seventeenth Annual Conference of the Cognitive Science Society* (pp. 170–175). Mahwah, NJ.: Lawrence Erlbaum Associates Inc.

McClelland, J. L. (1989). Parallel distributed processing: implications for cognition and development. In R. G. M. Morris (Ed.), *Parallel Distributed Processing: Implications for Psychology and Neurobiology*. Oxford: Clarendon Press.

McShane, J. (1979). The development of naming. *Linguistics, 17,* 879–905.

Piaget, J. (1952). *The origins of intelligence in the child.* New York: International Universities Press.

Piaget, J. (1955). Les stades du développement intellectual de l'enfant et de l'adolescent. In P. O. et al. (Ed.), *Le probleme des stades en psychologie de l'enfant.* Paris: Presses Universitaires de France.

Pinker, S., & Prince, A. (1988). On language and connectionism: Analysis of a parallel distributed processing model of language acquisition. *Cognition, 29,* 73–193.

Plaut, D. C., & Shallice, T. (1993). Deep dyslexia: A case study of connectionist neuropsychology. *Cognitive Neuropsychology, 10,* 377–500.

Plunkett, K. (1993). Lexical segmentation and vocabulary growth in early language acquisition, *Journal of Child Language, 20,* 43–60.

Plunkett, K. (1995). Connectionist approaches to language acquisition. In P. Fletcher & B. MacWhinney (Eds.), *Handbook of Child Language* (pp. 36–72). Oxford: Blackwell.

Plunkett, K., & Marchman, V. (1991). U-shaped learning and frequency effects in a multi-layered perceptron: Implications for child language acquisition. *Cognition, 38,* 43–102.

Plunkett, K., & Marchman, V. (1993). From rote learning to system building: acquiring verb morphology in children and connectionist nets. *Cognition, 48,* 1–49.

Plunkett, K., Sinha, C. G., Møller, M. F., & Strandsby (1992). Symbol grounding or the emergence of symbols? Vocabulary growth in children and a connectionist net. *Connection Science, 4,* 293–312.

Reznick, J. S., & Goldfield, B. A. (1992). Rapid change in lexical development in comprehension and production. *Developmental Psychology, 28,* 406–413.

Rumelhart, D. E., Hinton, G. E., & Williams, R. J. (1986). Learning internal representations by error propagation. In D. E. Rumelhart, J. L. McClelland, & PDP Research Group (Eds.), *Parallel distributed processing: Explorations in the microstructure of cognition, Vol 1. Foundations* (pp. 318–362). Cambridge, MA: MIT Press.

Rumelhart, D. E., & McClelland, J. L. (1986). On learning the past tense of English verbs. In J. L. McClelland & D. E. Rumelhart (Eds.), *Parallel distributed processing: explorations in the microstructure of cognition.* Cambridge, MA: MIT Press.

Siegler, R. (1981). Developmental sequences within and between concepts. *Monographs of the Society for Research in Child Development, 46,* Whole No. 2.

Smolensky, P. (1988). On the proper treatment of connectionism. *The Behavioral and Brain Sciences, 11,* 1–23.

Snow, C. E. (1977). Mothers' speech research: From input to interaction. In C. E. Snow & C. A. Ferguson (Eds.), *Talking to children: Language input and acquisition.* Cambridge: Cambridge University Press.

Spelke, E. S., Katz, G., Purcell, S. E., Ehrlich, S. M., & Breinlinger, K. (1994). Early knowledge of object motion: continuity and inertia. *Cognition, 51,* 131–176.

Ungerlieder, L. G., & Mishkin, M. (1982). Two cortical visual systems. In D. J. Ingle, M. A. Goodale, & Mansfield (Eds.), *Analysis of visual behavior.* Cambridge, MA: MIT Press.

van Geert, P. (1991). A dynamic systems model of cognitive and language growth. *Psychological Review, 98,* 3–53.

von Hofsten, C. (1989). Transition mechanisms in sensori-motor development. In A. de Ribaupierre (Ed.), *Transition mechanisms in child development: The longitudinal perspective* (pp. 223–259). Cambridge: Cambridge University Press.

Vygotsky, L. (1962). *Thought and language.* Cambridge, MA: MIT Press.

Author Index

Subject Index